CIVIL
AIRCRAFT MARKINGS
1984

D1335003

Alan J. Wright

LONDON

IAN ALLAN LTD

Introduction

The 'G' prefixed four letter registration system was adopted in 1919 after a short-lived spell of about three months with serial numbers beginning at K-100. Until July 1928 the UK allocations were in the G-Exxx range, but as a result of further International agreements, this series was ended at G-EBZZ, the replacement being G-Axxx. From this point the registrations were issued in a reasonably orderly manner through to G-AZZZ, reached in July 1972. There were two exceptions. To avoid possible confusion with signal codes, the G-AQxx sequence was omitted, while G-AUxx was reserved for Australian use originally. In recent years however, an individual request for a mark in the latter range has been granted by the Authorities.

Although the next logical sequence was started at G-Bxxx, it was not long before the strictly applied rules relating to aircraft registration began to be relaxed. Permission was readily given for personalised marks to be issued incorporating virtually any four letter combination, while re-registration has also become a common feature, a practice almost unheard of in the past. In this book, where this has taken place at some time, the previous UK civil identity appears in parenthesis after the owner's/operator's name. An example of this is One-Eleven G-BBMG which originally carried G-AWEJ.

Some aircraft have also been allowed to wear military markings without displaying their civil identity. In this case the serial number actually carried is shown in parenthesis after the type's name. For example Gladiator G-AMRK flies as L8082 in RAF colours. As an aid to the identification of these machines, a military conversion list is provided.

Other factors caused a sudden acceleration in the number of registrations allocated by the Civil Aviation Authority in the early 1980s. The first surge came with the discovery that it was possible to register plastic bags and other items even less likely to fly, on payment of the standard fee. This erosion of the main register was checked in early 1982 by the issue of a special sequence for such devices commencing at G-FYAA. Powered hang-gliders provided the second glut of allocations as a result of the decision that these types should be officially registered. Although a few of the early examples penetrated the normal in-sequence register, the vast majority were given marks in other special ranges, this time G-MBxx, G-MJxx and G-MMxx with G-MNxx, G-MVxx, G-MWxx, G-MYxx and G-MZxx reserved for future use. In practice not all microlights display their official identities.

Throughout the UK section of this book, there are many instances where the probable base of the aircraft has been included. This is positioned at the end of the owner/operator details preceded by an oblique stroke. It must of course be borne in mind that changes do take place and that no attempt has been made to record the residents at the many private strips. The base of airline equipment has been given as the company's headquarter's airport, although frequently aircraft are outstationed for long periods.

Non-airworthy preserved aircraft are shown with a star after the type.

Any new registrations issued by the CAA after this publication went to press will inevitably not be included until the next edition. To aid the recording of later marks logged, grids have been provided at the end of the book.

The two-letter codes used by airlines to prefix flight numbers in timetables, airport movements boards, etc are included for those carriers appearing in the book. Radio frequencies for the larger airfields/airports are also listed.

Acknowledgements

Once again thanks are extended to the Registration Department of the Civil Aviation Authority for their assistance and allowing access to their files. The comments and amendments flowing from Wal Gandy, Hans Kohne, David Lewis and Andrew Yarwood have as always proved of considerable value, while the help given by numerous airlines has been much appreciated. The work of A. S. Wright and C. P. Wright during the update of this edition must not go unrecorded, since without it, deadlines would probably become impossible.

AJW

Cover: *Lufthansa A310-203 Airbus.* Lufthansa

International Civil Aircraft Markings

A2-	Botswana	PH-	Netherlands
A3-	Tonga	PJ-	Netherlands Antilles
A5-	Bhutan	PK-, PT-	Indonesia and West Irian
A6-	United Arab Emirates	PP-, PT-	Brazil
A7-	Qatar	PZ-	Surinam
A9-	Bahrain	RDPL-	Laos
A40-	Oman	RP-	Philippine Republic
AP-	Pakistan	S2-	Bangladesh
B-	China/Taiwan	S7-	Seychelles
C-F, C-G	Canada	S9-	São Tomé
C2-	Nauru	SE-	Sweden
C5-	Gambia	SP-	Poland
C6-	Bahamas	ST-	Sudan
C9-	Mozambique	SU-	Egypt
CC-	Chile	SX-	Greece
CCCP-*	Soviet Union	T3-	Kiribati
CN-	Morocco	TC-	Turkey
CP-	Bolivia	TF-	Iceland
CR-	Portuguese Overseas Provinces	TG-	Guatemala
CS-	Portugal	TI-	Costa Rica
CU-	Cuba	TJ-	United Republic of Cameroon
CX-	Uruguay	TL-	Central African Republic
D-	German Federal Republic (West)	TN-	Republic of Congo (Brazzaville)
D2-	Angola	TR-	Gabon
D6-	Comores Islands	TS-	Tunisia
DDR-	German Democratic Republic (East)	TT-	Chad
DQ-	Fiji	TU-	Ivory Coast
EC-	Spain	TY-	Benin
EI-, EJ-	Republic of Ireland	TZ-	Mali
EL-	Liberia	V2-	Antigua
EP-	Iran	VH-	Australia
ET-	Ethiopia	VP-F	Falkland Islands
F-	France, Colonies and Protectorates	VP-H	Belize
G-	United Kingdom	VP-LKA/	
H4-	Solomon Islands	LLZ	St Kitts-Nevis
HA-	Hungarian People's Republic	VP-LMA/	
HB-	Switzerland and Liechtenstein	LUZ	Montserrat
HC-	Ecuador	VP-LVA/	
HH-	Haiti	LZZ	Virgin Islands
HI-	Dominican Republic	VP-V	St Vincent
HK-	Colombia	VQ-T	Turks & Caicos Islands
HL-	Korea (South)	VR-B	Bermuda
HP-	Panama	VR-C	Cayman Islands
HR-	Honduras	VR-G	Gibraltar (not used: present
HS-	Thailand		Gibraltar Airways aircraft
HZ-	Saudi Arabia		registered G-)
I-	Italy	VR-H	Hong Kong
J2-	Djibouti	VR-U	Brunei
J3-	Grenada	VT-	India
J5-	Guinea Bissau	XA-, XB-,	
J6-	St Lucia	XC-,	Mexico
JA-	Japan	XT-	Upper Volta
JY-	Jordan	XU-	Kampuchea (formerly Khmer
LN-	Norway		Republic)
LQ-, LV-	Argentine Republic	XV-	Vietnam
LX-	Luxembourg	XY-, XZ-	Burma
LZ-	Bulgaria	YA-	Afghanistan
MI-	Marshall Islands	YI-	Iraq
N-	United States of America	YJ-	Vanuatu
OB-	Peru	YK-	Syria
OD-	Lebanon	YN-	Nicaragua
OE-	Austria	YR-	Romania
OH-	Finland	YS-	El Salvador
OK-	Czechoslovakia	YU-	Yugoslavia
OO-	Belgium	YV-	Venezuela
OY-	Denmark	Z-	Zimbabwe
P-	Korea (North)	ZA-	Albania
P2-	Papua New Guinea	ZK-, ZL-,	
		ZM-	New Zealand
* Cyrillic letters for SSSR.		ZP-	Paraguay

ZS-, ZT-, ZU-	South Africa	6V-, 6W-	Senegal
3A-	Monaco	6Y-	Jamaica
3B-	Mauritius	7O-	Democratic Yemen
3C-	Equatorial Guinea	7P-	Lesotho
3D-	Swaziland	7Q-	Malawi
3X-	Guinea	7T-	Algeria
4R-	Sri Lanka	8P-	Barbados
4W-	Yemen Arab Republic	8Q-	Maldives
4X-	Israel	8R-	Guyana
5A-	Libya	9G-	Ghana
5B-	Cyprus	9H-	Malta
5H-	Tanzania	9J-	Zambia
5N-	Nigeria	9K-	Kuwait
5R-	Malagasy Republic (Madagascar)	9L-	Sierra Leone
5T-	Mauritania	9M-	Malaysia
5U-	Niger	9N-	Nepal
5V-	Togo	9Q-	Zaire
5W-	Western Somoa (Polynesia)	9U-	Burundi
5X-	Uganda	9V-	Singapore
5Y-	Kenya	9XR-	Rwanda
6O-	Somalia	9Y-	Trinidad and Tobago

Aircraft Type Designations

(eg PA-28 Piper Type 28)

A.	Beagle, Auster	GY	Gardan
AA-	American Aviation, Grumman American	H	Helio
		HM.	Henri Mignet
AB	Agusta-Bell	HP.	Handley Page
AS	Aerospatiale	HR.	Robin
A.S.	Airspeed	H.S.	Hawker Siddeley
A.W.	Armstrong Whitworth	IL	Ilyushin
B.	Blackburn, Bristol Boeing, Beagle	J.	Auster
		L.	Lockheed
BAC	British Aircraft Corporation	L.A.	Luton
BAe	British Aerospace	M.	Miles, Mooney
BN	Britten-Norman	MBB	Messerschmitt-Bölkow-Blohm
Bo	Bolkow	M.S.	Morane-Saulnier
Bu	Bucker	P.	Hunting (formerly Percival), Piaggio
C.H.	Chrislea	PA-	Piper
CLA	Comper	PC.	Pilatus
CP.	Piel	R.	Rockwell
D.	Druine	S.	Short, Sikorsky
DC-	Douglas Commercial	SA., SE, SO.	Sud-Aviation, Aérospatiale, Scottish Aviation
D.H.	de Havilland		
D.H.C.	de Havilland Canada	S.R.	Saunders-Roe, Stinson
DR.	Jodel (Robin-built)	ST	SOCATA
EP	Edgar Percival	T.	Tipsy
F.	Fairchild, Fokker	Tu	Tupolev
G.	Grumman	UH.	United Helicopters (Hiller)
GA	Gulfstream American	V.	Vickers-Armstrongs, BAC
G.A.L.	General Aircraft	V.S.	Vickers-Supermarine
G.C.	Globe	W.S.	Westland
		Z.	Zlin

British Civil Aircraft Registrations

Reg.	Type	Owner or Operator	Notes
G-EACN	BAT BK23 Bantam (KI23) ★	Shuttleworth Trust/O. Warden	
G-EAVX	Sopwith Pup (B1807)	K. A. M. Baker	
G-EBHX	D.H.53 Humming Bird	Shuttleworth Trust/O. Warden	
G-EBIA	S.E.5A (F904)	Shuttleworth Trust/O. Warden	
G-EBIB	S.E.5A (F939) ★	Science Museum	
G-EBIC	S.E.5A (F938) ★	RAF Museum	
G-EBIR	D.H.51	Shuttleworth Trust/O. Warden	
G-EBJG	Parnall Pixie III ★	Midland Aircraft Preservation Soc	
G-EBJO	ANEC II ★	Shuttleworth Trust/O. Warden	
G-EBKN	Avro 504K (E449) ★	RAF Museum	
G-EBKY	Sopwith Pup (N5180)	Shuttleworth Trust/O. Warden	
G-EBLV	D.H.60 Cirrus Moth	British Aerospace/Hatfield	
G-EBMB	Hawker Cygnet I ★	RAF Museum	
G-EBNV	English Electric Wren	Shuttleworth Trust/O. Warden	
G-EBQP	D.H.53 Humming Bird ★	Russavia Collection/Duxford	
G-EBWD	D.H.60X Hermes Moth	Shuttleworth Trust/O. Warden	
G-EBYY	Cierva C.8L ★	Musée de l'Air, Paris	
G-EBZM	Avro 594 Avian IIIA ★	Manchester Air & Space Museum	
G-AAAH	D.H.60G Gipsy Moth ★	Science Museum	
G-AACN	H.P.39 Gugnunc ★	Science Museum/Wroughton	
G-AAIN	Parnall Elf II	Shuttleworth Trust/O. Warden	
G-AAMY	D.H.60M Moth	C. C. & Mrs. J. M. Lovell	
G-AANG	Blériot Monoplane	Shuttleworth Trust/O. Warden	
G-AANH	Deperdussin Monoplane	Shuttleworth Trust/O. Warden	
G-AANI	Blackburn Monoplane	Shuttleworth Trust/O. Warden	
G-AANJ	L.V.G.-C VI (7198/19)	Shuttleworth Trust/O. Warden	
G-AAOK	Curtiss Wright Travel Air 12Q	Shipping & Airlines Ltd/Biggin Hill	
G-AAPZ	Desoutter I (mod.) ★	Shuttleworth Trust/O. Warden	
G-AAUP	Klemm L.25-IA	R. S. Russell	
G-AAVJ	D.H.60GMW Moth	R. I. & J. O. Souch	
G-AAWO	D.H.60G Gipsy Moth	J. F. W. Reid	
G-AAYX	Southern Martlet	Shuttleworth Trust/O. Warden	
G-AAZP	D.H.80A Puss Moth	R. P. Williams	
G-ABAA	Avro 504K (H2311) ★	RAF Museum	
G-ABAG	D.H.60G Moth	Shuttleworth Trust/O. Warden	
G-ABDW	D.H.80A Puss Moth	Museum of Flight/E. Fortune	
G-ABEE	Avro 594 Avian IVM (Sports) ★	Aeroplane Collection Ltd	
G-ABEV	D.H.60G Moth	R. I. & Mrs J. O. Souch	
G-ABLM	Cierva C.24 ★	Mosquito Aircraft Museum	
G-ABLS	D.H.80A Puss Moth	R. C. F. Bailey	
G-ABMR	Hart 2 (J9941) ★	RAF Museum	
G-ABNT	Civilian Coupe	Shipping & Airlines Ltd/Biggin Hill	
G-ABNX	Redwing 2	R. Nerou	
G-ABOI	Wheeler Slymph ★	Midland Air Museum	
G-ABTC	CLA.7 Swift	P. Channon/St. Just	
G-ABUS	CLA.7 Swift	R. C. F. Bailey	
G-ABUU	CLA.7 Swift	J. Pothecary	
G-ABVE	Arrow Active 2	J. D. Penrose	
G-ABWP	Spartan Arrow	R. E. Blain/Barton	
G-ABXL	Granger Archaeopteryx ★	Shuttleworth Trust/O. Warden	
G-ABYA	D.H.60G Gipsy Moth	Dr I. D. C. Hay & J. F. Moore	
G-ABZB	D.H.60G-III Moth Major	R. E. & B. A. Ogden	
G-ACCB	D.H.83 Fox Moth ★	Midland Aircraft Preservation Soc	
G-ACDC	D.H.82A Tiger Moth	Tiger Club Ltd/Redhill	
G-ACDJ	D.H.82A Tiger Moth	F. J. Terry	
G-ACGT	Avro 594 Avian IIIA ★	K. Smith	
G-ACIT	D.H.84 Dragon ★	Science Museum/Wroughton	
G-ACLL	D.H.85 Leopard Moth	H.L.S. Developments Ltd	
G-ACMA	D.H.85 Leopard Moth	S. J. Filhol/Sherburn	
G-ACMN	D.H.85 Leopard Moth	H. D. Labouchere	

Notes	Reg.	Type	Owner or Operator
	G-ACNB	Avro 504K (E3404)	Shuttleworth Trust/O. Warden
	G-ACSP	D.H.88 Comet ★	Veteran & Vintage Aircraft (Engineering) Ltd/Chirk
	G-ACSS	D.H.88 Comet ★	Shuttleworth Trust/O. Warden
	G-ACTF	CLA.7 Swift	A. J. Chalkley/Booker
	G-ACUS	D.H.85 Leopard Moth	C. W. Annis
	G-ACUU	Cierva C.30A ★	G. S. Baker/Duxford
	G-ACUX	S.16 Scion ★	Ulster Folk & Transport Museum
	G-ACVA	Kay Gyroplane ★	Glasgow Museum of Transport
	G-ACWP	Cierva C.30A (AP507) ★	Science Museum
	G-ACXE	B.K.L-25C Swallow	D. G. Ellis
	G-ADAH	D.H.89A Dragon Rapide ★	Museum of Flight/E. Fortune
	G-ADEL	Spartan Cruiser III ★	Museum of Flight/E. Fortune
	G-ADFV	Blackburn B-2 ★	Humberside Aircraft Preservation Soc
	G-ADGP	M.2L Hawk Speed Six	R. H. Reeves/O. Warden
	G-ADGT	D.H.82A Tiger Moth	D. R. & Mrs M. Wood
	G-ADIA	D.H.82A Tiger Moth	J. Beaty/Sywell
	G-ADJJ	D.H.82A Tiger Moth	J. M. Preston
	G-ADKC	D.H.87B Hornet Moth	E. J. Roe/Halfpenny Green
	G-ADKK	D.H.87B Hornet Moth	C. W. Annis
	G-ADKM	D.H.87B Hornet Moth	F. R. E. Hayter
	G-ADLY	D.H.87B Hornet Moth	P. & A. Wood
	G-ADMT	D.H.87B Hornet Moth	Scottish Aircraft Collection/Perth
	G-ADMW	M.2H Hawk Major (DG590) ★	RAF Museum
	G-ADND	D.H.87B Hornet Moth	Shuttleworth Trust/O. Warden
	G-ADNE	D.H.87B Hornet Moth	Shipping & Airlines Ltd/Biggin Hill
	G-ADNZ	D.H.82A Tiger Moth	R. W. & Mrs. S. Pullan
	G-ADOT	D.H.87B Hornet Moth ★	Mosquito Aircraft Museum
	G-ADPJ	B.A.C. Drone	P. G. Dunnington
	G-ADPR	P.3 Gull ★	Shuttleworth Trust Jean/O. Warden
	G-ADPS	Swallow 2	Strathallan Aircraft Collection
	G-ADRA	Pietenpol Aircamper	A. J. Mason & R. J. Barrett
	G-ADRC	K. & S. Jungster J-1	J. J. Penney & L. R. Williams
	G-ADRH	D.H.87B Hornet Moth	I. M. Callier
	G-ADRY	Pou-du-Ciel (Replica) (BAPC29) ★	P. Roberts
	G-ADUR	D.H.87B Hornet Moth	R. C. Lenton
	G-ADWO	D.H.82A Tiger Moth (BB807)	Wessex Aviation Soc
	G-ADXS	Pou-du-Ciel ★	Rebel Air Museum/Andrewsfield
	G-ADXT	D.H.82A Tiger Moth	J. & J. M. Pothecary
	G-ADYS	Aeronca C.3	J. Willmot
	G-AEBB	Pou-du-Ciel ★	Shuttleworth Trust/O. Warden
	G-AEBJ	Blackburn B-2	British Aerospace/Brough
	G-AEDB	B.A.C. Drone 2	M. C. Russell/Duxford
	G-AEEG	M.3A Falcon	Shipping & Airlines Ltd/Biggin Hill
	G-AEEH	Pou-du-Ciel ★	RAF/St Athan
	G-AEFT	Aeronca C-3	C. E. Humphreys & ptnrs/Henstridge
	G-AEGV	HM.14 Pou-du-Ciel ★	Midland Aircraft Preservation Soc
	G-AEHM	Pou-du-Ciel ★	Science Museum
	G-AEJR	B.A.C. Drone	P. G. Dunnington
	G-AEKR	Flying Flea (Replica) (BAPC 121) ★	S. Yorks Aviation Soc
	G-AEKV	Kronfield Drone	Wg Cdr J. E. McDonald
	G-AELO	D.H.87B Hornet Moth	S. N. Bostock
	G-AEML	D.H.89 Dragon Rapide	J. P. Filhol Ltd/St. Just
	G-AENP	Hawker Hind	Shuttleworth Trust/O. Warden
	G-AEOA	D.H.80A Puss Moth	P. & A. Wood/O. Warden
	G-AEOF†	HM.14 Pou-du-Ciel (BAPC22) ★	Newark Air Museum
	G-AEOF	Rearwin 8500	Shipping & Airlines Ltd/Biggin Hill
	G-AEOH	HM.14 Pou-du-Ciel ★	Midland Air Museum
	G-AEPH	Bristol F.2B (D8096)	Shuttleworth Trust/O. Warden
	G-AERD	P.3 Gull Six	N. C. Jensen/Redhill
	G-AERV	M.11A Whitney Straight ★	Ulster Folk & Transport Museum
	G-AESE	D.H.87B Hornet Moth	H. J. Shaw
	G-AETA	Caudron G.3 (3066) ★	RAF Museum
	G-AEUJ	M.11A Whitney Straight	R. E. Mitchell
	G-AEVS	Aeronca 100	R. & M. Nerou
	G-AEVZ	B.A. Swallow 2	J. O. Souch
	G-AEXD	Aeronca 100	Mrs M. A. & R. W. Mills

† False registration

Reg.	Type	Owner or Operator	Notes
G-AEXF	P.6 Mew Gull	T. M. Storey/Redhill	
G-AEXT	Dart Kitten II	A. E. Walsh & C. A. Stubbings	
G-AEXZ	Piper J-2 Cub	Mrs M. & J. R. Dowson/Leicester	
G-AEYY	Martin Monoplane ★	Martin Monoplane Syndicate	
G-AFBS	M14A Hawk Trainer ★-	G. D. Durbridge-Freeman (G-AKKU)/ Duxford	
G-AFCL	B. A. Swallow 2	A. M. Dowson/O. Warden	
G-AFDX	Hanriot HD.1 (75) ★	RAF Museum	
G-AFEL	Monocoupe 90A	Cillam Holdings Ltd	
G-AFFD	Percival Q-6 ★	K. Gomm	
G-AFFI	Pou-du-Ciel (BAPC76) ★	Nostell Aviation Museum	
G-AFGC	B. A. Swallow 2	H. Plain	
G-AFGD	B. A. Swallow 2	A. T. Williams & ptnrs/Shobdon	
G-AFGE	B. A. Swallow 2	Donald G. Ellis/Sandown	
G-AFGH	Chilton D.W.1.	M. L. & G. L. Joseph	
G-AFGI	Chilton D.W.1. ★	J. E. McDonald	
G-AFGM	Piper J-4A Cub Coupé	J. A. Thomas	
G-AFHA	Mosscraft M.A.1. ★	C. V. Butler	
G-AFIN	Chrislea Airguard ★	Aeroplane Collection Ltd	
G-AFIU	Parker C.A.4 Parasol (LA-3 Minor)	S. P. Connatty	
G-AFJA	Watkinson Dingbat ★	K. Woolley	
G-AFJB	Foster-Wickner G.M.1. Wicko (DR613) ★	K. Woolley	
G-AFJR	Tipsy Trainer 1	M. E. Vaisey	
G-AFJV	Mosscraft MA.2	C. V. Butler	
G-AFLW	M.17 Monarch	N. I. Dalziel/Biggin Hill	
G-AFNG	D.H.94 Moth Minor	R. W. Livett/Sywell	
G-AFNI	D.H.94 Moth Minor	B. M. Welford	
G-AFOB	D.H.94 Moth Minor	R. E. Ogden	
G-AFPN	D.H.94 Moth Minor	J. Black	
G-AFPR	D.H.94 Moth Minor	J. A. Livett	
G-AFRV	Tipsy Trainer 1	Capt R. C. F. Bailey	
G-AFRZ	M.17 Monarch	R. E. Mitchell (G-AIDE)	
G-AFSC	Tipsy Trainer 1	G. P. Hermer & ptnrs	
G-AFSV	Chilton D.W.1A	R. Nerou	
G-AFTA	Hawker Tomtit (K1786)	Shuttleworth Trust/O. Warden	
G-AFTN	Taylorcraft Plus C2 ★	Leicestershire County Council Museums	
G-AFVE	D.H.82 Tiger Moth	Swinstead Aviation Ltd	
G-AFVN	Tipsy Trainer 1	W. Callow & ptnrs	
G-AFWH	Piper J-4A Cub Coupé	G. R. S. Smith/Shobdon	
G-AFWI	D.H.82A Tiger Moth (BB8I4)	N. E. Rankin & ptnrs	
G-AFWT	Tipsy Trainer 1	J. S. Barker/Redhill	
G-AFYD	Luscombe 8E Silvaire	J. D. Iliffe	
G-AFYO	Stinson H.W.75	S. R. Clarke	
G-AFZE	Heath Parasol	K. C. D. St Cyrien	
G-AFZL	Porterfield CP.50	P. G. Lucas/White Waltham	
G-AFZN	Luscombe 8A	N. R. Haines/Thruxton	
G-AGBN	G.A.L.42 Cygnet 2	Museum of Flight/E. Fortune	
G-AGEG	D.H.82A Tiger Moth	P. Crispe	
G-AGFT	Avia FL.3	E. N. Grace	
G-AGIV	Piper J-3C-65 Cub	M. Pickering	
G-AGJG	D.H.89A Dragon Rapide	Aerial Enterprises Ltd/Duxford	
G-AGLK	Auster 5D	W. C. E. Tazewell	
G-AGNV	Avro 685 York 1 (MW100) ★	Aerospace Museum/Cosford	
G-AGOH	J/l Autocrat	Museum of Technology/Leicester	
G-AGOS	R.S.3 Desford I (VZ728)	Scottish Aircraft Collection/Perth	
G-AGOY	M.48 Messenger 3	T. Clark	
G-AGRU	V.498 Viking 1A ★	Aerospace Museum/Cosford	
G-AGSH	D.H.89A Dragon Rapide 6	Exeair Travel Ltd/Exeter	
G-AGTM	D.H.89A Dragon Rapide 6 (NF875)	Russavia Ltd/Duxford	
G-AGTO	J/l Autocrat	M. J. Barnett & D. J. T. Miller/Duxford	
G-AGTT	J/l Autocrat	C. Wilson	
G-AGVN	J/l Autocrat	P. J. Elliott/Leicester	
G-AGVV	Piper L-4H Cub	A. R. W. Taylor & D. Lofts/Sleap	
G-AGWE	Avro 19 Srs 2 ★	Loughborough & Leicester Air Museum	
G-AGXN	J/IN Alpha	P. A. Davey	

Notes	Reg.	Type	Owner or Operator
	G-AGXT	J/IN Alpha ★	The Aeroplane Collection
	G-AGXU	J/IN Alpha	Mrs J. Lewis
	G-AGXV	J/I Autocrat	F. Mumford
	G-AGYD	J/IN Alpha	P. Herring/Dishforth
	G-AGYH	J/IN Alpha	G. E. Twyman & P. J. Rae
	G-AGYK	J/I Autocrat	R. W. & Mrs N. M. Biggs/Rochester
	G-AGYT	J/IN Alpha	Portsmouth Naval Gliding Club/ Lee-on-Solent
	G-AGYU	DH.82A Tiger Moth (DE208)	P. & A. Wood
	G-AGYY	Ryan ST.3KR	D. S. & I. M. Morgan
	G-AGZZ	D.H.82A Tiger Moth	G. P. LaT. Shea-Simonds/Netheravon
	G-AHAL	J/IN Alpha	Skegness Air Taxi Services Ltd/ Ingoldmells
	G-AHAM	J/I Autocrat	D. W. Philip/Goodwood
	G-AHAU	J/I Autocrat	B. J. W. Foley/Panshanger
	G-AHAV	J/I Autocrat	R. H. G. Kingsmill/Headcorn
	G-AHBL	D.H.87B Hornet Moth	Dr Ursula H. Hamilton
	G-AHBM	D.H.87B Hornet Moth	P. A. & E. P. Gliddon
	G-AHCK	J/IN Alpha	P. A. Woodman/Shoreham
	G-AHCN	J/IN Alpha	FTS Flying Group
	G-AHCR	Gould-Taylorcraft Plus D Special	D. E. H. Balmford & D. R. Shepherd/ Yeovil
	G-AHED	D.H.89A Dragon Rapide (RL962) ★	RAF Museum (Cardington)
	G-AHGD	D.H.89A Dragon Rapide	M. R. L. Astor/Booker
	G-AHGW	Taylorcraft Plus D	C. V. Butler/Coventry
	G-AHGZ	Taylorcraft Plus D	S. J. Ball/Leicester
	G-AHHH	J/I Autocrat	D. Bridge/Coltishall
	G-AHHK	J/I Autocrat	W. J. Ogle (*Stored*)/Newtownards
	G-AHHN	J/I Autocrat	KK Aviation
	G-AHHT	J/IN Alpha	R.A.E. Aero Club/Farnborough
	G-AHIC	Avro 19 Srs 2 ★	G. M. K. Fraser/Bournemouth
	G-AHIZ	D.H.82A Tiger Moth	C.F.G. Flying Ltd/Cambridge
	G-AHKX	Avro 19 Srs 2	BAe (Manchester) Anson Preservation Group/Woodford
	G-AHKY	Miles M.18 Series 2	Scottish Aircraft Collection/Perth
	G-AHLI	Auster 3	G. A. Leathers
	G-AHLK	Auster 3	E. T. Brackenbury/Leicester
	G-AHLT	D.H.82A Tiger Moth	R. C. F. Bailey
	G-AHMJ	Cierva C.30A (K4235) ★	Shuttleworth Trust/O. Warden
	G-AHMN	D.H.82A Tiger Moth (N6985)	George House (Holdings) Ltd/ Compton Abbas
	G-AHRI	D.H.104 Dove 1 ★	Lincolnshire Aviation Museum
	G-AHRO	Cessna 140	R. H. Screen/Kidlington
	G-AHSA	Avro 621 Tutor (K3215)	Shuttleworth Trust/O. Warden
	G-AHSD	Taylorcraft Plus D	A. Tucker
	G-AHSO	J/IN Alpha	Skegness Air Taxi Services Ltd/ Ingoldmells
	G-AHSP	J/I Autocrat	F. A. L. Castleden & ptnrs/Andrewsfield
	G-AHSS	J/IN Alpha	Parker Airways Ltd/Denham
	G-AHST	J/IN Alpha	P. H. Lewis/Henstridge
	G-AHSW	J/I Autocrat	K. W. Brown/Sywell
	G-AHTE	P.44 Proctor V ★	S. Wales Historical Aircraft Preservation Soc
	G-AHTW	A.S.40 Oxford (V3388) ★	Skyfame Collection/Duxford
	G-AHUI	M.38 Messenger 2A ★	Humberside Aircraft Preservation Soc
	G-AHUJ	M.14A Hawk Trainer 3 (R1914)	Vintage Aircraft Team
	G-AHUV	D.H.82A Tiger Moth	W. G. Gordon
	G-AHVU	D.H.82A Tiger Moth	Parker Airways Ltd/Elstree
	G-AHVV	D.H.82A Tiger Moth	R. Jones
	G-AHWJ	Taylorcraft Plus D	A. Tucker
	G-AHXE	Taylorcraft Plus D (LB312)	Museum of Army Flying/Middle Wallop
	G-AIBE	Fulmar II (N1854) ★	F.A.A. Museum/Yeovilton
	G-AIBH	J/IN Alpha	A. J. Greenleaf
	G-AIBM	J/I Autocrat	J. L. Goodley
	G-AIBW	J/IN Alpha	Blackpool & Fylde Aero Club
	G-AIBX	J/I Autocrat	Wasp Flying Group/Panshanger
	G-AIBY	J/I Autocrat	D. Morris/Sherburn
	G-AIDL	D.H.89A Dragon Rapide 6	Southern Joyrides Ltd/Biggin Hill

Reg.	Type	Owner or Operator	Notes
G-AIDN	V.S.502 Spitfire T.8 (MT818)	G. F. Miller/Coventry	
G-AIDS	D.H.82A Tiger Moth	BSP Electric & Maintenance Co Ltd	
G-AIEK	M.38 Messenger 2A (RG333)	J. Buckingham	
G-AIFZ	J/1N Alpha	C. P. Humphries	
G-AIGD	J/1 Autocrat	A. G. Batchelor/Finmere	
G-AIGF	J/1N Alpha	A. R. C. Mathie/Coltishall	
G-AIGM	J/1N Alpha	S. T. Raby	
G-AIGR	J/1N Alpha	Aigret Aviation Ltd/Sywell	
G-AIGT	J/1N Alpha	B. D. Waller	
G-AIGU	J/1N Alpha	T. Pate	
G-AIIH	Piper L-4H Cub	J. A. de Salis	
G-AIIZ	D.H.82A Tiger Moth (T6645)	D. E. & J. A. Baker	
G-AIJI	J/1N Alpha ★	Humberside Aircraft Preservation Soc	
G-AIJM	Auster J/4	R. H. A. Thorne/Booker	
G-AIJR	Auster J/4	B. A. Harris/Halfpenny Green	
G-AIJT	Auster J/4	Aberdeen Auster Flying Group	
G-AILL	M.38 Messenger 2A	H. Best-Devereux	
G-AIPR	Auster J/4	MPM Flying Group/Booker	
G-AIPV	J/1 Autocrat	J. Linegar	
G-AIPW	J/1 Autocrat	J. Buckingham	
G-AIRC	J/1 Autocrat	A. G. Martlew/Liverpool	
G-AIRI	D.H.82A Tiger Moth	E. R. Goodwin	
G-AIRK	D.H.82A Tiger Moth	R. C. Teverson & ptnrs	
G-AISA	Tipsy B Srs 1	B. T. Morgan & A. Liddiard	
G-AISB	Tipsy B Srs 1	D. M. Fenton	
G-AISC	Tipsy B Srs 1	Wagtail Flying Group	
G-AIST	V.S.300 Spitfire IA (AR213)	The Hon P. Lindsay/Booker	
G-AISX	Piper J-3C-65 Cub	R. I. Souch/Hamble	
G-AITB	A.S.10 Oxford (MP425) ★	RAF Museum	
G-AITF	A.S.40 Oxford ★	RAF Museum/Henlow	
G-AITP	Piper J-3C-65 Cub	J. O. Souch/Hamble	
G-AIUA	M.14A Hawk Trainer 3 ★	Shuttleworth Trust/O. Warden	
G-AIUL	D.H.89A Dragon Rapide 6	A. F. Ward	
G-AIWA	P.28B Proctor 1 (R7524)	B. Wilmot/Biggin Hill	
G-AIXA	Taylorcraft Plus D	P. Stevens	
G-AIXD	D.H.82A Tiger Moth	D. L. Lloyd/Sywell	
G-AIXN	Benes-Mraz M.1c Sokol	J. F. Evetts & D. Patel	
G-AIYR	D.H.89A Dragon Rapide	C. D. Cyster & ptnrs	
G-AIYS	D.H.85 Leopard Moth	M. V. Gauntlett/Goodwood	
G-AIZE	F.24W Argus 2 ★	RAF Museum	
G-AIZG	V.S. Walrus (L2301) ★	F.A.A. Museum/Yeovilton	
G-AIZU	J/1 Autocrat	T. A. Collins & A. H. R. Stansfield	
G-AIZY	J/1 Autocrat	B. J. Richards	
G-AIZZ	J/1 Autocrat	S. E. Bond	
G-AJAB	J/1N Alpha	Air Farm Ltd	
G-AJAC	J/1N Alpha	R. C. Hibberd	
G-AJAE	J/1N Alpha	M. G. Stops	
G-AJAJ	J/1N Alpha	A. R. Milne & B. J. W. Thomas	
G-AJAM	J/2 Arrow	D. A. Porter/Sturgate	
G-AJAS	J/1N Alpha	C. J. Baker/Sturgate	
G-AJCP	D.31 Turbulent	H. J. Shaw	
G-AJDW	J/1 Autocrat	D. R. Hunt	
G-AJEB	J/1N Alpha ★	Aeroplane Collection Ltd	
G-AJEE	J/1 Autocrat	A. R. C. De Albanoz/Ronaldsway	
G-AJEH	J/1N Alpha	Astral Surveys Ltd/Fairoaks	
G-AJEI	J/1N Alpha	Skegness Air Taxi Services Ltd/Ingoldmells	
G-AJEM	J/1 Autocrat	H. A. Nind	
G-AJGJ	Auster 5	J. J. McLaughlin & ptnrs/Shoreham	
G-AJHO	D.H.89A Dragon Rapide ★	East Anglian Aviation Soc Ltd	
G-AJHS	D.H.82A Tiger Moth	W. G. Fisher/Sandown	
G-AJHU	D.H.82A Tiger Moth	F. P. Le Coyte	
G-AJID	J/1 Autocrat	D. J. Ronayne	
G-AJIH	J/1 Autocrat	D. F. Campbell & ptnrs	
G-AJIS	J/1N Alpha	A. Tucker	
G-AJIT	J/1 Kingsland Autocrat	Kingsland Aviation Ltd	
G-AJIU	J/1N Alpha	A. Murfin/Netherthorpe	
G-AJIW	J/1N Alpha	B. M. Baker (Hatfield) Ltd/Panshanger	
G-AJJP	Jet Gyrodyne (XJ389) ★	Aerospace Museum/Cosford	
G-AJKK	M.38 Messenger 2A ★	A. M. Lambourne & T. C. Eaves	

Notes	Reg.	Type	Owner or Operator
	G-AJOA	D.H.82A Tiger Moth (T5424)	F. P. Le Coyte
	G-AJOC	M.38 Messenger 2A ★	Ulster Folk & Transport Museum
	G-AJOE	M.38 Messenger 2A (RH378)	J. Eagles & P. C. Kirby/Staverton
	G-AJOV	Sikorsky S-51 ★	Aerospace Museum/Cosford
	G-AJOZ	F.24W Argus 2 ★	Lincolnshire Aviation Museum
	G-AJPI	F.24R-41a Argus 3	J. F. Read/Kidlington
	G-AJPZ	J/I Autocrat	K. Pyle
	G-AJRB	J/I Autocrat	S. C. Luck/Sywell
	G-AJRC	J/I Autocrat	S. W. Watkins & ptnrs
	G-AJRE	J/I Autocrat	D. J. Ronayne
	G-AJRH	J/IN Alpha	N. H. Ponsford
	G-AJRS	M.14A Hawk Trainer 3 (P6382)	Shuttleworth Trust/O. Warden
	G-AJTH	M.65 Gemini 1A	K. A. Learmonth
	G-AJUD	J/I Autocrat	C. L. Sawyer
	G-AJUE	J/I Autocrat	M. A. G. Westman
	G-AJUL	J/IN Alpha	M. J. Crees
	G-AJVE	D.H.82A Tiger Moth	M. J. Abbot & I. J. Jones
	G-AJVH	Swordfish (LS326)	F.A.A. Museum/Yeovilton
	G-AJVT	Auster 5	I. N. M. Cameron
	G-AJXC	Auster 5	J. E. Graves
	G-AJXV	Auster 4 (NJ695)	P. C. J. Farries/Tollerton
	G-AJYO	J/5B Autocar	A. H. Chaplin & ptnrs
	G-AKAA	Piper L-4H Cub	B. C. Cooper
	G-AKAT	M.14A Magister (T9738) ★	Newark Air Museum
	G-AKAZ	Piper J-3C-65 Cub	R. Mayo/Staverton
	G-AKBM	M.38 Messenger 2A ★	Bristol Plane Preservation Unit
	G-AKBO	M.38 Messenger 2A	J. R. A. Ramshaw
	G-AKDN	D.H.C. IA Chipmunk 10	K. R. Nunn/Seething
	G-AKEL	M.65 Gemini 1A	J. M. Bisco
	G-AKER	M.65 Gemini 1A ★	Vintage Aircraft Team
	G-AKEZ	M.38 Messenger 2A (RG333) ★	Wales Aircraft Museum
	G-AKGE	M.65 Gemini 3C	R. E. Winn
	G-AKHP	M.65 Gemini 1A	Fortresse Ltd/Biggin Hill
	G-AKHW	M.65 Gemini 1A	A. C. Pritchard
	G-AKHZ	M.65 Gemini 7 ★	Vintage Aircraft Team
	G-AKIF	D.H.89A Dragon Rapide	Airborne Taxi Services Ltd/Booker
	G-AKIN	M.38 Messenger 2A	A. J. Spiller/Sywell
	G-AKIU	Proctor V ★	N. Weald Aircraft Restoration Flight
	G-AKJU	J/IN Alpha	R. C. Lewis
	G-AKKB	M.65 Gemini 1A	S.A.C. Bristol Ltd/Staverton
	G-AKKH	M.65 Gemini 1A	M. C. Russell/Duxford
	G-AKKR	M.14A Magister (T9707) ★	Manchester Air & Space Museum
	G-AKNB	Dakota 4	Aces High Ltd/Blackpool
	G-AKOE	D.H.89A Dragon Rapide 4	J. E. Pierce
	G-AKOW	Auster 5 (TJ569)	Museum of Army Flying/Middle Wallop
	G-AKPF	M.14A Hawk Trainer (N3788) ★	L. N. D. Taylor
	G-AKPI	Auster 5 (NJ703)	B. H. Hargrave/Sherburn
	G-AKSZ	Auster 5	A. R. C. Mathie/ Upavon
	G-AKUW	C.H.3 Super Ace	C. V. Butler
	G-AKVF	C.H.3 Super Ace	P. V. B. Longthorp/White Waltham
	G-AKVZ	M.38 Messenger 4B	Shipping & Airlines Ltd/Biggin Hill
	G-AKWS	Auster 5	J. E. Homewood
	G-AKWT	Auster 5 (MT360) ★	Humberside Aircraft Preservation Soc
	G-AKXP	Auster 5	F. E. Telling
	G-AKXS	D.H.82A Tiger Moth	P. A. Colman
	G-AKZN	P.30 Proctor 2E (Z7197) ★	RAF Museum
	G-ALAH	M.38 Messenger 4A (RH377) ★	Aeroplane Collection Ltd
	G-ALAX	D.H.89A Dragon Rapide ★	Durney Aeronautical Collection
	G-ALBJ	Auster 5	R. H. Elkington
	G-ALBK	Auster 5	S. J. Wright & Co (Farmers) Ltd
	G-ALBN	Bristol 173 (XF785) ★	RAF Museum
	G-ALCK	P.34A Proctor 3 (LZ766) ★	Skyfame Collection/Duxford
	G-ALCS	M.65 Gemini 3C	R. E. Winn
	G-ALCU	D.H.104 Dove 2 ★	Midland Air Museum
	G-ALEH	PA-17 Vagabond	A. D. Pearce/Redhill
	G-ALFA	Auster 5	Alpha Flying Group/Leicester
	G-ALFT	D.H.104 Dove 6 ★	Torbay Aircraft Museum
	G-ALFU	D.H.104 Dove 6 ★	Imperial War Museum/Duxford
	G-ALGT	V.S.379 Spitfire 14 (RM619)	Rolls-Royce Ltd

Reg.	Type	Owner or Operator	Notes
G-ALIW	D.H.82A Tiger Moth	D. I. M. Geddes & F. Curry	
G-ALJF	P.34A Proctor 3	J. F. Moore/Biggin Hill	
G-ALNA	D.H.82A Tiger Moth	D. A. Lord/Shoreham	
G-ALND	D.H.82A Tiger Moth (N9191)	Arrow Air Services (Engineering) Ltd/ Shipdham	
G-ALOD	Cessna 140	J. R. Stainer	
G-ALRH	Eon Type 8 Baby	P. D. Moran	
G-ALSP	Bristol 171 (WV783) ★	RAF Museum	
G-ALSS	Bristol 171 (WA576) ★	—	
G-ALST	Bristol 171 (WA577) ★	N.E. Aircraft Museum	
G-ALSW	Bristol 171 (WT933) ★	Newark Air Museum	
G-ALSX	Bristol 171 (G-48-1) ★	Rotorcraft Museum/Duxford	
G-ALTO	Cessna 140	J. E. Cummings	
G-ALTW	D.H.82A Tiger Moth	C. J. Musk/(Stored)	
G-ALUC	D.H.82A Tiger Moth	D. R. & Mollie Wood	
G-ALUL	D.H.C.1 Chipmunk 22 (P-122)	G. Livett	
G-ALWB	D.H.C.1 Chipmunk 22A	Kelvin Aviation Ltd/Glasgow	
G-ALWC	Dakota 4	Clyde Surveys Ltd/White Waltham	
G-ALWF	V.701 Viscount ★	Viscount Preservation Trust/Duxford	
G-ALWW	D.H.82A Tiger Moth	F. W. Fay & ptnrs/Long Marston	
G-ALXT	D.H.89A Dragon Rapide ★	Science Museum/Wroughton	
G-ALXZ	Auster 5-150	T. Bessart & R. Witheridge	
G-ALYB	Auster 5	G. F. Kilsby	
G-ALYG	Auster 5D	A. L. Young	
G-ALZE	BN-1F ★	Aerospace Museum/Cosford	
G-ALZO	A.S.57 Ambassador ★	Dan-Air Preservation Group/Lasham	
G-AMAW	Luton L.A.4 Minor	J. R. Coates	
G-AMBB	D.H.82A Tiger Moth	J. Eagles/Staverton	
G-AMCA	Dakota 4	Air Atlantique Ltd/Jersey	
G-AMDA	Avro 652A Anson 1 (N4877)★	Skyfame Collection/Duxford	
G-AMDN	Hiller UH-12A	Bristow Helicopters Ltd	
G-AMEN	PA-19 Super Cub 95	A. Lovejoy & ptnrs/Lasham	
G-AMHJ	Dakota 6	Air Atlantique Ltd/Jersey	
G-AMIU	D.H.82A Tiger Moth	R. & Mrs J. L. Jones	
G-AMKU	J/IB Aiglet	Southdown Flying Group/Slinfold	
G-AMLK	B.170 Freighter 31M	Instone Air Line Ltd	
G-AMLZ	P.50 Prince 6E	J. F. Coggins/Coventry	
G-AMMS	J/5K Aiglet Trainer	D. Collyer	
G-AMOG	V.701 Viscount ★	Aerospace Museum/Cosford	
G-AMPO	Dakota 4	Air Atlantique Ltd/Jersey	
G-AMPP	Dakota 3 (G-AMSU) ★	Dan-Air Preservation Group/Lasham	
G-AMPW	J/5B Autocar	J. V. Inglis	
G-AMPY	Dakota 4	Air Atlantique Ltd/Jersey	
G-AMPZ	Dakota 4	Harvest Air Ltd/Southend	
G-AMRA	Dakota 6	Air Atlantique Ltd/Jersey	
G-AMRF	J/5F Aiglet Trainer	A. I. Topps/E. Midlands	
G-AMRK	G.37 Gladiator (L8032)	Shuttleworth Trust/O. Warden	
G-AMSG	SIPA 903	S. W. Markham/White Waltham	
G-AMSV	Dakota 4	Air Atlantique Ltd/Jersey	
G-AMSZ	Auster 5	G. & D. Knight & D. G. Pridham	
G-AMTA	J/5F Aiglet Trainer	H. J. Jauncey/Rochester	
G-AMTM	J/I Autocrat	R. Stobo & D. Clewley	
G-AMUF	D.H.C.I Chipmunk 21	Redhill Tailwheel Flying Club Ltd	
G-AMUH	D.H.C.I Chipmunk 21	W. A. Fernie/Biggin Hill	
G-AMVD	Auster 5	C. G. Clarke	
G-AMVP	Tipsy Junior	A. R. Wershat/Blackbushe	
G-AMVS	D.H.82A Tiger Moth	M. J. Abbott & R. J. W. Wood	
G-AMXA	D.H.106 Comet C2 (XK655) ★	Strathallan Aircraft Collection	
G-AMXT	D.H.104 Sea Devon C.20	Scoteroy Ltd	
G-AMYD	J/5L Aiglet Trainer	G. H. Maskell	
G-AMYJ	Dakota 6	Harvest Air Ltd/Southend	
G-AMZI	J/5F Aiglet Trainer	J. F. Moore/Biggin Hill	
G-AMZT	J/5F Aiglet Trainer	D. Hyde & J. W. Saull	
G-AMZU	J/5F Aiglet Trainer	R. N. Goode & ptnrs/White Waltham	
G-ANAF	Dakota 4	Air Atlantique Ltd/Jersey	
G-ANAP	D.H.104 Dove 6 ★	Brunel Technical College/Lulsgate	
G-ANCF	B.175 Britannia 308F	(Stored)/Manston	
G-ANCS	D.H.82A Tiger Moth	R. H. Reeves/Sywell	
G-ANCX	D.H.82A Tiger Moth	D. R. Wood/Biggin Hill	

Notes	Reg.	Type	Owner or Operator
	G-ANDE	D.H.82A Tiger Moth	Stapleford Tiger Group
	G-ANDM	D.H.82A Tiger Moth	J. Green
	G-ANDP	D.H.82A Tiger Moth	A. H. Diver
	G-ANEF	D.H.82A Tiger Moth (T5493)	RAF College Flying Club Co Ltd/ Cranwell
	G-ANEL	D.H.82A Tiger Moth (N9238)	W. P. Maynall
	G-ANEM	D.H.82A Tiger Moth	P. J. Benest
	G-ANEW	D.H.82A Tiger Moth	A. L. Young/Catterick
	G-ANEZ	D.H.82A Tiger Moth	D. G. Ellis & C. D. J. Bland/ Sandown
	G-ANFC	D.H.82A Tiger Moth (DE363) ★	Mosquito Aircraft Museum
	G-ANFH	Westland S.55 ★	British Rotorcraft Museum
	G-ANFI	D.H.82A Tiger Moth (DE623)	Ardentland Ltd
	G-ANFM	D.H.82A Tiger Moth	S. A. Brook & ptnrs/Booker
	G-ANFP	D.H.82A Tiger Moth ★	Mosquito Aircraft Museum
	G-ANFV	D.H.82A Tiger Moth (DF155)	R. A. L. Falconer/Inverness
	G-ANFW	D.H.82A Tiger Moth	G. M. Fraser/White Waltham
	G-ANHK	D.H.82A Tiger Moth	J. D. Iliffe
	G-ANHR	Auster 5	N. C. Jouanny/Jersey
	G-ANHS	Auster 4	G. A. Griffin
	G-ANHX	Auster 5D	D. J. Baker/(Stored)
	G-ANHZ	Auster 5	J. H. D. Newman/(Stored)
	G-ANIE	Auster 5	—
	G-ANIJ	Auster 5D	Museum of Army Flying/Middle Wallop
	G-ANIS	Auster 5	J. Clarke-Cockburn
	G-ANJA	D.H.82A Tiger Moth (N9389)	J. J. Young/Seething
	G-ANJD	D.H.82A Tiger Moth	H. J. Jauncey
	G-ANJK	D.H.82A Tiger Moth	Montgomery Ultra Light Flying Club
	G-ANJV	Westland S.55 Srs 3 ★	British Rotorcraft Museum
	G-ANKK	D.H.82A Tiger Moth (T5854)	P. W. Crispe/Halfpenny Green
	G-ANKT	D.H.82A Tiger Moth (T6818)	Shuttleworth Trust/O. Warden
	G-ANKZ	D.H.82A Tiger Moth	Cillam Holdings Ltd/Barton
	G-ANLS	D.H.82A Tiger Moth	P. A. Gliddon/Inverness
	G-ANLW	W.B.1. Widgeon (MD497) ★	Helicopter Hire Ltd
	G-ANMV	D.H.82A Tiger Moth (T7404)	George House (Holdings) Ltd/ Compton Abbas
	G-ANNK	D.H.82A Tiger Moth	Mrs P. J. Wilcox/Sywell
	G-ANOD	D.H.82A Tiger Moth	D. R. & Mrs M. Wood
	G-ANOH	D.H.82A Tiger Moth	D. H. Parkhouse & ptnrs/O. Warden
	G-ANOK	S.91 Safir ★	Museum of Flight/E. Fortune
	G-ANOM	D.H.82A Tiger Moth	P. A. Colman
	G-ANON	D.H.82A Tiger Moth (T7909)	A. C. Mercer/Sherburn
	G-ANOO	D.H.82A Tiger Moth	T. J. Hartwell & ptnrs
	G-ANOR	D.H.82A Tiger Moth	A. J. Cheshire/Shobdon
	G-ANOV	D.H.104 Dove 6 ★	Museum of Flight/E. Fortune
	G-ANPK	D.H.82A Tiger Moth	J. W. Benson
	G-ANPP	P.34A Proctor 3	C. P. A. & Mrs J. Jeffery/Duxford
	G-ANRF	D.H.82A Tiger Moth	C. D. Cyster
	G-ANRN	D.H.82A Tiger Moth	J. J. V. Elwes
	G-ANRP	Auster 5 (TW439) ★	Warnham War Museum
	G-ANRX	D.H.82A Tiger Moth ★	Mosquito Aircraft Museum
	G-ANSM	D.H.82A Tiger Moth	M. R. Vest & D. P. A. Bindon/ Dunkeswell
	G-ANSZ	D.H.114 Heron 1B/C	Hurst Rent-a-Car Ltd/Fairoaks
	G-ANTE	D.H.82A Tiger Moth	T. I. Sutton & B. J. Champion/ Chester
	G-ANTK	Avro 685 York ★	Dan Air Preservation Group/Lasham
	G-ANTS	D.H.82A Tiger Moth (N6532) ★	Strathallan Aircraft Collection
	G-ANUO	D.H.114 Heron 2D	Topflight Aviation Ltd/Fairoaks
	G-ANUW	D.H.104 Dove 6 ★	Civil Aviation Authority/Stansted
	G-ANVU	D.H.104 Dove 1B	T. D. Keegan/Southend
	G-ANWB	D.H.C.I Chipmunk 21	G. Briggs/Blackpool
	G-ANWX	J/5L Aiglet Trainer	Teesfare Holdings Ltd
	G-ANXB	D.H.114 Heron 1B ★	Newark Air Museum
	G-ANXR	P.31C Proctor 4 (RM221)	L. H. Oakins/Biggin Hill
	G-ANYP	P.31C Proctor 4 (NP184) ★	Torbay Aircraft Museum
	G-ANZJ	P.31C Proctor 4 (NP303) ★	P. Raymond
	G-ANZR	D.H.82A Tiger Moth	D. R. & Mrs. M. Wood
	G-ANZU	D.H.82A Tiger Moth	P. A. Jackson/Sibson
	G-ANZZ	D.H.82A Tiger Moth	Tiger Club Ltd

G-ALNA   D.H.82A Tiger Moth.

13

G-AOYP V.806 Viscount of Jersey Air Ferries.

14

Reg.	Type	Owner or Operator	Notes
G-AOAA	D.H.82A Tiger Moth	Tiger Club Ltd/Redhill	
G-AOAR	P.31C Proctor 4 (NP181)	Historic Aircraft Preservation Soc	
G-AOBH	D.H.82A Tiger Moth (T7997)	C. H. A. Bott	
G-AOBO	D.H.82A Tiger Moth	T. J. Bolt & J. N. Moore	
G-AOBU	P.84 Jet Provost ★	Shuttleworth Trust/O. Warden	
G-AOBV	J/5P Autocar	P. E. Champney	
G-AOBX	D.H.82A Tiger Moth (T7187)	M. Gibbs/Redhill	
G-AOCR	Auster 5D	C. E. Tyers	
G-AOCU	Auster 5	S. J. Ball/Leicester	
G-AODA	Westland S.55 Srs 3	Bristow Helicopters Ltd	
G-AODT	D.H.82A Tiger Moth	N. A. Brett & A. H. Warminger	
G-AOEG	D.H.82A Tiger Moth	Truman Aviation Ltd/Tollerton	
G-AOEH	Aeronca 7AC Champion	M. Weeks & ptnrs	
G-AOEI	D.H.82A Tiger Moth	C.F.G. Flying Ltd/Cambridge	
G-AOEL	D.H.82A Tiger Moth (N9510) ★	Museum of Flight/E. Fortune	
G-AOES	D.H.82A Tiger Moth	S. Haye & G. A. Cordery/Redhill	
G-AOET	D.H.82A Tiger Moth	Glylynn Ltd	
G-AOFE	D.H.C.1 Chipmunk 22A	B. Webster/Shobdon	
G-AOFJ	Auster 5	Miss M. R. Innocent/Perth	
G-AOFM	J/5P Autocar	C. M. Barnes/Popham	
G-AOFS	J/5L Aiglet Trainer	G. W. Howard/Stapleford	
G-AOGA	M.75 Aries	R. E. Winn	
G-AOGE	P.34A Proctor 3	N. I. Dalziel/Booker	
G-AOGI	D.H.82A Tiger Moth	W. J. Taylor	
G-AOGR	D.H.82A Tiger Moth	H. C. Adkins & E. Shipley/N. Denes	
G-AOGV	J/5R Alpine	ABH Aviation	
G-AOHK	V.802 Viscount ★	Hotel de France/St Helier, Jersey	
G-AOHL	V.802 Viscount ★	British Air Ferries (Cabin Trainer)/Southend	
G-AOHM	V.802 Viscount	British Air Ferries *Anne Marie*/Southend	
G-AOHT	V.802 Viscount	British Air Ferries/Southend	
G-AOHV	V.802 Viscount	Euroair Ltd/Gatwick	
G-AOHZ	J/5P Autocar	M. R. Gibbons & G. W. Brown/Popham	
G-AOIL	D.H.82A Tiger Moth	Shuttleworth Trust/(*Stored*)	
G-AOIM	D.H.82A Tiger Moth	R. M. Wade & F. J. Terry	
G-AOIR	Thruxton Jackaroo	Stevenage Flying Club/O. Warden	
G-AOIS	D.H.82A Tiger Moth	V. B. & R. G. Wheele/Shoreham	
G-AOIY	J/5G Autocar	P. E. Scott	
G-AOJC	V.802 Viscount ★	Wales Aircraft Museum	
G-AOJH	D.H.83C Fox Moth	J. S. Lewery/Bournemouth	
G-AOJJ	D.H.82A Tiger Moth	J. Austin	
G-AOKH	P.40 Prentice 1	J. F. Moore/Biggin Hill	
G-AOKL	P.40 Prentice 1 (VS610)	J. R. Batt/Southend	
G-AOKO	P.40 Prentice 1 ★	J. F. Coggins/Coventry	
G-AOKZ	P.40 Prentice 1 (VS623) ★	Midland Air Museum	
G-AOLK	P.40 Prentice 1	Hilton Aviation Ltd	
G-AOLU	P.40 Prentice 1 (VS356) ★	Scottish Aircraft Collection/Perth	
G-AORL	D.H.C.1 Chipmunk 22	D. Gardner	
G-AORR	D.H.C.1 Chipmunk 22A	R. E. Turner/Jersey	
G-AORW	D.H.C.1 Chipmunk 22A	D. C. Budd/Netherthorpe	
G-AOSK	D.H.C.1 Chipmunk 22	J. G. Cullen	
G-AOSO	D.H.C.1 Chipmunk 22	D. Blackburn	
G-AOSU	D.H.C.1 Chipmunk 22 (Lycoming)	RAFGSA/Bicester	
G-AOSY	D.H.C.1 Chipmunk 22	J. A. W. Clowes	
G-AOSZ	D.H.C.1 Chipmunk 22A	D. C. Flavell/Shoreham	
G-AOTD	D.H.C.1 Chipmunk 22	Shuttleworth Trust/(*Stored*)	
G-AOTF	D.H.C.1 Chipmunk 23	RAFGSA/Bicester	
G-AOTI	D.H.114 Heron 2D	Topflight Aviation Ltd/Fairoaks	
G-AOTK	D.53 Turbi	The T. K. Flying Group/Hatfield	
G-AOTR	D.H.C.1 Chipmunk 22	London Gliding Club (Pty) Ltd/Dunstable	
G-AOTY	D.H.C.1 Chipmunk 22A	West London Aero Services Ltd/White Waltham	
G-AOUJ	Fairey Ultra-Light ★	British Rotorcraft Museum	
G-AOUO	D.H.C.1 Chipmunk 22 (Lycoming)	RAFGSA/Bicester	
G-AOUP	D.H.C.1 Chipmunk 22	Wessex Flying Group/Hamble	
G-AOVF	B.175 Britannia 312F	(*Stored*)/Southend	
G-AOVT	B.175 Britannia 312F ★	Duxford Aviation Soc	
G-AOVW	Auster 5	B. Marriott	

Notes	Reg.	Type	Owner or Operator
	G-AOXG	D.H.82A Tiger Moth (XL717)	F.A.A. Museum/Yeovilton
	G-AOXN	D.H.82A Tiger Moth	S. L. G. Darch
	G-AOYG	V.806 Viscount	BAF Leasing Ltd/Southend
	G-AOYI	V.806 Viscount	Guernsey Airlines *Island of Guernsey*
	G-AOYJ	V.806 Viscount	BAF Leasing Ltd/Southend
	G-AOYL	V.806 Viscount	BAF Leasing Ltd/Southend
	G-AOYM	V.806 Viscount	BAF Leasing Ltd/Southend
	G-AOYN	V.806 Viscount	British Air Ferries/Southend
	G-AOYO	V.806 Viscount	BAF Leasing Ltd/Southend
	G-AOYP	V.806 Viscount	Jersey Air Ferries *Island of Jersey*
	G-AOYR	V.806 Viscount	BAF Leasing Ltd/Southend
	G-AOYS	V.806 Viscount (Cargo)	BAF Leasing Ltd/Southend
	G-AOZB	D.H.82A Tiger Moth	Structure Flex Ltd/Redhill
	G-AOZH	D.H.82A Tiger Moth (K2572)	V. B. & R. G. Wheele/Shoreham
	G-AOZL	J/5Q Alpine	L. C. Cole
	G-AOZP	D.H.C.1 Chipmunk 22	M. E. Darlington
	G-APAF	Auster 5	Globalpost Ltd/Goodwood
	G-APAH	Auster 5	Executive Flying Services Ltd
	G-APAM	Thruxton Jackaroo	R. P. Williams
	G-APAO	D.H.82A Tiger Moth	C. K. Irvine
	G-APAP	Thruxton Jackaroo	R. A. Slade
	G-APAS	D.H.106 Comet 1XB ★	Aerospace Museum/Cosford
	G-APBD	PA-23 Apache 160	E. A. Clack & T. Pritchard
	G-APBE	Auster 5	G. W. Clark/O. Warden
	G-APBI	D.H.82A Tiger Moth (EM903)	R. Devaney & ptnrs/Audley End
	G-APBO	D.53 Turbi	R. Johnson/Usworth
	G-APBW	Auster 5	J. R. Batt/Southend
	G-APCB	J/5Q Alpine	M. J. Wilson/Biggin Hill
	G-APCC	D.H.82A Tiger Moth	L. J. Rice/Henstridge
	G-APCU	D.H.82A Tiger Moth (N9508)	K. C. K. Virtue/Holland
	G-APCY	J/1N Alpha	J. R. Pearson
	G-APDB	D.H.106 Comet 4 ★	Duxford Aviation Soc
	G-APDT	D.H.106 Comet 4 ★	Fire School/Heathrow
	G-APDV	Hiller UH-12C	S. E. Davidson
	G-APEG	V.953C Merchantman	Air Bridge Carriers Ltd/E. Midlands
	G-APEJ	V.953C Merchantman	Air Bridge Carriers Ltd/E. Midlands
	G-APEK	V.953C Merchantman	Air Bridge Carriers Ltd/E. Midlands
	G-APEP	V.953C Merchantman	Air Bridge Carriers Ltd/E. Midlands
	G-APES	V.953C Merchantman	Air Bridge Carriers Ltd/E. Midlands
	G-APEX	V.806 Viscount	British Air Ferries/Southend
	G-APEY	V.806 Viscount	British Air Ferries/Southend
	G-APFA	D.54 Turbi	A. Eastelow & F. J. Keitch/Dunkeswell
	G-APFG	Boeing 707-436 ★	*Instructional airframe*/Stansted
	G-APFJ	Boeing 707-436 ★	Aerospace Museum/Cosford
	G-APFU	D.H.82A Tiger Moth	M. R. Coward & D. M. White/Bristol
	G-APGL	D.H.82A Tiger Moth (NM140) ★	Strathallan Aircraft Collection
	G-APHV	Avro 19 Srs 2 (VM360) ★	Museum of Flight/E. Fortune
	G-APIE	Tipsy Belfair B	J. J. Penney & ptnrs
	G-APIG	D.H.82A Tiger Moth	Evans Estates Ltd/Shoreham
	G-APIH	D.H.82A Tiger Moth (R5086)	A. J. Detheridge
	G-APIK	J/1N Alpha	T. D. Howe
	G-APIM	V.806 Viscount	BAF Leasing Ltd/Southend
	G-APIY	P.40 Prentice 1 (VR249) ★	Newark Air Museum
	G-APJB	P.40 Prentice 1	City Airways/Coventry
	G-APJJ	Fairey Ultra-light ★	Midland Aircraft Preservation Soc
	G-APJN	Hiller UH-12B	Bristow Helicopters Ltd
	G-APJO	D.H.82A Tiger Moth	D. R. & Mrs M. Wood
	G-APJZ	J/1N Alpha	L. Goddard & E. Amey
	G-APKH	D.H.85 Leopard Moth	P. Franklin (G-ACGS)/White Waltham
	G-APKM	J/1N Alpha	L. J. Barnes/Southend
	G-APKN	J/1N Alpha	Felthorpe Auster Group
	G-APKY	Hiller UH-12B	Sloane Helicopters Ltd
	G-APLG	J/5L Aiglet Trainer	B. Russel/Thruxton
	G-APLK	M-100 Student	Discovery (R&D) Ltd/Glasgow
	G-APLO	D.H.C.1 Chipmunk 22A	Channel Islands Aero Holdings Ltd
	G-APMH	J/1U Workmaster	R. E. Neal & S. R. Stevens
	G-APML	Dakota 6	Air Atlantique Ltd/Jersey
	G-APMM	D.H.82A Tiger Moth	R. K. J. Hadlow
	G-APMP	Hiller UH-12C	Morland Beazley Helicopters Ltd
	G-APMR	Hiller UH-12C	Bristow Helicopters Ltd

Reg.	Type	Owner or Operator	Notes
G-APMS	Hiller UH-12C	Bristow Helicopters Ltd	
G-APMX	D.H.82A Tiger Moth	K. B. Palmer/Headcorn	
G-APMY	PA-23 Apache 160 ★	Kelsterton College (instructional airframe)/Deeside	
G-APNJ	Cessna 310 ★	Chelsea College/Shoreham	
G-APNR	Hiller UH-12C	Bristow Helicopters Ltd	
G-APNS	Garland-Bianchi Linnet	The Tiger Zlin Group	
G-APNT	Currie Wot	L. W. Richardson & ptnrs	
G-APNZ	D.31 Turbulent	Tiger Club Ltd/Redhill	
G-APOA	J/1N Alpha	Bristow Helicopters Ltd	
G-APOD	Tipsy Belfair	A. J. Verlander/Wellesbourne	
G-APOI	Saro Skeeter Srs 8	B. G. Heron/Inverness	
G-APOL	D.36 Turbulent	J. H. Shearer & ptnrs	
G-APPL	P.40 Prentice 1	Miss S. J. Saggers/Biggin Hill	
G-APPM	D.H.C.1 Chipmunk 22	Southern Air/Shoreham	
G-APRF	Auster 5	P. Elliott & ptnrs/Biggin Hill	
G-APRJ	Avro 694 Lincoln B.2 (G-29-I) ★	D. W. Arnold	
G-APRL	AW650 Argosy 101	Air Bridge Carriers Ltd/E. Midlands	
G-APRN	AW650 Argosy 101	Air Bridge Carriers Ltd/E. Midlands	
G-APRO	Auster 6A	A. H. Wheeler	
G-APRR	Super Aero 45	P. J. P. Smyth	
G-APRT	Taylor JT-1 Monoplane	R. J. Moore/Coventry	
G-APRU	M.S.760 Paris	Cranfield Institute of Technology	
G-APSH	Hiller UH-12B	Bristow Helicopters Ltd	
G-APSO	D.H.104 Dove 5	Miss J. D. Baker	
G-APSZ	Cessna 172	M. J. Butler & ptnrs/Manchester	
G-APTH	Agusta-Bell 47J	W. R. Finance Ltd	
G-APTM	Hiller UH-12B	Bristow Helicopters Ltd	
G-APTP	PA-22 Tri-Pacer 150	J. R. Williams/Blackpool	
G-APTR	J/1N Alpha	C. J. & D. J. Baker	
G-APTS	D.H.C.1 Chipmunk 22A	B. R. Pickard/Biggin Hill	
G-APTU	Auster 5	P. Bowers	
G-APTW	W.B.1 Widgeon ★	Cornwall Air Park	
G-APTY	Beech G.35 Bonanza	G. E. Brennand & J. M. Fish/Blackpool	
G-APTZ	D.31 Turbulent	G. Edmiston	
G-APUD	Bensen B.7M (modified) ★	Manchester Air & Space Museum	
G-APUE	L-40 Meta Sokol	P. Phipps	
G-APUK	J/1 Autocrat	P. L. Morley	
G-APUP	Sopwith Pup (N5182) (replica)	RAF Museum	
G-APUR	PA-22 Tri-Pacer 160	G. A. Allen & ptnrs	
G-APUW	Auster J-5V-160	Anglia Auster Syndicate	
G-APUY	D.31 Turbulent	C. Jones & ptnrs/Barton	
G-APUZ	PA-24 Comanche 250	P. N. Martin & ptnrs/Elstree	
G-APVG	J/5L Aiglet Trainer	Cranfield Institute of Technology	
G-APVN	D.31 Turbulent	R. Sherwin/Shoreham	
G-APVS	Cessna 170B	P. E. L. Lamyman	
G-APVU	L-40 Meta-Sokol	D. Kirk	
G-APVV	Mooney M-20A	Telecon Associates/Barton	
G-APVY	PA-25 Pawnee 150	A.D.S (Aerial) Ltd/Southend	
G-APVZ	D.31 Turbulent	A. F. Bullock/Staverton	
G-APWA	HPR-7 Herald 100	BAF Leasing Ltd/Southend	
G-APWE	HPR-7 Herald 201	Air UK (Stored)/Norwich	
G-APWF	HPR-7 Herald 201	Air UK (Stored)/Jersey	
G-APWG	HPR-7 Herald 201	Air UK (Stored)/Jersey	
G-APWJ	HPR-7 Herald 201	Air UK/Norwich	
G-APWR	PA-22 Tri-Pacer 160	Bencray Ltd/Blackpool	
G-APWY	Piaggio P.166 ★	Science Museum/Wroughton	
G-APWZ	EP.9 Prospector	Sussex Agricultural Services/Shoreham	
G-APXJ	PA-24 Comanche 250	Tralnay Ltd/Birmingham	
G-APXR	PA-22 Tri-Pacer 160	D. F. Evans & S. F. Watts/Tollerton	
G-APXT	PA-22 Tri-Pacer 150	K. A. Goodchild/Southend	
G-APXU	PA-22 Tri-Pacer 125	I. V. & K. Fairhurst/Goodwood	
G-APXW	EP.9 Prospector	Sussex Agricultural Services/Shoreham	
G-APXX	D.H.A.3 Drover 2 (VH-FDT) ★	D. W. Arnold/Blackbushe	
G-APXY	Cessna 150	Merlin Flying Club Ltd/Hucknall	
G-APYB	T.66 Nipper 2	B. O. Smith	
G-APYD	D.H.106 Comet 4B ★	Science Museum Store/Wroughton	
G-APYG	D.H.C.1 Chipmunk 22	E. J. I. Musty & P. A. Colman	
G-APYI	PA-22 Tri-Pacer 135	Air Farm Ltd/Thruxton	
G-APYN	PA-22 Tri-Pacer 160	W. D. Stephens	
G-APYT	7FC Tri-Traveller	C. H. Morris & R. W. Brown	

Notes	Reg.	Type	Owner or Operator
	G-APYU	7FC Tri-Traveller	K. Collins
	G-APYW	PA-22 Tri-Pacer 150	B. G. Ell/Ipswich
	G-APYX	PA-23 Aztec 250	Tamavia Ltd/Biggin Hill
	G-APZE	PA-23 Apache 160	J. P. Dodd/Biggin Hill
	G-APZG	PA-24 Comanche 250	Steve Stephens Ltd
	G-APZJ	PA-18 Super Cub 150	Southern Sailplanes
	G-APZK	PA-18 Super Cub 95	W. T. Knapton
	G-APZL	PA-22 Tri-Pacer 160	M. R. & S. A. Coward/Lulsgate
	G-APZS	Cessna 175A	A. J. House
	G-APZU	D.H.104 Dove 6	Acraman Holdings Ltd
	G-APZX	PA-22 Tri-Pacer 150	M. G. Montgomerie & ptnrs
	G-ARAB	Cessna 150	A. H. Nicholas/Elstree
	G-ARAI	PA-22 Tri-Pacer 160	J. E. Fox
	G-ARAJ	PA-22 Tri-Pacer 160	Wearside Flying Group
	G-ARAM	PA-18 Super Cub 150	E. Sussex Gliding Club Ltd
	G-ARAN	PA-18 Super Cub 150	Yorkshire Gliding Club (Pty) Ltd
	G-ARAO	PA-18 Super Cub 95	G. Ashmore & ptnrs/Tollerton
	G-ARAP	7EC Traveller	P. J. Heron
	G-ARAS	7FC Tri-Traveller	A. Bruniges
	G-ARAT	Cessna 180C	R. E. Styles & ptnrs
	G-ARAU	Cessna 150	S. Lynn/Sibson
	G-ARAW	Cessna 182C Skylane	G. Grenall
	G-ARAX	PA-22 Tri-Pacer 150	Megacirc Ltd/Sywell
	G-ARAY	H.S.748 Srs 2	Dan-Air Services Ltd/Gatwick
	G-ARAZ	D.H.82A Tiger Moth (R4959)	M. V. Gauntlett/Goodwood
	G-ARBE	D.H.104 Dove 8	British Aerospace/Brough
	G-ARBG	T.66 Nipper 2	Felthorpe Tipsy Group
	G-ARBL	D.31 Turbulent	C. C. Taylor/Redhill
	G-ARBN	PA.23 Apache 160	H. Norden & H. J. Liggins
	G-ARBO	PA-24 Comanche 250	D. M. Harbottle/Blackpool
	G-ARBP	T.66 Nipper 2	A. Cambridge & D. B. Winstanley
	G-ARBS	PA-22 Tri-Pacer 160	Garb Enterprises/Southend
	G-ARBV	PA-22 Tri-Pacer 150	C. R. Turner
	G-ARBZ	D.31 Turbulent	D. G. H. Hilliard
	G-ARCC	PA-22 Tri-Pacer 150	Fainville Ltd
	G-ARCF	PA-22 Tri-Pacer 150	A. L. Scadding
	G-ARCI	Cessna 310D	Air Atlantique Ltd/Blackpool
	G-ARCL	Cessna 175A	C. E. Sharp Plant Hire and Sales Ltd/ Andrewsfield
	G-ARCS	Auster D6/180	E. A. Matty/Shobdon
	G-ARCT	PA-18 Super Cub 95	M. Kirk
	G-ARCV	Cessna 175A	W. F. H. Gough/Compton Abbas
	G-ARCW	PA-23 Apache 160	E. M. Brain & R. Chew/Wellesbourne
	G-ARCX	AW Meteor 14 ★	Museum of Flight/E. Fortune
	G-ARCZ	D.31 Turbulent	Stapleford Turbulent Group
	G-ARDB	PA-24 Comanche 250	G. K. Hare/Fenland
	G-ARDD	CP.301C1 Emeraude	A. Mackintosh/Shobdon
	G-ARDE	D.H.104 Dove 6	R. J. H. Small/Cranfield
	G-ARDG	EP.9 Prospector	Museum of Army Flying/Middle Wallop
	G-ARDJ	Auster D.6/180	J. D. H. Radford
	G-ARDO	Jodel D.112	P. J. H. McCraig
	G-ARDP	PA-22 Tri-Pacer 150	G. M. Jones
	G-ARDS	PA-22 Caribbean 150	D. V. Asher
	G-ARDT	PA-22 Tri-Pacer 160	A. A. Whiter
	G-ARDV	PA-22 Tri-Pacer 160	Exe International Ltd/Exeter
	G-ARDY	T.66 Nipper 2	R. & J. Thomas
	G-ARDZ	Jodel D.140A	W. R. Dryden
	G-AREA	D.H.104 Dove 8	British Aerospace/Hatfield
	G-AREB	Cessna 175B Skylark	R. J. Postlethwaite & ptnrs/ Wellesbourne
	G-AREE	PA-23 Aztec 250	W. C. C. Meyer/Stapleford
	G-AREF	PA-23 Aztec 250	Express Aviation Services Ltd/ Biggin Hill
	G-AREH	D.H.82A Tiger Moth	T. Pate
	G-AREI	Auster 3 (MT438)	R. Alliker & ptnrs/Bodmin
	G-AREJ	Beech 95 Travel Air	D. Huggett/Stapleford
	G-AREL	PA-22 Caribbean 150	H. H. Cousins/Fenland
	G-AREO	PA-I8 Super Cub 150	Lasham Gliding Soc Ltd
	G-ARET	PA-22 Tri-Pacer 160	P. & V. Slatterey
	G-AREV	PA-22 Tri-Pacer 160	Echo Victor Group/Barton

Reg.	Type	Owner or Operator	Notes
G-AREX	Aeronca 15AC Sedan	R. J. Middleton-Turnbull & P. Lowndes	
G-AREZ	D.31 Turbulent	J. St. Clair-Quentin/Staverton	
G-ARFB	PA-22 Caribbean 150	Borrowash Estates Ltd	
G-ARFD	PA-22 Tri-Pacer 160	C. Fergusson & ptnrs	
G-ARFG	Cessna 175A Skylark	C. S. & Mrs B. A. Frost/Elstree	
G-ARFH	PA-24 Comanche 250	L. M. Walton	
G-ARFL	Cessna 175B Skylark	A. R. Jay & L. G. Rawle	
G-ARFM	Cessna 175B Skylark	Foyle Aviation Ltd	
G-ARFO	Cessna 150A	A. R. Jay & L. G. Rawle	
G-ARFS	PA-22 Caribbean 150	M. H. Armstrong & C. McFadden	
G-ARFT	Jodel D.R. 1050	D. A. Willies/Cranwell	
G-ARFV	T.66 Nipper 2	C. G. Stone/Biggin Hill	
G-ARGB	Auster 6A	A. M. Witt	
G-ARGG	D.H.C.1 Chipmunk 22	Air Navigation&Trading Co Ltd/Blackpool	
G-ARGK	Cessna 210	G. H. K. Rogers	
G-ARGO	PA-22 Colt 108	B. E. Goodman/Liverpool	
G-ARGR	V.708 Viscount	(Stored)/Southend	
G-ARGV	PA-18 Super Cub 150	Deeside Gliding Club (Aberdeenshire) Ltd	
G-ARGY	PA-22 Tri-Pacer 160	D. H. Tanner & I. J. Enoch/Wellesbourne	
G-ARGZ	D.31 Turbulent	M. J. Sanders	
G-ARHB	Forney F-1A Aircoupe	J. T. Mountain	
G-ARHC	Forney F-1A Aircoupe	A. P. Gardner/Elstree	
G-ARHF	Forney F-1A Aircoupe	R. A. Nesbitt-Dufort	
G-ARHI	PA-24 Comanche 180	W. H. Entress/Swansea	
G-ARHL	PA-23 Aztec 250	J. J. Freeman & Co Ltd/Headcorn	
G-ARHM	Auster 6A	D. Hollowell & ptnrs	
G-ARHN	PA-22 Caribbean 150	P. H. Pickford/Henstridge	
G-ARHP	PA-22 Tri-Pacer 160	W. Wardle	
G-ARHR	PA-22 Caribbean 150	J. A. Hargraves/Fairoaks	
G-ARHT	PA-22 Caribbean 150	J. S. Lewery/Bournemouth	
G-ARHU	PA-22 Tri-Pacer 160	G. W. Worley/Fenland	
G-ARHW	D.H.104 Dove 8	British Aerospace/Woodford	
G-ARHZ	D.62 Condor	D. H. Wilson-Spratt	
G-ARIA	Bell 47G	Decca Navigator Co Ltd/Biggin Hill	
G-ARID	Cessna 172B	N. Law	
G-ARIE	PA-24 Comanche 250	W. Radwanski/Booker	
G-ARIF	O-H7 Minor Coupe	A. W. J. G. Ord-Hume	
G-ARIH	Auster 6A	B. D. Husband	
G-ARIK	PA-22 Caribbean 150	C. J. Berry	
G-ARIL	PA-22 Caribbean 150	G. N. Richardson Motors/Shoreham	
G-ARIN	PA-24 Comanche 250	Fisher Douglas Aviation Ltd/Elstree	
G-ARIR	V.708 Viscount	(Stored)/Aberdeen	
G-ARIU	Cessna 172B Skylark	P. A. Howell	
G-ARIV	Cessna 172B	J. A. Hood/Blackpool	
G-ARIW	CP.301B Emeraude	CJM Flying Group/Wellesbourne	
G-ARJE	PA-22 Colt 108	G. W. Doran	
G-ARJF	PA-22 Colt 108	R. A. Coombe	
G-ARJG	PA-22 Colt l08	Sqn Ldr G. R. Sharp	
G-ARJH	PA-22 Colt 108	A. Walmsley	
G-ARJR	PA-23 Apache 160	Instructional airframe/Kidlington	
G-ARJS	PA-23 Apache 160	Bencray Ltd/Blackpool	
G-ARJT	PA-23 Apache 160	R. D. Dickson	
G-ARJU	PA-23 Apache 160	Chantaco Ltd/Fairoaks	
G-ARJV	PA-23 Apache 160	Gordon King (Aviation) Ltd/Biggin Hill	
G-ARJW	PA-23 Apache 160	Gordon King (Aviation) Ltd/Biggin Hill	
G-ARJZ	D.31 Turbulent	N. H. Jones	
G-ARKG	J/5G Autocar	C. Thompson	
G-ARKJ	Beech N35 Bonanza	R. J. Guise/Blackpool	
G-ARKK	PA-22 Colt 108	A. W. Baxter/Tollerton	
G-ARKM	PA-22 Colt 108	L. E. Usher	
G-ARKN	PA-22 Colt 108	J. H. Underwood & A. J. F. Tabenor	
G-ARKP	PA-22 Colt 108	C. J. & J. Freeman/Headcorn	
G-ARKR	PA-22 Colt 108	H. L. Crawley/Staverton	
G-ARKS	PA-22 Colt 108	D. W. Mickleburgh/Leicester	
G-ARLB	PA-24 Comanche 250	Marine Acoustics/Blackbushe	
G-ARLD	H-395 Super Courier	P. H. Hall	
G-ARLG	Auster D.4/108	R. D. Hilliar-Symons	
G-ARLI	PA-23 Apache 150	(Stored)/Cowes	
G-ARLK	PA-24 Comanche 250	M. Walker & C. Robinson	
G-ARLL	PA-24 Comanche 250	E. J. Spiers/Coventry	

Notes	Reg.	Type	Owner or Operator
	G-ARLP	A.61 Terrier	J. M. Jones
	G-ARLR	A.61 Terrier	G. Griffith
	G-ARLT	Cessna 172B Skyhawk	A. R. German & Sons
	G-ARLU	Cessna 172B Skyhawk	*Instructional airframe*/Irish AC
	G-ARLV	Cessna 172B Skyhawk	A. C. Chaffey
	G-ARLW	Cessna 172B Skyhawk	S. Lancashire Flyers Ltd
	G-ARLX	Jodel D.140B	Meridian Drilling Co Ltd/Biggin Hill
	G-ARLY	J/5P Autocar	P. J. Elliott & G. Green/Leicester
	G-ARLZ	D.31A Turbulent	R. W. Rushton
	G-ARMA	PA-23 Apache 160	Oxford Air Training School Ltd/ Kidlington
	G-ARMB	D.H.C.1 Chipmunk 22A	College of Air Training/Hamble
	G-ARMC	D.H.C.1 Chipmunk 22A	W. London Aero Services Ltd
	G-ARMG	D.H.C.1 Chipmunk 22A	College of Air Training/Hamble
	G-ARMI	PA-23 Apache 160	Stapleford Flying Club Ltd
	G-ARMJ	Cessna 185 Skywagon	J. E. Tribe & ptnrs
	G-ARML	Cessna 175B Skylark	Woolmer Aircraft Ltd
	G-ARMN	Cessna 175B Skylark ★	Southall College of Technology
	G-ARMO	Cessna 172B Skyhawk	Sangria Designs Ltd & BRM Plastics Ltd/Booker
	G-ARMP	Cessna 172B	Southport & Merseyside Aero Club (1979) Ltd
	G-ARMR	Cessna 172B Skyhawk	J. Braithwaite/Kidlington
	G-ARMW	H.S.748 Srs 1	Dan-Air Services Ltd/Gatwick
	G-ARMZ	D.31 Turbulent	Frederick A. Shepherd
	G-ARNA	Mooney M.20B	R. Travers/Blackpool
	G-ARNB	J/5G Autocar	M. T. Jeffrey
	G-ARND	PA-22 Colt 108	Richard Rimington Ltd
	G-ARNE	PA-22 Colt 108	T. D. L. Bowden/Shipdham
	G-ARNI	PA-22 Colt 108	T. Rundle/Bodmin
	G-ARNJ	PA-22 Colt 108	MKM Flying Group/Leavesden
	G-ARNK	PA-22 Colt 108	D. P. Golding
	G-ARNL	PA-22 Colt 108	J. A. & J. A. Dodsworth/White Waltham
	G-ARNN	GC-1B Swift	K. E. Sword
	G-ARNO	A.61 Terrier	M. B. Hill
	G-ARNP	A.109 Airedale	D. W. Peckham/Shoreham
	G-ARNY	Jodel D.117	Inverness Flying Services Ltd
	G-ARNZ	D.31 Turbulent	P. L. Cox & ptnrs
	G-AROA	Cessna 172B Skyhawk	D. E. Partridge/Andrewsfield
	G-AROD	Cessna 175B	Medical Co Hospital Supplies Ltd
	G-AROE	Aero 145	G. S. & Mrs P. Galt/White Waltham
	G-AROF	L.40 Meta-Sokol	B. G. Barber/Stapleford
	G-AROJ	A.109 Airedale	D. J. Shaw
	G-AROK	Cessna 310F	S. E. Berry/Blackbushe
	G-ARON	PA-22 Colt 108	R. W. Curtis
	G-AROO	Forney F-1A Aircoupe	W. I. McMeekan
	G-AROR	Forney F-1A Aircoupe	Treswithick Air & Shipping Services Ltd
	G-AROW	Jodel D.140B	Kent Gliding Club Ltd
	G-AROY	Stearman A.75N.1	W. A. Jordan
	G-ARPD	H.S.121 Trident 1C ★	CAA Fire School, Tees-side
	G-ARPH	H.S.121 Trident 1C ★	Aerospace Museum, Cosford
	G-ARPK	H.S.121 Trident 1C ★	Manchester Airport Authority
	G-ARPL	H.S.121 Trident 1C ★	British Airports Authority/Edinburgh
	G-ARPN	H.S.121 Trident 1C ★	British Airports Authority/Aberdeen
	G-ARPO	H.S.121 Trident 1C ★	*Withdrawn*/Heathrow
	G-ARPP	H.S.121 Trident 1C ★	British Airports Authority/Glasgow
	G-ARPR	H.S.121 Trident 1C ★	CAA Fire School/Tees-side
	G-ARPW	H.S.121 Trident 1C ★	CAA Fire School/Tees-side
	G-ARPX	H.S.121 Trident 1C ★	Airwork Services Ltd/Perth
	G-ARPZ	H.S.121 Trident 1C ★	RFD Ltd/Dunsfold
	G-ARRD	Jodel DR.1050	N. L. E. Dupee/Dunkeswell
	G-ARRE	Jodel DR.1050	E. H. Ellis/Sherburn
	G-ARRF	Cessna 150A	Cornwall Flying Club/Bodmin
	G-ARRI	Cessna 175B Skylark	C. L. Thomas
	G-ARRL	J/1N Alpha	A. J. Brown
	G-ARRM	Beagle B.206-X ★	Brighton Transport Museum
	G-ARRP	PA.28 Cherokee 160	M. J. Flynn/Cardiff
	G-ARRS	CP-301A Emeraude	J. Y. Paxton/Sibson
	G-ARRT	Wallis WA-116-1	K. H. Wallis
	G-ARRU	D.31 Turbulent	J. R. Edwards & D. D. Smith
	G-ARRW	H.S.748 Srs 1	Dan-Air Services Ltd/Gatwick

Reg.	Type	Owner or Operator	Notes
G-ARRY	Jodel D.140B	R. G. Andrews/Southend	
G-ARRZ	D.31 Turbulent	C. C. Chandler/Redhill	
G-ARSB	Cessna 150A	B. T. White/Andrewsfield	
G-ARSG	Avro Triplane (replica)	Shuttleworth Trust/O. Warden	
G-ARSJ	CP.301-C2 Emeraude	J. R. Ware	
G-ARSL	A.61 Terrier	R. H. Perraton/Biggin Hill	
G-ARSP	L.40 Meta-Sokol	Classic Aerodrome Ltd/Staverton	
G-ARSU	PA-22 Colt 108	P. E. Palmer	
G-ARSW	PA-22 Colt 108	J. P. Smith/Shipdham	
G-ARSX	PA-22 Tri-Pacer 160	AF Aviation Ltd/Stansted	
G-ARTB	Mooney M.20B	R. E. Dagless/Shipdham	
G-ARTD	PA-23 Apache 160	Dr. D. A. Jones	
G-ARTF	D.31 Turbulent	J. R. D. Bygraves/O. Warden	
G-ARTG	Hiller UH-12C ★	Whitehorse Inn/Stockbridge	
G-ARTH	PA-12 Super Cruiser	R. Hornby	
G-ARTJ	Bensen B.8 ★	Museum of Flight/E. Fortune	
G-ARTL	D.H.82A Tiger Moth (T7281)	P. A. Jackson	
G-ARTT	M.S.880B Rallye Club	J. Berry	
G-ARUE	D.H.104 Dove 7	Staravia Ltd/Exeter	
G-ARUG	J/5G Autocar	N. P. Biggs	
G-ARUH	Jodel DR.1050	PFA Group/Denham	
G-ARUI	A.61 Terrier	D. C. Cullen	
G-ARUL	Cosmic Wind	J. Cull/Halfpenny Green	
G-ARUM	D.H.104 Dove 8	National Coal Board	
G-ARUO	PA-24 Comanche 180	Uniform Oscar Group/Elstree	
G-ARUR	PA-28 Cherokee 160	Falconash Ltd/Redhill	
G-ARUV	CP.301A Emeraude	J. Tanswell	
G-ARUY	J/1N Alpha	A. J. Brown	
G-ARUZ	Cessna 175C Skylark	J. E. Sansome & M. D. Faiers/Luton	
G-ARVF	V.1101 VC10 ★	Hermeskeil Museum (nr Trier)/ W. Germany	
G-ARVM	V.1101 VC10 ★	Aerospace Museum/Cosford	
G-ARVO	PA-18 Super Cub 95	R. H. Reeves/Barton	
G-ARVS	PA-28 Cherokee 160	Stapleford Flying Club Ltd	
G-ARVT	PA-28 Cherokee 160	C. R. Knapton	
G-ARVU	PA-28 Cherokee 160	M. S. Nazer	
G-ARVV	PA-28 Cherokee 160	R. J. Jackson/Sibson	
G-ARVW	PA-28 Cherokee 160	Bolton Air Training School Ltd/ Blackpool	
G-ARVZ	D62B Condor	T. B. McColl	
G-ARWB	D.H.C.1 Chipmunk 200	Aero-Bonner Co Ltd/Shoreham	
G-ARWC	Cessna 150B	Worldwide Wheels Ltd/Exeter	
G-ARWH	Cessna 172C Skyhawk	P. E. Nunn	
G-ARWM	Cessna 175C	Agricopters Ltd/Thruxton	
G-ARWO	Cessna 172C Skyhawk	T. A. Cox & R. C. Jackman/Bodmin	
G-ARWR	Cessna 172C Skyhawk	Cormack (Aircraft Services) Ltd/Glasgow	
G-ARWS	Cessna 175C Skylark	J. Mudd/Bodmin	
G-ARWW	Bensen B.8M	B. McIntyre	
G-ARWX	Luton LA-5A Major	A. G. Cameron	
G-ARWY	Mooney M.20A	B. P. Irish/Bodmin	
G-ARXD	A.109 Airedale	D. Howden	
G-ARXF	PA-23 Aztec 250B	Weendy Aviation (UK)	
G-ARXG	PA-24 Comanche 250	B. R. Grant & T. W. G. Frodsham/ Blackpool	
G-ARXH	Bell 47G	A.C.C. Builders & Capricorn Studios Ltd/Shoreham	
G-ARXN	Tipsy Nipper 2	Griffon Flying Group	
G-ARXP	Luton LA-4A Minor	W. C. Hymas/Stapleford	
G-ARXT	Jodel DR.1050	G. D. Bowd	
G-ARXU	Auster 6A	Bath & Wilts Gliding Club Ltd	
G-ARXW	M.S.885 Super Rallye	M. A. Jones	
G-ARXX	M.S.880B Rallye Club	M. S. Bird	
G-ARXY	M.S.880B Rallye Club	Horizon Flying Group	
G-ARYB	H.S.125 Srs 1 ★	British Aerospace PLC/Hatfield	
G-ARYC	H.S.125 Srs 1 ★	The Mosquito Aircraft Museum	
G-ARYD	Auster AOP.6 (WJ358)	Museum of Army Flying/Middle Wallop	
G-ARYF	PA.23 Aztec 250	I. J. T. Branson	
G-ARYH	PA-22 Tri-Pacer 160	Filtration (Water Treatment Engineers) Ltd/Blackpool	
G-ARYI	Cessna 172C	J. T. Parkins/Halfpenny Green	
G-ARYK	Cessna 172C	Mrs K. M. & T. Hemsley	

Notes	Reg.	Type	Owner or Operator
	G-ARYR	PA-28 Cherokee 180	Glenochill Engineering
	G-ARYS	Cessna 172C Skyhawk	K. J. Squires/Coventry
	G-ARYV	PA-24 Comanche 250	P. Meeson
	G-ARYZ	A.109 Airedale	J. D. Reid
	G-ARZA	Wallis WA.116 Srs 1	N. D. Z. de Ferranti/Leicester
	G-ARZB	Wallis WA.116 Srs 1	K. H. Wallis
	G-ARZF	Cessna 150B	M. M. James/Leicester
	G-ARZM	D.31 Turbulent	N. H. Jones/Redhill
	G-ARZN	Beech N35 Bonanza	Beech Aircraft Ltd/Elstree
	G-ARZP	A.109 Airedale	G. B. O'Neill/Biggin Hill
	G-ARZW	Currie Wot	D. F. Faulkner-Bryant/Redhill
	G-ARZX	Cessna 150B	E. T. Wicks
	G-ASAA	Luton LA-4A Minor	Four Counties Flying Syndicate
	G-ASAI	A.109 Airedale	A. C. Watt
	G-ASAJ	A.61 Terrier 2 (WE569)	R. Skingley
	G-ASAK	A.61 Terrier 2	Rochford Hundred Flying Group/Southend
	G-ASAL	SAL Bulldog 120	British Aerospace/Prestwick
	G-ASAM	D.31 Turbulent	Tiger Club Ltd/Redhill
	G-ASAN	A.61 Terrier 2	Truman Aviation Ltd/Tollerton
	G-ASAT	M.S.880B Rallye Club	M. S. McKean/(*Stored*)
	G-ASAU	M.S.880B Rallye Club	W. J. Armstrong
	G-ASAV	M.S.880B Rallye Club	McAully Flying Group/Little Snoring
	G-ASAX	A.61 Terrier 2	G. Strathdee
	G-ASAZ	Hiller UH-12 E4	Morland Beazley Helicopters Ltd
	G-ASBA	Currie Wot	M. A. Kaye
	G-ASBB	Beech 23 Musketeer	D. Silver/Southend
	G-ASBH	A.109 Airedale	Pyrochem (UK) Ltd
	G-ASBS	C.P.301A Emeraude	D. M. Upfield
	G-ASBU	A.61 Terrier 2	G. Strathdee
	G-ASBY	A.109 Airedale	A. Farrell
	G-ASCC	Beagle E.3 AOP Mk 11	M. D. N. & A. C. Fisher/Sibson
	G-ASCH	A.61 Terrier 2	Enstone Eagles Flying Group
	G-ASCJ	PA-24 Comanche 250	Telspec Ltd/Rochester
	G-ASCU	PA-18A-150 Super Cub	Farm Aviation Services Ltd
	G-ASCZ	CP.310A Emeraude	Hylton Flying Group/Usworth
	G-ASDA	Beech 65-80 Queen Air	Parker & Heard Ltd/Biggin Hill
	G-ASDL	A.61 Terrier 2	T. J. Rilley & C. E. Mason
	G-ASDY	Wallis WA-116/F	K. H. Wallis
	G-ASEA	Luton LA-4A Minor	A. Dunn/Shoreham
	G-ASEB	Luton LA-4A Minor	R. K. Lynn
	G-ASEE	J/IN Alpha	H. C. J. & Sara L. G. Williams
	G-ASEG	A.61 Terrier	J. T. Hogben/Liverpool
	G-ASEO	PA-24 Comanche 250	A. van Daalen
	G-ASEP	PA-23 Apache 235	G. R. Selbert
	G-ASEU	D.62A Condor	W. Grant & D. McNicholl
	G-ASEV	PA-23 Aztec 250	Selexpress Ltd
	G-ASFA	Cessna 172D	R. A. Marven
	G-ASFD	L-200A Morava	N. Price/Goodwood
	G-ASFK	J/5G Autocar	Orman (Carrolls Farm) Ltd
	G-ASFL	PA-28 Cherokee 180	K. Winfield & ptnrs/E. Midlands
	G-ASFX	D.31 Turbulent	E. F. Clapham & W. B. S. Dobie
	G-ASGC	V.1151 Super VC10 ★	Imperial War Museum/Duxford
	G-ASHA	Cessna F.172D	R. L. Fogg & Co Ltd & R. Soar
	G-ASHB	Cessna 182F	RN & R Marines Sport Parachute Association/Dunkeswell
	G-ASHH	PA-23 Aztec 250	G. Everington/Coventry
	G-ASHJ	Brantly B.2B	A. G. Dean
	G-ASHR	Beech B35-33 Debonair	C. M. Fraser & E. A. Perry/Blackpool
	G-ASHS	Stampe SV.4B	Tiger Club Ltd/Redhill
	G-ASHT	D.31 Turbulent	B. Houghton/Barton
	G-ASHU	PA-15 Vagabond	G. J. Romanes
	G-ASHV	PA-E23 Aztec 250	Haywards Aviation Ltd/Shoreham
	G-ASHW	D.H.104 Dove 8	L. de la Hay (Fishing & Marine) Salvage Ltd
	G-ASHX	PA-28 Cherokee 180	D. Morris
	G-ASIB	Cessna F.172D	K. D. Horton/Staverton
	G-ASII	PA-28 Cherokee 180	Worldwide Wheels Ltd & ptnrs/Lulsgate
	G-ASIJ	PA-28 Cherokee 180	M. Timmins
	G-ASIL	PA-28 Cherokee 180	F. W. Shaw & Sons (Worthing) Ltd/Shoreham

Reg.	Type	Owner or Operator	Notes
G-ASIS	Jodel D.112 Club	E. F. Hazell	
G-ASIT	Cessna 180	A. & P. A. Wood	
G-ASIY	PA-25 Pawnee 235	A.D.S (Aerial) Ltd/Southend	
G-ASJL	Beech H.35 Bonanza	P. M. Coulton	
G-ASJM	PA-30 Twin Comanche 160	Air & General Services Ltd/Biggin Hill	
G-ASJO	Beech B.23 Musketeer	A. H. Hunt & K. Parker/St. Just	
G-ASJU	Aero Commander 520	Interflight Ltd/Biggin Hill	
G-ASJV	V.S.361 Spitfire IX (MH434)	Nalfire Aviation Ltd/Booker	
G-ASJY	GY-80 Horizon 160	A. D. Hemley	
G-ASJZ	Jodel D.117A	Wolverhampton Ultra-light Flying Group	
G-ASKC	D.H.98 Mosquito 35 (TA719) ★	Skyfame Collection/Duxford	
G-ASKH	D.H.98 Mosquito T.3 (RR299)	British Aerospace/Chester	
G-ASKJ	A.61 Terrier 1	Norman Flying Group/Redhill	
G-ASKK	HPR-7 Herald 211	Air UK/Norwich	
G-ASKL	Jodel D.150A	J. M. Graty	
G-ASKM	Beech B.65-80 Queen Air	H. Williams & ptnrs	
G-ASKP	D.H.82A Tiger Moth	Tiger Club Ltd/Redhill	
G-ASKS	Cessna 336 Skymaster	M. J. Godwin	
G-ASKT	PA-28 Cherokee 180	Capel & Co (Printers) Ltd/Biggin Hill	
G-ASKV	PA-25 Pawnee 235	Southdown Gliding Club Ltd	
G-ASLA	PA-25 Pawnee 235	R. A. Bell	
G-ASLE	PA-30 Twin Comanche 160	Hampshire PVC Ltd/Bournemouth	
G-ASLF	Bensen B.7	S. R. Hughes	
G-ASLH	Cessna 182F	Celahurst Ltd/Southend	
G-ASLK	PA-25 Pawnee 235	Skegness Air Taxi Services Ltd/ Ingoldmells	
G-ASLN	Forney F.1A Aircoupe	Cornwall Flying Club/Bodmin	
G-ASLR	Agusta-Bell 47J-2	D. Jack	
G-ASLV	PA-28 Cherokee 235	C.S.E. (Aircraft Services) Ltd/Kidlington	
G-ASLX	CP.301A Emeraude	K. C. Green/Panshanger	
G-ASMA	PA-30 Twin Comanche 160	M. G. Edmunds/Biggin Hill	
G-ASMC	P.56 Provost T.1.	W. Walker	
G-ASME	Bensen B.8M	C. R. Pepper & A. J. Tabenor	
G-ASMF	Beech D.95A Travel Air	Hawk Aviation Ltd	
G-ASMG	D.H.104 Dove 8	British Aerospace/Dunsfold	
G-ASMJ	Cessna F.172E	J. B. Stocks & J. E. Tribe	
G-ASML	Luton LA-4A Minor	R. L. E. Horrell	
G-ASMM	D.31 Tubulent	Kenneth Browne	
G-ASMN	PA-23 Apache 160	W. London Aero Services Ltd/ White Waltham	
G-ASMO	PA-23 Apache 160	Aviation Enterprises/Fairoaks	
G-ASMS	Cessna 150A	K. R. & T. W. Davies	
G-ASMT	Fairtravel Linnet 2	R. D. Combes/Panshanger	
G-ASMU	Cessna 150D	Stapleford Flying Club Ltd	
G-ASMV	CP1310-C3 Super Emeraude	P. F. D. Waltham/Leicester	
G-ASMW	Cessna 150D	Yorkshire Light Aircraft Ltd/Leeds	
G-ASMY	PA-23 Apache 160	Thurston Aviation Ltd/Stansted	
G-ASMZ	A.61 Terrier 2	R. B. Humphries	
G-ASNA	PA-23 Aztec 250	Margate Motors Plant & Aircraft Hire Ltd/ Headcorn	
G-ASNB	Auster 6A	M. Pocock & ptnrs	
G-ASNC	Beagle D.5/180 Husky	Peterborough & Spalding Gliding Club/ Crowland	
G-ASND	PA-23 Aztec 250	Commercial Air (Woking) Ltd/ Fairoaks	
G-ASNE	PA-28 Cherokee 180	J. L. Dexter	
G-ASNF	Ercoupe 415-CD	Charles Robertson (Developments) Ltd	
G-ASNH	PA-23 Aztec 250	Derek Crouch (Contractors) Ltd	
G-ASNI	CP1310-C3 Super Emeraude	D. Chapman	
G-ASNK	Cessna 205	Transgap Ltd/Ringway	
G-ASNN	Cessna 182F Skylane	I. A. Louttit	
G-ASNP	Mooney M.20C Mark 21	W. Woodrum/Aberdeen	
G-ASNU	H.S.125 Srs. 1	Flintgrange Ltd	
G-ASNW	Cessna F.172E	S. J. A. Brown	
G-ASNY	Bensen B.8M	D. L. Wallis	
G-ASNZ	Bensen B.7M	W. H. Turner	
G-ASOB	PA-30 Twin Comanche 160	M. A. Grayburn/Southend	
G-ASOC	Auster 6A	Aquila Gliding Club	
G-ASOH	Beech B.55A Baron	Steer Aviation Ltd/Biggin Hill	
G-ASOI	A.61 Terrier 2	R. H. Jowett	
G-ASOK	Cessna F.172E	Okay Flying Group/Denham	

Notes	Reg.	Type	Owner or Operator
	G-ASON	PA-30 Twin Comanche 160	Roundham Garage Ltd/Bournemouth
	G-ASOO	PA-30 Twin Comanche 160	Glos-Air (Sales) Ltd/Bournemouth
	G-ASOV	PA-25 Pawnee 235	Welcross Aviation/Slinfold
	G-ASOX	Cessna 205A	Halfpenny Green Skydiving Club
	G-ASPF	Jodel D.120	W. S. Howell
	G-ASPI	Cessna F.172E	A. M. Castleton & ptnrs
	G-ASPK	PA-28 Cherokee 140	W. G. Glanville
	G-ASPP	Bristol Boxkite	Shuttleworth Trust/O. Warden
	G-ASPS	Piper J-3C-65 Cub	A. J. Chalkley
	G-ASPU	D.31 Turbulent	I. Maclennen/Redhill
	G-ASPV	D.H.82A Tiger Moth	B. S. Charters/Shipham
	G-ASPX	Bensen B-8S	L. D. Goldsmith/St Athan
	G-ASRB	D.62B Condor	Tiger Club Ltd (Stored)
	G-ASRC	D.62B Condor	Tiger Club Ltd/Husbands Bosworth
	G-ASRF	Jenny Wren	G. W. Gowland
	G-ASRH	PA-30 Twin Comanche 160	IOM & General Life Assurance Co Ltd & Bigland Holdings Ltd/Biggin Hill
	G-ASRI	PA-23 Aztec 250	Meridian Airmaps Ltd/Shoreham
	G-ASRO	PA-30 Twin Comanche 160	A. G. Perkins/Halfpenny Green
	G-ASRP	Jodel DR.1050	D. J. M. Edmondston
	G-ASRR	Cessna 182G	John V. White Ltd/Southend
	G-ASRT	Jodel D.150	H. M. Kendall
	G-ASRW	PA-28 Cherokee 180	K. R. Deering/Fairoaks
	G-ASRX	Beech 65 A80 Queen Air	Seismograph Service (England) Ltd & Parker & Heard Ltd/Biggin Hill
	G-ASSB	PA-30 Twin Comanche 160	E. Berks Boat Co Ltd/Booker
	G-ASSE	PA-22 Colt 108	J. B. King/Fairoaks
	G-ASSF	Cessna 182G Skylane	A. Newsham/Manchester
	G-ASSO	Cessna 150D	N. E. Sams/Cranfield
	G-ASSP	PA-30 Twin Comanche 160	The Mastermix Engineering Co Ltd/ Coventry
	G-ASSR	PA-30 Twin Comanche 160	Direct Air Ltd/Leavesden
	G-ASSS	Cessna 172E	D. H. N. Squires/Bristol
	G-ASST	Cessna 150D	F. R. H. Parker
	G-ASSU	CP.301A Emeraude	R. W. Millward/Redhill
	G-ASSW	PA-28 Cherokee 140	C. J. Plummer/Bembridge
	G-ASSY	D.31 Turbulent	G-ASSY Group/Redhill
	G-ASTA	D.31 Turbulent	D. J. R. Williams/Rochester
	G-ASTD	PA-23 Aztec 250	Peregrine Air Services Ltd/Inverness
	G-ASTG	Nord 1002	L. M. Walton
	G-ASTI	Auster 6A	M. Pocock
	G-ASTL	Fairey Firefly 1 (Z2033) ★	Skyfame Collection/Duxford
	G-ASTM	Hiller UH-12B	Bristow Helicopters Ltd
	G-ASTP	Hiller UH-12C	L. Goddard
	G-ASTR	Hiller UH-12B	Bristow Helicopters Ltd
	G-ASUB	Mooney M.20E Super 21	T. J. Pigott/Doncaster
	G-ASUD	PA-28 Cherokee 180	H. J. W. Ellison/Biggin Hill
	G-ASUE	Cessna 150D	D. Huckle/Panshanger
	G-ASUG	Beech E18S ★	Museum of Flight/E. Fortune
	G-ASUH	Cessna F.172E	G. H. Willson & E. Shipley/Felthorpe
	G-ASUI	A.61 Terrier 2	Dreiblaser Aviation Ltd
	G-ASUL	Cessna 182G Skylane	Halfpenny Green Parachute Centre Ltd
	G-ASUP	Cessna F.172E	W. T. Jenkins & M. Giles/Cardiff
	G-ASUR	Dornier Do 28A-1	Sheffair Ltd/Tollerton
	G-ASUS	Jurca MJ.2B Tempete	D. G. Jones/Coventry
	G-ASVG	CP.301B Emeraude	K. R. Jackson
	G-ASVH	Hiller UH-12B	P. W. Hicks
	G-ASVI	Hiller UH-12B	Bristow Helicopters Ltd
	G-ASVK	Hiller UH-12B	Bristow Helicopters Ltd
	G-ASVL	Hiller UH-12B	Bristow Helicopters Ltd
	G-ASVM	Cessna F.172E	J. White
	G-ASVN	Cessna U.206 Super Skywagon	British Skysports
	G-ASVO	HPR-7 Herald 214	British Air Ferries/Southend
	G-ASVP	PA-25 Pawnee 235	Welcross Aviation/Slinfold
	G-ASVZ	PA-28 Cherokee 140	J. Yourell/Luton
	G-ASWB	A.109 Airedale	Gainsborough Cars/Barton
	G-ASWF	A.109 Airedale	D. W. Wastell/Goodwood
	G-ASWG	PA-25 Pawnee 235	A.D.S. (Aerial) Ltd/Southend
	G-ASWH	Luton LA-5A Major	D. G. J. Chisholm
	G-ASWJ	Beagle 206 Srs 1 (8449M) ★	RAF Halton
	G-ASWL	Cessna F.172F	C. Wilson

Reg.	Type	Owner or Operator	Notes
G-ASWN	Bensen B.8M	D. R. Shepherd	
G-ASWP	Beech A.23 Musketeer	Tenair Ltd/Manchester	
G-ASWT	Aero 145 Series 20	A. C. Frost/Shoreham	
G-ASWW	PA-30 Twin Comanche 160	Bristol & Wessex Flying Club Ltd/Bristol	
G-ASWX	PA-28 Cherokee 180	H. I. Jones (Whitby Garage) Ltd	
G-ASXB	D.H.82A Tiger Moth	G. W. Bisshopp	
G-ASXC	SIPA 901	Waterside Flying Group	
G-ASXD	Brantley B2B	Brantley Enterprises	
G-ASXF	Brantley 305	Express Aviation Services Ltd/Biggin Hill	
G-ASXI	T.66 Nipper 2	D. Shrimpton	
G-ASXJ	Luton LA-4A Minor	P. D. Lee & E. A. Lingard	
G-ASXR	Cessna 210	Aberdeen Aviation Ltd	
G-ASXS	Jodel D.1050	C. J. J. Blyth	
G-ASXU	Jodel D.120A	R. W. & Mrs J. Thompsett/Fenland	
G-ASXX	Avro 683 Lancaster 7 (NX611) ★	RAF Scampton Gate Guard	
G-ASXY	Jodel D.117A	P. A. Davies & ptnrs/Cardiff	
G-ASXZ	Cessna 182G Skylane	P. M. Robertson/Perth	
G-ASYD	BAC One-Eleven 670	British Aerospace/Bournemouth	
G-ASYJ	Beech D.95A Travel Air	Crosby Aviation Ltd/Manchester	
G-ASYK	PA-30 Twin Comanche 160	G. C. Masterton	
G-ASYL	Cessna 150E	British Skysports	
G-ASYP	Cessna 150E	T. S. Quirk/Stapleford	
G-ASYV	Cessna 310G	R. E. Priestley & R. Jennings/Coventry	
G-ASYW	Bell 47G-2	Bristow Helicopters Ltd	
G-ASYZ	Victa Airtourer 100	R. Fletcher	
G-ASZB	Cessna 150E	H. J. Cox/Finmere	
G-ASZD	Bo 208A2 Junior	D. R. Elphick/O. Warden	
G-ASZE	A.61 Terrier 2	P. J. Moore	
G-ASZJ	S.C.7 Skyvan 3A-100	Short Bros Ltd/Sydenham	
G-ASZR	Fairtravel Linnet	H. C. D. & F. J. Garner/Shoreham	
G-ASZS	GY.80 Horizon 160	T. B. W. Jeremiah & ptnrs/Stapleford	
G-ASZU	Cessna 150E	D. C. Boyde	
G-ASZV	T.66 Nipper 2	R. L. Mitcham	
G-ASZX	A.61 Terrier	W. D. Hill/Fenland	
G-ATAA	PA-28 Cherokee 180	Brendair/Elstree	
G-ATAD	Mooney M.20C	H. W. Walker	
G-ATAF	Cesna F.172F	G. Bush	
G-ATAG	Jodel DR. 1050	T. J. N. H. Palmer & G. W. Oliver	
G-ATAH	Cessna 336 Skymaster	Alderney Air Charter/Bournemouth	
G-ATAI	D.H.104 Dove 8	Centrax Ltd	
G-ATAS	PA-28 Cherokee 180	D. R. Wood/Biggin Hill	
G-ATAT	Cessna 150E	The Derek Pointon Group/Coventry	
G-ATAU	D.62B Condor	M. A. Pearce/Redhill	
G-ATAV	D.62C Condor	The Condor Syndicate	
G-ATAW	A.109 Airedale	Jean Dalton	
G-ATBF	F-86E Sabre 4 (XB733) ★	Historic Aircraft Preservation Soc	
G-ATBG	Nord 1002	L. M. Walton	
G-ATBH	Aero 145	Colpak Aviation Ltd/Elstree	
G-ATBI	Beech A.23 Musketeer	R. F. G. Dent/Staverton	
G-ATBJ	Sikorsky S-61N	British Airways Helicopters Ltd/Aberdeen	
G-ATBK	Cessna F.172F	R. N. R. Bellamy/St Just	
G-ATBL	D.H.60G Moth	M. E. Vaisey	
G-ATBN	PA-28 Cherokee 140	M. R. McGregor/Stapleford	
G-ATBP	Fournier RF-3	C. Jacques & ptnrs	
G-ATBS	D.31 Turbulent	R. N. Crosland	
G-ATBU	A.61 Terrier 2	P. R. Anderson	
G-ATBW	T.66 Nipper 2	P. J. Dockerill	
G-ATBX	PA-20 Pacer 135	M. R. Smith/Staverton	
G-ATBZ	W.S-58 Wessex 60	Bristow Helicopters Ltd	
G-ATCC	A.109 Airedale	F. J. Lingham/Biggin Hill	
G-ATCD	D.5/180 Husky	Oxford Flying & Gliding Group	
G-ATCE	Cessna U.206	J. J. Aviation Ltd/Coventry	
G-ATCI	Victa Airtourer 100	B. & C. Building Materials (Canvey Island) Ltd	
G-ATCJ	Luton LA-4A Minor	R. M. Sharphouse	
G-ATCL	Victa Airtourer 100	D. Alexander/Leicester	

25

Notes	Reg.	Type	Owner or Operator
	G-ATCN	Luton LA-4A Minor	J. C. Gates & C. Neilson
	G-ATCR	Cessna 310	R. E. Daglass
	G-ATCU	Cessna 337	University of Cambridge
	G-ATCX	Cessna 182H Skylane	I. H. Sugden/Fairoaks
	G-ATCY	PA-23 Aztec 250	Window Machinery Sales Ltd/Coventry
	G-ATDA	PA-28 Cherokee 160	D. E. Siviter (Motors) Ltd/Coventry
	G-ATDB	Nord 1101 Noralpha	J. B. Jackson
	G-ATDC	PA-23 Aztec 250	Edinburgh Flying Services Ltd
	G-ATDN	A.61 Terrier 2	J. F. Moore
	G-ATDO	Bo 208C Junior	H. Swift
	G-ATDS	HPR.7 Herald 209	Express Air Services Ltd/Bournemouth
	G-ATDZ	Z326 Trener Master	P. A. Jackson
	G-ATED	Hiller UH-12E	North Scottish Helicopters Ltd
	G-ATEF	Cessna 150E	M. Smith & ptnrs/Blackbushe
	G-ATEG	Cessna 150E	Northair Aviation Ltd/Leeds
	G-ATEM	PA-28 Cherokee 180	G. Wyles & W. Adams
	G-ATEP	EAA Biplane	E. L. Martin
	G-ATES	PA-32 Cherokee Six 260	Aeroscot Ltd
	G-ATEV	Jodel DR.1050	B. A. Mills & G. W. Payne
	G-ATEW	PA-30 Twin Comanche 160	Air Northumbria Group/Newcastle
	G-ATEX	Victa Airtourer 100	D. C. Giles & ptnrs/Southend
	G-ATEZ	PA-28 Cherokee 140	J. A. Burton/E. Midlands
	G-ATFA	Bensen B-8	J. Butler
	G-ATFD	Jodel DR.1050	H. Fawcett & ptnrs/Tollerton
	G-ATFF	PA-23 Aztec 250	Tempus Aviation (Southern) Ltd/Luton
	G-ATFG	Brantley B2B	R. J. Chapman Ltd
	G-ATFK	PA-30 Twin Comanche 160	L. J. Martin/Redhill
	G-ATFL	Cessna F.172F	R. L. Beverley/Bournemouth
	G-ATFM	Sikorsky S-61N	British Airways Helicopters Ltd/ Aberdeen
	G-ATFR	PA-25 Pawnee 150	J. F. Pelham-Born & R. V. Miller/ Slinfold
	G-ATFU	D.H.85 Leopard Moth	A. H. Carrington & C. D. Duthy-James
	G-ATFV	Agusta/Bell 47J-2A	Alexander Warren & Co
	G-ATFW	Luton LA-4A Minor	S. R. Clarke
	G-ATFX	Cessna F.172G	M. J. J. Fenwick
	G-ATFY	Cessna F.172G	E. Cure Ltd/Tees-side
	G-ATGE	Jodel DR.1050	M. A. Roberts
	G-ATGF	M.S.892A Rallye Commodore 150	E. G. Bostock & R. A. Punter
	G-ATGG	M.S.885 Super Rallye	Southend Flying Club Ltd
	G-ATGH	Brantly B2B	R. Crook/Kidlington
	G-ATGO	Cessna F.172G	Hill Leigh Group Ltd/Bristol
	G-ATGP	Jodel DR.1050	W. M. Haley/Tees-side
	G-ATGY	GY.80 Horizon	P. W. Gibberson/Birmingham
	G-ATGZ	GH-4 Gyroplane	G. Griffiths
	G-ATHA	PA-23 Apache 235	Air Camelot/Bournemouth
	G-ATHD	D.H.C.1 Chipmunk 22	Spartan Flying Group Ltd/Denham
	G-ATHF	Cessna 150F	Cambridge Aero Club Ltd
	G-ATHG	Cessna 150F	G. T. Williams
	G-ATHJ	PA-23 Aztec 250	B. J. & A. K. Whitemore
	G-ATHK	Aeronca 7AC Champion	A. Corran/Denham
	G-ATHL	Wallis WA-116/F	W. Vinten Ltd
	G-ATHM	Wallis WA-116 Srs 1	Wallis Autogyros Ltd
	G-ATHN	Nord 1101 Noralpha	E. L. Martin
	G-ATHR	PA-28 Cherokee 180	Britannia Airways Ltd/Luton
	G-ATHT	Victa Airtourer 115	Southend District Flying Club
	G-ATHU	A.61 Terrier 1	Pinhoe Flying Club Ltd/Exeter
	G-ATHV	Cessna 150F	A. W. Pyle/Popham
	G-ATHW	Mooney Mk 20E	F. J. L. Aran/Sywell
	G-ATHX	Jodel DR.100A	T. S. Wilkins/Booker
	G-ATHZ	Cessna 150F	Rob-Air Ltd
	G-ATIA	PA-24 Comanche 260	India Alpha Partnership/Sywell
	G-ATIB	Bensen B.8M	K. J. Atkins
	G-ATIC	Jodel DR.1050	R. J. Hurstone & G. D. Kinnie
	G-ATID	Cessna 337	R.O. Air Services Ltd/Liverpool
	G-ATIE	Cessna 150F ★	*Parachute jump aircraft*/Chetwynd
	G-ATIG	HPR-7 Herald 214	Janus Airways Ltd/Lydd
	G-ATIN	Jodel D.117	Mrs M. J. Underhill/Shoreham
	G-ATIR	Stampe SV.4C	Mitchell Aviation/Halfpenny Green
	G-ATIS	PA-28 Cherokee 160	Oxford Educational Resources Ltd Kidlington

Reg.	Type	Owner or Operator	Notes
G-ATIZ	Jodel D.117	N. Chandler	
G-ATJA	Jodel DR.1050	Lesley Dee Fashions (Groby) Ltd/Leicester	
G-ATJC	Victa Airtourer 100	P. J. Petitt & ptnrs/Southend	
G-ATJL	PA-24 Comanche 260	M. W. Webb & M. J. Berry	
G-ATJM	Fokker DR.1 replica	R. Lamplough/Duxford	
G-ATJN	Jodel D.119	J. K. S. Wills/Biggin Hill	
G-ATJP	PA-23 Apache 160	T. Hood & A. Mattacks/Biggin Hill	
G-ATJR	PA-E23 Aztec 250	Bonaire/Bourn	
G-ATJT	GY.80 Horizon 160	M. Chamberlain/Fairoaks	
G-ATJV	PA-32 Cherokee Six 260	Ipswich Parachute Centre	
G-ATJW	Nord 1101 Noralpha	H. W. Elkin/Denham	
G-ATJX	Bu 131 Jungmann (AT+JX)	J. E. Fricker & G. H. A. Bird/Stapleford	
G-ATKC	Stampe S.V.4B	Tiger Club Ltd/Redhill	
G-ATKD	Cessna 150F	Rogers Aviation Ltd/Cranfield	
G-ATKE	Cessna 150F	Skegness Air Taxi Services Ltd	
G-ATKF	Cessna 150F	Rogers Aviation Ltd/Cranfield	
G-ATKG	Hiller UH-12B ★	Bickford Arms/Brandis Corner, Devon	
G-ATKH	Luton LA-4A Minor	L. Hepper/Rochester	
G-ATKI	Piper J-3C-65 Cub	A. C. Netting	
G-ATKS	Cessna F.172G	Rogers Aviation Ltd/Cranfield	
G-ATKT	Cessna F.172G	N. Y. Souster	
G-ATKU	Cessna F.172G	S. E. Ward & Sons (Engineers) Ltd/Doncaster	
G-ATKX	Jodel D.140C	Tiger Club Ltd/Redhill	
G-ATKY	Cessna 150F	R. L. Beverley	
G-ATKZ	T.66-2 Nipper	M. W. Knights/Felthorpe	
G-ATLA	Cessna 182J Skylane	Shefford Transport Engineers Ltd/Bourn	
G-ATLB	Jodel DR.1050-M1	Tiger Club Ltd/Redhill	
G-ATLC	PA-23 Aztec 250	Alderney Air Charter Ltd/Bournemouth	
G-ATLD	Cessna E-310K	Centreline Air Services Ltd/Biggin Hill	
G-ATLG	Hiller UH-12B	Bristow Helicopters Ltd	
G-ATLM	Cessna F.172G	Yorkshire Flying Services Ltd/Leeds	
G-ATLN	Cessna F.172G	Routair Aviation Services Ltd/Southend	
G-ATLP	Bensen B.8M	C. D. Julian	
G-ATLR	Cessna F.172G	A. Wood & R. F. Patmore/Andrewsfield	
G-ATLT	Cessna U-206A	W. Merriman/Sturgate	
G-ATLV	Jodel D.120	G. Dawes/Headcorn	
G-ATLW	PA-28 Cherokee 180	P. T. Unden & G. Corin/Shoreham	
G-ATMB	Cessna F.150F	The Prospect Group/Barton	
G-ATMC	Cessna F.150F	Rogers Aviation Ltd/Cranfield	
G-ATMG	M.S.893 Rallye Commodore 180	F. W. Fay & ptnrs/Long Marston	
G-ATMH	Beagle D.5/180 Husky	Devon & Somerset Gliding Club Ltd	
G-ATMI	H.S.748 Srs 2A	Dan-Air Services Ltd/Gatwick	
G-ATMJ	H.S.748 Srs 2A	British Airways/Glasgow	
G-ATMM	Cessna F.150F	Air Fenland Ltd	
G-ATMN	Cessna F.150F	Routair Flying Services Ltd/Southend	
G-ATMT	PA-30 Twin Comanche 160	D. H. T. Bain/Newcastle	
G-ATMU	PA-23 Apache 160	Southend Flying Club	
G-ATMW	PA-28 Cherokee 140	Bencray Ltd/Blackpool	
G-ATMX	Cessna F.150F	H. M. Synge/Sleap	
G-ATMY	Cessna 150F	J. C. D. Turner/Lee-on-Solent	
G-ATNB	PA-28 Cherokee 180	Chaplin Auto Preparation Ltd/Ipswich	
G-ATNE	Cessna F.150F	R. Gray/Leicester	
G-ATNI	Cessna F.150F	Rolim Ltd/Aberdeen	
G-ATNK	Cessna F.150F	Elliot Forbes (Kirkwall) Ltd/Aberdeen	
G-ATNL	Cessna F.150F	R & Mrs P. R. Budd/Goodwood	
G-ATNU	Cessna 182A	A. Bennett & W. W. Willis	
G-ATNV	PA-24 Comanche 260	Self-Fly Europe/Luton	
G-ATNX	Cessna F.150F	B. R. Walker/Halfpenny Green	
G-ATOA	PA-23 Apache 160	Aviation Enterprises/Fairoaks	
G-ATOD	Cessna F.150F	Cornwall Flying Club Ltd/Bodmin	
G-ATOE	Cessna F.150F	Argo Air Services Ltd/Shoreham	
G-ATOH	D.62B Condor	G. H. Daniels	
G-ATOI	PA-28 Cherokee 140	O. & E. Flying Ltd/Stapleford	
G-ATOJ	PA-28 Cherokee 140	O. T. Kernahan/Kidlington	
G-ATOK	PA-28 Cherokee 140	J. D. & M. Cheetham	
G-ATOL	PA-28 Cherokee 140	Tamar Flying Group/Bodmin	
G-ATOM	PA-28 Cherokee 140	A. Reynard/Kidlington	

Notes	Reg.	Type	Owner or Operator
	G-ATON	PA-28 Cherokee 140	A. Hall-Carpenter
	G-ATOO	PA-28 Cherokee 140	P. J. Stead/Cark
	G-ATOP	PA-28 Cherokee 140	A. J. McNeal
	G-ATOR	PA-28 Cherokee 140	T. A. J. Morgan & ptnrs/Shobdon
	G-ATOS	PA-28 Cherokee 140	AFT Craft Ltd/Halfpenny Green
	G-ATOT	PA-28 Cherokee 180	J. T. Turner/Halfpenny Green
	G-ATOU	Mooney M.20E Super 21	Charles Lock Motors Ltd/Stapleford
	G-ATOY	PA-24 Comanche 260 ★	Museum of Flight/E. Fortune
	G-ATPD	H.S.125 Srs 1B	Deribe Aviation Ltd/Luton
	G-ATPE	H.S.125 Srs 1B	Moseley Group (PSV) Ltd/E. Midlands
	G-ATPJ	BAC One-Eleven 301	Dan-Air Services Ltd/Gatwick
	G-ATPK	BAC One-Eleven 301	Bryan Aviation Ltd
	G-ATPL	BAC One-Eleven 301	Dan-Air Services Ltd/Gatwick
	G-ATPM	Cessna F.150F	Dan-Air Flying Club/Bournemouth
	G-ATPN	PA-28 Cherokee 140	D. A. Thompson & L. Martin/Southend
	G-ATPT	Cessna 182J Skylane	Western Models Ltd/Redhill
	G-ATPV	JB.01 Minicab	S. Russell
	G-ATRC	Beech B.95A Travel Air	Bulldog Aviation Ltd/Ipswich
	G-ATRG	PA-18 Super Cub 150	Lasham Gliding Soc Ltd
	G-ATRI	Bo 208C Junior	W. H. Jones/Shoreham
	G-ATRK	Cessna F.150F	A. B. Mills/Bourn
	G-ATRL	Cessna F.150F	Loganair Ltd/Glasgow
	G-ATRM	Cessna F.150F	J. W. C. A. Coulcutt/Sandown
	G-ATRN	Cessna F.150F	J. Gregson & L. Chiappi/Blackpool
	G-ATRO	PA-28 Cherokee 140	390th Flying Group
	G-ATRR	PA-28 Cherokee 140	Highland Aviation Ltd
	G-ATRU	PA-28 Cherokee 180	Britannia Airways Ltd/Luton
	G-ATRW	PA-32 Cherokee Six 260	Harvest Air Ltd/Southend
	G-ATRX	PA-32 Cherokee Six 260	R. F. Gibbs/Panshanger
	G-ATRY	Alon A-2 Aircoupe	B. W. George/Sandown
	G-ATSI	Bo 208C Junior	T. M. H. Paterson/Shoreham
	G-ATSL	Cessna F.172G	H. G. Le Cheminant
	G-ATSM	Cessna 337A	Tremletts (Skycraft) Ltd/Exeter
	G-ATSR	Beech M.35 Bonanza	Alstan Aviation Ltd/Swansea
	G-ATST	M.S.893A Rallye Commodore	Severnside International Aviation/Cardiff
	G-ATSU	Jodel D.140B	J. S. Burnett Ltd
	G-ATSX	Bo 208C Junior	N. M. G. Pearson/Lulsgate
	G-ATSY	Wassmer WA41 Super Baladou IV	D. R. Bull/Stapleford
	G-ATSZ	PA-30 Twin Comanche 160	Air Peterborough/Conington
	G-ATTB	Wallis WA.116-1	D. A. Wallis
	G-ATTD	Cessna 182J Skylane	Hanro Aviation Ltd/Leicester
	G-ATTF	PA-28 Cherokee 140	S. J. Green
	G-ATTG	PA-28 Cherokee 140	Arrow Air Services Engineering Ltd/Shipdham
	G-ATTI	PA-28 Cherokee 140	S. Mathews
	G-ATTK	PA-28 Cherokee 140	Andrewsfield Flying Club Ltd
	G-ATTM	Jodel DR.250-160	R. W. Tomkinson
	G-ATTP	BAC One-Eleven 207	Dan-Air Services Ltd/Gatwick
	G-ATTR	Bo 208C Junior 3	S. Luck
	G-ATTU	PA-28 Cherokee 140	Leith Air Ltd/Elstree
	G-ATTV	PA-28 Cherokee 140	B. W. Webb & R. J. Humphries/Lydd
	G-ATTX	PA-28 Cherokee 180	B. W. & D. C. P. Chaplin/Andrewsfield
	G-ATTY	PA-32 Cherokee Six 260	L. A. Dingemans & D. J. Everett/Stapleford
	G-ATUB	PA-28 Cherokee 140	J. E. Reid/Booker
	G-ATUC	PA-28 Cherokee 140	Airways Aero Associations Ltd/Booker
	G-ATUD	PA-28 Cherokee 140	Applyn Ltd/Bournemouth
	G-ATUF	Cessna F.150F	C. J. Lynn/Sibson
	G-ATUG	D.62B Condor	A. M. Hazell & C. B. Marsh/Rochester
	G-ATUH	T.66 Nipper	M. J. Smith
	G-ATUI	Bo 208C Junior	A. J. H. Martin/Southampton
	G-ATUL	PA-28 Cherokee 180	R. F. W. Warner
	G-ATVF	D.H.C.1 Chipmunk 22	RAFGSA
	G-ATVH	BAC One-Eleven 207	Dan-Air Services Ltd *City of Newcastle-upon-Tyne*/Gatwick
	G-ATVI	SIPA 903	J. Martin
	G-ATVK	PA-28 Cherokee 140	E. A. Clack/Southend
	G-ATVL	PA-28 Cherokee 140	West London Aero Services/White Waltham

G-ATIG HPR-7 Herald 214 of Janus Airways.

G-AVKZ PA-23 Aztec. *A. S. Wright*

30

Reg.	Type	Owner or Operator	Notes
G-ATVO	PA-28 Cherokee 140	E. C. Andrews/Stapleford	
G-ATVP	F.B.5 Gunbus (2345) ★	RAF Museum	
G-ATVS	PA-28 Cherokee 180	Marshalls Woodflakes Ltd/Lulsgate	
G-ATVW	D.62B Condor	J. R. Stanier & D. W. Evernden/ Panshanger	
G-ATVX	Bo 208C Junior	G. W. Stanmore/Rochester	
G-ATWA	Jodel DR.1050	R. S. Arbuthnot	
G-ATWB	Jodel D.117	T. Tabor & ptnrs	
G-ATWE	M.S.892A Rallye Commodore	D. I. Murray	
G-ATWJ	Cessna F.172F	C. J. & J. Freeman/Headcorn	
G-ATWL	Jodel D.120	T. A. S. Rosie	
G-ATWP	Alon A-2 Aircoupe	F. Bolton/Blackpool	
G-ATWR	PA-30 Twin Comanche 160	Lubair (Transport Services) Ltd E. Midlands	
G-ATWZ	M.S.892 Rallye Commodore	N. A. Hall & ptnrs/Bodmin	
G-ATXA	PA-22 Tri-Pacer 150	B. R. Gaunt	
G-ATXD	PA-30 Twin Comanche 160	Southwark Estates Ltd/Biggin Hill	
G-ATXF	GY-80 Horizon 150	A. I. Milne/Swanton Morley	
G-ATXM	PA-28 Cherokee 180	J. Khan/Stapleford	
G-ATXN	Mitchell-Proctor Kittiwake	D. W. Kent/Lasham	
G-ATXO	SIPA 903	M. Hillam/Sherburn	
G-ATXR	AFB 1 gas balloon	Mrs C. M. Bulmer *Omega One*	
G-ATXZ	Bo 208C Junior	J. K. Davies	
G-ATYA	PA-25 Pawnee 235	Skegness Air Taxi Services Ltd	
G-ATYM	Cessna F.150G	J. T. Tyer/Biggin Hill	
G-ATYN	Cessna F.150G	Skegness Air Taxi Services Ltd	
G-ATYS	PA-28 Cherokee 180	J. R. J. Bannochie/Biggin Hill	
G-ATYV	Bell 47G	Two Mile Oak Garage	
G-ATYZ	M.S.880B Rallye Club	Nylo Flying Group/Netherthorpe	
G-ATZA	Bo 208C Junior	W. C. Roberts	
G-ATZB	Hiller UH-12B	Bristow Helicopters Ltd	
G-ATZG	AFB2 gas balloon	Flt Lt S. Cameron *Aeolis*	
G-ATZK	PA-28 Cherokee 180	MGF Racing Sidecars/Andrewsfield	
G-ATZM	Piper J-3C-65 Cub	R. W. Davison	
G-ATZS	Wassmer WA41 Super Baladou IV	J. R. MacAlpine-Downie & P. A. May/ Manchester	
G-ATZU	PA-30 Twin Comanche 160	Routair Flying Services Ltd/Southend	
G-ATZV	PA-30 Twin Comanche 160	P. R. Lockwood/Guernsey	
G-ATZY	Cessna F.150G	P. P. D. Howard-Johnstone/Edinburgh	
G-ATZZ	Cessna F.150G	E. Greaves-Lord	
G-AUTO	Cessna 441 Conquest	Automobile Association Ltd/Coventry	
G-AVAA	Cessna F.150G	Argo Air Services Ltd/Shoreham	
G-AVAI	H.S.125 Srs 3B	Aravco Ltd/Heathrow	
G-AVAJ	Hiller UH-12B	Bristow Helicopters Ltd	
G-AVAK	M.S.893A Rallye Commodore 180	W. K. Anderson/Perth	
G-AVAP	Cessna F.150G	Seawing Flying Club Ltd/Southend	
G-AVAR	Cessna F.150G	Pembrokeshire Flying Club/ Haverfordwest	
G-AVAS	Cessna F.172H	Birmingham Aviation Ltd/ Halfpenny Green	
G-AVAU	PA-30 Twin Comanche 160	L. Batin/Fairoaks	
G-AVAW	D.62B Condor	Avato Flying Group	
G-AVAX	PA-28 Cherokee 180	College of Air Training/Hamble	
G-AVAY	PA-28 Cherokee 180	College of Air Training/Hamble	
G-AVAZ	PA-28 Cherokee 180	Intermark Ltd/Biggin Hill	
G-AVBA	PA-28 Cherokee 180 ★	*Engineering Trainer*/Hamble	
G-AVBB	PA-28 Cherokee 180	College of Air Training/Hamble	
G-AVBC	PA-28 Cherokee 180	College of Air Training/Hamble	
G-AVBE	PA-28 Cherokee 180	College of Air Training/Hamble	
G-AVBG	PA-28 Cherokee 180	College of Air Training/Hamble	
G-AVBH	PA-28 Cherokee 180	College of Air Training/Hamble	
G-AVBL	PA-30 Twin Comanche 160	Interavia 1983 Ltd/Ronaldsway	
G-AVBP	PA-28 Cherokee 140	Bristol & Wessex Aeroplane Club Ltd/Bristol	
G-AVBS	PA-28 Cherokee 180	I. J. James/Thruxton	
G-AVBT	PA-28 Cherokee 180	P. O. Hire & D. J. Spicer	
G-AVBU	PA-32 Cherokee Six 260	Tempus Aviation (Holdings) Ltd	
G-AVBZ	Cessna F.172H	J. Seville	

Notes	Reg.	Type	Owner or Operator
	G-AVCA	Brantly B.2B	M. J. & Mrs G. M. Page/Norwich
	G-AVCC	Cessna F.172H	Mercia Estates Ltd/Coventry
	G-AVCE	Cessna F.172H	Cleco Electrical Industries Ltd/Leicester
	G-AVCM	PA-24 Comanche 260	F. Smith & Sons Ltd/Stapleford
	G-AVCS	A.61 Terrier 1	L. M. Farrell & A. R. C. Hunter/Finmere
	G-AVCT	Cessna F.150G	Sierra Aviation Services
	G-AVCU	Cessna F.150G	P. R. Moss/Alderney
	G-AVCV	Cessna 182J Skylane	J. A. Moores/Barton
	G-AVCX	PA-30 Twin Comanche 160	F. J. Stevens/Leicester
	G-AVCY	PA-30 Twin Comanche 160	Thornhurst & Co/Halfpenny Green
	G-AVDA	Cessna 182K Skylane	J. W. Grant
	G-AVDE	Turner Gyroglider Mk 1	J. S. Smith
	G-AVDF	Beagle Pup 100 ★	Brighton Transport Musuem
	G-AVDG	Wallis WA-116 Srs 1	K. H. Wallis
	G-AVDR	Beech B80 Queen Air	Air Camelot/Bournemouth
	G-AVDS	Beech B80 Queen Air	Air Camelot/Bournemouth
	G-AVDT	Aeronca 7AC Champion	W. R. Prescott
	G-AVDV	PA-22 Tri-Pacer 150	S. C. Brooks/Slinfold
	G-AVDW	D.62B Condor	Essex Aviation/Andrewsfield
	G-AVDY	Luton LA-4A Minor	D. E. Evans & ptnrs
	G-AVDZ	PA-25 Pawnee 235	Skegness Air Taxi Services Ltd
	G-AVEB	Morane MS 230 Et 2	Hon P. Lindsay/Booker
	G-AVEC	Cessna F.172H	W. H. Ekin (Engineering) Co Ltd
	G-AVEF	Jodel D.150	Tiger Club Ltd/Redhill
	G-AVEG	SIAI-Marchetti S.205	G. Taylor/Sywell
	G-AVEH	SIAI-Marchetti S.205	K. D. Gomm
	G-AVEM	Cessna F.150G	C. P. Osbourne
	G-AVEN	Cessna F.150G	N. J. Rudd/Aberdeen
	G-AVER	Cessna F.150G	B. I. Chapman/Ipswich
	G-AVET	Beech C55 Baron	Spline Gauges Ltd/Coventry
	G-AVEU	Wassmer WA.41 Baladou	Baladou Flying Group/Aberdeen
	G-AVEX	D.62B Condor	Cotswold Roller Hire Ltd/Long Marston
	G-AVEY	Currie Super Wot	A. Eastelow/Dunkeswell
	G-AVEZ	HPR-7 Herald 210★	Norwich Aviation Museum
	G-AVFA	H.S.121 Trident 2E ★	British Airways (*ground school*) Heathrow
	G-AVFB	H.S.121 Trident 2E ★	Imperial War Museum/Duxford
	G-AVFE	H.S.121 Trident 2E	British Airways/Heathrow
	G-AVFF	H.S.121 Trident 2E	British Airways/Heathrow
	G-AVFG	H.S.121 Trident 2E	British Airways/Heathrow
	G-AVFL	H.S.121 Trident 2E	British Airways/Heathrow
	G-AVFM	H.S.121 Trident 2E	British Airways (WFU)/Heathrow
	G-AVFN	H.S.121 Trident 2E	British Airways/Heathrow
	G-AVFO	H.S.121 Trident 2E	British Airways/Heathrow
	G-AVFP	PA-28 Cherokee 140	H. D. Vince Ltd/Woodvale
	G-AVFR	PA-28 Cherokee 140	J. J. Ballagh
	G-AVFS	PA-32 Cherokee Six 300	Headcorn Parachute Club Ltd
	G-AVFU	PA-32 Cherokee Six 300	S. L. H. Construction Ltd/Biggin Hill
	G-AVFW	PA-30 Twin Comanche 160	Woodlands Investments Ltd/Ronaldsway
	G-AVFX	PA-28 Cherokee 140	J. E. Lawson
	G-AVFY	PA-28 Cherokee 140	F. Spencer-Jones/Sandown
	G-AVFZ	PA-28 Cherokee 140	Exe International Ltd/Exeter
	G-AVGA	PA-24 Comanche 260	W. B. Baillie/Tees-side
	G-AVGB	PA-28 Cherokee 140	B. Williams & G. Howells/Swansea
	G-AVGC	PA-28 Cherokee 140	B. A. Bennett/Redhill
	G-AVGD	PA-28 Cherokee 140	A. D. Wren/Southend
	G-AVGE	PA-28 Cherokee 140	A. G. Branch Contractors Ltd
	G-AVGH	PA-28 Cherokee 140	Mooney Aviation Ltd/Halfpenny Green
	G-AVGI	PA-28 Cherokee 140	F. Cooper
	G-AVGJ	Jodel DR.1050	G. D. Andrews/Lulsgate
	G-AVGK	PA-28 Cherokee 180	Liverpool Aero Club Ltd
	G-AVGP	BAC One-Eleven 408	British Airways *County of Nottinghamshire*/Birmingham
	G-AVGU	Cessna F.150G	G. R. W. Brown
	G-AVGV	Cessna F.150G	British Skysports
	G-AVGY	Cessna 182K Skylane	H. P. Nicholls
	G-AVGZ	Jodel DR.1050	D. C. Webb & S. P. Johnson
	G-AVHF	Beech A.23 Musketeer	R. W. Neale/Coventry
	G-AVHH	Cessna F.172H	V. W. Wharton & ptnrs
	G-AVHJ	Wassmer WA.41 Baladou	D. G. Pickering & ptnrs
	G-AVHL	Jodel DR.105A	G. L. Winterbourne/Booker

Reg.	Type	Owner or Operator	Notes
G-AVHM	Cessna F.150G	M. Tosh/Elstree	
G-AVHN	Cessna F.150G	Bristol and Wessex Aero Club Ltd/ Bristol	
G-AVHT	Auster AOP.9 (WZ711)	M. Somerton-Rayner/Middle Wallop	
G-AVHY	Fournier RF.4D	R. Swinn & J. Conolly	
G-AVIA	Cessna F.150G	P. N. Voltzenlogel	
G-AVIB	Cessna F.150G	W. K. Hadden & L. G. Edwards/ Halfpenny Green	
G-AVIC	Cessna F.172H	Pembrokeshire Air/Haverfordwest	
G-AVID	Cessna 182J	T. D. Boyle/Prestwick	
G-AVIE	Cessna F.172H	N. Denes Aerodrome Ltd	
G-AVIG	A-B 206B JetRanger	Bristow Helicopters Ltd	
G-AVII	A-B 206A JetRanger	Bristow Helicopters Ltd	
G-AVIL	Alon A.2 Aircoupe	D. W. Vernon/Woodvale	
G-AVIN	M.S.880B Rallye Club	D. R. F. Sapte/Elstree	
G-AVIO	M.S.880B Rallye Club	A. R. Johnston	
G-AVIP	Brantly B.2B	Cosworth Engineering Ltd	
G-AVIR	Cessna F.172H	W. Lancashire Aero Club Ltd/Woodvale	
G-AVIS	Cessna F.172H	Jon Paul Photography Ltd/Rochester	
G-AVIT	Cessna F.150G	Shropshire Aero Club Ltd/Sleap	
G-AVIZ	Scheibe SF.25A Motorfalke	D. C. Pattison & D. A. Wilson/Usworth	
G-AVJB	V.815 Viscount	British Air Ferries Jane/Southend	
G-AVJE	Cessna F.150G	P. R. Green & ptnrs/Popham	
G-AVJF	Cessna F.172H	J. A. & G. M. Rees/Haverfordwest	
G-AVJG	Cessna 337B	P. R. Moss/Bournemouth	
G-AVJH	D.62 Condor	Lleyn Flying Group/Mona	
G-AVJI	Cessna F.172H	Royal Artillery Aero Club Ltd/ Middle Wallop	
G-AVJJ	PA-30 Twin Comanche 160	A. H. Manser Ltd/Staverton	
G-AVJK	Jodel DR.1050 M.1	J. H. B. Urmston	
G-AVJN	Brantly B.2B	John Berry Ltd/Norwich	
G-AVJO	Fokker E.III Replica (422-15)	Personal Plane Services Ltd/Booker	
G-AVJU	PA-24 Comanche 260	Syd Ward (South Normanton)	
G-AVJV	Wallis WA-117 Srs 1	K. H. Wallis (G-ATCV)	
G-AVJW	Wallis WA-118 Srs 2	K. H. Wallis (G-ATPW)	
G-AVKB	MB.50 Pipistrelle	R. K. Haldenby & T. S. Warren/ Sandown	
G-AVKD	Fournier RF.4D	Lasham RF4 Group	
G-AVKE	Gadfly HDW.1 ★	British Rotorcraft Museum	
G-AVKG	Cessna F.172H	W. Lancs Aero Club Ltd/Woodvale	
G-AVKI	Nipper T.66 Srs 3	J. P. Tribe & K. D. G. Courtney/ Swansea	
G-AVKJ	Nipper T.66 Srs 3	P. W. Hunter/Booker	
G-AVKN	Cessna 401	Strand Furniture Ltd	
G-AVKP	A.109 Airedale	H. F. Igoe	
G-AVKR	Bo 208C Junior	D. F. Barley & D. A. Bishop/Redhill	
G-AVKS	Bell 47G-2	Rotor-Craft Services/Shoreham	
G-AVKX	Hiller UH-12E	Management Aviation Ltd/Bourn	
G-AVKY	Hiller UH-12E	Agricopters Ltd/Thruxton	
G-AVKZ	PA-23 Aztec 250	Volvo BM (UK) Ltd/Stansted	
G-AVLA	PA-28 Cherokee 140	C. Walker	
G-AVLB	PA-28 Cherokee 140	J. A. Overton Ltd	
G-AVLC	PA-28 Cherokee 140	F. C. V. Hopkins/Swansea	
G-AVLD	PA-28 Cherokee 140	AVLD Ltd	
G-AVLE	PA-28 Cherokee 140	P. A. Johnstone & E. J. Morgan	
G-AVLF	PA-28 Cherokee 140	W. London Aero Services Ltd/ White Waltham	
G-AVLG	PA-28 Cherokee 140	D. Golding & P. J. Pearce/Elstree	
G-AVLH	PA-28 Cherokee 140	T. L. Wilkinson	
G-AVLI	PA-28 Cherokee 140	R. P. I. Scott/Ipswich	
G-AVLN	B.121 Pup 2	C. B. G. Masefield/Woodford	
G-AVLO	Bo 208C Junior	J. A. Webb & K. F. Barnard/Lasham	
G-AVLP	PA-23 Aztec 250	B.K.S. Surveys Ltd	
G-AVLR	PA-28 Cherokee 140	E. Ford/Stapleford	
G-AVLS	PA-28 Cherokee 140	D. Charlton & ptnrs	
G-AVLT	PA-28 Cherokee 140	E. A. Clack & M. T. Pritchard/Southend	
G-AVLU	PA-28 Cherokee 140	I. K. George/Fairoaks	
G-AVLW	Fournier RF 4D	P. J. Sellar & B. M. O'Brien/Redhill	
G-AVLY	Jodel D.120A	R. Arbon & ptnrs/Tees-side	
G-AVMA	GY.80 Horizon 180	B. R. & S. Hildick	
G-AVMB	D.62B Condor	A. J. Starkey/Fairoaks	

Notes	Reg.	Type	Owner or Operator
	G-AVMD	Cessna 150G	K. J. Jarvis/Southend
	G-AVMF	Cessna F. 150G	J. F. Marsh & M. J. Oliver
	G-AVMH	BAC One-Eleven 510	British Airways/Manchester
	G-AVMI	BAC One-Eleven 510	British Airways *County of Merseyside*/Manchester
	G-AVMJ	BAC One-Eleven 510	British Airways/Manchester
	G-AVMK	BAC One-Eleven 510	British Airways/Manchester
	G-AVML	BAC One-Eleven 510	British Airways *County of Surrey*/Manchester
	G-AVMM	BAC One-Eleven 510	British Airways *County of Antrim*/Manchester
	G-AVMN	BAC One-Eleven 510	British Airways/Manchester
	G-AVMO	BAC One-Eleven 510	British Airways/Manchester
	G-AVMP	BAC One-Eleven 510	British Airways *Bailiwick of Jersey*/Manchester
	G-AVMR	BAC One-Eleven 510	British Airways *County of Tyne & Wear*/Manchester
	G-AVMS	BAC One-Eleven 510	British Airways/Manchester
	G-AVMT	BAC One-Eleven 510	British Airways *County of Glamorgan*/Manchester
	G-AVMU	BAC One-Eleven 510	British Airways/Manchester
	G-AVMV	BAC One-Eleven 510	British Airways *Greater Manchester County*/Manchester
	G-AVMW	BAC One-Eleven 510	British Airways *Grampian Region*/Manchester
	G-AVMX	BAC One-Eleven 510	British Airways *County of Nottingham*/Manchester
	G-AVMY	BAC One-Eleven 510	British Airways/Manchester
	G-AVMZ	BAC One-Eleven 510	British Airways/Manchester
	G-AVNB	Cessna F.150G	G. A. J. Bowles/Elstree
	G-AVNC	Cessna F.150G	Merrett Aviation Ltd
	G-AVNG	Beech A80 Queen Air	Parker & Heard Ltd/Biggin Hill
	G-AVNI	PA-30 Twin Comanche 160	D.P. Aviation/Coventry
	G-AVNL	PA-23 Aztec 250	Nalson Aviation Ltd/Biggin Hill
	G-AVNM	PA-28 Cherokee 180	Brands Hatch Circuit Ltd/Biggin Hill
	G-AVNN	PA-28 Cherokee 180	College of Air Training/Hamble
	G-AVNO	PA-28 Cherokee 180	College of Air Training/Hamble
	G-AVNP	PA-28 Cherokee 180	Magpie Flying Group/Glasgow
	G-AVNR	PA-28 Cherokee 180	Hamble Airfield Properties Ltd
	G-AVNS	PA-28 Cherokee 180	College of Air Training/Hamble
	G-AVNT	PA-28 Cherokee 180	College of Air Training/Hamble
	G-AVNU	PA-28 Cherokee 180	F. E. Gooding
	G-AVNV	PA-28 Cherokee 180	College of Air Training/Hamble
	G-AVNW	PA-28 Cherokee 180	College of Air Training/Hamble
	G-AVNX	Fournier RF-4D	O. C. Harris & C. G. Masterman
	G-AVNY	Fournier RF-4D	A. N. Mavrogordato/Biggin Hill
	G-AVNZ	Fournier RF-4D	Cobra Group/Usworth
	G-AVOA	Jodel DR.1050	I. MacPherson/Manchester
	G-AVOD	Beagle D5/180 Husky	D. Bonsall & ptnrs
	G-AVOE	BAC One-Eleven 416	British Aerospace (G-SURE)
	G-AVOF	BAC One-Eleven 416	British Aerospace (G-BMAN)
	G-AVOH	D.62B Condor	E. Shouler/Sturgate
	G-AVOI	H.S. 125 Srs 3B	Marstapool Aviation Ltd/Luton
	G-AVOM	Jodel DR.221	M. A. Mountford/Headcorn
	G-AVON	Luton LA-5A Major	G. R. Mee
	G-AVOO	PA-18-150 Super Cub	London Gliding Club Ltd/Dunstable
	G-AVOR	Lockspeiser LDA-01	D. Lockspeiser
	G-AVOZ	PA-28 Cherokee 180	Downley Garages Ltd/Booker
	G-AVPC	D.31 Turbulent	J. Sharp
	G-AVPD	D.9 Bebe	S. W. McKay
	G-AVPE	H.S.125 Srs 3B	British Aerospace/Filton
	G-AVPH	Cessna F.150G	W. Lancashire Aero Club/Woodvale
	G-AVPI	Cessna F.172H	R. Jones & J. Chancellor/Exeter
	G-AVPJ	D.H.82A Tiger Moth	R. W. Livett/Sywell
	G-AVPK	M.S.892A Rallye Commodore	Papa Kilo Flying Group/Usworth
	G-AVPM	Jodel D.117	J. Houghton/Sherburn
	G-AVPN	HPR.7 Herald 213	Air UK/Norwich
	G-AVPO	Hindustan HAL-26 Pushpak	A. & R. Rimington
	G-AVPR	PA-30 Twin Comanche 160	Cold Storage (Jersey) Ltd
	G-AVPS	PA-30 Twin Comanche 160	Russell Foster Holdings Ltd/Usworth

Reg.	Type	Owner or Operator	Notes
G-AVPT	PA-18 Super Cub 150	Tiger Club Ltd	
G-AVPU	PA-18 Super Cub 150	Scottish Gliding Union Ltd	
G-AVPV	PA-28 Cherokee 180	E. A. Clack/Southend	
G-AVPX	Taylor JT.1 Monoplane	S. M. Smith/Redhill	
G-AVRF	H.S.125 Srs 3B	Westland Helicopters Ltd	
G-AVRG	H.S.125 Srs 3B	Rogers Aviation Ltd/Cranfield	
G-AVRK	PA-28 Cherokee 180	Dollar Air Services Ltd/Coventry	
G-AVRL	Boeing 737-204	Britannia Airways Ltd *Sir Ernest Shackleton*/Luton	
G-AVRM	Boeing 737-204	Britannia Airways Ltd *James Watt*/Luton	
G-AVRN	Boeing 737-204	Britannia Airways Ltd *Capt James Cook*/Luton	
G-AVRO	Boeing 737-204	Britannia Airways Ltd *Sir Francis Drake*/Luton	
G-AVRP	PA-28 Cherokee 140	K. Cooper & N. D. Douglas/Halfpenny Green	
G-AVRS	GY.80 Horizon 180	Horizon Flyers Ltd/Denham	
G-AVRT	PA-28 Cherokee 140	F. Clarke/Stapleford	
G-AVRU	PA-28 Cherokee 180	Fenland Tractors Ltd	
G-AVRW	GY-20 Minicab	R. B. Pybus	
G-AVRY	PA-28 Cherokee 180	Roses Flying Group/Barton	
G-AVRZ	PA-28 Cherokee 180	Briglea Engineering Ltd/Guernsey	
G-AVSA	PA-28 Cherokee 180	Alliance Aviation Ltd/Barton	
G-AVSB	PA-28 Cherokee 180	White House Garage Ltd	
G-AVSC	PA-28 Cherokee 180	W. London Aero Services Ltd/White Waltham	
G-AVSD	PA-28 Cherokee 180	Famweld Engineering Ltd	
G-AVSE	PA-28 Cherokee 180	S E Aviation Ltd/Leeds	
G-AVSF	PA-28 Cherokee 180	Goodwood Terrena Ltd	
G-AVSH	PA-28 Cherokee 180	Elken Ltd/Ronaldsway	
G-AVSI	PA-28 Cherokee 140	E. P. van Mechelen/White Waltham	
G-AVSP	PA-28 Cherokee 180	Trig Engineering Ltd/Bristol	
G-AVSR	Beagle D 5/180 Husky	A. L. Young	
G-AVTB	Nipper T.66 Srs 3	S. Stride & J. Hobday/Long Marston	
G-AVTJ	PA-32 Cherokee Six 260	K. A. Goodchild/Southend	
G-AVTK	PA-32 Cherokee Six 260	Mannix Aviation Ltd	
G-AVTM	Cessna F.150H	J. K. Bamrah & J. B. Warwicker/Biggin Hill	
G-AVTP	Cessna F.172H	J. H. A. Clarke & ptnrs/Thruxton	
G-AVTT	Ercoupe 415D	L. C. Bourne/Andrewsfield	
G-AVTV	M.S.893A Rallye Commodore	Crowland Flying Group	
G-AVTX	Taylor JT.1 Monoplane	P. Lockwood	
G-AVUA	Cessna F.172H	Recreational Flying Centre (Popham) Ltd	
G-AVUD	PA-30 Twin Comanche 160B	F. M. Aviation/Biggin Hill	
G-AVUG	Cessna F.150H	Dukeries Aviation Ltd/Netherthorpe	
G-AVUH	Cessna F.150H	Sunderland Flying Club Ltd/Usworth	
G-AVUJ	F.8L Falco 4	M. Shield/Doncaster	
G-AVUL	Cessna F.172H	D. H. Stephens & D. J. Reason/Elstree	
G-AVUS	PA-28 Cherokee 140	Scandix Services Ltd/Biggin Hill	
G-AVUT	PA-28 Cherokee 140	Bencray Ltd/Blackpool	
G-AVUU	PA-28 Cherokee 140	Dane-Track Ltd/Goodwood	
G-AVUZ	PA-32 Cherokee Six 300	P. & Mrs M. E. Biggins/Guernsey	
G-AVVB	H.S. 125 Srs 3B	Brown & Root (UK) Ltd/Heathrow	
G-AVVE	Cessna F.150H	A. J. McDonald & H. P. Vox/Edinburgh	
G-AVVF	D.H.104 Dove 8	Martin Baker (Engineering) Ltd/Chalgrove	
G-AVVG	PA-28 Cherokee 180	604 Squadron Flying Club/Booker	
G-AVVI	PA-30 Twin Comanche 160B	Steepletone Products Ltd/Enstone	
G-AVVJ	M.S.893A Rallye Commodore	D. E. Schofield	
G-AVVL	Cessna F.150H	Chris-Air Ltd/Cranfield	
G-AVVM	Jodel D.117	R. R. Corker/Usworth	
G-AVVN	D.62C Condor	Avato Flying Group	
G-AVVO	Avro 652A Anson 19 (VL348) ★	Newark Air Museum	
G-AVVS	Hughes 269B	W. Holmes	
G-AVVT	PA-23 Aztec 250	Guernsey Airlines	
G-AVVV	PA-28 Cherokee 180	D. F. Field/Goodwood	
G-AVVX	Cessna F.150H	Hatfield Flying Club	
G-AVVY	Cessna F.150H	W. S. Davies	
G-AVWA	PA-28 Cherokee 140	W. London Aero Services Ltd/White Waltham	

Notes	Reg.	Type	Owner or Operator
	G-AVWD	PA-28 Cherokee 140	MSF Aviation Ltd/Manchester
	G-AVWE	PA-28 Cherokee 140	W. C. C. Meyer/Biggin Hill
	G-AVWF	PA-28 Cherokee 140	Liverpool Aero Club Ltd
	G-AVWG	PA-28 Cherokee 140	Bencray Ltd/Blackpool
	G-AVWH	PA-28 Cherokee 140	B. P. W. Faithfull/Biggin Hill
	G-AVWI	PA-28 Cherokee 140	L. M. Veitch/Newcastle
	G-AVWJ	PA-28 Cherokee 140	E.F.G. Flying Services Ltd/Biggin Hill
	G-AVWL	PA-28 Cherokee 140	Bristol & Wessex Aeroplane Club Ltd/Bristol
	G-AVWM	PA-28 Cherokee 140	Southend Flying Club
	G-AVWN	PA-28R Cherokee Arrow 180	L. Cooksey/Blackpool
	G-AVWO	PA-28R Cherokee Arrow 180	C & S Controls Ltd/Biggin Hill
	G-AVWR	PA-28R Cherokee Arrow 180	D. J. Cooper/Netherthorpe
	G-AVWT	PA-28R Cherokee Arrow 180	G. W. Barker & ptnrs/Leeds
	G-AVWU	PA-28R Cherokee Arrow 180	Horizon Flyers Ltd/Denham
	G-AVWV	PA-28R Cherokee Arrow 180	Mapair Ltd/Birmingham
	G-AVWW	Mooney M.20F	A. J. & G. Cullen
	G-AVWY	Fournier RF-4D	T. G. Hoult
	G-AVXA	PA-25 Pawnee 235	Howard Avis (Aviation) Ltd
	G-AVXB	PL-1 Gyroplane	C. Mowat
	G-AVXC	Nipper T.66 Srs 3	W. G. Wells & ptnrs
	G-AVXD	Nipper T.66 Srs 3	J. M. Murrie
	G-AVXF	PA-28R Cherokee-Arrow 180	J. G. Stewart & I. M. S. Ferriman/Cranfield
	G-AVXI	H.S.748 Srs 2A	Civil Aviation Authority/Stansted
	G-AVXJ	H.S.748 Srs 2A	Civil Aviation Authority/Stansted
	G-AVXV	Bleriot XI (BAPC 104) ★	Museum/RAF St Athan
	G-AVXW	D.62B Condor	M. D. Bailey/Rochester
	G-AVXX	Cessna FR.172E	Hadrian Flying Group/Newcastle
	G-AVXY	Auster AOP.9 (XK417)	R. Windley
	G-AVYE	H.S.121 Trident IE-140 ★	Science Museum Store/Wroughton
	G-AVYF	Beech A.23-24 Musketeer	Wearside Aviation Group/Usworth
	G-AVYK	A.61 Terrier 3	Airways Aero Associations Ltd/Booker
	G-AVYL	PA-28 Cherokee 180	Miller Aerial Spraying Ltd/Wickenby
	G-AVYM	PA-28 Cherokee 180	Carlisle Aviation Co Ltd/Crosby
	G-AVYO	PA-28 Cherokee 140	Noon Aircraft Leasing Ltd/Goodwood
	G-AVYP	PA-28 Cherokee 140	T. D. Reid (Braids) Ltd
	G-AVYR	PA-28 Cherokee 140	Dowty Rotol Flying Club/Staverton
	G-AVYS	PA-28R Cherokee Arrow 180	E. W. Passmore
	G-AVYT	PA-28R Cherokee Arrow 180	H. Stephenson/Tees-side
	G-AVYV	Jodel D.120	J. B. J. Berrow & M. A. Kaye/Shobdon
	G-AVYX	AB-206A JetRanger	S.W. Electricity Board/Bristol
	G-AVZA	IMCO Callair A-9	Arable & Bulb Chemicals Ltd
	G-AVZB	Aero Z-37 Cmelak	ADS (Aerial) Ltd/Southend
	G-AVZC	Hughes 269B	Ocean Rangers Charters Ltd/Thruxton
	G-AVZE	D.62B Condor	A. J. M. Trowbridge & J. Harris
	G-AVZI	Bo 208C Junior	C. F. Rogers
	G-AVZM	Beagle B.121 Pup 1	ARAZ Group/Elstree
	G-AVZN	Beagle B.121 Pup 1	W. E. Cro & Sons Ltd/Shoreham
	G-AVZO	Beagle B.121 Pup 1	Dungenair Ltd
	G-AVZP	Beagle B.121 Pup 1	T. A. White
	G-AVZR	PA-28 Cherokee 180	W. E. Lowe/Halfpenny Green
	G-AVZU	Cessna F.150H	E. J. R. McDowell
	G-AVZV	Cessna F.172H	Leisair Avionics Ltd
	G-AVZW	EAA Model P Biplane	R. G. Maidment & G. R. Edmundson/Goodwood
	G-AVZX	M.S.880B Rallye Club	Penbekon Contractors (Devon) Ltd/Plymouth
	G-AVZY	M.S.880B Rallye Club	R. McLindsay
	G-AWAA	M.S.880B Rallye Club	P. A. Cairns
	G-AWAC	GY-80 Horizon 180	Applied Sign Ltd
	G-AWAD	Beech D 55 Baron	College of Air Training/Bournemouth
	G-AWAE	Beech D 55 Baron	College of Air Training/Bournemouth
	G-AWAF	Beech D 55 Baron	College of Air Training/Bournemouth
	G-AWAG	Beech D 55 Baron	College of Air Training/Bournemouth
	G-AWAH	Beech D 55 Baron	College of Air Training/Bournemouth
	G-AWAI	Beech D 55 Baron	British Airways/Booker
	G-AWAJ	Beech D 55 Baron	College of Air Training/Bournemouth
	G-AWAK	Beech D 55 Baron	College of Air Training/Bournemouth
	G-AWAL	Beech D 55 Baron	College of Air Training/Bournemouth

Reg.	Type	Owner or Operator	Notes
G-AWAM	Beech D 55 Baron	College of Air Training/Bournemouth	
G-AWAN	Beech D 55 Baron	College of Air Training/Bournemouth	
G-AWAO	Beech D 55 Baron	College of Air Training/Bournemouth	
G-AWAT	D.62B Condor	Tiger Club Ltd/Redhill	
G-AWAU	Vickers F.B.27A Vimy (replica) (F8614) ★	RAF Museum	
G-AWAV	Cessna F.150F	J. F. Thurlow & J. H. Pickering/Ipswich	
G-AWAW	Cessna F.150F	G. J. Charlton	
G-AWAX	Cessna 150D	Cambridge Technical Developments (Leasing) Ltd	
G-AWAZ	PA-28R Cherokee Arrow 180	M. I. Edwards (Engineering) Ltd	
G-AWBA	PA-28R Cherokee Arrow 180	W. London Aero Services Ltd/ White Waltham	
G-AWBB	PA-28R Cherokee Arrow 180	Brian Neale Ltd/Sywell	
G-AWBC	PA-28R Cherokee Arrow 180	G. K. Furneaux/Blackbushe	
G-AWBE	PA-28 Cherokee 140	Aviation Technical Associates Ltd/ Jersey	
G-AWBG	PA-28 Cherokee 140	C. S. & B. A. Frost	
G-AWBH	PA-28 Cherokee 140	R. C. A. Mackworth	
G-AWBJ	Fournier RF-4D	The BJ Group/Redhill	
G-AWBL	BAC One-Eleven 416	British Airways County of Leicestershire/ Birmingham	
G-AWBM	D.31 Turbulent	J. T. S. Lewis	
G-AWBN	PA-30 Twin Comanche 160	Stourfield Investments Ltd/Jersey	
G-AWBP	Cessna 182L Skylane	A. H. & Mrs P. M. Butcher/Bournemouth	
G-AWBS	PA-28 Cherokee 140	W. London Aero Services Ltd/ White Waltham	
G-AWBT	PA-30 Twin Comanche 160	N. Y. Souster/Southampton	
G-AWBU	Morane-Saulnier N (replica) (M.S.50)	Personal Plane Services Ltd/Booker	
G-AWBV	Cessna 182L Skylane	Hunting Surveys & Consultants Ltd/ Manchester	
G-AWBW	Cessna F.172H ★	Brunel Technical College/Bristol	
G-AWBX	Cessna F.150H	D. F. Ranger & ptnrs	
G-AWCD	CEA DR.253	D. H. Smith	
G-AWCH	Cessna F.172H	M. Bua/Bournemouth	
G-AWCJ	Cessna F.150H	Transknight Ltd/Booker	
G-AWCL	Cessna F.150H	Signtest Ltd/Biggin Hill	
G-AWCM	Cessna F.150H	R. J. Jackson	
G-AWCN	Cessna FR.172E	LEC Refrigeration Ltd	
G-AWCP	Cessna F.150H (tailwheel)	Herefordshire Aero Club Ltd/Shobdon	
G-AWCW	Beech E.95 Travel Air	H. W. Astor/White Waltham	
G-AWCY	PA-32 Cherokee Six 260	Robinson & Carr Ltd/Wickenby	
G-AWDA	Nipper T.66 Srs. 3	D. F. Lea	
G-AWDD	Nipper T.66 Srs. 3	T. D. G. Roberts/Inverness	
G-AWDH	D.31 Turbulent	J. H. Tetley	
G-AWDI	PA-23 Aztec 250	Air Foyle Ltd/Luton	
G-AWDO	D.31 Turbulent	R. Watling-Greenwood	
G-AWDP	PA-28 Cherokee 180	Brian Ilston Ltd/Norwich	
G-AWDR	Cessna FR.172E	Levendene Ltd	
G-AWDU	Brantly B.2B	S. N. Cole	
G-AWDX	Beagle B.121 Pup 1	J. Pearse & O. D. West/Shoreham	
G-AWEF	Stampe SV-4B	Tiger Club Ltd/Redhill	
G-AWEG	Cessna 172G	H. Lawson/Usworth	
G-AWEI	D.62B Condor	M. A. Pearce/Redhill	
G-AWEL	Fournier RF.4D	A. B. Clymo/Halfpenny Green	
G-AWEM	Fournier RF.4D	B. J. Griffin/Wickenby	
G-AWEN	Jodel DR.1050	L. G. Earnshaw & ptnrs	
G-AWEO	Cessna F.150H	Banbury Plant Hire Ltd/Wellesbourne	
G-AWEP	JB-01 Minicab	P. H. Dyson & N. B. Gibbons/Barton	
G-AWER	PA-23 Aztec 250	Woodgate Air Services (IOM) Ltd	
G-AWES	Cessna 150H	Ralair Ltd/Edinburgh	
G-AWET	PA-28 Cherokee 180	Broadland Flying Group Ltd/ Swanton Morley	
G-AWEV	PA-28 Cherokee 140	Rite-Vent Ltd/Usworth	
G-AWEX	PA-28 Cherokee 140	R. V. Bowles	
G-AWEZ	PA-28R Cherokee Arrow 180	P. H. de Havilland/Cambridge	
G-AWFB	PA-28R Cherokee Arrow 180	Luke Aviation Ltd/Bristol	
G-AWFC	PA-28R Cherokee Arrow 180	K. A. Goodchild/Southend	
G-AWFD	PA-28R Cherokee Arrow 180	D. E. Roberts & J. G. Fisher/Birmingham	
G-AWFF	Cessna F.150H	Fowler Aviation Ltd/Elstree	

Notes	Reg.	Type	Owner or Operator
	G-AWFJ	PA-28R Cherokee Arrow 180	R. Watt
	G-AWFK	PA-28R Cherokee Arrow 180	J. A. Rundle (Holdings) Ltd/Kidlington
	G-AWFN	D.62B Condor	J. Guy
	G-AWFO	D.62B Condor	Cornwall Flying Group/St Just
	G-AWFP	D.62B Condor	Blackbushe Flying Club
	G-AWFT	Jodel D.9 Bebe	W. H. Cole
	G-AWFW	Jodel D.117	F. H. Greenwell
	G-AWFX	Sikorsky S-61N	British Airways Helicopters Ltd/ Aberdeen
	G-AWFY	SA.318C Alouette Astazou	N. Hutchings Ltd/Coventry
	G-AWFZ	Beech A23 Musketeer	R. Sweet & B D. Corbett/Thruxton
	G-AWGA	A.109 Airedale	RAFGSA/Bicester
	G-AWGD	Cessna F.172H	A. May/Biggin Hill
	G-AWGJ	Cessna F.172H	J. & C. J. Freeman/Headcorn
	G-AWGK	Cessna F.150H	Aerial Flying Group/Shoreham
	G-AWGL	Bensen B.8	M. H. J. Goldring
	G-AWGM	Mitchell-Procter Kittiwake 2	RAF Halton Flying Club Ltd
	G-AWGN	Fournier RF.4D	R. H. Ashforth/Staverton
	G-AWGR	Cessna F.172H	P. Bushell/Liverpool
	G-AWGU	AB-206B Jet Ranger 2	British Airways Helicopters Ltd/ Aberdeen
	G-AWGZ	Taylor JT.1 Monoplane	G. Jones
	G-AWHB	CASA 2.111 (6J+PR) ★	P. Raymond
	G-AWHV	Rollason Beta B.2A	Tiger Club Ltd/Redhill
	G-AWHW	Rollason Beta B.2A	C. E. Bellhouse/Redhill
	G-AWHX	Rollason Beta B.2	J. J. Cooke/Redhill
	G-AWIF	Brookland Mosquito	R. Watson
	G-AWIG	Jodel D.112	P. Hutchinson
	G-AWII	V.S.349 Spitfire VC (AR501)	Shuttleworth Trust/Duxford
	G-AWIJ	V.S.329 Spitfire IIA (P7350)	RAF Battle of Britain Historic Aircraft Flight/Coningsby
	G-AWIN	Campbell-Bensen B.8MC	M. J. Cuttel & J. Deane
	G-AWIO	Brantly B.2B	G. J. Ward & ptnrs/Staverton
	G-AWIP	Luton LA-4A Minor	J. Houghton/Doncaster
	G-AWIR	Midget Mustang	K. E. Sword/Leicester
	G-AWIT	PA-28 Cherokee 180	Faulkner & ptnrs/Goodwood
	G-AWIV	Storey TSR.3	C. J. Jesson/Redhill
	G-AWIW	Stampe SV.4B ★	Aerospace Museum/Cosford
	G-AWIY	PA-23 Aztec 250	Queen's University of Belfast
	G-AWJA	Cessna 182L Skylane	Mercia Aviation/Wellesbourne
	G-AWJC	Brighton gas balloon	P. D. Furlong *Slippery William*
	G-AWJE	Nipper T.66 Srs. 3	N. McArthur & T. Mosedale
	G-AWJF	Nipper T.66 Srs. 3	R. Wilcock/Shoreham
	G-AWJI	M.S.880B Rallye Club	D. V. Tyler/Ipswich
	G-AWJO	Tigercraft Tiger Mk. II	K. Aziz
	G-AWJT	Tigercraft Tiger Mk.I	J. H. Turner
	G-AWJV	D.H.98 Mosquito TT Mk.35 (TA634) ★	Mosquito Aircraft Museum
	G-AWJX	Z.526 Akrobat	Aerobatics International Ltd/ Farnborough
	G-AWJY	Z.526 Akrobat	Elco Manufacturing Co/Kidlington
	G-AWKB	M.J.5 Sirocco F2/39	G. D. Claxton
	G-AWKD	PA-17 Vagabond	A. T. & Mrs M. R. Dowie/ White Waltham
	G-AWKM	B.121 Pup 1	D. M. G. Jenkins/Swansea
	G-AWKO	B.121 Pup 1	S. G.Bailey & ptnrs/Luton
	G-AWKP	Jodel DR.253	R. C. Chandless
	G-AWKT	M.S.880B Rallye Club	D. C.Strain
	G-AWKW	PA-24 Comanche 180	F. J. Bellamy/St. Just
	G-AWKX	Beech A65 Queen Air	Westgate Shipping Ltd
	G-AWKZ	PA-23 Apache 160	E. A. Clack & T. Pritchard/Southend
	G-AWLA	Cessna F.150H	S. M. Bent & P. Thompson/Luton
	G-AWLB	D.31 Turbulent	A. E. Shouler
	G-AWLE	Cessna F.172H	Sunderland Flying Club Ltd
	G-AWLF	Cessna F.172H	Clement Spring Co Ltd/Coventry
	G-AWLG	SIPA 903	S. W. Markham
	G-AWLI	PA-22 Tri-Pacer 150	S. J. Saggers/Biggin Hill
	G-AWLJ	Cessna F.150H	D. S. Watts/Southend
	G-AWLL	AB-206B JetRanger 2	F. Lloyd (Penley) Ltd
	G-AWLM	Bensen B.8MS	C. J. E. Ashby
	G-AWLO	Boeing N2S-5 Kaydet	Warbirds of GB/Blackbushe

Reg.	Type	Owner or Operator	Notes
G-AWLP	Mooney M.20F	Siminco Ltd	
G-AWLR	Nipper T.66 Srs. 3	J. D. Lowther	
G-AWLS	Nipper T. 66 Srs. 3	D. W. Griffiths/Sibson	
G-AWLW	Hawker Hurricane IIB (P3308)	Davis Trust/Strathallan	
G-AWLY	Cessna F.150H	Banbury Plant Hire Ltd	
G-AWLZ	Fournier RF.4D	E. V. Goodwin & C. R. Williamson	
G-AWMC	Campbell-Bensen B.8MS	M. E. Sykes-Hankinson	
G-AWMD	Jodel D.11	J. Gilkspie	
G-AWMF	PA-18-150 Super Cub	Airways Aero Associations Ltd/Booker	
G-AWMI	Glos-Airtourer 115	Red Dragon Aviation Ltd	
G-AWMK	AB-206A JetRanger	Bristow Helicopters Ltd	
G-AWMM	M.S.893A Rallye Commodore 180	Tug 83 Group/Perranporth	
G-AWMN	Luton LA-4A Minor	R. E. R. Wilks	
G-AWMP	Cessna F.172H	W. Rennie-Roberts/Ipswich	
G-AWMR	D.31 Turbulent	P. R. M. Bowlan/Redhill	
G-AWMT	Cessna F.150H	R. V. Grocott/Sleap	
G-AWMU	Cessna F.172H	H. M. Jackson & B. D. Jones/Wellesbourne	
G-AWNA	Boeing 747-136	British Airways *Sir Richard Grenville*/Heathrow	
G-AWNB	Boeing 747-136	British Airways *City of Newcastle*/Heathrow	
G-AWNC	Boeing 747-136	British Airways *City of Belfast*/Heathrow	
G-AWND	Boeing 747-136	British Airways *Christopher Marlowe*/Heathrow	
G-AWNE	Boeing 747-136	British Airways *Sir Francis Drake*/Heathrow	
G-AWNF	Boeing 747-136	British Airways *City of Westminster*/Heathrow	
G-AWNG	Boeing 747-136	British Airways *City of London*/Heathrow	
G-AWNH	Boeing 747-136	British Airways *Sir Walter Raleigh*/Heathrow	
G-AWNJ	Boeing 747-136	British Airways *John Donne*/Heathrow	
G-AWNL	Boeing 747-136	British Airways *William Shakespeare*/Heathrow	
G-AWNM	Boeing 747-136	British Airways *City of Bristol*/Heathrow	
G-AWNN	Boeing 747-136	British Airways *Sebastian Cabot*/Heathrow	
G-AWNO	Boeing 747-136	British Airways *Sir Francis Bacon*/Heathrow	
G-AWNP	Boeing 747-136	British Airways *Sir John Hawkins*/Heathrow	
G-AWNT	BN-2A Islander	B.K.S. Surveys Ltd/Eglinton	
G-AWOA	M.S.880B Rallye Club	G. C. Taylor/Exeter	
G-AWOE	Aero Commander 680E	J. M. Houlder/Elstree	
G-AWOF	PA-15 Vagabond	R. A. & S. C. O'Neill	
G-AWOH	PA-17 Vagabond	K. M Bowen	
G-AWOL	Bell 206B JetRanger 2	Gemton Ltd/Liverpool	
G-AWOT	Cessna F.150H	I. R. Fraser	
G-AWOU	Cessna 170B	Red Fir Aviation Ltd/Clacton	
G-AWPH	P.56 Provost T.1	J. A. D. Bradshaw	
G-AWPJ	Cessna F.150H	W. J. Greenfield/Humberside	
G-AWPL	Bensen B.8	N. F. Higgins	
G-AWPN	Shield Xyla	T. Worrall/Finmere	
G-AWPP	Cessna F.150H	D. Williams	
G-AWPS	PA-28 Cherokee 140	Jakecourt Ltd/Bournemouth	
G-AWPU	Cessna F.150J	Light Planes (Lancashire) Ltd/Barton	
G-AWPW	PA-12 Super Cruiser	T. S. Warren & ptnrs/Sandown	
G-AWPX	Cessna 150E	W. R. Emberton/Southampton	
G-AWPZ	Andreasson BA-4B	S. A. W. Becker/Shoreham	
G-AWRB	B.121 Pup 1	P. O. P. Pulvermacher/Shoreham	
G-AWRK	Cessna F.150J	C. M. Evans/Wyberton	
G-AWRL	Cessna F.172H	R. D. Snow/Doncaster	
G-AWRS	Avro 19 Srs. 2 ★	N. E. Aircraft Museum	
G-AWRY	P.56 Provost T.1 (XF836)	Shuttleworth Trust/O. Warden	
G-AWRZ	Bell 47G-5	Land Air Services Ltd/Wellesbourne	
G-AWSA	Avro 652A Anson 19 (VL349) ★	Norfolk & Suffolk Aviation Museum	
G-AWSD	Cessna F.150J	Felthorpe Flying Group Ltd	

Notes	Reg.	Type	Owner or Operator
	G-AWSH	Z.526 Akrobat	Aerobatics International Ltd/Booker
	G-AWSL	PA-28 Cherokee 180D	Fascia Ltd/Southend
	G-AWSM	PA-28 Cherokee 235	Colton Aviation Services Ltd/Elstree
	G-AWSN	D.62B Condor	J. Leader
	G-AWSP	D.62B Condor	R. Q. & A. S. Bond/Enstone
	G-AWSS	D.62C Condor	J. L. Kinch
	G-AWST	D.62B Condor	Humberside Aviation
	G-AWSV	Skeeter 12 (XM553)	Maj. M. Somerton-Rayner/ Middle Wallop
	G-AWSY	Boeing 737-204	Britannia Airways Ltd General James Wolfe/Luton
	G-AWSZ	M.S.894A Rallye Minerva 220	D. Quinn & J. McCloskey
	G-AWTA	Cessna E.310N	A. H. Wiltshire/Fairoaks
	G-AWTJ	Cessna F.150J	Metropolitan Police Flying Club/ Biggin Hill
	G-AWTL	PA-28 Cherokee 180D	R. V. Longman/Stapleford
	G-AWTM	PA-28 Cherokee 140	Keenair Services Ltd/Liverpool
	G-AWTR	Beech A.23 Musketeer	J. & P. Donoher
	G-AWTV	Beech A.23 Musketeer	D. J. Johnson/Biggin Hill
	G-AWTW	Beech B.55 Baron	Worldwide Wheels Ltd/Bristol
	G-AWTX	Cessna F.150J	R. Pennington
	G-AWUA	Cessna P.206D	Balmar Aviation/Thruxton
	G-AWUB	GY.201-Minicab	H. P. Burrill
	G-AWUE	Jodel DR.1050	S. Bichan
	G-AWUF	H.S.125 Srs 1B	Goodman Air Taxis
	G-AWUG	Cessna F.150H	G. Hull
	G-AWUH	Cessna F.150H	M. J. Passingham/Hamble
	G-AWUJ	Cessna F.150H	R. J. Jones & J. M. Allen/Biggin Hill
	G-AWUL	Cessna F.150H	T. R. Sinclair/Kirkwall
	G-AWUN	Cessna F.150H	Northamptonshire School of Flying Ltd/ Sywell
	G-AWUO	Cessna F.150H	W. Todd
	G-AWUP	Cessna F.150H	R. H. Timmis/Bournemouth
	G-AWUS	Cessna F.150J	Recreational Flying Centre (Popham) Ltd
	G-AWUT	Cessna F.150J	T. I. Murtough/Tollerton
	G-AWUU	Cessna F.150J	S. G. McNulty
	G-AWUW	Cessna F.172H	T. A. Holding
	G-AWUX	Cessna F.172H	J. D. A. Shields & ptnrs/Lydd
	G-AWUY	Cessna F.172H	J. & B. Powell (Printers) Ltd/Manston
	G-AWUZ	Cessna F.172H	K. Wickenden/Shoreham
	G-AWVA	Cessna F.172H	R. G. F. Allwright
	G-AWVB	Jodel D.117	C. M. & T. R. C. Griffin/Swansea
	G-AWVC	B.121 Pup 1	S. W. Bates
	G-AWVE	Jodel DR.1050M.I	E. A. Taylor/Southend
	G-AWVF	P.56 Provost T.1	Rural Flying Corps/Bourn
	G-AWVG	AESL Airtourer T.2	R. S. Gibson/Goodwood
	G-AWVK	H.P.137 Jetstream	Decca Navigator Co Ltd/Biggin Hill
	G-AWVN	Aeronca 7AC Champion	Bowker Air Services Ltd/Rush Green
	G-AWVP	Brookland Hornet	Brookland Rotorcraft Ltd
	G-AWVS	Cessna 337D	Peterborough Aero Club Ltd/Sibson
	G-AWVZ	Jodel D.112	D. C. Stokes/Dunkeswell
	G-AWWE	B.121 Pup 2	G. J. Bunting
	G-AWWF	B.121 Pup 1	J. Pothecary
	G-AWWI	Jodel D.117	R. L. Sambell
	G-AWWM	GY-201 Minicab	J. S. Brayshaw
	G-AWWN	Jodel DR.1051	T. W. M. Beck & ptnrs/Shoreham
	G-AWWO	Jodel DR.1050	Whiskey Oscar Group/Barton
	G-AWWP	Woody Pusher III	M. S. Bird & Mrs R. D. Bird
	G-AWWT	D.31 Turbulent	J. C. Alderton & J. S. Moreton-Hale/ Redhill
	G-AWWU	Cessna FR.172F	Dowdeswell Engineering Co Ltd/ Coventry
	G-AWWV	Cessna FR.172F	I. R. Hamilton & J. P. M. Stewart/
	G-AWWW	Cessna 401	Westair Flying Services Ltd/Blackpool
	G-AWWX	BAC One-Eleven 509	Dan-Air Services Ltd/Gatwick
	G-AWWZ	BAC One-Eleven 509	Monarch Airlines Ltd/Luton
	G-AWXA	Cessna 182M Skylane	R. E. & Mrs U. C. Mankelow/Staverton
	G-AWXO	H.S.125 Srs. 400B	Alkharafi Aviation Ltd/Jersey
	G-AWXR	PA-28 Cherokee 180D	J. D. Williams
	G-AWXS	PA-28 Cherokee 180D	Rayhenro Flying Group/Shobdon

Reg.	Type	Owner or Operator	Notes
G-AWXU	Cessna F.150J	B. B. Burtenshaw & ptnrs/Breighton	
G-AWXV	Cessna F.172H	D. N. Forrest/Blackpool	
G-AWXX	Wessex Mk, 60 Srs. 1	Glos-Air (Services) Ltd/Bournemouth	
G-AWXY	M.S.885 Super Rallye	J. & B. Fowler	
G-AWXZ	SNCAN SV-4C	Personal Plane Services Ltd/Booker	
G-AWYB	Cessna FR.172F	C. W. Larkin/Southend	
G-AWYE	H.S.125 Srs 1B	Rolls-Royce Ltd/E. Midlands	
G-AWYF	G.159 Gulfstream 1	Ford Motor Co Ltd/Stansted	
G-AWYJ	B.121 Pup 2	H. C. Taylor/Southampton	
G-AWYL	Jodel DR.253B	Clarville Ltd/Headcorn	
G-AWYO	B.121 Pup 1	B. R. C. Wild/Popham	
G-AWYR	BAC One-Eleven 501	British Caledonian Airways *Isle of Tiree*/Gatwick	
G-AWYS	BAC One-Eleven 501	British Caledonian Airways *Isle of Bute*/Gatwick	
G-AWYT	BAC One-Eleven 501	British Caledonian Airways *Isle of Barra*/Gatwick	
G-AWYU	BAC One-Eleven 501	British Caledonian Airways *Isle of Colonsay*/Gatwick	
G-AWYV	BAC One-Eleven 501	British Caledonian Airways *Isle of Harris*/Gatwick	
G-AWYX	M.S.880B Rallye Club	Joy M. L. Edwards/Thruxton	
G-AWYY	T.57 Camel replica (C1701)	Leisure Sport Ltd/Thorpe Park	
G-AWYZ	H.S.121 Trident 3B	British Airways (*WFU*)/Heathrow	
G-AWZA	H.S.121 Trident 3B	British Airways (*WFU*)/Heathrow	
G-AWZB	H.S.121 Trident 3B	British Airways (*WFU*)/Heathrow	
G-AWZC	H.S.121 Trident 3B	British Airways/Heathrow	
G-AWZD	H.S.121 Trident 3B	British Airways/Heathrow	
G-AWZE	H.S.121 Trident 3B	British Airways (*WFU*)/Heathrow	
G-AWZF	H.S.121 Trident 3B	British Airways/Heathrow	
G-AWZG	H.S.121 Trident 3B	British Airways/Heathrow	
G-AWZH	H.S.121 Trident 3B	British Airways/Heathrow	
G-AWZI	H.S.121 Trident 3B	British Airways/Heathrow	
G-AWZJ	H.S.121 Trident 3B	British Airways/Heathrow	
G-AWZK	H.S.121 Trident 3B	British Airways/Heathrow	
G-AWZL	H.S.121 Trident 3B	British Airways (*WFU*)/Heathrow	
G-AWZM	H.S.121 Trident 3B	British Airways/Heathrow	
G-AWZN	H.S.121 Trident 3B	British Airways/Heathrow	
G-AWZO	H.S.121 Trident 3B	British Airways/Heathrow	
G-AWZP	H.S.121 Trident 3B	British Airways/Heathrow	
G-AWZR	H.S.121 Trident 3B	British Airways/Heathrow	
G-AWZS	H.S.121 Trident 3B	British Airways/Heathrow	
G-AWZU	H.S.121 Trident 3B	British Airways/Heathrow	
G-AWZV	H.S.121 Trident 3B	British Airways/Heathrow	
G-AWZW	H.S.121 Trident 3B	British Airways/Heathrow	
G-AWZX	H.S.121 Trident 3B	British Airways/Heathrow	
G-AWZZ	H.S.121 Trident 3B	British Airways/Heathrow	
G-AXAB	PA-28 Cherokee 140	Bencray Ltd/Blackpool	
G-AXAK	M.S.880B Rallye Club	R. L. & Mrs C. Stewart/Redhill	
G-AXAN	D.H.82A Tiger Moth	A. J. Cheshire/Staverton	
G-AXAO	Omega 56 balloon	P. D. Furlong *Renatus Cartesius*	
G-AXAS	Wallis WA-116T	K. H. Wallis (G-AVDH)	
G-AXAT	Jodel D.117A	J. F. Barber/Redhill	
G-AXAU	PA-30 Twin Comanche 160C	Bartcourt Ltd/Southampton	
G-AXAV	PA-30 Twin Comanche 160C	P. S. King/Guernsey	
G-AXAW	Cessna 421A	Airline Air Spares Ltd/Southend	
G-AXAX	PA-23 Aztec 250D	Euroair Transport Ltd/Biggin Hill	
G-AXAZ	PA-31 Navajo	Meridian Airmaps Ltd/Shoreham	
G-AXBB	BAC One-Eleven 409	British Island Airways *Island Entente*/Gatwick	
G-AXBG	Bensen B.8M	R. Curtis	
G-AXBH	Cessna F.172H	Farrowcrest Ltd/Bourn	
G-AXBJ	Cessna F.172H	K. M. Brennan & C. Mackay/Leicester	
G-AXBZ	D.H.82A Tiger Moth	D. H. McWhir	
G-AXCA	PA-28R Cherokee Arrow 200	J. A. Tooth/Halfpenny Green	
G-AXCC	Bell 47G-2	P. Lancaster/Shoreham	
G-AXCG	Jodel D.117	J. W. Hollingsworth & M. J. Doherty/Blackpool	
G-AXCI	Bensen B.8M ★	Loughborough & Leicester Aircraft Museum	

Notes	Reg.	Type	Owner or Operator
	G-AXCL	M.S.880B Rallye Club	Long Marston Flying Group
	G-AXCM	M.S.880B Rallye Club	M. A. Jones
	G-AXCN	M.S.880B Rallye Club	R. T. Griffiths/Swansea
	G-AXCP	BAC One-Eleven 401	Dan Air Services Ltd/Gatwick
	G-AXCX	B.121 Pup 2	A. C. Townend
	G-AXCY	Jodel D.117	R. M. Rennoldson
	G-AXCZ	Stampe SV-4C	Keenair Services Ltd/Liverpool
	G-AXDB	Piper L-4B Cub	N. D. Norman/Bembridge
	G-AXDC	PA-23 Aztec 250D	Trago Mills (South Devon) Ltd/Bodmin
	G-AXDE	Bensen B.8	T. J. Hartwell
	G-AXDH	BN-2A Islander	Parachute Regiment Freefall Club
	G-AXDI	Cessna F.172H	Jim Russell International Racing Drivers Ltd
	G-AXDK	Jodel DR.315	P. J. Checketts & T. J. Thomas/Sywell
	G-AXDL	PA-30 Twin Comanche 160C	Northern Executive Aviation Ltd/Manchester
	G-AXDM	H.S.125 Srs 400B	Ferranti Ltd/Edinburgh
	G-AXDN	BAC-Sud Concorde 01 ★	Duxford Aviation Soc
	G-AXDU	B.121 Pup 2	Deltair Ltd/Chester
	G-AXDV	B.121 Pup 1	R. A. Chappel/Thruxton
	G-AXDW	B.121 Pup 1	Cranfield Institute of Technology
	G-AXDY	Falconar F-II	G. K. Ellis
	G-AXDZ	Cassutt Racer Srs IIIM	A. Chadwick/Little Staughton
	G-AXEB	Cassutt Racer Srs IIIM	G. E. Horder/Denham
	G-AXEC	Cessna 182M	Sky-Ryte Promotions/White Waltham
	G-AXED	PA-25 Pawnee 235	Sprayfields (Scothern) Ltd/Wickenby
	G-AXEI	Ward Gnome ★	Lincolnshire Aviation Museum
	G-AXEO	Scheibe SF.25B Falke	D. Collinson/Usworth
	G-AXES	B.121 Pup 2	D. A. Lowe & A. Molesworth/Nairobi
	G-AXEU	B.121 Pup 2	Wings Flying Group/Swansea
	G-AXEV	B.121 Pup 2	B. Richardson/Southend
	G-AXEW	B.121 Pup 1	C. J. Spicer & A. A. Gray/Andrewsfield
	G-AXEX	B.121 Pup 1	Lubair (Transport Services) Ltd/E. Midlands
	G-AXFB	BN-3 Nymph	NDN Aircraft Ltd/Sandown
	G-AXFD	PA-25 Pawnee 235	J.E.F. Aviation Ltd
	G-AXFE	Beech B.90 King Air	GKN Contractors Ltd/Birmingham
	G-AXFG	Cessna 337D	Alfred Smith & Son (Penzance) Ltd/St Just
	G-AXFH	D.H.114 Heron 1B/C	Hurst Rent-a-Car Ltd/Fairoaks
	G-AXFN	Jodel D.119	D. C. Barber & B. Sleddon
	G-AXGA	PA-19 Super Cub 95	Felthorpe Flying Group Ltd
	G-AXGC	M.S.880B Rallye Club	K. M. & H. Bowen
	G-AXGD	M.S.880B Rallye Club	M. L. Goode/Stapleford
	G-AXGE	M.S.880B Rallye Club	R. P. Loxton
	G-AXGG	Cessna F.150J	A. R. Nicholls/Compton Abbas
	G-AXGP	Piper L-4B Cub	W. K. Butler
	G-AXGR	Luton LA-4A Minor	T. M. W. Webster/Long Marston
	G-AXGS	D.62B Condor	Tiger Club Ltd/Redhill
	G-AXGT	D.62B Condor	P. Simpson & ptnrs
	G-AXGU	D.62B Condor	Tiger Club Ltd/Redhill
	G-AXGV	D.62B Condor	R. J. Wrixon
	G-AXGX	Boeing 707-336C	Ruler of Qatar
	G-AXGZ	D.62B Condor	Lincoln Condor Group/Sturgate
	G-AXHA	Cessna 337A	S. E. Fellows/Southampton
	G-AXHC	Stampe SV-4C	BLS Aviation Ltd
	G-AXHE	BN-2A Islander	NW Parachute Centre/Cark
	G-AXHG	M.S.880B Rallye Club	The Rallye Groupe/Tees-side
	G-AXHI	M.S.880B Rallye Club	W. M. S. Innes & A. J. L. Evans
	G-AXHO	B.121 Pup 2	M. J. Steele/Andrewsfield
	G-AXHP	Piper L-4H Cub	R. Giles/Clacton
	G-AXHR	Piper L-4H Cub (329601)	D. E. Elphick/O. Warden
	G-AXHS	M.S.880B Rallye Club	R. Allan
	G-AXHT	M.S.880B Rallye Club	J. L. Osbourne & A. M. Sutton
	G-AXHV	Jodel D.117A	D. M. Cashmore & K. R. Payne
	G-AXHX	M.S.892A Rallye Commodore	G. A. Knight & W. Weever
	G-AXIA	B.121 Pup 1	Cranfield Institute of Technology
	G-AXIE	B.121 Pup 2	I. J. Ross & ptnrs/Ronaldsway
	G-AXIF	B.121 Pup 2	T. G. Hiscock
	G-AXIG	B.125 Bulldog 104	George House (Holdings) Ltd/Compton Abbas

G-AXMU   BAC One-Eleven 432 of British Island Airways.

44

Reg.	Type	Owner or Operator	Notes
G-AXIH	Bu 133 Jungmeister (AX+IH)	R. M. Stow/White Waltham	
G-AXIO	PA-28 Cherokee 140B	W. London Aero Services Ltd/ White Waltham	
G-AXIR	PA-28 Cherokee 140B	C. T. Brinson/Weston Zoyland	
G-AXIT	M.S.893A Rallye Commodore 180	South Wales Gliding Club Ltd	
G-AXIW	Scheibe SF.25B Falke	Herefordshire Gliding Club Ltd/Shobdon	
G-AXIX	Glos-Airtourer 150	I. Holden & M. Mann/Shotteswell	
G-AXIY	Bird Gyrocopter	Gerald Bird	
G-AXJB	Omega 84 balloon	Hot-air Group *Jester*	
G-AXJH	B.121 Pup 2	J. Pearce/Goodwood	
G-AXJI	B.121 Pup 2	Cole Aviation Ltd	
G-AXJJ	B.121 Pup 2	K. E. Buyer & ptnrs	
G-AXJK	BAC One-Eleven 501	British Caledonian Airways *Isle of Staffa*/Gatwick	
G-AXJM	BAC One-Eleven 501	British Caledonian Airways *Isle of Islay*/ Gatwick	
G-AXJN	B.121 Pup 2	J. B. Goodrich & D. M. Jenkins/ Shoreham	
G-AXJO	B.121 Pup 2	D. G. Chafferton/White Waltham	
G-AXJR	Scheibe SF.25B Falke	D. R. Chatterton/Staverton	
G-AXJV	PA-28 Cherokee 140B	Mona Aviation Ltd	
G-AXJW	PA-28 Cherokee 140B	D. L. Claydon	
G-AXJX	PA-28 Cherokee 140B	MSF Aviation Ltd/Manchester	
G-AXJY	Cessna U-206D	Hereford Parachute Club Ltd/Shobdon	
G-AXKD	PA-23 Aztec 250D	Jones & Bailey Contractors Ltd/ Glenrothes	
G-AXKH	Luton LA-4A Minor	M. E. Vaisey	
G-AXKI	Jodel D.9 Bebe	A. F. Cashin	
G-AXKJ	Jodel D.9 Bebe	C. H. Morris/Leavesden	
G-AXKK	Westland Bell 47G-4A	Bristow Helicopters Ltd	
G-AXKL	Westland Bell 47G-4A	Helicare Ltd/Liverpool	
G-AXKM	Westland Bell 47G-4A	Bristow Helicopters Ltd	
G-AXKN	Westland Bell 47G-4A	Helicare Ltd/Liverpool	
G-AXKO	Westland Bell 47G-4A	Bristow Helicopters Ltd	
G-AXKR	Westland Bell 47G-4A	Helicare Ltd/Liverpool	
G-AXKS	Westland Bell 47G-4A	Museum of Army Flying/Middle Wallop	
G-AXKU	Westland Bell 47G-4A	Bristow Helicopters Ltd	
G-AXKW	Westland Bell 47G-4A	Bristow Helicopters Ltd	
G-AXKX	Westland Bell 47G-4A	Bristow Helicopters Ltd	
G-AXKY	Westland Bell 47G-4A	Bristow Helicopters Ltd	
G-AXKZ	Westland Bell 47G-4A	Helicare Ltd/Liverpool	
G-AXLA	Westland Bell 47G-4A	Helicare Ltd/Liverpool	
G-AXLG	Cessna 310K	Smiths (Outdrives) Ltd	
G-AXLI	Nipper T.66 Srs 3	N. J. Arthur	
G-AXLL	BAC One-Eleven 523FJ	British Aerospace PLC	
G-AXLS	Jodel DR.105A	T. L. Giles/Doncaster	
G-AXLZ	PA-19 Super Cub 95	J. C. Quantrell/Ludham	
G-AXMA	PA-24 Comanche 180	Tegrel Products Ltd/Newcastle	
G-AXMB	Slingsby T.7 Motor Cadet	I. G. Smith/Langar	
G-AXMD	Omega 20 balloon	Nimble Bread Ltd *Nimble*	
G-AXME	SNCAN SV-4C	D. W. Hawthorne/Oporto	
G-AXMG	BAC One-Eleven 518	Monarch Airlines Ltd/Luton	
G-AXMN	J/5B Autocar	A. R. Norman/Bembridge	
G-AXMP	PA-28 Cherokee 180	D. J. Edensor	
G-AXMS	PA-30 Twin Comanche 160C	Ernest Green International Ltd/ Biggin Hill	
G-AXMT	Bu 133 Jungmeister	D. J. Berry/Hong Kong	
G-AXMU	BAC One-Eleven 432	British Island Airways *Island Esprit*/ Gatwick	
G-AXMW	B.121 Pup 1	DJP Engineering (Knebworth) Ltd	
G-AXMX	B.121 Pup 2	Susan A. Jones/France	
G-AXNA	Boeing 737-204C	Britannia Airways Ltd *Robert Clive of India*/Luton	
G-AXNB	Boeing 737-204C	Britannia Airways Ltd *Charles Darwin*/ Luton	
G-AXNC	Boeing 737-204	Britannia Airways Ltd *Isambard Kingdom Brunel*/Luton	
G-AXNJ	Wassmer Jodel D.120	Clive Flying Group/Sleap	
G-AXNK	Cessna F.150J	Mona Aviation Ltd	
G-AXNL	B.121 Pup 1	D. C. Barber/St Just	
G-AXNM	B.121 Pup 1	G. B. Knox	

Notes	Reg.	Type	Owner or Operator
	G-AXNN	B.121 Pup 2	Romney Marsh Flying Group/Lydd
	G-AXNP	B.121 Pup 2	Deltair Ltd/Chester
	G-AXNR	B.121 Pup 2	Specialised Mouldings Ltd & G. Broadley
	G-AXNS	B.121 Pup 2	S. J. Figures & N. Fields/Netherthorpe
	G-AXNW	SNCAN SV-4C	E. N. Grace
	G-AXNX	Cessna 182M	Machine Music Ltd/Blackbushe
	G-AXNZ	Pitts S.1C Special	W. A. Jordan
	G-AXOG	PA-23 Aztec 250D	R. W. Diggens/Denham
	G-AXOH	M.S.894 Rallye Minerva	Bristol Cars Ltd/White Waltham
	G-AXOI	Jodel D.9 Bebe	P. W. Thomas/Barton
	G-AXOJ	B.121 Pup 2	TM Air Ltd/Sywell
	G-AXOL	Currie Wot	J. A. Espin/Popham
	G-AXOR	PA-28 Cherokee 180D	P. D. Allum/Compton Abbas
	G-AXOS	M.S.894A Rallye Minerva	Seven Flying Group/Booker
	G-AXOT	M.S.893 Rallye Commodore 180	P. Evans & D. Riley
	G-AXOV	Beech B55A Baron	S. Brod/Elstree
	G-AXOW	PA-23 Aztec 250	G. Costello/Dublin
	G-AXOX	BAC One-Eleven 432	British Island Airways *Island Endeavour*/Gatwick
	G-AXOZ	B.121 Pup 1	P. R. Sexton & ptnrs/Shipdham
	G-AXPB	B.121 Pup 1	D. J. Sage/Cardiff
	G-AXPD	B.121 Pup 1	Surrey & Kent Flying Club Ltd/Biggin Hill
	G-AXPF	Cessna F.150K	Y. Newell/Booker
	G-AXPG	Mignet HM-293	W. H. Cole
	G-AXPM	B.121 Pup 1	D. Taylor/E. Midlands
	G-AXPN	B.121 Pup 2	Starline Elms Coaches/Elstree
	G-AXPZ	Campbell Cricket	W. R. Partridge
	G-AXRA	Campbell Cricket	L. E. Schnurr
	G-AXRB	Campbell Cricket	J. C. P. Thomas
	G-AXRC	Campbell Cricket	K. W. Hayr/(*Stored*)
	G-AXRD	Campbell Cricket	Glyndwr Rees
	G-AXRK	Practavia Sprite 115	E. G. Thale
	G-AXRL	PA-28 Cherokee 160	T. W. Clark/Headcorn
	G-AXRO	PA-30 Twin Comanche 160C	Havelet Aviation
	G-AXRP	SNCAN SV-4C	M. D. Tweedle & ptnrs
	G-AXRR	Auster AOP.9 (XR241)	British Aerial Museum/Duxford
	G-AXRS	Boeing 707-355C	British Caledonian Airways/Gatwick
	G-AXRT	Cessna FA.150K (tailwheel)	W. H. Milner/Brough
	G-AXRU	Cessna FA.150K	Arrival Enterprises Ltd
	G-AXSC	B.121 Pup 1	J. Hawkins/Manston
	G-AXSD	B.121 Pup 1	Surrey & Kent Flying Club Ltd/Biggin Hill
	G-AXSF	Nash Petrel	Nash Aircraft Ltd/Lasham
	G-AXSG	PA-28 Cherokee 180	Shropshire Aero Club Ltd/Sleap
	G-AXSH	PA-28 Cherokee 140	EAA Aviation Ltd/Fairoaks
	G-AXSJ	Cessna FA.150K	C. N. Peate & B. Maggs/Fairoaks
	G-AXSM	Jodel DR.1051	C. Cousten/White Waltham
	G-AXSR	Brantly B.2B ★	Museum of Flight/E. Fortune
	G-AXSV	Jodel DR.340	Leonard F. Jollye Ltd
	G-AXSW	Cessna FA.150K	Furness Aviation Ltd/Cark
	G-AXSX	Beech C.23 Musketeer	D. M. Balfour/Blackpool
	G-AXSZ	PA-28 Cherokee 140B	N. Cureton & R. B. Cheek/Sandown
	G-AXTA	PA-28 Cherokee 140B	Carlisle Aviation Co Ltd
	G-AXTC	PA-28 Cherokee 140B	A. Buczkowski & D. Rose/Booker
	G-AXTD	PA-28 Cherokee 140B	Vincent-Walker Engineering Ltd/Southend
	G-AXTE	PA-28 Cherokee 140B	N. Clayton
	G-AXTG	PA-28 Cherokee 140B	J. P. Pottier/Staverton
	G-AXTH	PA-28 Cherokee 140B	W. London Aero Services Ltd/White Waltham
	G-AXTI	PA-28 Cherokee 140B	I. K. George/Fairoaks
	G-AXTJ	PA-28 Cherokee 140B	S. G. Gibbons
	G-AXTK	PA-28 Cherokee 140B	Andrewsfield Flying Club Ltd
	G-AXTL	PA-28 Cherokee 140B	L. Williams/Elstree
	G-AXTO	PA-24 Comanche 260	Elecwind (Clay Cross) Ltd/E. Midlands
	G-AXTP	PA-28 Cherokee 180	E. R. Moore/Denham
	G-AXTX	Jodel D.112	J. J. Penney/Swansea
	G-AXUA	B.121 Pup 1	F. R. Blennerhassett & C. Wedlake/Tees-side

Reg.	Type	Owner or Operator	Notes
G-AXUB	BN-2A Islander	Headcorn Parachute Club	
G-AXUC	PA-12 Super Cruiser	V. N. Mukaloff/Manston	
G-AXUE	Jodel DR.105A	S•x Group/Netherthorpe	
G-AXUF	Cessna FA.150K	Turnhouse Flying Club Ltd	
G-AXUI	H.P.137 Jetstream 1	Cranfield Institute of Technology	
G-AXUJ	J/I Autocrat	R. G. Earp & J. W. H. Lee/Sibson	
G-AXUK	Jodel DR.1050	R. Pidcock & ptnrs/Sibson	
G-AXUM	H.P.137 Jetstream 1	Cranfield Institute of Technology	
G-AXUV	Cessna F.172H	F. A. & Mrs E. M. Smith/Shobdon	
G-AXUW	Cessna FA.150K	Coventry Air Training School	
G-AXUX	Beech B95 Travel Air	Melbren Air Ltd/Liverpool	
G-AXUZ	Practavia Sprite 125	B. Healey/Booker	
G-AXVB	Cessna F.172H	C. Gabbitas/Staverton	
G-AXVC	Cessna FA.150K	Rob Hughes Garages Ltd/Barton	
G-AXVG	H.S.748 Srs 2A	Dan-Air Services Ltd/Gatwick	
G-AXVK	Campbell Cricket	Campbell Gyroplanes Ltd	
G-AXVM	Campbell Cricket	D. M. Organ/Staverton	
G-AXVN	McCandless M.4	R. McCandless/(Stored)	
G-AXVS	Jodel DR.1050	F. W. Tilley/Rochester	
G-AXVU	Omega 84 balloon	Brede Balloons Ltd Henry VII	
G-AXVV	Piper L-4H Cub	J. MacCarthy	
G-AXVW	Cessna F.150K	R. Nichols/Elstree	
G-AXVX	Cessna F.172H	Staverton Flying Services Ltd	
G-AXWA	Auster AOP.9	T. Platt	
G-AXWB	Omega 65 balloon	A. Robinson & M. J. Moore Ezekiel	
G-AXWD	Jurca MJ 10	F.P.A. Group	
G-AXWE	Cessna F.150K	Light Planes (Lancashire) Ltd/Barton	
G-AXWF	Cessna F.172H	Redfir Aviation Ltd	
G-AXWH	BN-2A Islander	Telair Ltd/Liverpool	
G-AXWP	BN-2A Islander	Aurigny Air Services/Alderney	
G-AXWR	BN-2A Islander	Aurigny Air Services/Alderney	
G-AXWT	Jodel D.11	R. Owen/Shoreham	
G-AXWV	Jodel DR.253	Murray Motors/Southend	
G-AXWZ	PA-28R Cherokee Arrow 200	Niglon Ltd/Birmingham	
G-AXXC	CP.301B Emeraude	J. R. R. Gale & J. Tetley	
G-AXXG	BN-2A Islander	Air Camelot/Bournemouth	
G-AXXH	BN-2A Islander	Telair Ltd/Liverpool	
G-AXXJ	BN-2A Islander	Jersey European Airways Ltd	
G-AXXM	CP.301A Emeraude	Mrs P. H. Wren	
G-AXXN	WHE Airbuggy	R. Savage	
G-AXXV	D.H.82A Tiger Moth (DE992)	N. Smith/Wellesbourne	
G-AXXW	Jodel D.117	D. J. & M. Watson/Sherburn	
G-AXXY	Boeing 707-336B	British Airtours Ltd/Gatwick	
G-AXXZ	Boeing 707-336B	Zambia Airways	
G-AXYA	PA-31-300 Navajo	Air Foyle Ltd/Luton	
G-AXYD	BAC One-Eleven 509	Dan-Air Services Ltd/Gatwick	
G-AXYK	Taylor JT.1 Monoplane	C. Oakins	
G-AXYM	BN-2A Islander	Balmar Aviation/Thruxton	
G-AXYU	Jodel D.9 Bebe	D. P. Jones/Panshanger	
G-AXYX	WHE Airbuggy	R. T. Ginn	
G-AXYY	WHE Airbuggy	M. P. Chetwynd-Talbot	
G-AXYZ	WHE Airbuggy	W. H. Ekin	
G-AXZA	WHE Airbuggy	P. H. Dyson & W. B. Lumb	
G-AXZB	WHE Airbuggy	D. R. C. Pugh	
G-AXZD	PA-28 Cherokee 180E	College of Air Training/Hamble	
G-AXZE	PA-28 Cherokee 180E	College of Air Training/Hamble	
G-AXZF	PA-28 Cherokee 180E	E. P. C. & W. R. Rabson/Southampton	
G-AXZM	Slingsby Nipper T.66 Mk III	G. R. Harlow	
G-AXZO	Cessna 180	R.S.A. Parachute Club Ltd/Thruxton	
G-AXZP	PA-23 Aztec 250	White House Garage, Ashford Ltd/ Denham	
G-AXZR	Taylor JT.2 Titch	A. J. Fowler & D. E. Evans	
G-AXZT	Jodel D.117	H. W. Baines	
G-AXZU	Cessna 182N	R. Taylor & ptnrs/Leeds	
G-AYAA	PA-28 Cherokee 180E	Briskloom Ltd	
G-AYAB	PA-28 Cherokee 180E	J. A. & J. C. Cunningham	
G-AYAC	PA-28R Cherokee Arrow 200	Steer Aviation Ltd/Biggin Hill	
G-AYAE	Bell 47G-4A	Helicopter Hire Ltd/Southend	
G-AYAI	Fournier RF-5	Exeter RF Group	
G-AYAJ	Cameron O-84 balloon	E. T. Hall Flaming Pearl	

Notes	Reg.	Type	Owner or Operator
	G-AYAK	Yakovlev C-11(14)	Aero Vintage Ltd/Lydd
	G-AYAL	Omega 56 balloon	British Balloon Museum
	G-AYAN	Slingsby Motor Cadet Mk III	I. Stevenson/Sherburn
	G-AYAO	Cessna F.172H	Transmatic Fyllan Ltd/Little Staughton
	G-AYAP	PA-28 Cherokee 180E	E. F. S. & R. S. Chappell
	G-AYAR	PA-28 Cherokee 180E	College of Air Training/Hamble
	G-AYAS	PA-28 Cherokee 180E	College of Air Training/Hamble
	G-AYAT	PA-28 Cherokee 180E	College of Air Training/Hamble
	G-AYAU	PA-28 Cherokee 180E	Tiarco Ltd
	G-AYAV	PA-28 Cherokee 180E	College of Air Training/Hamble
	G-AYAW	PA-28 Cherokee 180E	College of Air Training/Hamble
	G-AYBD	Cessna F.150K	S. K. Bamrah/Biggin Hill
	G-AYBG	Scheibe SF.25B Falke	Doncaster Sailplane Services
	G-AYBK	PA-28 Cherokee 180E	College of Air Training/Hamble
	G-AYBO	PA-23 Aztec 250D	Twinguard Aviation Ltd/Elstree
	G-AYBP	Jodel D.112	F. H. French/Swansea
	G-AYBT	PA-28 Cherokee 180E	College of Air Training/Hamble
	G-AYBU	Western 84 balloon	D. R. Gibbons
	G-AYBV	Chasle Tourbillon	B. A. Mills
	G-AYCC	Campbell Cricket	K. W. E. Denson
	G-AYCE	CP.301C Emeraude	K. Webb/Bodmin
	G-AYCF	Cessna FA.150K	E. J. Atkins/Popham
	G-AYCG	SNCAN SV-4C	N. Bignall/Booker
	G-AYCJ	Cessna TP.206D	H. O. Holm
	G-AYCM	Bell 206A JetRanger	W.R. Finance Ltd
	G-AYCN	Piper L-4H Cub	W. R. & B. M. Young
	G-AYCO	CEA DR.360	L. M. Gould/Jersey
	G-AYCP	Jodel D.112	W. Hutchings
	G-AYCT	Cessna F.172H	Kontrox Ltd/Edinburgh
	G-AYDG	M.S.894A Rallye Minerva	R. Vaughan & F. T. Skipper (Electronics) Ltd/Goodwood
	G-AYDI	D.H.82A Tiger Moth	R. B. Woods & ptnrs
	G-AYDJ	Campbell Cricket	A. van Preussen
	G-AYDR	SNCAN SV-4C	R. A. Phillips
	G-AYDU	AJEP W.8 Tailwind (nosewheel)	AJEP Development Ltd
	G-AYDV	Coates SA.11-1 Swalesong	J. R. Coates/Rush Green
	G-AYDW	A.61 Terrier 2	J. S. Harwood
	G-AYDX	A.61 Terrier 2	D. C. Bonsall/Netherthorpe
	G-AYDY	Luton LA-4A Minor	C. R. Scott/Upavon
	G-AYDZ	Jodel DR.200	Don Martin (Car Sales) Ltd/Sywell
	G-AYEB	Jodel D.112	B. Ibbott
	G-AYEC	CP.301A Emeraude	A. P. Docherty & J. S. Barker/Redhill
	G-AYED	PA-24 Comanche 260	Patgrove Ltd
	G-AYEE	PA-28 Cherokee 180E	College of Air Training/Hamble
	G-AYEF	PA-28 Cherokee 180E	College of Air Training/Hamble
	G-AYEG	Falconar F-9	A. G. Thelwall
	G-AYEH	Jodel DR.1050	R. O. F. Harper & P. R. Skeels/Barton
	G-AYEI	PA-31-300 Navajo	Hubbard Air Ltd/Norwich
	G-AYEJ	Jodel DR.1050	G. Weaver
	G-AYEK	Jodel DR.1050	I. Shaw & B. Hanson/Sherburn
	G-AYEN	Piper L-4H Cub	P. Warde & C. F. Morris
	G-AYER	H.S.125 Srs 403B	MAM Aviation Ltd/Southampton
	G-AYES	M.S.892A Rallye Commodore 150	Waveney Flying Group
	G-AYET	M.S.892A Rallye Commodore 150	Lands End Flying Club/St Just
	G-AYEU	Brookland Hornet	J. B. Verney
	G-AYEV	Jodel DR.1050	M. R. Ireland/Redhill
	G-AYEW	Jodel DR.1051	D. G. Hammersley & R. E. Kendal/ Halfpenny Green
	G-AYEX	Boeing 707-355C	British Caledonian Airways Loch Leven/ Gatwick
	G-AYEY	Cessna F.150K	Gordon-Air Ltd
	G-AYFA	SA Twin Pioneer 3	Flight One Ltd/Shobdon
	G-AYFC	D.62B Condor	J. B. Randle/Redhill
	G-AYFD	D.62B Condor	Sherburn Aero Club
	G-AYFE	D.62C Condor	R. R. Harris
	G-AYFF	D.62B Condor	A. F. S. Caldecourt/Fairoaks
	G-AYFG	D.62C Condor	Wolds Gliding Club
	G-AYFJ	M.S.880B Rallye Club	G. W. G. C. Sudlow/Henstridge
	G-AYFP	Jodel D.140	S. K. Minocha/Sherburn

Reg.	Type	Owner or Operator	Notes
G-AYFS	Brookland Hornet	Brookland Rotorcraft Ltd	
G-AYFT	PA-39 Twin Comanche C/R	Kirby Oldham Ltd/Manchester	
G-AYFV	Crosby BA-4B	A. N. R. Houghton/Leicester	
G-AYFX	AA-I Yankee	P. A. Ellway & R. M. Bainbridge	
G-AYFY	EAA Biplane	H. Kuehling/(Stored)	
G-AYFZ	PA-31-300 Navajo	Exir Nominees Ltd	
G-AYGA	Jodel D.117	E. J. Baxter & pntrs/Stapleford	
G-AYGB	Cessna 310Q	Airwork Services Ltd/Perth	
G-AYGC	Cessna F.150K	D. W. Barron/Barton	
G-AYGD	Jodel DR.1051	I. S. Walsh	
G-AYGE	SNCAN SV-4C	The Hon A. M. J. Rothschild/Stapleford	
G-AYGG	Jodel D.120	J. E. Hobbs/Sandown	
G-AYGN	Cessna 210K	J. W. O'Sullivan/Jersey	
G-AYGX	Cessna FR.172G	J. A. Edwards	
G-AYGZ	Beech 58 Baron	General Engineering Co (Ilford) Ltd/ Stansted	
G-AYHA	AA-1 Yankee	P. Wilkinson & M. A. C. Stephenson	
G-AYHI	Campbell Cricket	E. Testo	
G-AYHX	Jodel D.117A	L. J. E. Goldfinch	
G-AYHY	Fournier RF-4D	Tiger Club Ltd/Redhill	
G-AYIB	Cessna 182N Skylane	R. M. Clarke	
G-AYIF	PA-28 Cherokee 140C	I. R. March/Elstree	
G-AYIG	PA-28 Cherokee 140C	Harris Aviation Services Ltd/Biggin Hill	
G-AYIH	PA-28 Cherokee 140C	B. Lince/Elstree	
G-AYII	PA-28R Cherokee Arrow 200	Devon Growers Ltd & A. L. Bacon/ Exeter	
G-AYIJ	SNCAN SV-4B	R. J. Maxey & N. J. Mathias/Panshanger	
G-AYIL	Scheibe SF.25B Falke	S. Evans & pntrs/Woodvale	
G-AYIO	PA-28 Cherokee 140C	A. P. Stone & pntrs/Blackpool	
G-AYIP	PA-39 Twin Comanche C/R	P. D. Lees & G. Pinkus/Elstree	
G-AYIT	D.H.82A Tiger Moth	R. L. H. Alexander & pntrs/ Newtownards	
G-AYJA	Jodel DR.1050	A. A. Alderdice & pntrs	
G-AYJB	SNCAN SV-4C	F. J. M. & J. P. Esson	
G-AYJD	Alpavia-Fournier RF-3	C. Wren/Southend	
G-AYJP	PA-28 Cherokee 140C	RAF Brize Norton Flying Club Ltd	
G-AYJR	PA-28 Cherokee 140C	RAF Brize Norton Flying Club Ltd	
G-AYJS	PA-28 Cherokee 140C	W. R. Griffiths & Sons (Office Furnishers) Ltd	
G-AYJT	PA-28 Cherokee 140C	Jennifer M. Lesslie/Enstone	
G-AYJU	Cessna TP-206A	J. E. Ball & R. W. F. Marsh/Thruxton	
G-AYJW	Cessna FR.172G	Alpine Press Ltd/Elstree	
G-AYJY	Isaacs Fury II	A. V. Francis	
G-AYKA	Beech 95-B55A Baron	Flockvale Ltd/Enstone	
G-AYKC	D.H.82A Tiger Moth	G. Freeman & pntrs	
G-AYKD	Jodel DR.1050	D. C. R. Writer/Biggin Hill	
G-AYKF	M.S.880B Rallye Club	Breen Aviation Ltd/Enstone	
G-AYKJ	Jodel D.117A	G. R. W. Monksfield/Stapleford	
G-AYKK	Jodel D.117	P. Cawkwell & pntrs/Crosland Moor	
G-AYKL	Cessna F.150L	Aero Group 78/Netherthorpe	
G-AYKS	Leopoldoff L-7	C. E. & W. B. Cooper	
G-AYKT	Jodel D.117	J. P. Owen-Jones/Glenrothes	
G-AYKU	PA-E23 Aztec 250D	Simulated Flight Training Ltd/Booker	
G-AYKV	PA-28 Cherokee 140C	W. A. G. Willbond	
G-AYKW	PA-28 Cherokee 140C	T. P. Sheff/Southend	
G-AYKX	PA-28 Cherokee 140C	M. J. Garland & pntrs	
G-AYKZ	SAI KZ-8	R. E. Mitchell/Coventry	
G-AYLA	Glos-Airtourer 115	Vagabond Flying Group	
G-AYLB	PA-39 Twin Comanche C/R	E. A. Radnall & Co Ltd/Birmingham	
G-AYLE	M.S.880B Rallye Club	J. E. Stephenson	
G-AYLF	Jodel DR.1051	W. A. G. Willbond & pntrs/Cambridge	
G-AYLK	Stampe SV-4C	R. W. & P. R. Budge	
G-AYLL	Jodel DR.1050	Firefly Aviation Ltd	
G-AYLO	AA-1 Yankee	J. A. & A. J. Boyd/Cardiff	
G-AYLP	AA-1 Yankee	D. Nairn & E. Y. Hawkins/Bournemouth	
G-AYLU	Pitts S-ID Special	I. M. G. Senior & J. G. Harper/Redhill	
G-AYLV	Jodel D.120	R. E. Wray/Stapleford	
G-AYLX	Hughes 269C	Feastlight Ltd	
G-AYLY	PA-23 Aztec 250	British Island Airways/Shoreham	
G-AYLZ	Super Aero 45 Srs 2	J. R. B. Aviation Ltd/Southend	
G-AYMA	Stolp Starduster Too	K. D. Ballinger & A. R. T. Jones/ Staverton	

Notes	Reg.	Type	Owner or Operator
	G-AYME	Fournier RF.5	R. D. Goodger/Biggin Hill
	G-AYMG	HPR-7 Herald 213	Securicor Ltd/Birmingham
	G-AYMK	PA-28 Cherokee 140C	The Piper Flying Group/Usworth
	G-AYML	PA-28 Cherokee 140C	J. M. Bendle/Elstree
	G-AYMM	Cessna 421B	Rogers Aviation Sales Ltd/Cranfield
	G-AYMN	PA-28 Cherokee 140C	F. R. Aviation Ltd/Coventry
	G-AYMO	PA-23 Aztec 250	Beechwood Properties Ltd
	G-AYMP	Currie Wot Special	H. F. Moffatt/Shobdon
	G-AYMR	Lederlin 380L Ladybug	J. S. Brayshaw
	G-AYMT	Jodel DR.1050	Merlin Flying Club Ltd
	G-AYMU	Jodel D.112	Shoreham Aero Club
	G-AYMV	Western 20 balloon	G. F. Turnbull & ptnrs *Tinkerbelle*
	G-AYMW	Bell 206A JetRanger 2	Wykeham Helicopters Ltd
	G-AYMX	Bell 206A JetRanger	W. Holmes
	G-AYMZ	PA-28 Cherokee 140C	D. Tuke/Crosby
	G-AYNA	Currie Wot	R. W. Hart/Redhill
	G-AYNB	PA-31-300 Navajo	B. Mendes/Southend
	G-AYNC	Wessex Mk 60 Srs 1	Glos-Air (Services) Ltd/Bournemouth
	G-AYND	Cessna 310Q	Source Premium & Promotional Consultants Ltd/Fairoaks
	G-AYNF	PA-28 Cherokee 140C	N. P. Bendle/Denham
	G-AYNJ	PA-28 Cherokee 140C	T. L. Deamer/Elstree
	G-AYNN	Cessna 185B Skywagon	Bencray Ltd/Blackpool
	G-AYNP	Westland S.55 Srs 3	Bristow Helicopters Ltd
	G-AYNS	Airmaster H2-B1	D. J. Fry/Blackbushe
	G-AYOD	Cessna 172	J. Vicary/Dunkeswell
	G-AYOL	GY-80 Horizon 180	J.B.D.R. Flying Group Ltd/Jersey
	G-AYOM	Sikorsky S-61N Mk 2	British Airways Helicopters Ltd/ Aberdeen
	G-AYOP	BAC One-Eleven 530	British Caledonian Airways *Isle of Hoy*/ Gatwick
	G-AYOW	Cessna 182N Skylane	D. P. H. Lennox/Shobdon
	G-AYOX	V.814 Viscount	British Midland Airways Ltd/E. Midlands
	G-AYOY	Sikorsky S-61N Mk 2	British Airways Helicopters Ltd/ Aberdeen
	G-AYOZ	Cessna FA.150L	Exeter Flying Club Ltd
	G-AYPB	Beech C-23 Musketeer	Robin G. Motors Ltd/Doncaster
	G-AYPC	Beech 70 Queen Air	Vernair Transport Services/Liverpool
	G-AYPD	Beech 95 B.55 Baron	Sir W. S. Dugdale/Birmingham
	G-AYPE	Bo 209 Monsun	Papa Echo Ltd/Biggin Hill
	G-AYPF	Cessna F.177RG	H.W. Structures Ltd/Southend
	G-AYPG	Cessna F.177RG	J. T. Duffin
	G-AYPH	Cessna F.177RG	G. A. Witherington/Shoreham
	G-AYPI	Cessna F.177RG	Cardinal Aviation Ltd/Guernsey
	G-AYPM	PA-19 Super Cub 95	C. H. A. Bott
	G-AYPO	PA-19 Super Cub 95	Mrs J. E. Mavrogordato/Shobdon
	G-AYPP	PA-19 Super Cub 95	M. Kirk
	G-AYPR	PA-19 Super Cub 95	R. J. Vessall
	G-AYPS	PA-19 Super Cub 95	Tony Dyer Television
	G-AYPT	PA-19 Super Cub 95	Laarbruch Flying Club
	G-AYPU	PA-28R Cherokee Arrow 200	Alpine Ltd/Jersey
	G-AYPV	PA-28 Cherokee 140D	Meeting Point Ltd/Newcastle
	G-AYPZ	Campbell Cricket	A. Melody/Lasham
	G-AYRB	Campbell Cricket	Campbell Gyroplanes Ltd
	G-AYRC	Campbell Cricket	G. A. Coventry
	G-AYRF	Cessna F.150L	Northern Auto Salvage/Inverness
	G-AYRG	Cessna F.172K	J. F. Bennett
	G-AYRH	M.S.892A Rallye Commodore 150	J. D. Watt
	G-AYRI	PA-28R Cherokee Arrow 200	K. R. Tools & Delta Motor Co Ltd/ White Waltham
	G-AYRK	Cessna 150J	K. A. Learmonth/Southend
	G-AYRL	Fournier SFS.31 Milan	W. A. L. Mitchell/Plymouth
	G-AYRM	PA-28 Cherokee 140D	E. S. Dignam/Biggin Hill
	G-AYRN	Schleicher ASK-14	V. J. F. Falconer/Dunstable
	G-AYRO	Cessna FA.150L Aerobat	Red Fir Aviation Ltd/Clacton
	G-AYRP	Cessna F.150L Aerobat	Banff Flying Club/Boyndie
	G-AYRT	Cessna F.172K	W. A. Webb/Southampton
	G-AYRU	BN-2A-6 Islander	Joint Services Parachute Centre/ Netheravon
	G-AYSA	PA-23 Aztec 250C	RTH Aircraft

Reg.	Type	Owner or Operator	Notes
G-AYSB	PA-30 Twin Commanche 160C	Sandcliffe Aviation/Biggin Hill	
G-AYSD	Slingsby T.67A Falke	J. Conolly/Tees-side	
G-AYSG	Cessna F.172K	Aircraft Mart Ltd/Staverton	
G-AYSK	Luton L.A.4A Minor	P. F. Bennison & ptnrs/Barton	
G-AYSX	Cessna F.177RG	Nasaire Ltd/Liverpool	
G-AYSY	Cessna F.177RG	R. Chown/Tees-side	
G-AYSZ	Cessna FA.150L Aerobat	J. R. Richardson	
G-AYTA	M.S.880B Rallye Club	Willoughby Farms Ltd	
G-AYTC	PA-E23 Aztec 250C	New Guarantee Trust Finance Ltd/ E. Midlands	
G-AYTD	PA-23 Aztec 250C	F. C. Ellwood/Southend	
G-AYTF	Bell 206B JetRanger 2	D. W. Smith/Booker	
G-AYTJ	Cessna 207 Super Skywagon	Foxair/Glenrothes	
G-AYTN	Cameron O-65 balloon	P. G. Hall & R. F. Jessett *Prometheus*	
G-AYTP	PA-23E Aztec 250E	J. Traynor/Birmingham	
G-AYTR	CP.301A Emeraude	M. C. Wroe	
G-AYTT	Phoenix PM-3 Duet	Gp Capt A. S. Knowles/Fairoaks	
G-AYTV	MJ.2A Tempete	P. Russell/Netherthorpe	
G-AYTY	Bensen B.8	J. H. Wood	
G-AYUB	CEA DR.253B	D. J. Brook/Shoreham	
G-AYUC	Cessna F.150L	Lincoln Aero Club Ltd/Sturgate	
G-AYUH	PA-28 Cherokee 180F	M. S. Bayliss/Coventry	
G-AYUI	PA-28 Cherokee 180	Routair Aviation Services Ltd/Southend	
G-AYUJ	Evans VP.1 Volksplane	J. A. Wills/Dundee	
G-AYUL	PA-23 Aztec 250E	Kattan (GB) Ltd/Manchester	
G-AYUM	Slingsby T-61A Falke	Doncaster & District Gliding Club	
G-AYUN	Slingsby T-61A Falke	C. W. Vigar & R. J. Watts	
G-AYUP	Slingsby T-61A Falke	Cranwell Gliding Club	
G-AYUR	Slingsby T-61A Falke	W. A Urwin	
G-AYUS	Taylor JT.1 Monoplane	R. R. McKinnon & A. D. Lincoln/ Southampton	
G-AYUT	Jodel DR.1050	R. Norris	
G-AYUV	Cessna F.172H	S. W. Wilson/Halfpenny Green	
G-AYUX	D.H.82A Tiger Moth (PG651)	P. R. Harris/Booker	
G-AYUY	Cessna FA.150L Aerobat	J. A. Wills/Dundee	
G-AYVA	Cameron O-84 balloon	A. Kirk *April Fool*	
G-AYVB	Cessna F.172K	Botsford & Willard Ltd/Panshanger	
G-AYVF	H.S.121 Trident 3B	British Airways/Heathrow	
G-AYVI	Cessna T.210H	Trident Marine Ltd/Edinburgh	
G-AYVO	Wallis WA120 Srs 1 ★	Science Museum/London	
G-AYVP	Woody Pusher	J. R. Wraight	
G-AYVT	Brochet MB.84	Dunelm Flying Group	
G-AYVU	Cameron O-56 balloon	Shell-Mex & B.P. Ltd *Hot Potato*	
G-AYVY	D.H.82A Tiger Moth (PG617)	G. Smith/Ronaldsway	
G-AYWA	Avro 19 Srs 2 ★	Strathallan Aircraft Collection	
G-AYWD	Cessna 182N	Trans Para Aviation Ltd/Barton	
G-AYWE	PA-28 Cherokee 140C	John Ridgway Engineering Ltd/Booker	
G-AYWF	PA-23 Aztec 250C	Peregrine Air Services Ltd/Inverness	
G-AYWG	PA-E23 Aztec 250C	G.D. Air Services/Manston	
G-AYWH	Jodel D.117A	J. M. Knapp & ptnrs	
G-AYWI	BN-2A Mk III-I Trislander	Aurigny Air Services/Alderney	
G-AYWM	Glos-Airtourer Super 150	F. B. Miles/Staverton	
G-AYWT	Stampe SV-4B	B. K. Lecomber/Tees-side	
G-AYWU	Cessna 150G	C. L. Duke/USA	
G-AYWW	PA-28R Cherokee Arrow 200D	J. A. Butterfield & ptnrs/Leicester	
G-AYXO	Luton LA-5A Major	A. C. T. Broomcroft	
G-AYXP	Jodel D.117A	G. N. Davies/Shobdon	
G-AYXS	SIAI-Marchetti S205-18R	W. F. South/Liverpool	
G-AYXT	Westland Sikorsky S-55 Srs 2	J. E. Wilkie	
G-AYXU	Champion 7KCAB Citabria	H. Fould & ptnrs	
G-AYXV	Cessna FA.150L	Leo Designs	
G-AYXW	Evans VP.1 Volksplane	J. S. Penny/Doncaster	
G-AYYD	M.S.894A Rallye Minerva	G. Lyons	
G-AYYF	Cessna F.150L	Falcon Aero Club/Swansea	
G-AYYK	Slingsby T-61A Falke	Cornish Gliding & Flying Club Ltd/ Perranporth	
G-AYYN	PA-28R Cherokee Arrow 200B	W. & R. Leggott Ltd/Leeds	
G-AYYO	Jodel DR.1050/M1	Bustard Flying Club Ltd/Old Sarum	
G-AYYT	Jodel DR.1050/M1	T. S. Warren & ptnrs/Sandown	
G-AYYU	Beech C23 Musketeer	A. F. Clements/Andrewsfield	

Notes	Reg.	Type	Owner or Operator
	G-AYYX	M.S.880B Rallye Club	D. Hall & V. Thompson/Usworth
	G-AYYY	M.S.880B Rallye Club	T. W. Heffer/Panshanger
	G-AYYZ	M.S.880B Rallye Club	R. J. Napp/Southend
	G-AYZC	PA-E23 Aztec 250D	N. W. Aero Services Ltd/Liverpool
	G-AYZE	PA-39 Twin Comanche 160 C/R	Melbourns Brewery Ltd/East Midlands
	G-AYZH	Taylor JT-2 Titch	K. J. Munro
	G-AYZI	Stampe SV-4C	F. M. Barrett
	G-AYZJ	Westland Sikorsky S-55 (XM685) ★	Newark Air Museum
	G-AYZK	Jodel DR.1050/M1	G. S. Claybourn/Doncaster
	G-AYZN	PA-E23 Aztec 250	Central Air Services (Air Envoy) Ltd/Birmingham
	G-AYZS	D.62B Condor	A. M. & M. J. Cherry-Downes
	G-AYZT	D.62B Condor	R. R. Harris
	G-AYZU	Slingsby T.61A Falke	The Falcon Gliding Group
	G-AYZW	Slingsby T.61A Falke	J. A. Dandie & R. J. M. Clement
	G-AYZY	PA-39 Twin Comanche 160 C/R	C. & M. Thomas/Cardiff
	G-AZAB	PA-30 Twin Comanche 160	T. W. P. Sheffield/Humberside
	G-AZAD	Jodel DR.1051	I. C. Young & J. S. Paget/Bodmin
	G-AZAJ	PA-28R Cherokee Arrow 200B	Driscoll Tyres Ltd & J. McHugh & Son (Civil Engineers) Ltd/Stapleford
	G-AZAV	Cessna 337F	W. T. Johnson & Sons (Huddersfield) Ltd
	G-AZAW	GY-80 Horizon 160	Scottish Electric Ltd/Dundee
	G-AZAZ	Bensen B.8M	FAA Museum/Yeovilton
	G-AZBA	T.66 Nipper 3	I. McKenzie
	G-AZBB	MBB Bo 209 Monsun 160FV	Cheyne Motors Ltd/Biggin Hill
	G-AZBC	PA-39 Twin Comanche 160 C/R	Dennis Silver & Co/Southend
	G-AZBE	Glos-Airtourer Super 150	S. A. Warwick/Staverton
	G-AZBI	Jodel D.150	T. A. Rawson & K. H. Siorpaes
	G-AZBK	PA-E23 Aztec 250E	Qualitair Engineering Ltd/Blackbushe
	G-AZBL	Jodel D.9 Bebe	West Midlands Flying Group/Halfpenny Green
	G-AZBN	AT-16 Harvard 2B (FT391)	Colt Car Co Ltd/Staverton
	G-AZBT	Western O-65 balloon	D. J. Harris *Hermes*
	G-AZBU	Auster AOP.9	K. H. Wallis
	G-AZCB	Stampe SV-4B	M. J. Coburn
	G-AZCH	H.S.125 Srs 3B/RA	Leopard Aviation Ltd/Cranfield
	G-AZCI	Cessna 320A Skyknight	Landsurcon (Air Survey) Ltd/Staverton
	G-AZCK	B.121 Pup 2	Wickenby Flying Club Ltd
	G-AZCL	B.121 Pup 2	Cameron Rainwear Ltd
	G-AZCP	B.121 Pup 1	M. M. Pepper/Sibson
	G-AZCT	B.121 Pup 1	Trent Aviation Services/Cranfield
	G-AZCU	B.121 Pup 1	Leyline Aviation Ltd/Tees-side
	G-AZCZ	B.121 Pup 2	B. Rogalewski/Booker
	G-AZDA	B.121 Pup 1	G. H. G. Bishop & K. E. Fehrenbach/Shoreham
	G-AZDD	MBB Bo 209 Monsun 150FF	E. M. Emerson & N. Hughes-Narborough/Biggin Hill
	G-AZDE	PA-28R Cherokee Arrow 200B	Electro-Motion UK (Export) Ltd/Tollerton
	G-AZDF	Cameron O-84 balloon	K. L. C. M. Busemeyer
	G-AZDK	Beech B55 Baron	Burton Metal Fabrications Ltd/E. Midlands
	G-AZDW	PA-28 Cherokee 180F	DFS Aviation Ltd/Goodwood
	G-AZDX	PA-28 Cherokee 180F	Anglo-Dansk Marine Engineering Co Ltd/Humberside
	G-AZDY	D.H.82A Tiger Moth	B. A. Mills
	G-AZEA	Cessna 182N	R-T Stuart Ltd/Perth
	G-AZED	BAC One-Eleven 414	Dan-Air Services Ltd/Gatwick
	G-AZEE	M.S.880B Rallye Club	P. L. Clements
	G-AZEF	Jodel D.120	P. Cawkwell & G. Firth/Sherburn
	G-AZEG	PA-28 Cherokee 140D	J. W. Simmons/Barrow
	G-AZER	Cameron O-42 balloon	M. P. Dokk-Olsen & P. L. Jaye *Shy Tot*
	G-AZEU	B.121 Pup 2	J. N. Russell/Aberdeen
	G-AZEV	B.121 Pup 2	G. P. Martin/Shoreham
	G-AZEW	B.121 Pup 2	Deltair Ltd/Chester
	G-AZFA	B.121 Pup 2	K. F. Plummer/Sywell
	G-AZFB	Boeing 720-051B	Monarch Airlines Ltd/Luton

Reg.	Type	Owner or Operator	Notes
G-AZFC	PA-28 Cherokee 140D	A. H. Lavender	
G-AZFE	PA-23 Aztec 250D	Air Charter (Scotland) Ltd/Glasgow	
G-AZFF	Jodel D.112	J. M. Newbold	
G-AZFI	PA-28R Cherokee Arrow 200B	Hawksworth Garage Ltd	
G-AZFM	PA-28R Cherokee Arrow 200B	Linco Poultry Machinery Ltd/Biggin Hill	
G-AZFO	PA-39 Twin Comanche 160 C/R	Handhorn Ltd	
G-AZFP	Cessna F.177RG	Afronix (UK) Ltd/Bournemouth	
G-AZFR	Cessna 401B	Shorrock Security Systems Ltd/Blackpool	
G-AZFS	Beech B80 Queen Air	Globetrotter Survey Co Ltd/Southampton	
G-AZFZ	Cessna 414	J. Rowe/Manchester	
G-AZGA	Jodel D.120	M. A. Webb/Finmere	
G-AZGB	PA-E23 Aztec 250D	Qualitair Engineering Ltd/Blackbushe	
G-AZGC	Stampe SV-4C (No 120)	The Hon Patrick Lindsay/Booker	
G-AZGE	Stampe SV-4A	M. R. L. Astor/Booker	
G-AZGF	B.121 Pup 2	S. Kirkpatrick & ptnrs/Leeds	
G-AZGH	M.S.880B Rallye Club	R. G. Moore	
G-AZGI	M.S.880B Rallye Club	G. E. M. Hallett & ptnrs/Newcastle	
G-AZGJ	M.S.880B Rallye Club	S. C. Howes & E. T. French	
G-AZGL	M.S.894A Rallye Minerva	The Cambridge Aero Club Ltd	
G-AZGY	CP.301B Emeraude	Rodingair Flying Group/Stapleford	
G-AZGZ	D.H.82A Tiger Moth (NM181)	F. R. Manning	
G-AZHA	PA-E23 Aztec 250E	Air Charter (Scotland) Ltd/Glasgow	
G-AZHB	Robin HR 100-200	W. H. Everett & Son Ltd/Lydd	
G-AZHC	Jodel D.112	J. A. Summer & A. Burton/Netherthorpe	
G-AZHD	Slingsby T.61A Falke	West Wales Gliding Co Ltd	
G-AZHF	Cessna 150L	P. H. Dance & Son Ltd	
G-AZHH	SA 102.5 Cavalier	D. W. Buckle *Time*	
G-AZHI	Glos-Airtourer Super 150	R. E. Charleton & ptnrs	
G-AZHJ	S.A. Twin Pioneer Srs 3	Flight One Ltd/Shobdon	
G-AZHK	Robin HR 100-200	J. J. Woodhouse	
G-AZHL	PA-31-300 Navajo	BAC Aviation Ltd/Stapleford	
G-AZHM	Cassutt Racer	J. A. H. Chadwick	
G-AZHO	Jodel DR.1050	S. Alexander	
G-AZHR	Piccard Ax6 balloon	J. W. Moss *Happiness*	
G-AZHT	Glos-Airtourer T.3	D. C. Giles	
G-AZHU	Luton LA-4A Minor	F. Didsbury/Netherthorpe	
G-AZIB	ST-10 Diplomate	Wilmslow Audio Ltd/Barton	
G-AZID	Cessna FA.150L	Oldment Ltd/Brough	
G-AZII	Jodel D.117A	J. S. Brayshaw	
G-AZIJ	Jodel DR.360	K. H. Tostevin/Guernsey	
G-AZIK	PA-34-200 Seneca	C.S.E. (Aircraft Services) Ltd/Kidlington	
G-AZIL	Slingsby T.61A Falke	I. Jamieson	
G-AZIO	SNCAN SV-4C	Rollason Aircraft & Engines Ltd/(*Stored*)	
G-AZIP	Cameron O-65 balloon	Dante Balloon Group *Dante*	
G-AZIR	Stampe SV-4C	Rollason Aircraft & Engines Ltd	
G-AZJB	PA-34-200 Seneca	G. Gamble & Sons Ltd/E. Midlands	
G-AZJC	Fournier RF-5	J. J. Butter	
G-AZJD	AT-6D Harvard III	Meridian Drilling Co Ltd/Biggin Hill	
G-AZJE	JB-01 Minicab	J. B. Evans/Sandown	
G-AZJI	Western O-65 balloon	W. Davison *Peek-a-Boo*	
G-AZJN	Robin DR 300/140	Wright Farm Eggs Ltd	
G-AZJV	Cessna F.172L	The JV Group/Denham	
G-AZJW	Cessna F.150L	T. G. Aviation Ltd/Manston	
G-AZJY	Cessna FRA.150L	Shropshire Aero Club Ltd/Sleap	
G-AZJZ	PA-23 Aztec 250E	Air Commuter Ltd/Coventry	
G-AZKC	M.S.880B Rallye Club	L. J. Martin/Fairoaks	
G-AZKD	M.S.880B Rallye Club	O. G. Stuart-Lee/Fairoaks	
G-AZKE	M.S.880B Rallye Club	D. H. Tonkin & B. H. Cook/Bodmin	
G-AZKG	Cessna F.172L	Wycombe Air Centre Ltd/Booker	
G-AZKI	AT-16 Harvard IIB (FT229)	Noblair Ltd	
G-AZKK	Cameron O-56 balloon	Gemini Balloon Group *Gemini*	
G-AZKN	Robin HR.100/200	K. Marriott/Tollerton	
G-AZKO	Cessna F.337F	Crispair Aviation Services Ltd	
G-AZKP	Jodel D.117	J. Lowe/Tollerton	
G-AZKR	PA-24 Comanche 180	B. J. Boughton	
G-AZKS	AA-1A Trainer	J. G. Hill	
G-AZKV	Cessna FRA.150L	Penguin Flight/Bodmin	
G-AZKW	Cessna F.172L	Banbury Plant Hire Ltd/Hinton-in-the-Hedges	

Notes	Reg.	Type	Owner or Operator
	G-AZKZ	Cessna F.172L	Sprowston Engineering Ltd/Norwich
	G-AZLE	Boeing N2S-5 Kaydet	A. E. Poulson
	G-AZLF	Jodel D.120	J. Brooks
	G-AZLH	Cessna F.150L	M. Bonsall/E. Midlands
	G-AZLJ	BN-2A-1 Mk III Trislander	Aurigny Air Services/Alderney
	G-AZLK	Cessna F.150L	A. D. M. Edie/Shoreham
	G-AZLL	Cessna FRA.150L	Airwork Ltd/Bournemouth
	G-AZLM	Cessna F.172L	J. F. Davis & Q. J. Rigby
	G-AZLN	PA-28 Cherokee 180F	D. H. L. Wigan/Swanton Morley
	G-AZLO	Cessna F.337F	Leasetec Ltd
	G-AZLP	V.813 Viscount	British Midland Airways Ltd/E. Midlands
	G-AZLR	V.813 Viscount	British Midland Airways Ltd/E. Midlands
	G-AZLS	V.813 Viscount	British Midland Airways Ltd/E. Midlands
	G-AZLV	Cessna 172K	J. Braithwaite (Aerial Photography) Ltd/Hinton-in-the-Hedges
	G-AZLY	Cessna F.150L	Cleveland Flying School Ltd/Tees-side
	G-AZLZ	Cessna F.150L	H. Carolan/Stapleford
	G-AZMA	Jodel D.140B	I. J. Bishop & M. Kirk
	G-AZMB	Bell 47G-3B	Helicopter Farming Ltd
	G-AZMC	Slingsby T.61A Falke	Essex Gliding Club Ltd/N. Weald
	G-AZMD	Slingsby T.61C Falke	P. J. Moss & ptnrs/Long Marston
	G-AZMF	BAC One-Eleven 530	British Caledonian Airways/Gatwick
	G-AZMH	Morane-Saulnier M.S.500 (7A+WN)	Hon P. Lindsay/Booker
	G-AZMJ	AA-5 Traveler	R. T. Love/Bodmin
	G-AZMK	PA-23 Aztec 250	Andrew Edie Aviation/Shoreham
	G-AZMN	Glos-Airtourer T.5	R. G. Lowerson & T. Ellefson/ Usworth
	G-AZMO	PA-32 Cherokee Six 260	Dateline International Dating Systems Ltd & Grangewood Press Ltd/ Elstree
	G-AZMV	D.62C Condor	Ouse Gliding Club Ltd/Rufforth
	G-AZMX	PA-28 Cherokee 140 ★	Kelsterton College (instructional airframe)/Deeside
	G-AZMY	SIAI Marchetti SF-260	Miss W. M. Miller/Fairoaks
	G-AZMZ	M.S.893A Rallye Commodore 150	W. A. L. Mitchell
	G-AZNA	V.813 Viscount	Manx Airlines/Ronaldsway
	G-AZNB	V.813 Viscount	British Midland Airways Ltd/E. Midlands
	G-AZNC	V.813 Viscount	British Midland Airways Ltd/E. Midlands
	G-AZNF	Stampe SV-4C	H. J. Smith/Booker
	G-AZNI	S.A.315B Lama	Dollar Air Services Ltd (G-AWLC)/ Coventry
	G-AZNJ	M.S.880B Rallye Club	Miss J. G. White/Shipdham
	G-AZNK	Stampe SV-4A	A. E. Hutton/Duxford
	G-AZNL	PA-28R Cherokee Arrow 200D	C. W. Middlemiss/Biggin Hill
	G-AZNO	Cessna 182P	M&D Aviation/Bournemouth
	G-AZNT	Cameron O-84 balloon	Cameron Balloons Ltd Oberon
	G-AZNY	PA-E23 Aztec 250E	Eastern Airways/Humberside
	G-AZNZ	Boeing 737-222	Britannia Airways Ltd Henry Hudson/ Luton
	G-AZOA	MBB Bo 209 Monsun 150FF	Dr G. R. Outwin/Doncaster
	G-AZOB	MBB Bo 209 Monsun 150FF	G. N. Richardson
	G-AZOD	PA-23 Aztec 250D	Peregrine Air Services Ltd/Inverness
	G-AZOE	Glos-Airtourer 115	Victa Flying Group/Usworth
	G-AZOF	Glos-Airtourer Super 150	Hampshire Aeroplane Co Ltd/St Just
	G-AZOG	PA-28R Cherokee Arrow 200D	Winchfield Enterprises Ltd
	G-AZOH	Beech 65-B90 Queen Air	Clyde Surveys Ltd/White Waltham
	G-AZOL	PA-34-200 Seneca	MTV Design Ltd
	G-AZOM	MBB Bo 105D	Bristow Helicopters Ltd/Aberdeen
	G-AZON	PA-34-200-2 Seneca	Willowvale Electronics Ltd/Blackbushe
	G-AZOO	Western O-65 balloon	Southern Balloon Group Carousel
	G-AZOS	MJ.5-F1 Sirocco	R. Wells/Usworth
	G-AZOT	PA-34-200-2 Seneca	L. G. Payne/Elstree
	G-AZOU	Jodel DR.1051	T. W. Jones & ptnrs/Slinfold
	G-AZOZ	Cessna FRA.150L	L. C. Cole
	G-AZPA	PA-25 Pawnee 235	Black Mountain Gliding Co Ltd
	G-AZPC	Slingsby T.61C Falke	B. C. Dixon
	G-AZPF	Fournier RF-5	R. Pye/Barton
	G-AZPH	Craft-Pitts S-1S Special	Aerobatics International Ltd/ Farnborough

Reg.	Type	Owner or Operator	Notes
G-AZPV	Luton LA-4A Minor	J. Scott/Slinfold	
G-AZPX	Western O-31 balloon	E. R. McCosh	
G-AZPZ	BAC One-Eleven 515	British Caledonian Airways Ltd/Gatwick	
G-AZRA	MBB Bo 209 Monsun	Alpha Flying Group Ltd/Biggin Hill	
G-AZRD	Cessna 401B	John Finlan Ltd/Liverpool	
G-AZRF	Sikorsky S-61N	Bristow Helicopters *Pitcaple*	
G-AZRG	PA-23 Aztec 250D	Woodgate Aviation (IOM) Ltd/ Ronaldsway	
G-AZRH	PA-28 Cherokee 140D	Newcastle-upon-Tyne Aero Club Ltd	
G-AZRI	Payne balloon	G. F. Payne *Shoestring*	
G-AZRK	Fournier RF-5	Strathtay Flying Group/Perth	
G-AZRL	PA-19 Super Cub 95	S. J. & L. M. Harmer	
G-AZRM	Fournier RF-5	Miss R. S. A. Lloyd-Bostock	
G-AZRN	Cameron O-84 balloon	M. Yarrow *Gravida II*	
G-AZRP	Glos-Airtourer 115	Tudor Flying School/Wellesbourne	
G-AZRR	Cessna 310Q	Ames Company (Transport) Ltd/ Liverpool	
G-AZRS	PA-22 Tri-Pacer 150	E. A. Harrhy/Shoreham	
G-AZRU	AB-206B JetRanger 2	Dollar Air Services Ltd/Coventry	
G-AZRV	PA-28R Cherokee Arrow 200B	S. G. Daniel	
G-AZRW	Cessna T.337C	A.D.S. (Aerial) Ltd/Southend	
G-AZRX	GY-80 Horizon 160	J. B. McBride/Aldergrove	
G-AZRZ	Cessna U-206F	Army Parachute Association/ Netheravon	
G-AZSA	Stampe SV-4B	J. K. Faulkner/Biggin Hill	
G-AZSC	AT-16 Harvard IIB (FT323)	D. W. Arnold/Blackbushe	
G-AZSD	Slingsby T.29B Motor Tutor	R. G. Boynton	
G-AZSE	PA-28R Cherokee Arrow 200D	Northlink Storage Systems Ltd/Aberdeen	
G-AZSF	PA-28R Cherokee Arrow 200D	P. Blamire/Coventry	
G-AZSG	PA-28 Cherokee 180E	Cherokee Flying Group/Netherthorpe	
G-AZSH	PA-28R Cherokee Arrow 180	C. R. Hayward	
G-AZSK	Taylor JT.1 Monoplane	R. R. Lockwood	
G-AZSM	PA-28R Cherokee Arrow 180	Winchlond Ltd	
G-AZSN	PA-28R Cherokee Arrow 200	S. G. Hoole	
G-AZSS	Jodel D.9 Bebe	M. W. Rice	
G-AZSU	H.S.748 Srs 2A	British Airways/Glasgow	
G-AZSW	Beagle 121 Pup 1	Northamptonshire School of Flying Ltd/Sywell	
G-AZSX	Beagle 121 Pup 1	P. W. Hunter/Elstree	
G-AZSZ	PA-23 Aztec 250	Air Kilroe/Manchester	
G-AZTA	MBB Bo 209 Monsun 150FF	R. S. Perks/Elstree	
G-AZTD	PA-32 Cherokee Six 300	Presshouse Publications Ltd/Enstone	
G-AZTF	Cessna F.177RG	Carentals Ltd/Shoreham	
G-AZTK	Cessna F.172F	C. C. Donald	
G-AZTM	Glos-Airtourer 115	I. J. Smith	
G-AZTO	PA-34-200-2 Seneca	E. W. Noakes	
G-AZTR	SNCAN SV.4C	D. J. Shires/Stapleford	
G-AZTS	Cessna F.172L	Transgap Ltd/Manchester	
G-AZTT	PA-28R Cherokee Arrow 200	Rivermill Pyford Ltd/Fairoaks	
G-AZTV	Stolp SA.500 Starlet	The Stolp Group	
G-AZTW	Cessna F.177RG	R. M. Clarke/Leicester	
G-AZUM	Cessna F.172L	Shetland Flying Club Ltd	
G-AZUO	Cessna F.177RG	Newbury Sand and Gravel Co Ltd	
G-AZUP	Cameron O-65 balloon	C. M. G. Ellis & ptnrs	
G-AZUT	M.S.893A Rallye Commodore 180	Rallye Flying Group	
G-AZUV	Cameron O-65 balloon ★	British Balloon Museum	
G-AZUX	Western O-56 balloon	H. C. J. & Mrs S. L. G. Williams *Slow Djinn*	
G-AZUY	Cessna E.310L	Grimwood Marketing Services/ Denham	
G-AZUZ	Cessna FRA.150L	D. J. Parker/Netherthorpe	
G-AZVA	MBB Bo 209 Monsun 150FF	K. H. Wallis	
G-AZVB	MBB Bo 209 Monsun 150FF	P. C. Logsdon/Dunkeswell	
G-AZVC	MBB Bo 209 Monsun 150FF	G. E. Horder & D. Cockcroft Ltd/Popham	
G-AZVE	AA-5 Traveler	P. E. Nunn	
G-AZVF	M.S.894A Rallye Minerva	R. J. Cole & W. G. Gregory/Cardiff	
G-AZVG	AA-5 Traveler	W. B. J. & A. M. Davis/Newtownards	
G-AZVH	M.S.894A Rallye Minerva	C. H. T. Trace	
G-AZVI	M.S.892A Rallye Commodore	Agricultural & Industrial Services (Wiltshire) Ltd & J. F. Snook	
G-AZVJ	PA-34-200-2 Seneca	Business Air Travel Ltd/Lydd	

Notes	Reg.	Type	Owner or Operator
	G-AZVL	Jodel D.119	C. Drinkwater/Stapleford
	G-AZVM	Hughes 369HS	Diagnostic Reagents Ltd
	G-AZVP	Cessna F.177RG	R. W. Martin & R. G. Saunders/ Biggin Hill
	G-AZVR	Cessna F.150L	E. P. Collier/Ipswich
	G-AZVS	H.S.125 Srs 3B	Eastern Airways
	G-AZVT	Cameron O-84 balloon	Sky Soarer Ltd *Jules Verne*
	G-AZVV	PA-28 Cherokee 180G	Woodgate Air Services (IOM) Ltd/ Ronaldsway
	G-AZVW	Bell 47G-5A	Adela Aerial Services International Ltd
	G-AZVX	Bell 47G-5A	Adela Aerial Services Internatinoal Ltd
	G-AZVZ	PA-28 Cherokee 140	Gordon King (Aviation) Ltd/Biggin Hill
	G-AZWB	PA-28 Cherokee 140	MSF Aviation Ltd/Manchester
	G-AZWD	PA-28 Cherokee 140	Airways Aero Associations Ltd/Booker
	G-AZWE	PA-28 Cherokee 140	Airways Aero Associations Ltd/Booker
	G-AZWF	SAN Jodel DR.1050	D. C. Shiells/Sywell
	G-AZWS	PA-28R Cherokee Arrow 180	Thames Estuary Flying Club/Southend
	G-AZWT	Westland Lysander III (V9441)	Strathallan Aircraft Collection
	G-AZWW	PA-23 Aztec 250E	Phoenix Aviation (Bedford) Ltd/ Cranfield
	G-AZWY	PA-24 Comanche 260	Keymer Son & Co Ltd/Biggin Hill
	G-AZXA	Beechcraft 95-C55 Baron	Flight Refuelling Ltd/Bournemouth
	G-AZXB	Cameron O-65 balloon	London Balloon Club Ltd *London Pride II*
	G-AZXC	Cessna F.150L	Magpie Service Station/Doncaster
	G-AZXD	Cessna F.172L	Birdlake Ltd/Wellesbourne
	G-AZXE	Jodel D.120A	Kestrel Flying Group/Hucknall
	G-AZXG	PA-23 Aztec 250	K. J. Le Fevre/Norwich
	G-AZXH	PA-34-200-2 Seneca	Carentals Ltd
	G-AZXM	H.S.121 Trident 2E	British Airways/Heathrow
	G-AZYA	GY-80 Horizon 160	T. Poole & G. L. Newbrook/Sywell
	G-AZYB	Bell 47H-1	G. Watt
	G-AZYD	M.S.893A Rallye Commodore	Deeside Gliding Club
	G-AZYF	PA-28 Cherokee 180	J. C. Glynn/E. Midlands
	G-AZYG	PA-E23 Aztec 250	F. M. Barrett/Elstree
	G-AZYK	Cessna 310Q	M. E. Stone/Exeter
	G-AZYL	Portslade School free balloon	R. M. Glover *Mercury*
	G-AZYM	Cessna E-310Q	Grimward Marketing Services
	G-AZYR	Cessna 340	Exeair Travel Ltd/Exeter
	G-AZYS	CP.301C-1 Emeraude	J. R. Hughes/Stapleford
	G-AZYU	PA-E23 Aztec 250	Thinair Ltd/Fairoaks
	G-AZYV	Burns O-77 balloon	B. F. G. Ribbans *Contrary Mary*
	G-AZYX	M.S.893A Rallye Commodore	Black Mountain Gliding Co Ltd/ Shobdon
	G-AZYY	Slingsby T.61A Falke	J. A. Towers
	G-AZYZ	WA.51A Pacific	A. E. O'Broin
	G-AZZA	PA-E23 Aztec 250	Air Charter (Scotland) Ltd/Glasgow
	G-AZZB	AB-206B JetRanger 2	Air Hanson Ltd/Brooklands
	G-AZZF	M.S.880B Rallye Club	I. C. Davies/Swansea
	G-AZZG	Cessna 188 Agwagon	Farm Supply Co (Thirsk) Ltd
	G-AZZH	Practavia Pilot Sprite 115	K. G. Stewart
	G-AZZK	Cessna 414	Unifix Air Ltd/Stansted
	G-AZZO	PA-28 Cherokee 140	G. D. Macro & A. R. Chambers Stapleford
	G-AZZP	Cessna F.172H	Glos-Air (Services) Ltd/Bournemouth
	G-AZZR	Cessna F.150L	Herefordshire Aero Club Ltd/Shobdon
	G-AZZS	PA-34-200-2 Seneca	Margate Motors Ltd/Manston
	G-AZZT	PA-28 Cherokee 180 ★	*Ground instruction airframe*/Cranfield
	G-AZZV	Cessna F.172L	Linskill Air Charter Ltd/Tees-side
	G-AZZW	Fournier RF-5	Gloster Aero Group/Staverton
	G-AZZX	Cessna FRA.150L	J. E. Uprichard & ptnrs/Newtownards
	G-AZZZ	D.H.82A Tiger Moth	S. W. McKay
	G-BAAD	Evans Super VP-1	R. W. Husband/Netherthorpe
	G-BAAF	Manning-Flanders MF1 replica	D. E. Bianchi/Booker
	G-BAAG	Beechcraft B.55 Baron	Mannin Aviaiton Ltd/Blackpool
	G-BAAH	Coates SA.III Swalesong	J. R. Coates
	G-BAAI	M.S.893A Rallye Commodore	A. F. Butcher
	G-BAAK	Cessna 207	Sunderland Parachute Centre Ltd/ Usworth

Reg.	Type	Owner or Operator	Notes
G-BAAL	Cessna 172A	V. H. Bellamy/St Just	
G-BAAP	PA-28R Cherokee Arrow 200	Shirley A. Shelley/Ford	
G-BAAR	PA-28R Cherokee Arrow 200	Diplomatic & Consular Yearbook Ltd/ Elstree	
G-BAAT	Cessna 182P Skylane	S. J. Martin Ltd/Newtownards	
G-BAAU	Enstrom F-28C-UK	Norman Bailey Helicopters Ltd/ Blackbushe	
G-BAAW	Jodel D.119	J. M. Alexander & R. J. Allan/Aberdeen	
G-BAAX	Cameron O-84 balloon	The New Holker Estate Co Ltd Holker Hall	
G-BAAY	Valtion Viima II (BA+AY)	A. M. Stow/White Waltham	
G-BAAZ	PA-28A Cherokee Arrow 200D	A. W. Rix/Guernsey	
G-BABA	D.H.82A Tiger Moth	S. W. McKay	
G-BABB	Cessna F.150L	George House Holdings Ltd/ Compton Abbas	
G-BABC	Cessna F.150L	E. P. Collier/Ipswich	
G-BABD	Cessna FRA.150L	Leaf Puma Ltd/Cranfield	
G-BABE	Taylor JT.2 Titch	J. Berry	
G-BABG	PA-28 Cherokee 180	R. W. Scott/Biggin Hill	
G-BABH	Cessna F.150L	N.F. O'Neil &E. J. Leathem/Newtownards	
G-BABK	PA-34-200-2 Seneca	D. F. J. & N. R. Flashman/Biggin Hill	
G-BABY	Taylor JT.2 Titch	J. R. D. Bygraves/O. Warden	
G-BACA	BAC Petrel	British Aircraft Corporation Ltd/Warton	
G-BACB	PA-34-200-2 Seneca	Ernair Ltd	
G-BACC	Cessna FRA.150L	Chainrose Ltd/Little Staughton	
G-BACE	Fournier RF-5	R. W. K. Stead	
G-BACH	Enstrom F.28A	Finload Ltd	
G-BACJ	Jodel D.120	Wearside Flying Association/Usworth	
G-BACK	D.H.82A Tiger Moth (DF130)	G. R. French & ptnrs	
G-BACL	Jodel D.150	G. R. French	
G-BACM	Cessna F.150L	Air Compton Ltd/Compton Abbas	
G-BACN	Cessna FRA.150L	Airwork Ltd/Perth	
G-BACO	Cessna FRA.150L	R. A. Bowes & P. A. Crawford/ Plymouth	
G-BACP	Cessna FRA.150L	Norfolk & Norwich Aero Club Ltd/ Swanton Morley	
G-BADC	Luton Beta B.2A	H. M. Mackenzie	
G-BADE	PA-23 Aztec 250	Thurston Aviation Ltd/Stansted	
G-BADF	PA-34-200-2 Seneca	Strata Surveys Ltd/Manchester	
G-BADH	Slingsby T.61A Falke	E. M. Andrew & ptnrs/Yeovilton	
G-BADI	PA-E23 Aztec 250	W. London Aero Services Ltd/ White Waltham	
G-BADJ	PA-E23 Aztec 250	J. G. Hogg/Rochester	
G-BADK	BN-2A-8 Islander	P. R. Eurosalve Ltd/Lydd	
G-BADL	PA-34-200-2 Seneca	Cartographical Services (Southampton) Ltd/Birmingham	
G-BADO	PA-32 Cherokee Six 300	D. Russell	
G-BADP	Boeing 737-204	Britannia Airways Ltd Sir Arthur Whitten Brown/Luton	
G-BADR	Boeing 737-204	Britannia Airways Ltd Capt Robert Falconer Scott/Luton	
G-BADT	Cessna 402B	British Aircraft Corp Ltd/Warton	
G-BADU	Cameron O-56 balloon	J. Philp Dream Machine	
G-BADV	Brochet MB-50	P. A. Cairns/Dunkeswell	
G-BADW	Pitts S-2A Special	Aerospace Museum/Cosford	
G-BADY	Pitts S-2A Special	Comed Aviation Ltd/Blackpool	
G-BADZ	Pitts S-2A Special	A. L. Brown & ptnrs/Luton	
G-BAEB	Robin DR.400/160	Bracknell Refrigeration Services Ltd/ Fairoaks	
G-BAEC	Robin HR.100/210	Autographics Ltd/White Waltham	
G-BAED	PA-E23 Aztec 250	Auxair International Ltd/Stapleford	
G-BAEE	Jodel DR.1050/M1	Group JJ/White Waltham	
G-BAEF	Boeing 727-46	Dan-Air Services Ltd/Gatwick	
G-BAEM	Robin DR.400/125	Store Equipment (London) Ltd/ Biggin Hill	
G-BAEN	Robin DR.400/180	Trans Europe Air Charter Ltd/Booker	
G-BAEP	Cessna FRA.150L	Balgin Ltd	
G-BAER	Cosmic Wind	R. S. Voice/Redhill	
G-BAES	Cessna 337A	Page & Moy Ltd & High Voltage Applications Ltd/Leicester	
G-BAET	Piper L-4H Cub	C. M. G. Ellis	
G-BAEU	Cessna F.150L	Skyviews & General Ltd/Sherburn	

Notes	Reg.	Type	Owner or Operator
	G-BAEV	Cessna FRA.150L	South Midland Communications Ltd/ Popham
	G-BAEW	Cessna F.172M	Northamptonshire School of Flying Ltd/ Sywell
	G-BAEX	Cessna F.172M	D. H. Stephenson & ptnrs
	G-BAEY	Cessna F.172M	R. Fursman/Southampton
	G-BAEZ	Cessna FRA.150L	J. C. Glyn/E. Midlands
	G-BAFA	AA-5 Traveler	L. H. Mayall/Ronaldsway
	G-BAFD	MBB Bo 105D	British Caledonian Helicopters Ltd
	G-BAFG	D.H.82A Tiger Moth	C. D. Cyster
	G-BAFH	Evans VP-1 Volksplane	R. H. W. Beath/Dunkeswell
	G-BAFI	Cessna F.177RG	Nottingham Building Soc/Tollerton
	G-BAFL	Cessna 182P	Ingham Aviation Ltd/Lulsgate
	G-BAFM	AT-16 Harvard IIB	J. Parks/Southampton
	G-BAFP	Robin DR.400/160	C. J. Halsey/Headcorn
	G-BAFS	PA-18 Super Cub 150	Doncaster & District Gliding Club
	G-BAFT	PA-18 Super Cub 150	Cambridge University Gliding Trust Ltd/ Duxford
	G-BAFU	PA-28 Cherokee 140	Goshawk Aviation Ltd/Southend
	G-BAFV	PA-18 Super Cub 95	P. Elliott/Biggin Hill
	G-BAFW	PA-28 Cherokee 140	K. McCann
	G-BAFX	Robin DR.400/140	Copthorne Precision Products Ltd/ Headcorn
	G-BAFZ	Boeing 727-46	Dan-Air Services Ltd/Gatwick
	G-BAGA	Cessna 182A Skylane	Peterborough Parachute Centre Ltd/ Sibson
	G-BAGB	SIAI-Marchetti SF.260	British Midland Airways Ltd/ E. Midlands
	G-BAGC	Robin DR.400/140	Hempalm Ltd/Headcorn
	G-BAGF	Jodel D.92 Bebe	G. R. French & J. D. Watt
	G-BAGG	PA-32 Cherokee Six 300E	Hornair Ltd/Jersey
	G-BAGI	Cameron O-31 balloon	Cameron Balloons Ltd *Vital Spark*
	G-BAGL	SA.341 G. Gazelle Srs 1	Westland Helicopters Ltd/Yeovil
	G-BAGN	Cessna F.177RG	M. L. Rhodes/Halfpenny Green
	G-BAGO	Cessna 421B	Banline Aviation Ltd/E. Midlands
	G-BAGR	Robin DR.400/125	F. C. Aris & ptnrs/Mona
	G-BAGS	Robin DR.400/180 2+2	Headcorn Flying School Ltd
	G-BAGT	Helio H.295 Courier	B. J. C. Woodhall Ltd
	G-BAGU	Luton LA-5A Major	J. Gawley
	G-BAGV	Cessna U.206F	W. W. Dickson
	G-BAGX	PA-28 Cherokee 140	M. F. Bruce/Liverpool
	G-BAGY	Cameron O-84 balloon	P. G. Dunnington *Beatrice*
	G-BAHC	PA-23 Aztec 250	Berkeley Hotel Ltd/Coventry
	G-BAHD	Cessna 182P Skylane	S. Brunt (Silverdale Staffs) Ltd/Sleap
	G-BAHE	PA-28 Cherokee 140	A. H. Evans & A. O. Jones
	G-BAHF	PA-28 Cherokee 140	RJS Aviation Ltd
	G-BAHG	PA-24 Comanche 260	Friendly Aviation (Jersey) Ltd
	G-BAHH	Wallis WA.121	K. H. Wallis
	G-BAHI	Cessna F.150H	B. Jones/E. Midlands
	G-BAHJ	PA-24 Comanche 250	Videovision/Elstree
	G-BAHL	Robin DR.400/160	Norvett Electronics Ltd
	G-BAHN	Beech 58 Baron	British Midland Airways/E. Midlands
	G-BAHO	Beech C.23 Sundowner	Fairflight Ltd/Biggin Hill
	G-BAHP	Volmer VJ.22 Sportsman	M. T. Moore & E. P. Beck
	G-BAHS	PA-28R Cherokee Arrow 200-II	A. A. Wild & ptnrs
	G-BAHU	Enstrom F-28A	Anvil Aviation Ltd/Blackbushe
	G-BAHX	Cessna 182P	S. Shorrock/Barton
	G-BAHZ	PA-28R Cherokee Arrow 200-II	C. McFadden/Newtownards
	G-BAIA	PA-32 Cherokee Six 300E	Langham International (Aircraft) Ltd/ Southend
	G-BAIB	Enstrom F-28A	C.S.E. Aviation Ltd/Kidlington
	G-BAIF	Western O-65 balloon	B. M. Smith *Captain Starlight*
	G-BAIH	PA-28R Cherokee Arrow 200-II	J. Pemberton/Cambridge
	G-BAII	Cessna FRA.150L	Taurus Trading Ltd/Denham
	G-BAIK	Cessna F.150L	Wickenby Aviation Ltd
	G-BAIL	Cessna FR.172J	Red Fir Aviation Ltd/Clacton
	G-BAIM	Cessna 310Q	Airwork Services Ltd/Perth
	G-BAIN	Cessna FRA.150L	Airwork Services Ltd/Perth
	G-BAIP	Cessna F.150L	W. D. Cliffe & ptnrs/Wellesbourne
	G-BAIR	Thunder Ax7-77 balloon	P. A. & Mrs M. Hutchins

G-BAHN   Beech 58 Baron of British Midland Airways.   *S. G. Richards*

59

Reg.	Type	Owner or Operator	Notes
G-BAIS	Cessna F.177RG	I. H. Bewley	
G-BAIU	Hiller UH-12E (Soloy)	Heliwork Finance Ltd/Thruxton	
G-BAIW	Cessna F.172M	Thoresway Growers/Humberside	
G-BAIX	Cessna F.172M	John Cordery Aviation Ltd/Elstree	
G-BAIY	Cameron O-65 balloon	Budget Rent A Car (UK) Ltd *Lady Budget*	
G-BAIZ	Slingsby T.61A Falke	W. L. C. O'Neill & ptnrs/Sywell	
G-BAJA	Cessna F.177RG	Don Ward Productions Ltd/Biggin Hill	
G-BAJB	Cessna F.177RG	Brittfish (Hull) Ltd/Humberside	
G-BAJC	Evans VP-1	J. R. Clements/Headcorn	
G-BAJE	Cessna 177 Cardinal	Triavia Ltd/Biggin Hill	
G-BAJN	AA-5 Traveler	Janacrew Ltd/Sherburn	
G-BAJO	AA-5 Traveler	A. Towns	
G-BAJR	PA-28 Cherokee 180	K. P. Davison/Shobdon	
G-BAJT	PA-28R Cherokee Arrow 200-II	M. G. Edmonds	
G-BAJU	PA-23 Aztec 250	Aircraft Mart (Staverton) Ltd	
G-BAJW	Boeing 727-46	Dan-Air Services Ltd/Gatwick	
G-BAJX	PA-E23 Aztec 250	A. J. Walgate & Son Ltd/Humberside	
G-BAJY	Robin DR.400/180	Rolincs Aviation/Sturgate	
G-BAJZ	Robin DR.400/125	Readwell Aviation/Rochester	
G-BAKA	Sikorsky S-61N	Bristow Helicopters Ltd *West Sole*	
G-BAKB	Sikorsky S-61N	Bristow Helicopters Ltd *Montrose*	
G-BAKC	Sikorsky S-61N	Bristow Helicopters Ltd *Forties*	
G-BAKD	PA-34-200-2 Seneca	NIC Instruments Ltd/Manston	
G-BAKF	Bell 206B JetRanger 2	M. J. K. Belmont/Coventry	
G-BAKG	Hughes 269C	W. R. Finance Ltd	
G-BAKH	PA-28 Cherokee 140	Woodgate Air Services (IoM) Ltd/Ronaldsway	
G-BAKJ	PA-30 Twin Comanche 160	Kwik Air Services Ltd	
G-BAKK	Cessna F.172H	C. M. Hampson/Coventry	
G-BAKL	F.27 Friendship 200	Air UK/Norwich	
G-BAKM	Robin DR.400/140	F. Goodison/Netherthorpe	
G-BAKN	SNCAN SV-4C	M. Holloway	
G-BAKO	Cameron O-84 balloon	D. C. Dokk-Olsen *Pied Piper*	
G-BAKP	PA-E23 Aztec 250	J. J. Woodhouse	
G-BAKR	Jodel D.117	A. B. Bailey/White Waltham	
G-BAKS	A-B 206B JetRanger 2	G. M. H. Willis/Coventry	
G-BAKT	A-B 206B JetRanger 2	Burnthills Plant Hire Ltd/Glasgow	
G-BAKV	PA-18 Super Cub 150	Pounds Marine Shipping Ltd/Goodwood	
G-BAKW	B.121 Pup 2	J. Trevor-Hicks Ltd/Goodwood	
G-BAKY	Slingsby T.61C Falke	G. Hill & P. Shepherd	
G-BALB	Air & Space Model 18A	Interflight Ltd	
G-BALC	Bell 206B JetRanger 2	Dollar Air Services Ltd/Coventry	
G-BALE	Enstrom F.28A	C.S.E. Aviation Ltd/Kidlington	
G-BALF	Robin DR.400/140	F. A. Spear/Panshanger	
G-BALG	Robin DR.400/180	R. Jones	
G-BALH	Robin DR.400/140B	Pennine Leisure Ltd/Blackpool	
G-BALI	Robin DR.400 2+2	G. R. Page/Biggin Hill	
G-BALJ	Robin DR.400/180	Barlodz Ltd/Headcorn	
G-BALK	SNCAN SV-4C	J. C. Brierley/Liverpool	
G-BALL	Bede BD-5	J. P. Turner	
G-BALM	Cessna 340	Manro Transport Ltd/Manchester	
G-BALN	Cessna T.310Q	O'Brien Properties Ltd/Shoreham	
G-BALP	PA-39 Twin Comanche 160 C/R	Maynards (Heels) Ltd/Stapleford	
G-BALS	Nipper T.66 Mk 3	L. W. Shaw	
G-BALT	Enstrom F28A	W. Gray/Cambridge	
G-BALU	PA-E23 Aztec 250C	Jabrest Ltd (G-BADD)/Biggin Hill	
G-BALW	PA-28R Cherokee Arrow 200-II	H. R. Fenwick/Glasgow	
G-BALX	D.H.82A Tiger Moth (N6848)	C. P. B. Horsley & R. G. Annis/Fairoaks	
G-BALY	Practavia Pilot Sprite 150	A. L. Young	
G-BALZ	Bell 212	B.E.A.S. Ltd/Redhill	
G-BAMB	Slingsby T.61C Falke	Universities of Glasgow & Strathclyde Gliding Club/Strathaven	
G-BAMC	Cessna F.150L	D. R. Calo & M. McDonald/Elstree	
G-BAME	Volmer VJ-22 Sportsman	V. H. Bellamy/St Just	
G-BAMF	MBB Bo 105D	Management Aviation Ltd/Bourn	
G-BAMG	Avions Lobet Ganagobie	J. A. Brompton	
G-BAMI	Beech 95-B55 Baron	Less Now Ltd	
G-BAMJ	Cessna 182P	Motionster Ltd/Blackbushe	
G-BAMK	Cameron D.96 hot-air airship	Cameron Balloons Ltd	
G-BAML	Bell 206A JetRanger	Blue Star Ship Management Ltd	

Notes	Reg.	Type	Owner or Operator
	G-BAMM	PA-28 Cherokee 235	E. R. Walters/Sherburn
	G-BAMN	Cessna U.206 Super Skywagon	M. E. Robinson/Langar
	G-BAMR	PA-16 Clipper	H. Boyce
	G-BAMS	Robin DR.400/160	G-BAMS Ltd/Biggin Hill
	G-BAMU	Robin DR.400/160	Anvil Flying Group
	G-BAMV	Robin DR.400/180	W. J. Gooding
	G-BAMY	PA-28R Cherokee Arrow 200-II	B. Gittins & ptnrs/Birmingham
	G-BANA	Robin DR.221	G. T. Pryor/Felthorpe
	G-BANB	Robin DR.400/180	Time Electronics Ltd/Headcorn
	G-BANC	GY-201 Minicab	C. D. B. Trollope
	G-BAND	Cameron O-84 balloon	Mid-Bucks Farmers Balloon Group *Clover*
	G-BANE	Cessna FRA.150L	D. J. Park & A. P. Clarke/Blackpool
	G-BANF	Luton LA-4A Minor	D. W. Bosworth/Shobdon
	G-BANK	PA-34-200-2 Seneca	Edmondson Freightliners Ltd/Blackpool
	G-BANL	BN-2A-8 Islander	Loganair Ltd/Glasgow
	G-BANS	PA-34-200-2 Seneca	G. Knowles/Halfpenny Green
	G-BANU	Wassmer Jodel D.120	C. E. McKinney
	G-BANV	Phoenix Currie Wot	K. Knight/Shobdon
	G-BANW	CP-1330 Super Emeraude	J. D. McCracker & ptnrs/E. Fortune
	G-BANX	Cessna F.172M	S. Martin & T. Hawthorne/Newtownards
	G-BAOB	Cessna F.172M	Gordon King (Aviation) Ltd/Biggin Hill
	G-BAOC	M.S.894E Rallye Minerva	P. V. & Mrs E. M. Gilliar/Southend
	G-BAOG	M.S.880B Rallye Club	W. A. McCartney & T. A. Pugh
	G-BAOH	M.S.880B Rallye Club	S. P. Bryant & ptnrs/Shobdon
	G-BAOJ	M.S.880B Rallye Club	D. W. Busby & J. L. Howard
	G-BAOM	M.S.880B Rallye Club	G. Avery & ptnrs/Ipswich
	G-BAOP	Cessna FRA.150L	F. W. Bennett/Halfpenny Green
	G-BAOS	Cessna F.172M	M. E. Aldridge
	G-BAOT	M.S.880B Rallye Club	Cormack (Aircraft Services) Ltd/ Glasgow
	G-BAOU	AA-5 Traveler	W. H. Ingram/St Just
	G-BAOV	AA-5 Traveler	G. K. Ellerker
	G-BAOW	Cameron O-65 balloon	P. A. White *Winslow Boy*
	G-BAOY	Cameron S-31 balloon	Shell-Mex BP Ltd *New Potato*
	G-BAPA	Fournier RF-5B Sperber	R. Pasold & D. Stuynor/Booker
	G-BAPB	DHC-1 Chipmunk 22	R. C. P. Brookhouse/Panshanger
	G-BAPC	Luton LA-4A Minor	Midland Aircraft Preservation Soc
	G-BAPF	V.814 Viscount	British Midland Airways Ltd/E. Midlands
	G-BAPG	V.814 Viscount	Philstone International Ltd/Exeter
	G-BAPH	Cessna FRA.150L	E. Shipley
	G-BAPI	Cessna FRA.150L	Industrial Supplies (Peterborough) Ltd
	G-BAPJ	Cessna FRA.150L	M. D. Page/Manston
	G-BAPK	Cessna F.150L	Justgold Ltd/Blackpool
	G-BAPL	PA-23 Aztec 250E	Scottish Malt Distillers Ltd/Lossiemouth
	G-BAPM	Fuji FA.200-160	Falcon Aero Club/Swansea
	G-BAPN	PA-28 Cherokee 180	J. O. Carlisle/E. Midlands
	G-BAPP	Evans VP-1	N. Crow
	G-BAPR	Jodel D.11	E. W. Osborn & ptnrs
	G-BAPS	Campbell Cougar ★	British Rotorcraft Museum
	G-BAPT	Fuji FA.200-180	J. F. Thurlow & J. H. Pickering
	G-BAPV	Robin DR.400/160	J. D. Millne & ptnrs
	G-BAPW	PA-28R Cherokee Arrow 180	G. & R. Consultants Ltd/E. Midlands
	G-BAPX	Robin DR.400/160	R. R. Hall & R. H. Richards
	G-BAPY	Robin HR.100/210	Engineering Appliances Ltd/Booker
	G-BARB	PA-34-200-2 Seneca	Maykind Ltd/Leavesden
	G-BARC	Cessna FR.172J	C. Porter & ptnrs/Defford
	G-BARD	Cessna 337C	Europa Aviation Ltd
	G-BARF	Jodel D.112 Club	J. E. Shepherd & ptnrs
	G-BARG	Cessna E.310Q	Nottingham Building Soc Ltd/ E. Midlands
	G-BARH	Beech C.23 Sundowner	Hadley Green Garage Ltd/Leavesden
	G-BARJ	Bell 212	B.E.A.S. Ltd/Redhill
	G-BARN	Taylor JT.2 Titch	R. G. W. Newton
	G-BARP	Bell 206B JetRanger 2	S.W. Electricity Board/Bristol
	G-BARR	H.S.125 Srs 600B	Rolls-Royce Ltd/E. Midlands
	G-BARS	D.H.C.1. Chipmunk 22	T. I. Sutton/Chester
	G-BART	H.S.125 Srs 600B	Crossoceans Ltd
	G-BARV	Cessna 310Q	Old England Watches Ltd/Elstree
	G-BARX	Bell 206B JetRanger 2	W. R. Finance Ltd
	G-BARY	CP.301A Emeraude	W. C. C. Meyer

Reg.	Type	Owner or Operator	Notes
G-BARZ	Scheibe SF.28A Tandem Falke	J. A. Fox & ptnrs/Upavon	
G-BASB	Enstrom F-28A	Southern Air/Shoreham	
G-BASD	B.121 Pup 2	C. C. Brown/Leicester	
G-BASE	Bell 206B JetRanger 2	Air Hanson Ltd/Brooklands	
G-BASG	AA-5 Traveler	C. & M. J. Deane	
G-BASH	AA-5 Traveler	M. J. Metham/Blackbushe	
G-BASI	PA-28 Cherokee 140	Melbren Air Ltd/Liverpool	
G-BASJ	PA-28 Cherokee 180	J. J. Smyth	
G-BASL	PA-28 Cherokee 140	Air Navigation & Trading Ltd/Blackpool	
G-BASM	PA-34-200-2 Seneca	Bird Aviation Ltd/Stapleford	
G-BASN	Beech C.23 Sundowner	M. F. Fisher	
G-BASO	Lake LA-4 Amphibian	P. B. W. Spearing & H. W. A. Deacon	
G-BASP	B.121 Pup 1	Northamtonshire School of Flying Ltd/Sywell	
G-BASU	PA-31-350 Navajo Chieftain	Casair Aviation Ltd/Tees-side	
G-BASX	PA-34-200-2 Seneca	Willowvale Electronics Ltd/Blackbushe	
G-BASY	Jodel D.9 Bebe	R. L. Sambell	
G-BATA	H.S.125 Srs 403B	Aravia (CI) Ltd	
G-BATC	MBB Bo 105D	Management Aviation Ltd/Bourn	
G-BATH	Cessna F.337G	Pegasus Profiles Ltd	
G-BATJ	Jodel D.119	E. G. Waite	
G-BATM	PA-32 Cherokee Six 300	Patgrove Ltd & J. Wakeman & Co	
G-BATN	PA-E23 Aztec 250	Marshall of Cambridge Ltd	
G-BATR	PA-34-200-2 Seneca	Executive Aviation Ltd/Birmingham	
G-BATS	Taylor JT.1 Monoplane	J. Jennings	
G-BATT	Hughes 269C	Farm Supply (Thirsk) Ltd	
G-BATU	Enstrom F.28A-UK	Stewart Air Ltd/Elstree	
G-BATV	PA-28 Cherokee 180D	The Scoresby Flying Group	
G-BATW	PA-28 Cherokee 140	J. E. Shepherd	
G-BATX	PA-23 Aztec 250E	Tayside Aviation Ltd/Dundee	
G-BAUA	PA-E23 Aztec 250	David Parr & Associates Ltd/Shobdon	
G-BAUC	PA-25 Pawnee 235	P. M. Charles/Little Snoring	
G-BAUD	Robin DR.400/160	Triton Air Travel Ltd/Shoreham	
G-BAUE	Cessna 310Q	A. J. Dyer/Elstree	
G-BAUH	Jodel D.112	I. G. & Mrs M. Glenn	
G-BAUI	PA-E23 Aztec 250	Simulated Flight Training Ltd/Stansted	
G-BAUJ	PA-E23 Aztec 250	Voyager Enterprises Ltd/Ronaldsway	
G-BAUK	Hughes 269C	Curtis Engineering (Frome) Ltd	
G-BAUR	F.27 Friendship Mk 200	Air UK Ltd/Norwich	
G-BAUV	Cessna F.150L	Cooper Airmotive (UK) Ltd/Kidlington	
G-BAUW	PA-E23 Aztec 250	R. E. Myson/Stapleford	
G-BAUX	Limba Lapwing	B. J. Jacobson & R. M. Fisher	
G-BAUY	Cessna FRA.150L	Inverness Flying Services Ltd	
G-BAUZ	Nord NC.854S	W. A. Ashley & D. Horne	
G-BAVB	Cessna F.172M	Hudson Bell Aviation/Southend	
G-BAVC	Cessna F.150L	Elles Aviation/Biggin Hill	
G-BAVE	Beech A.100 King Air	Vernair Transport Services/Liverpool	
G-BAVF	Beech 58 Baron	Fergabrook Ltd/Elstree	
G-BAVG	Beech E.90 King Air	Bass Ltd/Leeds	
G-BAVH	D.H.C.1 Chipmunk 22	Portsmouth Naval Gliding Club/Lee-on-Solent	
G-BAVL	PA-E23 Aztec 250	Shipboard Maintenance Ltd/Usworth	
G-BAVM	PA-31-350 Navajo Chieftain	Air Commuter Ltd/Coventry	
G-BAVN	Boeing Stearman PT-17	P. D. Evans & Co Ltd	
G-BAVO	Boeing Stearman N2S (26)	Keenair Services Ltd/Liverpool	
G-BAVR	AA-5 Traveler	Rabhart Ltd/Prestwick	
G-BAVS	AA-5 Traveler	Crystal Heart Salad Co Ltd/Brough	
G-BAVU	Cameron A-105 balloon	J. D. Michaelis	
G-BAVX	HPR-7 Herald 214	British Air Ferries Ltd/Southend	
G-BAVZ	PA-E23 Aztec 250	Merseyside Air Charter Ltd/Liverpool	
G-BAWA	PA-28R-200-2 Cherokee Arrow	A. Somerville/Blackbushe	
G-BAWB	PA-E23 Aztec 250	Sutaberry Ltd	
G-BAWG	PA-28R-200-2 Cherokee Arrow	South Coast Aero Club/Southampton	
G-BAWI	Enstrom F-28A-UK	Red Baron Properties Ltd	
G-BAWK	PA-28 Cherokee 140	Newcastle-Upon-Tyne Aero Club Ltd	
G-BAWL	Airborne Industries gas airship	A. F. J. Smith *The Santos-Dumont*	
G-BAWN	PA-30C Twin Comanche 160	J. & Y. Plastics (Aviation) Ltd/Manchester	
G-BAWR	Robin HR.100/210	Kinchplan Ltd/Biggin Hill	
G-BAWU	PA-30 Twin Comanche 160	Tiger Club Displays Ltd/Redhill	

Notes	Reg.	Type	Owner or Operator
	G-BAWV	PA-E23 Aztec 250	Merseyside Commercial Sales & Service Ltd/Liverpool
	G-BAWW	Thunder Ax7-77 balloon	Miss M. L. C. Hutchins *Taurus*
	G-BAWX	PA-28 Cherokee 180	Beavergrain Ltd
	G-BAWZ	Cessna 402B	Culinair Ltd/Biggin Hill
	G-BAXD	BN-2A Mk III Trislander	Aurigny Air Services/Guernsey
	G-BAXE	Hughes 269A	Reethorpe Engineering Ltd
	G-BAXF	Cameron O-77 balloon	R. D. Sargeant & M. F. Casson
	G-BAXH	Cessna 310Q	D. A. Williamson
	G-BAXJ	PA-32 Cherokee Six 300	UK Parachute Services/Ipswich
	G-BAXK	Thunder Ax7-77 balloon	Newbury Balloon Group *Jack O'Newbury*
	G-BAXL	H.S.125 Srs 3B	Dennis Vanguard International (Switchgear) Ltd/Coventry
	G-BAXM	Beech B.24R Sierra	Strangford Flying Group/Newtownards
	G-BAXN	PA-34-200-2 Seneca	Ards Aviation/Newtownards
	G-BAXP	PA-E23 Aztec 250	Peregrine Air Services Ltd/Inverness
	G-BAXR	Beech B.55 Baron	N. F. Parker/Elstree
	G-BAXS	Bell 47G-5	T. C. Barton
	G-BAXT	PA-28R-200 Cherokee Arrow	Williams & Griffin Ltd
	G-BAXU	Cessna F.150L	W. Lancs Aero Club Ltd/Woodvale
	G-BAXV	Cessna F.150L	Cardiff Aviation Ltd
	G-BAXY	Cessna F.172M	The Bearing Mart Ltd/Manchester
	G-BAXZ	PA-28 Cherokee 140	A. J. Smith & D. Norris
	G-BAYC	Cameron O-65 balloon	D. Whitlock & R. T. F. Mitchell
	G-BAYL	Nord 1203/III Norecrin	D. M. Fincham/Bodmin
	G-BAYO	Cessna 150L	Cheshire Air Training School Ltd/ Liverpool
	G-BAYP	Cessna 150L	T. G. Aviation Ltd/Manston
	G-BAYR	Robin HR.100/210	Gilbey Warren Co Ltd/Stapleford
	G-BAYX	Bell 47G-5	Helicopter Hire Ltd/Southend
	G-BAYY	Cessna 310C	Allen Baker Aviation Ltd/Coventry
	G-BAYZ	Bellanca 7GC BC Citabria	Cambridge University Gliding Trust Ltd/ Duxford
	G-BAZA	H.S.125 Srs 403B	Northern Engineering Industries Ltd/ Newcastle
	G-BAZB	H.S.125 Srs 400B	Short Bros Ltd/Sydenham
	G-BAZC	Robin DR.400/160	Greatascot Ltd/Biggin Hill
	G-BAZF	AA-5 Traveler	N. London Flying Club/Elstree
	G-BAZG	Boeing 737-204	Britannia Airways Ltd *Florence Nightingale*/Luton
	G-BAZH	Boeing 737-204	Britannia Airways Ltd *Sir Frederick Handley Page*/Luton
	G-BAZI	Boeing 737-204	Britannia Airways Ltd *Sir Walter Raleigh*/Luton
	G-BAZJ	HPR-7 Herald 209	Air UK/Norwich
	G-BAZM	Jodel D.11	Bingley Flying Group/Leeds
	G-BAZN	Bell 206B JetRanger 2	Somerton-Rayner Helicopters Ltd/ Thruxton
	G-BAZS	Cessna F.150L	Sherburn Aero Club Ltd
	G-BAZT	Cessna F.172M	Murray Fraser (Aviation) Ltd/Exeter
	G-BAZU	PA-28R-200 Cherokee Arrow	Andytruc Ltd/White Waltham
	G-BAZV	PA-E23 Aztec 250	Wings International/Elstree
	G-BBAE	L.1011-385 TriStar	British Airways *The Stargazer Rose*/ Heathrow
	G-BBAF	L.1011-385 TriStar	British Airways *The Coronation Gold Rose*/Heathrow
	G-BBAG	L.1011-385 TriStar	British Airways *The Caroline Davison Rose*/Heathrow
	G-BBAH	L.1011-385 TriStar	British Airways *The Sunsilk Rose*/ Heathrow
	G-BBAI	L.1011-385 TriStar	British Airways *The Molly McGredy Rose*/Heathrow
	G-BBAJ	L.1011-385 TriStar	British Airtours Ltd *The Elizabeth Harkness Rose*/Gatwick
	G-BBAK	M.S.894A Rallye Minerva	Scramble Flying Group
	G-BBAR	Jodel D.117	J. F. Wright
	G-BBAU	Enstrom F.28A	Norman Bailey Helicopters Ltd/ Southampton
	G-BBAW	Robin HR.100/210	Scoba Ltd/Biggin Hill
	G-BBAX	Robin DR.400/140	S. R. Young

Reg.	Type	Owner or Operator	Notes
G-BBAY	Robin DR.400/140	G. A. Pentelow & D. B. Roadnight/ Sywell	
G-BBAZ	Hiller UH-12E	Management Aviation Ltd/Bourn	
G-BBBA	Hiller UH-12E	Management Aviation Ltd/Bourn	
G-BBBB	Taylor JT.1 Monoplane	S. A. MacConnacher	
G-BBBC	Cessna F.150L	I. M. Williamson/Biggin Hill	
G-BBBI	AA-5 Traveler	Hornet Aviation Ltd	
G-BBBK	PA-28 Cherokee 140	Bolton Air Training School Ltd/ Blackpool	
G-BBBL	Cessna 337B	Alderney Air Charter Ltd	
G-BBBM	Bell 206B JetRanger 2	Keluma Ltd	
G-BBBN	PA-28 Cherokee 180	B. R. Rossiter/White Waltham	
G-BBBO	SIPA 903	D. A. C. Clissett & L. L. Vickers/ Stapleford	
G-BBBW	FRED Series 2	D. L. Webster/Sherburn	
G-BBBX	Cessna E310L	Air Atlantique Ltd/Jersey	
G-BBBY	PA-28 Cherokee 140	R. A. E. Tremlett/Guernsey	
G-BBCA	Bell 206B JetRanger 2	Harvest Aviation Ltd	
G-BBCB	Western O-65 balloon	M. Westwood *Cee Bee*	
G-BBCC	PA-E23 Aztec 250	Goodridge (UK) Ltd/Exeter	
G-BBCD	Beech 95-B55 Baron	J. H. Jackson (Estate Agents) Ltd/ Biggin Hill	
G-BBCF	Cessna FRA.150L	Cheshire Air Training School/Liverpool	
G-BBCG	Robin DR.400/2+2	Headcorn Flying School Ltd	
G-BBCH	Robin DR. 400/2+2	Headcorn Flying School Ltd	
G-BBCI	Cessna 150H	N. R. Windley	
G-BBCJ	Cessna 150J	Eastern Diving & Aviation Services Ltd	
G-BBCK	Cameron O-77 balloon	R. J. Leathart *The Mary Gloster*	
G-BBCM	PA-E23 Aztec 250	Keenair Services Ltd/Liverpool	
G-BBCN	Robin HR.100/210	M. B. Aviation Ltd/Humberside	
G-BBCP	Thunder Ax6-56 balloon	J. M. Robinson *Jack Frost*	
G-BBCS	Robin DR.400/140	Headcorn Flying School Ltd	
G-BBCW	PA-E23 Aztec 250	Deborah Services Ltd/Sturgate	
G-BBCX	Airship (hot-air) radio-controlled	E. A. Wills & G. W. Moger *Dew Drop*	
G-BBCY	Luton LA-4A Minor	C. H. Difford/Dunkeswell	
G-BBCZ	AA-5 Traveler	Stronghill Flying Group/Bournemouth	
G-BBDA	AA-5 Traveler	David Burke Marine Ltd	
G-BBDB	PA-28 Cherokee 180	T. D. Strange/Newtownards	
G-BBDC	PA-28 Cherokee 140	MSF Aviation Ltd/Manchester	
G-BBDD	PA-28 Cherokee 140	FR Aviation/Coventry	
G-BBDE	PA-28R-200-2 Cherokee Arrow	S. P. Hales	
G-BBDG	Concorde 100	British Aerospace PLC/Filton	
G-BBDH	Cessna F.172M	G. Jones	
G-BBDI	PA-18-150 Super Cub	Scottish Gliding Union Ltd	
G-BBDJ	Thunder Ax6-56 balloon	S. W. D. & H. B. Ashby *Jack Tar*	
G-BBDK	V.808F Viscount Cargomaster	British Air Ferries/Southend	
G-BBDL	AA-5 Traveler	J. Jones/Halfpenny Green	
G-BBDM	AA-5 Traveler	E. M. Pettit Construction Ltd/Stapleford	
G-BBDN	Taylor JT.1 Monoplane	D. A. Nice	
G-BBDO	PA-E23 Aztec 250	R. Long/Bristol	
G-BBDP	Robin DR.400/160	Jarrett & Plumb Aviation (Rochester) Ltd	
G-BBDS	PA-31 Navajo	Broad Oak Air Services/Rochester	
G-BBDT	Cessna 150H	J. M. McCloy/Sherburn	
G-BBDU	PA-31 Navajo	ITT Components Ltd/Stansted	
G-BBDV	SIPA S.903	A. W. Webster	
G-BBEA	Luton LA-4A Minor	D. J. Wells & ptnrs/Fenland	
G-BBEB	PA-28R-200-2 Cherokee Arrow	Scoutside Ltd	
G-BBEC	PA-28 Cherokee 180	P. F. Blake	
G-BBED	M.S.894B Rallye Minerva	Trago Mills Ltd/Bodmin	
G-BBEF	PA-28 Cherokee 140	Air Navigation & Trading Co Ltd/ Blackpool	
G-BBEI	PA-31 Navajo	BKS Surveys Ltd/Exeter	
G-BBEJ	PA-31-350 Navajo Chieftain	Eastern Airways/Humberside	
G-BBEL	PA-28R Cherokee Arrow 180	J. M. McRitchie/Newtownards	
G-BBEM	Beech B.55 Baron	M. J. Coburn & L. C. G. Hughes/Luton	
G-BBEN	Bellanca 7GCBC Citabria	Ulster Gliding Club Ltd	
G-BBEO	Cessna FRA.150L	Granair Ltd	
G-BBEP	H.S.125 Srs 600B		
G-BBEU	Bell 206B JetRanger 2	Air Hanson Ltd/Brooklands	
G-BBEV	PA-28 Cherokee 140	Keenair Services Ltd/Liverpool	

Notes	Reg.	Type	Owner or Operator
	G-BBEW	PA-E23 Aztec 250	Eastern Airways/Humberside
	G-BBEX	Cessna 185A Skywagon	R. G. Brooks & D. E. Wilson/Dunkeswell
	G-BBEY	PA-E23 Aztec 250	Berrard Aviation/Blackbushe
	G-BBFC	AA-1B Trainer	R. C. Gillingham & G. Mobey
	G-BBFD	PA-28R-200-2 Cherokee Arrow	F. T. Holdcraft
	G-BBFE	Bell 206 JetRanger	Specialist Flying Training Ltd/Hamble
	G-BBFL	GY-201 Minicab	M. F. Coy/Wellesbourne
	G-BBFS	Van Den Bemden gas balloon	A. J. F. Smith *Le Tomate*
	G-BBFT	Cessna A.188B Ag Truck	Mindacre Ltd
	G-BBFU	PA-E23 Aztec 250	Ulmke Metals Ltd/Birmingham
	G-BBFV	PA-32 Cherokee Six 260	Southend Securities Ltd
	G-BBFW	PA-E23 Aztec 250B	T. Bartlett/Stapleford
	G-BBFX	PA-34-200-2 Seneca	C. D. Weiswall/Elstree
	G-BBFZ	PA-28R-200-2 Cherokee Arrow	Larkfield Garage (Chepstow) Ltd
	G-BBGB	PA-E23 Aztec 250	Lassair International Ltd/Bristol
	G-BBGC	M.S.893E Rallye Commodore 180	A. Somerville/Alderney
	G-BBGE	PA-E23 Aztec 250	Dollar Air Services Ltd/Coventry
	G-BBGF	Cessna 340	Hillair Ltd & Lawrence Wilson & Son Ltd/Leeds
	G-BBGH	AA-5 Traveler	London Aerial Tours Ltd
	G-BBGI	Fuji FA.200-160	Scottish Airways Flyers (Prestwick) Ltd
	G-BBGJ	Cessna 180	Med-Co Hospital Supplies Ltd
	G-BBGL	Baby Great Lakes	P. W. Thomas/Barton
	G-BBGR	Cameron O-65 balloon	Thames Valley Balloon Group
	G-BBGS	Sikorsky S-61N	Bristow Helicopters Ltd *Indefatigable*
	G-BBGX	Cessna 182P Skylane	H. I. Williams & ptnrs/Sleap
	G-BBGZ	CHABA 42 balloon	British Balloon Museum *Phlogiston*
	G-BBHB	PA-31-300 Navajo	Kondair/Stansted
	G-BBHC	Enstrom F-28A	Dumbrill Plant & Engineering Co Ltd/Swansea
	G-BBHD	Enstrom F-28A	Stott Demolition Ltd
	G-BBHE	Enstrom F-28A	C. Leonard
	G-BBHF	PA-23 Aztec 250E	Bevan Lynch Aviation Ltd/Coventry
	G-BBHG	Cessna E-310Q	Airwork Services Ltd/Perth
	G-BBHI	Cessna 177RG	Economeats & Foods (Wholesale & Retail) Ltd/Jersey
	G-BBHJ	Piper J-3C-65 Cub	R. V. Miller & R. H. Heath
	G-BBHK	AT-16 Harvard IIB	Bob Warner Aviation/Long Marston
	G-BBHL	Sikorsky S-61N Mk II	Bristow Helicopters Ltd *Glamis*
	G-BBHM	Sikorsky S-61N Mk II	Bristow Helicopters Ltd *Braemar*
	G-BBHU	SA.341G Gazelle 1	Solaria Investments Ltd/Jersey
	G-BBHW	SA.341G Gazelle 1	McAlpine Aviation Ltd/Hayes
	G-BBHX	M.S.893E Rallye Commodore	P. J. Pitts/Alderney
	G-BBHY	PA-28 Cherokee 180	Air Operations Ltd/Guernsey
	G-BBIA	PA-28R-200 Cherokee Arrow	A. G. (Commodities) Ltd/Stapleford
	G-BBIC	Cessna 310Q	Hanro Aviation Ltd/E. Midlands
	G-BBID	PA-28 Cherokee 140	T. K. Aero Enterprises Ltd/Elstree
	G-BBIF	PA-E23 Aztec 250	Northern Executive Aviation Ltd/Manchester
	G-BBIH	Enstrom F-28A	Norman Bailey Helicopters Ltd/Southampto
	G-BBII	Fiat G-46-3B	The Hon Patrick Lindsay/Booker
	G-BBIJ	Cessna 421B	Exeair Travel Ltd/Exeter
	G-BBIL	PA-28 Cherokee 140	Daryll Group
	G-BBIN	Enstrom F28A	Southern Air Ltd/Shoreham
	G-BBIO	Robin HR.100/210	R. A. King/Headcorn
	G-BBIT	Hughes 269B	Contract Development & Projects (Leeds) Ltd
	G-BBIV	Hughes 269C	W. R. Finance Ltd
	G-BBIW	Hughes 269C	W. R. Finance Ltd
	G-BBIX	PA-28 Cherokee 140	R. C. Harvey & W. G. Best/Biggin Hill
	G-BBJB	Thunder Ax7-77 balloon	St Crispin Balloon Group *Dick Darby*
	G-BBJI	Isaacs Spitfire	A. N. R. Houghton & ptnrs
	G-BBJT	Robin HR.200/100	M. J. McRobert/Headcorn
	G-BBJU	Robin DR.400/140	J. C. Lister
	G-BBJV	Cessna F.177RG	Pilot Magazine/Biggin Hill
	G-BBJW	Cessna FRA.150L	J. G. Johnston/Biggin Hill
	G-BBJX	Cessna F.150L	Yorkshire Flying Services Ltd/Leeds
	G-BBJY	Cessna F.172M	J. Lucketti/Barton
	G-BBJZ	Cessna F.172M	AM Flight Services Ltd
	G-BBKA	Cessna F.150L	Sherburn Aero Club Ltd

Reg.	Type	Owner or Operator	Notes
G-BBKB	Cessna F.150L	Shoreham Flight Simulation Ltd	
G-BBKC	Cessna F.172M	D. E. H. Designs Ltd/Bournemouth	
G-BBKE	Cessna F.150L	Wickenby Aviation Ltd	
G-BBKF	Cessna FRA.150L	George House Holdings Ltd/ Compton Abbas	
G-BBKG	Cessna FR.172J	D. A. D. T. Telfer-Smollett/Bourn	
G-BBKI	Cessna F.172M	B. C. Lemon & D. Godfrey/ Crowland	
G-BBKJ	Cessna FT.337G	Carter Aviation Ltd/E. Midlands	
G-BBKL	CP.301A Emeraude	W. J. Walker	
G-BBKO	Thunder Ax7-77 balloon	J. A. Clarke	
G-BBKR	Scheibe SF.24A Motorspatz	P. I. Morgans	
G-BBKU	Cessna FRA.150L	Balgin Ltd/Bourn	
G-BBKV	Cessna FRA.150L	Laarbruch Flying Club	
G-BBKX	PA-28 Cherokee 180	P. E. Eglington	
G-BBKY	Cessna F.150L	W. of Scotland Flying Club Ltd/Glasgow	
G-BBKZ	Cessna 172M	Exeter Flying Club Ltd	
G-BBLA	PA-28 Cherokee 140	Southport Aviation Co Ltd/Woodvale	
G-BBLC	Hiller UH-12E	Agricopters Ltd/Thruxton	
G-BBLE	Hiller UH-12E	Agricopters Ltd/Thruxton	
G-BBLG	Hiller UH-12E	Sloane Aviation Ltd/Sywell	
G-BBLH	Piper O-59A Grasshopper	P. A. Mann/Biggin Hill	
G-BBLL	Cameron O-84 balloon	University of East Anglia Hot-Air Ballooning Club Boadicea	
G-BBLM	MS.880 Rallye 100 Sport	R. J. Lewis & P. Walker/Shoreham	
G-BBLP	PA-E23 Aztec 250D	Banline Aviation Ltd/E. Midlands	
G-BBLS	AA-5 Traveler	Prestwick Flying Club	
G-BBLU	PA-34-200-2 Seneca	F. Tranter/Manchester	
G-BBMB	Robin DR.400/180	R. B. Tyler	
G-BBME	BAC One-Eleven 401	British Airways County of Shropshire (G-AZMI)/Birmingham	
G-BBMF	BAC One-Eleven 401	British Airways County of Worcestershire (G-ATVU)/Birmingham	
G-BBMG	BAC One-Eleven 408	British Airways County of Gloucestershire (G-AWEJ)/Birmingham	
G-BBMH	E.A.A. Sports Biplane Model P.1.	K. Dawson	
G-BBMJ	PA-E23 Aztec 250	Fras-Air Ltd	
G-BBMK	PA-31-300 Navajo	Steer Aviation Ltd/Biggin Hill	
G-BBMN	D.H.C.I Chipmunk 22	R. Steiner/Panshanger	
G-BBMO	D.H.C.I Chipmunk 22	A. J. Hurst/Holland	
G-BBMR	D.H.C.I Chipmunk T.10 ★ (WB763)	Southall Technical College	
G-BBMT	D.H.C.I Chipmunk 22	A. T. Letts & ptnrs/Bourn	
G-BBMV	D.H.C.I Chipmunk 22 (WG348)	M. D. Payne/White Waltham	
G-BBMW	D.H.C.I Chipmunk 22	Andrew Edie Aviation/Shoreham	
G-BBMX	D.H.C.I Chipmunk 22	W. Damms	
G-BBMZ	D.H.C.I Chipmunk 22	A. J. Baggarley	
G-BBNA	D.H.C.I Chipmunk 22 (Lycoming)	Coventry Gliding Club Ltd/Husbands Bosworth	
G-BBNC	D.H.C.I Chipmunk T.10 ★ (WP790)	Mosquito Aircraft Museum	
G-BBND	D.H.C.I Chipmunk 22	West Johnson Property Holdings/Bourn	
G-BBNG	Bell 206B JetRanger 2	Bristow Helicopters Ltd	
G-BBNH	PA-34-200-2 Seneca	Lawrence Goodwin Machine Tools Ltd Wellesbourne	
G-BBNI	PA-34-200-2 Seneca	Colneray Ltd/Guernsey	
G-BBNJ	Cessna F.150L	K. D. Wickenden/Shoreham	
G-BBNM	PA-23 Aztec 250	Philstone International Ltd	
G-BBNN	PA-E23 Aztec 250D	British Caledonian Airways Ltd/Gatwick	
G-BBNO	PA-E23 Aztec 250E	Kondair/Stansted	
G-BBNR	Cessna 340	J. Lipton/Elstree	
G-BBNT	PA-31-350 Navajo Chieftain	Northern Executive Aviation Ltd/ Manchester	
G-BBNV	Fuji FA.200-160	C.S.E. (Aircraft Services) Ltd/Kidlington	
G-BBNX	Cessna FRA.150L	Three Counties Aero Club Ltd/ Blackbushe	
G-BBNY	Cessna FRA.150L	Fairoaks Aviation Services Ltd	
G-BBNZ	Cessna F.172M	Lunnons Commercials/Stapleford	
G-BBOA	Cessna F.172M	George House (Holdings) Ltd/ Compton Abbas	
G-BBOB	Cessna 421B	Exe International Ltd/Exeter	
G-BBOC	Cameron O-77 balloon	Bacchus Balloons Bacchus	

Notes	Reg.	Type	Owner or Operator
	G-BBOD	Thunder 005 balloon	Thunder Balloons Ltd *Eric the Lad*
	G-BBOE	Robin HR.200/100	R. D. V. Kite & J. G. Anderson
	G-BBOH	Pitts S-1S Special	P. Meeson
	G-BBOI	Bede BD-5B	Heather V. B. Wheeler/Greenland
	G-BBOL	PA-18-150 Super Cub	Lakes Gliding Club Ltd/Barrow
	G-BBOM	PA-E23 Aztec 250E	Maldocrest Ltd/Lulsgate
	G-BBOO	Thunder Ax6-56 balloon	K. Meehan *Tigerjack*
	G-BBOR	Bell 206B JetRanger 2	J. M. V. Butterfield
	G-BBOX	Thunder Ax7-77 balloon	R. C. Weyda *Rocinante*
	G-BBOY	Thunder Ax6-56A balloon	N. C. Faithfull *Eric of Titchfield*
	G-BBPJ	Cessna F.172M	Simmette Ltd/Exeter
	G-BBPK	Evans VP-1	P. D. Kelsey
	G-BBPM	Enstrom F-28A	Source Promotions & Premium Consultants Ltd
	G-BBPN	Enstrom F-28A	C.S.E. Aviation Ltd/Kidlington
	G-BBPO	Enstrom F-28A	M. Page
	G-BBPP	PA-28 Cherokee 180	J. H. Nightingale Ltd/Blackpool
	G-BBPU	Boeing 747-136	British Airways *Henry Hudson*/Heathrow
	G-BBPW	Robin HR.100/210	Parlway Ltd/Biggin Hill
	G-BBPX	PA-34-200-2 Seneca	Richel Investments Ltd/Guernsey
	G-BBPY	PA-28 Cherokee 180	Ulster Flying Club (1961) Ltd/Newtownards
	G-BBRA	PA-E23 Aztec 250E	Kraken Air Ltd/Cardiff
	G-BBRB	D.H.82A Tiger Moth (DF198)	R. Barham
	G-BBRC	Fuji FA.200-180	W. & L. Installations & Co Ltd/Fairoaks
	G-BBRE	Fuji FA.200-160	M. R. Howse/Wellesbourne
	G-BBRI	Bell 47G-5A	Camlet Helicopters Ltd/Fairoaks
	G-BBRN	Procter Kittiwake	RNGSA/Yeovilton
	G-BBRV	D.H.C.I Chipmunk 22	HSA (Chester) Sports & Social Club
	G-BBRW	PA-28 Cherokee 140	March Flying Group/Stapleford
	G-BBRX	SIAI-Marchetti S.205-18F	W. Chrystal/Usworth
	G-BBRZ	AA-5 Traveler	M. J. Coleman/Jersey
	G-BBSA	AA-5 Traveler	J. H. Ashcroft/Netherthorpe
	G-BBSB	Beech C23 Sundowner	Sundowner Group/Manchester
	G-BBSC	Beech B24R Sierra	Beechcombers Flying Group
	G-BBSE	D.H.C. I Chipmunk 22	Hartley House Investments Ltd
	G-BBSF	Cessna 310Q	Wilkinson Developments (Yorkshire) Ltd
	G-BBSM	PA-32 Cherokee Six 300	Plentglen Ltd/Halfpenny Green
	G-BBSN	PA-E23 Aztec 250	Burnthills (Contractors) Ltd/Glasgow
	G-BBSO	PA-28 Cherokee 140	K. Edwards/Coventry
	G-BBSR	PA-E23 Aztec 250D	LDL Enterprises/Elstree
	G-BBSS	D.H.C.IA Chipmunk 22	Northumbria Gliding Club Ltd
	G-BBST	PA-E23 Aztec 250	Thurston Aviation Ltd/Stansted
	G-BBSU	Cessna 421B	Fisons Ltd/E. Midlands
	G-BBSV	Cessna 421B	D. M. Coombs
	G-BBSW	Pietenpol Air Camper	J. K. S. Wills
	G-BBTB	Cessna FRA.150L	George House (Holdings) Ltd/Compton Abbas
	G-BBTG	Cessna F.172M	D. H. Laws
	G-BBTH	Cessna F.172M	H. J. C. Townley & ptnrs/Newtownards
	G-BBTJ	PA-E23 Aztec 250E	Milford Haven Dry Dock Ltd/Cambridge
	G-BBTK	Cessna FRA.150L	Airwork Services Ltd/Perth
	G-BBTL	PA-E23 Aztec 250C	Air Navigation & Trading Co Ltd/Blackpool
	G-BBTS	Beech V35B Bonanza	Charles Lock Motors Ltd/Elstree
	G-BBTU	ST-10 Diplomate	P. Campion/Stapleford
	G-BBTW	PA-31P Navajo	M. G. Tyrell & Co Ltd
	G-BBTX	Beech C23 Sundowner	Celahurst Ltd
	G-BBTY	Beech C23 Sundowner	Torlid Ltd/Biggin Hill
	G-BBTZ	Cessna F.150L	Woodgate Air Services Ltd
	G-BBUD	Sikorsky S-61N Mk II	British Airways Helicopters Ltd/Aberdeen
	G-BBUE	AA-5 Traveler	C. A. Arnold/Southend
	G-BBUF	AA-5 Traveler	Eglinton Flying Club
	G-BBUG	PA-16 Clipper	I. M. Callier & G. V. Harfield
	G-BBUJ	Cessna 421B	The Automobile Association/Coventry
	G-BBUL	Mitchell-Procter Kittiwake 1	R. Bull
	G-BBUO	Cessna 150L	Exeter Flying Club Ltd
	G-BBUP	B.121 Pup 1	C. C. Brown/Leicester
	G-BBUT	Western O-65 balloon	Wg. Cdr. G. F. Turnbull & Mrs K. Turnbull *Christabelle II*

Reg.	Type	Owner or Operator	Notes
G-BBUU	Piper L-4B Cub	Cooper Bros/Little Snoring	
G-BBUY	Bell 206B JetRanger 2	Helicopter Hire Ltd/Southend	
G-BBVA	Sikorsky S-61N Mk. II	Bristow Helicopters Ltd *Vega*	
G-BBVE	Cessna 340	R. M. Cox Ltd/Biggin Hill	
G-BBVF	SA Twin Pioneer III ★	Museum of Flight/E. Fortune	
G-BBVG	PA-E23 Aztec 250D	R. F. Wanbon & P. G. Warmerdan/ Panshanger	
G-BBVH	V.807 Viscount	GB Airways Ltd/Gibraltar	
G-BBVI	Enstrom F-28A ★	*Ground trainer*/Kidlington	
G-BBVJ	Beech B24R Sierra	D. J. Pemberton & R. N. Evans/ Netherthorpe	
G-BBVM	Beech A.100 King Air	Vernair Transport Services/Liverpool	
G-BBVO	Isaacs Fury II	D. B. Wilson/Jersey	
G-BBVP	Westland-Bell 47G-3BI	Freemans of Bewdley (Aviation) Ltd	
G-BBWM	PA-E23 Aztec 250E	Alidair Ltd/E. Midlands	
G-BBWN	D.H.C.I Chipmunk 22	G. R. Tait & J. Ripley/Elstree	
G-BBWZ	AA-1B Trainer	Warner Aviation/Sherburn	
G-BBXA	Beech B.55 Baron	Crevet Holdings Ltd/Guernsey	
G-BBXB	Cessna FRA.150L	M. L. Swain/Bourn	
G-BBXG	PA-34-200-2 Seneca	Ann Green Manufacturing Co	
G-BBXH	Cessna FR.172F	Vale Hire & Contracting Co Ltd	
G-BBXI	HPR-7 Herald 203	Air UK/Norwich	
G-BBXK	PA-34-200-2 Seneca	J. A Galt/Sandown	
G-BBXL	Cessna E310Q	SMC Leisure Ltd/Stapleford	
G-BBXO	Enstrom F-28A	C.S.E. Aviation Ltd/Kidlington	
G-BBXR	PA-31-350 Navajo Chieftain	Rolls-Royce Ltd/E. Midlands	
G-BBXS	Piper J-3C-65 Cub	N. Simpson (G-ALMA)/Cranwell	
G-BBXT	Cessna F.172M	I. B. Wilkens/Southampton	
G-BBXU	Beech B24R Sierra	Glidegold Ltd/Goodwood	
G-BBXV	PA-28-151 Warrior	Beechwood Marine Ltd/Staverton	
G-BBXW	PA-28-151 Warrior	3D Aluminium Ltd/Kidlington	
G-BBXX	PA-31-350 Navajo Chieftain	Natural Environment Research Council	
G-BBXY	Bellanca 7GC BC Citabria	Peter Hilton (Wickham) Ltd/Goodwood	
G-BBXZ	Evans VP-1	J. A. Naughton/Long Marston	
G-BBYB	PA-18 Super Cub 95	Hornet Aviation Ltd/Sherburn	
G-BBYE	Cessna 195	Wilrow Products Ltd	
G-BBYH	Cessna 182P	Sanderson (Forklifts) Ltd	
G-BBYK	PA-E23 Aztec 250	Flash Virgo Ltd/Swansea	
G-BBYL	Cameron O-77 balloon	Buckingham Balloon Club *Jammy*	
G-BBYM	H.P.137 Jestream 200	Rig Design Services Ltd (G-AYWR)	
G-BBYN	PA-30 Twin Comanche 160	Express Aviation Services Ltd	
G-BBYO	BN-2A Mk. III Trislander	Aurigny Air Services (G-BBWR)/Alderney	
G-BBYP	PA-28 Cherokee 140	Wear Ltd/Jersey	
G-BBYR	Cameron O-65 balloon	D. M. Winder *Phoenix*	
G-BBYS	Cessna 182P Skylane	Forth Engineering Ltd/Coventry	
G-BBYU	Cameron O-56 balloon	C. J. T. Davey *Chieftain*	
G-BBYW	PA-28 Cherokee 140	C.S.E. (Aircraft Services) Ltd/Kidlington	
G-BBZF	PA-28 Cherokee 140	R. F. Grute & M. K. Taylor/Wellesbourne	
G-BBZH	PA-28R-200 Cherokee Arrow	George House (Holdings) Ltd/ Compton Abbas	
G-BBZI	PA-31-310 Navajo	Air Messenger/Manston	
G-BBZJ	PA-34-200-2 Seneca	C.S.E. (Aircraft Services) Ltd/Kidlington	
G-BBZN	Fuji FA.200-180	J. Brown & D. W. Parfrey	
G-BBZO	Fuji FA.200-160	D. G. Foreman/Biggin Hill	
G-BBZS	Enstrom F-28A	Spooner Aviation (Enstrom Helicopters) Ltd/Shoreham	
G-BBZV	PA-28R-200-2 Cherokee Arrow	Unicol Engineering/Kidlington	
G-BCAC	M.S.894A Rallye Minerva 220	C. H. Royal	
G-BCAD	M.S.894A Rallye Minerva 220	G. W. Lloyd/Staverton	
G-BCAH	D.H.C.I Chipmunk 22 (WG316)	P. D. Southerington/Cranfield	
G-BCAN	Thunder Ax7-77 balloon	D. & L. Cole *Billboard*	
G-BCAR	Thunder Ax7-77 balloon	T. J. Woodbridge/Australia	
G-BCAS	Thunder Ax7-77 balloon	Zebedee Balloon Service *Drifter*	
G-BCAT	PA-31-310 Turbo Navajo	David Martin Couriers Ltd	
G-BCAZ	PA-12 Super Cruiser	A. D. Williams	
G-BCBD	Bede BD-5B	Brockmore-Bede Aircraft (UK) Ltd/ Shobdon	
G-BCBG	PA-E23 Aztec 250	M. J. L. Barr/Booker	
G-BCBH	Fairchild 24R-46A Argus III	Bluegale Ltd/Biggin Hill	
G-BCBI	Cessna 402B	C. M. Vlieland-Boddy	

Notes	Reg.	Type	Owner or Operator
	G-BCBJ	PA-25 Pawnee 235	CKS Air Ltd/Southend
	G-BCBK	Cessna 421B	Lloyds & Scottish Development Ltd/ Luton
	G-BCBL	Fairchild 24R-46A Argus III (HB751)	Battle of Britain Prints International Ltd/ Benson
	G-BCBN	Scheibe SF.27M-Ci	D. B. James/Booker
	G-BCBP	M.S.880B Rallye 100S Sport	A. A. Thomas/Dunkeswell
	G-BCBR	AJEP/Wittman W.8 Tailwind	G. McMillan
	G-BCBV	PA-25 Pawnee 235	Farmair Ltd/Headcorn
	G-BCBW	Cessna 182P	Davison & Co Ltd
	G-BCBX	Cessna F.150L	Woodgate Air Services Ltd/Aldergrove
	G-BCBY	Cessna F.150L	R. A. Ranscombe/Ronaldsway
	G-BCBZ	Cessna 337C	H. Tempest Ltd/Bodmin
	G-BCCB	Robin HR.200/100	Tradebase Ltd
	G-BCCC	Cessna F.150L	J. C. Glynn
	G-BCCD	Cessna F.172M	Spooner Aviation (Engineering) Ltd/ Shoreham
	G-BCCE	PA-E23 Aztec 250	House of Brazil Ltd/Biggin Hill
	G-BCCF	PA-28 Cherokee 180	J. T. Friskney Ltd
	G-BCCG	Thunder Ax7-65 balloon	N. H. Ponsford
	G-BCCJ	AA-5 Traveler	T. Needham & ptnrs/Manchester
	G-BCCK	AA-5 Traveler	Donald Healey Motor Co Ltd/Staverton
	G-BCCP	Robin HR. 200/100	Northampton School of Flying Ltd/ Sywell
	G-BCCR	CP.301B Emeraude	A. B. Fisher/Stapleford
	G-BCCX	D.H.C.I Chipmunk 22 (Lycoming)	RAFGSA/Bicester
	G-BCCY	Robin HR.200/100	D. S. Farler/Lulsgate
	G-BCDA	Boeing 727-46	Dan-Air Services Ltd/Gatwick
	G-BCDB	PA-34-200-2 Seneca	C.S.E. (Aircraft Services) Ltd/Kidlington
	G-BCDC	PA-18 Super Cub 95	ALY Aviation Ltd
	G-BCDH	MBB Bo 105D	North-Scottish Helicopters Ltd
	G-BCDJ	PA-28 Cherokee 140	Andrewsfield Flying Club Ltd
	G-BCDK	Partenavia P.68B	Peak Aviation International Ltd
	G-BCDL	Cameron O-42 balloon	D. P. & Mrs B. O. Turner Chums
	G-BCDN	F.27 Friendship Mk. 200	Air UK/Norwich
	G-BCDO	F.27 Friendship Mk. 200	Air UK/Norwich
	G-BCDR	Thunder Ax7-77 balloon	W. G. Johnston & ptnrs Obelix
	G-BCDS	PA-E23 Aztec 250	Hamilton Aviation Ltd/Jersey
	G-BCDY	Cessna FRA.150L	Airwork Ltd
	G-BCDZ	H.S.748 Srs 2A	British Aerospace/Woodford
	G-BCEA	Sikorsky S-61N Mk. II	British Airways Helicopters Ltd/ Aberdeen
	G-BCEB	Sikorsky S-61N Mk. II	British Airways Helicopters Ltd/ Penzance
	G-BCEC	Cessna F.172M	Great Consall Copper Mine Co Ltd
	G-BCEE	AA-5 Traveler	Echo Echo Ltd/Compton Abbas
	G-BCEF	AA-5 Traveler	Echo Fox Ltd/Jersey
	G-BCEN	BN-2A Islander	Horizon Holdings Ltd/Bournemouth
	G-BCEO	AA-5 Traveler	Hudson Forge Ltd
	G-BCEP	AA-5 Traveler	Nottingham Industrial Cleaners Ltd/ Tollerton
	G-BCER	GY-201 Minicab	D. Beaumont
	G-BCEU	Cameron O-42 balloon	Entertainment Services Ltd Harlequin
	G-BCEX	PA-E23 Aztec 250	Weekes Bros (Welling) Ltd/Biggin Hill
	G-BCEY	D.H.C.1 Chipmunk 22	D. O. Wallis
	G-BCEZ	Cameron O-84 balloon	Anglia Aeronauts Ascension Assocation Stars and Bars
	G-BCFB	Cameron O-77 balloon	J. J. Harris & P. Pryce-Jones Teutonic Turkey
	G-BCFC	Cameron O-65 balloon	B. H. Mead Candy Twist
	G-BCFD	West balloon	British Balloon Museum Hellfire
	G-BCFE	Odyssey 4000 balloon	R. M. Glover Odyssey
	G-BCFF	Fuji FA-200-160	P. Barnes/Southampton
	G-BCFN	Cameron O-65 balloon	W. G. Johnson & H. M. Savage
	G-BCFO	PA-18-150 Super Cub	Bristol & Gloucestershire Gliding Club (Pty) Ltd/Nympsfield
	G-BCFP	Enstrom F-28A	GCS Leisure Ltd/Blackbushe
	G-BCFR	Cessna FRA.150L	J. J. Baumhardt Associates Ltd/ Southend
	G-BCFW	Saab 91D Safir	D. R. Williams
	G-BCFY	Luton LA-4A Minor	D. V. Magee

Reg.	Type	Owner or Operator	Notes
G-BCFZ	Cameron A-500 balloon	C. J. T. Davy & ptnrs *Le Geant*	
G-BCGB	Bensen B.8	A. Melody	
G-BCGC	D.H.C.I Chipmunk 22	Culdrose Gliding Club	
G-BCGD	PA-28R-200-2 Cherokee Arrow	BLA Ltd	
G-BCGG	Jodel DR.250 Srs 160	C. G. Gray (G-ATZL)	
G-BCGH	Nord NC.854S	G. T. Roberts & A. W. Hughes	
G-BCGI	PA-28 Cherokee 140	G. W. Peace/Kidlington	
G-BCGJ	PA-28 Cherokee 140	I. T. D. Hall & B. R. Sedgeman Tees-side	
G-BCGK	PA-28 Cherokee 140	CSE (Aircraft Services) Ltd/Kidlington	
G-BCGL	Jodel D.112	R. A. Lock	
G-BCGM	Jodel D.120	I. E. Fisher/Wick	
G-BCGN	PA-28 Cherokee 140	Oxford Flyers Ltd/Kidlington	
G-BCGS	PA-28R-200 Cherokee Arrow	D. W. Hermiston-Hooper/Sandown	
G-BCGT	PA-28 Cherokee 140	I. M. Fieldsend/Ipswich	
G-BCGW	Jodel D.11	G. H. & M. D. Chittenden/Panshanger	
G-BCGX	Bede BD-5A/B	R. Hodgson	
G-BCHK	Cessna F.172H	N. Yorks Aviation Ltd	
G-BCHL	D.H.C.I Chipmunk 22A	B. D. Bate & R. Rutherford/Sleap	
G-BCHM	SA.341G Gazelle	Westland Helicopters Ltd/Yeovil	
G-BCHP	CP.1310C-3 Super Emeraude	P. D. Wheatland (G-JOSI)/Barton	
G-BCHT	Schleicher ASK.16	K. M. Barton & ptnrs/Dunstable	
G-BCHU	Dawes VP-2	G. Dawes	
G-BCHV	D.H.C.I Chipmunk 22	N. F. Charles/Cranwell	
G-BCHX	SF.23A Sperling	R. L. McClean/Doncaster	
G-BCID	PA-34-200-2 Seneca	Comanche Air Services Ltd/Lydd	
G-BCIE	PA-28-151 Warrior	Bryan Goss Motorcycles Ltd	
G-BCIF	PA-28 Cherokee 140	Fryer-Robins Aviation Ltd/E. Midlands	
G-BCIH	D.H.C.I Chipmunk 22 (WD363)	J. M. Hosey & R. A. Schofield/Stansted	
G-BCIJ	AA-5 Traveler	Crosby Agents & Brokers Ltd/ Humberside	
G-BCIK	AA-5 Traveler	W. Nutt & Son Ltd	
G-BCIL	AA-1B Trainer	Hirflire/Sherburn	
G-BCIM	AA-1B Trainer	R. H. Partington & R. J. Bourner/Strubby	
G-BCIN	Thunder Ax7-77 balloon	P. G & R. A. Vale	
G-BCIR	PA-28-151 Warrior	Call Sign Aviation/Leavesden	
G-BCIT	CIT/AI Srs 1	Cranfield Institute of Technology	
G-BCIW	D.H.C.I Chipmunk 22 (WZ868)	R. K. J. Hadlow & ptnrs/Holland	
G-BCJF	Beagle B.206 Srs 1	A. A. Mattacks/Biggin Hill	
G-BCJH	Mooney M.20F	S. R. Cannell/Luton	
G-BCJL	PA-28 Cherokee 140	P. B. Donoghue/Stapleford	
G-BCJM	PA-28 Cherokee 140	Pearson Charlton Engineers Ltd	
G-BCJN	PA-28 Cherokee 140	A. J. Steed/Dunkeswell	
G-BCJO	PA-28R-200 Cherokee Arrow	G. I. Cooper	
G-BCJP	PA-28 Cherokee 140	G. C. Smith/Stapleford	
G-BCJR	PA-E23 Aztec 250	Severnside International Aviation/Cardiff	
G-BCJS	PA-E23 Aztec 250	Woodgate Air Services (IOM) Ltd/ Ronaldsway	
G-BCKC	R. Thrush Commander 600	ADS (Aerial) Ltd/Southend	
G-BCKD	PA-28R-200-2 Cherokee Arrow	A. B. Plant (Aviation) Ltd/Bristol	
G-BCKF	SA.102.5 Cavalier	K. Fairness	
G-BCKJ	PA-23 Aztec 250	Jonas Travel Services Ltd	
G-BCKM	Cessna 500 Citation	Comet Radiovision Services Ltd/ Humberside	
G-BCKN	D.H.C.I A Chipmunk 22	RAFGSA/Cranwell	
G-BCKO	PA-E23 Aztec 250	Fras-Air Ltd	
G-BCKP	Luton LA-5A Major	J. R. Callow	
G-BCKS	Fuji FA.200-180	J. T. Hicks/Shoreham	
G-BCKT	Fuji FA.200-180	Littlewick Green Service Station Ltd/ Booker	
G-BCKU	Cessna FRA.150L	Airwork Services Ltd/Perth	
G-BCKV	Cessna FRA.150L	Airwork Services Ltd/Perth	
G-BCLA	Sikorsky S-61N	Bristow Helicopters Ltd	
G-BCLC	Sikorsky S-61N	Bristow Helicopters Ltd *Craigievar*	
G-BCLD	Sikorsky S-61N	Bristow Helicopters Ltd *Slains*	
G-BCLI	AA-5 Traveler	C. G. Whittaker (Commercials) Ltd/ Netherthorpe	
G-BCLJ	AA-5 Traveler	C. P. W. Villa & ptnrs/Shoreham	
G-BCLL	PA-28 Cherokee 180	Stu Davidson & Son Plant Hire Ltd/ Doncaster	
G-BCLS	Cessna 170B	C. W. Proffitt-White/Shotteswell	

Notes	Reg.	Type	Owner or Operator
	G-BCLU	Jodel D.117	N. A. Wallace
	G-BCLV	Bede BD-5A	R. A. Gardiner
	G-BCLW	AA-1B Trainer	Whisky Flying Group Ltd/Manchester
	G-BCMB	Partenavia P.68B	DK Aviation Ltd/Birmingham
	G-BCMC	Bell 212	Bristow Helicopters Ltd
	G-BCMD	PA-19 Super Cub 95	R. G. Brooks/Henstridge
	G-BCMF	Levi Go-Plane RL-6 Srs 1	R. Levi
	G-BCMJ	SA.102.5 Cavalier (tailwheel)	T. Fox & D. A. Thorpe/ Crowland
	G-BCMR	Robin HR.100/285	D. Betts
	G-BCMT	Isaacs Fury II	M. H. Turner
	G-BCNC	GY.201 Minicab	J. R. Wraight
	G-BCNP	Cameron O-77 balloon	J. E. H. Quilliam & ptnrs
	G-BCNR	Thunder Ax7-77A balloon	S. J. Miliken & ptnrs *Howdy*
	G-BCNS	Cameron O-77 balloon	Cathay Pacific Airways Ltd *Cathay I*
	G-BCNT	Partenavia P.68B	Cillam Holdings Ltd/Denham
	G-BCNX	Piper J.3C-65 Cub	N. J. R. Empson & ptnrs
	G-BCNZ	Fuji FA.200-160	P. R. Fabish
	G-BCOA	Cameron O-65 balloon	W. J. Hill *Bunny*
	G-BCOB	Piper J-3C-65 Cub	R. W. & Mrs J. W. Marjoram
	G-BCOE	HS.748 Srs 2A	British Airways/Glasgow
	G-BCOF	HS.748 Srs 2A	British Airways/Glasgow
	G-BCOG	Jodel D.112	B. A. Bower & ptnrs
	G-BCOH	Avro 683 Lancaster 10	Strathallan Aircraft Collection
	G-BCOI	D.H.C.I Chipmunk 22	D. S. McGregor & A. T. Letham
	G-BCOJ	Cameron O-56 balloon	T. J. Knott & M. J. Webber
	G-BCOL	Cessna F.172M	J. Birkett/Wickenby
	G-BCOM	Piper J-3C-65 Cub	P. M. Whitlock & J. P. Whitham/ Sywell
	G-BCOO	D.H.C.I Chipmunk 22	T. G. Fielding & M. S. Morton/Woodvale
	G-BCOP	PA-28R-200 Cherokee Arrow	J. H. Parker & ptnrs/Halfpenny Green
	G-BCOR	SOCATA Rallye 100ST	H. J. Pincombe/Dunkeswell
	G-BCOT	Enstrom F-28C-UK	P. J. Skinner/Panshanger
	G-BCOU	D.H.C.I Chipmunk 22	P. J. Loweth
	G-BCOV	Hawker Sea Fury TT.20 (VX302)	D. W. Arnold/Blackbushe
	G-BCOX	Bede BD-5A	H. J. Cox
	G-BCOY	D.H.C.I Chipmunk 22	Coventry Gliding Club Ltd/ Husbands Bosworth
	G-BCPA	SA.315B Alouette II	Dollar Air Services Ltd/Coventry
	G-BCPB	Howes radio-controlled model free balloon	R. B. & Mrs C. Howes *Posbee 1*
	G-BCPD	GY-201 Minicab	A. H. K. Denniss/Halfpenny Green
	G-BCPE	Cessna F.150M	Channel Islands Aero Holdings Ltd/ Jersey
	G-BCPF	PA-23 Aztec 250	M. A. Bonsall
	G-BCPG	PA-28R-200 Cherokee Arrow	Progressive Business Services Ltd/ Birmingham
	G-BCPH	Piper J-3C-65 Cub	J. J. Anziani/Booker
	G-BCPJ	Piper J-3C-65 Cub	M. C. Barraclough & T. M. Storey
	G-BCPK	Cessna F.172M	Skegness Air Taxi Services Ltd
	G-BCPN	AA-5 Traveler	B.W. Agricultural Equipments Ltd
	G-BCPO	Partenavia P.68B	N. C. N. Housden
	G-BCPU	D.H.C.I Chipmunk T.10	P. Waller/Booker
	G-BCPX	Szep HFC.125	A. Szep/Netherthorpe
	G-BCRA	Cessna F.150M	Three Counties Aero Club/Blackbushe
	G-BCRB	Cessna F.172M	F. D. & M. D. Forbes/Biggin Hill
	G-BCRE	Cameron O-77 balloon	A. R. Langston & R. J. Fuller *Snapdragon*
	G-BCRH	Alaparma Baldo B.75	A. L. Scadding/(*Stored*)
	G-BCRI	Cameron O-65 balloon	V. J. Thorne *Joseph*
	G-BCRJ	Taylor JT.1 Monoplane	Canary Flying Group
	G-BCRK	SA.102.5 Cavalier	J. M. Evans/Wyberton
	G-BCRL	PA-28-151 Warrior	F. N. Garland/Biggin Hill
	G-BCRN	Cessna FRA.150L	Airwork Services Ltd/Perth
	G-BCRP	PA-E23 Aztec 250	LEC Refrigeration Ltd/Bognor
	G-BCRR	AA-5B Tiger	Travelworth Ltd
	G-BCRT	Cessna F.150M	R. J. Everett Engineering Ltd/Ipswich
	G-BCRX	D.H.C.I Chipmunk 22	J. P. V. Hunt & P. G. H. Tory/Denham
	G-BCSA	D.H.C.I Chipmunk 22	RAFGSA/Dishforth
	G-BCSB	D.H.C.I Chipmunk 22	RAFGSA/Cosford

Reg.	Type	Owner or Operator	Notes
G-BCSL	D.H.C.I Chipmunk 22	Jalawain Ltd/Barton	
G-BCSM	Bellanca 8GC BC Scout	CKS Air Ltd/Southend	
G-BCST	M.S.893A Rallye Commodore 180	P. J. Wilcox/Cranfield	
G-BCSV	Cessna 421B	Northair Aviation Ltd/Leeds	
G-BCSX	Thunder Ax7-77 balloon	A. T. Wood *Whoopski*	
G-BCSY	Taylor JT.2 Titch	P. L. Mines/Sywell	
G-BCSZ	PA-28R-200 Cherokee Arrow	T. L. P. Delaney/White Waltham	
G-BCTA	PA-28-151 Warrior	T. G. Aviation Ltd/Manston	
G-BCTF	PA-28-151 Warrior	D. R. Stanley	
G-BCTI	Schleicher ASK.16	R. J. Steward	
G-BCTJ	Cessna 310Q	Airwork Services Ltd/Perth	
G-BCTK	Cessna FR.172J	Shobdon Aviation Co Ltd	
G-BCTR	Taylor JT.2 Titch	T. Reagan/Redhill	
G-BCTT	Evans VP-1	B. J. Boughton	
G-BCTU	Cessna FRA.150M	Mona Aviation Ltd	
G-BCTV	Cessna F.150M	Andrewsfield Flying Club Ltd	
G-BCTW	Cessna F.150M	Woodgate Air Services Ltd/Aldergrove	
G-BCUB	Piper J-3C-65 Cub	M. J. Mead/Bourn	
G-BCUF	Cessna F.172M	G. H. Kirke Ltd	
G-BCUH	Cessna F.150M	Gordon King (Aviation) Ltd/Biggin Hill	
G-BCUI	Cessna F.172M	Hillhouse Estates Ltd	
G-BCUJ	Cessna F.150M	G. Stewart/Humberside	
G-BCUK	Cessna F.172M	Q. Quitmann Ltd/Biggin Hill	
G-BCUL	SOCATA Rallye 100ST	C. B. Dew	
G-BCUM	Stinson HW-75	P. J. Sellar/Biggin Hill	
G-BCUW	Cessna F.177RG Cardinal	Martin J. Storey Ltd/Ipswich	
G-BCUY	Cessna FRA.150M	R. T. Williams & R. J. Meyer	
G-BCUZ	Beech A200 Super King Air	Allied Breweries (UK) Ltd/Tatenhill	
G-BCVA	Cameron O-65 balloon	J. C. Bass & ptnrs *Crepe Suzette*	
G-BCVB	PA-17 Vagabond	A. T. Nowak & B. Holland/Popham	
G-BCVC	SOCATA Rallye 100ST	Brettshire Ltd/Southend	
G-BCVE	Evans VP-2	D. Masterson	
G-BCVF	Practavia Pilot Sprite	G. B. Castle/Elstree	
G-BCVG	Cessna FRA.150L	Airwork Ltd/Perth	
G-BCVH	Cessna FRA.150L	W. Lancs Aero Club Ltd/Woodvale	
G-BCVI	Cessna FR.172J	B. D. & Mrs W. Phillips/Biggin Hill	
G-BCVJ	Cessna F.172M	J. Males/Manchester	
G-BCVV	PA-28-151 Warrior	Channel Islands Aero Holdings Ltd/ Jersey	
G-BCVW	GY-80 Horizon 180	P. M. A. Parrett/Bristol	
G-BCVX	Jodel DR.1050	E. W. Bradbury	
G-BCVY	PA-34-200T Seneca	Dawson Keith Hire Ltd	
G-BCWA	BAC One-Eleven 518	Dan-Air Services Ltd (G-AXMK)/ Gatwick	
G-BCWB	Cessna 182P	Environmental Services Ltd	
G-BCWE	HPR-7 Herald 206	Chemco Equipment Finance Ltd Southend	
G-BCWF	S.A. Twin Pioneer 1	Flight One Ltd (G-APRS)/Shobdon	
G-BCWH	Practavia Pilot Sprite	R. Tasker/Warton	
G-BCWI	Bensen B.8M	C. J. Blundell	
G-BCWK	Alpavia Fournier RF-3	D. I. Nickolls & ptnrs	
G-BCWL	Westland Lysander III (V9281)	D. W. Arnold/Blackbushe	
G-BCWM	AB-206B JetRanger 2	Helicare Ltd/Liverpool	
G-BCWW	HP.137 Jetstream 200	The Distillers Co Ltd (G-AXUN)/ Bournemouth	
G-BCXB	SOCATA Rallye 100ST	Inchberry Ltd/Swanton Morley	
G-BCXE	Robin DR.400/2+2	Headcorn Flying School Ltd	
G-BCXF	H.S.125 Srs 600B	Beecham International Aviation Ltd/ Luton	
G-BCXH	PA-28 Cherokee 140F	Airborne Electronics Ltd/Blackbushe	
G-BCXJ	Piper J-3C-65 Cub	W. F. Stockdale/Compton Abbas	
G-BCXN	D.H.C.I Chipmunk 22	J. D. Scott/Swanton Morley	
G-BCXO	MBB Bo 105D	Management Aviation Ltd/Bourn	
G-BCXR	BAC One-Eleven 517	Dan-Air Services Ltd (G-BCCV)/Gatwick	
G-BCXT	Cessna F.150M	Peterborough Aero Club Ltd/Sibson	
G-BCXZ	Cameron O-56 balloon	Olives from Spain Ltd *Olives from Spain*	
G-BCYE	D.H.C.I Chipmunk 22 (WG350)	L. T. Mersh/Biggin Hill	
G-BCYF	Dassault Mystère 20	Nidiva Services (UK) Ltd/Heathrow	
G-BCYH	DAW Privateer Mk. 2	D. B. Limbert	
G-BCYI	Schleicher ASK-16	J. Fox & J. Harding/Lasham	
G-BCYJ	D.H.C.I Chipmunk 22 (WG307)	R. A. L. Falconer	

Notes	Reg.	Type	Owner or Operator
	G-BCYK	Avro CF.100 Mk 4 Canuck (18393) ★	Imperial War Museum/Duxford
	G-BCYL	D.H.C.I Chipmunk 22	P. C. Henry/Denham
	G-BCYM	D.H.C.I Chipmunk 22	C. R. R. Eagleton
	G-BCYP	AB-206B JetRanger 2	Alan Mann Helicopters Ltd/Fairoaks
	G-BCYR	Cessna F.172M	Laxtonbridge Ltd/Leicester
	G-BCYY	Westland-Bell 47G-3B1	Astoncroft Ltd
	G-BCYZ	Westland-Bell 47G-3B1	Helicrops Ltd
	G-BCZF	PA-28 Cherokee 180	Hartmann Ltd/Ronaldsway
	G-BCZH	D.H.C.I Chipmunk 22	The London Gliding Club (Pty) Ltd/ Dunstable
	G-BCZI	Thunder Ax7-77 balloon	Motor Tyres & Accessories *Motorway for Tyres*
	G-BCZM	Cessna F.172M	I. J. Norman & ptnrs
	G-BCZN	Cessna F.150M	T. M. G. Hanley/Manchester
	G-BCZO	Cameron O-77 balloon	W. O. T. Holmes *Leo*
	G-BDAB	SA.102.5 Cavalier	A. H. Brown
	G-BDAC	Cameron O-77 balloon	D. Fowler & J. Goody *Chocolate Ripple*
	G-BDAD	Taylor JT.1 Monoplane	Rochester Flying Group
	G-BDAE	BAC One-Eleven 518	Dan-Air Services Ltd (G-AXMI)/Gatwick
	G-BDAG	Taylor JT.1 Monoplane	R. S. Basinger
	G-BDAH	Evans VP-1	R. W. Lowe/Popham
	G-BDAI	Cessna FRA.150M	Tractreed Ltd/Bristol
	G-BDAJ	R. Commander 112A	Ortonpost Ltd
	G-BDAK	R. Commander 112A	T. E. Abell
	G-BDAL	R. 500S Shrike Commander	Micro Consultants Ltd/Biggin Hill
	G-BDAM	AT-16 Harvard IIB (FE992)	M. V. Gauntlett/Booker
	G-BDAP	AJEP Tailwind	J. Whiting
	G-BDAR	Evans VP-1	S. C. Foggin & M. T. Dugmore
	G-BDAS	BAC One-Eleven 518	Dan-Air Services Ltd (G-AXMH)/ Gatwick
	G-BDAT	BAC One-Eleven 518	Dan-Air Services Ltd (G-AYOR)/ Gatwick
	G-BDAU	Cessna FRA.150M	Airwork Services Ltd/Perth
	G-BDAV	PA-23 Aztec 250	Air Ipswich
	G-BDAW	Enstrom F-28A	Usoland Ltd/Elstree
	G-BDAX	PA-E23 Aztec 250	R. Phillips/Biggin Hill
	G-BDAY	Thunder Ax5-42A balloon	T. M. Donnelly *Tom's Balloon*
	G-BDBD	Wittman W.8 Tailwind	R. W. L. Breckell/Woodvale
	G-BDBF	FRED Srs 2	W. T. Morrell
	G-BDBH	Bellanca 7GCBC Citabria	Inkpen Gliding Club Ltd/Thruxton
	G-BDBI	Cameron O-77 balloon	Robert Pooley Ltd
	G-BDBJ	Cessna 182P	I. I. Woollacott
	G-BDBL	D.H.C.I Chipmunk 22	Wycombe Gliding School Syndicate/ Booker
	G-BDBP	D.H.C.I Chipmunk 22	Sherwood Flying Club Ltd/Tollerton
	G-BDBR	AB-206B JetRanger 2	P.L.M. Helicopters Ltd/Inverness
	G-BDBS	Short SD3-30	Short Bros Ltd/Sydenham
	G-BDBU	Cessna F.150M	Channel Islands Aero Holdings Ltd/ Jersey
	G-BDBV	Jodel D.11A	J. P. de Hevingham
	G-BDBW	Heintz Zenith 100 A18	D. B. Winstanley
	G-BDBX	Evans VP-1	Montgomeryshire Ultra-Light Flying Club
	G-BDBZ	WS.55 Whirlwind Srs 2 ★	*Ground instruction airframe*/Kidlington
	G-BDCA	SOCATA Rallye 150ST	B. W. J. Pring & ptnrs/Dunkeswell
	G-BDCB	D.H.C.I Chipmunk 22	D. R. Hodgson/Swanton Morley
	G-BDCC	D.H.C.I Chipmunk 22	Coventry Gliding Club Ltd/ Husbands Bosworth
	G-BDCD	Piper J-3C-65 Cub	Suzanne C. Brooks/Slinfold
	G-BDCE	Cessna F.172H	H. A. Baillie/Blackbushe
	G-BDCI	CP.301A Emeraude	H. A. R. Horesign
	G-BDCK	AA-5 Traveler	Sequoia Air Ltd/Aberdeen
	G-BDCM	Cessna F.177RG	Park Plant Ltd/Wickenby
	G-BDCO	B.121 Pup 1	Dr R. D. H. & Mrs K. N. Maxwell/Leeds
	G-BDCP	AB-206B JetRanger 2	Ben Turner & Sons (Helicopters) Ltd
	G-BDCS	Cessna 421B	Marchwiel Aviation Ltd/ Halfpenny Green
	G-BDCT	PA-25 Pawnee 235C	Sprayfields (Scothern) Ltd/Bardney
	G-BDCU	Cameron O-77 balloon	Swanflight Balloon Group

Reg.	Type	Owner or Operator	Notes
G-BDDA	Sikorsky S-61N Mk II	British Airways Helicopters Ltd/ Aberdeen	
G-BDDD	D.H.C.I Chipmunk 22	RAE Aero Club Ltd/Farnborough	
G-BDDF	Jodel D.120	Sywell Skyriders Flying Group	
G-BDDG	Jodel D.112	A. C. Watt & T. C. Greig/Perth	
G-BDDH	F.27 Friendship Mk 200	Air UK Ltd/Norwich	
G-BDDJ	Luton LA-4A Minor	D. D. Johnson	
G-BDDS	PA-25 Pawnee 235	Farm Air (Shropshire) Ltd	
G-BDDT	PA-25 Pawnee 235	Farm Aviation Services Ltd/Enstone	
G-BDDX	Whittaker MW.2B Excalibur ★	Cornwall Aero Park/Helston	
G-BDDZ	CP.301A Emeraude	D. L. Sentance	
G-BDEB	SOCATA Rallye 100ST	W. G. Dunn & ptnrs/Dunkeswell	
G-BDEC	SOCATA Rallye 100ST	Cambridge Chemical Co Ltd	
G-BDEF	PA-34-200T-2 Seneca	European Paper Sales Ltd/Biggin Hill	
G-BDEH	Jodel D.120A	R. E. Figg	
G-BDEI	Jodel D.9 Bebe	P. J. Griggs/Fenland	
G-BDEJ	R. Commander 112	R. W. Fairless	
G-BDEN	SIAI-Marchetti SF.260	Micro Consultants Ltd/Biggin Hill	
G-BDER	Auster AOP.9 (WZ672)	K. D. J. Ecclestone	
G-BDES	Sikorsky S-61N Mk II	British Airways Helicopters Ltd/ Aberdeen	
G-BDET	D.H.C.I Chipmunk 22	A. J. C. Plowman & ptnrs/Stapleford	
G-BDEU	D.H.C.I Chipmunk 22 (WP808)	A. Taylor/Sibson	
G-BDEV	Taylor JT.1 Monoplane	P. J. Houston	
G-BDEW	Cessna FRA.150M	George House (Holdings) Ltd/ Compton Abbas	
G-BDEX	Cessna FRA.150M	George House (Holdings) Ltd/ Compton Abbas	
G-BDEY	Piper J-3C-65 Cub	Ducksworth Flying Club	
G-BDEZ	Piper J-3C-65 Cub	P. Elliott/Biggin Hill	
G-BDFB	Currie Wot	D. F. Faulkner-Bryant/Shoreham	
G-BDFC	R. Commander 112A	Lemrest Ltd/Biggin Hill	
G-BDFE	HPR-7 Herald 206	BAF Leasing/Janus Airways	
G-BDFG	Cameron O-65 balloon	N. A. Robertson Golly II	
G-BDFH	Auster AOP.9 (XR240)	R. O. Holden/Booker	
G-BDFI	Cessna F.150M	Coventry Civil Aviation Ltd	
G-BDFJ	Cessna F.150M	Coventry Civil Aviation Ltd	
G-BDFM	Caudron C.270 Luciole	G. V. Gower	
G-BDFO	Hiller UH-12E	Heliscot Ltd & F. F. Chamberlain/ Inverness	
G-BDFR	Fuji FA.200-160	C.S.E. (Aircraft Services) Ltd/Kidlington	
G-BDFS	Fuji FA.200-160	D. J. Carding/Halfpenny Green	
G-BDFT	V.668 Varsity T.1 (WJ897)	Leicester Aircraft Preservation Group	
G-BDFU	Dragonfly MPA Mk 1 ★	Museum of Flight/E. Fortune	
G-BDFW	R. Commander 112A	T. D. C. Lloyd & D. A. Wilkins/ Birmingham	
G-BDFX	Auster 5	K. E. Ballington	
G-BDFY	AA-5 Traveler	E. O. Liebert/Jersey	
G-BDFZ	Cessna F.150M	Skyviews & General Ltd/Sherburn	
G-BDGA	Bushby-Long Midget Mustang	J. R. Owen	
G-BDGB	GY-20 Minicab	D. G. Burden	
G-BDGH	Thunder Ax7-77 balloon	The London Balloon Club Ltd London Pride III	
G-BDGK	Beechcraft D.17S	P. M. J. Wolf/Biggin Hill	
G-BDGL	Cessna U.206 Super Skywagon	C. Wren	
G-BDGM	PA-28-151 Warrior	Channel Islands Aero Holdings Ltd/ Jersey	
G-BDGN	AA-5B Tiger	Hamblin & Glover Oil Field (Services) Ltd	
G-BDGO	Thunder Ax7-77 balloon	International Distillers & Vintners Ltd J. & B. Rare	
G-BDGP	Cameron V-65 balloon	P. G. Dunnington	
G-BDGY	PA-28 Cherokee 140	R. E. Woolridge/Staverton	
G-BDHB	Isaacs Fury II	D. H. Berry	
G-BDHJ	Pazmany PL.1	P. Richardson	
G-BDHK	Piper J-3C-65 Cub (329417)	A. Liddiard	
G-BDHL	PA-E23 Aztec 250E	Air Northwest Ltd/Manchester	
G-BDHM	SA.102.5 Cavalier	D. H. Mitchell/Hong Kong	
G-BDIC	D.H.C.1 Chipmunk 22	T. Bibby & D. Halliwell	
G-BDID	D.H.C.1 Chipmunk 22	Coventry Gliding Club Ltd/ Husbands Bosworth	
G-BDIE	R. Commander 112A	Time Out (Ashby) Ltd/E. Midlands	

Notes	Reg.	Type	Owner or Operator
	G-BDIG	Cessna 182P	A. W. Saxon/Elstree
	G-BDIH	Jodel D.117	J. Chisholm
	G-BDII	Sikorsky S-61N Mk II	Bristow Helicopters Ltd *Drum*
	G-BDIM	D.H.C.1 Chipmunk 22	L. W. Gruber & ptnrs/Goodwood
	G-BDIT	D.H.106 Comet 4C ★	D. W. Arnold/Blackbushe
	G-BDIV	D.H.106 Comet 4C ★	Dan-Air Preservation Group/Lasham
	G-BDIW	D.H.106 Comet 4C ★	Air Classik/Dusseldorf
	G-BDIX	D.H.106 Comet 4C ★	Museum of Flight/E. Fortune
	G-BDIY	Luton LA-4A Minor	M. A. Musselwhite
	G-BDJB	Taylor JT.1 Monoplane	J. F. Barber
	G-BDJC	AJEP W.8 Tailwind	A. Whiting
	G-BDJD	Jodel D.112	J. V. Derrick/Goodwood
	G-BDJF	Bensen B.8MV	R. P. White
	G-BDJN	Robin HR.200/100	Northampton School of Flying Co Ltd/ Sywell
	G-BDJP	Piper J-3C-65 Cub	Mrs J. M. Pothecary/Slinfold
	G-BDJR	Nord NC.858	R. F. M. Marson & ptnrs
	G-BDKC	Cessna A185F	Bridge of Tilt Co Ltd/Perth
	G-BDKD	Enstrom F-28A	D. Philp/Goodwood
	G-BDKH	CP.301A Emeraude	R. F. Bridge/Goodwood
	G-BDKI	Sikorsky S-61N MK II	British Airways Helicopters Ltd/ Aberdeen
	G-BDKJ	SA.102.5 Cavalier	H. B. Yardley
	G-BDKK	Bede BD-5B	A. W. Odell
	G-BDKM	SIPA 903	S. W. Markham/White Waltham
	G-BDKS	Pitts S-2A Special	Airmiles Ltd/Cardiff
	G-BDKU	Taylor JT.1 Monoplane	A. C. Dove
	G-BDKV	PA-28R-200-2 Cherokee Arrow	Trucks Bristol Ltd/Lulsgate
	G-BDKW	R. Commander 112A	Denny Bros Printing Ltd
	G-BDLO	AA-5A Cheetah	T. Booth & P. Hopkins
	G-BDLR	AA-5B Tiger	Coldmix Ltd/Elstree
	G-BDLS	AA-1B Trainer	M. Brown
	G-BDLT	R. Commander 112A	Wintergrain Ltd/Exeter
	G-BDLV	Chilton DW.1A	R. E. Nerou
	G-BDLY	SA.102.5 Cavalier	B. S. Reeve/Popham
	G-BDMB	Robin HR.100/210	R. J. Hitchman & Son
	G-BDMC	MBB Bo 105D	Management Aviation Ltd/Bourn
	G-BDME	Robin DR.400/140B	Miss S. A. Pound/Fairoaks
	G-BDMM	Jodel D.11	D. M. Metcalf
	G-BDMO	Thunder Ax7-77A balloon	H. G. Twilley Ltd *Flash Harry*
	G-BDMS	Piper J-3C-65 Cub	A. T. H. Martin & K. G. Harris
	G-BDMW	Jodel DR.100	J. T. Nixon/Blackpool
	G-BDNC	Taylor JT.1 Monoplane	N. J. Cole/Lydd
	G-BDNF	Bensen B.8M	W. F. O'Brien
	G-BDNG	Taylor JT.1 Monoplane	D. J. Phillips/Long Marston
	G-BDNO	Taylor JT.1 Monoplane	W. R. Partridge/Bodmin
	G-BDNP	BN-2A Islander ★	*Ground parachute trainer*/Headcorn
	G-BDNR	Cessna FRA.150M	Cheshire Air Training School Ltd/ Liverpool
	G-BDNT	Jodel D.92	E. R. Gourd
	G-BDNU	Cessna F.172M	Trans Europe Air Charter Ltd
	G-BDNW	AA-1B Trainer	T. K. Norten & I. J. Turner
	G-BDNX	AA-1B Trainer	R. M. North
	G-BDNY	AA-1B Trainer	M. R. Langford/Doncaster
	G-BDNZ	Cameron O-77 balloon	N. R. Page *Winston Churchill*
	G-BDOC	Sikorsky S-61N Mk II	Bristow Helicopters Ltd *Tolquhoun*
	G-BDOD	Cessna F.150M	Latharp Ltd/Booker
	G-BDOE	Cessna FR.172J	P.A.V.H. (International) Ltd/Bodmin
	G-BDOF	Cameron O-56 balloon	New Holker Estates Co *Fred Cavendish*
	G-BDOG	SA Bullfinch Srs 2100	I. Drake/Netherthorpe
	G-BDOI	Hiller UH-12E	Heli-Spray Ltd
	G-BDOL	Piper J-3C-65 Cub	Allman & Son (Redhill) Ltd/Shoreham
	G-BDON	Thunder Ax7-77A balloon	J. R. Henderson & ptnrs
	G-BDOO	Thunder Ax7-77 balloon	Thunder Balloons Ltd
	G-BDOR	Thunder Ax6-56A balloon	G. R. Quaife
	G-BDOS	BN-2A Mk III-2 Trislander	Kondair/Stansted
	G-BDOU	Cessna FRA.150M	D. Telfer-Smollett
	G-BDOW	Cessna FRA.150M	Stornoway Flying Club
	G-BDOY	Hughes 369HS	Cosworth Engineering Ltd/Sywell
	G-BDPA	PA-28-151 Warrior	Noon (Aircraft Leasing) Ltd/ Shoreham

Reg.	Type	Owner or Operator	Notes
G-BDPB	Falconar F-II-3	A. E. Pritchard	
G-BDPC	Bede BD-5A	P. R. Cremer	
G-BDPF	Cessna F.172M	Huntara House/Shoreham	
G-BDPH	Cessna F.172M	True-Flight (UK) Ltd/Birmingham	
G-BDPI	PA-25 Pawnee 235B	Farmair Ltd	
G-BDPK	Cameron O-56 balloon	Manpower Ltd *Manpower*	
G-BDPL	Falconar F-II	P. J. Shone & D. L. Scott/Popham	
G-BDPV	Boeing 747-136	British Airways *City of Aberdeen*/ Heathrow	
G-BDRB	AA-5B Tiger	Northern Strip Mining Ltd/Netherthorpe	
G-BDRC	V.724 Viscount	(*Stored*)/Guernsey	
G-BDRD	Cessna FRA.150M	Airwork Services Ltd/Perth	
G-BDRE	AA-1B Trainer	M. C. Hastings & ptnrs/Elstree	
G-BDRF	Taylor JT.1 Monoplane	R. A. Codling/Croft	
G-BDRG	Taylor JT.2 Titch	D. R. Gray	
G-BDRI	PA-34-200T-2 Seneca	D. J. Parry/Southend	
G-BDRJ	D.H.C.I Chipmunk 22 (WP857)	J. K. Avis/Felthorpe	
G-BDRK	Cameron O-65 balloon	D. L. Smith *Smirk*	
G-BDRL	Stitts SA-3 Playboy	D. L. MacLean/Rochester	
G-BDRO	BN-2A-21 Islander	Aerogulf Services (UK) Ltd/ Goodwood	
G-BDRY	Hiller UH-12E	G. & S. G. Neal (Helicopters) Ltd/ Fenland	
G-BDSB	PA-28-181 Archer II	BDSB Ltd/Fairoaks	
G-BDSC	Cessna F.150M	B. J. M. Vermilio/Andrewsfield	
G-BDSD	Evans VP-1	J. E. Worthington	
G-BDSE	Cameron O-77 balloon	British Airways *Concorde*	
G-BDSF	Cameron O-56 balloon	A. R. Greensides & B. H. Osbourne	
G-BDSH	PA-28 Cherokee 140	Bamberhurst Ltd/Tollerton	
G-BDSK	Cameron O-65 balloon	Southern Balloon Group *Carousel II*	
G-BDSL	Cessna F.150M	Cleveland Flying School Ltd/Tees-side	
G-BDSM	Slingsby/Kirby Cadet Mk 3	D. W. Savage	
G-BDSN	Wassmer WA.52 Europa	E. A. Lawton (G-BADN)/Redhill	
G-BDSO	Cameron O-31 balloon	Budget Rent-a-Car *Baby Budget*	
G-BDSP	Cessna U.206F Stationair	White, Morgan & Co Ltd/Biggin Hill	
G-BDSR	PA-25 Pawnee 235	A. G. Edwards	
G-BDSZ	BN-2A Islander	Fletcher & Stewart Ltd/Tollerton	
G-BDTB	Evans VP-1	T. E. Boyes/Usworth	
G-BDTL	Evans VP-1	A. K. Lang/Dunkeswell	
G-BDTT	Bede BD-5	The TT Group	
G-BDTU	Omega III gas balloon	Mrs K. E. Turnbull *Omega II*	
G-BDTV	Mooney M.20F	J. P. McDermott & ptnrs	
G-BDTW	Cassutt Racer	B. E. Smith & C. S. Thompson/Redhill	
G-BDTX	Cessna F.150M	A. A. & R. N. Croxford/Biggin Hill	
G-BDUI	Cameron V-56 balloon	G. H. Dorrell *Pig Bucket*	
G-BDUJ	PA-31-310 Navajo	Vickers Shipbuilding Group Ltd/Barrow	
G-BDUL	Evans VP-1	C. Goodman/Sibson	
G-BDUM	Cessna F.150M	Swanton Morley Flying Group	
G-BDUO	Cessna F.150M	Fishbourne Garage Ltd/Shoreham	
G-BDUP	B.175 Britannia 253	Afrek Ltd/Athens	
G-BDUR	B.175 Britannia 253	Afrek Ltd/Athens	
G-BDUX	Slingsby T.31B motor glider	J. C. Anderson/Southend	
G-BDUY	Robin DR.400/140B	Waveney Flying Group/Seething	
G-BDUZ	Cameron V-56 balloon	Balloon Stable Ltd *Hot Lips*	
G-BDVA	PA-17 Vagabond	Mrs H. S. & I. M. Callier	
G-BDVB	PA-15 (PA-17) Vagabond	S. Lowe	
G-BDVC	PA-17 Vagabond	B. G. Ell/Ipswich	
G-BDVG	Thunder Ax6-56A balloon	R. F. Pollard *Argonaut*	
G-BDVH	H.S.748 Srs 2A	British Aerospace/Woodford	
G-BDVJ	Westland-Bell 47G-3BI	Hawkspare Ltd	
G-BDVS	F.27 Friendship 200	Air UK/Norwich	
G-BDVT	F.27 Friendship 200	Air UK/Norwich	
G-BDVU	Mooney M.20F	Videochord Ltd/Stapleford	
G-BDVW	BN-2A Islander	Loganair Ltd/Glasgow	
G-BDWA	SOCATA Rallye 150ST	H. Cowan/Newtownards	
G-BDWB	SOCATA Rallye 150ST	P. H. Johnson/Kirkbymoorside	
G-BDWE	Flaglor Scooter	D. W. Evernden	
G-BDWG	BN-2A Islander	Kingsmetal Ltd/Lydd	
G-BDWH	SOCATA Rallye 150ST	J. Scott	
G-BDWI	PA-34-200T-2 Seneca	Rentons Garages Ltd/Blackpool	
G-BDWJ	SE-5A Replica (F4650)	S. M. Smith	

Notes	Reg.	Type	Owner or Operator
	G-BDWK	Beech 95-B58 Baron	David Huggett Motor Factors Ltd/ Stapleford
	G-BDWL	PA-25 Pawnee 235	Summerhouse Farm Ltd/Sherburn
	G-BDWM	Mustang replica	D. C. Bonsall
	G-BDWN	SA.318C Alouette II	AB Aviation Holdings Ltd/Denham
	G-BDWO	Howes Ax6 balloon	R. B. & Mrs C. Howes *Griffin*
	G-BDWP	PA-32R-300 Cherokee Lance	Starline (Sails Ideas) Ltd/Blackpool
	G-BDWW	Cameron O-77 balloon	Dan-Air Hot-Air Balloon Group *Dan-Air*
	G-BDWX	Jodel D.120A	J. P. Lassey
	G-BDWY	PA-28 Cherokee 140	Tees-side Aviation Ltd
	G-BDXA	Boeing 747-236B	British Airways *City of Cardiff*/Heathrow
	G-BDXB	Boeing 747-236B	British Airways *City of Liverpool*/ Heathrow
	G-BDXC	Boeing 747-236B	British Airways *City of Manchester*/ Heathrow
	G-BDXD	Boeing 747-236B	British Airways *City of Plymouth*/ Heathrow
	G-BDXE	Boeing 747-236B	British Airways *City of Glasgow*/ Heathrow
	G-BDXF	Boeing 747-236B	British Airways *City of York*/Heathrow
	G-BDXG	Boeing 747-236B	British Airways *City of Oxford*/ Heathrow
	G-BDXH	Boeing 747-236B	British Airways *City of Edinburgh*/ Heathrow
	G-BDXI	Boeing 747-236B	British Airways *City of Cambridge*/ Heathrow
	G-BDXJ	Boeing 747-236B	British Airways *City of Birmingham*/ Heathrow
	G-BDXK	Boeing 747-236B	British Airways/Heathrow
	G-BDXL	Boeing 747-236B	British Airtours *City of Winchester*/ Gatwick
	G-BDXW	PA-28R-200 Cherokee Arrow	M. D. Joy/Fairoaks
	G-BDXX	Nord NC.858S	A. F. Cashin
	G-BDXY	Auster AOP.9 (XR269)	Tyre & Tyne Transport Ltd
	G-BDXZ	Pitts S-1S Special	P. Meeson
	G-BDYB	AA-5B Tiger	M. D. Joy/S. Lowe/Elstree
	G-BDYC	AA-1B Trainer	H. Preston & D. Mallinson
	G-BDYD	R. Commander 114	SRJ Aviation
	G-BDYF	Cessna 421C	Mining Suppliers Ltd/Sturgate
	G-BDYG	Percival Provost T.1 (WV493)	Museum of Flight/E. Fortune
	G-BDYH	Cameron V-56 balloon	I. S. & S. W. Matthews
	G-BDYL	Beech C23 Sundowner	J. M. Yendall
	G-BDYM	Skysales S-31 balloon	Miss A. I. Smith & M. J. Moore *Cheeky Devil*
	G-BDYY	Hiller UH-12E	AGN Helicopters Ltd
	G-BDYZ	MBB Bo 105D	Management Aviation Ltd/Bourn
	G-BDZA	Scheibe SF.25E Super Falke	Norfolk Gliding Club Ltd/Tibenham
	G-BDZB	Cameron S-31 balloon	Kenning Motor Group Ltd *Kenning*
	G-BDZC	Cessna F.150M	Air Tows Ltd/Blackbushe
	G-BDZD	Cessna F.172M	M. T. Hodges/Blackbushe
	G-BDZF	G.164 Ag-Cat B	Miller Aerial Spraying Ltd/Wickenby
	G-BDZS	Scheibe SF.25E Super Falke	A. D. Gubbay/Panshanger
	G-BDZU	Cessna 421C	Page & Moy Ltd & ptnrs
	G-BDZW	PA-28 Cherokee 140	Oldbus Ltd/Shoreham
	G-BDZX	PA-28-151 Warrior	Lyndair Aviation Ltd/Biggin Hill
	G-BDZY	Phoenix LA-4A Minor	P. J. Dalby
	G-BEAA	Taylor JT.1 Monoplane	R. C. Hobbs/Bembridge
	G-BEAB	Jodel DR.1051	S. M. Burrows
	G-BEAC	PA-28 Cherokee 140	Eileen R. Purfield/Biggin Hill
	G-BEAE	PA-25 Pawnee 235	R. V. Miller & J. F. P. Burn/Slinfold
	G-BEAG	PA-34-200T-2 Seneca	Paucrister Ltd/Gibraltar
	G-BEAH	J/2 Arrow	W. J. & Mrs M. D. Horler
	G-BEAK	L-1011-385 TriStar	British Airways *The Northern Lights Rose*/Heathrow
	G-BEAL	L-1011-385 TriStar	British Airways *The Red Devil Rose*/ Heathrow
	G-BEAM	L-1011-385 TriStar	British Airtours Ltd *The Silver Jubilee Rose*/Gatwick
	G-BEAR	Viscount V.5 balloon	B. Hargraves & B. King
	G-BEAU	Pazmany PL.4A	B. H. R. Smith

Reg.	Type	Owner or Operator	Notes
G-BEBA	H.S.748 Srs 2	Dan-Air Services Ltd/Gatwick	
G-BEBB	HPR-7 Herald 214	BAF Leasing/Janus Airways	
G-BEBC	WS.55 Whirlwind 3 (XP355) ★	Norwich Aviation Museum	
G-BEBE	AA-5A Cheetah	G. N. Smith/Netherthorpe	
G-BEBF	Auster AOP.9	M. D. N. & Mrs A. C. Fisher	
G-BEBG	WSK-PZL SDZ-45A Ogar	D. S. McKay & ptnrs/Booker	
G-BEBI	Cessna F.172M	Calder Equipment Ltd/Luton	
G-BEBK	PA-31-300 Turbo Navajo	Vange Scaffolding & Engineering Co Ltd	
G-BEBL	Douglas DC-10-30	British Caledonian Airways *Sir Alexander Flemming-The Scottish Challenger*/Gatwick	
G-BEBM	Douglas DC-10-30	British Caledonian Airways *Robert Burns-The Scottish Bard*/Gatwick	
G-BEBN	Cessna 177B	J. M. Nichol/Hamble	
G-BEBO	Turner TSW-2 Wot	E. Newsham & ptnrs	
G-BEBR	GY-201 Minicab	A. S. Jones & D. R. Upton	
G-BEBS	Andreasson BA-4B	D. M. Fenton	
G-BEBT	Andreasson BA-4B	D. M. Fenton	
G-BEBU	R. Commander 112A	Judd Studios Ltd/Biggin Hill	
G-BEBZ	PA-28-151 Warrior	Goodwood Terrena Ltd/Goodwood	
G-BECA	SOCATA Rallye 100ST	Goricstar Ltd	
G-BECB	SOCATA Rallye 100ST	A. Devery	
G-BECC	SOCATA Rallye 150ST	Air Touring Services Ltd/Biggin Hill	
G-BECD	SOCATA Rallye 150ST	J. B. Roberts/Denham	
G-BECF	Scheibe SF.25A Falke	D. A. Wilson & ptnrs/Usworth	
G-BECG	Boeing 737-204ADV	Britannia Airways Ltd *Amy Johnson*/Luton	
G-BECH	Boeing 737-204ADV	Britannia Airways Ltd *Viscount Montgomery of Alamein*/Luton	
G-BECJ	Partenavia P.68B	Hereford Parachute Club Ltd/Shobdon	
G-BECK	Cameron V-56 balloon	K. H. Greenaway	
G-BECL	C.A.S.A. C.352L (N9+AA)	Warbirds of Great Britain Ltd/Blackbushe	
G-BECM	Aerotec Pitts S-2A Special	Airmiles Ltd/Cardiff	
G-BECN	Piper J-3C-65 Cub	Harvest Air Ltd/Southend	
G-BECO	Beech A.36 Bonanza	Thorney Machinery Co Ltd	
G-BECP	PA-31-310 Turbo Navajo	Moseley Group (PSV) Ltd/E. Midlands	
G-BECT	C.A.S.A.1.131 Jungmann	Rendermere Ltd/Shoreham	
G-BECW	C.A.S.A.1.131 Jungmann	N. C. Jensen/Redhill	
G-BECZ	CAARP CAP.10B	Aerobatic Associates Ltd/Booker	
G-BEDA	C.A.S.A.1.131 Jungmann	M. G. Kates & D. J. Berry/Hong Kong	
G-BEDB	Nord 1203 Norecrin	B. F. G. Lister	
G-BEDD	Jodel D.117A	A. T. Croy/Kirkwall	
G-BEDE	Bede BD-5A	Biggin Hill BD5 Syndicate	
G-BEDF	Boeing B-17G-105-VE (485784)	M. H. Campbell/Duxford	
G-BEDG	R. Commander 112A	Elken Ltd	
G-BEDH	R. Commander 114	Glenroy Investments Ltd	
G-BEDI	Sikorsky S-61N Mk II	British Airways Helicopters Ltd/Aberdeen	
G-BEDJ	Piper J-3C-65 Cub	D. J. Elliott & A. E. Molton	
G-BEDK	Hiller UH-12E	T. C. Jay/Bourn	
G-BEDL	Cessna T.337D	John Bisco (Cheltenham) Ltd	
G-BEDO	BN-2A Mk III-2 Trislander	BN (Bembridge) Ltd	
G-BEDS	Thunder Ax7-77 balloon	Thunder Balloons Ltd	
G-BEDU	Scheibe SF.23C Sperling	Doncaster & District Gliding Club Ltd	
G-BEDV	V.668 Varsity T.1 (WJ945)	D. S. Selway/Duxford	
G-BEDZ	BN-2A Islander	Loganair Ltd/Glasgow	
G-BEEA	SOCATA Rallye 235E	Snowden Aviation Ltd	
G-BEEE	Thunder Ax6-56A balloon	I. R. M. Jacobs *Avia*	
G-BEEG	BN-2A Islander	Loganair Ltd/Glasgow	
G-BEEH	Cameron V-56 balloon	J. M. Langley *Kaleidoscope*	
G-BEEI	Cameron N-77 balloon	D. W. A. Legg *Master McGrath*	
G-BEEJ	Cameron O-77 balloon	DAL (Builders Merchants) Ltd *Dal's Pal*	
G-BEEL	Enstrom F-280C-UK-2 Shark	Slea Aviation Ltd	
G-BEEN	Cameron O-56 balloon	Swire Bottlers Ltd *Coke*/Hong Kong	
G-BEEP	Thunder Ax5-42 balloon	Mrs B. C. Faithful *Also Kenneth*	
G-BEER	Isaacs Fury II	M. J. Clark/Bournemouth	
G-BEEU	PA-28 Cherokee 140E	Berkshire Aviation Services Ltd/Fairoaks	

Notes	Reg.	Type	Owner or Operator
	G-BEEV	PA-28 Cherokee 140E	K. W. Watts/Andrewsfield
	G-BEEW	Taylor JT.1 Monoplane	K. Wigglesworth
	G-BEFA	PA-28-151 Warrior	A. J. Blois-Brooke/Dubai
	G-BEFC	AA-5B Tiger	A. G. McLeod/Shobdon
	G-BEFF	PA-28 Cherokee 140	Sherwood Flying Club Ltd/Tollerton
	G-BEFH	Nord 3202	F&H Aircraft Ltd/Sibson
	G-BEFR	Fokker DR.I Replica (F1425/17)	Leisure Sport Ltd/Thorpe Park
	G-BEFT	Cessna 421C	Eclipsol Oil Co Ltd
	G-BEFV	Evans VP-2	Yeadon Aeroplane Group/Leeds
	G-BEFW	PA-39 Twin Comanche C/R	Warnell Motors Ltd (G-AYZP)/Stapleford
	G-BEFX	Hiller UH-12E	Agricopters Ltd
	G-BEFY	Hiller UH-12E	Heliscot Ltd/Inverness
	G-BEFZ	H.S.125 Srs 700B	McAlpine Aviation Ltd/Luton
	G-BEGA	Westland Bell 47G-3B1	P. Pilkington & K. M. Armitage/Coventry
	G-BEGG	Scheibe SF.25E Super Falke	RAFGSA/Bicester
	G-BEGV	PA-23 Aztec 250F	ATS Air Charter/Blackbushe
	G-BEHC	BN-2A Mk. III-2 Trislander	BN (Bembridge) Ltd
	G-BEHD	BN-2A Mk. III-2 Trislander	Adam & Harvey Ltd
	G-BEHG	AB-206B JetRanger 2	Compass Helicopters/Bristol
	G-BEHH	PA-32R-300 Cherokee Lance	SMK Engineering Ltd/Leeds
	G-BEHJ	Evans VP-1	K. Heath
	G-BEHK	Agusta-Bell 47G-3B1 (Soloy)	Dollar Air Services Ltd/Coventry
	G-BEHM	Taylor JT-1 Monoplane	H. McGovern
	G-BEHN	Westland Bell 47G-3B1 (Soloy)	Dollar Air Services Ltd/Coventry
	G-BEHS	PA-25 Pawnee 260C	Farm Aviation Services Ltd/Enstone
	G-BEHU	PA-34-200T-2 Seneca	Thomas Long & Sons Ltd/Tollerton
	G-BEHV	Cessna F.172N	L. Mitchell
	G-BEHW	Cessna F.150M	S. R. Taylor/Leeds
	G-BEHX	Evans VP-2	G. S Adams
	G-BEHY	PA-28-181 Archer II	Q. P. Cope/Dubai
	G-BEIA	Cessna FRA.150M	Airwork Services Ltd/Perth
	G-BEIB	Cessna F.172N	R. L. Orsborn & Son Ltd/Sywell
	G-BEIC	Sikorsky S-61N	British Airways Helicopters Ltd/Aberdeen
	G-BEID	Sikorsky S-61N	British Airways Helicopters Ltd/Aberdeen
	G-BEIE	Evans VP-2	F. G. Morris
	G-BEIF	Cameron O-65 balloon	C. Vening
	G-BEIG	Cessna F.150M	Gordon King (Aviation) Ltd/Biggin Hill
	G-BEIH	PA-25 Pawnee 235D	Farmair Ltd
	G-BEII	PA-25 Pawnee 235D	Miller Aerial Spraying Ltd/Wickenby
	G-BEIK	Beech A.36 Bonanza	Scot-Stock Ltd/Inverness
	G-BEIL	SOCATA Rallye 150T	D. H. Tonkin/Bodmin
	G-BEIP	PA-28-181 Archer II	M. Ferguson Ltd/Newtownards
	G-BEIS	Evans VP-1	D. J. Park
	G-BEIZ	Cessna 500 Citation	Keenair Services Ltd/Liverpool
	G-BEJA	Thunder Ax6-56A balloon	P. A. Hutchins *Jackson*
	G-BEJB	Thunder Ax6-56A balloon	International Distillers & Vinters Ltd *Baby J. & B.*
	G-BEJD	H.S.748 Srs 1	Dan-Air Services Ltd/Gatwick
	G-BEJE	H.S.748 Srs 1	Dan-Air Services Ltd/Gatwick
	G-BEJK	Cameron S-31 balloon	Esso Petroleum Ltd
	G-BEJL	Sikorsky S-61N	British Airways Helicopters Ltd/Aberdeen
	G-BEJM	BAC One-Eleven 423	Ford Motor Co Ltd/Stansted
	G-BEJO	Saffrey S.250 free balloon	Cupro Sapphire Ltd *Firefly*
	G-BEJP	D.H.C.-6 Twin Otter 310	Manx Airlines Ltd/Ronaldsway
	G-BEJT	PA-23 Aztec 250F	Acey Global Ltd
	G-BEJV	PA-34-200T-2 Seneca	C.S.E. Aviation Ltd/Kidlington
	G-BEJW	BAC One-Eleven 423	Ford Motor Co Ltd/Stansted
	G-BEKA	BAC One-Eleven 520	Dan-Air Services Ltd/Gatwick
	G-BEKB	PA-23 Aztec 250	Alidair Ltd/E. Midlands
	G-BEKC	H.S.748 Srs 1	Dan-Air Services Ltd/Gatwick
	G-BEKE	H.S.748 Srs 1	Dan-Air Services Ltd/Gatwick
	G-BEKH	AB-206B JetRanger 2	W. R. Finance Ltd
	G-BEKL	Bede BD-4E	G. A. Hodges
	G-BEKM	Evans VP-1	G. J. McDill
	G-BEKN	Cessna FRA.150M	Balgin/Bourn
	G-BEKO	Cessna F.182Q	D. W. Clark Land Drainage Ltd

Reg.	Type	Owner or Operator	Notes
G-BEKR	Rand KR-2	K. B. Raven	
G-BEKS	PA-25 Pawnee 235D	Farmair (Kent) Ltd/Headcorn	
G-BELK	BN-2A Islander	Brown Root (UK) Ltd/Bournemouth	
G-BELP	PA-28-151 Warrior	Environmental Equipments Ltd/ Blackbushe	
G-BELR	PA-28 Cherokee 140	Woodgate Air Services (IOM) Ltd/ Ronaldsway	
G-BELT	Cessna F.150J	Yorkshire Light Aircraft Ltd (G-AWUV)/ Leeds	
G-BELX	Cameron V-56 balloon	W.H. & Mrs J. P. Morgan *Topsy*	
G-BEMA	Cessna 310R II	Westair Flying Services Ltd/ Blackpool	
G-BEMB	Cessna F.172M	Northair Aviation Ltd/Fairoaks	
G-BEMC	Cessna F.172M	Seven Seas Finance Ltd	
G-BEMD	Beech 95-B55 Baron	Vaux (Aviation) Ltd/Usworth	
G-BEMF	Taylor JT.1 Monoplane	J. Simpson	
G-BEMM	Slingsby T.31B Motor Cadet	M. N. Martin	
G-BEMT	Bede BD-5G	G. Smith	
G-BEMU	Thunder Ax5-42 balloon	P. J. Langford	
G-BEMV	PA-28 Cherokee 140	Jersey European Airways Ltd	
G-BEMW	PA-28-181 Archer II	Encee Services/Cardiff	
G-BEMY	Cessna FRA.150M	T. G. Aviation/Manston	
G-BEND	Cameron V-56 balloon	Dante Balloon Group *Le Billet*	
G-BENE	Cessna 402B	Greenline Refrigerated Transport Ltd/ Liverpool	
G-BENF	Cessna T.210L	Laughton Aviation Ltd	
G-BENH	Phoenix LA-5A Major	C. D. Macartney/Newtownards	
G-BENK	Cessna F.172M	Capeston Aviation Ltd	
G-BENL	PA-25 Pawneee 235D	Yorkshire Gliding Club (Pty) Ltd	
G-BENM	PA-31-325 Navajo	Gull Air Ltd	
G-BENN	Cameron V-56 balloon	S. L. G. & H. C. J. Williams/Ipswich	
G-BENO	Enstrom F-280C Shark	H. M. Stevenson (Glenochil) & Co Ltd	
G-BENS	Saffrey S.330 balloon	D. Whitlock *Hot Plastic*	
G-BENT	Cameron N-77 balloon	N. Tasker	
G-BEOD	Cessna 180	Midland Parachute Centre/Long Marston	
G-BEOE	Cessna FRA.150M	Johtyne Ltd	
G-BEOH	PA-28R-201T Turbo Arrow III	P. C. Roberts	
G-BEOI	PA-18-150 Super Cub	S. Down Gliding Club Ltd	
G-BEOK	Cessna F.150M	Gordon King (Aviation) Ltd/Biggin Hill	
G-BEOO	Sikorsky S-61N Mk. II	British Airways Helicopters Ltd/Aberdeen	
G-BEOT	PA-25 Pawnee 235D	Moonraker Aviation Ltd/Thruxton	
G-BEOV	PA-28 Cherokee 140	N. R. R. Dessauki/Dubai	
G-BEOW	PA-28 Cherokee 140	S. G. Hayman/Dubai	
G-BEOX	L-414 Hudson IV (A16-199) ★	RAF Museum	
G-BEOY	Cessna FRA.150L	Fowler Aviation Ltd	
G-BEOZ	A.W.650 Argosy 101	Air Bridge Carriers Ltd/E. Midlands	
G-BEPB	Pereira Osprey II	J. J. & A. J. C. Zwetsloot	
G-BEPC	SNCAN SV-4C	M. Harbron/Bodmin	
G-BEPD	SA.102.5 Cavalier	P. & Mrs E. A. Donaldson	
G-BEPE	SC.5 Belfast	HeavyLift Cargo Airlines Ltd (G-ASKE)/ Stansted	
G-BEPF	SNCAN SV-4A	M. Stelfox & R. G. Harrington	
G-BEPI	BN-2A Mk. III-2 Trislander	Aurigny Air Services Ltd/Guernsey	
G-BEPJ	BN-2A Mk. III-2 Trislander	BN (Bembridge) Ltd	
G-BEPK	BN-2A Mk. III-2 Trislander	BN (Bembridge) Ltd	
G-BEPO	Cameron N-77 balloon	P. C. C. Clarke	
G-BEPP	AB-206B JetRanger 2	Travel Centre (Norwich) Ltd	
G-BEPS	SC.5 Belfast	HeavyLift Cargo Airlines Ltd/Stansted	
G-BEPV	Fokker S.11-I Instructor	Strathallan Aircraft Collection	
G-BEPY	R. Commander 112B	D. S. Thomas/Booker	
G-BEPZ	Cameron D-96 hot-air airship	IAZ International (UK) Ltd	
G-BERA	SOCATA Rallye 150ST	B. J. Durrant-Peatfield	
G-BERB	SOCATA Rallye 150ST	Martin Ltd/Biggin Hill	
G-BERC	SOCATA Rallye 150ST	T. I. Evans & W. S. Finney	
G-BERD	Thunder Ax6-56A balloon	H. G. Twilley Ltd	
G-BERI	R. Commander 114	Ryan Fishing Co Ltd/Leeds	
G-BERJ	Bell 47G-4A	Hon. G. M. H. Wills/Coventry	
G-BERK	Osprey Mk. 6 balloon	A. P. Chown & ptnrs	
G-BERL	AA-5B Tiger	Scotia Safari Ltd/Edinburgh	
G-BERM	AA-5A Cheetah	John Farbon & Co Ltd/Elstree	
G-BERN	Saffrey S.330 balloon	B. Martin *Beeze*	

Notes	Reg.	Type	Owner or Operator
	G-BERT	Cameron V-56 balloon	Southern Balloon Group *Bert*
	G-BERW	R. Commander 114	Allison (Contractors) Ltd/Conington
	G-BERY	AA-1B Trainer	P. R. Botterill
	G-BESO	BN-2A Islander	John Jolly (1978) Ltd/Kirkwall
	G-BESS	Hughes 369D	Rassler Aero Services
	G-BETA	Rollason B.2A Beta	J. L. Kinch
	G-BETD	Robin HR.200/100	R. A. Parsons
	G-BETE	Rollason B.2A Beta	T. M. Jones
	G-BETF	Cameron 'Champion' balloon	Balloon Stable Ltd *Champion*
	G-BETG	Cessna 180K Skywagon	D. Adlington
	G-BETH	Thunder Ax6-56A balloon	Debenhams Ltd *Debenhams I*
	G-BETI	Pitts S-1D Special	P. Metcalfe/Tees-side
	G-BETJ	Douglas DC-8-33 ★	*Derelict at Stansted*
	G-BETL	PA-25 Pawnee 235D	Crop Aviation (UK) Ltd/Wyberton
	G-BETM	PA-25 Pawnee 235D	Crop Aviation (UK) Ltd/Wyberton
	G-BETO	MS.885 Super Rallye	A. Somerville
	G-BETP	Cameron O-65 balloon	J. R. Rix & Sons Ltd
	G-BETS	Cessna A.188B Ag Truck	J. H. Farrar/Blackbushe
	G-BETT	PA-34-200-2 Seneca	Andrews Professional Colour Laboratories Ltd/Stansted
	G-BETU	Piper J-3C-65 Cub	M. J. Curran & R. G. Fitton
	G-BETV	HS.125 Srs 600B	Tenneco Aviation Ltd/Luton
	G-BETW	Rand KR-2	T. A. Wiffen
	G-BEUA	PA-18-150 Super Cub	London Gliding Club (Pty) Ltd/ Dunstable
	G-BEUC	PA-28-161 Warrior II	P. C. T. Warner/Fairoaks
	G-BEUD	Robin HR.100/285R	E. A. & L. M. C. Payton
	G-BEUI	Piper J-3C-65 Cub	J. P. Turner/Booker
	G-BEUK	Fuji FA-200-160	C.S.E Aviation Ltd/Kidlington
	G-BEUL	Beech 95-58 Baron	Basic Metal Co Ltd/Denham
	G-BEUM	Taylor JT.1 Monoplane	P. J. Hart
	G-BEUN	Cassutt Racer IIIm	R. S. Voice/Redhill
	G-BEUP	Robin DR.400/180	J. Button/Rochester
	G-BEUR	Cessna F.172M	G. A. Locke & Sons Ltd
	G-BEUS	SNCAN SV-4C	G. V. Gower
	G-BEUU	PA-19 Super Cub 95	W. B. & C. E. Cooper
	G-BEUV	Thunder Ax6-56A balloon	Thunder Balloons Ltd *Debenhams II*
	G-BEUW	AA-5A Cheetah	D. Speed/Denham
	G-BEUX	Cessna F.172N	Light Planes (Lancashire) Ltd/Barton
	G-BEUY	Cameron N-31 balloon	Southern Balloon Group
	G-BEVA	SOCATA Rallye 150ST	P. T. Bolton
	G-BEVB	SOCATA Rallye 150ST	T. R. Sinclair
	G-BEVC	SOCATA Rallye 150ST	B. W. Walpole
	G-BEVE	Thunder Ax7-77A balloon	Thunder Balloons Ltd
	G-BEVG	PA-34-200T-2 Seneca	Plastfurn Ltd/Stapleford
	G-BEVH	Holland D.700 balloon	D. I. Holland *Sally*
	G-BEVI	Thunder Ax7-77A balloon	The Painted Clouds Balloon Co Ltd
	G-BEVJ	Cessna U-206F Stationair	Twinguard Aviation Ltd
	G-BEVL	Cessna 421C	Arbor Finance Ltd
	G-BEVO	Sportavia-Pützer RF-5	D. Lister & R. F. Bradshaw
	G-BEVP	Evans VP-2	C. F. Bloyce
	G-BEVR	BN-2A Mk III-2 Trislander	Adam & Harvey Ltd
	G-BEVS	Taylor JT.1 Monoplane	D. Hunter
	G-BEVT	BN-2A Mk. III-2 Trislander	Aurigny Air Services Ltd/ Guernsey
	G-BEVV	BN-2A Mk. III-2 Trislander	Air Camelot Ltd/Bournemouth
	G-BEVW	SOCATA Rallye 150ST	P. C. Goodwin & M. G. Wiltshire
	G-BEVY	BN-2A Mk. III-2 Trislander	Adam & Harvey Ltd
	G-BEWJ	Westland-Bell 47G-3B1	G. Tanner & P. O. Wicks Ltd/Luton
	G-BEWL	Sikorsky S-61N Mk. II	British Airways Helicopters Ltd/ Aberdeen
	G-BEWM	Sikorsky S-61N Mk. II	British Airways Helicopters Ltd/ Aberdeen
	G-BEWN	D.H.82A Tiger Moth	H. D. Labouchere
	G-BEWO	Zlin 326 Trener Master	R. C. Poolman & K. D. Ballinger/ Staverton
	G-BEWR	Cessna F.172N	Mersey Flying Club Ltd/Liverpool
	G-BEWS	Cameron 56 'Lamp Bulb' hot-air balloon	Osram (GEC) Ltd *Osram*
	G-BEWW	HS.125 Srs 600B	Truzone Ltd (G-AZUF)/Luton
	G-BEWX	PA-28R-201 Arrow III	Gidney & Kirby Holdings Ltd/Biggin Hill

Reg.	Type	Owner or Operator	Notes
G-BEWY	Bell 206B JetRanger 2	Bristow Helicopters Ltd	
G-BEWZ	PA-32-300 Cherokee Six C	Sherwood Car Hire (Mansfield) Ltd	
G-BEXK	PA-25 Pawnee 235D	Howard Avis (Aviation) Ltd	
G-BEXL	PA-25 Pawnee 235D	Aerial Farm Assistance Ltd	
G-BEXN	AA-1C Lynx	Scotia Safari Ltd/Prestwick	
G-BEXO	PA-23 Apache 160	B. Burton/Bournemouth	
G-BEXR	Mudry/CAARP CAP-10B	R. P. Lewis/Redhill	
G-BEXS	Cessna F.150M	Wholegreen Ltd/Coventry	
G-BEXW	PA-28-181 Archer II	J. Coyle	
G-BEXX	Cameron V-56 balloon	A. Tyler & ptnrs *Rupert of Rutland*	
G-BEXY	PA-28 Cherokee 140	A-One Transport (Leeds) Ltd	
G-BEXZ	Cameron N-56 balloon	M. J. Moroney *Valor*	
G-BEYA	Enstrom F-280C Shark	Guy Morton & Sons Ltd	
G-BEYB	Fairey Flycatcher (replica) (S1287)	John S. Fairey/Yeovilton	
G-BEYD	HPR-7 Herald 401	BAF Leasing Ltd/Southend	
G-BEYE	HPR-7 Herald 401	BAF Leasing Ltd/Southend	
G-BEYF	HPR-7 Herald 401	BAF Leasing Ltd/Southend	
G-BEYJ	HPR-7 Herald 401	BAF Leasing Ltd/Southend	
G-BEYK	HPR-7 Herald 401	Air UK/Norwich	
G-BEYL	PA-28 Cherokee 180	B. G. & G. Airlines Ltd/Jersey	
G-BEYM	Cessna F.150M	Anglian Flight Training Ltd/Seething	
G-BEYN	Evans VP-2	C. D. Denham	
G-BEYO	PA-28 Cherokee 140	Rimmer Scaffolding/White Waltham	
G-BEYP	Fuji FA-200-180AO	A. C. Pritchard/Booker	
G-BEYV	Cessna T.210M	Northair Aviation Ltd	
G-BEYW	Taylor JT.I Monoplane	E. M. Pearson	
G-BEYY	PA-31-310 Turbo Navajo	Trans Europe Air Charters Ltd/ Biggin Hill	
G-BEYZ	Jodel DR.1051/MI	M. J. McCarthy & S. Aarons/ Biggin Hill	
G-BEZA	Zlin 226T Trener	L. Bezak	
G-BEZB	HPR-7 Herald 209	Express Air Services (CI) Ltd/ Bournemouth	
G-BEZC	AA-5 Traveler	R. M. Gosling & P. J. Schwind/ Andrewsfield	
G-BEZE	Rutan VariEze	M. F. Sharples & ptnrs/Blackpool	
G-BEZF	AA-5 Traveler	KAL Aviation/Coventry	
G-BEZG	AA-5 Traveler	Melbron Air Ltd/Liverpool	
G-BEZH	AA-5 Traveler	H. & L. Sims Ltd	
G-BEZI	AA-5 Traveler	M. J. Bennett	
G-BEZJ	MBB Bo 105D	Management Aviation Ltd/Bourn	
G-BEZK	Cessna F.172H	R. J. Lock & ptnrs/Andrewsfield	
G-BEZL	PA-31-310 Navajo	Barratt Developments (Northern) Ltd/ Newcastle	
G-BEZM	Cessna F.182Q	Walton Summit Truck Centre Ltd/ Blackpool	
G-BEZO	Cessna F.172M	Rogers Aviation Ltd/Cranfield	
G-BEZP	PA-32-300D Cherokee Six	Falcon Styles Ltd/Kidlington	
G-BEZR	Cessna F.172M	Kirmington Aviation Ltd/Humberside	
G-BEZU	PA-31-350 Navajo Chieftain	Commercial & Capital Leasing Ltd	
G-BEZV	Cessna F.172M	S. G. Brady/Aberdeen	
G-BEZW	Practavia Pilot Sprite	T. S. Wilkins & ptnrs	
G-BEZY	Rutan VariEze	R. J. Jones	
G-BEZZ	Jodel D.112	A. J. Stevens & ptnrs/Barton	
G-BFAA	GY-80 Horizon 160	Mary Poppins Ltd	
G-BFAB	Cameron N-56 balloon	Phonogram Ltd *Phonogram*	
G-BFAC	Cessna F.177 RG	J. J. Baumhardt Associates Ltd/ Ipswich	
G-BFAD	PA-28-161 Warrior II	Elso Properties Ltd/Newcastle	
G-BFAF	Aeronca 7BCM	D. C. W. Harper/Finmere	
G-BFAH	Phoenix Currie Wot	J. F. Dowe	
G-BFAI	R. Commander 114	Ringwood Ltd	
G-BFAK	MS.892A Rallye Commodore 150	R. Jennings & ptnrs/Alderney	
G-BFAM	PA-31P Navajo	Video Unlimited Motion Pictures	
G-BFAN	H.S.125 Srs 600F	British Aerospace (G-AZHS)/Hatfield	
G-BFAO	PA-20 Pacer 135	W. Hinchcliffe & A. Akroyd/Denham	
G-BFAP	SIAI-Marchetti S.205-20R	Miss M. A. Eccles	
G-BFAR	Cessna 500-1 Citation	Fairflight Ltd/Biggin Hill	

Notes	Reg.	Type	Owner or Operator
	G-BFAS	Evans VP-1	A. I. Sutherland
	G-BFAV	Orion model free balloon	D. C. Boxall
	G-BFAW	D.H.C.1 Chipmunk 22	G. Jones & ptnrs/Cardiff
	G-BFAX	D.H.C.1 Chipmunk 22 (WG422)	P. G. D. Bell/Sibson
	G-BFBA	Jodel DR.100A	Wasp Flying Group/Redhill
	G-BFBB	PA-23 Aztec 250E	Worldair Sales Ltd/Jersey
	G-BFBC	Taylor JT.1 Monoplane	A. Brooks
	G-BFBD	Partenavia P.68B	Pegasus Aviation Ltd/Ronaldsway
	G-BFBE	Robin HR.200/100	Charles Major Ltd/Blackpool
	G-BFBF	PA-28 Cherokee 140	J. J. Donnelly
	G-BFBH	PA-31-325 Turbo Navajo	Civil Aviation Authority/Stansted
	G-BFBJ	PA-34-200T-2 Seneca	Shorgard Ltd/Edinburgh
	G-BFBK	Agusta-Bell 47G-3B1	Dollar Air Services Ltd/Coventry
	G-BFBM	Saffery S.330 balloon	B. Martin *Beeze II*
	G-BFBN	PA-25 Pawnee 235D	J. E. F. Aviation Ltd
	G-BFBR	PA-28-161 Warrior II	Linvic Ltd/Fairoaks
	G-BFBS	Boeing 707-351B	IEA Europe Ltd
	G-BFBU	Partenavia P.68B	Nordic Oil Services Ltd/Glasgow
	G-BFBV	Brügger Colibri M.B.2	J. D. Hutton & ptnrs/Netherthorpe
	G-BFBW	PA-25 Pawnee 235D	A & A Aviation Services Ltd/Staverton
	G-BFBX	PA-25 Pawnee 235D	Bowker Aircraft Services Ltd/Rush Greer
	G-BFBY	Piper J-3C-65 Cub	L. W. Usherwood
	G-BFBZ	Boeing 707-351B	IEA Europe Ltd
	G-BFCT	Cessna TU-206F	Cecil Aviation Ltd/Cambridge
	G-BFCX	BN-2A Islander	Loganair Ltd/Glasgow
	G-BFCY	AB-206B JetRanger 2	Window Boxes Ltd/Blackbushe
	G-BFCZ	Sopwith Camel (B7270)	Leisure Sport Ltd
	G-BFDA	PA-31-350 Navajo Chieftain	Air Charter (Scotland) Ltd/Glasgow
	G-BFDC	D.H.C.1 Chipmunk 22	Aldhaven Ltd/Newtownards
	G-BFDD	BN-2A Mk III-2 Trislander	BN (Bembridge) Ltd
	G-BFDE	Sopwith Tabloid (replica) (168) ★	Bomber Command Museum/Hendon
	G-BFDF	SOCATA Rallye 235E	J. H. Atkinson
	G-BFDG	PA-28R-201T Turbo-Arrow III	Noblair Ltd
	G-BFDI	PA-28-181 Archer II	Reedtrend Ltd
	G-BFDK	PA-28-161 Warrior II	C.S.E. Aviation Ltd/Kidlington
	G-BFDL	Piper L-4J Cub (454537)	R. W. H. Watson/Prestwick
	G-BFDM	Jodel D.120	Worcestershire Gliding Ltd/ Wellesbourne
	G-BFDN	PA-31-350 Navajo Chieftain	Topflight Aviation Ltd/Fairoaks
	G-BFDO	PA-28R-201T Turbo-Arrow III	Grangewood Press Ltd/Elstree
	G-BFDP	CP.301A Emeraude	J. P. McGrath & J. Robson/Barton
	G-BFDZ	Taylor JT.1 Monoplane	D. C. Barber
	G-BFEB	Jodel D.150	D. Aldersea & ptnrs/Sherburn
	G-BFEC	PA-23 Aztec 250F	Milford Docks Air Services Ltd/ Cambridge
	G-BFEE	Beech 95-E55 Baron	MLP Aviation Ltd/Elstree
	G-BFEF	Agusta-Bell 47G-3B1	Autair Ltd/Luton
	G-BFEG	Westland-Bell 47G-3B1	Trent Helicopters Ltd
	G-BFEH	Jodel D.117A	N. W. Charles
	G-BFEI	Westland-Bell 47G-3B1	Autair Ltd/Luton
	G-BFEJ	Agusta-Bell 47G-3B1	Copley Farms Ltd/Cambridge
	G-BFEK	Cessna F.152	Staverton Flying Services Ltd
	G-BFEL	Cessna F.150M	A. L. Strongman/Norwich
	G-BFEO	Boeing 707-323C	Tradewinds Airways Ltd/Gatwick
	G-BFER	Bell 212	Bristow Helicopters Ltd
	G-BFES	Bell 212	Bristow Helicopters Ltd
	G-BFEV	PA-25 Pawnee 235	Bowker Aircraft Services Ltd/ Rush Green
	G-BFEW	PA-25 Pawnee 235	Agricola Aerial Work Ltd
	G-BFEX	PA-25 Pawnee 235	CKS Air Ltd/Southend
	G-BFEY	PA-25 Pawnee 235	Harvest Air Ltd/Southend
	G-BFFB	Evans VP-2	D. Bradley
	G-BFFC	Cessna F.152-II	Yorkshire Flying Services Ltd/Leeds
	G-BFFD	Cessna F.152-II	Hartmann Ltd/Ronaldsway
	G-BFFE	Cessna F.152-II	Vectstar Ltd/Doncaster
	G-BFFF	Cessna 188B Ag Truck	Plains Aerial Spraying Ltd/ Compton Abbas
	G-BFFG	Beech 95-B55 Baron	J. J. Donn
	G-BFFJ	Sikorsky S-61N Mk II	British Airways Helicopters Ltd/ Aberdeen

Reg.	Type	Owner or Operator	Notes
G-BFFK	Sikorsky S.61N Mk II	British Airways Helicopters Ltd/Aberdeen	
G-BFFP	PA-18-150 Super Cub	Airways Aero Associations Ltd/Booker	
G-BFFT	Cameron V-56 balloon	R. I. M. Kerr & D. C. Boxall	
G-BFFW	Cessna F.152	Sir Philip G. Suttie/Aberdeen	
G-BFFY	Cessna F.150M	H. Rothwell/Dundee	
G-BFFZ	Cessna FR.172 Hawk XP	Autair Ltd/Luton	
G-BFGA	SOCATA Rallye 150ST	The BBC Club/Denham	
G-BFGC	Cessna F.150M	Northair Aviation Ltd/Edinburgh	
G-BFGD	Cessna F.172N-II	Wickwell (UK) Ltd/Southampton	
G-BFGE	Cessna F.172N-II	Scottish Aero Club Ltd/Perth	
G-BFGF	Cessna F.177RG	Victree (V.M.) Ltd	
G-BFGG	Cessna FRA.150M	Airwork Services Ltd/Perth	
G-BFGH	Cessna F.337G	Waneprod Engineering Co Ltd/Blackpool	
G-BFGI	Douglas DC-10-30	British Caledonian Airways *David Livingstone — The Scottish Explorer*/Gatwick	
G-BFGK	Jodel D.117	H. A. Jones/Coltishall	
G-BFGL	Cessna FA.152	Yorkshire Flying Services Ltd/Leeds	
G-BFGM	Boeing 727-095	Dan-Air Services Ltd/Gatwick	
G-BFGO	Fuji FA.200-160	Hillcrest Garage (Heseldon) Ltd/Usworth	
G-BFGP	D.H.C.6 Twin Otter 310	Spacegrand Ltd/Blackpool	
G-BFGS	MS.893E Rallye 180GT	P. A. Cairns/Dunkeswell	
G-BFGW	Cessna F.150H	J. F. Morgan	
G-BFGX	Cessna FRA.150M	Airwork Services Ltd/Perth	
G-BFGY	Cessna F.182P	Oxford Controls Ltd/Kidlington	
G-BFGZ	Cessna FRA.150M	Airwork Services Ltd/Perth	
G-BFHD	C.A.S.A. C.352L (N8+AA)	Warbirds of Great Britain Ltd/Blackbushe	
G-BFHF	C.A.S.A. C.352L	Warbirds of Great Britain Ltd/Blackbushe	
G-BFHG	C.A.S.A. C.352L	Warbirds of Great Britain Ltd/Blackbushe	
G-BFHH	D.H.82A Tiger Moth	P. Harrison & M. J. Gambrell	
G-BFHI	Piper J-3C-65 Cub	J. M. Robinson	
G-BFHK	Cessna F.177RG-II	T. Midgley & Sons Ltd/Humberside	
G-BFHM	Steen Skybolt	N. M. Bloom	
G-BFHN	Scheibe SF.25E Super Falke	W. J. Dyer & R. D. C. Hart	
G-BFHP	Champion 7GCAA Citabria	Buckminster Gliding Club Ltd	
G-BFHR	Jodel DR.220/2+2	J. B. Keith & J. Bugg/Fenland	
G-BFHT	Cessna F.152-II	Riger Ltd/Luton	
G-BFHU	Cessna F.152-II	Air Continental Securities Ltd/Luton	
G-BFHV	Cessna F.152-II	RJS Aviation	
G-BFHX	Evans VP-1	P. Johnson/Hamble	
G-BFIB	PA-31-310 Turbo Navajo	Mann Aviation Ltd/Fairoaks	
G-BFID	Taylor JT.2 Titch Mk III	W. F. Adams	
G-BFIE	Cessna FRA.150M	Rural Flying Club/Bourn	
G-BFIF	Cessna FR.172K XPII	Cambrian Air Charter Ltd/Cardiff	
G-BFIG	Cessna FR.172K XPII	D. M. Balfour/Blackpool	
G-BFII	PA-23 Aztec 250E	Budleigh Estates Ltd/Guernsey	
G-BFIJ	AA-5A Cheetah	T. Saveker Ltd	
G-BFIK	AA-5A Cheetah	Communication Techniques Aviation Ltd/Elstree	
G-BFIL	AA-5A Cheetah	Paine Electrics/Elstree	
G-BFIM	AA-5A Cheetah	D. E. Nixon & C. Heathcote /Elstree	
G-BFIN	AA-5A Cheetah	Shep-Air Aviation/Kidlington	
G-BFIP	Wallbro Monoplane 1909 Replica	K. H. Wallis	
G-BFIR	Avro 652A Anson 21 (WD413)	G. M. K. Fraser/Bournemouth	
G-BFIT	Thunder Ax6-56Z balloon	R. J. Nicholson & C. MacKinnon	
G-BFIU	Cessna FR.172K XP	Fletcher Bakeries Ltd/Netherthorpe	
G-BFIV	Cessna F.177RG	C. Fisher/Blackbushe	
G-BFIX	Thunder Ax7-77A balloon	E. Sawden Ltd	
G-BFJA	AA-5B Tiger	G. W. Hind/Perth	
G-BFJH	SA.102-5 Cavalier	B. F. J. Hope	
G-BFJI	Robin HR.100/250	H. Deville & C. J. Lear	
G-BFJJ	Evans VP-1	P. R. Pykett & B. J. Dyke/Thruxton	
G-BFJK	PA-23 Aztec 250E	Drive Petroleum Co Ltd	
G-BFJM	Cessna F.152	Pegasus Aviation Ltd/Aberdeen	
G-BFJN	Westland-Bell 47G-3B1	Nordic Oil Services Ltd	

Notes	Reg.	Type	Owner or Operator
	G-BFJO	G.164B Ag-Cat 450	Summer House Farm Ltd/Sherburn
	G-BFJR	Cessna F.337G	John Roberts Services Ltd/Sturgate
	G-BFJV	Cessna F.172H	G. J. Keating
	G-BFJW	AB-206B JetRanger 2	Dollar Air Services Ltd/Coventry
	G-BFJZ	Robin DR.400/140B	Forge House Restaurant Ltd/Biggin Hill
	G-BFKA	Cessna F.172N	C. Blackburn/Sherburn
	G-BFKB	Cessna F.172N	N. Denes Aerodrome Ltd
	G-BFKC	Rand KR.2	K. K. Cutt
	G-BFKD	R. Commander 114B	K. W. Ford & S. R. Whitehead/Guernsey
	G-BFKF	Cessna FA.152	Klingair Ltd/Conington
	G-BFKG	Cessna F.152	Wickwell (UK) Ltd/Southampton
	G-BFKH	Cessna F.152	RJS Aviation Ltd
	G-BFKJ	PA-31-310 Navajo	J. T. Duffin/Sywell
	G-BFKL	Cameron N-56 balloon	Merrythought Toys Ltd *Merrythought*
	G-BFKM	Westland-Bell 47G-3B1	Heliwork Ltd/Thruxton
	G-BFKN	PA-23 Aztec 250F	Air Envoy Ltd/Birmingham
	G-BFKP	Partenavia P.68B	Curry & Pennick (Builders) Ltd
	G-BFKT	Cessna F.172M	Wycombe Air Centre Ltd/Booker
	G-BFKV	PA-25 Pawnee 235D	Moonraker Aviation Co Ltd/Thruxton
	G-BFKY	PA-34-200 Seneca	S.L.H. Construction Ltd/Biggin Hill
	G-BFLC	Cessna 210L	R. J. Gibson & ptnrs/Blackbushe
	G-BFLD	Boeing 707-338C	British Midland Airways Ltd/E. Midlands
	G-BFLE	Boeing 707-338C	British Midland Airways Ltd/E. Midlands
	G-BFLH	PA-34-200T-2 Seneca	C.S.E. (Aircraft Services) Ltd/Kidlington
	G-BFLI	PA-28R-201T Turbo Arrow III	Peter Walker (Heritage) Ltd
	G-BFLK	Cessna F.152	Gordon King (Aviation) Ltd/Biggin Hill
	G-BFLL	H.S.748 Srs 2A	British Airways/Glasgow
	G-BFLM	Cessna 150M	Cornwall Flying Club Ltd/Bodmin
	G-BFLN	Cessna 150M	Sherburn Aero Club Ltd
	G-BFLO	Cessna F.172M	W. A. Cook & K. Dando/Sherburn
	G-BFLP	Amethyst Ax6 balloon	K. J. Hendry *Amethyst*
	G-BFLR	Hiller UH-12E	Heliscot Ltd & Major F. F. Chamberlain/Inverness
	G-BFLT	—	—
	G-BFLU	Cessna F.152	Inverness Flying Services Ltd
	G-BFLV	Cessna F.172N	N. Denes Aerodrome Ltd
	G-BFLW	PA-39 Twin Comanche 160CR	Harris Aviation Services Ltd/Biggin Hill
	G-BFLX	AA-5A Cheetah	Sheffield Auto Hire/Netherthorpe
	G-BFLZ	Beech 95-A55 Baron	K. K. Demel Ltd/Elstree
	G-BFMC	BAC One-Eleven 414	Ford Motor Co Ltd/Stansted
	G-BFME	Cameron V-56 balloon	Warwick Balloons Ltd
	G-BFMF	Cassutt Racer Mk III	P. H. Lewis
	G-BFMG	PA-28-161 Warrior II	K. J. Hardware/Fairoaks
	G-BFMH	Cessna 177B	Span Aviation/Usworth
	G-BFMJ	AA-5B Tiger	John Farbon & Co Ltd/Halfpenny Green
	G-BFMK	Cessna FA.152	RAF Halton Aeroplane Club Ltd
	G-BFMM	PA-28-181 Archer II	Bristol & Wessex Aeroplane Club Ltd/Bristol
	G-BFMR	PA-20 Pacer 125	S. B. Reay & ptnrs/Popham
	G-BFMS	MS.893E Rallye 180GT	Air Space Advertising Ltd
	G-BFMT	Robin HR.200/100	Eagle Forms (GB) Ltd/Biggin Hill
	G-BFMU	AA-5A Cheetah	Tentergate Trading/Elstree
	G-BFMW	V.735 Viscount	(*Stored*)/E. Midlands
	G-BFMX	Cessna F.172N	Bletchley Motor (Rentals) Ltd
	G-BFMY	Sikorsky S-61N	Bristow Helicopters Ltd
	G-BFMZ	Payne Ax6 balloon	G. F. Payne
	G-BFNB	PA-25 Pawnee 235D	A. G. Edwards/Wickenby
	G-BFNC	AS.350B Ecureuil	A. Pilkington & K. M. Armitage/Coventry
	G-BFNE	C.A.S.A. 1.131 Jungmann	J. Lipton/Booker
	G-BFNG	Jodel D.112	K. D. Bass/Andrewsfield
	G-BFNH	Cameron V-77 balloon	P. O. Atkins & R. Emms *Red Pepper*
	G-BFNI	PA-28-161 Warrior II	C.S.E. (Aircraft Services) Ltd/Kidlington
	G-BFNJ	PA-28-161 Warrior II	C.S.E. (Aircraft Services) Ltd/Kidlington
	G-BFNK	PA-28-161 Warrior II	C.S.E. (Aircraft Services) Ltd/Kidlington
	G-BFNM	Globe GC.1 Swift	Nottingham Flying Group/Hucknall
	G-BFNU	BN-2B Islander	Fairoaks Aviation Services Ltd/Blackbushe
	G-BFNV	BN-2A Islander	Loganair Ltd/Glasgow
	G-BFOD	Cessna F.182Q	Graphiking Publicity Ltd/Staverton

Reg.	Type	Owner or Operator	Notes
G-BFOE	Cessna F.152	Armstrong Whitworth Flying Group/ Coventry	
G-BFOF	Cessna F.152	Staverton Flying School Ltd	
G-BFOG	Cessna 150M	Zincraft Ltd/Biggin Hill	
G-BFOH	Westland-Bell 47G-3B1	Helicopter Hire Ltd/Southend	
G-BFOI	Westland-Bell 47G-3B1	CKS Air Ltd/Southend	
G-BFOJ	AA-1 Yankee	A. J. Morten & M. T. Voile/Bournemouth	
G-BFOM	PA-31-325 Navajo	Brew Bros Ltd/Blackbushe	
G-BFON	PA-31-310 Navajo	Air Kilroe/Manchester	
G-BFOP	Jodel D.120	H. Cope/Stapleford	
G-BFOS	Thunder Ax6-56A balloon	N. T. Petty	
G-BFOT	Thunder Ax6-56A balloon	Thunder Balloons Ltd	
G-BFOU	Taylor JT.1 Monoplane	G. Bee/Tees-side	
G-BFOV	Cessna F.172N	Gooda Walker Ltd/Shoreham	
G-BFOW	Cessna F.172N	Lobby Ticketing Ltd/Shoreham	
G-BFOX	D.H.83 Fox Moth Replica	R. K. J. Hadlow	
G-BFOY	Cessna A.188B AgTruck	Plains Aerial Spraying Ltd/ Compton Abbas	
G-BFOZ	Thunder Ax6-56 balloon	Motorway Tyres *Motorway II*	
G-BFPA	Scheibe SF.25B Super Falke	Yorkshire Gliding Club (Pty) Ltd	
G-BFPB	AA-5B Tiger	Seatoller Ltd/Guernsey	
G-BFPD	AA-5A Cheetah	Scotia Safari Ltd/Halfpenny Green	
G-BFPF	Sikorsky S-61N	British Caledonian Helicopters Ltd	
G-BFPH	Cessna F.172K	Air Fenland Ltd/Fenland	
G-BFPI	H.S.125 Srs 700B	McAlpine Aviation Ltd/Luton	
G-BFPJ	Procter Petrel	S. G. Craggs	
G-BFPK	Beech A.23 Musketeer	Five Octa Flying Group/Biggin Hill	
G-BFPL	Fokker D.VII Replica (4253/18)	Leisure Sport Ltd/Thorpe Park	
G-BFPM	Cessna F.172M	Abbey Windows Ltd	
G-BFPO	R. Commander 112B	Millet Shipping Ltd/Biggin Hill	
G-BFPP	Bell 47J-2	Avon Electrics (Wholesale) Ltd	
G-BFPS	PA-25 Pawnee 235D	Bowker Aviation Services Ltd/ Rush Green	
G-BFPX	Taylor JT.1 Monoplane	E. A. Taylor	
G-BFPZ	Cessna F.177RG	S. R. Cherry-Downes	
G-BFRA	R. Commander 114	Sabre Engines Ltd/Bournemouth	
G-BFRB	Cessna F.152	W. Shyvers Ltd/Lydd	
G-BFRC	AA-5A Cheetah	Northgleam Ltd/Manchester	
G-BFRD	Bowers Flybaby 1A	F. R. Donaldson	
G-BFRF	Taylor JT.1 Monoplane	E. R. Bailey	
G-BFRI	Sikorsky S-61N	Bristow Helicopters Ltd	
G-BFRJ	HPR-7 Herald 209	Elan International Ltd/E. Midlands	
G-BFRK	HPR-7 Herald 209	Elan International Ltd/E. Midlands	
G-BFRL	Cessna F.152	J. J. Baumhardt Associates Ltd/ Southend	
G-BFRM	Cessna 550 Citation II	Marshall of Cambridge (Engineering) Ltd	
G-BFRO	Cessna F.150M	Skyviews & General Ltd	
G-BFRR	Cessna FRA.150M	M.O.M. Aberdeen (Offshore) Ltd	
G-BFRS	Cessna F.172N	Poplar Toys Ltd	
G-BFRT	Cessna FR.172K XP II	B. J. Sharpe	
G-BFRV	Cessna FA.152	Rogers Aviation Ltd/Cranfield	
G-BFRY	PA-25 Pawnee 260	C. J. Pearce/Shoreham	
G-BFSA	Cessna F.182Q	Clark Masts Ltd/Sandown	
G-BFSB	Cessna F.152	R. M. Clarke/Leicester	
G-BFSC	PA-25 Pawnee 235D	Farm Aviation Services Ltd/Enstone	
G-BFSD	PA-25 Pawnee 235D	Farm Aviation Services Ltd/Enstone	
G-BFSJ	Westland-Bell 47G-3B1	R.K.B. Leasing Services/Shobdan	
G-BFSK	PA-23 Apache 160 ★	Oxford Air Training School/Kidlington	
G-BFSL	Cessna U.206F Stationair	Range Air	
G-BFSO	H.S.125 Srs 700B	Dravidian Air Services Ltd/Heathrow	
G-BFSP	H.S.125 Srs 700B	Dravidian Air Services Ltd/Heathrow	
G-BFSR	Cessna F.150J	Norfolk & Norwich Aero Club Ltd/ Swanton Morley	
G-BFSS	Cessna FR.172G	Minerva Services	
G-BFST	Partenavia P.68B	Autofarm Ltd/Booker	
G-BFSY	PA-28-181 Archer II	K. F. Davison/Birmingham	
G-BFTA	PA-28-161 Warrior II	N. Clayton	
G-BFTC	PA-28R-201T Turbo Arrow II	Albert J. Parsons & Sons Ltd	
G-BFTE	AA.5A Cheetah	B. Refson/Elstree	
G-BFTF	AA-5B Tiger	F. C. Burrow Ltd/Leeds	

Notes	Reg.	Type	Owner or Operator
	G-BFTG	AA-5B Tiger	PJW Consultants/Sibson
	G-BFTH	Cessna F.172N	The Hamper People Ltd/Norwich
	G-BFTR	Bell 206L Long Ranger	Air Hanson Ltd/Brooklands
	G-BFTT	Cessna 421C	P&B Metal Components Ltd/Manston
	G-BFTU	Cessna FA.152	J. H. Wilmshurst Ltd/Shoreham
	G-BFTW	PA-23 Aztec 250F	Southampton Airport Ltd
	G-BFTX	Cessna F.172N	Telepoint Ltd/Manchester
	G-BFTY	Cameron V-77 balloon	Regal Motors (Bilston) Ltd *Regal Motors*
	G-BFTZ	MS.880B Rallye Club	R. & B. Legge Ltd
	G-BFUB	PA-32RT-300 Turbo Lance II	Bumbles Ltd/Jersey
	G-BFUD	Scheibe SF.25E Super Falke	R. C. Bull/Barrow
	G-BFUG	Cameron N-77 balloon	Aeolus Balloons
	G-BFUZ	Cameron V-77 balloon	Skysales Ltd
	G-BFVA	Boeing 737-204ADV	Britannia Airways Ltd *Sir John Alcock*/Luton
	G-BFVB	Boeing 737-204DV	Britannia Airways Ltd *Sir Thomas Sopwith*/Luton
	G-BFVF	PA-38-112 Tomahawk	Ipswich School of Flying
	G-BFVG	PA-28-181 Archer II	P. A. Cornah & S. Reed/Blackpool
	G-BFVH	D.H.2 Replica (5894)	Leisure Sport Ltd/Thorpe Park
	G-BFVI	H.S.125 Srs 700B	Bristow Helicopters Ltd
	G-BFVM	Westland-Bell 47G-3B1	Gleneagle Helicopters Ltd/Perth
	G-BFVO	Partenavia P.68B	P. Meeson
	G-BFVP	PA-23 Aztec 250	Dukes Transport (Craigavon) Ltd/Newtownards
	G-BFVS	AA-5B Tiger	S. W. Biroth & ptnrs/Denham
	G-BFVU	Cessna 150L	I. R. Ferrars
	G-BFVV	SA.365 Dauphin 2	Management Aviation Ltd/Bourn
	G-BFVW	SA.365 Dauphin 2	Management Aviation Ltd/Bourn
	G-BFVX	Beech C90 King Air	Vernair Transport Services/Liverpool
	G-BFVY	Beech C90 King Air	Vernair Transport Services/Liverpool
	G-BFWB	PA-28-161 Warrior II	C.S.E. (Aircraft Services) Ltd/Kidlington
	G-BFWD	Currie Wot	F. E. Nuthall/Popham
	G-BFWE	PA-23 Aztec 250	Air Navigation & Trading Co Ltd/Blackpool
	G-BFWF	Cessna 421B	Alcon Oil Ltd/Staverton
	G-BFWG	R. Commander 112A	Southern Air Ltd/Shoreham
	G-BFWK	PA-28-161 Warrior II	Woodgate Air Services (IOM) Ltd/Ronaldsway
	G-BFWL	Cessna F.150L	J.Dolan
	G-BFWM	Hiller UH-12D	Management Aviation Ltd/Bourn
	G-BFWW	Robin HR.100/210	Willingair Ltd
	G-BFXC	Mooney M.20C	A. H. Faulkner
	G-BFXD	PA-28-161 Warrior II	C.S.E. (Aircraft Services) Ltd/Kidlington
	G-BFXE	PA-28-161 Warrior II	C.S.E. (Aircraft Services) Ltd/Kidlington
	G-BFXF	Andreasson BA.4B	A. Brown/Sherburn
	G-BFXG	D.31 Turbulent	S. Griffin
	G-BFXH	Cessna F.152	RJS Aviation Ltd/Halfpenny Green
	G-BFXI	Cessna F.172M	Thanet Electronics/Manston
	G-BFXK	PA-28 Cherokee 140	G. S. & Mrs M. T. Pritchard/Southend
	G-BFXL	Albatross D.5A (D5397/17)	Leisure Sport Ltd/Thorpe Park
	G-BFXM	Jurca MJ.5 Sirocco	D. I. & W. A. Barker
	G-BFXN	PA-36-375 Brave	Farm Aviation Services Ltd/Enstone
	G-BFXO	Taylor JT.1 Monoplane	A. S. Nixon
	G-BFXR	Jodel D.112	R. E. Walker & M. Riddin/Netherthorpe
	G-BFXS	R. Commander 114	European Steel Sheets Ltd/Birmingham
	G-BFXT	H.S.125 Srs 700B	Coca Cola Export Corporation
	G-BFXU	American Beta Z Airship	G. Turnbull
	G-BFXW	AA-5B Tiger	Terry Giles Ltd/Doncaster
	G-BFXX	AA-5B Tiger	Lewis Flying Group Ltd/Ronaldsway
	G-BFXY	AA-5A Cheetah	Kaal Electrics Ltd/Elstree
	G-BFXZ	PA-28-181 Archer II	Cleanacres Ltd/Staverton
	G-BFYA	MBB Bo 105D	Helicopter Hire Ltd/Southend
	G-BFYB	PA-28-161 Warrior II	C.S.E. (Aircraft Services) Ltd/Shoreham
	G-BFYC	PA-32RT-300 Lance II	Avingate/Blackpool
	G-BFYE	Robin HR.100/285	Tollbridge Machine Tool Co Ltd/Fairoaks
	G-BFYF	Westland-Bell 47G-3B1	H. J. Hofman
	G-BFYI	Westland-Bell 47G-3B1	Dollar Air Services Ltd/Coventry
	G-BFYJ	Hughes 369HE	Wilford Aviation Ltd/Fairoaks

Reg.	Type	Owner or Operator	Notes
G-BFYL	Evans VP.2	A. G. Wilford	
G-BFYM	PA-28-161 Warrior II	C.S.E. (Aircraft Services) Ltd/Kidlington	
G-BFYN	Cessna FA.152	Phoenix Flying Services Ltd	
G-BFYO	Spad XIII (replica) (3398)	Leisure Sport Ltd/Thorpe Park	
G-BFYP	Bensen B.7	A. J. Philpotts	
G-BFYU	SC.5 Belfast	HeavyLift Cargo Airlines Ltd/Stansted	
G-BFZA	Alpavia Fournier RF-3	T. J. Hartwell & D. R. Wilkinson	
G-BFZB	Piper J-3C-85 Cub	Zebedee Flying Group/Shoreham	
G-BFZD	Cessna FR.182RG	R. B. Lewis & Co	
G-BFZE	AS.350B Ecureuil	TBF Transport Ltd/Tollerton	
G-BFZF	Boeing 707-321C	(stored)/Lasham	
G-BFZG	PA-28-161 Warrior II	C.S.E. (Aircraft Services) Ltd/Kidlington	
G-BFZH	PA-28R-200 Cherokee Arrow	J. M. Arthurs/Usworth	
G-BFZK	EMB-110P2 Bandeirante	Fairflight Ltd/Air Ecosse/Aberdeen	
G-BFZL	V.836 Viscount	British Midland Airways Ltd/E. Midlands	
G-BFZM	R. Commander 112TC	Rolls-Royce Ltd/Filton	
G-BFZN	Cessna F.152	Leicestershire Aero Club Ltd	
G-BFZO	AA-5A Cheetah	Heald Air Ltd/Manchester	
G-BFZP	AA-5B Tiger	Scotia Safari Ltd/Prestwick	
G-BFZS	Cessna F.152	R. T. Haddow/Southampton	
G-BFZT	Cessna FA.152	Shirlstar Container Transport Ltd/ Southampton	
G-BFZU	Cessna FA.152	W. D. & P. M. Jasper/Goodwood	
G-BGAA	Cessna 152 II	Solent Flight Centre/Southampton	
G-BGAB	Cessna F.152 II	G. Capes/Humberside	
G-BGAD	Cessna F.152 II	R. F. Howard/Biggin Hill	
G-BGAE	Cessna F.152 II	Northfield Garage (Cowdenbeath) Ltd	
G-BGAF	Cessna FA.152	E. P. Collier/Ipswich	
G-BGAG	Cessna F.172N	Adifer Ltd	
G-BGAH	FRED Srs 2	G. A. Harris	
G-BGAJ	Cessna F.182Q II	Channel Islands Aero Holdings Ltd/ Jersey	
G-BGAK	Cessna F.182Q II	R&L Aviation Ltd	
G-BGAL	Saffery S.330 balloon	A. M. Lindsay English Lady	
G-BGAT	Douglas DC-10-30	British Caledonian Airways James Watt — The Scottish Engineer/Gatwick	
G-BGAU	Rearwin 9000L	Shipping & Airlines Ltd/Biggin Hill	
G-BGAV	Rearwin 8135T	Shipping & Airlines Ltd/Biggin Hill	
G-BGAX	PA-28 Cherokee 140	D. E. Nicholl/Aberdeen	
G-BGAY	Cameron O-77 balloon	Dante Balloon Group Antonia	
G-BGAZ	Cameron V-77 balloon	Cameron Balloons Ltd Silicon Chip	
G-BGBA	Robin R.2100A	D. Faulkner/Redhill	
G-BGBB	L.1011-385 TriStar 200	British Airways The Lakeland Rose/ Heathrow	
G-BGBC	L.1011-385 TriStar 200	British Airways The Shot Silk Rose/ Heathrow	
G-BGBE	Jodel DR.1050	D. G. Perry/Stapleford	
G-BGBF	D.31A Turbulent	R. Cole/Bodmin	
G-BGBG	PA-28-181 Archer II	Harlow Printing Ltd/Newcastle	
G-BGBI	Cessna F.150L	Air Fenland Ltd	
G-BGBK	PA-38-112 Tomahawk	Sandtoft Air Services Ltd	
G-BGBN	PA-38-112 Tomahawk	R. G. I. & H. T. D. Phillips	
G-BGBP	Cessna F.152	Sheffield Aero Club Ltd/Netherthorpe	
G-BGBR	Cessna F172N	Steer Aviation Ltd/Biggin Hill	
G-BGBT	Partenavia P.68B	Francis Mander Aviation	
G-BGBU	Auster AOP.9	P. Neilson	
G-BGBW	PA-38-112 Tomahawk	Spatial Air Brokers & Forwarders Ltd Tollerton	
G-BGBX	PA-38-112 Tomahawk	Ipswich School of Flying	
G-BGBY	PA-38-112 Tomahawk	Cheshire Flying Services Ltd/ Manchester	
G-BGBZ	R. Commander 114	R. S. Fenwick/Rochester	
G-BGCA	Slingsby T.65A Vega	E. C. Neighbour	
G-BGCB	Slingsby T.65A Vega	D. J. Dawson/Lasham	
G-BGCC	PA-31-325 Navajo	Foster Associates Ltd	
G-BGCD	Cameron A-140 balloon	Skysales Ltd Maxim	
G-BGCH	PA-38-112 Tomahawk	Micro Installation Services Ltd	
G-BGCL	AA-5A Cheetah	Goddard Aviation/Elstree	
G-BGCM	AA-5A Cheetah	Air Consultants/Elstree	
G-BGCO	PA-44-180 Seminole	J. R. Henderson	

Notes	Reg.	Type	Owner or Operator
	G-BGCS	EMB-110P1 Bandeirante	Genair/Humberside
	G-BGCV	AS.350B Ecureuil	Cezanne Ltd/Ronaldsway
	G-BGCX	Taylor JT.1 Monoplane	G. M. R. Walters
	G-BGCY	Taylor JT.1 Monoplane	R. L. A. Davies
	G-BGDA	Boeing 737-236	British Airways *River Tamar*/Heathrow
	G-BGDB	Boeing 737-236	British Airways *River Tweed*/Heathrow
	G-BGDC	Boeing 737-236	British Airways *River Humber*/Heathrow
	G-BGDD	Boeing 737-236	British Airways *River Tees*/Heathrow
	G-BGDE	Boeing 737-236	British Airways *River Avon*/Heathrow
	G-BGDF	Boeing 737-236	British Airways *River Thames*/Heathrow
	G-BGDG	Boeing 737-236	British Airways *River Medway*/Heathrow
	G-BGDH	Boeing 737-236	British Airways *River Clyde*/Heathrow
	G-BGDI	Boeing 737-236	British Airways *River Ouse*/Heathrow
	G-BGDJ	Boeing 737-236	British Airways *River Trent*/Heathrow
	G-BGDK	Boeing 737-236	British Airways *River Mersey*/Heathrow
	G-BGDL	Boeing 737-236	British Airways *River Don*/Heathrow
	G-BGDN	Boeing 737-236	British Airways *River Tyne*/Heathrow
	G-BGDO	Boeing 737-236	British Airways *River Usk*/Heathrow
	G-BGDP	Boeing 737-236	British Airways *River Taff*/Heathrow
	G-BGDR	Boeing 737-236	British Airways *River Bann*/Heathrow
	G-BGDS	Boeing 737-236	British Airways *River Severn*/Heathrow
	G-BGDT	Boeing 737-236	British Airways *River Forth*/Heathrow
	G-BGDU	Boeing 737-236	British Airways *River Dee*/Heathrow
	G-BGDV	—	British Airways
	G-BGDW	—	British Airways
	G-BGDX	—	British Airways
	G-BGDY	—	British Airways
	G-BGDZ	—	British Airways
	G-BGEA	Cessna F.150M	R. L. Beverley/Bournemouth
	G-BGED	Cessna U.206F	Midland Parachute Centre/Long Marston
	G-BGEE	Evans VP-1	A. Morris/Fairoaks
	G-BGEF	Jodel D.112	G. G. Johnson & S. J. Davies
	G-BGEH	Monnet Sonerai II	G. K. Penson
	G-BGEI	Baby Great Lakes	D. H. Greenwood/Barton
	G-BGEK	PA-38-112 Tomahawk	Cheshire Flying Services Ltd/Manchester
	G-BGEL	PA-38-112 Tomahawk	Cheshire Flying Services Ltd/Manchester
	G-BGEM	Partenavia P.68B	Hosking Equipment Ltd
	G-BGEN	D.H.C.-6 Twin Otter 310	Loganair Ltd/Glasgow
	G-BGEO	PA-31-350 Navajo Chieftain	Christian Salveson (Cold Storage) Ltd/Edinburgh
	G-BGEP	Cameron D-38 balloon	Cameron Balloons Ltd
	G-BGES	Currie Wot	K. E. Ballington
	G-BGET	PA-38-112 Tomahawk	Liverpool Aero Club Ltd
	G-BGEV	PA-38-112 Tomahawk	R. Heron
	G-BGEW	Nord NC.854S	R. A. Yates/Wyberton
	G-BGEX	Brookland Mosquito 2	R. T. Gough/Shobdon
	G-BGFC	Evans VP-2	R. W. Eastman & J. A. Roberts
	G-BGFD	PA-32-300 Cherokee Six	City Roads Ltd/Manchester
	G-BGFF	FRED Srs 2	G. R. G. Smith
	G-BGFG	AA-5A Cheetah	Warner Aviation/Elstree
	G-BGFH	Cessna F.182Q	Mindon Engineering (Nottingham) Ltd/Tollerton
	G-BGFI	AA-5A Cheetah	Maston Property Holdings Ltd
	G-BGFJ	Jodel D.9 Bebe	C. M. Fitton
	G-BGFK	Evans VP-1	D. Beaumont
	G-BGFM	Rollason-Luton Beta 4	G. H. C. Jiggins
	G-BGFN	PA-25 Pawnee 235	Farmwork Services (Eastern) Ltd
	G-BGFS	Westland-Bell 47G-3B1	G. S. Mason
	G-BGFT	PA-34-200T-2 Seneca	C.S.E. (Aircraft Services) Ltd/Kidlington
	G-BGFX	Cessna F.152	A. W. Fay/Southampton
	G-BGGA	Bellanca 7GCBC Citabria	A. G. Forshaw/Barton
	G-BGGB	Bellanca 7GCBC Citabria	R. J. W. Wood
	G-BGGC	Bellanca 7GCBC Citabria	R. P. Ashfield & B. A. Jesty
	G-BGGD	Bellanca 8GCBC Scout	Bristol & Gloucestershire Gliding Club/Nympsfield
	G-BGGE	PA-38-112 Tomahawk	C.S.E. (Aircraft Services) Ltd/Kidlington
	G-BGGF	PA-38-112 Tomahawk	C.S.E. (Aircraft Services) Ltd/Kidlington
	G-BGGG	PA-38-112 Tomahawk	C.S.E. (Aircraft Services) Ltd/Kidlington
	G-BGGI	PA-38-112 Tomahawk	C.S.E. (Aircraft Services) Ltd/Kidlington
	G-BGGJ	PA-38-112 Tomahawk	C.S.E. (Aircraft Services) Ltd/Kidlington

Reg.	Type	Owner or Operator	Notes
G-BGGK	PA-38-112 Tomahawk	C.S.E. (Aircraft Services) Ltd/Kidlington	
G-BGGL	PA-38-112 Tomahawk	C.S.E. (Aircraft Services) Ltd/Kidlington	
G-BGGM	PA-38-112 Tomahawk	C.S.E. (Aircraft Services) Ltd/Kidlington	
G-BGGN	PA-38-112 Tomahawk	C.S.E. (Aircraft Services) Ltd/Kidlington	
G-BGGO	Cessna F.152	E. Midlands Aviation Ltd	
G-BGGP	Cessna F.152	E. Midlands Aviation Ltd	
G-BGGT	Zenith CH.200	P. R. M. Nind	
G-BGGU	Wallis WA-116R-R	K. H. Wallis	
G-BGGV	Wallis WA-120 Srs 2	K. H. Wallis	
G-BGGW	Wallis WA-112	K. H. Wallis	
G-BGGY	AB-206B JetRanger 3	Mann Aviation Ltd/Fairoaks	
G-BGHA	Cessna F.152	Wickwell (UK) Ltd/Shoreham	
G-BGHC	Saffery Hot Pants Firefly balloon	H. C. Saffery *Petuniga*	
G-BGHD	Saffery Helios Blister balloon	H. C. Saffery	
G-BGHE	Convair L-13A	J. Davis/USA	
G-BGHF	Westland WG.30	Westland Helicopters Ltd/Yeovil	
G-BGHI	Cessna F.152	Taxon Ltd/Shoreham	
G-BGHJ	Cessna F.172N	P.A.C.K. Enterprises (Sussex) Ltd/ Shoreham	
G-BGHK	Cessna F.152	Solent Flight Centre/Southampton	
G-BGHL	GA-7 Cougar	Peacock Salt Ltd/Glasgow	
G-BGHM	Robin R.1180T	Copeland Properties Ltd/Southend	
G-BGHO	Agusta-Bell 47G-3B1	M. H. Wills/Coventry	
G-BGHP	Beech 76 Duchess	J. J. Baumhardt Associates Ltd	
G-BGHS	Cameron N-31 balloon	Balloon Stable Ltd	
G-BGHT	Falconar F-12	T. K. Baillie	
G-BGHU	T-6G Harvard	S. M. & P. S. Warner/Wellesbourne	
G-BGHV	Cameron V-77 balloon	E. Davies	
G-BGHW	Thunder Ax8-90 balloon	Edinburgh University Balloon Group *James Tytler*	
G-BGHX	Chasle YC-12 Tourbillon	C. Clark	
G-BGHY	Taylor JT.1 Monoplane	J. Prowse	
G-BGHZ	FRED Srs 3	T. A. Timms	
G-BGIA	Cessna 152 II	Southern Air Ltd/Shoreham	
G-BGIB	Cessna 152 II	K. D. Wickenden/Shoreham	
G-BGIC	Cessna 172N	Colour Library International Ltd/ Fairoaks	
G-BGID	Westland-Bell 47G-3B1	A. E. & B. G. Brown	
G-BGIG	PA-38-112 Tomahawk	Apollo Leasing Ltd/Glasgow	
G-BGIH	Rand KR-2	G. & D. G. Park	
G-BGII	PA-32-300 Cherokee Six	Rosefair Electronics Ltd/Elstree	
G-BGIJ	Cameron O-77 balloon	H. P. Carlton	
G-BGIK	Taylor JT.1 Monoplane	J. H. Medforth	
G-BGIM	AS.350B Ecureuil	Lord Glendyne/Hayes	
G-BGIO	Bensen B.8M	C. G. Johns	
G-BGIP	Colt 56A balloon	Lipton Export Ltd	
G-BGIS	Boeing 707-321C	Tradewinds Ltd/Gatwick	
G-BGIU	Cessna F.172H	Metro Equipment (Chesham) Ltd/ Panshanger	
G-BGIV	Bell 47G-5	Helicopter Farming Ltd	
G-BGIW	Bell 47G-2	Autair Ltd/Panshanger	
G-BGIX	H.295 Super Courier	Nordic Oil Services Ltd/Edinburgh	
G-BGIY	Cessna F.172N	McArthur Properties Ltd/Cranfield	
G-BGIZ	Cessna F.152	S. E. Stafford	
G-BGJA	Cessna FA.152	D. G. Crabtree	
G-BGJB	PA-44-180 Seminole	Air & General Services Ltd/Biggin Hill	
G-BGJE	Boeing 737-236	British Airways *Sandpiper*/Gatwick	
G-BGJF	Boeing 737-236	British Airways *Skylark*/Gatwick	
G-BGJG	Boeing 737-236	British Airways *Kingfisher*/Gatwick	
G-BGJH	Boeing 737-236	British Airways *Wren*/Gatwick	
G-BGJI	Boeing 737-236	British Airways *Swallow*/Gatwick	
G-BGJJ	Boeing 737-236	British Airways *Kestrel*/Gatwick	
G-BGJK	Boeing 737-236	British Airways *Firecrest*/Gatwick	
G-BGJL	Boeing 737-236	British Airways *Goldfinch*/Gatwick	
G-BGJM	Boeing 737-236	British Airways *Curlew*/Gatwick	
G-BGJN	—	—	
G-BGJO	—	—	
G-BGJP	—	—	
G-BGJR	—	—	
G-BGJS	—	—	
G-BGJT	—	—	

Notes	Reg.	Type	Owner or Operator
	G-BGJU	Cameron V-65 Balloon	D. T. Watkins *Spoils*
	G-BGJV	H.S.748 Srs 2B	British Aerospace PLC/Woodford
	G-BGJW	GA-7 Cougar	Trent Air Services Ltd/Cranfield
	G-BGKA	P.56 Provost T.1 (XF690)	D. W. Mickleburgh/Leicester
	G-BGKB	SOCATA Rallye 110ST	Air Westward Co Ltd
	G-BGKC	SOCATA Rallye 110ST	Martin Ltd/Biggin Hill
	G-BGKD	SOCATA Rallye 110ST	Air Westward Co Ltd/Dunkeswell
	G-BGKE	BAC One Eleven 539	British Airways *County of West Midlands*/Birmingham
	G-BGKF	BAC One-Eleven 539	British Airways *County of Stafford*/Birmingham
	G-BGKG	BAC One-Eleven 539	British Airways *County of Warwick*/Birmingham
	G-BGKH	Cessna A.188B AgTruck	Miller Aerial Spraying Ltd/Wickenby
	G-BGKI	Cessna A.188B AgTruck	Miller Aerial Spraying Ltd/Wickenby
	G-BGKJ	MBB Bo 105C	North Scottish Helicopters Ltd
	G-BGKM	SA.365C Dauphin	Management Aviation Ltd/Bourn
	G-BGKO	GY-20 Minicab	R. B. Webber
	G-BGKP	MBB Bo 105C	Management Aviation Ltd/Bourn
	G-BGKR	PA-28-161 Warrior II	J. E. Cannings/Kidlington
	G-BGKS	PA-28-161 Warrior II	Woodgate Air Services (IOM) Ltd/Ronaldsway
	G-BGKT	Auster AOP.9	K. H. Wallis
	G-BGKU	PA-28R-201 Arrow III	Farr (Metal Fabrications) Ltd
	G-BGKV	PA-28R-201 Arrow III	G. E. Salter Industrial Enterprises Ltd/Shipdham
	G-BGKW	Evans VP-1	I. W. Black
	G-BGKX	PA-38-112 Tomahawk	Cambrian Aviation Ltd/Cardiff
	G-BGKY	PA-38-112 Tomahawk	J. D. Apthorp/Elstree
	G-BGKZ	J/5F Aiglet Trainer	R. C. H. Hibberd/Dunkeswell
	G-BGLA	PA-38-112 Tomahawk	Moore House Freight/Bournemouth
	G-BGLB	Bede BD-5B	W. Sawney
	G-BGLD	Beech 76 Duchess	A. E. C. Cohen & D. R. Brown
	G-BGLE	Saffrey S.330 Balloon	C. J. Dodd & ptnrs
	G-BGLF	Evans VP-1	E. F. Fryer
	G-BGLG	Cessna 152	Skyviews & General Ltd/Stapleford
	G-BGLH	Cessna 152	Deltair Ltd/Chester
	G-BGLI	Cessna 152	G. Capes/Humberside
	G-BGLK	Monnet Sonerai II	G. L. Kemp & J. Beck
	G-BGLN	Cessna FA.152	Shoreham Flight Simulation Ltd/Bournemouth
	G-BGLO	Cessna F.172N	A. H. Slaughter/Southend
	G-BGLR	Cessna F.152	Auxair International/Stapleford
	G-BGLS	Baby Great Lakes	D. S. Morgan/Lasham
	G-BGLW	PA-34-200 Seneca	Adrian Alan Ltd/Shoreham
	G-BGLX	Cameron N-56 balloon	Sara A. G. Williams
	G-BGLZ	Stits SA-3A Playboy	P. E. Barker
	G-BGMA	D.31 Turbulent	G. C. Masterson
	G-BGMB	Taylor JT.2 Titch	E. M. Bourne
	G-BGMC	D.H.C.-6 Twin Otter 310	Jersey European Airways
	G-BGMD	D.H.C.-6 Twin Otter 310	Spacegrand Ltd/Blackpool
	G-BGME	SIPA S.903	M. Emery (G-BCML)/Redhill
	G-BGMJ	GY-201 Minicab	H. P. Burrill
	G-BGMM	PA-28-181 Archer II	Allen Technical Services Ltd
	G-BGMP	Cessna F.172G	Norvic Racing Engines Ltd/Little Staughton
	G-BGMR	GY-201 Minicab	T. J. D. Hodge & A. B. Holloway/Southend
	G-BGMS	Taylor JT.2 Titch	M. A. J. Spice
	G-BGMT	MS.894E Rallye 235GT	M. E. Taylor
	G-BGMU	Westland Bell 47G-3B1	W. A. Braim Ltd
	G-BGMV	Scheibe SF.25B Falke	Wolds Gliding Club Ltd/Pocklington
	G-BGMW	Edgeley EA-7 Optica	Edgeley Aircraft Ltd/Cranfield
	G-BGMX	Enstrom F-280C-UK-2 Shark	Barry Sheene Racing Ltd
	G-BGNA	Short SD3-30	Air Ecosse Ltd/Aberdeen
	G-BGND	Cessna F.172N	A. J. Freeman & ptnrs/Stansted
	G-BGNL	Hiway Super Scorpion	G. Breen/Enstone
	G-BGNM	SA.365C Dauphin	Management Aviation Ltd/Bourn
	G-BGNN	AA-5A Cheetah	Caslon Ltd/Elstree
	G-BGNO	AA-5A Cheetah	Noscar Aviation/Biggin Hill
	G-BGNP	Saffrey S.200 balloon	N. H. Ponsford

Reg.	Type	Owner or Operator	Notes
G-BGNR	Cessna F.172N	Bevan Lynch Aviation Ltd	
G-BGNS	Cessna F.172N	Wickwell (UK) Ltd/Shoreham	
G-BGNT	Cessna F.152	Solent Flight Centre/Southampton	
G-BGNU	Beech E90 King Air	Norwich Union Fire Insurance Ltd/ Norwich	
G-BGNV	GA-7 Cougar	H. Snelson (Engineers) Ltd	
G-BGNW	Boeing 737-219ADV	Britannia Airways Ltd George Stephenson/Luton	
G-BGNZ	Cessna FRA.150L	Kingsmetal Ltd/Lydd	
G-BGOA	Cessna FR.182RG	The Forestry Commission/Fairoaks	
G-BGOC	Cessna F.152	Elliot Forbes Ltd/Aberdeen	
G-BGOD	Colt 77A balloon	Aquarious Balloon School Ltd	
G-BGOE	Beech 76 Duchess	B. D. Steel (Holdings) Ltd/E. Midlands	
G-BGOF	Cessna F.152	Kingsmetal Ltd/Lydd	
G-BGOG	PA-28-161 Warrior II	M. J. Cowham	
G-BGOH	Cessna F.182Q	Zonex Ltd/Blackpool	
G-BGOI	Cameron O-56 balloon	Balloon Stable Ltd Skymaster	
G-BGOL	PA-28R-201T Turbo Arrow IV	M. G. Tyrrell & Co Ltd/Booker	
G-BGOM	PA-31-310 Navajo	Sun Valley Poultry Ltd/Shobdon	
G-BGON	GA-7 Cougar	Sefact (Hire) Ltd/Elstree	
G-BGOO	Colt 56 SS balloon	British Gas Corporation	
G-BGOP	Dassault Falcon 20F	Datsun (UK) Ltd/Heathrow	
G-BGOR	AT-6D Harvard III	M. L. Sargeant	
G-BGOU	AT-6C Harvard IIA	A. P. Snell	
G-BGOX	PA-31-350 Navajo Chieftain	Berrard Ltd/Blackbushe	
G-BGOY	PA-31-350 Navajo Chieftain	Berrard Ltd/Blackbushe	
G-BGOZ	Westland-Bell 47G-3B1	GSM Helicopters	
G-BGPA	Cessna 182Q	R. A. Robinson	
G-BGPB	AT-16 Harvard IV (385)	A. G. Walker & R. Lamplough/Duxford	
G-BGPC	D.H.C.-6 Twin Otter 310	Nordic Oil Services Ltd/Glasgow	
G-BGPD	Piper L-4H Cub	P. D. Whiteman	
G-BGPE	Thunder Ax6-56 balloon	C. Wolstenholme Sergeant Pepper	
G-BGPF	Thunder Ax6-56Z balloon	Thunder Balloons Ltd Pepsi	
G-BGPG	AA-5B Tiger	Tentergate Aviation/Elstree	
G-BGPH	AA-5B Tiger	Peter Turnbull (York) Ltd	
G-BGPI	Plumb BGP-1	B. G. Plumb	
G-BGPJ	PA-28-161 Warrior II	R. P. Maughan & A. E. Hart/ Biggin Hill	
G-BGPK	AA-5B Tiger	Ann Green Manufacturing Co Ltd/ Elstree	
G-BGPL	PA-28-161 Warrior II	Cormack (Aircraft Services) Ltd/ Glasgow	
G-BGPM	Evans VP-2	T. G. Painter	
G-BGPN	PA-18-150 Super Cub	Roy Moore Ltd/Blackpool	
G-BGPO	PA-25 Pawnee 235	CKS Air Ltd/Southend	
G-BGPP	PA-25 Pawnee 235	Sprayfields (Scothern) Ltd/Bardney	
G-BGPS	Aero Commander 200D	K. Davison/Shobdon	
G-BGPT	Parker Teenie Two	K. Atkinson	
G-BGPU	PA-28 Cherokee 140	Air Navigation & Trading Co Ltd/ Blackpool	
G-BGPZ	MS.890A Rallye Commodore	J. R. Espin/Popham	
G-BGRA	Taylor JT.2 Titch	J. R. C. Thompson	
G-BGRC	PA-28 Cherokee 140	G. Rowe/Headcorn	
G-BGRE	Beech A200 Super King Air	Dowty Group Services Ltd/Staverton	
G-BGRF	Beech 95-58P Baron	Hitchins (Hatfield) Ltd/Leavesden	
G-BGRG	Beech 76 Duchess	Lambson Holdings Ltd/Leeds	
G-BGRH	Robin DR.400/2+2	A. Taylor & ptnrs/Headcorn	
G-BGRI	Jodel DR.1051	R. M. McEwan/Fenland	
G-BGRJ	Cessna T.310R	Gledhill Water Storage Ltd/Blackpool	
G-BGRK	PA-38-112 Tomahawk	Goodwood Terrena Ltd	
G-BGRL	PA-38-112 Tomahawk	Goodwood Terrena Ltd	
G-BGRM	PA-38-112 Tomahawk	Goodwood Terrena Ltd	
G-BGRN	PA-38-112 Tomahawk	Goodwood Terrena Ltd	
G-BGRO	Cessna F.172M	Citation Flying Services Ltd/Humberside	
G-BGRR	PA-38-112 Tomahawk	Cormack (Aircraft Services) Ltd/ Glasgow	
G-BGRS	Thunder Ax7-77Z balloon	P. Hassall Ltd	
G-BGRT	Steen Skybolt	R. C. Teverson	
G-BGRX	PA-38-112 Tomahawk	Flamingo Aviation Ltd/Leavesden	
G-BGSA	MS.892E Rallye 150GT	G. A. Schulz & ptnrs/Leicester	
G-BGSC	Ayres S2R-T34 Turbo Thrush 500	Farmair Ltd/Headcorn	

Notes	Reg.	Type	Owner or Operator
	G-BGSE	Pitts S-2A Special	P. H. Meeson/Blackbushe
	G-BGSG	PA-44-180 Seminole	Contropol Ltd/Goodwood
	G-BGSH	PA-38-112 Tomahawk	Apollo Leasing Ltd/Edinburgh
	G-BGSI	PA-38-112 Tomahawk	Burnthills Plant Hire Ltd/Glasgow
	G-BGSJ	Piper J-3C-65 Cub	H. A. Bridgman/Dunkeswell
	G-BGSK	AA-5A Cheetah	G. W. Plowman & Son Ltd/Fenland
	G-BGSL	AA-5A Cheetah	R. M. de Garston/Biggin Hill
	G-BGSM	MS.892E Rallye 150GT	Tyre & Tune Service Station
	G-BGSN	Enstrom F-28C-UK-2	Nicelynn Ltd
	G-BGSO	PA-31-310 Navajo	Ulmke Metals Ltd/Birmingham
	G-BGSS	PA-38-112 Tomahawk	Cambrian Flying Club/Cardiff
	G-BGST	Thunder Ax7-65 balloon	L. H. T. Large & ptnrs *Eclipse*
	G-BGSV	Cessna F.172N	Wickenby Flying Club Ltd
	G-BGSW	Beech F33 Debonair	D. J. Shires/Stapleford
	G-BGSX	Cessna F.152	RJS Aviation Ltd/Coventry
	G-BGSY	GA-7 Cougar	I. T. Evans & M. S. Little/Southampton
	G-BGTA	Firebird Bunce B.500 balloon	S. J. Bunce
	G-BGTB	SOCATA TB.10 Tobago ★	S. Yorks Aviation Soc
	G-BGTC	Auster AOP.9 (XP282)	P. J. Marsham/Felthorpe
	G-BGTD	H.S.125 Srs.700B	Rank Zerox (UK) Ltd/Luton
	G-BGTF	PA-44-180 Seminole	New Guarantee Trust Ltd/Jersey
	G-BGTG	PA-23 Aztec 250	Hockstar Ltd/Biggin Hill
	G-BGTH	PA-23 Aztec 250F	Scotia Safari Ltd/Prestwick
	G-BGTI	Piper J-3C-65 Cub	W. J. Clarke & A. C. Broad
	G-BGTJ	PA-28 Cherokee 180	Serendipity Aviation/Staverton
	G-BGTK	Cessna F.182RG	Kestrel Air Services Ltd/Denham
	G-BGTL	GY-20 Minicab	A. K. Lang
	G-BGTM	Thunder Ax6-56Z balloon	Engineering Polymers Ltd
	G-BGTP	Robin HR.100/210	A. E. James & P. Houghton/Southend
	G-BGTR	PA-28 Cherokee 140	Keenair Services Ltd/Liverpool
	G-BGTS	PA-28 Cherokee 140	Keenair Services Ltd/Liverpool
	G-BGTT	Cessna 310R	Air Atlantique/Jersey
	G-BGTU	BAC One-Eleven 409	Turbo Union Ltd/Filton
	G-BGTV	Boeing 737-2T5	Orion Airways Ltd/E. Midlands
	G-BGTW	Boeing 737-2T5	Orion Airways Ltd/E. Midlands
	G-BGTX	Jodel D.117	Madley Flying Group
	G-BGTY	Boeing 737-2Q8	Orion Airways Ltd/E. Midlands
	G-BGUA	PA-38-112 Tomahawk	Truman Aviation Ltd/Tollerton
	G-BGUB	PA-32-300 Cherokee Six	J. Beckers & ptnrs/Gamston

NOTE: The G-BGUx sequence will not be issued unless specifically requested

Notes	Reg.	Type	Owner or Operator
	G-BGUY	Cameron V-56 balloon	G. V. Beckwith
	G-BGVA	Cessna 414A	Clymsil Holdings Ltd
	G-BGVB	Robin DR.315	J. R. D. Bygraves/O. Warden
	G-BGVE	CP1310-C3 Super Emeraude	C. Watson
	G-BGVF	Colt 77A balloon	Hot Air Balloon Co Ltd
	G-BGVH	Beech 76 Duchess	Laura Ashley Ltd/Staverton
	G-BGVI	Cessna F.152	Farr (Metal Fabrications) Ltd
	G-BGVJ	PA-28 Cherokee 180	H. Devonish/Southend
	G-BGVL	PA-38-112 Tomahawk	Cambrian Flying Club/Cardiff
	G-BGVM	Wilson Cassutt 3M	J. T. Mirley/Halfpenny Green
	G-BGVN	PA-28RT-201 Arrow IV	Essex Aviation Ltd/Stapleford
	G-BGVP	Thunder Ax6-56Z balloon	Hot Air Balloon Co Ltd
	G-BGVR	Thunder Ax6-56Z balloon	A. N. G. Howie
	G-BGVS	Cessna F.172M	P. D. A. Aviation Ltd/Tollerton
	G-BGVT	Cessna R.182RG	Barnes Reinforced Plastics Ltd
	G-BGVU	PA-28 Cherokee 180	Solair Ltd/Biggin Hill
	G-BGVV	AA-5A Cheetah	B. D. Greenwood
	G-BGVW	AA-5A Cheetah	Goddard Aviation Ltd/White Waltham
	G-BGVX	Cessna P.210N	Industrial Pharmaceutical Service Ltd/Manchester
	G-BGVY	AA-5B Tiger	M. J. Lawrence/Denham
	G-BGVZ	PA-28-181 Archer II	Robinson-Wyllie Ltd
	G-BGWA	GA-7 Cougar	Lough Erne Aviation Ltd
	G-BGWC	Robin DR.400/180	E. F. Braddon/Rochester
	G-BGWD	Robin HR.100/285	Hordell Engineering Ltd/Fairoaks
	G-BGWF	PA-18-150 Super Cub	Farmair Ltd
	G-BGWG	PA-18-150 Super Cub	Farmair Ltd

Reg.	Type	Owner or Operator	Notes
G-BGWH	PA-18-150 Super Cub	Farmair Ltd	
G-BGWI	Cameron V-65 balloon	Army Balloon Club	
G-BGWJ	Sikorsky S-61N	Bristow Helicopters Ltd	
G-BGWK	Sikorsky S-61N	British Executive Air Services Ltd	
G-BGWM	PA-28-181 Archer II	Zitair Flying Club Ltd	
G-BGWN	PA-38-112 Tomahawk	Apollo Leasing Ltd/Glasgow	
G-BGWO	Jodel D.112	A. J. Court	
G-BGWP	MBB Bo 105C	Management Aviation Ltd/Bourn	
G-BGWR	Cessna U.206A	Cecil Aviation Ltd/Cambridge	
G-BGWS	Enstrom F-280C Shark	G. Firbank & N. M. Grimshaw	
G-BGWT	WS-58 Wessex 60 Srs 1	Bristow Helicopters Ltd	
G-BGWU	PA-38-112 Tomahawk	Burnthills Aviation Ltd/Glasgow	
G-BGWV	Aeronca 7AC Champion	RFC Flying Group/Popham	
G-BGWW	PA-23 Aztec 250E	Chargewell Ltd/Biggin Hill	
G-BGWY	Thunder Ax6-56Z balloon	Dinal (Car Care) UK Ltd	
G-BGWZ	Eclipse Super Eagle ★	FAA Museum/Yeovilton	
G-BGXA	Piper J-3C-65 Cub	P. E. & J. A. Bates	
G-BGXB	PA-38-112 Tomahawk	Keenair Services Ltd/Liverpool	
G-BGXC	SOCATA TB.10 Tobago	A. J. Halliday/Shoreham	
G-BGXD	SOCATA TB.10 Tobago	Selles Dispensing Chemists Ltd	
G-BGXJ	Partenavia P.68B	Wickenby Aviation Ltd	
G-BGXK	Cessna 310R	McCarthy & Stone (Developments) PLC/Bournemouth	
G-BGXL	Bensen B.8MV	H. A. Bancroft-Wilson	
G-BGXN	PA-38-112 Tomahawk	Keats Web Offset Ltd/Denham	
G-BGXO	PA-38-112 Tomahawk	G. C. F. Moffatt & Co Ltd	
G-BGXP	Westland-Bell 47G-3B1	B. A. Hogan & ptnrs	
G-BGXR	Robin HR.200/100	J. H. Spanton	
G-BGXS	PA-28-236 Dakota	Debian Car Hire Ltd/Jersey	
G-BGXT	SOCATA TB.10 Tobago	County Aviation Ltd/Halfpenny Green	
G-BGXU	WMB-1 balloon	C. J. Dodd & ptnrs	
G-BGXV	Piper J-3C-65 Cub	G. Cormack/Glasgow	
G-BGXX	Jodel DR.1051M1	P. Evans	
G-BGXZ	Cessna FA.152	Kingsmetal Ltd/Lydd	
G-BGYG	PA-28-161 Warrior II	C.S.E. (Aircraft Services) Ltd/Kidlington	
G-BGYH	PA-28-161 Warrior II	C.S.E. (Aircraft Services) Ltd/Kidlington	
G-BGYJ	Boeing 737-204	Britannia Airways Ltd *Sir Barnes Wallis*/Luton	
G-BGYK	Boeing 737-204	Britannia Airways Ltd *R. J. Mitchell*/Luton	
G-BGYL	Boeing 737-204	Britannia Airways Ltd *Jean Batten*/Luton	
G-BGYN	PA-18-150 Super Cub	A. G. Walker	
G-BGYP	GA-7 Cougar	Bambair & Nixon Aviation/Netherthorpe	
G-BGYR	H.S.125 Srs 600B	British Aerospace/Warton	
G-BGZC	C.A.S.A. 1.131 Jungmann	J. E. Douglas	
G-BGZE	PA-38-112 Tomahawk	Manchester School of Flying Ltd	
G-BGZF	PA-38-112 Tomahawk	Shirlster Container Transport Ltd/Cardiff	
G-BGZG	PA-38-112 Tomahawk	Kilmartin Leasing & Finance/Leavesden	
G-BGZH	PA-38-112 Tomahawk	Norwich Air Training	
G-BGZJ	PA-38-112 Tomahawk	Wickwell (UK) Ltd/Southampton	
G-BGZK	Westland-Bell 47G-3B1	K. McDonald	
G-BGZL	Eiri PIK-20E	D. I. Liddell-Grainger	
G-BGZN	WMB.2 Windtracker balloon	S. R. Woolfries	
G-BGZO	M.S.880B Rallye Club	W. G. R. Wunderlich/Biggin Hill	
G-BGZP	D.H.C.6 Twin Otter 310	Spacegrand Ltd/Blackpool	
G-BGZR	Meagher Model balloon Mk.1	S. C. Meagher	
G-BGZS	Keirs Heated Air Tube	M. N. J. Kirby	
G-BGZW	PA-38-112 Tomahawk	Nottingham School of Flying Ltd/Tollerton	
G-BGZX	PA-32 Cherokee Six 260	R. H. R. Rue/Stapleford	
G-BGZY	Jodel D.120	P. J. Sebastian/Popham	
G-BGZZ	Thunder Ax6-56 balloon	J. M. Robinson	
G-BHAA	Cessna 152	Herefordshire Aero Club Ltd/Shobdon	
G-BHAB	Cessna 152	Herefordshire Aero Club Ltd/Shobdon	
G-BHAC	Cessna A.152	Herefordshire Aero Club Ltd/Shobdon	
G-BHAD	Cessna A.152	Shropshire Aero Club Ltd/Sleap	
G-BHAF	PA-38-112 Tomahawk	R. Colin Snow/Doncaster	
G-BHAG	Scheibe SF.25E Super Falke	British Gliding Association/Lasham	

Notes	Reg.	Type	Owner or Operator
	G-BHAI	Cessna F.152	Channel Islands Aero Holdings Ltd/ Jersey
	G-BHAJ	Robin DR.400/160	Crocker Aviation Services/Biggin Hill
	G-BHAL	Rango Saffery S.200 SS	A. M. Lindsay *Anneky Panky*
	G-BHAM	Thunder Ax6-56 balloon	D. Sampson
	G-BHAR	Westland-Bell 47G-3B1	E. A. L. Sturmer
	G-BHAT	Thunder Ax7-77 balloon	C. P. Witter Ltd *Witter*
	G-BHAU	B.175 Britannia 253F	(*Stored*) Manston
	G-BHAV	Cessna F.152	Essenlynn Enterprises Ltd
	G-BHAW	Cessna F.172N	J. M. Boucher/Jersey
	G-BHAX	Enstrom F-28C-UK-2	Flairair/Shoreham
	G-BHAY	PA-28RT-201 Arrow IV	Chiltern Aviation/Denham
	G-BHBA	Campbell Cricket	S. M. Irwin
	G-BHBB	Colt 77A balloon	S. D. Bellew/USA
	G-BHBE	Westland Bell 47G-3B1 (Soloy)	Fosse Helicopter Services Ltd
	G-BHBF	Sikorsky S-76A	Bristow Helicopters Ltd
	G-BHBG	PA-32R-300 Lance	D. A. Stewart/Birmingham
	G-BHBI	Mooney M.20J	B. K. Arthur
	G-BHBJ	Cameron D.96 airship	Buckfame Ltd
	G-BHBK	Viscount V-5 balloon	B. Hargraves & B. King
	G-BHBL	L.1011-385 TriStar 200	British Airways *The Red Ensign Rose*/ Heathrow
	G-BHBM	L.1011-385 TriStar 200	British Airways *The Piccadilly Rose*/ Heathrow
	G-BHBN	L.1011-385 TriStar 200	British Airways *The Fragrant Star Rose*/ Heathrow
	G-BHBO	L.1011-385 TriStar 200	British Airways *The Morning Jewel Rose*/Heathrow
	G-BHBP	L.1011-385 TriStar 200	British Airways *Osprey*/Heathrow
	G-BHBR	L.1011-385 TriStar 200	British Airways *Golden Eagle*/Heathrow
	G-BHBS	PA-28RT-201T Turbo Arrow IV	Zipmaster Ltd/Denham
	G-BHBT	MA.5 Charger	R. G. & C. J. Maidment/Goodwood
	G-BHBU	Westland Bell 47G-3B1 (Soloy)	Heliwork Ltd/Thruxton
	G-BHBW	Westland Bell 47G-3Bl	Heliwork Ltd/Thruxton
	G-BHBX	Agusta Bell 47G-3B1	Heliwork Ltd/Thruxton
	G-BHBY	Westland Bell 47G-3B1	Heliwork Ltd/Thruxton
	G-BHBZ	Partenavia P.68B	Insituform Holdings Ltd/Jersey
	G-BHCB	AA-5A Cheetah	Huronair/Doncaster
	G-BHCC	Cessna 172M	A. Potter & Jearide Ltd/Bournemouth
	G-BHCE	Jodel D.112	G. F. M. Garner
	G-BHCF	WMB.2 Windtracker balloon	C. J. Dodd & ptnrs
	G-BHCJ	H.S.748 Srs 2A	Dan-Air Services Ltd/Gatwick
	G-BHCK	AA-5A Cheetah	Crispex (Foods) Ltd/Biggin Hill
	G-BHCM	Cessna F.172H	The English Connection Ltd/Panshanger
	G-BHCP	Cessna F.152	Neptune Securities Ltd/Shoreham
	G-BHCT	PA-23 Aztec 250	Colt Transport Ltd/Goodwood
	G-BHCW	PA-22 Tri-Pacer 150	B. Brooks
	G-BHCX	Cessna F.152	Light Planes (Lancs) Ltd/Barton
	G-BHCZ	PA-38-112 Tomahawk	Simulated Flight Training Ltd/ Bournemouth
	G-BHDA	Shultz balloon	G. F. Fitzjohn
	G-BHDB	Maule M5-235 Lunar Rocket	Cleanacres Ltd/Staverton
	G-BHDD	V.668 Varsity T.1 (WL626)	G. & F. W. Vale/E. Midlands
	G-BHDE	SOCATA TB.10 Tobago	B. D. Glynn/Biggin Hill
	G-BHDH	Douglas DC-10-30	British Caledonian Airways *Sir Walter Scott*/Gatwick
	G-BHDI	Douglas DC-10-30	British Caledonian Airways/Gatwick
	G-BHDJ	Douglas DC-10-30	British Caledonian Airways/Gatwick
	G-BHDK	Boeing B-29A-BN (461748) ★	Imperial War Museum/Duxford
	G-BHDM	Cessna F.152 II	Tayside Aviation Ltd/Dundee
	G-BHDO	Cessna F.182Q II	S. Richman & ptnrs/Bodmin
	G-BHDP	Cessna F.182Q II	Rimmer Aviation Ltd/Elstree
	G-BHDR	Cessna F.152 II	G. Apes
	G-BHDS	Cessna F.152 II	Tayside Aviation Ltd/Dundee
	G-BHDT	SOCATA TB.10 Tobago	Property Associates Ltd/Ipswich
	G-BHDU	Cessna F.152 II	P. N. Voysey/Sandown
	G-BHDV	Cameron V-77 balloon	D. E. P. Price
	G-BHDW	Cessna F.152	A. G. Chrismas Ltd/Shoreham
	G-BHDX	Cessna F.172N	D. M. Slama & T. Parsons/Sandown
	G-BHDZ	Cessna F.172N	Repclif Aviation Services Ltd/Liverpool
	G-BHEC	Cessna F.152	Wickwell (UK) Ltd/Southampton

Reg.	Type	Owner or Operator	Notes
G-BHED	Cessna FA.152	P. Skinner/Doncaster	
G-BHEG	Jodel D.150	P. R. Underhill	
G-BHEH	Cessna 310G	P. D. Higgs/Elstree	
G-BHEK	CP.1315C-3 Super Emeraude	D. B. Winstanley/Barton	
G-BHEL	Jodel D.117	J. C. Jefferies	
G-BHEM	Bensen B.8M	E. Kenny	
G-BHEN	Cessna FA.152	Leicestershire Aero Club Ltd	
G-BHEO	Cessna FR.182RG	Cosworth Engineering Ltd/Coventry	
G-BHEP	Cessna 172 RG Cutlass	Memec Systems Ltd/Booker	
G-BHER	SOCATA TB.10 Tobago	W. R. M. Dury/Biggin Hill	
G-BHET	SOCATA TB.10 Tobago	Dickens & Cartwright (Nottingham) Ltd/ Tollerton	
G-BHEU	Thunder Ax7-65 balloon	M. H. R. Govett *Polo Moche*	
G-BHEV	PA-28R Cherokee Arrow 200	C. A. Savile	
G-BHEW	Sopwith Triplane Replica (N5430)	The Hon Patrick Lindsay/Booker	
G-BHEX	Colt 56A balloon	A. S. Dear & ptnrs *Super Wasp*	
G-BHEY	Pterodactyl O.R.	High School of Hang Gliding Ltd	
G-BHEZ	Jodel D.150	E. J. Horsfall/Blackpool	
G-BHFA	Pterodactyl O.R.	High School of Hang Gliding Ltd	
G-BHFB	Pterodactyl O.R.	High School of Hang Gliding Ltd	
G-BHFC	Cessna F.152	T. G. Aviation Ltd/Manston	
G-BHFD	D.H.C.-6 Twin Otter 310	Metropolitan Airways Ltd/Bournemouth	
G-BHFF	Jodel D.112	A. J. Maxwell	
G-BHFG	SNCAN SV-4C (45)	R. J. Godfrey/Enstone	
G-BHFH	PA-34-200T-2 Seneca	Heltor Ltd/Exeter	
G-BHFI	Cessna F.152	The BAE (Warton) Flying Group/ Blackpool	
G-BHFK	PA-28-151 Warrior	Ilkeston Car Sales Ltd	
G-BHFL	PA-28 Cherokee 180	R. & C. Lord/Coventry	
G-BHFM	Murphy S.200 balloon	M. Murphy	
G-BHFN	Eiri PIK-20E-1	B. A. Eastwell/Shoreham	
G-BHFR	Eiri PIK-20E-1	G. Mackie	
G-BHFS	Robin DR.400/180	Flair (Soft Drinks) Ltd/Shoreham	
G-BHFU	Saffery S.330 balloon	N. H. Ponsford *Jennie Toyhill*	
G-BHFY	Beech 95-B58 Baron	Kebbell Holdings Ltd/Leavesden	
G-BHFZ	Saffery S.200 balloon	D. Morris	
G-BHGA	PA-31-310 Navajo	Heltor Ltd	
G-BHGC	PA-18-150 Super Cub	Herefordshire Gliding Club Ltd/ Shobdon	
G-BHGF	Cameron V-56 balloon	I. T. & H. Seddon *Biggles*	
G-BHGG	Cessna F.172N	Tosair Ltd/Denham	
G-BHGI	—	—	
G-BHGJ	Jodel D.120	C. E. M. Davies/Shobdon	
G-BHGK	Sikorsky S-76	North Scottish Helicopters Ltd/ Peterhead	
G-BHGM	Beech 76 Duchess	R. J. A. Brown/Guernsey	
G-BHGN	Evans VP-1	A. R. Cameron	
G-BHGO	PA-32 Cherokee Six 260	L. J. Steward/Kidlington	
G-BHGP	SOCATA TB.10 Tobago	J. McLeary & ptnrs	
G-BHGR	Robin DR.315	Headcorn Flying School Ltd	
G-BHGS	PA-31-350 Navajo Chieftain	Jersey European Airways	
G-BHGT	Beech B90 King Air	Navigations Ltd/Elstree	
G-BHGU	WMB.2 Windtracker balloon	I. D. Bamber & ptnrs	
G-BHGV	Keirs captive balloon	K. J. Faulkoner	
G-BHGW	Colt 14A balloon	Colt Balloons Ltd	
G-BHGX	Colt 56B balloon	S. Doyle *Vomibag*	
G-BHGY	PA-28R Cherokee Arrow 200	Luca Marketing Ltd/Southend	
G-BHHA	EMB-110P1 Bandeirante	Loganair Ltd/Glasgow	
G-BHHB	Cameron V-77 balloon	I. G. N. Franklin	
G-BHHE	Jodel DR.1051/M1	B. E. Lowe-Lauri	
G-BHHG	Cessna F.152	Northamptonshire School of Flying Ltd/ Sywell	
G-BHHH	Thunder Ax7-65 balloon	C. A. Hendley (Essex) Ltd	
G-BHHI	Cessna F.152	Air Navigation & Trading Co Ltd/ Blackpool	
G-BHHJ	Cessna F.152	Leicestershire Aero Club Ltd	
G-BHHK	Cameron N-77 balloon	S. Bridge & ptnrs	
G-BHHN	Cameron V-77 balloon	Itchen Valley Balloon Group	
G-BHHO	PA-28 Cherokee 180	Peter Clifford Aviation Ltd/Kidlington	
G-BHHR	Robin DR.400/180R	R. Jones/Bidford	

Notes	Reg.	Type	Owner or Operator
	G-BHHX	Jodel D.112	C. F. Walter
	G-BHHY	G.164 Turbo AgCat D	Miller Aerial Spraying Ltd/Wickenby
	G-BHHZ	Rotorway Scorpion 133	P. A. Gunn & D. Willingham
	G-BHIA	Cessna F.152	W. H. Wilkins Ltd
	G-BHIB	Cessna F.182Q	ISF Aviation Ltd/Leicester
	G-BHIC	Cessna F.182Q	General Building Services Ltd/Leeds
	G-BHID	SOCATA TB.10 Tobago	W. B. Pinckney & Sons Farming Co Ltd/Coventry
	G-BHIF	Colt 160A balloon	Colt Balloons Ltd
	G-BHIH	Cessna F.172N	Watkins Group Aviation Ltd/Biggin Hill
	G-BHII	Cameron V-77 balloon	Zebedee Balloon Services
	G-BHIJ	Eiri PIK-20E-1	R. W. Hall & ptnrs/Swanton Morley
	G-BHIK	Adam RA-14 Loisirs	P. J. H. McCaig
	G-BHIL	PA-28-161 Warrior II	Simulated Flight Training Ltd/Booker
	G-BHIM	Jodel D.112	I. B. & J. M. Grace
	G-BHIN	Cessna F.152	Kestrel Air Services/Denham
	G-BHIR	PA-28R Cherokee Arrow 200	ISS Industrial & Scientific Services Ltd/Manchester
	G-BHIS	Thunder Ax7-65 balloon	Hedgehoppers Balloon Group
	G-BHIT	SOCATA TB.9 Tampico	Prices Supreme Coaches/Coventry
	G-BHIV	AS.350B Ecureuil	Marley Tile Co Ltd
	G-BHIW	—	
	G-BHIY	Cessna F.150K	W. H. Cole
	G-BHIZ	PA-31 Navajo	L. J. Steward/Kidlington
	G-BHJA	Cessna A.152	Hartmann Ltd/Ronaldsway
	G-BHJB	Cessna A.152	E. E. Fenning & Son
	G-BHJF	SOCATA TB.10 Tobago	G. S. Goodsir & ptnrs/Biggin Hill
	G-BHJI	Mooney 20J	T. R. Bamber & B. Refson/Elstree
	G-BHJK	Maule M5-235C Lunar Rocket	G. A. & B. J. Finch
	G-BHJN	Fournier RF-4D	G. G. Milton/Sibson
	G-BHJO	PA-28-161 Warrior II	Nairn Flying Services Ltd/Inverness
	G-BHJP	Partenavia P-68C	Shirlstar Container Transport Ltd/Edinburgh
	G-BHJR	Saffery S.200 balloon	R. S. Sweeting
	G-BHJS	Partenavia P-68B	Fairoaks Aviation Services Ltd/Blackbushe
	G-BHJU	Robin DR.400/2+2	Harlow Transport Services Ltd/Headcorn
	G-BHJW	Cessna F.152	Leicestershire Aero Club Ltd
	G-BHJY	EMB-110P1 Bandeirante	Euroair Transport Ltd/Gatwick
	G-BHJZ	EMB-110P2 Bandeirante	Jersey European Airways
	G-BHKA	Evans VP-1	M. L. Perry
	G-BHKB	Westland-Bell 47G-3B1 (Soloy)	Helinorth Ltd
	G-BHKC	Westland-Bell 47G-3B1 (Soloy)	Heliwork Finance Ltd/Thruxton
	G-BHKE	Bensen B.8MV	V. C. Whitehead
	G-BHKH	Cameron O-65 balloon	D. G. Body
	G-BHKI	Cessna 402C	B. K. Aviation Ltd/Goodwood
	G-BHKJ	Cessna 421C	Northair Aviation Ltd
	G-BHKL	Colt Flying Bottle 1A balloon	J. R. Parkington & Co Ltd
	G-BHKM	Colt 14A balloon	Hot-Air Balloon Co Ltd
	G-BHKN	Colt 14A balloon	Hot-Air Balloon Co Ltd
	G-BHKO	Colt 14A balloon	Hot-Air Balloon Co Ltd
	G-BHKP	Colt 14A balloon	Hot-Air Balloon Co Ltd
	G-BHKR	Colt 14A balloon	Hot-Air Balloon Co Ltd
	G-BHKS	Beech E90 King Air	The Plessey Co Ltd/Stansted
	G-BHKT	Jodel D.112	G. V. Harfield & J. R. Nutter/Thruxton
	G-BHKU	AA-5A Cheetah	Urban & City Properties Ltd/Biggin Hill
	G-BHKV	AA-5A Cheetah	T. & J. Bowers/Doncaster
	G-BHKW	Westland-Bell 47G-3B1	M. Burgin & K. Rix
	G-BHKX	Beech 76 Duchess	R. M. English & Son Ltd
	G-BHKY	Cessna 310R II	Airwork Ltd/Perth
	G-BHLA	Cessna 421C	Stewart Singleton Fabrics Ltd/Cardiff
	G-BHLE	Robin DR.400/180	B. A. Eastwell
	G-BHLF	H.S.125 Srs 700B	The Marconi Co Ltd/Luton
	G-BHLH	Robin DR.400/180	Trinecare Ltd/Southend
	G-BHLI	R. Turbo Commander 690B	Flightline International Ltd/Bournemouth
	G-BHLJ	Saffery-Rigg S.200 balloon	I. A. Rigg
	G-BHLK	GA-7 Cougar	Cougar Flying Group/Prestwick
	G-BHLM	Cessna 421C	Brush Electrical Co Ltd/E. Midlands

Reg.	Type	Owner or Operator	Notes
G-BHLO	Cessna 441	McAlpine Aviation Ltd/Luton	
G-BHLP	Cessna 441	Automobile Association/Coventry	
G-BHLT	D.H.82A Tiger Moth	R. L. Godwin	
G-BHLU	Fournier RF-3	G. G. Milton/Felthorpe	
G-BHLV	CP.301A Emeraude	K. E. Armstrong	
G-BHLW	Cessna 120	Wichita Flying Group	
G-BHLX	AA-5B Tiger	Tiger Aviation Ltd (Jersey)	
G-BHLY	Sikorsky S-76A	Bristow Helicopters Ltd	
G-BHLZ	GY-30 Supercab	C. R. & M. C. Sims/Goodwood	
G-BHMA	SIPA 903	Fairwood Flying Group/Swansea	
G-BHMC	M.S.880B Rallye Club	Trago Stadium Ltd/Bodmin	
G-BHMD	Rand KR-2	W. D. Francis	
G-BHME	WMB.2 Windtracker balloon	I. R. Bell & ptnrs	
G-BHMF	Cessna FA.152	Denham Flying Training School Ltd	
G-BHMG	Cessna FA.152	Denham Flying Training School Ltd	
G-BHMH	Cessna FA.152	Denham Flying Training School Ltd	
G-BHMI	Cessna F.172N	Howard, Richard & Co Ltd/Denham	
G-BHMJ	Avenger T.200-2112 balloon	R. Light *Lord Anthony 1*	
G-BHMK	Avenger T.200-2112 balloon	P. Kinder *Lord Anthony 2*	
G-BHML	Avenger T.200-2112 balloon	L. Caulfield *Lord Anthony 3*	
G-BHMM	Avenger T.200-2112 balloon	M. Murphy *Lord Anthony 4*	
G-BHMO	PA-20M Cerpa Special (Pacer)	J. D. Campbell	
G-BHMR	Stinson 108-3	J. R. Rowell/Sandown	
G-BHMT	Evans VP-1	P. E. J. Sturgeon	
G-BHMU	Colt 21A balloon	J. M. Parkington & Co Ltd	
G-BHMV	Bell 206A JetRanger 2	Bristow Helicopters Ltd	
G-BHMW	F.27 Friendship Mk 200	Air UK/Norwich	
G-BHMX	F.27 Friendship Mk 200	Air UK/Norwich	
G-BHMY	F.27 Friendship Mk 200	Air UK/Norwich	
G-BHMZ	F.27 Friendship Mk 200	Air UK/Norwich	
G-BHNA	Cessna F.152	W. E. B. Wordsword/Stapleford	
G-BHNC	Cameron O-65 balloon	D. & C. Bareford	
G-BHND	Cameron N-65 balloon	Hunter & Sons (Mells) Ltd	
G-BHNE	Boeing 727-2J4	Dan-Air Services Ltd/Gatwick	
G-BHNF	Boeing 727-2J4	Dan-Air Services Ltd/Gatwick	
G-BHNG	PA-23 Aztec 250	Southern Wings Ltd/Guernsey	
G-BHNH	Cessna 404 Titan	Northair Aviation Ltd/Leeds	
G-BHNI	Cessna 404 Titan	Donington Aviation Ltd/E. Midlands	
G-BHNK	Jodel D.120A	G. N. Smith	
G-BHNL	Jodel D.112	J. A. Harding	
G-BHNM	PA-44-180 Seminole	Cearte Tiles Ltd	
G-BHNN	PA-32R-301 Saratoga SP	Messenger Newspaper Group/Manchester	
G-BHNO	PA-28-181 Archer II	Davison Plant Hire Co/Compton Abbas	
G-BHNP	Eiri PIK-20E-1	M. Astley/Husbands Bosworth	
G-BHNR	Cameron N-77 balloon	Bath University Hot-Air Balloon Club	
G-BHNS	PA-28R-201 Arrow III	M. Dukes/Biggin Hill	
G-BHNT	Cessna F.172N	Kestrel Air Services Ltd/Denham	
G-BHNU	Cessna F.172N	B. Swindell (Haulage) Ltd/Barton	
G-BHNV	Westland-Bell 47G-3B1	Leyline Helicopters Ltd	
G-BHNW	—	—	
G-BHNX	Jodel D.117	A. Scott & O. M. Hammond	
G-BHNY	Cessna 425	Sinclair Research Ltd/Cambridge	
G-BHOA	Robin DR.400/160	M. F. Bunn	
G-BHOC	R. Commander 112A	Gordon Davis (Chemists) Ltd/Leicester	
G-BHOE	—	—	
G-BHOF	Sikorsky S-61N	Bristow Helicopters Ltd	
G-BHOG	Sikorsky S-61N	Bristow Helicopters Ltd	
G-BHOH	Sikorsky S-61N	Bristow Helicopters Ltd	
G-BHOI	Westland-Bell 47G-3B1	Helicopter Hire Ltd/Southend	
G-BHOJ	Colt 14A balloon	Hot Air Balloon Co Ltd	
G-BHOL	Jodel DR.1050	B. D. Deubelbeiss/Panshanger	
G-BHOM	PA-18 Super Cub 95	W. J. C. Scrope	
G-BHON	Rango NA.6 balloon	Rango Kite Co *Rosamund Hine*	
G-BHOO	Thunder Ax7-65 balloon	D. Livesey & J. M. Purves *Scraps*	
G-BHOP	Thunder Ax3 balloon	R. G. Griffin & R. Blackwell	
G-BHOR	PA-28-161 Warrior II	H. Young Transport Ltd/Southampton	
G-BHOT	Cameron V-65 balloon	Dante Balloon Group	
G-BHOU	Cameron V-65 balloon	D. I. Gray-Fisk	
G-BHOW	Beech 95-58P Baron	Anglo-African Machinery Ltd/Birmingham	

99

Notes	Reg.	Type	Owner or Operator
	G-BHOZ	SOCATA TB.9 Tampico	J. R. Bone/Bournemouth
	G-BHPJ	Eagle Microlite	G. Breen/Enstone
	G-BHPK	Piper J-3C-65 Cub (479865)	J. A. Verlander/Wellesbourne
	G-BHPL	C.A.S.A. 1.131 Jungmann	M. G. Jefferies
	G-BHPM	PA-18 Super Cub 95	P. Morgans
	G-BHPO	Colt 14A balloon	C. Boxall
	G-BHPS	Jodel D.120A	C. J. & S. E. Francis/Swansea
	G-BHPT	Piper J-3C-65 Cub	Anvil Aviation Ltd
	G-BHPV	Cessna U.206G	Balfour Beatty Construction Ltd/ Biggin Hill
	G-BHPX	Cessna 152	A. G. Chrismas Ltd/Shoreham
	G-BHPY	Cessna 152	Wickwell (UK) Ltd/Southampton
	G-BHPZ	Cessna 172N	O'Brian Properties Ltd/Shoreham
	G-BHRA	R. Commander 114A	Anglian Double Glazing Co Ltd/ Norwich
	G-BHRB	Cessna F.152	Light Planes (Lancashire) Ltd/Barton
	G-BHRC	PA-28-161 Warrior II	Sherwood Flying Club Ltd/Tollerton
	G-BHRD	D.H.C.1 Chipmunk 22 (WP977)	B. C. Heywood & ptnrs/ Hinton-in-the-Hedges
	G-BHRE	Persephone S.200 balloon	Cupro-Sapphire Ltd
	G-BHRF	Airborne Industries AB400 gas balloon	Balloon Stable Ltd
	G-BHRG	—	
	G-BHRH	Cessna FA.150K	Merlin Flying Club Ltd/E. Midlands
	G-BHRI	Saffery S.200 balloon	Cupro-Sapphire Ltd *Can-Can*
	G-BHRM	Cessna F.152	Channel Islands Aero Club (Guernsey) Ltd
	G-BHRN	Cessna F.152	Channel Islands Aero Holdings Ltd/ Jersey
	G-BHRO	R. Commander 112A	John Raymond Transport Ltd/Cardiff
	G-BHRP	PA-44-180 Seminole	Rosemount Aviation/Biggin Hill
	G-BHRR	CP.301A Emeraude	W. H. Cole
	G-BHRS	ICA IS-28M2	British Aerospace Aircraft Group/ Woodford
	G-BHRU	Saffery S.1000 balloon	Cupro-Sapphire Ltd *Petunia*
	G-BHRV	Mooney M.20J	Tecnovil Equipamentos Industriales
	G-BHRW	Jodel DR.221	J. T. M. Ball/Redhill
	G-BHRY	Colt 56A balloon	Hot Air Balloon Co Ltd
	G-BHSA	Cessna 152	Skyviews & General Ltd/Sherburn
	G-BHSB	Cessna 172N	W. R. Craddock & Son Ltd/Sturgate
	G-BHSC	—	
	G-BHSD	Scheibe SF.25E Super Falke	Lasham Gliding Soc Ltd
	G-BHSE	R. Commander 114	B.C.C. (Decorations) Ltd/Staverton
	G-BHSF	AA-5A Cheetah	D.S. Plant Hire Ltd (G-BHAS)
	G-BHSG	AB-206A JetRanger	Specialist Flying Training Ltd/Hamble
	G-BHSI	Jodel D.9	J. H. Betton
	G-BHSL	C.A.S.A. 1.131 Jungmann	Cotswold Flying Group/Staverton
	G-BHSM	AB-206B JetRanger 2	Dollar Air Services Ltd/Coventry
	G-BHSN	Cameron N-56 balloon	Ballooning Endeavours Ltd
	G-BHSP	Thunder Ax7-77Z balloon	Chicago Instruments Ltd
	G-BHSR	—	
	G-BHSS	Pitts S-1C Special	J. Eisdon-Davies/Bembridge
	G-BHST	Hughes 369D	Abbey Hill Vehicle Services
	G-BHSU	H.S.125 Srs 700B	Shell Aircraft Ltd/Heathrow
	G-BHSV	H.S.125 Srs 700B	Shell Aircraft Ltd/Heathrow
	G-BHSW	H.S.125 Srs 700B	Shell Aircraft Ltd/Heathrow
	G-BHSX	—	
	G-BHSY	Jodel DR.1050	S. R. Orwin & T. R. Allebone
	G-BHSZ	Cessna 152	Millet Shipping Ltd/Coventry
	G-BHTA	PA-28-236 Dakota	Stenloss Ltd/Sywell
	G-BHTB	Monnet Sonerai II	R. H. Thring
	G-BHTC	Jodel DR.1050/M1	T. A. Carpenter/Popham
	G-BHTD	Cessna T.188C AgHusky	Dallah-ADS Ltd
	G-BHTF	Enstrom F-28C-UK	Southern Air/Shoreham
	G-BHTG	Thunder Ax6-56 balloon	F. R. & Mrs S. H. MacDonald
	G-BHTH	T-6G Texan (2807)	Keenair Services Ltd/Liverpool
	G-BHTI	SA.102.5 Cavalier	R. Cochrane
	G-BHTK	D.H.C.-6 Twin Otter 310	Loganair Ltd/Glasgow
	G-BHTM	Cameron 80 Can SS balloon	BP Oil Ltd
	G-BHTO	—	
	G-BHTP	PA-31T-500 Cheyenne I	Ugland (UK) Ltd

Reg.	Type	Owner or Operator	Notes
G-BHTR	Bell 206B JetRanger 3	J. S. Bloor Ltd	
G-BHTT	Cessna 500 Citation	Lucas Industries Ltd/Birmingham	
G-BHTV	Cessna 310R	Air Atlantique Ltd/Jersey	
G-BHTW	Cessna FR.172J	Apollo Manufacturing (Derby) Ltd/ E. Midlands	
G-BHUB	Douglas C-47 (315509)	Imperial War Museum/Duxford	
G-BHUE	Jodel DR.1050	G. A. Mason	
G-BHUF	PA-18-150 Super Cub	T. A. McMullin/Dunstable	
G-BHUG	Cessna 172N	B. Giles/Barton	
G-BHUH	Cremer PC.14 balloon	P. A. Cremer	
G-BHUI	Cessna 152	J. MacDonald	
G-BHUJ	Cessna 172N	Three Counties Aero Club Ltd/ Blackbushe	
G-BHUL	Beech E90 King Air	Cega Aviation Ltd (G-BBKM)/Goodwood	
G-BHUM	D.H.82A Tiger Moth	S. G. Towers	
G-BHUN	PZL-104 Wilga 35	W. Radwanski/Booker	
G-BHUO	Evans VP-2	R. A. Povall	
G-BHUP	Cessna F.152	Light Planes (Lancs) Ltd/Barton	
G-BHUR	Thunder Ax3 balloon	B. F. G. Ribbons	
G-BHUU	PA-25 Pawnee 235	Farmwork Services (Eastern) Ltd	
G-BHUV	PA-25 Pawnee 235	Farmwork Services (Eastern) Ltd	
G-BHVA	—		
G-BHVB	PA-28-161 Warrior II	Norwich Air Training Ltd	
G-BHVC	Cessna 172RG Cutlass	Ian Willis Publicity Ltd/Panshanger	
G-BHVE	Saffery S.330 balloon	P. M. Randles	
G-BHVF	Jodel D.150A	C. A. Parker/Sywell	
G-BHVG	Boeing 737-2T5	Orion Airways Ltd/E. Midlands	
G-BHVH	Boeing 737-2T5	Orion Airways Ltd/E. Midlands	
G-BHVI	Boeing 737-2T5	Orion Airways Ltd/E. Midlands	
G-BHVM	Cessna 152	K. R. Whyham/Blackpool	
G-BHVN	Cessna 152	Three Counties Aero Club Ltd/ Blackbushe	
G-BHVP	Cessna 182Q	Air Tows/Lasham	
G-BHVR	Cessna 172N	F. & S. E. Horridge	
G-BHVS	Enstrom F-28A-UK	Southern Air Ltd/Shoreham	
G-BHVT	Boeing 727-212	Dan-Air Services Ltd/Gatwick	
G-BHVU	Cessna 414A	Stewart Air Ltd/Elstree	
G-BHVV	Piper J-3C-65 Cub	I. S. Hodge	
G-BHVY	AA-5B Tiger	Track Z Ltd/Elstree	
G-BHVZ	Cessna 180	R. Moore/Blackpool	
G-BHWA	Cessna F.152	Wickenby Aviation Ltd	
G-BHWB	Cessna F.152	Wickenby Aviation Ltd	
G-BHWE	Boeing 737-204ADV	Britannia Airways Ltd *Sir Sidney Camm*/ Luton	
G-BHWF	Boeing 737-204ADV	Britannia Airways Ltd *Lord Brabazon of Tara*/Luton	
G-BHWG	Mahatma S.200SR balloon	H. W. Gandy *Spectrum*	
G-BHWH	Weedhopper JC-24A	G. A. Clephane	
G-BHWK	M.S.880B Rallye Club	T. M. W. Webster & ptnrs/Pershore	
G-BHWL	—		
G-BHWN	WMB.3 Windtracker 200 balloon	C. J. Dodd & G. J. Luckett	
G-BHWO	WMB.4 Windtracker II balloon	C. J. Dodd	
G-BHWR	AA-5A Cheetah	Gulfstream School of Flying Ltd/ Denham	
G-BHWS	Cessna F.152	Shirlstar Container Transport Ltd/ Stapleford	
G-BHWW	Cessna U.206G	Sir G. P. Grant-Suttie/E. Fortune	
G-BHWY	PA-28R-200 Cherokee Arrow	Marplane Ltd/Barton	
G-BHWZ	PA-28-181 Archer II	Symtec Computer Service Ltd	
G-BHXD	Jodel D.120	P. R. Powell/Shobdon	
G-BHXE	Thunder Ax3 balloon	C. Benning	
G-BHXG	D.H.C.-6 Twin Otter 310	Loganair Ltd/Glasgow	
G-BHXI	BN-2B Islander	Euroair Transport Ltd/Biggin Hill	
G-BHXJ	Nord 1203/2 Norecrin	R. E. Coates/Popham	
G-BHXK	PA-28 Cherokee 140	I. R. F. Hammond	
G-BHXL	Evans VP-2	J. J. Fitzgerald	
G-BHXN	Van's RV.3	P. R. Hing	
G-BHXO	Colt 14A balloon	Colt Balloons Ltd	
G-BHXP	—		
G-BHXR	Thunder Ax7-65 balloon	Thunder Balloons Ltd	

Notes	Reg.	Type	Owner or Operator
	G-BHXS	Jodel D.120	K. Fox & J. Smith/Fenland
	G-BHXT	Thunder Ax6-56Z balloon	Ocean Traffic Services Ltd
	G-BHXU	AB-206B JetRanger 3	Castle Air Charters Ltd
	G-BHXX	PA-23 Aztec 250	R. Walker (Food Merchants) Ltd
	G-BHXY	Piper J-3C-65 Cub	D. S. Morgan
	G-BHYA	Cessna R.182RG II	MLP Aviation Ltd/Elstree
	G-BHYB	Sikorsky S-76A	British Airways Helicopters Ltd/Beccles
	G-BHYC	Cessna 172RG Cutlass	TDS Circuits (Blackburn) Ltd/Blackpool
	G-BHYD	Cessna R.172K XP	Sylmar Aviation Services Ltd
	G-BHYE	PA-34-200T-2 Seneca	C.S.E. Aviation Ltd/Kidlington
	G-BHYF	PA-34-200T-2 Seneca	C.S.E. Aviation Ltd/Kidlington
	G-BHYG	PA-34-200T-2 Seneca	C.S.E. Aviation Ltd/Kidlington
	G-BHYI	Stampe SV-4A	D. E. Starkey & M. Heudebourck/Booker
	G-BHYN	Evans VP-2	A. B. Cameron
	G-BHYO	Cameron N-77 balloon	C. Sisson
	G-BHYP	Cessna F.172M	J. Burgess & ptnrs/Barton
	G-BHYR	Cessna F.172M	J. Lloyd
	G-BHYS	PA-28-181 Archer II	Minstrel Kitchens Ltd/Tollerton
	G-BHYT	EMB-110P2 Bandeirante	Genair/Humberside
	G-BHYU	Beech A200 Super King Air	Kenton Utilities & Developments Ltd/ Tees-side
	G-BHYV	Evans VP-1	L. Chiappi
	G-BHYW	AB-206B JetRanger	Gleneagles Helicopter Services (Scotland) Ltd
	G-BHYX	Cessna 152	Tradecliff Ltd/Blackbushe
	G-BHZA	Piper J-3C-65 Cub	A. J. Hyatt & J. R. Wraight
	G-BHZD	PA-38-112 Tomahawk	Cormack (Aircraft Services) Ltd/Glasgow
	G-BHZE	PA-28-181 Archer II	E. O. Smith & Co Ltd
	G-BHZF	Evans VP-2	D. Silsbury
	G-BHZG	Monnet Sonerai II	R. A. Gardiner & B. Chapman/Prestwick
	G-BHZH	Cessna F.152	Shoreham Flight Simulation Ltd/ Bournemouth
	G-BHZI	Thunder Ax3 balloon	Thunder Balloons Ltd
	G-BHZJ	Hughes Stratosphere 150 balloon	P. J. Hughes
	G-BHZK	AA-5B Tiger	Achandunie Farming Co
	G-BHZL	AA-5A Cheetah	N. London Flying Club Ltd
	G-BHZM	Jodel DR.1050	G. H. Wylde/Manchester
	G-BHZN	AA-5B Tiger	Peacock Salt Ltd/Halfpenny Green
	G-BHZO	AA-5A Cheetah	Peacock Salt Ltd/Glasgow
	G-BHZU	Piper J-3C-65 Cub	J. K. Tomkinson
	G-BHZV	Jodel D.120A	W. C. Forster/Popham
	G-BHZX	Thunder Ax7-65A balloon	Thermark (Plastic Processing) Ltd
	G-BHZY	Monnet Sonerai II	C. A. Keech
	G-BIAA	SOCATA TB.9 Tampico	O. G. Owen
	G-BIAB	SOCATA TB.9 Tampico	Meridian Aviation/Biggin Hill
	G-BIAC	M.S.894E Rallye Minerva	Brencham Ltd
	G-BIAH	Jodel D.112	M. N. Mahony
	G-BIAI	WMB.2 Windtracker balloon	I. Chadwick
	G-BIAK	SOCATA TB.10 Tobago	Trent Combustion Components Ltd/ E. Midlands
	G-BIAL	Rango NA.8 balloon	A. M. Lindsay
	G-BIAO	Evans VP-2	J. Stephenson/Tees-side
	G-BIAP	PA-16 Clipper	I. M. Callier & P. J. Bish/White Waltham
	G-BIAR	Rigg Skyliner II balloon	I. A. Rigg
	G-BIAT	Sopwith Pup Replica	G. A. Black
	G-BIAU	Sopwith Pup Replica ★ (N6452)	Whitehall Theatre of War
	G-BIAV	Sikorsky S-76A	British Airways Helicopters Ltd/ Aberdeen
	G-BIAW	Sikorsky S-76A	British Airways Helicopters Ltd/ Aberdeen
	G-BIAX	Taylor JT.2 Titch	G. F. Rowley
	G-BIAY	AA-5 Traveler	Brackley Motors Ltd/ Hinton-in-the-Hedges
	G-BIBA	SOCATA TB.9 Tampico	Channel Aviation Ltd/Guernsey
	G-BIBB	Mooney M.20C	Gloucestershire Flying Club/Staverton
	G-BIBC	Cessna 310R	Airwork Ltd/Perth
	G-BIBD	Rotec Rally 2B	A. Clarke/Sturgate
	G-BIBE	EMB-110P1 Bandeirante	Loganair Ltd/Glasgow
	G-BIBF	Smith A12 Sport balloon	T. J. Smith

Reg.	Type	Owner or Operator	Notes
G-BIBG	Sikorsky S-76A	British Caledonian Helicopters Ltd/ Aberdeen	
G-BIBJ	Enstrom F-280C-UK Shark	W. W. Kedrick & Sons Ltd/ Halfpenny Green	
G-BIBK	Taylor JT.2 Titch	T. Corbett	
G-BIBL	Taylor JT.2 Titch	J. Sharp	
G-BIBM	AA-5A Cheetah	J. Apthorp Aviation & Leasing/ Leavesden	
G-BIBN	Cessna FA.150K	P. H. Lewis	
G-BIBO	Cameron V-65 balloon	Southern Balloon Group	
G-BIBP	AA-5A Cheetah	Peacock Salt Ltd/Glasgow	
G-BIBS	Cameron P-20 balloon	Cameron Balloons Ltd	
G-BIBT	AA-5B Tiger	Fergusons (Blyth) Ltd	
G-BIBU	Morris Ax7-77 balloon	K. Morris	
G-BIBV	WMB.3 Windtracker balloon	P. B. Street	
G-BIBW	Cessna F.172N	Deltair Ltd/Liverpool	
G-BIBX	WMB.2 Windtracker balloon	I. A. Rigg	
G-BIBY	Beech F33A Bonanza	Carl Peterson Ltd/Bournemouth	
G-BIBZ	Thunder Ax3 balloon	F. W. Barnes	
G-BICA	—		
G-BICB	Rotec Rally 2B	J. D. Lye & A. P. Jones	
G-BICC	Vulture Tx3 balloon	C. P. Clitheroe	
G-BICD	Auster 5	J. A. S. Baldry & ptnrs	
G-BICE	AT-6C Harvard IIA	C. M. L. Edwards	
G-BICF	GA-7 Cougar	Apollo Leasing Ltd/Glasgow	
G-BICG	Cessna F.152	R. M. Clarke/Coventry	
G-BICI	Cameron R-833 balloon	Ballooning Endeavours Ltd	
G-BICJ	Monnet Sonerai II	J. R. S. Heaton	
G-BICM	Colt 56A balloon	T. A. R. & S. Turner	
G-BICN	F.8L Falco	R. J. Barber	
G-BICO	Neal Mitefly balloon	T. J. Neale	
G-BICP	Robin DR.360	I. H. Thompson/Coventry	
G-BICR	Jodel D.120A	S. W. C. Hall & ptnrs/Redhill	
G-BICS	Robin R.2100A	Tredair/Cardiff	
G-BICT	Evans VP-1	A. S. Coombe & D. L. Tribe	
G-BICU	Cameron V-56 balloon	I. S. Clark	
G-BICW	PA-28-161 Warrior II	Fastraven Ltd/Luton	
G-BICX	Maule M5-235C Lunar Rocket	Sexton & Sons	
G-BICY	PA-23 Apache 160	Allen Technical Services Ltd/Luton	
G-BIDA	SOCATA Rallye Club 100ST	B. R. Spooner/Fairoaks	
G-BIDB	BAe 167 Strikemaster	British Aerospace/Bournemouth	
G-BIDD	Evans VP-1	A. R. Bender	
G-BIDE	CP.301A Emeraude	D. Elliott	
G-BIDF	Cessna F.172P	Horizon Flying Club/Ipswich	
G-BIDG	Jodel D.150A	D. R. Gray	
G-BIDH	Cessna 152	Birmingham Aerocentre Ltd	
G-BIDI	PA-28R-201 Arrow III	M. J. Webb/Birmingham	
G-BIDJ	PA-18-150 Super Cub	Marchington Gliding Club	
G-BIDK	PA-18-150 Super Cub	Holding & Barnes Ltd	
G-BIDM	Cessna F.172H	J. F. Packaging/Ingoldmells	
G-BIDN	P-57 Sea Prince T.1 (WF133)	Atlantic & Caribbean Aviation Ltd/ Staverton	
G-BIDO	CP.301A Emeraude	N. B. Gray/Barton	
G-BIDP	PA-28-181 Archer II	MAP Aviation Ltd	
G-BIDR	—		
G-BIDT	Cameron A375 balloon	Ballooning Endeavours Ltd	
G-BIDU	Cameron V-77 balloon	E. Eleazor	
G-BIDV	Colt 14A balloon	International Distillers & Vintners (House Trade) Ltd	
G-BIDW	Sopwith 1½ Strutter replica (A8226)	RAF Museum	
G-BIDX	Jodel D.112	H. N. Nuttall & R. P. Walley	
G-BIDY	WMB.2 Windtracker balloon	D. M. Campion	
G-BIDZ	Colt 21A balloon	Hot Air Balloon Co Ltd	
G-BIEB	Agusta-Bell 47G-3B1	Agricopters Ltd	
G-BIEC	AB-206A JetRanger 2	Autair Helicopters Ltd/Luton	
G-BIED	Beech F90 King Air	United Biscuits (Foods) Ltd/Denham	
G-BIEF	Cameron V-77 balloon	D. S. Bush	
G-BIEH	Sikorsky S-76A	Management Aviation Ltd/Bourn	
G-BIEJ	Sikorsky S-76A	Bristow Helicopters Ltd	
G-BIEK	WMB.4 Windtracker balloon	P. B. Street	

Notes	Reg.	Type	Owner or Operator
	G-BIEL	WMB.4 Windtracker balloon	A. T. Walden
	G-BIEM	D.H.C.-6 Twin Otter 310	Loganair Ltd/Glasgow
	G-BIEN	Jodel D.120A	J. C. Mansell & R. V. Smith
	G-BIEO	Jodel D.112	P. Bourne/Sibson
	G-BIER	Rutan Long-Eze	V. Mossor
	G-BIES	Maule M5-235C Lunar Rocket	William Proctor Farms
	G-BIET	Cameron O-77 balloon	G. M. Westley
	G-BIEV	AA-5A Cheetah	Abraxas Aviation Ltd/Denham
	G-BIEW	Cessna U.206G	G. D. Atkinson/Guernsey
	G-BIEX	Andreasson BA-4B	H. P. Burrill/Sherburn
	G-BIEY	PA-28-151 Warrior	Noblair Ltd
	G-BIEZ	Beech F90 King Air	Eagle Aircraft Services Ltd/Leavesden
	G-BIFA	Cessna 310R-II	Land & Estates Consultants Ltd/ Biggin Hill
	G-BIFB	PA-28 Cherokee 150	C. J. Reed/Elstree
	G-BIFC	Colt 14A balloon	Colt Balloons Ltd
	G-BIFD	R. Commander 114	D. H. MacDonald
	G-BIFE	Cessna A.185F	Conguess Aviation Ltd/Conington
	G-BIFF	AA-5A Cheetah	Mission Control Music Ltd/Elstree
	G-BIFM	—	—
	G-BIFN	Bensen B.8M	K. Willows
	G-BIFO	Evans VP-1	P. Raggett/Filton
	G-BIFP	Colt 56C balloon	J. Philp
	G-BIFT	Cessna F.150L	Leaf Puma Ltd/Cranfield
	G-BIFU	Short Skyhawk balloon	D. K. Short
	G-BIFV	Jodel D.150	J. H. Kirkham/Barton
	G-BIFW	Scruggs BL.2 Wunda balloon	D. Morris
	G-BIFY	Cessna F.150L	Leaf Puma Ltd/Cranfield
	G-BIFZ	Partenavia P.68C	Abbey Hill Vehicle Services
	G-BIGB	Bell 212	Bristow Helicopters Ltd
	G-BIGC	Cameron O-42 balloon	C. M. Moroney
	G-BIGD	Cameron V-77 balloon	D. L. Clark
	G-BIGE	Champion Cloudseeker balloon	A. Foster
	G-BIGF	Thunder Ax7-77 balloon	M. D. Stever & C. A. Allen
	G-BIGG	Saffery S.200 balloon	R. S. Sweeting
	G-BIGH	Piper L-4H Cub	R. Warwick
	G-BIGI	Mooney M.20J	Melinco Marketing (Jersey) Ltd
	G-BIGJ	Cessna F.172M	Essex Aero Services Ltd/Southend
	G-BIGK	Taylorcraft BC-12D	J. Rowell/Sandown
	G-BIGL	Cameron O-65 balloon	A. H. K. Olpin *Scorpio*
	G-BIGM	Avenger T.200-2112 balloon	M. Murphy
	G-BIGN	Attic Srs 1 balloon	G. Nettleship
	G-BIGP	Bensen B.8M	R. H. S. Cooper
	G-BIGR	Avenger T.200-2112 balloon	R. Light
	G-BIGU	Bensen B.8M	J. R. Martin
	G-BIGX	Bensen B.8M	J. R. Martin
	G-BIGY	Cameron V-65 balloon	Dante Balloon Group
	G-BIGZ	Scheibe SF.25B Falke	K. Ballington
	G-BIHB	Scruggs BL.2 Wunda balloon	D. Morris
	G-BIHC	Scruggs BL.2 Wunda balloon	P. D. Kiddell
	G-BIHD	Robin DR.400/160	G. R. Pope & ptnrs/Biggin Hill
	G-BIHE	Cessna FA.152	Inverness Flying Services Ltd
	G-BIHF	SE-5A Replica	K. J. Garrett
	G-BIHG	PA-28 Cherokee 140	T. Parmenter/Clacton
	G-BIHH	Sikorsky S-61N	British Caledonian Helicopters Ltd/ Aberdeen
	G-BIHI	Cessna 172M	J. H. A. Rogers/Ingoldmells
	G-BIHN	Skyship 500 airship	Airship Industries Ltd/Cardington
	G-BIHO	D.H.C.-6 Twin Otter 310	Brymon Aviation Ltd/Plymouth
	G-BIHP	Van Den Bemden gas balloon	J. J. Harris
	G-BIHR	WMB.2 Windtracker balloon	A. F. Langhelt
	G-BIHT	PA-17 Vagabond	G. D. Thomson/Wellesbourne
	G-BIHU	Saffery S.200 balloon	A. F. Langhelt
	G-BIHV	WMB.2 Windtracker balloon	T. H. W. Bradley
	G-BIHW	Aeronca A65TAC (2-7767)	W. F. Crozier & ptnrs/Glasgow
	G-BIHX	Bensen B.8M	C. C. Irvine
	G-BIHY	Isaacs Fury	D. E. Olivant
	G-BIIA	Fournier RF-3	M. K. Field/Enstone
	G-BIIB	Cessna F.172M	S. L. Hawkins/Biggin Hill
	G-BIIC	Scruggs BL.2 Wunda balloon	S. J. Hodder & D. Cockerill
	G-BIID	PA-18 Super Cub 95	The Tiger Zlin Group/Farnborough

Reg.	Type	Owner or Operator	Notes
G-BIIE	Cessna F.172P	Shoreham Flight Simulation Ltd/ Bournemouth	
G-BIIF	Fournier RF-4D	A. P. Walsh (G-BVET)/Swanton Morley	
G-BIIG	Thunder Ax-6-56Z balloon	The Larter Group Ltd	
G-BIIH	Scruggs BL.2T Turbo balloon	B. M. Scott	
G-BIIJ	Cessna F.152	Leicestershire Aero Club Ltd	
G-BIIK	M.S.883 Rallye 115	H. Russell & ptnrs	
G-BIIL	Thunder Ax6-56 balloon	G. W. Reader	
G-BIIM	Scruggs BL.2A Wunda balloon	K. D. Head	
G-BIIT	PA-28-161 Warrior II	Tayside Aviation Ltd/Dundee	
G-BIIV	PA-28-181 Archer II	Stratton Motor Co Ltd/Seething	
G-BIIW	Rango NA.10 balloon	Rango Kite Co	
G-BIIX	Rango NA.12 balloon	Rango Kite Co	
G-BIIZ	Great Lakes 2T-1A Sport Trainer	Hon P. Lindsay/Booker	
G-BIJA	Scruggs BL.2A Wunda balloon	P. L. E. Bennett	
G-BIJB	PA-18-150 Super Cub	Essex Gliding Club/North Weald	
G-BIJC	AB-206A JetRanger	Specialist Flying Training Ltd/ Hamble	
G-BIJD	Bo 208C Junior	D. J. Dulborough/Redhill	
G-BIJE	Piper L-4A Cub	J. H. T. Davies & ptnrs	
G-BIJS	Luton LA-4A Minor	I. J. Smith	
G-BIJT	AA-5A Cheetah	G. W. Plowman & Son Ltd	
G-BIJU	CP.301A Emeraude	C. J. Norman & M. Howard (G-BHTX)/ Fairoaks	
G-BIJV	Cessna F.152	Civil Service Flying Club Ltd/ Biggin Hill	
G-BIJW	Cessna F.152	Civil Service Flying Club Ltd/ Biggin Hill	
G-BIJX	Cessna F.152	Civil Service Flying Club Ltd/ Biggin Hill	
G-BIJZ	Skyventurer Mk 1 balloon	R. Sweeting	
G-BIKA	Boeing 757-236	British Airways *Dover Castle*/ Heathrow	
G-BIKB	Boeing 757-236	British Airways *Windsor Castle*/ Heathrow	
G-BIKC	Boeing 757-236	British Airways *Edinburgh Castle*/ Heathrow	
G-BIKD	Boeing 757-236	British Airways *Caernarvon Castle*/ Heathrow	
G-BIKE	PA-28R Cherokee Arrow 200	R. V. Webb Ltd	
G-BIKF	Boeing 757-236	British Airways *Carrikfergus Castle*/ Heathrow	
G-BIKG	Boeing 757-236	British Airways *Stirling Castle*/ Heathrow	
G-BIKH	Boeing 757-236	British Airways *Richmond Castle*/ Heathrow	
G-BIKI	Boeing 757-236	British Airways *Tintagel Castle*/ Heathrow	
G-BIKJ	Boeing 757-236	British Airways *Conway Castle*/ Heathrow	
G-BIKK	Boeing 757-236	British Airways *Eilean Donan Castle*/ Heathrow	
G-BIKL	Boeing 757-236	British Airways *Nottingham Castle*/ Heathrow	
G-BIKM	Boeing 757-236	British Airways *Glamis Castle*/ Heathrow	
G-BIKN	Boeing 757-236	British Airways *Bodiam Castle*/ Heathrow	
G-BIKO	Boeing 757-236	British Airways *Enniskillen Castle*/ Heathrow	
G-BIKP	Boeing 757-236	British Airways *Corfe Castle*/ Heathrow	
G-BIKR	Boeing 757-236	British Airways *Braemar Castle*/ Heathrow	
G-BIKS	Boeing 757-236	British Airways *Carrisbrooke Castle*/ Heathrow	
G-BILA	Daletol DM.165L Viking	R. Lamplough/Duxford	
G-BILB	WMB.2 Windtracker balloon	A. F. Langhelt	
G-BILE	Scruggs BL.2B balloon	P. D. Ridout	
G-BILF	Practavia Sprite 125	G. Harfield	
G-BILG	Scruggs BL.2B balloon	P. D. Ridout	

Notes	Reg.	Type	Owner or Operator
	G-BILI	Piper J-3C-65 Cub	A. Dodd/Cranwell
	G-BILJ	Cessna FA.152	Shoreham Flight Simulation Ltd/ Bournemouth
	G-BILK	Cessna FA.152	A. Blair
	G-BILL	PA-25 Pawnee 235	Bowker Air Services Ltd/Rush Green
	G-BILP	Cessna 152	Skyviews & General Ltd
	G-BILR	Cessna 152	Skyviews & General Ltd
	G-BILS	Cessna 152	Skyviews & General Ltd
	G-BILT	Cessna F.172P	Denham Flying Training School Ltd
	G-BILU	Cessna 172RG	Propex (UK) Ltd
	G-BILX	Colt 31A balloon	Hot Air Balloon Co Ltd
	G-BILZ	Taylor JT.1 Monoplane	G. Beaumont
	G-BIMK	Tiger T.200 Srs 1 balloon	M. K. Baron
	G-BIML	Turner Super T.40A	R. T. Callow
	G-BIMM	PA-18 Super Cub 135	D. S. & I. M. Morgan
	G-BIMN	Steen Skybolt	C. R. Williamson
	G-BIMO	Stampe SV-4C	R. K. G. Hannington/Middle Wallop
	G-BIMT	Cessna FA.152	Staverton Flying Services Ltd
	G-BIMU	Sikorsky S-61N	British Caledonian Helicopters Ltd/ Aberdeen
	G-BIMW	D.H.C.-6 Twin Otter 310	Metropolitan Airways/Bournemouth
	G-BIMX	Rutan Vari-Eze	A. S. Knowles
	G-BIMZ	Beech 76 Duchess	Barrein Engineers Ltd/Lulsgate
	G-BINA	Saffery S.9 balloon	A. P. Bashford
	G-BINB	WMB.2A Windtracker balloon	S. R. Woolfries
	G-BINC	Tour de Calais balloon	Cupro Sapphire Ltd
	G-BIND	M.S.894E Rallye 235	G. Archer
	G-BINE	Scruggs BL.2A Wunda balloon	M. Gilbey
	G-BINF	Saffery S.200 balloon	T. Lewis
	G-BING	Cessna F.172P	J. E. M. Patrick/Humberside
	G-BINH	D.H.82A Tiger Moth	Arrow Air Services (Engineering) Ltd/ Felthorpe
	G-BINI	Scruggs BL.2C balloon	S. W. Woolfries
	G-BINJ	Rango NA.12 balloon	M. R. Haslam
	G-BINL	Scruggs BL.2B balloon	P. D. Ridout
	G-BINM	Scruggs BL.2B balloon	P. D. Ridout
	G-BINN	Unicorn UE.1A balloon	Unicorn Group
	G-BINO	Evans VP-1	J. I. Visser
	G-BINR	Unicorn UE.1A balloon	Unicorn Group
	G-BINS	Unicorn UE.2A balloon	Unicorn Group
	G-BINT	Unicorn UE.1A balloon	Unicorn Group
	G-BINU	Saffery S.200 balloon	T. Lewis
	G-BINV	Saffery S.200 balloon	R. S. Harris
	G-BINW	Scruggs BL.2B balloon	P. G. Mackin
	G-BINX	Scruggs BL.2B balloon	P. D. Ridout
	G-BINY	Oriental balloon	J. L. Morton
	G-BINZ	Rango NA.8 balloon	T. J. Sweeting & M. O. Davies
	G-BIOA	Hughes 369D	Weetabix Ltd/Sywell
	G-BIOB	Cessna F.172P	Hunting Surveys & Consultants Ltd
	G-BIOC	Cessna F.150L	T. E. Abell
	G-BIOI	Jodel DR.1051-M	R. Cochrane/Stapleford
	G-BIOJ	R. Commander 112TCA	N. J. Orr/Denham
	G-BIOK	Cessna F.152	Hartmann Ltd/Booker
	G-BIOL	Colt 77A balloon	Colt Balloons Ltd
	G-BIOM	Cessna F.152	Shetland Flying Club
	G-BION	Cameron V-77 balloon	Elliott's Pharmacy Ltd
	G-BIOO	Unicorn UE.2B balloon	Unicorn Group
	G-BIOP	Scruggs BL.2D balloon	J. P. S. Donnellan
	G-BIOR	M.S.880B Rallye Club	C. R. Galloway/Kidlington
	G-BIOS	Scruggs BL.2B balloon	D. Eaves
	G-BIOT	Bensen B.8M	M. W. & J. A. Joynes
	G-BIOU	Jodel D.117A	M. S. Printing & Graphics Machinery Ltd/Booker
	G-BIOW	Slingsby T.67A	Slingsby Aviation Ltd/Kirkbymoorside
	G-BIOX	Potter Crompton PRO.1 balloon	G. M. Potter
	G-BIOY	PAC-14 Special Shape balloon	P. A. Cremer
	G-BIPA	AA-5B Tiger	J. Campbell/Barrow
	G-BIPB	Weedhopper JC-24B	E. H. Moroney
	G-BIPC	PAC-14 Hefferlump balloon	P. A. Cremer
	G-BIPF	Scruggs BL.2C balloon	D. Morris

Reg.	Type	Owner or Operator	Notes
G-BIPG	Global Mini balloon	P. Globe	
G-BIPH	Scruggs BL.2B balloon	C. M. Dewsnap	
G-BIPI	Everett Blackbird Mk 1	R. J. Everett (Engineering) Ltd	
G-BIPJ	PA-36-375 Brave	G. B. Pearce/Shoreham	
G-BIPK	Saffery S.200 balloon	P. J. Kelsey	
G-BIPL	AA-5A Cheetah	Parspex Ltd/Denham	
G-BIPM	Flamboyant Ax7-65 balloon	Pepsi Cola International Ltd	
G-BIPN	Fournier RF-3	Syerston Soaring Group	
G-BIPO	Mudry/CAARP CAP.20LS-200	Personal Plane Services Ltd/Booker	
G-BIPS	SOCATA Rallye 100ST	Operation Sky Quest Ltd	
G-BIPT	Jodel D.112	C. K. Farley/Bournemouth	
G-BIPU	AA-5B Tiger	Aero Group 78/Netherthorpe	
G-BIPV	AA-5B Tiger	I. D. Longfellow/Southampton	
G-BIPW	Avenger T.200-2112 balloon	A. F. Langhelt	
G-BIPX	Saffery S.9 balloon	J. R. Havers	
G-BIPY	Bensen B.8	A. J. Wood	
G-BIPZ	McCandless Mk 4-4	B. McIntyre	
G-BIRA	SOCATA TB.9 Tampico	Goldangel Ltd/Swansea	
G-BIRB	M.S.880B Rallye 100T	E. Smith	
G-BIRD	Pitts S-1C Special	R. N. York/Cranfield	
G-BIRE	Colt 56 Bottle balloon	Hot Air Balloon Co Ltd	
G-BIRG	M.S.880B Rallye Club	Air Touring Services Ltd/Biggin Hill	
G-BIRH	PA-18 Super Cub 135	I. R. F. Hammond/Lee-on-Solent	
G-BIRI	C.A.S.A. 1.131E Jungmann	L. B. Jefferies	
G-BIRK	Avenger T.200-2112 balloon	D. Harland	
G-BIRL	Avenger T.200-2112 balloon	R. Light	
G-BIRM	Avenger T.200-2112 balloon	P. Higgins	
G-BIRN	Short SD3-30	Loganair Ltd/Glasgow	
G-BIRO	Cessna 172P	M. C. Grant/Elstree	
G-BIRP	Arena Mk 17 Skyship balloon	A. S. Viel	
G-BIRS	Cessna 182P	D. P. Cranston (G-BBBS)/Cranfield	
G-BIRT	Robin R.1180TD	W. D'A. Hall/Kidlington	
G-BIRU	H.S.125 Srs 700B	MAM Aviation Ltd/Southampton	
G-BIRV	Bensen B.8MV	R. Hart	
G-BIRW	M.S.505 Criquet (F+IS)	Museum of Flight/E. Fortune	
G-BIRX	Scruggs RS.5000 balloon	J. H. Searle	
G-BIRY	Cameron V-77 balloon	J. J. Winter	
G-BIRZ	Zenair CH.250	B. A. Arnall & M. Hanley	
G-BISA	Hase IIIT balloon	M. A. Hase	
G-BISB	Cessna F.152	Sheffield Aero Club Ltd/Netherthorpe	
G-BISC	Robinson R-22	H. E. Bland/Sywell	
G-BISD	Enstrom F-280C-UK-2	W. H. & J. J. Gadsby	
G-BISF	Robinson R-22	Compuster Ltd	
G-BISG	FRED Srs 3	R. A. Coombe	
G-BISH	Cameron O-42 balloon	Zebedee Balloon Service	
G-BISI	Robinson R-22	Sloane Helicopters Ltd/Luton	
G-BISJ	Cessna 340A	Castle Aviation/Leeds	
G-BISK	R. Commander 112B	Rogers Auto's Ltd/Denham	
G-BISL	Scruggs BL.2B balloon	P. D. Ridout	
G-BISM	Scruggs BL.2B balloon	P. D. Ridout	
G-BISN	Boeing Vertol 234LR Chinook	British Airways Helicopters Ltd/ Aberdeen	
G-BISO	Boeing Vertol 234LR Chinook	British Airways Helicopters Ltd/ Aberdeen	
G-BISP	Boeing Vertol 234LR Chinook	British Airways Helicopters Ltd/ Aberdeen	
G-BISR	Boeing Vertol 234LR Chinook	British Airways Helicopters Ltd/ Aberdeen	
G-BISS	Scruggs BL.2C balloon	P. D. Ridout	
G-BIST	Scruggs BL.2C balloon	P. D. Ridout	
G-BISU	B.170 Freighter 31M	Instone Air Line Ltd/Stansted	
G-BISV	Cameron O-65 balloon	Hylne Rabbits Ltd	
G-BISW	Cameron O-65 balloon	Hylne Rabbits Ltd	
G-BISX	Colt 56A balloon	Long John International Ltd	
G-BISY	Scruggs BL.2C balloon	P. T. Witty	
G-BISZ	Sikorsky S-76A	Bristow Helicopters Ltd	
G-BITA	PA-18-150 Super Cub	V. E. Dickson	
G-BITE	SOCATA TB.10 Tobago	I. M. White/Fairoaks	
G-BITF	Cessna F.152	Bristol & Wessex Aeroplane Club/ Bristol	
G-BITG	Cessna F.152	Bristol & Wessex Aeroplane Club/ Bristol	

Notes	Reg.	Type	Owner or Operator
	G-BITH	Cessna F.152	Bristol & Wessex Aeroplane Club/Bristol
	G-BITI	Scruggs RS.5000 balloon	A. E. Smith
	G-BITK	FRED Srs 2	B. J. Miles
	G-BITL	Horncastle LL-901 balloon	M. J. Worsdell
	G-BITM	Cessna F.172P	Pleusque Ltd/Bournemouth
	G-BITN	Short Albatross balloon	D. K. Short
	G-BITO	Jodel D.112D	A. Dunbar/Barton
	G-BITR	Sikorsky S.76A	Bristow Helicopters Ltd
	G-BITS	Drayton B-56 balloon	M. J. Betts
	G-BITT	Bo 208C Junior	T. R. & E. A. Wiltshire/Popham
	G-BITV	Short SD3-30	—
	G-BITX	Short SD3-30	Guernsey Airlines Ltd
	G-BITY	FD.31T balloon	A. J. Bell
	G-BITZ	Cremer Sandoe PACDS.14 balloon	P. A. Cremer & C. D. Sandoe
	G-BIUE	BN-2A Islander	Pilatus BN Ltd/Bembridge
	G-BIUG	BN-2A Islander	Pilatus BN Ltd/Bembridge
	G-BIUH	BN-2A Islander	Pilatus BN Ltd/Bembridge
	G-BIUI	Cessna F.152	Cleveland Flying School Ltd/Tees-side
	G-BIUL	Cameron 60 SS balloon	Engineering Appliances Ltd
	G-BIUM	Cessna F.152	Sheffield Aero Club Ltd/Netherthorpe
	G-BIUN	Cessna F.152	Sheffield Aero Club Ltd/Netherthorpe
	G-BIUO	R. Commander 112A	K. D. Pryce & C. Hain
	G-BIUP	SNCAN NC.854C	J. A. Coghlan
	G-BIUR	Boeing 727-155C	Dan-Air Services Ltd/Gatwick
	G-BIUT	Scruggs BL.2C balloon	N. J. Ball
	G-BIUU	PA-23 Aztec 250	Kingsmetal Ltd/Lydd
	G-BIUV	H.S.748 Srs 2A	Dan-Air Services Ltd (G-AYYH)/Gatwick
	G-BIUW	PA-28-161 Warrior II	Staeng Ltd/Bodmin
	G-BIUX	PA-28-161 Warrior II	C.S.E. Aviation Ltd/Kidlington
	G-BIUY	PA-28-181 Archer II	Mega Yield Ltd
	G-BIUZ	Slingsby T.67B	Slingsby Aviation Ltd/Kirkbymoorside
	G-BIVA	Robin R.2112	Cotswold Aero Club Ltd/Staverton
	G-BIVB	Jodel D.112	C. & T. Wright/Shoreham
	G-BIVC	Jodel D.112	The Harrier Flying Group
	G-BIVF	CP.301C-3 Emeraude	J. Casker
	G-BIVG	Thunder Ax3 balloon	Thunder Balloons Ltd
	G-BIVI	Cremer PAC.500 airship	P. A. Cremer
	G-BIVJ	Cessna F.152	Wickwell (UK) Ltd/Southampton
	G-BIVK	Bensen B.8	J. G. Toy
	G-BIVL	Bensen B.8	T. E. Davies
	G-BIVO	G.164D Ag-Cat	Miller Aerial Spraying Ltd/Wickenby
	G-BIVR	Featherlight Mk 1 balloon	A. P. Newman & N. P. Kemp
	G-BIVS	Featherlight Mk 2 balloon	J. M. J. Roberts & S. R. Rushton
	G-BIVT	Saffery S.80 balloon	L. F. Guyot
	G-BIVU	AA-5A Cheetah	Rowan Consultants International Ltd
	G-BIVV	AA-5A Cheetah	MLP Aviation Ltd/Elstree
	G-BIVW	Z.326 Trener Master	Tiger Zlin Group/Redhill
	G-BIVX	Saffery S.80 balloon	P. T. Witty
	G-BIVY	Cessna 172N	R. J. Scott/Blackbushe
	G-BIVZ	D.31A Turbulent	N. Jones
	G-BIWA	Stevendon Skyreacher balloon	S. D. Barnes
	G-BIWB	Scruggs RS.5000 balloon	P. D. Ridout
	G-BIWC	Scruggs RS.5000 balloon	P. D. Ridout
	G-BIWD	Scruggs RS.5000 balloon	D. Eaves
	G-BIWE	Scruggs BL.2D balloon	M. D. Saunders
	G-BIWF	Warren balloon	P. D. Ridout
	G-BIWG	Zelenski Mk 2 balloon	P. D. Ridout
	G-BIWH	Cremer Super Fliteliner balloon	G. Lowther
	G-BIWI	Cremer WS.1 balloon	P. A. Cremer
	G-BIWJ	Unicorn UE.1A balloon	A. F. Langhelt
	G-BIWK	Cameron V-65 balloon	I. R. Williams & R. G. Bickerdale
	G-BIWL	PA-32-301 Saratoga	R. Arnold & ptnrs/Staverton

Reg.	Type	Owner or Operator	Notes
G-BIWN	Jodel D.112	E. J. Kemp/Bristol	
G-BIWO	Scruggs RS.5000 balloon	D. Morris	
G-BIWP	Mooney M.20J	Tropair Cooling Ltd/Biggin Hill	
G-BIWR	Mooney M.20F	C. W. Yarnton & J. D. Heykoop/ Redhill	
G-BIWS	Cessna 182R	Rogers Aviation Sales Ltd/ Cranfield	
G-BIWU	Cameron V-65 balloon	J. T. Whicker & J. W. Unwin	
G-BIWV	Cremer PAC-550T balloon	P. A. Rutherford	
G-BIWW	AA-5 Traveler	R. Davis	
G-BIWX	AT-16 Harvard IV (FT239)	A. E. Hutton/Duxford	
G-BIWY	Westland WG.30	British Airways Helicopters Ltd/ Beccles	
G-BIXA	SOCATA TB.9 Tampico	McClean & Gibson (Engineers) Ltd	
G-BIXB	SOCATA TB.9 Tampico	Ferrymen Holdings Ltd/Blackbushe	
G-BIXH	Cessna F.152	Cambridge Aero Club Ltd	
G-BIXI	Cessna 172RG Cutlass	J. F. P. Lewis/Sandown	
G-BIXJ	Saffery S.40 balloon	T. M. Pates	
G-BIXK	Rand KR.2	R. G. Cousins	
G-BIXL	P-51D Mustang (472216)	R. Lamplough/Duxford	
G-BIXM	Beech C90 King Air	Eagle Aircraft Services Ltd/ Leavesden	
G-BIXN	Boeing A.75N1 Stearman	Evans Estates Ltd/Shoreham	
G-BIXP	V.S.361 Spitfire IX	R. Lamplough/Duxford	
G-BIXR	Cameron A-140 balloon	Skysales Ltd	
G-BIXS	Avenger T.200-2112 balloon	M. Stuart	
G-BIXT	Cessna 182R	W. Lipka	
G-BIXU	AA-5B Tiger	Peacock Salt Ltd/Glasgow	
G-BIXV	Bell 212	Bristow Helicopters Ltd	
G-BIXW	Colt 56B balloon	Lighter-Than-Air Ltd	
G-BIXX	Pearson Srs 2 balloon	D. Pearson	
G-BIXY	Piper J-3C-90 Cub	M. Johnson/Barton	
G-BIXZ	Grob G-109	K. E. White/Booker	
G-BIYI	Cameron V-65 balloon	Sarnia Balloon Group	
G-BIYJ	PA-19 Super Cub 95	S. Russell	
G-BIYK	Isaacs Fury	R. S. Martin	
G-BIYM	PA-32R-301 Saratoga SP	Marlow Chemical Co Ltd/Booker	
G-BIYN	Pitts S-1S Special	R. P. Lewis/Shoreham	
G-BIYO	PA-31-310 Turbo Navajo	Northern Executive Aviation Ltd/ Manchester	
G-BIYP	PA-20 Pacer 135	R. A. Lloyd-Hubbard & R. J. Whitcombe	
G-BIYR	PA-18 Super Cub 135	Truman Aviation Ltd/Tollerton	
G-BIYT	Colt 17A balloon	E. T. Houten	
G-BIYU	Fokker S.11.1 Instructor (E-15)	H. R. Smallwood/Blackbushe	
G-BIYV	Cremer 14.700-15 balloon	G. Lowther & ptnrs	
G-BIYW	Jodel D.112	W. J. Tanswell/Redhill	
G-BIYX	PA-28 Cherokee 140	C. C. Butt/Liverpool	
G-BIYY	PA-19 Super Cub 95	A. E. & W. J. Taylor/Wyberton	
G-BIYZ	Cessna 182R	Northair Aviation Ltd/Leeds	
G-BIZB	AB-206 JetRanger 3	Martin Butler Associates Ltd	
G-BIZC	AB-206 JetRanger 3	Alan Mann Helicopters Ltd/ Fairoaks	
G-BIZD	AB-206 JetRanger 3	Alan Mann Helicopters Ltd/ Fairoaks	
G-BIZE	SOCATA TB.9 Tampico	M. J. Reid	
G-BIZF	Cessna F.172P	C. M. Vlieland-Boddy	
G-BIZG	Cessna F.152	Aero Group 78	
G-BIZI	Robin DR.400/120	Headcorn Flying School Ltd	
G-BIZJ	Nord 3202	Keenair Services Ltd/Liverpool	
G-BIZK	Nord 3202	Keenair Services Ltd/Liverpool	
G-BIZL	Nord 3202	Keenair Services Ltd/Liverpool	
G-BIZM	Nord 3202	Keenair Services Ltd/Liverpool	
G-BIZN	Slingsby T.67A	Specialist Flying Training Ltd/ Hamble	
G-BIZO	PA-28R Cherokee Arrow 200	Aviation Advisory Services Ltd/ Stapleford	
G-BIZP	Pilatus PC.6-B2/H2 Porter	Peterborough Parachute Centre Ltd/ Sibson	
G-BIZR	SOCATA TB.9 Tampico	Martin Ltd	
G-BIZT	Bensen B.80D	J. Ferguson	

Notes	Reg.	Type	Owner or Operator
	G-BIZU	Thunder Ax6-56Z balloon	S. L. Leigh
	G-BIZV	PA-19 Super Cub 95	A. A. Rae & M. J. Darlington
	G-BIZW	Champion 7GCBC Citabria	R. Windley
	G-BIZX	Beech B200 Super King Air	Eagle Aircraft Services Ltd/Leavesden
	G-BIZY	Jodel D.112	L. B. Jefferies
	G-BIZZ	Cessna 500 Citation	Vickers Ltd
	G-BJAA	Unicorn UE.1A balloon	K. H. Turner
	G-BJAB	Ayres S2R Thrush Commander	Ag-Air
	G-BJAC	Boeing Vertol 234LR Chinook	British Airways Helicopters Ltd/ Aberdeen
	G-BJAD	FRED Srs 2	C. Allison
	G-BJAE	Starck AS.80 Lavadoux	D. J. & S. A. E. Phillips/Coventry
	G-BJAF	Piper J-3C-65 Cub	P. J. Cottle
	G-BJAG	PA-28-181 Archer II	N. C. P. & A. Buddin/Tees-side
	G-BJAH	Unicorn UE.1A balloon	A. D. Hutchings
	G-BJAJ	AA-5B Tiger	Batrade Ltd/Denham
	G-BJAK	Mooney M.20C	D. B. Jay/Stapleford
	G-BJAL	C.A.S.A. 1.131E Jungmann	Buccaneer Aviation Ltd/Booker
	G-BJAN	SA.102-5 Cavalier	J. Powlesland
	G-BJAO	Bensen B.8M	G. L. Stockdale
	G-BJAP	D.H.82A Tiger Moth	J. Pothecary
	G-BJAR	Unicorn UE.3A balloon	Unicorn Group
	G-BJAS	Rango NA.9 balloon	A. Lindsay
	G-BJAU	PZL-104 Wilga 35	Anglo Polish Sailplanes Ltd/Booker
	G-BJAV	GY-80 Horizon 160	R. Pickett/Leicester
	G-BJAW	Cameron V-65 balloon	G. W. McCarthy
	G-BJAX	Pilatus P2-05 (J-108)	Lea Aviation/Redhill
	G-BJAY	Piper J-3C-65 Cub	K. L. Clarke/Ingoldmells
	G-BJAZ	Thunder Ax7-77 balloon	R. C. Weyda
	G-BJBA	Cessna 152	J. P. Pottier/Staverton
	G-BJBB	Cessna 152	J. P. Pottier/Staverton
	G-BJBI	Cessna 414A	Fosters Shopfitters (Southern) Ltd
	G-BJBJ	Boeing 737-2T5	Orion Airways Ltd/E. Midlands
	G-BJBK	PA-19 Super Cub 95	J. D. Campbell/White Waltham
	G-BJBL	Unicorn UE.1A balloon	Unicorn Group
	G-BJBM	Monnet Sonerai 1	J. Pickerell & ptnrs
	G-BJBN	Ball JB.980 balloon	J. D. Ball
	G-BJBO	Jodel DR.250/160	T. P. Bowen
	G-BJBP	Beech A200 Super King Air	Chiglow Ltd (G-HLUB)
	G-BJBR	Robinson R-22	Findon Air Services/Shoreham
	G-BJBS	Robinson R-22	Cosworth Engineering Ltd
	G-BJBU	PA-23 Aztec 250	Harvest Air Ltd/Southend
	G-BJBV	PA-28-161 Warrior II	C.S.E. Aviation Ltd/Kidlington
	G-BJBW	PA-28-161 Warrior II	C.S.E. Aviation Ltd/Kidlington
	G-BJBX	PA-28-161 Warrior II	C.S.E. Aviation Ltd/Kidlington
	G-BJBY	PA-28-161 Warrior II	C.S.E. Aviation Ltd/Kidlington
	G-BJBZ	Rotorway 133 Executive	Rotorway (UK) Ltd
	G-BJCA	PA-28-161 Warrior II	J. T. Duffin/Coventry
	G-BJCC	Unicorn UE.1A balloon	R. J. Pooley
	G-BJCD	Bede BD-5BH	Brockmoor-Bede Aircraft (UK) Ltd
	G-BJCE	Cessna F.172P	N. T. Smith/Southampton
	G-BJCF	CP.1310-C3 Super Emeraude	M. W. Wooldridge & P. Palmer/ Felthorpe
	G-BJCH	Ocset 1 balloon	B.H.M.E.D. Balloon Group
	G-BJCI	PA-18-150 Super Cub	The Borders (Milfield) Aero-Tour Club Ltd
	G-BJCJ	PA-28-181 Archer II	Golden River Co Ltd
	G-BJCL	Morane Saulnier M.S.230 (1049)	B. J. S. Grey/Booker
	G-BJCM	FRED Srs 2	J. C. Miller
	G-BJCN	Cessna T.337H	Afro-Asia Investment Co Ltd/Jersey
	G-BJCP	Unicorn UE.2B balloon	Unicorn Group
	G-BJCR	Partenavia P.68C	Avionics Research Ltd/ Little Staughton
	G-BJCS	Meagher Mk 2 balloon	S. A. Fowler
	G-BJCT	Boeing 737-204ADV	Britannia Airways Ltd Hon C. S. Rolls/Luton
	G-BJCU	Boeing 737-204ADV	Britannia Airways Ltd Sir Henry Royce/Luton
	G-BJCV	Boeing 737-204ADV	Britannia Airways Ltd Viscount Trenchard/Luton

Reg.	Type	Owner or Operator	Notes
G-BJCW	PA-32R-301 Saratoga SP	Viscount Chelsea/Kidlington	
G-BJCX	—	—	
G-BJCY	Slingsby T.67A	Slingsby Aviation Ltd/Kirkbymoorside	
G-BJCZ	—	—	
G-BJDC	SC.7 Skyvan Srs 3	Short Bros Ltd/Sydenham	
G-BJDE	Cessna F.172M	Sibson Aero Sales Ltd	
G-BJDF	M.S.880B Rallye 100T	D. M. Leonard/Tees-side	
G-BJDG	SOCATA TB.10 Tobago	Sutton Windows Ltd/Biggin Hill	
G-BJDI	Cessna FR.182RG	Spoils Kitchen Reject Shops Ltd/ Ipswich	
G-BJDJ	H.S.125 Srs 700B	Consolidated Contractors (UK) Services Ltd/Heathrow	
G-BJDK	European E.14 balloon	Aeroprint Tours	
G-BJDL	Rango NA.9 balloon	D. Lawrence	
G-BJDM	SA.102-5 Cavalier	J. D. McCracken	
G-BJDO	AA-5A Cheetah	Border Transport/Southampton	
G-BJDP	Cremer Cloudcruiser balloon	P. J. Petitt & M. J. Harper	
G-BJDR	Fokker S.11-1 Instructor	J. D. Read	
G-BJDS	British Bulldog balloon	A. J. Cremer	
G-BJDT	SOCATA TB.9 Tampico	Wingspeed Ltd/Southampton	
G-BJDU	Scruggs BL.2B-2 balloon	C. D. Ibell	
G-BJDV	Kingram balloon	T. J. King & S. Ingram	
G-BJDW	Cessna F.172M	E. P. Collier/Ipswich	
G-BJDX	Scruggs BL.2D-2 balloon	A. R. Maple	
G-BJDZ	Unicorn UE.1A balloon	A. P. & K. E. Chown	
G-BJEE	BN-2B Islander	Pilatus BN Ltd/Bembridge	
G-BJEF	BN-2B Islander	Pilatus BN Ltd/Bembridge	
G-BJEG	BN-2B Islander	Pilatus BN Ltd/Bembridge	
G-BJEI	PA-19 Super Cub 95	H. J. Cox & D. Platt/Bicester	
G-BJEJ	BN-2B Islander	Pilatus BN Ltd/Bembridge	
G-BJEL	Nord NC.854	J. P. Taylor/Lulsgate	
G-BJEM	Cube balloon	A. J. Cremer	
G-BJEN	Scruggs RS.5000 balloon	N. J. Richardson	
G-BJES	Scruggs RS.5000 balloon	J. E. Christopher	
G-BJET	Cessna 425	Gatwick Air Taxis Ltd	
G-BJEU	Scruggs BL.2D-2 balloon	G. G. Kneller	
G-BJEV	Aeronca 11AC Chief	M. A. Musselwhite	
G-BJEW	Cremer balloon	C. D. Sandoe	
G-BJEX	Bo 208C Junior	C. D. H. Crawford/Thruxton	
G-BJEY	BHMED Srs 1 balloon	D. R. Meades & J. S. Edwards	
G-BJEZ	Cameron O-105 balloon	Cameron Balloons Ltd	
G-BJFB	Mk 1A balloon	Aeroprint Tours	
G-BJFC	European E.8 balloon	P. D. Ridout	
G-BJFD	BHMED Srs 1 balloon	D. G. Dance & I. R. Bell	
G-BJFE	PA-19 Super Cub 95 (L-18C)	C. C. Lovell	
G-BJFF	Enstrom F-28C-UK-2	A. D. M. Edie/Shoreham	
G-BJFH	Boeing 737-2S3	Air Europe Ltd *Roma*/Gatwick	
G-BJFK	Short SD3-30	British Midland Airways/E. Midlands	
G-BJFL	Sikorsky S-76A	Bristow Helicopters Ltd	
G-BJFM	Jodel D.120	M. L. Smith & ptnrs/Popham	
G-BJFN	Mk IV balloon	Windsor Balloon Group	
G-BJFO	Mk II balloon	Windsor Balloon Group	
G-BJFP	Mk III balloon	Windsor Balloon Group	
G-BJFR	Mk IV balloon	Windsor Balloon Group	
G-BJFS	Mk IV balloon	Windsor Balloon Group	
G-BJFT	Mk IV balloon	Windsor Balloon Group	
G-BJFU	Mk IV balloon	Windsor Balloon Group	
G-BJFV	Mk V balloon	Windsor Balloon Group	
G-BJFW	Mk V balloon	Windsor Balloon Group	
G-BJFX	Mk V balloon	Windsor Balloon Group	
G-BJFY	Mk I balloon	Windsor Balloon Group	
G-BJFZ	Mk II balloon	Windsor Balloon Group	
G-BJGA	Mk IV balloon	Windsor Balloon Group	
G-BJGB	Mk I balloon	Windsor Balloon Group	
G-BJGC	Mk IV balloon	Windsor Balloon Group	
G-BJGD	Mk IV balloon	Windsor Balloon Group	
G-BJGE	Thunder Ax3 balloon	C. E. Weston-Baker	
G-BJGF	Mk 1 balloon	D. & D. Eaves	
G-BJGG	Mk 2 balloon	D. & D. Eaves	
G-BJGH	Slingsby T.67A	Slingsby Engineering Ltd/Kirkbymoorside	
G-BJGK	Cameron V-77 balloon	A. T. Willmer	

Notes	Reg.	Type	Owner or Operator
	G-BJGL	Cremer balloon	G. Lowther
	G-BJGM	Unicorn UE.1A balloon	D. Eaves & P. D. Ridout
	G-BJGN	Scruggs RS.5000 balloon	K. H. Turner
	G-BJGO	Cessna 172N	Golf Oscar Ltd/Birmingham
	G-BJGS	Cremer balloon	C. A. Larkins
	G-BJGT	Mooney M.20K	Cooper Merseyside Ltd
	G-BJGW	M.H.1521M Broussard (31-GW)	G. A. Warner/Duxford
	G-BJGX	Sikorsky S-76A	Bristow Helicopters Ltd
	G-BJGY	Cessna F.172P	Derek Crouch PLC
	G-BJHA	Cremer balloon	G. Cope
	G-BJHB	Mooney M.20J	TII Services Ltd
	G-BJHC	Swan 1 balloon	C. A. Swan
	G-BJHD	Mk 3B balloon	S. Meagher
	G-BJHE	Osprey 1B balloon	R. B. Symonds & J. M. Hopkins
	G-BJHF	Osprey 1B balloon	K. R. Bundy
	G-BJHG	Cremer balloon	P. A. Cremer & H. J. A. Green
	G-BJHJ	Osprey 1C balloon	D. Eaves
	G-BJHK	EAA Acro Sport	J. H. Kimber
	G-BJHL	Osprey 1C balloon	E. Bartlett
	G-BJHM	Osprey 1B balloon	W. P. Fulford
	G-BJHN	Osprey 1B balloon	J. E. Christopher
	G-BJHO	Osprey 1C balloon	G. G. Kneller
	G-BJHP	Osprey 1C balloon	N. J. Richardson
	G-BJHR	Osprey 1B balloon	J. E. Christopher
	G-BJHS	S.25 Sunderland V	Sunderland Ltd
	G-BJHT	Thunder Ax7-65 balloon	A. H. & L. Symonds
	G-BJHU	Osprey 1C balloon	G. G. Kneller
	G-BJHV	Voisin Replica	M. P. Sayer/O. Warden
	G-BJHW	Osprey 1C balloon	N. J. Richardson
	G-BJHX	Osprey 1C balloon	A. B. Gulliford
	G-BJHY	Osprey 1C balloon	T. J. King & S. Ingram
	G-BJHZ	Osprey 1C balloon	M. Christopher
	G-BJIA	Allport balloon	D. J. Allport
	G-BJIB	D.31 Turbulent	N. H. Lemon
	G-BJIC	Dodo 1A balloon	P. D. Ridout
	G-BJID	Osprey 1B balloon	P. D. Ridout
	G-BJIE	Sphinx balloon	P. T. Witty
	G-BJIF	Bensen B.8M	H. Redwin
	G-BJIG	Slingsby T.67A	Slingsby Engineering Ltd/Kirkbymoorside
	G-BJIH	Solent balloon	K. Andrews & S. C. Jerrim
	G-BJII	Sphinx balloon	I. French
	G-BJIJ	Osprey 1B balloon	R. Hownsell
	G-BJIL	Cessna 550 Citation II	RTZ Services Ltd/Biggin Hill
	G-BJIM	—	
	G-BJIP	Osprey 1B balloon	A. P. & K. E. Chown
	G-BJIR	Cessna 550 Citation II	Royco Homes Ltd/Kidlington
	G-BJIS	Mk 1 balloon	P. Paine
	G-BJIU	Bell 212	Bristow Helicopters Ltd
	G-BJIV	PA-18-150 Super Cub	M. T. A. Sands
	G-BJIW	T-1 balloon	S. Holland & G. Watmore
	G-BJIX	T-1 balloon	S. Holland & G. Watmore
	G-BJIY	Cessna T337D	Shaun Wilson (Sale) Ltd
	G-BJJA	Kingram 01 balloon	A. P. & K. E. Chown
	G-BJJB	Kingram 01 balloon	A. P. & K. E. Chown
	G-BJJC	Dodo Mk 1 balloon	A. P. & K. E. Chown
	G-BJJE	Dodo Mk 3 balloon	D. Eaves
	G-BJJF	Dodo Mk 4 balloon	D. Eaves
	G-BJJG	Dodo Mk 5 balloon	D. Eaves
	G-BJJI	SAS balloon	R. Hounsell & M. R. Rooke
	G-BJJJ	Bitterne balloon	A. P. & K. E. Chown
	G-BJJK	Bitterne balloon	R. Hounsell & M. R. Rooke
	G-BJJL	SAS balloon	M. R. Rooke
	G-BJJN	Cessna F.172M	C. P. Hawker/Stapleford
	G-BJJO	Bell 212	Bristow Helicopters Ltd
	G-BJJP	Bell 212	Bristow Helicopters Ltd
	G-BJJR	Bell 212	Bristow Helicopters Ltd
	G-BJJS	Sphinx balloon	C. N. Childs
	G-BJJT	Mabey balloon	M. W. Mabey
	G-BJJU	Sphinx balloon	T. M. Bates
	G-BJJV	Beech B200 Super King Air	Eagle Aircraft Services Ltd/Leavesden
	G-BJJW	Mk B balloon	S. Meagher

Reg.	Type	Owner or Operator	Notes
G-BJJX	Mk B balloon	S. Meagher	
G-BJJY	Mk B balloon	S. Meagher	
G-BJJZ	Unicorn UE.1A balloon	R. Woodley	
G-BJKA	SA.365C Dauphin 2	Management Aviation Ltd/Bourn	
G-BJKB	SA.365C Dauphin 2	Management Aviation Ltd/Bourn	
G-BJKC	Mk B balloon	S. Meagher	
G-BJKD	Mk B balloon	S. Meagher	
G-BJKE	Mk A balloon	D. Addison	
G-BJKF	SOCATA TB.9 Tampico	Martin Ltd	
G-BJKG	Mk A balloon	D. Addison	
G-BJKH	Mk A balloon	D. Addison	
G-BJKI	Mk A balloon	D. Addison	
G-BJKJ	Mk A balloon	D. Addison	
G-BJKK	Mk A balloon	D. Addison	
G-BJKL	Mk A balloon	D. Addison	
G-BJKM	Mk II balloon	S. Meagher	
G-BJKN	Mk 1 balloon	D. Addison	
G-BJKO	Mk 1 balloon	D. Addison	
G-BJKP	Mk 7 balloon	D. Addison	
G-BJKR	Mk 1 balloon	D. Addison	
G-BJKS	Mk 1 balloon	D. Addison	
G-BJKT	Mk B balloon	S. Meagher	
G-BJKU	Osprey 1B balloon	S. A. Dalmas & P. G. Tarr	
G-BJKV	Opsrey 1F balloon	B. Diggle	
G-BJKW	Wills Aera II	J. K. S. Wills	
G-BJKX	Cessna F.152	Eglinton Flying Club	
G-BJKY	Cessna F.152	Westair Flying Services Ltd/Blackpool	
G-BJKZ	Osprey 1F balloon	M. J. N. Kirby	
G-BJLA	Osprey 1B balloon	D. Lawrence	
G-BJLB	Nord NC.854S	M. J. Barnby/Cardiff	
G-BJLC	Monnet Sonerai IIL	J. P. Whitham	
G-BJLD	Eagle 8 Mk 2 balloon	R. M. Richards	
G-BJLE	Osprey 1B balloon	I. Chadwick	
G-BJLF	Unicorn UE.1C balloon	I. Chadwick	
G-BJLG	Unicorn UE.1B balloon	I. Chadwick	
G-BJLH	PA-19 Super Cub 95 (K-33)	Keenair Services Ltd/Liverpool	
G-BJLJ	Cameron D-50 balloon	Cameron Balloons Ltd	
G-BJLM	Short SD3-30	Short Bros Ltd	
G-BJLN	Featherlight Mk 3 balloon	A. P. Newman & T. J. Sweeting	
G-BJLO	PA-31-310 Navajo	Linco (Poultry Machinery) Ltd/ Biggin Hill	
G-BJLP	Featherlight Mk 3 balloon	N. P. Kemp & M. O. Davies	
G-BJLR	Featherlight Mk 3 balloon	M. O. Davies & S. R. Roberts	
G-BJLT	Featherlight Mk 3 balloon	J. M. J. Roberts & C. C. Marshall	
G-BJLU	Featherlight Mk 3 balloon	T. J. Sweeting & N. P. Kemp	
G-BJLV	Sphinx balloon	L. F. Guyot	
G-BJLW	Gleave CJ-I balloon	C. J. Gleave	
G-BJLX	Cremer balloon	P. W. May	
G-BJLY	Cremer balloon	P. Cannon	
G-BJLZ	Cremer balloon	S. K. McLean	
G-BJMA	Colt 21A balloon	Colt Balloons Ltd	
G-BJMB	Osprey 1B balloon	S. Meagher	
G-BJMG	European E.26C balloon	D. Eaves & A. P. Chown	
G-BJMH	Osprey Mk 3A balloon	D. Eaves	
G-BJMI	European E.84 balloon	D. Eaves	
G-BJMJ	Bensen B.8M	P. R. Snowdon	
G-BJMK	Cremer balloon	B. J. Larkins	
G-BJML	Cessna 120	C. C. Lovell	
G-BJMM	Cremer balloon	M. J. Larkins	
G-BJMO	Taylor JT.1 Monoplane	R. C. Mark	
G-BJMP	Brugger Colibri M.B.2	F. Skinner	
G-BJMR	Cessna 310R	A-One Transport (Leeds) Ltd/Sherburn	
G-BJMT	Osprey Mk 1E balloon	M. J. Sheather	
G-BJMU	European E.157 balloon	A. C. Mitchell	
G-BJMV	BAC One-Eleven 531FS	Dan-Air Services Ltd/Gatwick	
G-BJMW	Thunder Ax8-105 balloon	G. M. Westley	
G-BJMX	Jarre JR.3 balloon	P. D. Ridout	
G-BJMZ	European EA.8A balloon	P. D. Ridout	
G-BJNA	Arena Mk 117P balloon	P. D. Ridout	
G-BJNB	WAR F4U Corsair	A. V. Francis	
G-BJNC	Osprey Mk 1E balloon	G. Whitehead	

Notes	Reg.	Type	Owner or Operator
	G-BJND	Osprey Mk 1E balloon	A. Billington & D. Whitmore
	G-BJNE	Osprey Mk 1E balloon	D. R. Sheldon
	G-BJNF	Cessna F.152	Exeter Flying Club Ltd
	G-BJNG	Slingsby T.67A	Slingsby Aviation Ltd/Kirkbymoorside
	G-BJNH	Osprey Mk 1E balloon	D. A. Kirk
	G-BJNI	Osprey Mk 1C balloon	M. J. Sheather
	G-BJNJ	Bell 206B JetRanger 3	Petrochemical Supplies Ltd
	G-BJNL	Evans VP-2	K. Morris
	G-BJNN	PA-38-112 Tomahawk	Apollo Leasing Ltd/Glasgow
	G-BJNO	AA-5B Tiger	Kaal Electrics Ltd/Elstree
	G-BJNP	Rango NA.32 balloon	N. H. Ponsford
	G-BJNW	EAA Sport Biplane P.2	A. R. Thompson & M. J. Barton
	G-BJNX	Cameron O-65 balloon	B. J. Petteford
	G-BJNY	Aeronca 11CC Super Chief	R. A. C. Hoppenbrouwers
	G-BJNZ	PA-23 Aztec 250	Distance No Object Ltd (G-FANZ)
	G-BJOA	PA-28-181 Archer II	C.S.E. Aviation Ltd/Kidlington
	G-BJOB	Jodel D.140C	B. E. Cotton/Shoreham
	G-BJOC	Colt 240A balloon	Colt Balloons Ltd
	G-BJOD	Hollman HA-2M Sportster	H. J. Goddard
	G-BJOE	Jodel D.120A	B. F. E. Thornton & J. Smith
	G-BJOG	BN-2T Turbo Islander	Pilatus BN Ltd/Bembridge
	G-BJOI	Isaacs Special	J. O. Isaacs
	G-BJOK	BN-2B Islander	Pilatus BN Ltd/Bembridge
	G-BJON	BN-2B Islander	Pilatus BN Ltd/Bembridge
	G-BJOO	BN-2B Islander	Pilatus BN Ltd/Bembridge
	G-BJOP	BN-2B Islander	Pilatus BN Ltd/Bembridge
	G-BJOT	Jodel D.117	F. M. Ward
	G-BJOV	Cessna F.150K	Falcon Flying Services/Biggin Hill
	G-BJOX	—	
	G-BJOZ	Scheibe SF.25B Falke	P. W. Hextall
	G-BJPA	Osprey Mk 3A balloon	N. D. Brabham
	G-BJPB	Osprey Mk 4A balloon	C. B. Rundle
	G-BJPC	Cremer 1 gyroplane	P. A. Cremer
	G-BJPD	Osprey Mk 4D balloon	E. L. Fuller
	G-BJPE	Osprey Mk 1E balloon	M. A. Hase
	G-BJPH	Osprey Mk 3G balloon	K. R. Bundy
	G-BJPI	BD.5-G	M. D. McQueen
	G-BJPJ	Osprey Mk 3A	K. R. Bundy
	G-BJPK	Osprey Mk 1B balloon	G. M. Hocquard
	G-BJPL	Osprey Mk 4A balloon	M. Vincent
	G-BJPM	Bursell PW.1 balloon	I. M. Holdsworth
	G-BJPN	JK Mk 1 balloon	A. Kaye & J. Corcoran
	G-BJPO	B&C balloon	S. Browne & J. Cheetham
	G-BJPS	Osprey Mk 4B balloon	S. A. Hassell
	G-BJPU	Osprey Mk 4B balloon	P. Globe
	G-BJPV	Haigh balloon	M. J. Haigh
	G-BJPW	Osprey Mk 1C balloon	P. J. Cooper & M. Draper
	G-BJPX	Phoenix balloon	Cupro Sapphire Ltd
	G-BJPY	Cremer balloon	P. A. Cremer & P. V. M. Green
	G-BJPZ	Osprey Mk 1C balloon	C. E. Newman
	G-BJRA	Osprey Mk 4B balloon	E. Osborn
	G-BJRB	European E.254 balloon	D. Eaves
	G-BJRC	European E.84R balloon	D. Eaves
	G-BJRD	European E.84R balloon	D. Eaves
	G-BJRF	Saffery S.80 balloon	C. F. Chipping
	G-BJRG	Osprey Mk 4B balloon	A. de Gruchy
	G-BJRH	Rango NA.36 balloon	N. H. Ponsford
	G-BJRI	Osprey Mk 4D balloon	G. G. Kneller
	G-BJRJ	Osprey Mk 4D balloon	G. G. Kneller
	G-BJRK	Osprey Mk 1E balloon	G. G. Kneller
	G-BJRL	Osprey Mk 4B balloon	G. G. Kneller
	G-BJRN	Graham balloon	D. G. Goose
	G-BJRO	Osprey Mk 4D balloon	M. Christopher
	G-BJRP	Cremer balloon	M. Williams
	G-BJRR	Cremer balloon	M. Wallbank
	G-BJRS	Cremer balloon	M. Wallbank
	G-BJRT	BAC One-Eleven 528	British Caledonian Airways Ltd/Gatwick
	G-BJRU	BAC One-Eleven 528	British Caledonian Airways Ltd/Gatwick
	G-BJRV	Cremer balloon	M. D. Williams

Reg.	Type	Owner or Operator	Notes
G-BJRW	Cessna U.206G	A. I. Walgate & Son Ltd	
G-BJRX	RMB Mk 1 balloon	R. J. MacNeil	
G-BJRY	PA-28-151 Warrior	Eastern Counties Aero Club Ltd/ Southend	
G-BJRZ	Partenavia P.68C	Fletcher Rentals (TV) Ltd	
G-BJSA	BN-2A Islander	Harvest Air Ltd/Southend	
G-BJSC	Osprey Mk 4D balloon	N. J. Richardson	
G-BJSD	Osprey Mk 4D balloon	N. J. Richardson	
G-BJSE	Osprey Mk 1E balloon	J. E. Christopher	
G-BJSF	Osprey Mk 4B balloon	N. J. Richardson	
G-BJSG	V.S.361 Spitfire LF.IXE (ML417)	B. J. S. Grey/Booker	
G-BJSH	Sindlinger Hurricane 5/8 scale replica	A. F. Winstanley	
G-BJSI	Osprey Mk 1E balloon	N. J. Richardson	
G-BJSJ	Osprey Mk 1E balloon	M. Christopher	
G-BJSK	Osprey Mk 4B balloon	J. E. Christopher	
G-BJSL	Flamboyant Ax7-65 balloon	Pepsi Cola International Ltd	
G-BJSM	Bursell Mk 1 balloon	M. C. Bursell	
G-BJSP	Guido 1A Srs 61 balloon	G. A. Newsome	
G-BJSR	Osprey Mk 4B balloon	C. F. Chipping	
G-BJSS	Allport balloon	D. J. Allport	
G-BJST	CCF Harvard 4	V. Norman & M. Lawrence	
G-BJSU	Bensen B.8M	J. D. Newlyn	
G-BJSV	PA-28-161 Warrior II	A. F. Aviation Ltd/Stansted	
G-BJSW	Thunder Ax7-65 balloon	Sandcliffe Garage Ltd	
G-BJSX	Unicorn UE-1C balloon	N. J. Richardson	
G-BJSY	Beech E90 King Air	Allcharter Ltd	
G-BJSZ	Piper J-3C-65 Cub	H. Gilbert	
G-BJTA	Osprey Mk 4B balloon	C. F. Chipping	
G-BJTB	Cessna A.150M	Leisure Lease Aviation/Southend	
G-BJTD	Colt AS-90 airship	Colt Balloons Ltd	
G-BJTF	Skyrider Mk 1 balloon	D. A. Kirk	
G-BJTG	Osprey Mk 4B balloon	M. Millen	
G-BJTH	Kestrel AC Mk 1 balloon	G. Whitehead	
G-BJTI	Woodie K2400J-2 balloon	M. J. Woodward	
G-BJTJ	Osprey Mk 4B balloon	G. Hocquard	
G-BJTK	Taylor JT.1 Monoplane	P. J. Hart (G-BEUM)	
G-BJTN	Osprey Mk 4B balloon	M. Vincent	
G-BJTO	Piper L-4H Cub	K. R. Nunn	
G-BJTP	PA-19 Super Cub 95	J. T. Parkins/Wellesbourne	
G-BJTS	Osprey Mk 4B balloon	G. Hocquard	
G-BJTT	Sphinx SP.2 balloon	N. J. Godfrey	
G-BJTU	Cremer Cracker balloon	D. R. Green	
G-BJTV	M.S.880B Rallye Club	J. M. Kirk	
G-BJTW	European E.107 balloon	C. J. Brealey	
G-BJTX	PA-31-325 Turbo Navajo	Truvelo Manufacturers Ltd	
G-BJTY	Osprey Mk 4B balloon	A. E. de Gruchy	
G-BJTZ	Osprey Mk 4A balloon	M. J. Sheather	
G-BJUA	Sphinx SP.12 balloon	T. M. Pates	
G-BJUB	BVS Special 01 balloon	P. G. Wild	
G-BJUC	Robinson R-22	Jones & Brooks Ltd	
G-BJUD	Robin DR.400/180R	Southern Sailplanes Ltd	
G-BJUE	Osprey Mk 4B balloon	M. Vincent	
G-BJUG	SOCATA TB.9 Tampico	Martin Ltd	
G-BJUH	Unicorn UE.1C balloon	A. P. Chown	
G-BJUI	Osprey Mk 4B balloon	B. A. de Gruchy	
G-BJUL	Short SD3-30	Short Bros Ltd	
G-BJUM	Unicorn UE.1C balloon	S. A. Hassell	
G-BJUN	Unicorn UE.1C balloon	K. R. Bundy	
G-BJUP	Osprey Mk 4B balloon	W. J. Pill	
G-BJUR	PA-38-112 Tomahawk	Truman Aviation Ltd/Tollerton	
G-BJUS	PA-38-112 Tomahawk	C.S.E. Aviation Ltd/Kidlington	
G-BJUU	Osprey Mk 4B balloon	M. Vincent	
G-BJUV	Cameron V-20 balloon	Cameron Balloons Ltd	
G-BJUW	Osprey Mk 4B balloon	C. F. Chipping	
G-BJUX	Bursell balloon	I. M. Holdsworth	
G-BJUY	Colt Ax-77 balloon	Colt Balloons Ltd	
G-BJUZ	BAT Mk II balloon	A. R. Thompson	
G-BJVA	BAT Mk I balloon	B. L. Thompson	
G-BJVB	Cremcorn Ax1.4 balloon	P. A. Cremer & I. Chadwick	
G-BJVC	Evans VP-2	R. G. Fenn	

Notes	Reg.	Type	Owner or Operator
	G-BJVE	—	—
	G-BJVF	Thunder Ax3 balloon	A. G. R. Calder & F. J. Spite
	G-BJVG	Thunder Ax8-105 balloon	Thunder Balloons Ltd
	G-BJVH	Cessna F.182Q	A. R. G. Brooker Engineering Ltd
	G-BJVI	Osprey Mk 4D balloon	S. M. Colville
	G-BJVJ	Cessna F.152	Cambridge Aero Club Ltd
	G-BJVK	Grob G-109	B. Kimberley/Enstone
	G-BJVL	Saffery Hermes balloon	Cupro Sapphire Ltd
	G-BJVM	Cessna 172M	P. Blundell & C. Wright/Coventry
	G-BJVN	—	—
	G-BJVO	Cameron D-50 balloon	Cameron Balloons Ltd
	G-BJVS	CP.1315C-3 Super Emeraude	Victor Sierra Aero Club
	G-BJVT	Cessna F.152	Cambridge Aero Club Ltd
	G-BJVU	Thunder Ax6-56 balloon	G. V. Beckwith
	G-BJVV	Robin R.1180	Medway Flying Group Ltd/Rochester
	G-BJVX	Sikorsky S-76A	Bristow Helicopters Ltd
	G-BJVZ	Sikorsky S-76A	Bristow Helicopters Ltd
	G-BJWB	H.S.125 Srs 700B	Opencity Ltd
	G-BJWC	Saro Skeeter AOP.12	J. E. Wilkie
	G-BJWD	Zenith CH.300	D. Winton
	G-BJWF	Ayres S2R-R3S Thrush Commander	Farmair Ltd/Headcorn
	G-BJWH	Cessna F.152	K. W. & W. R. Norris/Bournemouth
	G-BJWI	Cessna F.172P	A&G Aviation Ltd/Bournemouth
	G-BJWJ	Cameron V-65 balloon	R. G. Turnbull & S. G. Forse
	G-BJWL	BN-2A-8 Islander	Harvest Air Ltd (G-BBMC)/Southend
	G-BJWM	BN-2A-26 Islander	Harvest Air Ltd (G-BCAE)/Southend
	G-BJWN	BN-2A-8 Islander	Harvest Air Ltd (G-BALO)/Southend
	G-BJWO	BN-2A-8 Islander	Harvest Air Ltd (G-BAXC)/Southend
	G-BJWP	BN-2A-26 Islander	Harvest Air Ltd (G-BCEJ)/Southend
	G-BJWR	D.H.82A Tiger Moth	D. R. Whitby & ptnrs
	G-BJWT	Wittman W.10 Tailwind	J. F. Bakewell & R. A. Shelley
	G-BJWU	Thunder Ax7-65Z balloon	Thunder Balloons Ltd
	G-BJWV	Colt 17A balloon	Lighter-Than-Air Ltd
	G-BJWW	Cessna F.172N	Westair Flying Services Ltd/Blackpool
	G-BJWX	PA-19 Super Cub 95	D. E. Lamb/Wyberton
	G-BJWY	Sikorsky S-55 Whirlwind 21	J. E. Wilkie
	G-BJWZ	PA-19 Super Cub 95	G. V. Harfield
	G-BJXA	Slingsby T.67A	I. C. Fallows/Leeds
	G-BJXB	Slingsby T.67A	Slingsby Aviation Ltd/Kirkbymoorside
	G-BJXD	Colt 17A balloon	Hot Air Balloon Co Ltd
	G-BJXJ	Boeing 737-219	Dan-Air Services Ltd/Gatwick
	G-BJXK	Fournier RF-5	P. Storey & ptnrs
	G-BJXL	Boeing 737-2T4	Dan-Air Services Ltd/Gatwick
	G-BJXN	Boeing 747-230B	British Caledonian Airways *Mungo Park — The Scottish Explorer*/Gatwick
	G-BJXO	Cessna 441	Hatfield Executive Aviation Ltd Cranfield
	G-BJXP	Colt 56B balloon	Lighter-Than-Air Ltd
	G-BJXR	Auster AOP.9 (XR267)	Cotswold Aircraft Restoration Group
	G-BJXU	Thunder Ax7-77 balloon	Perdix Ltd
	G-BJXW	PA28R Cherokee Arrow 200	J. B. Anderson/Newtownards
	G-BJXX	PA-23 Aztec 250	New Venture Carpets Ltd/ Halfpenny Green
	G-BJXZ	Cessna 172N	J. R. Kettle/Wellesbourne
	G-BJYB	Cessna 441	McAlpine Aviation Ltd/Luton
	G-BJYC	Cessna 425	Northern Air Taxis Ltd/Leeds
	G-BJYD	Cessna F.152 II	Cleveland Flying School Ltd/ Tees-side
	G-BJYF	Colt 56A balloon	Hot Air Balloon Co Ltd
	G-BJYG	PA-28-161 Warrior II	C.S.E. Aviation Ltd/Kidlington
	G-BJYK	Jodel D.120A	D. R. Emmett
	G-BJYL	BAC One-Eleven 515FB	Dan-Air Services Ltd (G-AZPE)/Gatwick
	G-BJYM	BAC One-Eleven 531FS	Dan-Air Services Ltd/Gatwick
	G-BJYN	PA-38-112 Tomahawk	Panshanger School of Flying Ltd (G-BJTE)
	G-BJYO	PA-38-112 Tomahawk	Panshanger School of Flying Ltd
	G-BJYU	BN-2B Islander	Pilatus BN Ltd/Bembridge
	G-BJYV	BN-2B Islander	Pilatus BN Ltd/Bembridge
	G-BJYW	BN-2B Islander	Pilatus BN Ltd/Bembridge
	G-BJYX	BN-2B Islander	Pilatus BN Ltd/Bembridge

G-BJWZ   PA-19 Super Cub 95.

117

G-BJZE   Doulgas DC-10-30 of British Caledonian Airways.

118

Reg.	Type	Owner or Operator	Notes
G-BJYY	BN-2B Islander	Pilatus BN Ltd/Bembridge	
G-BJYZ	BN-2B Islander	Pilatus BN Ltd/Bembridge	
G-BJZA	Cameron N-65 balloon	E. J. Aldrich Ltd	
G-BJZB	Evans VP-2	A. Graham	
G-BJZC	Thunder Ax7-65Z balloon	Greenpeace (UK) Ltd	
G-BJZD	Douglas DC-10-10	British Caledonian Airways (G-GSKY)/ Gatwick	
G-BJZE	Douglas DC-10-10	British Caledonian Airways (G-GFAL)/ Gatwick	
G-BJZF	D.H.82A Tiger Moth	C. A. Parker/Sywell	
G-BJZH	Colt 77B balloon	Colt Balloons Ltd	
G-BJZK	Cessna T.303	Standard Aviation Ltd/Usworth	
G-BJZL	Cameron V-65 balloon	S. L. G. Williams	
G-BJZM	Slingsby T.67A	Slingsby Aviation Ltd/Kirkbymoorside	
G-BJZN	Slingsby T-67A	Slingsby Aviation Ltd/Kirkbymoorside	
G-BJZO	Cessna R.182	Northair Aviation Ltd/Staverton	
G-BJZR	Colt 42A balloon	C. F. Sisson	
G-BJZT	Cessna FA.152	Denham Flying Training School Ltd	
G-BJZU	Cessna FA.152	Denham Flying Training School Ltd	
G-BJZX	Grob G.109	Sport Flying Ltd/Enstone	
G-BJZY	Bensen B.8MV	D. E. & M. A. Cooke	
G-BJZZ	Hispano HA.1112 (14) ★	Whitehall Theatre of War	
G-BKAA	H.S.125 Srs 700B	Aravco Ltd	
G-BKAB	ICA Brasov IS-28M2	Weslake Air Services Ltd/Biggin Hill	
G-BKAC	Cessna F.150L	Andrewsfield Flying Club Ltd (G-BAIO)	
G-BKAD	—	—	
G-BKAE	Jodel D.120	J. S. Lewer	
G-BKAF	FRED Srs 2	L. G. Millen	
G-BKAG	Boeing 727-217	Dan-Air Services Ltd/Gatwick	
G-BKAI	SA.330J Puma	Bristow Helicopters Ltd	
G-BKAJ	H.S.125 Srs 400B	McAlpine Aviation Ltd (G-AYNR)/Luton	
G-BKAK	Beech C90 King Air	Airmore Sales Ltd/Elstree	
G-BKAL	H.S. 748 Srs. 2	British Aerospace PLC/Woodford	
G-BKAM	Slingsby T.67M Firefly	Slingsby Aviation Ltd/Kirkbymoorside	
G-BKAN	Cessna 340A	Northair Aviation Ltd/Leeds	
G-BKAO	Jodel D.112	E. Carter & G. Higgins	
G-BKAP	Boeing 737-2L9	Orion Airways Ltd/E. Midlands	
G-BKAR	PA-38-112 Tomahawk	C.S.E. Aviation Ltd/Kidlington	
G-BKAS	PA-38-112 Tomahawk	C.S.E. Aviation Ltd/Kidlington	
G-BKAT	Pitts S-1C Special	I. M. G. Senior & J. G. Harper	
G-BKAY	R. Commander 114	Costello Gears Ltd	
G-BKAZ	Cessna 152	Skyviews & General Ltd/Leeds	
G-BKBA	H.S.125 Srs 403B	McAlpine Aviation Ltd (G-BBGU)/Luton	
G-BKBB	Hawker Fury replica	The Hon P. Lindsay/Booker	
G-BKBC	D.H.C.-6 Twin Otter 310	Jersey European Airways/Jersey	
G-BKBD	Thunder Ax3 balloon	D. Clark	
G-BKBE	AA-5A Cheetah	G. W. Plowman & Sons Ltd/Elstree	
G-BKBF	M.S.894A Rallye Minerva 220	Callow Aviation/Staverton	
G-BKBI	Quickie Q.2	R. H. Gibbs	
G-BKBK	Stampe SV-4A	Skyfever Aviation/Biggin Hill	
G-BKBL	Westland WG.13 Lynx 87	Westland Helicopters Ltd/Yeovil	
G-BKBM	H.S.125 Srs 600B	R. Hitchin & Co Ltd (G-BCCL)/Luton	
G-BKBN	SOCATA TB.10 Tobago	Martin Ltd	
G-BKBO	Colt 17A balloon	Courage Eastern Ltd	
G-BKBP	Bellanca 7GCBC Scout	L. B. Jefferies	
G-BKBR	Cameron Chateau 84 balloon	Cameron Balloons Ltd	
G-BKBS	Bensen B.8	C. R. Dawe	
G-BKBV	SOCATA TB.10 Tobago	J. Be	
G-BKBW	SOCATA TB.10 Tobago	P. Murphy/Blackbushe	
G-BKBX	CP.301A Emeraude	R. Yates	
G-BKBY	Bell 206B JetRanger 3	Real Time Control Ltd	
G-BKCB	PA-28R Cherokee Arrow 200	G. C. Smith	
G-BKCC	PA-28 Cherokee 180	Classic Aeroplane Ltd	
G-BKCD	H.S.125 Srs 600B	McAlpine Aviation Ltd (G-BDOA)/Luton	
G-BKCE	Cessna F.172P-II	A. N. J. & S. L. Palmer/Norwich	
G-BKCF	Rutan LongEze	I. C. Fallows	
G-BKCG	Boeing 727-117	Dan-Air Services Ltd/Gatwick	
G-BKCH	Thompson Cassutt	S. C. Thompson	
G-BKCI	Brugger M.B.2 Colibri	E. R. Newall	
G-BKCJ	Oldfield Baby Great Lakes	S. V. Roberts	

Notes	Reg.	Type	Owner or Operator
	G-BKCK	CCF Harvard IV	E. T. & T. C. Webster
	G-BKCL	PA-30 Twin Comanche 160	Jubilee Airways Ltd (G-AXSP)/Fairoaks
	G-BKCM	Bell 206B JetRanger 3	S. W. Electricity Board/Lulsgate
	G-BKCN	Currie Wot	S. E. Tomlinson
	G-BKCP	—	
	G-BKCR	SOCATA TB.9 Tampico	Air Touring Services Ltd/Biggin Hill
	G-BKCS	Cessna T.207	Blackbushe Engineering Co Ltd
	G-BKCT	Cameron V-77 balloon	Quality Products General Engineering (Wickwat) Ltd
	G-BKCU	Sequoia F.8L Falco	J. J. Anziani & D. F. Simpson
	G-BKCV	EAA Acro Sport II	M. J. Clark
	G-BKCW	Jodel D.120	T. Rayner & P. McIntosh/Dundee
	G-BKCX	Mudry CAARP CAP.10	Roger Knights Ltd/Booker
	G-BKCY	PA-38-112 Tomahawk II	Norwich Air Training Ltd
	G-BKCZ	Jodel D.120A	P. Penn-Sayers Model Services Ltd/ Shoreham
	G-BKDA	AB-206B JetRanger	Rotair Ltd/Panshanger
	G-BKDC	Monnet Sonerai II	J. Boobyer
	G-BKDD	Bell 206B JetRanger	Dollar Air Services Ltd/Coventry
	G-BKDE	Kendrick I Motorglider	J. K. Rushton
	G-BKDF	Kendrick II Motorglider	J. K. Rushton
	G-BKDG	PA-19 Super Cub 95	M. Fleetwood
	G-BKDH	Robin DR.400/120	Wickwell Aviation Ltd/Southampton
	G-BKDI	Robin DR.400/120	Wickwell Aivation Ltd/Southampton
	G-BKDJ	Robin DR.400/120	Wickwell Aviation Ltd/Southampton
	G-BKDK	Thunder Ax7-77Z balloon	Thunder Balloons Ltd
	G-BKDN	Short SD3-30	Air UK Ltd *Enterprise*/Norwich
	G-BKDO	Short SD3-30	Genair/Humberside
	G-BKDP	FRED Srs 3	M. Whittaker
	G-BKDR	Pitts S.1S Special	T. R. G. Barnby
	G-BKDS	Colt 14A balloon	Colt Balloons Ltd
	G-BKDT	S.E.5A replica	J. H. Tetley & W. A. Sneesby
	G-BKDV	Beech B80 Queen Air	Samtanus (UK) Ltd
	G-BKDW	K.1260/3 Stu balloon	P. C. Carlton
	G-BKDX	Jodel DR.1050	M. H. Simms
	G-BKDY	Jodel D.120A	J. J. Pratt & A. Lumley/ Humberside
	G-BKEA	BN-2B Islander	Pilatus BN Ltd/Bembridge
	G-BKEB	BN-2B Islander	Pilatus BN Ltd/Bembridge
	G-BKED	BN-2B Islander	Pilatus BN Ltd/Bembridge
	G-BKEE	BN-2B Islander	Pilatus BN Ltd/Bembridge
	G-BKEF	BN-2B Islander	Pilatus BN Ltd/Bembridge
	G-BKEG	BN-2B Islander	Pilatus BN Ltd/Bembridge
	G-BKEH	BN-2B Islander	Pilatus BN Ltd/Bembridge
	G-BKEI	BN-2B Islander	Pilatus BN Ltd/Bembridge
	G-BKEJ	BN-2B Islander	Pilatus BN Ltd/Bembridge
	G-BKEK	PA-32 Cherokee Six 300	Cruspane Ltd/Stapleford
	G-BKEL	—	
	G-BKEM	SOCATA TB.9 Tampico	D. V. D. Reed/Exeter
	G-BKEN	SOCATA TB.10 Tobago	Berglen Products Ltd
	G-BKEO	Cameron House SS 60 balloon	Cameron Balloons Ltd
	G-BKEP	Cessna F.172M	Reedtrend Ltd
	G-BKER	S.E.5A replica (F5447)	N. K. Geddes
	G-BKES	Cameron SS bottle balloon	Lighter-Than-Air Ltd
	G-BKET	PA-19 Super Cub 95	G. R. Lennon
	G-BKEU	Taylor JT.1 Monoplane	R. J. Whybrow & J. M. Springham
	G-BKEV	Cessna F.172M	W. H. Wilkins Ltd
	G-BKEW	Bell 206B JetRanger 3	N. R. Foster/Fairoaks
	G-BKEX	Rich Prototype glider	D. B. Rich
	G-BKEY	FRED Srs 3	G. S. Taylor
	G-BKEZ	PA-19 Super Cub 95	A. N. G. Gardiner
	G-BKFA	Monnet Sonerai IIL	R. F. Bridge
	G-BKFB	AS.350B Ecureuil	T. W. Walker Ltd
	G-BKFC	Cessna F.152-II	D. W. Walton/Sywell
	G-BKFG	Thunder Ax3 balloon	Thunder Balloons Ltd
	G-BKFI	Evans VP-1	F. A. R. de Lavergne
	G-BKFK	Isaacs Fury II	G. C. Jones
	G-BKFL	Aerosport Scamp	I. D. Daniels
	G-BKFM	Rutan Quickie	R. I. Davidson & P. J. Cheyney
	G-BKFN	Bell 214ST	British Caledonian Helicopters Ltd
	G-BKFP	Bell 214ST	British Caledonian Helicopters Ltd

Reg.	Type	Owner or Operator	Notes
G-BKFR	CP.301C Emeraude	I. N. Jennison/Barton	
G-BKFT	Cessna F.152-II	Rogers Aviation Ltd/Cranfield	
G-BKFV	Rand KR.2	F. H. French	
G-BKFW	P.56 Provost T.1	M. Howson	
G-BKFX	Colt 17A balloon	Colt Balloons Ltd	
G-BKFY	Beech C90 King Air	Medop Ltd	
G-BKFZ	PA-28R Cherokee Arrow 200	L & M Food Group Ltd/Stapleford	
G-BKGA	M.S.892E Rallye 150GT	Harwoods of Essex Ltd/Ipswich	
G-BKGB	Jodel D.120	R. W. Greenwood	
G-BKGC	Maule M.6	Stol-Air Ltd	
G-BKGD	Westland WG.30 Srs 100	British Airways Helicopters Ltd (G-BKBJ)/Beccles	
G-BKGE	Evans VP-2	D. Johnstone & L. Ward	
G-BKGF	Saxon II	Saxon Aircraft Co	
G-BKGH	Bell 205A-1	Rotair Ltd	
G-BKGJ	—		
G-BKGK	PA-31T3 T1040	Vickers Shipbuilding & Engineering Ltd/Barrow	
G-BKGL	Beech 18 (164)	G. A. Warner/Duxford	
G-BKGM	Beech 18	G. A. Warner/Duxford	
G-BKGN	Cessna U.206-II	Westair Flying Services Ltd/Blackpool	
G-BKGO	Piper J-3C-65 Cub	J. A. S. & I. K. Baldry	
G-BKGP	Thunder Ax6-56Z balloon	M. L. Faithful	
G-BKGR	Cameron O-65 balloon	S. R. Bridge	
G-BKGS	M.S.892A Rallye Commodore 150	B. A. Mills	
G-BKGT	SOCATA Rallye 110ST	Cambridge Discount Heating & Plumbing Ltd	
G-BKGU	Boeing 737-204	Britannia Airways Ltd/Luton	
G-BKGV	Boeing 737-204	Britannia Airways Ltd/Luton	
G-BKGW	Cessna F.152-II	Leicestershire Aero Club Ltd	
G-BKGX	Isaacs Fury	I. L. McMahon	
G-BKGZ	Bensen B.8	C. F. Simpson	
G-BKHA	WS.55 Whirlwind HAR.10	R. Windley	
G-BKHB	WS.55 Whirlwind HAR.10	R. Windley	
G-BKHC	WS.55 Whirlwind HAR.10	R. Windley	
G-BKHD	Baby Great Lakes	P. J. Tanulak	
G-BKHE	Boeing 737-204	Britannia Airways Ltd/Luton	
G-BKHF	Boeing 737-204	Britannia Airways Ltd/Luton	
G-BKHG	Piper J-3C-65 Cub	K. G. Wakefield/Cardiff	
G-BKHH	Thunder Ax10-140 balloon	R. Carr	
G-BKHI	SA Jetstream 3101	Peregrine Air Services Ltd/Edinburgh	
G-BKHJ	Cessna 182P	Augur Films Ltd/Ipswich	
G-BKHL	Thunder Ax9-140 balloon	R. Carr	
G-BKHM	Ben Air Sparrowhawk VL12/35	Ben Air Ltd	
G-BKHN	—		
G-BKHO	Boeing 737-2T4	Orion Airways Ltd/E. Midlands	
G-BKHP	P.56 Provost T.1 (WW397)	M. J. Crymble	
G-BKHR	Luton LA-4 Minor	R. J. Parkhouse	
G-BKHS	PA-34-220T-3 Seneca	C.S.E. Aviation Ltd/Kidlington	
G-BKHT	BAe 146-100	Dan-Air Services Ltd/Gatwick	
G-BKHV	Taylor JT.2 Titch	P. D. Holt	
G-BKHW	Stoddard-Hamilton Glassair SH.2	N. Clayton	
G-BKHX	Bensen B.8M	D. H. Greenwood	
G-BKHY	Taylor JT.1 Monoplane	J. Hall	
G-BKHZ	Cessna F.172P	Rogers Aviation Ltd/Cranfield	
G-BKIA	SOCATA TB.10 Tobago	Air Touring Services Ltd/Biggin Hill	
G-BKIB	SOCATA TB.9 Tampico	Bobbington Aviation Ltd/Halfpenny Green	
G-BKIC	Cameron V-77 balloon	C. A. Butter	
G-BKID	Beech C90 King Air	Airmore Sales Ltd/Elstree	
G-BKIE	Short SD3-30	Genair/Humberside	
G-BKIF	Fournier RF-6B	G. G. Milton/Sibson	
G-BKIH	AS.355F Twin Squirrel	McAlpine Helicopters Ltd/Hayes	
G-BKII	Cessna F.172M	M. S. Knight	
G-BKIJ	Cessna F.172M	WTFA Ltd/Stapleford	
G-BKIK	Cameron DG-10 airship	Cameron Balloons Ltd	
G-BKIL	—		
G-BKIM	Unicorn UE.5A balloon	I. Chadwick & K. H. Turner	

Notes	Reg.	Type	Owner or Operator
	G-BKIN	Alon A.2A Aircoupe	A. D. Lovell-Spencer/Elstree
	G-BKIP	Beech C90-1 King Air	Reckitt & Colman Products Ltd/ Norwich
	G-BKIR	Jodel D.117	R. Shaw & D. M. Hardaker
	G-BKIS	SOCATA TB.10 Tobago	Air Touring Services Ltd/Biggin Hill
	G-BKIT	SOCATA TB.9 Tampico	Martin Ltd
	G-BKIU	Colt 17A balloon	Robert Pooley Ltd
	G-BKIV	Colt 21A balloon	Colt Balloons Ltd
	G-BKIX	Cameron V-31 balloon	P. G. Dunnington
	G-BKIY	Thunder Ax3 balloon	A. Horn
	G-BKIZ	Cameron V-31 balloon	A. P. Greathead
	G-BKJB	PA-18 Super Cub 135	Cormack (Aircraft Services) Ltd/ Glasgow
	G-BKJD	Bell 214ST	British Caledonian Helicopters Ltd/ Aberdeen
	G-BKJE	Cessna 172N	Kilby Bros Property Ltd
	G-BKJF	M.S.880B Rallye 100T	R. W. H. Watson/Prestwick
	G-BKJG	BN-2B Islander	Pilatus BN Ltd/Bembridge
	G-BKJH	BN-2B Islander	Pilatus BN Ltd/Bembridge
	G-BKJI	BN-2B Islander	Pilatus BN Ltd/Bembridge
	G-BKJJ	BN-2B Islander	Pilatus BN Ltd/Bembridge
	G-BKJK	BN-2B Islander	Pilatus BN Ltd/Bembridge
	G-BKJL	BN-2B Islander	Pilatus BN Ltd/Bembridge
	G-BKJM	BN-2B Islander	Pilatus BN Ltd/Bembridge
	G-BKJN	BN-2B Islander	Pilatus BN Ltd/Bembridge
	G-BKJO	BN-2B Islander	Pilatus BN Ltd/Bembridge
	G-BKJP	BN-2B Islander	Pilatus BN Ltd/Bembridge
	G-BKJR	Hughes 269C	Thirsk Aero Services Ltd
	G-BKJS	Jodel D.120A	S. Walmsley/Blackpool
	G-BKJT	Cameron O-65 balloon	K. A. Ward
	G-BKJU	Sikorsky S-76A	Bristow Helicopters Ltd
	G-BKJW	PA-23 Aztec 2150	Alan Williams Enterprises Ltd
	G-BKJZ	G.159 Gulfstream 1	Rolls-Royce Ltd/E. Midlands
	G-BKKA	Cessna A.188B	Northair Aviation Ltd/Leeds
	G-BKKB	Cessna A.188B	Northair Aviation Ltd/Leeds
	G-BKKC	Cessna A.188B	Northair Aviation Ltd/Leeds
	G-BKKD	Cessna A.188B	Northair Aviation Ltd/Leeds
	G-BKKE	Cessna A.188B	Northair Aviation Ltd/Leeds
	G-BKKF	Cessna A.188B	Northair Aviation Ltd/Leeds
	G-BKKG	Cessna A.188B	Northair Aviation Ltd/Leeds
	G-BKKH	Cessna A.188B	Northair Aviation Ltd/Leeds
	G-BKKI	Westland WG.30 Srs 100	Westland Helicopters Ltd/Yeovil
	G-BKKJ	Cessna TU.206G	VW PLC
	G-BKKK	—	
	G-BKKL	—	
	G-BKKM	Aeronca 7AC Champion	M. McChesney
	G-BKKN	Cessna 182R	Northair Aviation Ltd/Leeds
	G-BKKO	Cessna 182R	Northair Aviation Ltd/Leeds
	G-BKKP	Cessna 182R	Bramall & Ogden Ltd/Doncaster
	G-BKKR	Rand KR-2	D. R. Trouse
	G-BKKS	Mercury Dart Srs 1	B. A. Mills
	G-BKKT	Short SD3-60	Genair/Humberside
	G-BKKY	BAe Jetstream 3102	Peregrine Air Services Ltd/Inverness
	G-BKKZ	Pitts S-1D Special	G. C. Masterson
	G-BKLA	SOCATA TB.20 Trinidad	E. Bilney Garage Ltd/Shipdham
	G-BKLB	—	
	G-BKLC	Cameron V-56 balloon	B. J. & L. A. Workman
	G-BKLJ	Westland Scout AH.1	J. E. Wilkie
	G-BKLK	Thunder Ax9-140-2 balloon	Thunder Balloons Ltd
	G-BKLO	Cessna F.172M	Reedtrend Ltd
	G-BKLP	Cessna F.172N	Reedtrend Ltd
	G-BKLR	—	
	G-BKLS	SA.341G Gazelle	Helicopter Services Ltd
	G-BKLT	SA.341G Gazelle	Helicopter Services Ltd
	G-BKLU	SA.341G Gazelle	Helicopter Services Ltd
	G-BKLV	SA.341G Gazelle	Helicopter Services Ltd
	G-BKLW	SA.341G Gazelle	Helicopter Services Ltd
	G-BKLX	Colt 105A balloon	Colt Balloons Ltd
	G-BKLY	Cameron A-140 balloon	S. P. Cymru
	G-BKLZ	Vinten-Wallis WA-116MC	W. Vinten Ltd
	G-BKMA	Mooney M.20J Srs 201	Clement Garage Ltd/Stapleford

G-BKDN   Short SD3-30 of Air UK.

123

G-BKWA Cessna 404 Titan

124

Reg.	Type	Owner or Operator	Notes
G-BKMB	Mooney M.20J Srs 201	R. Matthews	
G-BKMD	SC.7 Skyvan Srs 3	Trojan Air Services Ltd (G-BAHK)	
G-BKME	SC.7 Skyvan Srs 3	Trojan Air Services Ltd	
G-BKMF	SC.7 Skyvan Srs 3	Trojan Air Services Ltd	
G-BKMG	Handley Page 0/400 replica	M. G. King	
G-BKMH	Flamboyant Ax7-65 balloon	Pepsi-Cola International Ltd	
G-BKMI	V.S.359 Spitfire HF VIII	Fighter Wing Display Ltd	
G-BKMJ	Bell 206L-1 LongRanger	Air Hanson Sales Ltd/Weybridge	
G-BKMK	PA-38-112 Tomahawk	Cormack (Aircraft Services) Ltd/Glasgow	
G-BKML	Cessna 210H	John Bisco (Cheltenham) Ltd/Staverton	
G-BKMM	Cessna 180A	J. D. Brook	
G-BKMN	BAe 146-100	Dan-Air Services Ltd (G-ODAN)/ Gatwick	
G-BKMP	—	—	
G-BKMR	Thunder Ax3 balloon	B. F. G. Ribbons	
G-BKMS	Boeing 737-2K8	Orion Airways Ltd/E. Midlands	
G-BKMT	PA-32R-301 Saratoga SP	Hillary Investments Ltd	
G-BKMW	Short SD3-30	Short Bros Ltd/Sydenham	
G-BKMX	Short SD3-60	Loganair Ltd/Glasgow	
G-BKNA	Cessna 421	Star Paper Ltd	
G-BKNB	Cameron V-42 balloon	S. A. Burnett	
G-BKND	Colt 56A balloon	Hot Air Balloon Co Ltd	
G-BKNE	PA-28-161 Warrior II	J. R. Coughlan/Stapleford	
G-BKNF	Westland Bell 47G-3B1	Rotair Ltd/Panshanger	
G-BKNG	Boeing 727-217	Dan-Air Services Ltd/Gatwick	
G-BKNH	Boeing 737-2E7	Dan-Air Services Ltd/Gatwick	
G-BKNI	GY-80 Horizon 160D	A. Hartigan & ptnrs	
G-BKNJ	Grob G.109	Oxfordshire Sport Flying Ltd/Enstone	
G-BKNK	Rutan Vari-Eze	P. & S. H. Sutcliffe	
G-BKNN	Cameron Minar E Pakistan balloon	Forbes Europe Ltd	
G-BKNO	Monnet Sonerai IIL	S. Tattersfield & K. Bailey	
G-BKNR	Agusta-Bell 412	Alan Mann Helicopters Ltd	
G-BKNS	Agusta-Bell 412	Alan Mann Helicopters Ltd	
G-BKNT	Agusta-Bell 412	Alan Mann Helicopters Ltd	
G-BKNU	Agusta-Bell 412	Alan Mann Helicopters Ltd	
G-BKNX	SA.102.5	G. D. Horn	
G-BKNY	Bensen B.8M-P-VW	D. A. C. MacCormack	
G-BKOA	M.S.893E Rallye 180GT	Airborne Advertising Ltd/Blackpool	
G-BKOO	Barnes 7B balloon	Robert Pooley Ltd	
G-BKOP	Barnes 65 balloon	Robert Pooley Ltd	
G-BKOR	Barnes 77 balloon	Robert Pooley Ltd	
G-BKOS	P.56 Provost T.51	J. G. Cassidy	
G-BKOT	—	—	
G-BKOU	P.84 Jet Provost T.3	A. Topen	
G-BKOV	Jodel DR.220A	M. Edgerton	
G-BKOW	—	—	
G-BKOX	—	—	
G-BKOY	—	—	
G-BKOZ	—	—	
G-BKPA	Hoffman H-36 Dimona	Airmark Aviation Ltd	
G-BKPB	Aerosport Scamp	R. Scroby	
G-BKPC	Cessna A.185F	Black Knights Parachute Centre	
G-BKPD	Viking Dragonfly	P. E. J. Sturgeon	
G-BKPE	Jodel DR.250/160	H. Best-Devereux/Panshanger	
G-BKPG	Luscombe Rattler Strike	Luscombe Aircraft Ltd/Ashford	
G-BKPH	Luscombe Valiant	Luscombe Aircraft Ltd/Ashford	
G-BKPI	Piper J-3C-65 Cub	J. L. & D. S. Petty	
G-BKPJ	Colt 77B balloon	Colt Balloons Ltd	
G-BKPK	Campbell Cricket	J. C. McHugh	
G-BKPL	SOCATA TB.9 Tampico	G. P. Waudby	
G-BKPM	Schempp-Hirth HS.5 Nimbus 2	J. L. Rolls	
G-BKPN	Cameron N-77 balloon	Flamboyant Promotions Ltd	
G-BKPS	AA-5B Tiger	Eyewitness Ltd/Southampton	
G-BKPT	M.H.1521M Broussard	Lea Aviation/Redhill	
G-BKPU	M.H.1521M Broussard	Lea Aviation/Redhill	
G-BKPV	Stevex 250.1	A. F. Stevens	
G-BKPW	Boeing 767-204	Britannia Airways Ltd *Sir Winston Churchill*/Luton	
G-BKPX	—	—	
G-BKPY	Saab 91B/2 Safir ★	Newark Air Museum Ltd	

Notes	Reg.	Type	Owner or Operator
	G-BKPZ	Pitts S-1 Special	P. G. Kynsey & J. Harper
	G-BKRA	AT-6G Harvard	T. S. Warren/Sandown
	G-BKRB	Cessna 172N	Saunders Caravans Ltd
	G-BKRC	Robin R.2160	B. A. Mills
	G-BKRD	Cessna 320E	MLP Aviation Ltd/Elstree
	G-BKRE	—	
	G-BKRF	PA-18 Super Cub 95	N. R. Windley
	G-BKRG	Beechcraft C-45G	Aces High Ltd/Duxford
	G-BKRH	Brugger MB.2 Colibri	M. R. Benwell
	G-BKRI	Cameron V-77 balloon	J. R. Lowe & R. J. Fuller
	G-BKRJ	Colt 105A balloon	Owners Abroad Group PLC
	G-BKRK	SNCAN Stampe SV-4C	J. M. Alexander & ptnrs
	G-BKRL	Designability Leopard	Chichester-Miles Consultants Ltd
	G-BKRM	Boeing 757-236	Air Europe Ltd/Gatwick
	G-BKRN	Beechcraft D.18S	Scottish Aircraft Collection/Perth
	G-BKRP	S2R Thrush Commander	D. W. Craig
	G-BKRR	Cameron N-56 balloon	S. L. G. Williams
	G-BKRS	Cameron V-56 balloon	M. Z. & L. A. Rawson
	G-BKRT	PA-34-220T-3 Seneca	C.S.E. Aviation Ltd/Kidlington
	G-BKRU	Ensign Crossley Racer	M. Crossley
	G-BKRV	Hovey Beta Bird	A. V. Francis
	G-BKRW	Cameron O-160 balloon	Bondbaste Ltd
	G-BKRX	Cameron O-160 balloon	Bondbaste Ltd
	G-BKRY	Thunder Ax6-56Z balloon	Thunder Balloons Ltd
	G-BKRZ	Dragon 77 balloon	Anglia Balloon School Ltd
	G-BKSA	Cessna 425	Northair Aviation Ltd/Leeds
	G-BKSB	Cessna T.310Q	P. S. King
	G-BKSC	Saro Skeeter AOP.12	J. Powell & K. Abbott
	G-BKSD	Colt 56A balloon	Colt Balloons Ltd
	G-BKSE	Quickie Quickie	C. G. Taylor & M. DeLisle
	G-BKSG	Hoffman H-36	B. J. Wilson & F. C. Y. Cheung
	G-BKSH	Colt 21A balloon	Greenham Trading Ltd
	G-BKSI	Cessna P.206E	J. W. Van Staveren/Dubai
	G-BKSJ	—	
	G-BKSK	Quickie Q-2	M. J. Sullivan
	G-BKSO	Cessna 421C	Anglian Double Glazing Co Ltd/Norwich
	G-BKSP	Schleicher ASK.14	M. R. Shelton
	G-BKSR	Cessna 550 Citation II	Sarpenden Ltd
	G-BKSS	Jodel D.150	D. H. Wilson-Spratt
	G-BKST	Rutan Vari-Eze	R. Towle
	G-BKSU	Short SD3-30	Air UK Ltd/Norwich
	G-BKSV	Short SD3-30	Short Bros Ltd/Sydenham
	G-BKSW	Bensen B.8M	E. Kelly
	G-BKSX	SNCAN Stampe SV-4C	W. N. Blair-Hickman
	G-BKSY	Fouga CM.170-II Magister	B. J. S. Grey
	G-BKSZ	Cessna P.210N	Clarks Mast Ltd/Sandown
	G-BKTA	PA-18 Super Cub 95	ISI Sales & Marketing Ltd
	G-BKTB	Mooney M.20E	A. T. Bruce
	G-BKTC	Pitts S-2E	E. B. Bray
	G-BKTD	Partenavia P.68C	Alvair Aircraft Sales Ltd/Coventry
	G-BKTE	Colt AS-105 airship	Thunder Balloons Ltd
	G-BKTF	H.S.125 Srs 800A	British Aerospace PLC/Chester
	G-BKTG	Enstrom F-280 Shark	Trowell Plant Sales Ltd
	G-BKTH	CCF Hawker Sea Hurricane IB	Shuttleworth Trust/Duxford
	G-BKTI	—	
	G-BKTJ	Cessna 404 Titan	Donington Aviation Ltd/E. Midlands
	G-BKTK	Hughes 369HS	Suflinks Holdings Ltd
	G-BKTM	PZL SZD-45A Ogar	Anglo-Polish Sailplanes Ltd/Booker
	G-BKTN	BAe Jetstream 3102	McAlpine Aviation Ltd/Luton
	G-BKTO	—	
	G-BKTP	Colt AS-105 airship	Colt Balloons Ltd
	G-BKTR	Cameron V-77 balloon	G. F. & D. D. Bouten
	G-BKTS	Cameron O-65 balloon	C. H. Pearce & Sons (Contractors) Ltd
	G-BKTT	Cessna F.152	Stapleford Flying Club Ltd
	G-BKTU	Colt 56A balloon	E. Ten Houten
	G-BKTV	Cessna F.152	London Flight Centre Ltd/Stapleford
	G-BKTW	Cessna 404 Titan II	Hawk Aviation Ltd (G-WTVE)
	G-BKTX	—	
	G-BKTY	SOCATA TB.10 Tobago	Air Touring Services Ltd/Biggin Hill
	G-BKTZ	Slingsby T.67M Firefly	Slingsby Aviation Ltd (G-SFTV)/ Kirkbymoorside

Reg.	Type	Owner or Operator	Notes
G-BKUA	Bell 206A JetRanger	Rotair Ltd/Panshanger	
G-BKUB	Bell 206A JetRanger	Rotair Ltd/Panshanger	
G-BKUC	Mudry/CAARP CAP.10B	D. M. Britten	
G-BKUD	Cameron O-65 balloon	Cameron Balloons Ltd	
G-BKUE	SOCATA TB.9 Tampico	Air Touring Services Ltd/Biggin Hill	
G-BKUI	D.31 Turbulent	A. Onoufriou	
G-BKUJ	Thunder Ax6-56 balloon	J. M. Albury	
G-BKUL	AS.355F Twin Squirrel	McAlpine Helicopters Ltd/Hayes	
G-BKUM	AS.350B Ecureuil	McAlpine Helicopters Ltd/Hayes	
G-BKUN	Cessna 404 Titan	E. Midlands Aviation Ltd	
G-BKUO	Monnet Moni	F. S. Beckett	
G-BKUP	—		
G-BKUR	CP.301A Emeraude	P. Gilmour	
G-BKUS	Bensen B.80	J. F. MacKay	
G-BKUT	M.S.880B Rallye Club	J. J. Hustwitt	
G-BKUU	Thunder Ax7-77-1 balloon	Thunder Balloons Ltd	
G-BKUV	—		
G-BKUW	H.S.125 Srs 800A	British Aerospace PLC/Chester	
G-BKUX	Beech C90 King Air	Marchwiel Aviation Ltd/ Halfpenny Green	
G-BKUY	BAe Jetstream 3102	McAlpine Aviation Ltd/Luton	
G-BKUZ	Zenair CH.250	K. Morris	
G-BKVA	SOCATA Rallye 180T	R. Evans	
G-BKVB	SOCATA Rallye 110ST	Martin Ltd	
G-BKVC	SOCATA TB.9 Tampico	Martin Ltd	
G-BKVE	Rutan Vari-Eze	H. R. Rowley	
G-BKVF	FRED Srs 3	N. E. Johnson	
G-BKVG	Scheibe SF.25E Super Falke	Westland Flying Club Ltd/Yeovil	
G-BKVH	Cessna 404 Titan	E. Midlands Aviation Ltd (G-WTVA)	
G-BKVI	—		
G-BKVJ	Colt 21A balloon	Colt Balloons Ltd	
G-BKVK	Auster AOP.9	J. Powell & ptnrs	
G-BKVL	Robin DR.400/160	The Cotswold Aero Club Ltd/Staverton	
G-BKVM	PA-18 Super Cub 150	N. D. Meredith-Hardy	
G-BKVN	PA-23 Aztec 250F	VG Instruments Ltd/Headcorn	
G-BKVO	Pietenpol Aircamper	M. J. Honeychurch	
G-BKVP	Pitts S-21D Special	P. J. Leggo	
G-BKVR	PA-28 Cherokee 140	Aviamar Ltd	
G-BKVS	Bensen B.8M	V. Scott	
G-BKVT	—		
G-BKVV	Beech 95-B55 Baron	L. Mc. G. Tulloch	
G-BKVW	—		
G-BKVX	—		
G-BKVY	Airtour 31 balloon	Airtour Balloon Co Ltd	
G-BKVZ	Boeing 767-204	Britannia Airways Ltd *Viscount Mountbatten of Burma*/Luton	
G-BKWA	Cessna 404 Titan	Hawk Aviation Ltd (G-BELV)/ E. Midlands	
G-BKWB	EMB-110P2 Bandeirante	Euroflite Ltd (G-CHEV)/Luton	
G-BKWC	—		
G-BKWD	Taylor JT.2 Titch	E. Shouler	
G-BKWE	Colt 17A balloon	Hot-Air Balloon Co Ltd	
G-BKWF	—		
G-BKWG	PZL-104 Wilga	Anglo-Polish Sailplanes Ltd/Booker	
G-BKWH	Cessna F.172P	W. H. & J. Rogers Group Ltd/Cranfield	
G-BKWI	Pitts S-2A	G. C. Masterson	
G-BKWL	Short SD3-60	Short Bros Ltd/Sydenham	
G-BKWO	—		
G-BKWR	Cameron V-65 balloon	April & Gilbert Games Photographers	
G-BKWS	EMB-110P1 Bandeirante	Olsencrest Ltd (G-CTLN)	
G-BKWT	Airbus A.310-203	British Caledonian Airways Ltd/Gatwick	
G-BKWU	Airbus A.310-203	British Caledonian Airways Ltd/Gatwick	
G-BKWV	Colt 105A balloon	Lighter-Than-Air Ltd	
G-BKWW	Cameron O-77 balloon	A. M. Marten	
G-BKWX	Cessna 421C	Northair Aviation Ltd/Leeds	
G-BKWY	Cessna F.152	Cambridge Aero Club	
G-BKWZ	—		
G-BKXA	Robin R.2100	G. J. Anderson & ptnrs	
G-BKXB	Steen Skybolt	P. W. Scott	
G-BKXC	Cameron V-77 balloon	P. Sarrett	
G-BKXD	SA.365N Dauphin 2	Management Aviation Ltd/Aberdeen	

Notes	Reg.	Type	Owner or Operator
	G-BKXE	SA.365N Dauphin 2	Management Aviation Ltd/Aberdeen
	G-BKXF	PA-28R Cherokee Arrow 200	Aviation Sales (Guernsey) Ltd
	G-BKXG	Cessna T.303	Rogers Aviation Ltd/Cranfield
	G-BKXH	Robinson R-22	March Helicopters Ltd/Sywell
	G-BKXI	Cessna T.303	Northair Aviation Ltd/Leeds
	G-BKXJ	Rutan Vari-Eze	B. Wronski
	G-BKXK	SA.365N Dauphin 2	McAlpine Helicopters Ltd/Hayes
	G-BKXL	Cameron Bottle 70 balloon	Cameron Balloons Ltd
	G-BKXM	Colt 17A balloon	R. G. Turnbull
	G-BKXN	ICA IS-28M2A	British Aerospace PLC
	G-BKXO	Rutan Long-Eze	P. J. Wareham
	G-BKXP	Auster AOP.6	R. Skingley
	G-BKXR	D.31 Turbulent	G. L. Owens
	G-BKXS	Colt 56A balloon	Hot-Air Balloon Co Ltd
	G-BKXT	Cameron D-50 airship	Cameron Balloons Ltd
	G-BKXU	Cameron Dairy Queen Cone balloon	Cameron Balloons Ltd
	G-BKXV	SA.365C Dauphin	Management Aviation Ltd/Aberdeen
	G-BKXW	TB-25J Mitchell	Aces High Ltd/Duxford
	G-BKXX	Cameron V-65 balloon	P. G. Dunnington
	G-BKXY	Westland WG.30 Srs 100	Westland Helicopters Ltd/Yeovil
	G-BKYA	—	British Airways/Heathrow
	G-BKYB	—	British Airways/Heathrow
	G-BKYC	—	British Airways/Heathrow
	G-BKYD	—	British Airways/Heathrow
	G-BKYE	—	British Airways/Heathrow
	G-BKYF	—	British Airways/Heathrow
	G-BKYG	—	British Airways/Heathrow
	G-BKYH	—	British Airways/Heathrow
	G-BKYI	—	British Airways/Heathrow
	G-BKYJ	—	British Airways/Heathrow
	G-BKYK	—	British Airways/Heathrow
	G-BKYL	—	British Airways/Heathrow
	G-BKYM	—	British Airways/Heathrow
	G-BKYN	—	British Airways/Heathrow
	G-BKYO	—	British Airways/Heathrow
	G-BKYP	—	British Airways/Heathrow
	G-BKYR	—	British Airways/Heathrow
	G-BKYS	—	British Airways/Heathrow
	G-BKYT	—	British Airways/Heathrow
	G-BKYU	—	British Airways/Heathrow
	G-BKYV	—	British Airways/Heathrow
	G-BKYW	—	British Airways/Heathrow
	G-BKYX	—	British Airways/Heathrow
	G-BKYY	—	British Airways/Heathrow
	G-BKYZ	—	British Airways/Heathrow

The G-BKYA-YZ batch will be used for 14 Boeing 737-200s from late 1984. Another 17 will follow probably allocated in this and the G-BLBx sequence.

	G-BKZA	Cameron N-77 balloon	University of Bath Students Union
	G-BKZB	Cameron V-77 balloon	A. J. Montgomery
	G-BKZC	Cessna A.152	Montaguis Ltd
	G-BKZD	Cessna A.152	Montaguis Ltd
	G-BKZE	AS.332L Super Puma	British Airways Helicopters/Aberdeen
	G-BKZF	Cameron V-56 balloon	G. M. Hobster
	G-BKZG	AS.332L Super Puma	British Airways Helicopters/Aberdeen
	G-BKZH	AS.332L Super Puma	British Airways Helicopters/Aberdeen
	G-BKZI	Bell 206B JetRanger	Helicrops Ltd
	G-BKZJ	Bensen B.8V	S. H. Kirkby
	G-BKZK	Robinson R-22A	Sloane Helicopters Ltd
	G-BKZL	Colt AS-42 airship	Colt Balloons Ltd
	G-BKZM	Isaacs Fury II	R. J. Smyth
	G-BKZR	Short SD3-60	Genair/Humberside
	G-BKZS	Short SD3-60	Short Bros Ltd/Sydenham
	G-BKZT	FRED Srs 2	A. E. Morris
	G-BKZU	Colt 105A balloon	Colt Balloons Ltd
	G-BKZV	—	—
	G-BKZW	Beech C90 King Air	Airmore Sales Ltd/Elstree
	G-BKZX	EMB110P1 Bandeirante	C.S.E. Aviation Ltd/Kidlington
	G-BKZY	—	—

Reg.	Type	Owner or Operator	Notes
G-BKZZ	Cessna 404 Titan	Airmore Sales Ltd/Elstree	
G-BLAA	Fournier RF-5	A. D. Wren	
G-BLAB	DG.400	R. L. McLean	
G-BLAC	Cessna FA.152	Lancashire Aero Club/Barton	
G-BLAD	Thunder Ax7-77-1 balloon	Thunder Balloons Ltd	
G-BLAE	Beech 200 Super King Air	Airmore Aviation Ltd/Elstree	
G-BLAF	Stolp V-Star SA.900	J. E. Malloy	
G-BLAG	Pitts S-1D Special	J. A. Lowe	
G-BLAH	Thunder Ax7-77-1 balloon	T. Donnelly	
G-BLAI	Monnet Sonerai IIL	T. Simpson	
G-BLAJ	Pazmany PL.4A	J. D. LePine	
G-BLAK	Jodel DR.220	E. J. Horsfall/Blackpool	
G-BLAL	—	—	
G-BLAM	—	—	
G-BLAN	SA.341G Gazelle	Specialist Flying Training Ltd/Hamble	
G-BLAO	SA.341G Gazelle	Specialist Flying Training Ltd/Hamble	
G-BLAP	SA.341G Gazelle	Specialist Flying Training Ltd/Hamble	
G-BLAR	—		
G-BLAS	V.S.361 Spitfire F.IX	Aero Vintage Ltd	
G-BLAT	—		
G-BLAU	Bell 47G4	Bridge Helicopters Ltd	
G-BLAV	—		
G-BLAW	PA-28-181 Archer II	Express Aviation Services Ltd/ Biggin Hill	
G-BLAX	Cessna FA.152	A. & G. Aviation Ltd	
G-BLAY	—		
G-BLAZ	Cessna 421B	R. J. S. McMillan	

The G-BLBA-BZ batch has been reserved for British Airways.

G-BLCA	Bell 206B JetRanger	RNH Stainless Ltd	
G-BLCB	BAe Jetstream 3102	British Aerospace PLC/Prestwick	
G-BLCC	Thunder Ax7-77Z balloon	Thunder Balloons Ltd	
G-BLCD	PA-34-200-2 Seneca	Air Charter Scotland Ltd/Glasgow	
G-BLCE	Cessna 402C	Cecil Aviation Ltd/Cambridge	
G-BLCF	EAA Acrosport 2	M. J. Watkins & ptnrs	
G-BLCG	SOCATA TB.10 Tobago	Crescent Leasing	
G-BLCH	Colt 65D balloon	A. D. McCutcheon	
G-BLCI	—		
G-BLCJ	Cessna 441	Northair Aviation Ltd/Leeds	
G-BLCK	V.S.361 Spitfire F.IX	Aero Vintage Ltd	
G-BLCL	Cessna 441	Northair Aviation Ltd/Leeds	
G-BLCM	SOCATA TB.9 Tampico	Repclif Aviation Ltd/Liverpool	
G-BLCN	Short SD3-60	Short Bros Ltd/Sydenham	
G-BLCS	Short SD3-60	Short Bros Ltd/Sydenham	
G-BLCT	Jodel DR.220	R. W. H. Cole	
G-BLCU	Scheibe SF.25B Falke	B. Lumb & ptnrs	
G-BLCV	—		
G-BLCW	Evans VP-1	K. D. Pearce	
G-BLCX	—		
G-BLCY	Thunder Ax7-65Z balloon	Thunder Balloons Ltd	
G-BLCZ	Cessna 441	Northair Aviation Ltd/Leeds	
G-BLDA	SOCATA Rallye 110ST	Martin Ltd	
G-BLDB	Taylor JT.1 Monoplane	C. J. Bush	
G-BLDC	K&S Jungster 1	C. A. Laycock	
G-BLDD	Aero Trainer	C. A. Laycock	
G-BLDE	Boeing 737-2E7	Dan-Air Services Ltd/Gatwick	
G-BLDF	Bell 47G5	Helitech (Luton) Ltd	
G-BLDG	PA-25 Pawnee 260C	L. G. & M. Appelbeck	
G-BLDH	BAC One-Eleven 475EZ	British Aerospace PLC	
G-BLDI	Douglas C-47A	Aces High Ltd/Duxford	
G-BLDJ	PA-28-161 Warrior II	Simulated Flight Training Ltd	
G-BLDK	Robinson R-22A	Sloane Helicopters Ltd	
G-BLDL	Cameron Truck 56 balloon	Cameron Balloons Ltd	
G-BLDM	Hiller UH-12E	Gand S. G. Neal (Helicopters) Ltd	
G-BLDN	Rand KR-2	K. Y. Kendal	
G-BLDO	BAe Jetstream 3102	McAlpine Aviation Ltd/Luton	
G-BLDP	Slingsby T.67M Firefly	Cavendish Aviation Ltd	
G-BLDR	SA.365N Dauphin 2	McAlpine Helicopters Ltd/Hayes	
G-BLDS	BN-2B Islander	Pilatus BN Ltd/Bembridge	

Notes	Reg.	Type	Owner or Operator
	G-BLDT	BN-2B Islander	Pilatus BN Ltd/Bembridge
	G-BLDU	BN-2B Islander	Pilatus BN Ltd/Bembridge
	G-BLDV	BN-2B Islander	Pilatus BN Ltd/Bembridge
	G-BLDW	BN-2B Islander	Pilatus BN Ltd/Bembridge
	G-BLDX	BN-2B Islander	Pilatus BN Ltd/Bembridge
	G-BLDY	Bell 212	Bristow Helicopters Ltd
	G-BLDZ	Cameron N-77 balloon	Flamboyant Promotions Ltd
	G-BLEA	—	—
	G-BLEB	Colt 69A balloon	I. R. M. Jacobs
	G-BLEC	BN-2B-27 Islander	LEC Refrigeration PLC
	G-BLED	Short SD3-60	Short Bros Ltd/Sydenham
	G-BLEE	Short SD3-60	Short Bros Ltd/Sydenham
	G-BLEF	Short SD3-60	Short Bros Ltd/Sydenham
	G-BLEG	Short SD3-60	Short Bros Ltd/Sydenham
	G-BLEH	Short SD3-60	Short Bros Ltd/Sydenham
	G-BLEI	—	—
	G-BLEJ	—	—
	G-BLEK	—	—
	G-BLEL	Ax7-77-245 balloon	T. S. Price
	G-BLEM	—	—
	G-BLEN	Piper J-3C-65 Cub	C. H. A. Bott
	G-BLEO	Westland WG.30 Srs 100	Westland Helicopters Ltd (G-VAJC)
	G-BLEP	—	—
	G-BLER	—	—
	G-BLES	SA.750 Acroduster Too	W. G. Hosie & ptnrs
	G-BLET	—	—
	G-BLEU	—	—
	G-BLEV	—	—
	G-BLEW	Cessna F.182Q	Interair Aviation Ltd
	G-BLEX	—	—
	G-BLEY	SA.365N Dauphin 2	Management Aviation Ltd
	G-BLEZ	SA.365N Dauphin 2	Managament Aviation Ltd
	G-BLFA	—	—
	G-BLFB	—	—
	G-BLFC	—	—
	G-BLFD	—	—
	G-BLGS	SOCATA Rallye 180T	Lasham Gliding Society Ltd
	G-BLGW	F-27 Friendship Mk 200	British Midland Airways/Air UK
	G-BLHN	Robin HR100/285	H. M. Bouquiere
	G-BLJM	Beech 95-B55 Baron	Advanced Marketing Management Ltd
	G-BLPG	J/1N Alpha	L. A & P. Groves (G-AZIH)
	G-BLPP	Cameron V-77 balloon	L. P. Purfield
	G-BLRJ	Jodel DR.1051	M. P. Hallam
	G-BLSF	AA-5A Cheetah	G. W. Plowman & Sons Ltd (G-BGCK)
	G-BLST	Cessna 421C	Cecil Aviation Ltd/Cambridge
	G-BLUE	Colting 77 balloon	M. R. & C. Cumpston

Out-of-Sequence Registrations

Reg.	Type	Owner or Operator	Notes
G-BMAA	Douglas DC-9-15	British Midland Airways Ltd *Dovedale* (G-BFIH)/E. Midlands	
G-BMAB	Douglas DC-9-15	British Midland Airways Ltd *Ulster*/ E. Midlands	
G-BMAC	Douglas DC-9-15	British Midland Airways Ltd/E. Midlands	
G-BMAE	F.27 Friendship Mk 200	British Midland Airways Ltd/E. Midlands	
G-BMAF	Cessna 180F	N. F. Hemming (G-BDVR)/Staverton	
G-BMAG	Douglas DC-9-15	British Midland Airways Ltd/E. Midlands	
G-BMAH	Douglas DC-9-14	British Midland Airways Ltd/E. Midlands	
G-BMAI	Douglas DC-9-14	British Midland Airways Ltd/E. Midlands	
G-BMAJ	Short SD3-60	British Midland Airways Ltd (G-BKPO)/ E. Midlands	
G-BMAK	Douglas DC-9-30	British Midland Airways Ltd/E. Midlands	
G-BMAL	Sikorsky S-76A	N. Scottish Helicopters/Aberdeen	
G-BMAM	Douglas DC-9-30	British Midland Airways Ltd/E. Midlands	
G-BMAP	F-27 Friendship Mk 200	British Midland Airways Ltd/E. Midlands	
G-BMAR	—		
G-BMAT	V.813 Viscount	British Midland Airways Ltd (G-AZLT)/ E. Midlands	
G-BMAU	F-27 Friendship Mk 200	British Midland Airways Ltd/E. Midlands	
G-BMAV	AS.350B Ecureuil	Timothy Laing Aviation	
G-BMAW	F-27 Friendship Mk 200	British Midland Airways Ltd/E. Midlands	
G-BMAX	FRED Srs 2	P. Cawkwell	
G-BMAZ	Boeing 707-321C	British Midland Airways/E. Midlands	
G-BMCA	Beech A200 Super King Air	Marchwiel Aviation Ltd/ Halfpenny Green	
G-BMCL	Cessna 550 Citation II	Osiwell Ltd/Leavesden	
G-BMCP	Maule M5-235C Lunar Rocket	M. C. Pierce	
G-BMEC	Boeing 737-2S3	Air Europe Ltd *Joy*/Gatwick	
G-BMEL	PA-23 Aztec 250	M. C. Harrington	
G-BMFD	PA-23 Aztec 250	Bomford & Evershed Ltd (G-BGYY)/ Coventry	
G-BMHC	Cessna U.206F	D. R. Bromiley	
G-BMHG	Boeing 737-2S3	Air Europe Ltd *Adam*/Gatwick	
G-BMID	Jodel D.120	A. W. Cooke/Sywell	
G-BMIP	Jodel D.112	M. T. Kinch	
G-BMLM	Beech 95-58 Baron	Mowlem Construction (Plant Hire) Ltd (G-BBJF)/Fairoaks	
G-BMON	Boeing 737-2K9	Monarch Airlines Ltd/Luton	
G-BMOR	Boeing 737-2S3	Air Europe Ltd *Eve*/Gatwick	
G-BMSB	V.S.509 Spitfire IX	M. S. Bayliss/Coventry	
G-BMSC	Evans VP-2	G. J. Taylor	
G-BMSF	PA-38-112 Tomahawk	MSF Aviation Ltd/Manchester	
G-BMSM	Boeing 737-253	Air Europe Ltd *Roma*/Gatwick	
G-BMTC	AS.355F Twin Squirrel	The Marley Tile Co Ltd (G-BKUK)	
G-BMUD	Cessna 182P	J. Lloyd/Lulsgate	
G-BMVV	Rutan Vari-Viggen	G. B. Morris	
G-BMYU	Jodel D.120	G. Davies	
G-BNBH	Hughes 269C	Norman Bailey Helicopters Ltd/ Blackbushe	
G-BNBY	Beech 95-B55A Baron	E. L. Klinge (G-AXXR)	
G-BNDX	H.S.125 Srs 600B	Goodman Air Taxis (G-BAYT)	
G-BNHP	Saffrey S.330 balloon	N. H. Ponsford *Alpha II*	
G-BNJF	PA-32RT-300 Turbo Lance II	Academy Fork Lifts Ltd & Phennicus Ltd	
G-BNOC	EMB-110P1 Bandeirante	Fairflight Ltd/Air Ecosse/Aberdeen	
G-BNPD	PA-23 Aztec 250	Fras-Air Ltd	
G-BNSH	Sikorsky S-76A	N. Scottish Helicopters/Aberdeen	
G-BOAA	Concorde 102	British Airways (G-N94AA)/Heathrow	
G-BOAB	Concorde 102	British Airways (G-N94AB)/Heathrow	
G-BOAC	Concorde 102	British Airways (G-N81AC)/Heathrow	
G-BOAD	Concorde 102	British Airways (G-N94AD)/Heathrow	
G-BOAE	Concorde 102	British Airways (G-N94AE)/Heathrow	
G-BOAF	Concorde 102	British Airways (G-N94AF/G-BFKX)/ Heathrow	
G-BOAG	Concorde 102	British Airways (G-BFKW)/Heathrow	
G-BOBI	Cessna 152	R. M. Seath (G-BHJD)/Sherburn	
G-BOBS	Quickie Q.2	R. Stevens	

Notes	Reg.	Type	Owner or Operator
	G-BOBY	Monnet Sonerai II	R. G. Hallam/Sleap
	G-BOLT	R. Commander 114	Hooper & Jones Ltd/Kidlington
	G-BOMB	Cassutt Racer	R. W. L. Breckell
	G-BOND	Sikorsky S-76	N. Scottish Helicopters Ltd/Peterhead
	G-BONE	Pilatus P2-06 (U-142)	Aeromech Ltd/Booker
	G-BOOB	Cameron N-65 balloon	I. J. Sadler
	G-BOOK	Pitts S-1S Special	B. K. Lecomber/Denham
	G-BOOM	Hunter T.7	Brencham Ltd/Bournemouth
	G-BOOZ	Cameron N-77 balloon	J. A. F. Croft
	G-BOSS	PA-34-200T Seneca	Messenger Newspaper Group Ltd/Manchester
	G-BOTL	Colt 42R balloon	Colt Balloons Ltd
	G-BPAH	Colt 69A balloon	International Distillers & Vintners Ltd
	G-BPAJ	D.H.82A Tiger Moth	P. A. Jackson (G-AOIX)/Sibson
	G-BPAM	Jodel D.150A	A. J. Symes-Bullen
	G-BPAR	PA-31-350 Navajo Chieftain	Air Charter (Scotland) Ltd/Glasgow
	G-BPAV	FRED Srs 2	P. A. Valentine
	G-BPBP	Brugger Colibri Mk II	B. Perkins
	G-BPEG	Currie Wot	D. M. Harrington
	G-BPFA	Knight Swallow GK-2	G. Knight & D. G. Pridham
	G-BPGW	Boeing 757-236	Air Europe Ltd Anna-Marie/Gatwick
	G-BPJH	PA-19 Super Cub 95	P. J. Heron
	G-BPMB	Maule M5-235C Lunar Rocket	P. M. Breton
	G-BPMN	Super Coot Model A	P. Napp
	G-BPOP	Aircraft Designs Sheriff	Sheriff Aerospace Ltd/Sandown
	G-BPPN	Cessna F.182Q	Hunt Norris Ltd/Shoreham
	G-BPUF	Thunder Ax6-56Z balloon	Buf-Puf Balloon Group Buf-Puf
	G-BPYN	Piper J-3C-65 Cub	D. W. Stubbs & ptnrs/Popham
	G-BPZD	Nord NC.858S	S. O. Ghose/Shoreham
	G-BRAD	Beech 95-B55 Baron	Finrad Ltd/Biggin Hill
	G-BRAF	V. S. Spitfire 18 (SM969)	D. W. Arnold/Blackbushe
	G-BRAG	Taylor JT.2 Titch	A. R. Greenfield
	G-BRAL	G.159 Gulfstream 1	Ford Motor Co Ltd/Stansted
	G-BREF	Cessna 421C	Refair Ltd/Jersey
	G-BREL	Cameron O-77 balloon	BICC Research & Engineering Ltd
	G-BREW	PA-31-350 Navajo Chieftain	Whitbread & Co Ltd/Biggin Hill
	G-BRFC	P.57 Sea Prince T.1 (WP321)	Rural Naval Air Service/Bourn
	G-BRGH	FRED Srs 2	F. G. Hallam
	G-BRGV	PA-31-350 Navajo Chieftain	Centreline Air Services Ltd/Biggin Hill
	G-BRGW	GY-201 Minicab	R. G. White
	G-BRIC	Cameron V-65 balloon	E. D. P. Price
	G-BRIK	Tipsy Nipper 3	C. W. R. Piper
	G-BRIT	Cessna 421C	Britannia Airways Ltd/Luton
	G-BRIX	PA-32-301 Saratoga SP	Taylor Maxwell & Co Ltd/Bristol
	G-BRJP	Boeing 737-2S3	Air Europe Ltd (Louise)/Gatwick
	G-BRJW	Bellanca 7GCBC Citabria	Comarket/Staverton
	G-BRMA	WS-51 Dragonfly Mk 5 (WG719) ★	British Rotorcraft Museum
	G-BRMB	B.192 Belvedere Mk 1 (XG452) ★	British Rotorcraft Museum
	G-BRMC	Stampe SV-4B	A. Cullen/Booker
	G-BRMH	Bell 206B JetRanger 2	R. M. H. Stainless Ltd (G-BBUX)
	G-BROM	ICA IS-28M2	Westlake & Co Ltd
	G-BRSL	Cameron N-56 balloon	Balloon Stable Ltd Boris
	G-BRUX	PA-44-180 Seminole	Hambrair Ltd/Tollerton
	G-BRWG	Maule M5-235C Lunar Rocket	R. W. Gaskell/Exeter
	G-BRYA	D.H.C. 7-110 Dash Seven	Brymon Aviation Ltd/Plymouth
	G-BRYB	D.H.C. 7-110 Dash Seven	Brymon Aviation Ltd/Plymouth
	G-BRYC	D.H.C. 7-110 Dash Seven	Brymon Aviation Ltd/Plymouth
	G-BSAA	H.S.125 Srs 3B	Finevale Ltd/Heathrow
	G-BSAL	G.1159 Gulfstream 3	Shell Aviation Ltd/Heathrow
	G-BSAN	G.1159A Gulfstream 3	Shell Aviation Ltd/Heathrow
	G-BSBH	Short SD3-30	Short Bros Ltd/Sydenham
	G-BSDL	SOCATA TB.10 Tobago	Systems Designers Aviation Ltd/Blackbushe
	G-BSEL	Slingsby T-61G	RAFGSA/Bicester
	G-BSFC	PA-38-112 Tomahawk	Sherwood Flying Club Ltd/Tollerton
	G-BSFL	PA-23 Aztec 250	T. Kilroe & Sons Ltd/Manchester
	G-BSFT	PA-31-300 Navajo	Simulated Flight Training Ltd (G-AXYC)/Stansted

Reg.	Type	Owner or Operator	Notes
G-BSFZ	PA-25 Pawnee 235	Skegness Air Taxi Services Ltd (G-ASFZ)/Wyberton	
G-BSHL	H.S.125 Srs 600B	S. H. Services Ltd (G-BBMD)/Luton	
G-BSIS	Pitts S-1S Special	R. A. Mills	
G-BSPC	Jodel D.140C	B. E. Cotton/Shoreham	
G-BSPE	Cessna F.172P	Sceptre Precision Engineers/Bournemouth	
G-BSSL	Beech B80 Queen Air	Southern Air Ltd (G-BFEP)/Shoreham	
G-BSST	Concorde 002 ★	Fleet Air Arm Museum	
G-BSUS	Taylor JT.1 Monoplane	R. Parker	
G-BSVP	PA-23 Aztec 250F	Cladrose Ltd	
G-BTAL	Cessna F.152	TG Aviation Ltd	
G-BTAN	Thunder Ax7-65Z balloon	The BTAN Balloon Group	
G-BTBM	Grumman TBM-3W2 Avenger ★	War Birds of GB Ltd/Blackbushe	
G-BTCG	PA-23 Aztec 250	Eagle Tugs Ltd (G-AVRX)	
G-BTDK	Cessna 421B	Surplus Machinery Exports Ltd/Manchester	
G-BTEA	Cameron N-105 balloon	Southern Balloon Group	
G-BTFC	Cessna F.152 II	Tayside Aviation Ltd/Dundee	
G-BTFH	Cessna 414A	C. Taylor & Co Ltd/Birmingham	
G-BTGS	Smyth Sidewinder	T. G. Soloman	
G-BTHL	PA-31-350 Navajo Chieftain	Air Charter (Scotland) Ltd/Glasgow	
G-BTHS	PA-23 Aztec 250F	Partlease Ltd/Stansted	
G-BTIE	SOCATA TB.10 Tobago	Southern Aviation Services/Biggin Hill	
G-BTJM	Taylor JT.2 Titch	T. J. Miller/Dunkeswell	
G-BTLE	PA-31-350 Navajo Chieftain	Merlix Air Ltd/Blackbushe	
G-BTOM	PA-38-112 Tomahawk	Channel Aviation Ltd/Guernsey	
G-BTOW	SOCATA Rallye 180T	Aerospecial Ltd	
G-BTSC	Evans VP-2	D. W. Burrell	
G-BTSF	Evans VP-2	D. W. Burrell	
G-BTSH	Evans VP-2	B. P. Irish	
G-BTUG	SOCATA Rallye 180T	Lasham Gliding Soc Ltd	
G-BTWA	Bell 206B JetRanger 2	C. Hughesdon	
G-BTWT	D.H.C.-6 Twin Otter 310	Tulip Holdings Ltd	
G-BUCK	C.A.S.A. 1.131E Jungmann (BU+CK)	E. J. F. Lusted/White Waltham	
G-BUDY	Colt 17A balloon	Bondbaste Ltd	
G-BUFF	Jodel D.112	D. J. Buffham/Fenland	
G-BUMP	PA-28-181 Archer II	Autofarm Ltd/Leavesden	
G-BURD	Cessna F.172N	Volstatic Aviation Ltd/Denham	
G-BURT	PA-28-161 Warrior II	A. T. Howarth/Biggin Hill	
G-BUSA	AS.355F Twin Squirrel	Barratt Developments Ltd	
G-BUSY	Thunder Ax6-56A balloon	B. R. & Mrs M. Boyle Busy Bodies	
G-BUZZ	AB-206B JetRanger 2	Adifer Ltd	
G-BVMM	Robin HR.200/100	M. G. Owen	
G-BVPI	Evans VP-1	N. L. E. & R. A. Dupee/Dunkeswell	
G-BVPM	Evans VP-2	P. Marigold	
G-BWAL	PA-31-350 Navajo Chieftain	Marshall Sons & Co Ltd/Wickenby	
G-BWEC	Cassutt-Colson Variant	W. E. Colson/Redhill	
G-BWFC	Boeing Vertol 234LR Chinook	British Airways Helicopters Ltd/Aberdeen	
G-BWFJ	Evans VP-1	W. F. Jones	
G-BWHO	Thunder Ax6-56Z balloon	Thunder Balloons Ltd (G-BJZP)	
G-BWIG	G.17S replica	K. Wigglesworth	
G-BWJB	Thunder Ax8-105 balloon	Justerini & Brooks Ltd Whiskey J. & B.	
G-BWKK	Auster AOP.9 (XP279)	G. F. Kilsby	
G-BWKS	Lake LA-4-200 Buccaneer	Newell Aircraft & Tool Co Ltd (G-BDDI)/Headcorn	
G-BWMB	Jodel D.119	Tony Dyer Television	
G-BWRB	D.H.C.-6 Twin Otter 310	Brymon Aviation Ltd/Plymouth	
G-BWWW	BAe Jetstream 3102	The Distillers Co PLC/Bournemouth	
G-BXNW	SNCAN SV-4C	A. J. Ditheridge/Ipswich	
G-BXPU	H.S.125 Srs 3B/RA	McAlpine Aviation Ltd (G-AXPU/G-IBIS)/Luton	
G-BXYZ	R. Turbo Commander 690C	British Airports Authority/Gatwick	
G-BYRD	Mooney M.20K	Birds Garage Ltd/Denham	
G-BYSE	AB-206B JetRanger 2	Bewise Ltd (G-BFND)	
G-BZAC	Sikorsky S-76A	British Airways Helicopters Ltd/Aberdeen	
G-BZBH	Thunder Ax6-65 balloon	R. S. Whittaker & P. E. Sadler	

Notes	Reg.	Type	Owner or Operator
	G-BZBY	Colt 56 Buzby balloon	British Telecom
	G-BZKK	Cameron V-56 balloon	P. J. Green & C. Bosley *Gemini II*
	G-BZZZ	Enstrom F-28C-UK	Hampden Bottom Farm Ltd (G-BBBZ)
	G-CALL	PA-23 Aztec 250F	City Air Links/Ronaldsway
	G-CBEA	BAe Jetstream 3102-01	Birmingham Executive Airways Ltd
	G-CBIA	BAC One-Eleven 416	British Island Airways (G-AWXJ) *Island Ensign*/Gatwick
	G-CBIL	Cessna 182K	J. G. Reeves/Liverpool
	G-CCAA	H.S.125 Srs 700B	Civil Aviation Authority (G-DBBI)/Stansted
	G-CCAR	Cameron N-77 balloon	Colt Car Co Ltd *Colt*
	G-CCCC	Cessna 172H	P. D. Higgs/Elstree
	G-CCOZ	Monnet Sonerai II	P. R. Cozens
	G-CCUB	Piper J-3C-65 Cub	Cormack (Aircraft Services) Ltd
	G-CDAH	Taylor Super Coot A	D. A. Hood
	G-CDAN	V.S.361 Spitfire LF.16C	J. Parks & W. Francis
	G-CDGA	Taylor JT.1 Monoplane	D. G. Anderson (*stored*)/Prestwick
	G-CDGL	Saffery S.330 balloon	C. J. Dodd & G. J. Luckett *Penny*
	G-CEGA	PA-34-200T-2 Seneca	Cega Aviation Ltd/Goodwood
	G-CELT	EMB-110P2 Bandeirante	Fairflight Ltd/Air Ecosse/Aberdeen
	G-CETA	Cessna E.310Q	CETA Video Ltd (G-BBIM)/Elstree
	G-CETC	Aeronca 15AC Sedan	G. Churchill
	G-CEZY	Thunder Ax9-140 balloon	R. Carr
	G-CFLY	Cessna 172F	J. A. Clegg
	G-CGHM	PA-28 Cherokee 140	CGH Managements Ltd/Elstree
	G-CHIK	Cessna F.152	Wickwell (UK) Ltd (G-BHAZ)/Shoreham
	G-CHIP	PA-28-181 Archer II	R. H. Howard/Leeds
	G-CHOP	Westland Bell 47G-3B1	Time Choppers Ltd
	G-CITY	PA-31-350 Navajo Chieftain	City Air Links Ltd/Ronaldsway
	G-CJAN	PA-28-181 Archer II	J. Traynor/E. Midlands
	G-CJBC	PA-28 Cherokee 180	J. B. Cave/Halfpenny Green
	G-CJCB	Bell 206L LongRanger	J. C. Bamford (Excavators) Ltd (G-LIII)/E. Midlands
	G-CJDH	Pitts S.1S Special	C. J. D. Hackett
	G-CJHI	Bell 206B JetRanger	Tudorbury Air Services Ltd (G-BBFB)
	G-CJIM	Taylor JT.1 Monoplane	J. Crawford
	G-CLAN	PA-31-350 Navajo Chieftain	Bioplan Ltd/Bournemouth
	G-CLEA	PA-28-161 Warrior II	Roger Head Motors/Staverton
	G-CLEM	Bo 208A2 Junior	G. Clements (G-ASWE)
	G-CLUB	Cessna FRA.150M	B.L.A. Ltd
	G-CLUX	Cessna F.172N	N. J. Hebditch/Compton Abbas
	G-CNIS	Partenavia P.68B	White Withers & Co (G-BJOF/G-PAUL)
	G-COAL	Bell 206B JetRanger 3	NSM Aviation Ltd
	G-COCO	Cessna F.172M	Capel Aviation/Ipswich
	G-COLD	Cessna T.337D	Coldspec Ltd/Goodwood
	G-COLL	Enstrom F-280C	Capel & Co (Printers) Ltd
	G-COMM	PA-23 Aztec 250	Commair Aviation Ltd (G-AZMG)/E. Midlands
	G-CONI	L.749A-79 Constellation ★	Science Museum/Wroughton
	G-COOL	Cameron O-31 balloon	Swire Bros *Sprite*
	G-COOP	Cameron N-31 balloon	Balloon Stable Ltd *Co-op*
	G-COPE	Enstrom F-280C-UK-2 Shark	A. Cope
	G-COPS	Piper J-3C-65 Cub	W. T. Sproat
	G-COPY	AA-5A Cheetah	Gotelee Printing Ltd (G-BIEU)/Biggin Hill
	G-CORR	AS.355F Twin Squirrel	Colt Car Co Ltd/Staverton
	G-COTT	Cameron 60 SS balloon	Nottingham Building Soc
	G-CPAC	PA-28R Cherokee Arrow 200	D. McSorley
	G-CPFC	Cessna F.152	Central Air Services/Birmingham
	G-CPPC	PA-23 Aztec 250	Executive Air Ltd (G-BGBH)/Birmingham
	G-CPTS	AB-206B JetRanger 2	A. R. B. Aspinall
	G-CRAN	Robin R.1180T	Slea Aviation Ltd
	G-CRIC	Colomban Cri-Cri MC-15	A. J. Maxwell
	G-CRIL	R. Commander 112B	K. Cochrane
	G-CRIS	Taylor JT.1 Monoplane	C. J. Bragg
	G-CRTI	PA-28RT-201 Arrow IV	Hulbritts Developments Ltd
	G-CRZY	Thunder Ax8-105 balloon	R. Carr
	G-CSBM	Cessna F.150M	Coventry (Civil) Aviation Ltd
	G-CSFC	Cessna 150L	D. G. Jones & A. T. Jay/Mona
	G-CSKY	AB-206B JetRanger 3	Skyline Helicopters Ltd (G-TALY)/Booker

Reg.	Type	Owner or Operator	Notes
G-CSNA	Cessna 421C	Armstrong Aviation Ltd/Brough	
G-CSSC	Cessna F.152	K. H. Bunt/Shoreham	
G-CSZB	V.807SB Viscount	(Stored) (G-AOXU)/Exeter	
G-CTKL	AT-6 Harvard IIA	C. T. K. Lane	
G-CTRN	Enstrom F-28C-UK	Southern Charters Ltd/Shoreham	
G-CTSI	Enstrom F-280C Shark	Lemlyne Ltd (G-BKIO)	
G-CUBB	PA-18-150 Super Cub	Booker Gliding Club Ltd	
G-CUBI	PA-18-135 Super Cub	Hambletons Gliding Club Ltd	
G-CUBJ	PA-18 Super Cub 150	A. K. Leasing (Jersey) Ltd	
G-CUKL	Beech 200 Super King Air	Conoco (UK) Ltd (G-CNSI/G-OSKA)/ Luton	
G-CWOT	Currie Wot	D. A. Lord	
G-CXMF	G.1159 Gulfstream 2	Fay Air (Jersey) Ltd	
G-CYMA	GA-7 Cougar	CYMA Petroleum Ltd (G-BKOM)/Elstree	
G-DAAH	PA-28R-201T Turbo Arrow IV	A. A. Hunter	
G-DACA	P.57 Sea Prince T.1	Atlantic & Caribbean Aviation Ltd/ Staverton	
G-DAJW	K & S Jungster 1	A. J. Walters	
G-DAKS	Dakota 3	Aviation Enterprises/Duxford	
G-DAND	SOCATA TB.10 Tobago	Whitemoor Engineering Co Ltd	
G-DANN	Stampe SV-4B (Coupé)	D. R. Scott-Songhurst/White Waltham	
G-DART	Rollason Beta B2	M. G. Ollis	
G-DASI	Short SD3-60	Manx Airlines Ltd (G-BKKW)/ Ronaldsway	
G-DATA	EMB-110P2 Bandeirante	Fairflight Ltd/Air Ecosse (G-BGNK)/ Aberdeen	
G-DAVE	Jodel D.112	D. A. Porter/Sturgate	
G-DAVY	Evans VP-2	D. Morris	
G-DCAN	PA-38-112 Tomahawk	Airways Aero Associations Ltd/Booker	
G-DCAT	G.164D Ag-Cat	Miller Aerial Spraying Ltd/Wickenby	
G-DCCC	H.S.125 Srs 800B	British Aerospace PLC/Chester	
G-DCIO	Douglas DC-10-30	British Caledonian Airways *Flora McDonald — The Scottish Heroine*	
G-DCKK	Cessna F.172N	Bulldog Aviation Ltd/Andrewsfield	
G-DDDV	Boeing 737-2S3	Air Europe Ltd/Gatwick	
G-DEBS	Colt AA-150 gas balloon	Hot-Air Balloon Co Ltd	
G-DELI	Thunder Ax7-77 balloon	C. Delius	
G-DEVA	PA-23 Aztec 250	Eyelure Ltd/Panshanger	
G-DFIN	SA.365N Dauphin 2	McAlpine Helicopters Ltd/Hayes	
G-DFLY	PA-38-112 Tomahawk	Airways Aero Associations Ltd/Booker	
G-DFTS	Cessna FA.152	Denham Flying Training School Ltd	
G-DFUB	Boeing 737-2K9	Monarch Airlines Ltd/Luton	
G-DGDG	Glaser-Dirks DG-400/17	I. L. McKelvie & ptnrs	
G-DGDP	Boeing 737-2T7	Monarch Airlines Ltd/Luton	
G-DICK	Thunder Ax6-56Z balloon	Bandag Tyre Co	
G-DINA	AA-5B Tiger	Simon Deverall Print Ltd/Compton Abbas	
G-DIPS	Taylor JT.1 Monoplane	B. J. Halls	
G-DIVE	BN-2A-26 Islander	RAF Parachute Association (G-BEXA)/ Weston-on-the-Green	
G-DJBE	Cessna 550 Citation II	Paul Sykes Organisation Ltd/ Leeds	
G-DJHB	Beech A23-19 Musketeer	D. J. Bruce (G-AZZE)	
C-DJHH	Cessna 550 Citation II	York Aviation Ltd/Humberside	
G-DJIM	DHCA-I	J. Crawford	
G-DMAN	H.S.125 Srs 600B	McAlpine Aviation Ltd/Luton	
G-DMCH	Hiller UH-12E	D. McK. Carnegie & ptnrs	
G-DODD	Cessna F.172P-II	Northair Aviation Ltd/Leeds	
G-DOGS	Cessna R.182RG	Newbranch Ltd/Elstree	
G-DOLL	Thunder Ax6-56 S.I. balloon	Zebedee Balloon Service	
G-DORE	Partenavia P.68C	W. N. & H. E. Dore	
G-DOVE	Cessna 182Q	S. G. Lawrence	
G-DRAY	Taylor JT.1 Monoplane	L. J. Dray	
G-DTOO	PA-38-112 Tomahawk	Airways Aero Associations Ltd/Booker	
G-DUET	Wood Duet	C. Wood	
G-DUNN	Zenair CH.250	A. Dunn	
G-DUVL	Cessna F.172N	Duval Studios Ltd/Denham	
G-DWHH	Boeing 737-2T7	Monarch Airlines Ltd/Luton	
G-DWMI	Bell 206L-1 LongRanger	Glenwood Helicopters Ltd	
G-DYOU	PA-38-112 Tomahawk	Airways Aero Associations Ltd/Booker	
G-EAGL	Cessna 421C	Systime Ltd/Leeds	

Notes	Reg.	Type	Owner or Operator
	G-EASI	Short SD3-30	Genair (G-BITW)/Humberside
	G-EBJI	Hawker Cygnet Replica	A. V. Francis
	G-ECCO	GA-7 Cougar	M. J. Sparshatt-Warley Ltd/ Southampton
	G-ECGC	Cessna F.172N-II	Leicestershire Aero Club Ltd
	G-ECHO	Enstrom F-280C-UK-2 Shark	Litton Heating & Plumbing Ltd (G-LONS/G-BDIB)/Shoreham
	G-ECMA	PA-31-325 Navajo	Elliot Bros (London) Ltd/Rochester
	G-ECOX	Pietenpol Aircamper GN.I	H. C. Cox
	G-EDDY	PA-28RT-201 Arrow IV	Supaglide Ltd/Stapleford
	G-EDEN	SOCATA TB.10 Tobago	Tobago Air Services/Elstree
	G-EDHE	PA-24 Comanche 180	Hughes Engineers (Devon) Ltd (G-ASFH)
	G-EDIF	Evans VP-2	R. Simpson
	G-EEEE	Slingsby T.31 Motor Glider	R. F. Selby
	G-EENY	GA-7 Cougar	A. J. Hows/Elstree
	G-EEUP	SNCAN SV-4C	Meridian Drilling Co Ltd
	G-EEZE	Rutan Vari-Eze	A. J. Nurse
	G-EGEE	Cessna 310Q	Trent Park Stables Ltd (G-AZVY)
	G-EGGS	Robin DR.400/180	R. Foot/Compton Abbas
	G-EGLE	Christen Eagle II	Airmore Aviation Ltd/Elstree
	G-EHAP	Sportavia-Pützer RF.7	M. J. Revill/Exeter
	G-EIIR	Cameron N-77 balloon	Major C. J. T. Davey Silver Jubilee
	G-ELEC	Westland WG.30 Srs 200	Westland Helicopters Ltd (G-BKNV)/ Yeovil
	G-EMKM	Jodel D.120A	C. R. Davey/Inverness
	G-EMMA	Cessna F.182Q	Watkiss Group Aviation
	G-EMMS	PA-38-112 Tomahawk	Surrey & Kent Flying Club Ltd/ Biggin Hill
	G-EMMY	Rutan Vari-Eze	M. J. Tooze
	G-ENIE	Nipper T.66 Srs 3	C. N. Harrison
	G-ENII	Cessna F.172M	M. S. Knight/Goodwood
	G-ENOA	Cessna F.172F	Genoa Precision Engineers Ltd (G-ASZW)/Bournemouth
	G-ENSI	Beech F33A Bonanza	F. B. Gibbons & Sons Ltd
	G-EOFF	Taylor JT.2 Titch	G. Wylde
	G-EORG	PA-38-112 Tomahawk	Cormack (Aircraft Services) Ltd/ Glasgow
	G-EPDI	Cameron N-77 balloon	E.P.D. Containers & Supply Co Ltd & Pegasus Aviation Ltd Pegasus
	G-ERDB	Hawker Cygnet Replica	R. D. Bertram
	G-ERIC	R. Commander 112TC	DJF (Jersey) Ltd/Shobdon
	G-ERMS	Thunder AS33 Airship	Thunder Balloons Ltd
	G-ERTY	D.H.82A Tiger Moth	E. R. Thomas (G-ANDC)
	G-ESSX	PA-28-161 Warrior II	S. Harcourt (G-BHYY)/Stapleford
	G-ETUP	Cessna F.150L	Crepshaw Ltd/Leeds
	G-EURA	Agusta-Bell 47J-2	Eurospace Aviation Ltd (G-ASNV)
	G-EVAN	Taylor JT.2 Titch	E. Evans
	G-EVNS	Cessna 441	Northair Aviation Ltd/Leeds
	G-EWBJ	SOCATA TB.10 Tobago	Crocker Air Services/Biggin Hill
	G-EWIZ	Pitts S-2E Special	J. E. Davies
	G-EXEC	PA-34-200 Seneca	Capros Ltd
	G-EXEX	Cessna 404	Mills Aviation Ltd/Norwich
	G-EXIT	SOCATA Rallye 180GT	G-Exit Ltd/Rochester
	G-EZEE	Rutan Vari-Eze	M. G. E. Hutton
	G-EZLT	Rutan Vari-Eze	M. G. E. Hutton
	G-EZOS	Rutan Vari-Eze	O. Smith/Tees-side
	G-FAIR	SOCATA TB.10 Tobago	Sally Marine Ltd/Guernsey
	G-FALC	Aviamilano F.8L Falco	P. W. Hunter (G-AROT)
	G-FALK	Sequoia F.8L Falco 4	I. Chancellor
	G-FALL	Cessna 182L	D. M. Penny
	G-FANG	AA-5A Cheetah	Reedtrend Ltd
	G-FANL	Cessna FR.172K XP-II	J. Woodhouse & Co/Staverton
	G-FARM	SOCATA Rallye 235GT	M. J. Jardine-Paterson
	G-FARR	Jodel D.150	G. H. Farr
	G-FAYE	Cessna F.150M	Cheshire Air Training School Ltd/ Liverpool
	G-FBDC	Cessna 340A	Food Brokers Ltd (G-BFJS)
	G-FBWH	PA-28R Cherokee Arrow 180	Servicecentre Systems (Cambs) Ltd
	G-FCAS	PA-23 Aztec 250	E. L. Becker & J. Harper/Ronaldsway
	G-FCHJ	Cessna 340A	Telspec Ltd (G-BJLS)/Southend

Reg.	Type	Owner or Operator	Notes
G-FDGM	Beech B60 Duke	Fisher & Donaldson (G-BFEZ)	
G-FERY	Cessna 550 Citation II	European Ferries Ltd (G-DJBI)	
G-FFEN	Cessna F.150M	E. P. Collier/Ipswich	
G-FFLY	Slingsby T.67M Firefly	Slingsby Aviation Ltd/ Kirkbymoorside	
G-FHAS	Scheibe SF.25E Super Falke	Fourth Harrow Aviation/Booker	
G-FIRE	V.S.379 Spitfire XIVc	Classic Air Displays Ltd	
G-FISH	Cessna 310R-II	Boston Deep Sea Fisheries Ltd/ Humberside	
G-FIST	Fieseler Fi.156C Storch	Spoils Kitchen Reject Shops Ltd	
G-FIVE	H.S.125 Srs 1	Euroair Ltd (G-ASEC)/Gatwick	
G-FIZZ	PA-28-161 Warrior II	J. G. Fairhurst/Headcorn	
G-FJKI	Cessna 404 Titan	Countland House (Holdings) Ltd (G-VWGB)	
G-FLCH	AB-206B JetRanger 3	Fletchair (G-BGGX)/Leeds	
G-FLCO	Sequoia F.8L Falco	J. B. Mowforth	
G-FLEA	SOCATA TB.10 Tobago	Scientific & General Productions (Penzance) Ltd	
G-FLIC	Cessna FA.152	Birmingham Aviation Ltd (G-BILV)	
G-FLIK	Pitts S.1S Special	R. P. Millinship	
G-FLIP	Cessna F.152	Brailsford Aviation Ltd/Netherthorpe	
G-FLIX	Cessna E.310P	Peter Long International Services Ltd (G-AZFL)	
G-FLPI	R. Commander 112A	Tuscany Ltd/Leicester	
G-FLYI	PA-34-200 Seneca	G. R. T. Catering Ltd (G-BHVO)/Elstree	
G-FMFC	EMB-110P2 Bandeirante	Fairflight Ltd/Air Ecosse/Aberdeen	
G-FMUS	Robinson R-22	F. M. Usher-Smith (G-BJBT)	
G-FOAM	M.S.892A Rallye Commodore	Precision Foam (G-AVPL)/Lt. Staughton	
G-FOCK	Focke-Wulf Fw.190-A	P. R. Underhill	
G-FOIL	PA-31-310 Navajo	Air Foyle Ltd/Luton	
G-FORD	SNCAN SV-4B	P. Meeson	
G-FOTO	PA-23 Aztec 250	Davis Gibson Advertising Ltd (G-BJDH/ G-BDXV)/Booker	
G-FOUX	AA-5A Cheetah	Baryn Finance Ltd/Denham	
G-FOYL	PA-23 Aztec 250	Foyle Aviation (Leasing) Co (G-AVNK)/Luton	
G-FRAG	PA-32-300 Cherokee Six	R. Goodwin & Co Ltd/Southend	
G-FRED	FRED Srs 2	R. Cox	
G-FRJB	Britten Sheriff SA-1	Air Bembridge (IOW) Ltd	
G-FRST	PA-44T Turbo Seminole 180	Frost & Frost	
G-FSDA	AB-206B JetRanger 2	Flair (Soft Drinks) Ltd (G-AWJW)/ Shoreham	
G-FSPL	PA-32R-300 Lance	R. E. Husband & A. D. Widdows/ Staverton	
G-FUEL	Robin DR.400/180	R. Darch/Compton Abbas	
G-FUJI	Fuji FA200-180	S. T. Newington/Sibson	
G-FUND	Thunder Ax7-65Z balloon	Schroder Life Assurance Ltd	
G-FUZZ	PA-19 Super Cub 95	G. W. Cline	
G-FVEE	Monnet Sonerai I	D. R. Sparke	
G-FWRP	Cessna 421C	Vange Scaffolding & Engineering Co Ltd	
G-FXIV	V.S.379 Spitfire FR.XIV (MV370) ★	Whitehall Theatre of War	
G-FZZZ	Colt 56A balloon	Hot-Air Balloon Co Ltd	
G-GABD	GA-7 Cougar	Scotia Safari Ltd/Prestwick	
G-GACA	P.57 Sea Prince T.1	Atlantic & Caribbean Aviation Ltd/ Staverton	
G-GAEL	H.S.125 Srs 800B	Heron Management Ltd	
G-GALE	PA-34-200-2 Seneca	Gale Construction Ltd/Norwich	
G-GAMA	Beech B58 Baron	Gama Aviation Ltd (G-BBSD)/Fairoaks	
G-GAME	Cessna T.303	Lindsay Advertising Ltd	
G-GAYL	Learjet 35A	Heron Management PLC (G-ZING)/ Leavesden	
G-GBAO	Robin R.1180TD	J. Kay-Movat	
G-GBSL	Beech 76 Duchess	George Barlow & Sons Ltd (G-BGVG)/ Leavesden	
G-GCAT	PA-28 Cherokee 140B	Cheshire Air Training School Ltd (G-BFRH)/Liverpool	
G-GCKI	Mooney M.20K	Imperial Group Ltd/Biggin Hill	
G-GDAM	PA-18 Super Cub 135	Citation Flying Services Ltd	
G-GEAR	Cessna FR.182Q	Ranelagh Garage Ltd/Bodmin	
G-GEEP	Robin R.1180T	Organic Concentrates Ltd/Booker	

Notes	Reg.	Type	Owner or Operator
	G-GEES	Cameron N-77 balloon	Mark Jarvis Ltd *Mark Jarvis*
	G-GENE	Cessna 501 Citation	ABI Caravans Ltd/Leavesden
	G-GEOF	Pereira Osprey 2	G. Crossley
	G-GEUP	Cameron N-77 balloon	Colt Car Co Ltd
	G-GFLY	Cessna F.150K	Bolton Air Training School/ Blackpool
	G-GGGG	Thunder Ax7-77A balloon	Test Valley Balloon Group
	G-GHNC	AA-5A Cheetah	Chamberlain Leasing/Andrewsfield
	G-GHRW	PA-28RT-201 Arrow IV	Distance No Object Ltd (G-ONAB/ G-BHAK)
	G-GIGI	M.S.893A Rallye Commodore	Holding & Barnes Ltd (G-AYVX)/Southend
	G-GILL	Cessna 402C	Gill Aviation Ltd/Newcastle
	G-GINA	AS.350B Ecureuil	Endeavour Aviation Ltd/Shoreham
	G-GKNB	Beech 200 Super King Air	GKN Group Services Ltd
	G-GLEN	Bell 212	Autair International Ltd
	G-GLOS	H.P.137 Jetstream 200	Sabre Engines Ltd (G-BCGU/G-AXRI)/ Bournemouth
	G-GLUE	Cameron N-65 balloon	M. F. Glue
	G-GMSI	SOCATA TB.9 Tampico	A. H. McVicar & N. Hamilton/Prestwick
	G-GNAT	H.S. Gnat T.1 (XS101)	Ruanil Investments Ltd/Cranfield
	G-GOGO	Hughes 369D	A. W. Alloys Ltd
	G-GOLD	Thunder Ax6-56A balloon	John Terry & Sons Ltd
	G-GOLF	SOCATA TB.10 Tobago	K. Piggott
	G-GOMM	PA-32R-300 Lance	Embermere Ltd/Blackbushe
	G-GOOS	Cessna F.182Q	R. Clark (Airtransport Ltd)
	G-GOSS	Jodel DR.221	M. I. Goss
	G-GRAY	Cessna 172N	Buddale Ltd/Doncaster
	G-GRIF	R. Commander 112TCA	Z. I. Bilbeisi (G-BHXC)
	G-GROB	Grob G.109	Soaring (Oxford) Ltd/Enstone
	G-GROW	Cameron N-77 balloon	Derbyshire Building Society
	G-GTPL	Mooney M.20K	Valencienne Ltd (G-BHOS)/Biggin Hill
	G-GUNN	Cessna F.172H	J. G. Gunn (G-AWGC)
	G-GWYN	Cessna F.172M	G. P. Owen/White Waltham
	G-GYRO	Bensen B.8	The G-GYRO Group
	G-HADI	G.1159 Gulfstream 2	Arab Express Ltd/Heathrow
	G-HALL	PA-22 Tri-Pacer 160	F P. Hall (G-ARAH)
	G-HALP	SOCATA TB.10 Tobago	D. Halpern (G-BITD)/Elstree
	G-HANK	Cessna FR.172H	J. H. & R. Hankinson (G-AYTH)
	G-HANS	Robin DR.400 2+2	Headcorn Flying School Ltd
	G-HAPR	B.171 Sycamore HC.14 (XG547) ★	British Rotorcraft Museum
	G-HARV	PA-23 Aztec 250	Kraken Air Ltd/Cardiff
	G-HAWK	H.S.1182 Hawk	British Aerospace/Dunsfold
	G-HBUS	Bell 206B LongRanger	Toleman Delivery Service Ltd
	G-HEAD	Colt 56 balloon	Colt Balloons Ltd
	G-HELI	Saro Skeeter Mk 12 (XM556) ★	British Rotorcraft Museum
	G-HELY	Agusta 109A	Barratt Developments Ltd/Newcastle
	G-HENS	Cameron N-65 balloon	Horrells Dairies Ltd
	G-HEWS	Hughes 369D	Carroll Industries Leasing Ltd/ Stansted
	G-HFCI	Cessna F.150L	Horizon Flying Club Ltd/Ipswich
	G-HFCT	Cessna F.152	Horizon Flying Club Ltd/Ipswich
	G-HGGS	EMP-110P1 Bandeirante	Euroair Transport Ltd/Biggin Hill
	G-HGPC	BN-2A-27 Islander	Pilatus BN Ltd (G-FANS)/Bembridge
	G-HHOI	H.S.125 Srs 700B	Trust House Forte Airport Services Ltd (G-BHTJ)/Heathrow
	G-HIFI	PA-28R-201 Arrow III	Partipak Ltd/White Waltham
	G-HIGH	Cessna FT.337GP	P. L. Builder/Jersey
	G-HILR	Hiller UH-12E	G. & S. G. Neal (Helicopters) Ltd
	G-HIRE	GA-7 Cougar	London Aerial Tours Ltd (G-BGSZ)/ Biggin Hill
	G-HLFT	SC.5 Belfast (XR365)	HeavyLift Cargo Airlines Ltd/Southend
	G-HOLS	Warner Special	J. O. C. Warner
	G-HOLT	Taylor JT.1 Monoplane	K. D. Holt
	G-HOME	Colt 77A balloon	Anglia Balloon School *Tardis*
	G-HOOK	Hughes 369D	Auto Alloys (Helicopters) Ltd
	G-HOPE	Beech F33A Bonanza	Eurohaul Ltd/Southampton
	G-HOPL	BN-2T Islander	Anglo-Thai Corporation Ltd (G-BJBE)
	G-HORN	Cameron V-77 balloon	G. J. E. Horn
	G-HOSE	Cessna 152 II	Rustington Autos/Shoreham
	G-HOSK	PA-32R-301 Saratoga SP	Hosking Equipment Ltd/Norwich

Reg.	Type	Owner or Operator	Notes
G-HOST	Cameron N-77 balloon	A. J. Clarke & J. M. Hallam	
G-HOTS	Thunder Colt AS-80 airship	Thunder Balloons Ltd	
G-HOUL	FRED Srs 2	D. M. M. Richardson	
G-HOUS	Colt 31A balloon	Anglia Balloons Ltd	
G-HOVA	Enstrom F-280C-UK Shark	Supaglide Ltd (G-BEYR)	
G-HPVC	Partenavia P.68	Hampshire Pipelines Valves & Components Ltd	
G-HRLM	Brugger MB.2 Colibri	R. A. Harris	
G-HRZN	Colt 77A balloon	D. Gaze	
G-HSON	Cessna 441	Paul Sykes Group Ltd/Leeds	
G-HUBB	Partenavia P.68B	Hubbardair Ltd/Norwich	
G-HUFF	Cessna 182P	Robert Herbert (Holdings) Ltd/Liverpool	
G-HUGH	PA-32RT-300T Turbo Lance II	Mann Aviation Sales Ltd (G-IFLY)/ Fairoaks	
G-HULL	Cessna F.150M	Oldment Ltd/Netherthorpe	
G-HUNT	Hunter F.51	M. R. Carlton/Bournemouth	
G-HUNY	Cessna F.150G	T. J. Lynn (G-AVGL)	
G-HURI	CCF Hawker Hurricane IIB	B. J. S. Grey	
G-HWAY	PA-28R-200-2 Cherokee Arrow	Highway Windscreens (UK) Ltd (G-JULI)	
G-HWBK	Agusta A.109A	Willowbrook International Ltd/Fairoaks	
G-HYDE	AB-206B JetRanger 3	Hyde Helicopters Ltd	
G-IAHL	BN-2T Islander	Pilatus BN Ltd (G-IACL/G-BJYS)/ Bembridge	
G-IBFW	PA-28R-201 Arrow III	B. Walker & Co (Dursley) Ltd & J. & C. Ward (Holdings) Ltd/ Staverton	
G-ICES	Thunder Ax6-56SS balloon	Lighter-Than-Air Ltd	
G-ICRU	Bell 206A JetRanger	Specialist Flying Training Ltd/ Hamble	
G-ICUB	Piper J-3C-65 Cub	G. Cormack/Glasgow	
G-IDDY	D.H.C.I Super Chipmunk	N. A. Brendish (G-BBMS)/Southend	
G-IDJB	Cessna 150L	Leisure Lease Aviation/Southend	
G-IDWR	Hughes 369HS	Ryburn Air Ltd (G-AXEJ)	
G-IESH	D.H.82A Tiger Moth	I. E. S. Huddleston (G-ANPE)/Southend	
G-IFLI	AA-5A Cheetah	London Aviation Ltd/Biggin Hill	
G-IHDH	PA-28RT-201 Arrow IV	H.D.H. Cleaners Ltd (G-MRJV)	
G-IIIA	Swearingen Merlin IIIB	Willowbrook International Ltd/Fairoaks	
G-IKIS	Cessna 210M	Bob Crowe Aircraft Sales Ltd	
G-ILFC	Boeing 737-2U4	Dan-Air Services Ltd (G-BOSL)/Gatwick	
G-ILLY	PA-28-181 Archer II	A. G. & K. M. Spiers/Booker	
G-IMBE	PA-31-310 Navajo	T. Beattie Edwards & Co Ltd (G-BXYB/G-AXYB)/Biggin Hill	
G-IMLH	Bell 206A JetRanger 3	Sabaru (UK) Ltd	
G-INDC	Cessna T.303	Northair Aviation Ltd (G-BKFH)/ Leeds	
G-INMO	PA-31-310 Turbo Navajo	Sabaru (UK) Ltd/Coventry	
G-INNY	SE-5A Replica	R. M. Ordish	
G-IOMA	F.27 Friendship Mk 100	Loganair Ltd/Glasgow	
G-IOOO	Gulfstream Commander 1000	Mann Aviation Ltd/Fairoaks	
G-IOSI	Jodel DR.1051	R. G. E. Simpson & A. M. Alexander/ Panshanger	
G-IPPM	SA.102-5 Cavalier	I. D. Perry & P. S. Murfitt	
G-IPRA	Beech A200 Super King Air	J. H. Ritblat (G-BGRD)/Stansted	
G-IPSY	Rutan Vari-Eze	R. A. Fairclough	
G-IRLS	Cessna FR.172J	Starvillas Ltd/Luton	
G-ISIS	D.H.82A Tiger Moth	D. R. & M. Wood (G-AODR)	
G-IVAN	Rutan Vari-Eze	I. Shaw	
G-IWPL	Cessna F.172M	Reedy Supplies Ltd/Exeter	
G-JADE	Beech 95-58 Baron	Liaison & Consultant Services Ltd	
G-JAKE	D.H.C.I Chipmunk 22	J.M.W.Henstock (G-BBMY)/Netherthorpe	
G-JAKK	AA-5B Tiger	Sefact Message Centres Ltd (G-BHWI)	
G-JAKO	Cessna TU.206G	New Hatherley Garage/Ipswich	
G-JAKY	PA-31-325 Navajo	Ace Aviation Ltd/Glasgow	
G-JANE	Cessna 340A	Malcolm Air Ltd	
G-JANS	Cessna FR.172J	I. G. Aizlewood/Luton	
G-JASP	PA-23 Aztec 250	Landsurcon (Air Survey) Ltd/Staverton	
G-JAWS	Enstrom F-280C Shark	GPS (Print) Ltd	
G-JAZZ	AA-5A Cheetah	Fenchurch Leasing Ltd/Elstree	

Notes	Reg.	Type	Owner or Operator
	G-JBUS	FRED Srs 2	R. V. Joyce
	G-JCUB	PA-18 Super Cub 135	Piper Cub Consortium Ltd/Jersey
	G-JDST	PA-31-350 Navajo Chieftain	Jack Tighe Ltd/Sturgate
	G-JEAN	Cessna 500 Citation	Castlewood Air Services Ltd/Leavesden
	G-JEFF	PA-38-112 Tomahawk	Channel Aviation Ltd/Guernsey
	G-JENA	Mooney M.20K	Express Aviation Services Ltd/ Biggin Hill
	G-JENN	AA-5B Tiger	Charles Henry Leasing/Elstree
	G-JENS	SOCATA Rallye 100ST	B. H. Burnet (G-BDEG)/Dunkeswell
	G-JENY	Baby Great Lakes	J. M. C. Pothecary
	G-JETA	Cessna 550 Citation II	IDS Aircraft Ltd/Heathrow
	G-JETC	Cessna 550 Citation II	IDS Aircraft Ltd/Heathrow
	G-JETD	Cessna 550 Citation II	IDS Aircraft Ltd/Heathrow
	G-JETH	Hawker Sea Hawk FGA.6	Brencham Ltd
	G-JETM	Gloster Meteor T.7	Brencham Ltd
	G-JETP	Hunting Jet Provost T.52A	Brencham Ltd/Bournemouth
	G-JETS	A.61 Terrier 2	J. E. Tootell (G-ASOM)
	G-JETT	T-33 Mk 3 Silver Star	Anvil Aviation (Aircraft Restoration) Ltd/ (G-OAHB)
	G-JFWI	Cessna F.172N	J. F. Wallis/Goodwood
	G-JGCL	Cessna 414A	Johnson Group Management Services Ltd/Blackpool
	G-JGFF	AB-206B JetRanger 3	S.W. Electricity Board/Lulsgate
	G-JILL	R. Commander 112TCA	Hanover Estates Co (Property) Ltd/ Elstree
	G-JIMS	Cessna 340A-II	Granpack Ltd (G-PETE)/Leavesden
	G-JIMY	PA-28 Cherokee 140	J. C. Kumar (G-AYUG)/Coventry
	G-JJSG	Learjet 35A	Smurfit Ltd
	G-JLBI	Bell 206L-1 Long Ranger	Towers Transport Co
	G-JLCO	AS.355F Twin Squirrel	John Laing Construction Ltd
	G-JMCC	Beech 95-58 Baron	Ibis Enterprises Ltd
	G-JMFW	Taylor JT.1 Monoplane	G. J. M. F. Winder
	G-JMSO	Mitsubishi MU.300 Diamond	Colt Car Co Ltd
	G-JMVB	AB-206B JetRanger 3	J. M. V. Butterfield (G-OIML)
	G-JMWT	SOCATA TB.10 Tobago	Halton Communications Ltd/Liverpool
	G-JOAN	AA-5B Tiger	Oldment Ltd (G-BFML)/Netherthorpe
	G-JOEY	BN-2A Mk III-2 Trislander	Aurigny Air Services (G-BDGG)/ Alderney
	G-JOHN	PA-28R-201T Turbo Arrow III	Fairoaks Flight Centre
	G-JOLY	Cessna 120	E. J. F. Lusted/White Waltham
	G-JONE	Cessna 172M	Glibbery Electronics Ltd
	G-JONS	PA-31-350 Navajo Chieftain	Topflight Aviation
	G-JOON	Cessna 182D	Allen Technical Services/Luton
	G-JORR	AS.350B Ecureuil	Colt Car Co Ltd (G-BJMY)/Staverton
	G-JOSE	Cessna U.206G	Safari Skylink Enterprises Ltd
	G-JRCM	Hawker Fury Mk I Replica	J. R. C. Morgan
	G-JRMM	R. Turbo Commander 690B	R. B. Tyler (Plant) Ltd/Stansted
	G-JRSY	F-27 Friendship Mk 200	Jersey European Airways (For sale)
	G-JSAX	H.S.125 Srs 3BRA	Saxon Air Services Ltd (G-GGAE)
	G-JSBA	BAe Jetstream 3102-01	British Aerospace PLC/Prestwick
	G-JSSD	SA. Jetstream 3001	British Aerospace (G-AXJZ)/Prestwick
	G-JTCA	PA-23 Aztec 250	J. D. Tighe & Co Ltd (G-BBCU)/Sturgate
	G-JTIE	Cessna 421C	Eastern Air Executive (G-RBBE)/Sturgate
	G-JUDI	AT-6 Harvard III (FX301)	A. Haig-Thomas
	G-JUDY	AA-5A Cheetah	W. H. & J. M. Gadsby/Netherthorpe
	G-JULY	AA-5A Cheetah	W. H. Wilkins Ltd (G-BHTZ)/Biggin Hill
	G-JUNE	PA-28-161 Warrior II	Allen Technical Services Ltd/Luton
	G-JURG	R. Commander 114	Maronco Ltd/Leeds
	G-JVMR	Partenavia P.68B	Matthew Royce Ltd (G-JCTI/G-OJOE)
	G-JWIV	Jodel DR.1051	J. W. West
	G-KAFC	Cessna 152	King Air Flying Club/Biggin Hill
	G-KAIR	PA-28-181 Archer II	Academy Lithoplates Ltd/Aldergrove
	G-KASH	AA-5 Traveler	Karen Peters Knitware Ltd (G-AZUG)/ Elstree
	G-KATE	Westland WG.30 Srs 100	Helicopter Hire Ltd/Southend
	G-KATH	Cessna P.210N	HM Machinery Ltd/Humberside
	G-KATS	PA-28 Cherokee 140	J. R. Burgess (G-BIRC)
	G-KBPI	PA-28-161 Warrior II	K. B. Page (Aviation) Ltd (G-BESZ)/ Shoreham
	G-KCIG	Sportavia RF-5B	Executive Air Sport Ltd/Exeter
	G-KDFF	Scheibe SF.25E Super Falke	Booker Gliding Club Ltd

Reg.	Type	Owner or Operator	Notes
G-KDIX	Jodel D.9 Bebe	K. Barlow	
G-KEEN	Stolp SA.300 Starduster Too	F. Holmes/Panshanger	
G-KENY	Enstrom F-280C-UK-2	Decoy Engineering Project Ltd/ Birmingham	
G-KERC	Nord NC.854S	Kirk Aviation	
G-KERR	Cessna FR.172K-XP	A. G. Chrismas Ltd/Shoreham	
G-KERY	PA-28 Cherokee 180	Kerrytype Ltd (G-ATWO)/Shoreham	
G-KEYS	PA-23 Aztec 250	Ferguson Aviation/Newtownards	
G-KFIT	Beech F90 King Air	Kwik Fit Euro Ltd (G-BHUS)/Edinburgh	
G-KHRE	M.S.893E Rallye 150SV	Kenlyn Enterprises Ltd	
G-KIDS	PA-34-220T-3 Seneca	Holding & Barnes Ltd	
G-KILT	AA-5A Cheetah	Apollo Leasing Ltd (G-BJFA)/Glasgow	
G-KINE	AA-5A Cheetah	Audio Kinectic (UK) Ltd/Elstree	
G-KING	PA-38-112 Tomahawk	Gordon King (Aviation) Ltd/Biggin Hill	
G-KIRK	Piper J-3C-65 Cub	M. Kirk	
G-KISS	Rand KR-2	A. C. Waller	
G-KLAY	Enstrom F-280C Shark	Apollo Manufacturing (Derby) Ltd (G-BGZD)	
G-KOOL	D.H.104 Devon C.2	J. D. Rees/Biggin Hill	
G-KRIS	Maule M5-235C Lunar Rocket	Lord Howard of Walden	
G-KSBF	Hughes 369D	Ken Stokes (Business Forms) Ltd (G-BMJH)	
G-KUKU	Pfalzkuku (BS676)	A. D. Lawrence	
G-KUTU	Quickie Q2	M. S. Evans & ptnrs	
G-KWAX	Cessna 182E Skylane	E. W. Duck	
G-KWIK	Partenavia P.68B	Birchwood Aviation Ltd	
G-KYAK	Yakolev C-11 (00)	R. Lamplough/Duxford	
G-LADE	PA-32 Cherokee Six 300E	Appleby Glade Ltd/E. Midlands	
G-LAKI	Jodel DR.1050	V. Panteli	
G-LANA	SOCATA TB.10 Tobago	Pektron Ltd	
G-LANE	Cessna F.172N	Mark Laing Aviation Ltd	
G-LASH	Monnet Sonerai II	A. Lawson	
G-LASS	Rutan Vari-Eze	G. Lewis	
G-LATC	EMB-110P1 Bandeirante	Euroair Transport Ltd/Biggin Hill	
G-LAZE	Jodel DR.1050	N. B. Holmes	
G-LDYS	Colt 56A balloon	A. Green	
G-LEAM	PA-28-236 Dakota	Clutchstar Ltd (G-BHLS)/Fairoaks	
G-LEAN	Cessna FR.182	Velcourt (East) Ltd & Maidenhill Holdings Ltd (G-BGAP)	
G-LEAR	Learjet 35A	David Pratt & ptnrs Ltd (G-ZEST)/ Manchester	
G-LEAU	Cameron N-31 balloon	Balloon Stable Ltd	
G-LENS	Thunder Ax7-77Z balloon	Island Airship Co Ltd	
G-LEON	PA-31-350 Navajo Chieftain	Air Charter (Scotland) Ltd/Glasgow	
G-LEXI	Cameron N-77 balloon	R. H. Welch	
G-LEZE	Rutan Long Eze	K. G. M. Loyal & ptnrs	
G-LFCA	Cessna F.152	G. Capes/Humberside	
G-LFIX	V.S.509 Spitfire LF.IX	Island Trading Ltd	
G-LIDD	D.H.104 Dove 8A	Acme Jewellery Ltd (G-ARSN)/Coventry	
G-LIDE	PA-31-350 Navajo Chieftain	Mont Arthur Finance Ltd/Jersey	
G-LIFE	Thunder Ax6-56Z balloon	Schroder Life Assurance Ltd	
G-LIMA	R. Commander 114	Cargo Care Ltd/Ronaldsway	
G-LING	Thunder Ax7-65 balloon	Bridges Van Hire Ltd	
G-LINK	Sikorsky S-61N	British Caledonian Airways/Gatwick	
G-LINT	Pitts S.1S Special	P. L. Moss	
G-LIOA	Lockheed 10A Electra ★	Science Museum/Wroughton	
G-LION	PA-18-135 Super Cub	Holding & Barnes Ltd	
G-LITE	R. Commander 112A	Rhoburt Ltd/Manchester	
G-LLAI	Colt 21A balloon	Lighter-Than-Air Ltd	
G-LOAG	Cameron N-77 balloon	Matthew Gloag & Son Ltd	
G-LONG	Bell 206L LongRanger	Air Hanson Ltd/Brooklands	
G-LOOK	Cessna F.172M	Laarbruch Flying Club	
G-LOOP	Pitts S-1C Special	P. Meeson/Headcorn	
G-LORI	H.S.125 Srs 403B	Re-Enforce Trading Co Ltd (G-AYOJ)	
G-LORY	Thunder Ax4-31Z balloon	Thunder Balloons Ltd	
G-LOTI	Bleriot XI (replica)	M. L. Beach	
G-LOVO	Cessna 414A	Lovaux Ltd (G-KENT)/Blackbushe	
G-LOWE	Monnet Sonerai II	P. Archer	
G-LRII	Bell 206L LongRanger	Castle Air Charters Ltd	
G-LSMI	Cessna F.152	Hartmann Ltd	
G-LUAR	SOCATA TB.10 Tobago	Specialist Flying Training Ltd/ Hamble	

Notes	Reg.	Type	Owner or Operator
	G-LUCK	Cessna F.150M	M. Carrigan/Humberside
	G-LUCY	PA-30 Twin Comanche 160	Business Aviation Services (Selair) Ltd (G-AVCP)
	G-LULU	Grob G.109	Deltabond Ltd/Booker
	G-LUNA	PA-32RT-300T Turbo Lance II	Everest Aviation Ltd
	G-LYDE	Eiri PIK-20E	J. F. McAulay
	G-LYNN	PA-32RT-300 Lance II	P. Avery & R. J. Stanley (G-BGNY)
	G-LYNX	Westland WG.13 Lynx	Westland Helicopters Ltd/Yeovil
	G-MABI	Cessna F.150L	M. A. Berriman (G-BGOJ)/Andrewsfield
	G-MACH	SIAI-Marchetti SF.260	R. A. Sareen/Booker
	G-MACK	PA-28R Cherokee Arrow 200	Grumman Travel (Surrey) Ltd
	G-MADI	Cessna 310R II	IBC Transport Containers Ltd/Fairoaks
	G-MAFF	BN-2T Islander	Ministry of Agriculture, Food & Fisheries (G-BJEO)
	G-MAGG	Pitts S-1S Special	R. J. Pickin
	G-MAGI	AS.350B Ecureuil	Anglian Double Glazing Ltd (G-BHLR)/ Norwich
	G-MAGS	Cessna 340A	Goldstar Publications Ltd/Biggin Hill
	G-MAGY	AS.350B Ecureuil	Quantel Ltd (G-BIYC)
	G-MAIL	D.H.C.-6 Twin Otter 310	Fairflight Ltd/Air Ecosse/Aberdeen
	G-MALA	PA-28-181 Archer II	M. A. Lenhian & Associates (G-BIIU)/ Doncaster
	G-MALC	AA-5 Traveler	Air Coventry Ltd (G-BCPM)/Coventry
	G-MALK	Cessna F.172N	D. Bardsky/Barton
	G-MANX	FRED Srs 2	P. Williamson
	G-MARC	AS.350B Ecureuil	Denis Ferranti Hoverknights Ltd (G-BKHU)
	G-MARG	PA-31-350 Navajo Chieftain	M. Ferguson (Newtownards) Ltd
	G-MARK	Cessna F.337H	Denis Ferranti Hoverknights Ltd
	G-MARY	Cassutt Special 1	J. Chadwick/Redhill
	G-MAUL	Maule M5-235C Lunar Rocket	Capital Aviation Sales (UK) Ltd/ Staverton
	G-MAWL	Maule M4-210C Rocket	Hawk Aero Services Ltd/ Andrewsfield
	G-MAXI	PA-34-200T-2 Seneca	Auxili-Air Aviation Ltd
	G-MAXY	Cessna 210L	Lodge Flying Ltd/Elstree
	G-MAYO	PA-28-161 Warrior II	J. E. Greenall/Fairoaks
	G-MCAH	AS.355 Twin Squirrel	McAlpine Helicopters Ltd
	G-MCAR	PA-32 Cherokee Six 300D	Miller Aerial Spraying Ltd (G-LADA/G-AYWK)
	G-MCDS	Cessna 210N	Merseyside Car Delivery (G-BHNB)/ Liverpool
	G-MCEO	Beech A200 Super King Air	Colt Car Co Ltd (G-BILY)/Staverton
	G-MCOX	Fuji FA.200-180AO	W. Surrey Engineering (Shepperton) Ltd
	G-MDAS	PA-31-310 Navajo	Crosbyglow Ltd (G-BCJZ)
	G-MEBC	Cessna 310-1	Rogers Aviation Ltd (G-ROGA/G-ASVV)/ Cranfield
	G-MELT	Cessna F.172H	Alvair Aviation (Sales) Ltd (G-AWTI)/ Coventry
	G-MERI	PA-28-181 Archer II	Peacock Salt Ltd/Glasgow
	G-META	Bell 222	The Metropolitan Police/Lippitts Hill
	G-METB	Bell 222	The Metropolitan Police/Lippitts Hill
	G-METC	Bell 222	The Metropolitan Police (G-JAMC)/ Lippitts Hill
	G-MFEU	H.S.125 Srs 600B	Clartacrest Ltd/Cranfield
	G-MFMM	Scheibe SF-25C Falke	Derby & Lancs Gliding Club Ltd
	G-MICK	Cessna F.172N	J. W. Barwell/Leicester
	G-MIKE	Hornet Gyroplane	M. H. J. Goldring
	G-MILK	SOCATA TB.10 Tobago	G. Whincup
	G-MINI	Currie Wot	D. Collinson
	G-MINT	Pitts S-1S Special	T. G. Anderson
	G-MISS	Taylor JT.2 Titch	A. Brennan
	G-MIST	Cessna T.210K	Allzones Travel Ltd (G-AYGM)/ Biggin Hill
	G-MKAY	Cessna 172N	Air & General Services Ltd
	G-MKEE	EAA Acro Sport	G. M. McKee
	G-MKIV	Bristol Blenheim IV	G. A. Warner/Duxford
	G-MKIX	V.S.361 Spitfire F.IX	D. W. Arnold/Blackbushe
	G-MLAS	Cessna 182E	Mark Luton Aviation Services
	G-MLCS	Cessna 414A	Mountleigh Air Services (G-MGHI/ G-BHKK)/Leeds

Reg.	Type	Owner or Operator	Notes
G-MOBL	EMB-110P2 Bandeirante	Fairflight Ltd/Air Ecosse/Aberdeen	
G-MOGG	Cessna F.172N	J. G. James (G-BHDY)	
G-MOLY	PA-23 Apache 160	A. H. Hunt & ptnrs (G-APFV)/ St Just	
G-MONA	M.S.880B Rallye Club	K. S. Pattinson (G-AWJK)	
G-MONB	Boeing 757-2T7	Monarch Airlines Ltd/Luton	
G-MONC	Boeing 757-2T7	Monarch Airlines Ltd/Luton	
G-MOND	Boeing 757-2T7	Monarch Airlines Ltd/Luton	
G-MONO	Taylor JT.1 Monoplane	A. Doughty	
G-MORR	AS.350B Ecureuil	Colt Car Co Ltd (G-BHIU)/Staverton	
G-MOSI	D.H.98 Mosquito 35	D. W. Arnold (G-ASKA)/Blackbushe	
G-MOTH	D.H.82A Tiger Moth (K2567)	M. C. Russell/Duxford	
G-MOVE	Aerostar 601P	Red Dragon Travel Ltd/Cardiff	
G-MOXY	Cessna 441	Moxy Dump Trucks Ltd (G-BHLN)	
G-MOZY	D.H.98 (replica)	J. Beck & G. L. Kemp	
G-MPWI	Robin HR.100/210	MPW Aviation Ltd/Booker	
G-MSDS	Cessna 404	Elecwind (Clay Cross) Ltd/ E. Midlands	
G-MSFY	H.S.125 Srs 700B	Aravco Ltd/Heathrow	
G-MUSO	Rutan Long-Eze	M. Moran	
G-MXIV	V.S.379 Spitfire FR.XIV (NH749)	A. Wickenden	
G-NAIR	Cessna 421B	Genair (G-KACT)/Humberside	
G-NASH	AA-5A Cheetah	T. R. Bamber/Southampton	
G-NATT	R. Commander 114A	Northgleam Ltd	
G-NAVY	D.H.104 Sea Devon C.20 (XJ348)	J. S. Flavell & K. Fehrenbach (G-AMXX)/Shoreham	
G-NBSI	Cameron N-77 balloon	Nottingham Building Soc	
G-NDGC	Grob G.109	Soaring Southwest	
G-NDNI	NDN-1 Firecracker	Norman Marsh Aircraft Ltd/Goodwood	
G-NEAL	PA-32 Cherokee Six 260	C. Goodliffe Neal & Co Ltd (G-BFPY)	
G-NEIL	Thunder Ax3 balloon	Islington Motors (Trowbridge) Ltd	
G-NELL	R. Commander 112A	Arcdeal Ltd/E. Midlands	
G-NEUS	Brugger MB.2 Colibri	G. S. Smeaton	
G-NEWR	PA-31-350 Navajo Chieftain	Aaronite Equipment Ltd	
G-NEWS	Bell 206B JetRanger 3	Peter Press Ltd	
G-NEWU	Partenavia P.68C	Biograft Private Clinic Ltd (G-BHJX)/ Leeds	
G-NHRH	PA-28 Cherokee 140	H. Dodd	
G-NHVH	Maule M5-235C Lunar Rocket	Commercial Go-Karts Ltd/Exeter	
G-NICE	Short SD3-30	Genair/Humberside	
G-NICK	PA-19 Super Cub 95	J. G. O'Donnell & I. Woolacott/ Rochester	
G-NILE	Colt 77A balloon	I. J. McDonnell & A. Gray	
G-NITE	PA-31-350 Navajo Chieftain	WT Shipping Group Ltd/Luton	
G-NIUS	Cessna F.172N	Horizon Lighting Products Ltd/ Coventry	
G-NJAG	Cessna 207	G. H. Nolan Ltd/Biggin Hill	
G-NJAP	Cessna T.207A	N. Otaqui/Saudi Arabia	
G-NMAN	PA-31 Turbo Navajo	Machine Music Ltd (G-AXDD)/ Blackbushe	
G-NNAC	PA-18 Super Cub 135	Norwich & Norfolk Aero Club Ltd/ Swanton Morley	
G-NOBY	Rand KR-2	N. P. Rieser	
G-NODE	AA-5B Tiger	Curd & Green Ltd/Elstree	
G-NOEL	AB-206B JetRanger 2	N. Edmonds & Direct Produce Supplies Ltd	
G-NOME	Baby Great Lakes	J. B. Scott	
G-NORC	Cessna 425	Norcross Ltd/Blackbushe	
G-NORD	Nord NC.854	R. G. E. Simpson & A. M. Alexander/ Panshanger	
G-NORM	Bell 206B JetRanger 3	Norman Bailey Helicopters Ltd (G-BKPF)	
G-NOVA	Cessna T.337H	C. C. Deane/Blackpool	
G-NRDC	NDN-6 Fieldmaster	NDN Aeroculture Ltd/Sandown	
G-NUIT	Beech 99	Nightflight Ltd/Luton	
G-NUTS	Cameron 35SS balloon	The Balloon Stable Ltd	
G-NWPB	Thunder Ax7-77Z balloon	Lighter-Than-Air Ltd	
G-OABI	Cessna 421C	Mont Arthur Finance Ltd	
G-OADE	Cessna F.177RG	A. R. Gurney & ptnrs (G-AZKH)	
G-OAIM	Hughes 369HS	J. E. Clarke (G-BDFP)/Bournemouth	

Notes	Reg.	Type	Owner or Operator
	G-OAKL	Beech 200 Super King Air	T. Kilroe & Sons (G-BJZG)/Manchester
	G-OAKS	Cessna 421C	Barratt Developments Ltd/Newcastle
	G-OAMH	Agusta 109A	Goodman Air Taxis
	G-OAPA	Pilatus PC-6/B2-H2 Porter	Army Parachute Association/ Netheravon
	G-OATS	PA-38-112 Tomahawk	P. L. Brunton
	G-OAUS	Sikorsky S-76A	Ashton Upthorpe Stud & Farms Ltd
	G-OBAC	AS.350B Ecureuil	BAC Aviation Ltd (G-EORR/G-FERG/ G-BGCW)
	G-OBAT	Cessna F.152	J. J. Baumhardt Associates Ltd
	G-OBCA	Cessna 421C	British Car Auctions Ltd/Southampton
	G-OBEA	BAe Jetstream 3102-01	Birmingham Executive Airways Ltd
	G-OBEY	PA-23 Aztec 250	S. Warwickshire Flying School (G-BAAJ)/ Wellesbourne
	G-OBLE	C.A.S.A. 1.131 Jungmann	A.J.D. Securities Ltd/Elstree
	G-OBMW	AA-5 Traveler	Fretcourt Ltd (G-BDPV)
	G-OCAL	Partenavia P.68B	Grosvenor Aviation Services Ltd (G-BGMY)/Manchester
	G-OCAS	Short SD3-30	Genair (G-BJUK)/Humberside
	G-OCAT	Eiri PIK-20E	D. S. Innes
	G-OCPC	Cessna FA.152	Hampshire Aeroplane Co Ltd/ St Just
	G-OCUB	Piper J-3C-90 Cub	W. Savin & A. Buchanan
	G-ODAS	Cessna 404 Titan	Hubbardair Ltd
	G-ODAY	Cameron N-56 balloon	C. O. Day (Estate Agents)
	G-ODEL	Falconar F-II-3	A. Brinkley
	G-ODJM	Cessna 401	DJM Construction Ltd (G-BSIX/G-CAFE/ G-AWXM)/Jersey
	G-ODON	AA-5B Tiger	Moynihan Motor Engineering Ltd/ Elstree
	G-OEMA	Cessna 404 Titan	Kilby Bros (Property) Ltd
	G-OEZE	Rutan Vari-Eze	S. Stride & ptnrs
	G-OFAR	Cessna 402C	Wm Leach (Builders) Ltd/Newcastle
	G-OFBL	Beech C90 King Air	Food Brokers Ltd (G-MEDI)
	G-OFCM	Cessna F172L	W. B. Garnham & P. J. Woodland (G-AZUN)/Guernsey
	G-OFED	Enstrom F-280C-UK-2 Shark	Bellus Ltd
	G-OFHS	Hughes 369E	A. & P. M. Ford
	G-OFLY	Cessna 210L	A. P. Mothew/Stapleford
	G-OFRL	Cessna 414A	Flight Refuelling Ltd/Bournemouth
	G-OGAS	Westland WG.30 Srs 100	Bristol Helicopters Ltd (G-BKNW)
	G-OGDN	Beech A200 Super King Air	A. Ogden & Sons Ltd/Leeds
	G-OGET	PA-39 Twin Commanche 160 C/R	R. E. Lundquist (G-AYXY)
	G-OGKN	Quickie Q.2	Quickie Aircraft (Europe) Ltd
	G-OGOJ	AA-5A Cheetah	Publishing Innovations Leasing Ltd/ Elstree
	G-OHCA	SC.5 Belfast (XR363)	HeavyLift Cargo Airlines Ltd/Southend
	G-OHTL	Sikorsky S-76A	Air Hanson Ltd/Brooklands
	G-OIAN	M.S.880B Rallye Club	Ian Richard Transport Services Ltd
	G-OIAS	PA-31-350 Navajo Chieftain	Inkerman Air Services Ltd
	G-OIFR	Cessna 172RG	J. J. Baumhardt Associates (G-BHJG)
	G-OILS	Cessna T.210L	Machine Music Ltd (G-BCZP)/ Blackbushe
	G-OINK	Piper J-3C-65 Cub	A. R. Harding (G-BILD/G-KERK)
	G-OIOO	PA-23 Aztec 250	A. A. Kelly (G-AVLV)/Glasgow
	G-OJCB	AB-206B JetRanger 3	Air Hanson Ltd/Weybridge
	G-OJCT	Partenavia P.68C	Rockville Motors Ltd (G-BHOV)/Leeds
	G-OJCW	PA-32RT-300 Lance II	J. C. Walsh Contractors & Plant Hire Ltd/Woodvale
	G-OJEA	D.H.C.-6 Twin Otter 310	Jersey European Airways
	G-OJEE	Bede BD-4	G. Hodges
	G-OJON	Taylor JT.2 Titch	J. H. Fell
	G-OJVC	J/1N Alpha	R. W. J. Holland (G-AHCL)
	G-OJVH	Cessna F.150H	Westshells Ltd (G-AWJZ)/Sherburn
	G-OKAY	Pitts S-1E Special	Sky Fever (Aviation Enterprises)/Redhill
	G-OLDI	Ayres S2R-T-15/500 Thrush Commander	Farm Aviation Services Ltd
	G-OLDS	Colt AS-105 airship	Hot-Air Balloon Co Ltd
	G-OLDY	Luton LA-5 Major	M. P. & A. P. Sargent
	G-OLEE	Cessna F.152	Birmingham Aviation Ltd
	G-OLEN	Cessna 425	L. Shaw/Guernsey

Reg.	Type	Owner or Operator	Notes
G-OLIN	PA-30 Twin Comanche 160	Skyhawk Ltd (G-AWMB)/Stapleford	
G-OLLI	Cameron O-31 SS balloon	N. A. Robertson	
G-OLLY	PA-31-350 Navajo Chieftain	Robertson Foods Ltd (G-BCES)/Bristol	
G-OLVR	FRED Srs 2	A. R. Oliver	
G-OMAN	F.27 Friendship Mk 100	Manx Airlines/Air UK (G-SPUD)	
G-OMAV	AS.355F Twin Squirrel	Massellas Helicopters Ltd/Jersey	
G-OMCL	Cessna 550 Citation II	Micro Consultants Ltd/Biggin Hill	
G-OMET	Beech C90 King Air	Aerotime Ltd (G-COTE/G-BBKN)	
G-OMHC	PA-28RT-201 Arrow IV	M. H. Cundley/Redhill	
G-OMJH	Hughes 369E	M. Hughes	
G-ONTA	Hughes 369D	Southern Air/Shoreham	
G-ONPN	H.S.125 Srs 1B	Avonmore International Ltd (G-BAXG)	
G-ONPP	Hughes 369HS	Flintgrange Ltd	
G-OODE	SNCAN SV-4A	V. S. E. Norman (G-AZNN)	
G-OODI	Pitts S-1D Special	R. N. Goode (G-BBBU)/White Waltham	
G-OODO	Stephens Akro	R. N. Goode/White Waltham	
G-OODY	PA-28R Cherokee Arrow 200	J. Traynor Ltd/E. Midlands	
G-OOFY	Rollason Beta	G. Staples	
G-OOSE	Rutan Vari-Eze	J. A. Towers	
G-OPAT	Beech 76 Duchess	Ray Holt (Land Drainage) Ltd/(G-BHAO)	
G-OPBN	BN-2T Islander	Pilatus BN Ltd (G-BJOH)/Bembridge	
G-OPEL	Cessna F.172G	Concord Motor Services Ltd/Stansted	
G-OPIK	Eiri PIK-20E	R. L. McLean & ptnrs	
G-OPJT	Enstrom F-280C Shark	Sutton Windows Ltd (G-BKCO)	
G-OPSF	PA-38-112 Tomahawk	Panshanger School of Flying (G-BGZI)	
G-ORAV	Cessna 337D	R. J. Everett Engineering Ltd (G-AXGJ)/ Ipswich	
G-ORMC	Beech A200 Super King Air	RMC Group Services Ltd (G-BEST)/ Biggin Hill	
G-OROY	Partenavia P.68B	Astra Design Consultants Ltd (G-BFSU)/ Guernsey	
G-OSAL	Cessna 421C	Swinstead Aviation Ltd	
G-OSAM	H.S.125 Srs 700B	RSM Holdings (G-BKHK)/Heathrow	
G-OSKY	Cessna 172M	R. T. Pritchard/Coventry	
G-OSPL	Cessna P.210N	Saint Piran Ltd	
G-OTOW	Cessna 175B	S. R. Taylor (G-AROC)/Crosland Moor	
G-OTRG	Cessna TR.182RG	G. F. Holdings (Contractors) Ltd/ Manchester	
G-OTTA	Colt 1.5 MCB balloon	Colt Balloons Ltd	
G-OTUG	PA-18 Super Cub 150	Holding & Barnes Ltd	
G-OTUX	PA-28R-201T Turbo Arrow III	M. A. M. Quadrini/Newcastle	
G-OTVS	BN-2T Islander	TVS Television Ltd (G-BPBN/G-BCMY)/ Southampton	
G-OULD	Gould Mk I balloon	C. A. Gould	
G-OVFR	Cessna F.172N	B. Mitton/Leeds	
G-OVMC	Cessna F.152 II	Staverton Flying Services Ltd	
G-OWAC	Cessna F.152	Birmingham Aviation Ltd (G-BHEB)/ Birmingham	
G-OWAK	Cessna F.152	Warwickshire Aero Club (G-BHEA)/ Birmingham	
G-OWEN	K & S Jungster	R. C. Owen	
G-OWIN	BN-2A-8 Islander	London Parachuting Ltd (G-AYXE)	
G-OWJM	AB-206B JetRanger 3	J. M. Gow (G-BHXV)	
G-PACE	Robin R.1180T	Millicron Instruments Ltd/Coventry	
G-PACY	Rutan Vari-Viggen	E. Pace	
G-PADY	R. Commander 114	Wyndley Nurseries Ltd/Coventry	
G-PAGE	Cessna F.150L	Page Vehicle Hire (Strumpshaw) Ltd/ Seething	
G-PALS	Enstrom F-280C-UK-2 Shark	Southern Air/Shoreham	
G-PARA	Cessna 207	MacPara Ltd/Shobdon	
G-PARI	Cessna 172RG Cutlass	Frank Slowey Ltd/Inverness	
G-PARK	Lake LA-4-200 Buccaneer	Leisure Sport Ltd (G-BBGK)/ Thorpe Park	
G-PARS	Evans VP-2	A. Parsfield	
G-PATT	Cessna 404 Titan	Casair Aviation Ltd (G-BHGL)/ Tees-side	
G-PAWL	PA-28 Cherokee 140	P. Lodge (G-AWEU)/Liverpool	
G-PAWS	AA-5A Cheetah	Reedtrend Ltd	
G-PAXX	PA-20 Pacer 135	D. W. & M. R. Grace	
G-PCUB	PA-18 Super Cub 135 (L-21B) (54-2474)	M. J. Wilson/Biggin Hill	

Notes	Reg.	Type	Owner or Operator
	G-PDON	WMB.2 Windtracker balloon	P. Donnellan
	G-PEET	Cessna 401A	J. R. Fuller
	G-PENN	AA-5B Tiger	Wendexim Trading Co Ltd
	G-PENY	Sopwith LC-IT Triplane	J. S. Penny
	G-PERR	Cameron 60 bottle balloon	The Balloon Stable Ltd
	G-PFAA	EAA Model P biplane	P. E. Barker
	G-PFAB	FRED Srs 2	P. E. Barker
	G-PFAC	FRED Srs 2	M. Boulton & L. G. Carvall
	G-PFAD	Wittman W.8 Tailwind	M. R. Stamp
	G-PFAE	Taylor JT.1 Monoplane	G. Johnson
	G-PFAF	FRED Srs 2	D. H. Handley
	G-PFAG	Evans VP-1	N. S. Giles-Townsend
	G-PFAH	Evans VP-1	J. A. Scott
	G-PFAI	Clutton EC.2 Easy Too	E. Clutton & A. Tabenor
	G-PFAL	FRED Srs 2	A. Troughton
	G-PFAM	FRED Srs 2	W. C. Rigby
	G-PFAN	Avro 558 (replica)	N. P. Harrison
	G-PFAO	Evans VP-1	P. W. Price
	G-PFAP	Currie Wot/SE-5A (C1904)	P. G. Abbey
	G-PFAR	Isaacs Fury II	C. J. Repik
	G-PFAS	GY-20 Minicab	J. Sproston & F. W. Speed
	G-PFAT	Monnet Sonerai II	H. B. Carter
	G-PFAU	Rand KR-2	D. E. Peace
	G-PFAV	D.31 Turbulent	B. A. Luckins
	G-PFAW	Evans VP-1	R. F. Shingler
	G-PFAX	FRED Srs 2	A. J. Dunston
	G-PFAY	EAA Biplane	A. K. Lang & A. L. Young
	G-PFAZ	Evans VP-1	B. Kylo
	G-PHIL	Hornet Gyroplane	A. J. Philpotts
	G-PICS	Cessna 182F	Astral Aerial Surveys Ltd (G-ASHO)
	G-PIED	PA-23 Aztec 250	Air London (Executive Travel) Ltd/ Biggin Hill
	G-PIES	Thunder Ax7-77Z balloon	Pork Farms Ltd
	G-PIGN	Bolmet Paloma Mk 1	T. P. Metson & J. A. Bollen
	G-PINT	Cameron 65 SS balloon	Charles Wells Ltd
	G-PIPE	Cameron N-56 SS balloon	Carreras Rothmans Ltd
	G-PLAN	Cessna F.150L	S. S. Padam/Denham
	G-PLAY	Robin R.2100A	Cotswold Aero Club Ltd/Staverton
	G-PLEV	Cessna 340	KJ Bill Aviation Ltd/Birmingham
	G-PLIV	Pazmany PL.4	B. P. North
	G-PLOW	Hughes 269B	March Helicopters Ltd (G-AVUM)/ Sywell
	G-PLUM	Bell 206L LongRanger	PLM Helicopters Ltd
	G-PLUS	PA-34-200T-2 Seneca	C. G. Strasser/Jersey
	G-PMCN	Monnet Sonerai II	P. J. McNamee
	G-POKE	Pitts S-1E Special	D. C. Purley/Goodwood
	G-POLO	PA-31-350 Navajo Chieftain	Grosvenor Aviation Services Ltd/ Manchester
	G-POLY	Cameron N-77 balloon	A. J. Bingley Ltd Polywallets
	G-PONY	Colt 31A balloon	Lighter-Than-Air Ltd
	G-POOH	Piper J-3C-65 Cub	P. Robinson
	G-POPE	Eiri PIK-20E-1	J. T. Pope/Booker
	G-PORR	AS.350B Ecureuil	Colt Car Co Ltd/Staverton
	G-POST	EMB-110P1 Bandeirante	Fairflight Ltd/Air Ecosse/Aberdeen
	G-POWA	PA-24 Comanche 400	G. F. Miller/Cardiff
	G-POWL	Cessna 182R	Northair Aviation Ltd/Leeds
	G-PPLI	Pazmany PL.1	G. Anderson
	G-PRAG	Brugger MB.2 Colibri	R. J. Hodder
	G-PROV	Hunting Jet Provost T.52A	Brencham Ltd/Bournemouth
	G-PRXI	V.S.365 Spitfire PR.XI	Trent Aero Engineering Ltd
	G-PSID	P-51D Mustang	Fairoaks Aviation Services Ltd/ Blackbushe
	G-PSPS	Thundercolt AS-80 airship	Lighter-Than-Air Ltd
	G-PTER	Beech C90 King Air	Colt Car Co Ltd (G-BIEE)/Staverton
	G-PTWO	Pilatus P2-05 (RF+16)	R. Lamplough/Duxford
	G-PUBS	Colt 56 SS balloon	Lighter-Than-Air Ltd
	G-PUFF	Thunder Ax7-77A balloon	Intervarsity Balloon Club Puffin II
	G-PULL	PA-18 Super Cub 150	G. R. Janney
	G-PUMA	AS.332L Super Puma	Management Aviation Ltd
	G-PUMB	AS.332L Super Puma	Management Aviation Ltd
	G-PUMD	AS.332L Super Puma	Management Aviation Ltd

G-MONB   Boeing 757-2T7 of Monarch Airlines.

147

G-PFAG   Evans VP-1.

G-TJET   Lockheed T-33A-1-LO.

Reg.	Type	Owner or Operator	Notes
G-PUME	AS.332L Super Puma	Management Aviation Ltd	
G-PUMG	AS.332L Super Puma	Management Aviation Ltd	
G-PUMH	AS.332L Super Puma	Management Aviation Ltd	
G-PURR	AA-5A Cheetah	W. H. Wilkins Ltd (G-BJDN)/Biggin Hill	
G-PUSH	Rutan Long-Eze	E. G. Peterson	
G-PVAF	PA-44-180 Seminole	Pincus Vidler Arthur Fitzgerald Ltd/ Shoreham	
G-PVAM	Port Victoria 7 Grain Kitten	A. J. Manning	
G-PYRO	Cameron N-65 balloon	Masts Engineering Ltd	
G-RACA	P.57 Sea Prince T.1	Atlantic & Caribbean Aviation Ltd/ Staverton	
G-RADE	Cessna 210L	R. J. Herbert (G-CENT)	
G-RAEM	Rutan LongEze	G. F. H. Singleton	
G-RAFC	Robin R.2112	RAF Cranwell Flying Club	
G-RAFE	Thunder Ax7-77 balloon	A. J. W. Rose	
G-RAFT	Rutan Long-Eze	D. G. Foreman	
G-RAIN	Maule M5-235C Lunar Rocket	J. S. Mehew	
G-RAMS	PA-32R-301 Saratoga SP	Peacock & Archer Ltd/Manchester	
G-RAND	Rand KR-2	R. L. Wharmby	
G-RAPA	BN-2T Islander	Rhine Army Parachute Association	
G-RARE	Thunder Ax5-42 SS balloon	International Distillers & Vintners Ltd	
G-RASC	Evans VP-2	R. A. Codling	
G-RAYS	Zenair CH.250	R. E. Delves	
G-RBIN	Robin DR.400/2+2	Headcorn Flying School Ltd	
G-RBLA	D.H.C.-6 Twin Otter 310	Express Air Services Ltd/Bournemouth	
G-RBOS	Colt AS-105 airship	Royal Bank of Scotland	
G-RDON	WMB.2 Windtracker balloon	P. J. Donnellan (G-BICH)	
G-REAT	GA-7 Cougar	Lessnow Ltd	
G-REEK	AA-5A Cheetah	JT Aviation Ltd/Denham	
G-REES	Jodel D.140C	J. D. Rees/Biggin Hill	
G-REID	Rotorway Scorpion 133	J. Reid (G-BGAW)	
G-REIS	PA-28R-201T Turbo Arrow III	H. Reis (Hard Chrome) Ltd/ Halfpenny Green	
G-RENO	SOCATA TB.10 Tobago	Tyler International Ltd	
G-REST	Beech P35 Bonanza	C. R. Taylor (G-ASFJ)	
G-RETA	C.A.S.A. 1.131 Jungmann	C. Maron/Booker	
G-REXS	PA-28-181 Archer II	Channel Islands Aero Holdings (Jersey) Ltd	
G-RHCN	Cessna FR.182RG	R. H. C. Neville	
G-RHFI	Alexander Todd Skybolt	RHF (Estates) Ltd/Andrewsfield	
G-RHHT	PA-32RT-300 Lance II	H. T. Air Freight Ltd/Staverton	
G-RIDE	Stephens Akro	R. Mitchell/Coventry	
G-RIGS	Aerostar 601P	Rigs Design Services Ltd/Fairoaks	
G-RILL	Cessna 421C	Maxwell Restaurants Ltd (G-BGZM)/ Elstree	
G-RILY	Monnet Sonerai II	K. D. Riley	
G-RIND	Cessna 335	ATA Grinding Processes/Leavesden	
G-RIST	Cessna 310R-II	Velcourt (East) Ltd & ptnrs (G-DATS)/ Staverton	
G-RJMI	AA-5A Cheetah	R. J. Mole	
G-RLAY	EMB-110P1 Bandeirante	Genair/Humberside	
G-RMAE	PA-31 Turbo Navajo	Cooper Merseyside Ltd (G-BAEG)	
G-RMAM	Musselwhite MAM.1	M. A. Musselwhite	
G-RMSS	Short SD3-60	Air Ecosse Ltd (G-BKKU)/Aberdeen	
G-RNAS	D.H.104 Sea Devon C.20	D. W. Hermiston-Hooper/Sandown	
G-RNSY	F.27 Friendship Mk 200	Jersey European Airways (For sale)	
G-ROAN	Boeing E.75N-1 Stearman	R. & A. Windley	
G-ROAR	Cessna 401	Salon Productions Ltd (G-BZFL/ G-AWSF)/Biggin Hill	
G-ROBI	Grob G.109B	Soaring (Oxford) Ltd	
G-ROBK	Cessna R.182RG	Northair Aviation Ltd/Leeds	
G-ROBN	Robin R.1180T	F. J. Franklin/Booker	
G-ROBY	Colt 17A balloon	Colt Balloons Ltd	
G-RODI	Isaacs Fury	J. R. C. Morgan	
G-ROGR	Bell 206A JetRanger	Direct Rentals (G-AXMM)	
G-ROLF	PA-28R-301 Saratoga SP	R. W. Burchardt	
G-ROLL	Pitts S-2A Special	G. Lynn	
G-RONW	Fred Srs 2	P. J. D. Granow	
G-ROOK	Cessna F.172P	Cejam Electronics Ltd	
G-ROOM	Short SD3-60	Short Bros Ltd (G-BSBL)/Sydenham	
G-ROOT	AB-206B JetRanger	Godfrey Hope Aviation Ltd (G-JETR)	

Notes	Reg.	Type	Owner or Operator
	G-RORO	Cessna 337B	Ronageny (Shipping) Ltd (G-AVIX)/ Ronaldsway
	G-ROSE	Evans VP-1	W. K. Rose
	G-ROSS	Practavia Pilot Sprite	F. M. T. Ross
	G-ROUS	PA-34-200T-2 Seneca	Casair Aviation Ltd/Tees-side
	G-ROVE	PA-18 Super Cub 135	East Air Travel Ltd
	G-ROWL	AA-5B Tiger	BLS Aviation Ltd
	G-ROWS	PA-28-151 Warrior	E. S. F. & R. S. Chappell
	G-ROYL	Taylor JT.1 Monoplane	R. L. Wharmby
	G-ROYS	D.H.C.I Chipmunk T.10	R. W. & S. Pullan
	G-RPAH	Rutan Vari-Eze	B. Hanson
	G-RRRR	Privateer Motor Glider	R. F. Selby
	G-RTHL	Leivers Special	R. Leivers
	G-RUBB	AA-5B Tiger	Grubb Aviation Ltd
	G-RUDD	Cameron V-65 balloon	R. J. Apsey
	G-RUIA	Cessna F.172M	Delamere & Norley Finance Ltd/Barton
	G-RUMN	AA-1A Trainer	Reefly Ltd
	G-RUNT	Cassutt IIIM	N. A. Brendish
	G-RUSH	Cessna 404	Kondair (G-BEMX)/Stansted
	G-RUSS	Cessna 172N	Leisure Lease/Southend
	G-RVIP	EMB-110P2 Bandeirante	Genair/Humberside
	G-RYAN	PA-28R-201T Turbo Arrow III	Lancing Service Station Ltd (G-BFMN)/ Shoreham
	G-SAAB	R. Commander 112TC	Continental Cars Ltd (G-BEFS)/Stansted
	G-SAAS	Ayres S2R-T34 Thrush Commander	Farmair Ltd/Headcorn
	G-SABA	PA-28R-201T Turbo Arrow III	Barlow Tyrie Ltd
	G-SACD	Cessna F.172H	Southern Air Ltd (G-AVCD)/Shoreham
	G-SAFE	Cameron N-77 balloon	Derbyshire Building Soc
	G-SAHI	Trago Mills SAH-1	Trago Mills Ltd/Bodmin
	G-SAIL	Boeing 707-323C	Tradewinds Ltd/Gatwick
	G-SALA	PA-32-300 Cherokee Six	Rodney Saunders Associates/Elstree
	G-SALL	Cessna F.150L	Citation Flying Services Ltd
	G-SALY	Hawker Sea Fury FB.11	T. P. Luscombe & ptnrs/Ashford
	G-SAMS	M.S.880B Rallye Club	H. F. Hambling/Fenland
	G-SARA	PA-28-181 Archer II	R. H. Ford/Elstree
	G-SARO	Saro Skeeter Mk 12	F. F. Chamberlain/Inverness
	G-SATO	PA-23 Aztec 250	Linskill Air Charter Ltd (G-BCXP)/ Tees-side
	G-SAVE	PA-31-350 Navajo Chieftain	Securicor Ltd/Birmingham
	G-SBRV	BRV Special	B. R. Vickers
	G-SCAH	Cameron V-77 balloon	S. C. A. Howarth
	G-SCAN	Vinten-Wallis WA-116/100	W. Vinten Ltd
	G-SCOT	PA-31-350 Navajo Chieftain	ATS Air Charter Ltd
	G-SCUB	PA-18-135 Super Cub (542447)	N. D. Needham Farms
	G-SEAH	Hawker Sea Hawk FB.3	Brencham Ltd/Bournemouth
	G-SEAR	Pazmany PL.4	A. J. Sear
	G-SEED	Piper J-3C-65 Cub	J. H. Seed
	G-SEEK	Cessna T.210N	Northair Aviation Ltd/Leeds
	G-SEJW	PA-28-161 Warrior II	Truman Aviation Ltd/Tollerton
	G-SEWL	PA-28-151 Warrior	A. R. Sewell & Sons/Andrewsfield
	G-SEXY	AA-I Yankee	W. Davies (G-AYLM)/Cardiff
	G-SFHR	PA-23 Aztec 250	E. L. Becker & J. Harper (G-BHSO)/ Blackpool
	G-SFTA	SA.341G Gazelle Srs 1	Specialist Flying Training Ltd/Hamble
	G-SFTC	SA.341G Gazelle Srs 1	Specialist Flying Training Ltd/Hamble
	G-SFTD	SA.341G Gazelle Srs 1	Specialist Flying Training Ltd/Hamble
	G-SFTE	SA.341G Gazelle Srs 1	Specialist Flying Training Ltd/Hamble
	G-SFTF	SA.341G Gazelle Srs 1	Specialist Flying Training Ltd/Hamble
	G-SFTG	SA.341G Gazelle Srs 1	Specialist Flying Training Ltd/Hamble
	G-SFTR	NDN-1T Turbo Firecracker	Specialist Flying Training Ltd/Hamble
	G-SFTS	NDN-1T Turbo Firecracker	Specialist Flying Training Ltd/Hamble
	G-SFTT	NDN-1T Turbo Firecracker	Specialist Flying Training Ltd/Hamble
	G-SFTW	Slingsby T.67M Firefly	Specialist Flying Training Ltd/Hamble
	G-SFTX	Slingsby T.67M Firefly	Specialist Flying Training Ltd/Hamble
	G-SFAY	Slingsby T.67M Firefly	Specialist Flying Training Ltd/Hamble
	G-SFTZ	Slingsby T.67M Firefly	Specialist Flying Training Ltd/Hamble
	G-SHAW	PA-30 Twin Comanche 160	Micro Metalsmiths Ltd
	G-SHEL	Cameron O-56 balloon	The Shell Company of Hong Kong Ltd
	G-SHIP	PA-23 Aztec 250	Birmingham Aerocentre Ltd

Reg.	Type	Owner or Operator	Notes
G-SHOE	Cessna 421C-II	Shuimpex Services Ltd (G-BHGD)/ Biggin Hill	
G-SHOT	Cameron V-77 balloon	Mabey Construction Co Ltd	
G-SIGN	PA-39 Twin Comanche C/R	K. W. Hawes (Electrical) Ltd/Leavesden	
G-SILK	Aerostar 601P	Centreline Air Services Ltd/Biggin Hill	
G-SILV	Cessna 340A	Superprime Ltd/Elstree	
G-SIME	J/1N Alpha	J. T. Sime (G-AHHP)/Perth	
G-SIPA	SIPA 903	V. M. C. Van Den Bergh & ptnrs (G-BGBM)	
G-SIXA	Douglas DC-6B	Bowden Grange Enterprise Ltd (G-ARXZ)/Manston	
G-SJAB	PA-39 Twin Comanche 160 C/R	G. L. Owens	
G-SKIM	AS.350B Ecureuil	Ernest George Aviation Ltd (G-BIVP)	
G-SKIP	Cameron N-77 balloon	Skipton Building Soc	
G-SKSA	Airship Industries SKS.500	Airship Industries Ltd/Cardington	
G-SKSB	Airship Industries SKS.500	Airship Industries Ltd/Cardington	
G-SKSC	Airship Industries SKS.600	Airship Industries Ltd/Cardington	
G-SKSD	Airship Industries SKS.600	Airship Industries Ltd/Cardington	
G-SKSE	Airship Industries SKS.600	Airship Industries Ltd/Cardington	
G-SKSF	Airship Industries SKS.600	Airship Industries Ltd/Cardington	
G-SKYE	Cessna TU.206G	RAF Sport Parachute Association	
G-SKYH	Cessna 172N	Elgor Hire Purchase & Credit Ltd/ Southend	
G-SKYM	Cessna F.337E	Bencray Ltd (G-AYHW)/Blackpool	
G-SLEA	Mudry/CAARP CAP.10B	C. J. Else & Co Ltd/Sturgate	
G-SLIK	Taylor JT.2 Titch	J. Jennings	
G-SMHK	Cameron D-38 airship	San Miguel Brewery Ltd	
G-SMIG	Cameron 0-65 balloon	G. Green & R. W. Taafe/Hong Kong	
G-SMIT	Messerschmitt Bf.109G	Fairoaks Aviation Services Ltd/ Australia	
G-SMJJ	Cessna 414A	Gull Air Ltd/Guernsey	
G-SMRI	Westland-Bell 47G-3B1 (Soloy)	Helicrops Ltd (G-BHBV)	
G-SNIP	Cessna F.172H	IWT Sheetmetal Ltd (G-AXSI)	
G-SNOW	Cameron V-77 balloon	M. J. Snow	
G-SOAR	Eiri PIK-20E	P. Rees	
G-SOFA	Cameron N-65 balloon	Northern Upholstery Ltd	
G-SOLO	Pitts S-2S Special	Avalanche Promotions/Booker	
G-SOLY	Westland Bell 47G-3B1 (Soloy)	Heliwork Ltd/Thruxton	
G-SONA	SOCATA TB.10 Tobago	Sonardyne Ltd (G-BIBI)/Blackbushe	
G-SONG	Beech A200 Super King Air	Tembo Records Ltd (G-BKTI)/Leavesden	
G-SOOO	PA-30 Twin Comanche 160	Leisair Avionics Ltd (G-AXMY)/ Humberside	
G-SORR	AS.350B Ecureuil	Colt Car Co Ltd (G-BKMO)/Staverton	
G-SPEY	AB-206B JetRanger 3	Castle Air Charters Ltd (G-BIGO)	
G-SPIN	Pitts S-2A Special	R. N. Goode/White Waltham	
G-SPIT	V.S.379 Spitfire XIV (MV293)	D. W. Arnold (G-BGHB)/Blackbushe	
G-SPOT	Partenavia P.68B Observer	J.&C.J. Freeman (G-BCDK)/ (1) Headcorn	
G-SSBS	Colting Ax77 balloon	R. J. Barr	
G-SSCH	BAe.146-100	British Aerospace Ltd (G-BIAF)/Hatfield	
G-SSHH	BAe.146-100	British Aerospace Ltd (G-BIAE)/Hatfield	
G-SSSH	BAe.146-100	British Aerospace Ltd (G-BIAD)/Hatfield	
G-STAG	Cameron 0-65 balloon	Holker Estates Ltd	
G-STAN	F.27 Friendship Mk.200	Air UK/Norwich	
G-STAT	Cessna U.206F	E. A. Black/Ashford	
G-STEV	Jodel DR.221	S. W. Talbot/Long Marston	
G-STIO	ST.10 Diplomate	M. O. Webb & K. R. Parkinson	
G-STMP	SNCAN Stampe SV-4A	W. Partridge	
G-STOL	M.S.894A Rallye Minerva	Cole Cutters Ltd	
G-SUES	AT-6D Harvard III (133854)	P. W. Leaney Automatic Transmissions Ltd/Biggin Hill	
G-SUPA	PA-18-150 Super Cub	Yorkshire Gliding Club (Pty) Ltd	
G-SUZY	Taylor JT.1 Monoplane	S. A. Kanick	
G-SVHA	Partenavia P.68B	W. P. J. Davison	
G-SWOT	Currie Super Wot	S.T.A. Albu	
G-SWPR	Cameron N-56 balloon	Balloon Stable Ltd	
G-SYFW	Focke-Wulf Fw.190 replica	M. R. Parr	
G-TACA	P.57 Sea Prince T.1	Atlantic & Caribbean Aviation Ltd/ Staverton	
G-TACE	H.S.125 Srs 403B	Lynx Aviation Ltd (G-AYIZ)/Cranfield	
G-TALI	AS.355F Twin Squirrel	The Duke of Westminster	
G-TAMY	Cessna 421B	Abbergail Ltd/Luton	

Notes	Reg.	Type	Owner or Operator
	G-TAPE	PA-23 Aztec 250	Redapple Ltd (G-AWVW)
	G-TATI	Hughes 369HS	Jack Tatties Ltd
	G-TATT	GY-20 Minicab	L. Tattershall
	G-TAXI	PA-23 Aztec 250	Northern Executive Aviation Ltd/ Manchester
	G-TAXY	PA-31 Navajo	Air Continental Securities Ltd/Luton
	G-TBCA	Bell 206L LongRanger	British Car Auctions Ltd (G-BFAL)
	G-TBIO	SOCATA TB.10 Tobago	Buchanan Electronics
	G-TBXX	SOCATA TB.20 Trinidad	Air Touring Services Ltd/Biggin Hill
	G-TCAT	G.164D Ag-Cat	Miller Aerial Spraying Ltd/Wickenby
	G-TDAA	Cessna U.206G	Edward & Susan Dexter Ltd/Denham
	G-TEAC	AT-6C Harvard IIA (MC280)	E. C. English
	G-TEAM	Cessna 414A	Imperial Brewing & Leisure Ltd/ (G-BHJT)
	G-TEDS	SOCATA TB.10 Tobago	E. M. Fleet (G-BHCO)
	G-TEFC	PA-28 Cherokee 140	Thames Estuary Flying Club/Southend
	G-TEFH	Cessna 500 Citation	T. B. T. (Transport) Ltd (G-BCII)/ E. Midlands
	G-TESS	Quickie Q.2	D. Evans
	G-TFCI	Cessna FA.152	Tayside Aviation Ltd/Dundee
	G-THAM	Cessna F.182Q	German Tourist Facilities Ltd/Luton
	G-THEA	Boeing E75 Stearman	L. M. Walton
	G-THOM	Thunder Ax6-56 balloon	T. H. Wilson
	G-THOR	Thunder Ax8-105 balloon	N. C. Faithful *Turncoat*
	G-THSL	PA-28R-201 Arrow II	G. Fearnley/Southend
	G-TIGB	AS.332L Super Puma	Bristow Helicopters Ltd (G-BJXC)
	G-TIGC	AS.332L Super Puma	Bristow Helicopters Ltd (G-BJYH)
	G-TIGE	AS.332L Super Puma	Bristow Helicopters Ltd (G-BJYJ)
	G-TIGF	AS.332L Super Puma	Bristow Helicopters Ltd
	G-TIGG	AS.332L Super Puma	Bristow Helicopters Ltd
	G-TIGH	AS.332L Super Puma	Bristow Helicopters Ltd
	G-TIGI	AS.332L Super Puma	Bristow Helicopters Ltd
	G-TIGJ	AS.332L Super Puma	Bristow Helicopters Ltd
	G-TIGK	AS.332L Super Puma	Bristow Helicopters Ltd
	G-TIGL	AS.332L Super Puma	Bristow Helicopters Ltd
	G-TIGM	AS.332L Super Puma	Bristow Helicopters Ltd
	G-TIGN	AS.332L Super Puma	Bristow Helicopters Ltd
	G-TIGO	AS.332L Super Puma	Bristow Helicopters Ltd
	G-TIGP	AS.332L Super Puma	Bristow Helicopters Ltd
	G-TIGR	AS.332L Super Puma	Bristow Helicopters Ltd
	G-TIGS	AS.332L Super Puma	Bristow Helicopters Ltd
	G-TIGT	AS.332L Super Puma	Bristow Helicopters Ltd
	G-TIME	Aerostar 601P	Marlborough Fine Art (London) Ltd
	G-TIMK	PA-28-181 Archer II	T. Kilroe & Sons Ltd/Manchester
	G-TINA	SOCATA TB.10 Tobago	A. Lister
	G-TJCB	H.S.125 Srs 700B	J. C. Bamford (Excavators) Ltd/ E. Midlands
	G-TJET	Lockheed T-33A-1-LO	Aces High Ltd/Duxford
	G-TKHM	AB-206B JetRanger 3	T. Kilroe & Sons Ltd (G-MKAN/ G-DOUG)/Manchester
	G-TLOL	Cessna 421C	Littlewoods Organisation Ltd/ Manchester
	G-TOBY	Cessna 172B	J. A. Kelman (G-ARCM)/Elstree
	G-TOFF	AS.355F Twin Squirrel	Atlantic Computer Leasing PLC (G-BKJX)
	G-TOGA	PA-32-301 Saratoga	D. C. Luffingham/Staverton
	G-TOMF	PA-34-220T-3 Seneca	Lane Investment Co Ltd (G-BJEO)/ Guernsey
	G-TOMS	PA-38-112 Tomahawk	Channel Aviation Ltd/Guernsey
	G-TONI	Cessna 421C	Rassler Aero Services/Booker
	G-TOUR	Robin R.2112	Finncharter Services
	G-TOYS	Enstrom F-280C-UK-2	AB Gee of Ripley (G-BISE)/Shoreham
	G-TPTR	AB-206B JetRanger 3	Alan Mann Helicopters Ltd (G-LOCK)/ Fairoaks
	G-TREV	Saffery S.330 balloon	T. W. Gurd
	G-TRIX	V.S.509 Spitfire T.IX	S. Atkins
	G-TSIX	AT-6C Harvard IIA	D. Taylor/E. Midlands
	G-TTAM	Taylor JT.2 Titch	A. J. Manning
	G-TTWO	Colt 56A balloon	Talbot Motor Co Ltd
	G-TUBY	Cessna 310J	A. H. Bower (G-ASZZ)
	G-TUGG	PA-18 Super Cub 150	Holding & Barnes Ltd

Reg.	Type	Owner or Operator	Notes
G-TUKE	Robin DR.400/160	Tukair/Headcorn	
G-TURB	D.31 Turbulent	P. S. E. Clifton	
G-TVKE	Cessna 310R	Ewart & Co (Studio) Ltd (G-EURO)/ Elstree	
G-TVSI	Campbell Cricket	K. Aziz (G-AYHH)	
G-TWEL	PA-28-181 Archer II	T. W. Electrical Ltd/Sywell	
G-TWIN	PA-44-180 Seminole	Osiwell Ltd/Leavesden	
G-TYGA	AA-5B Tiger	Rosemount Aviation Ltd (G-BHNZ)/ Aberdeen	
G-TYME	R. Commander 690B	Marlborough (London) Ltd	
G-TYRE	Cessna F.172M	Watts Aviation Ltd/Staverton	
G-UBHL	Beech B200 Super King Air	United Biscuits (UK) Ltd/Denham	
G-UIDE	Jodel D.120	S. T. Gilbert/Popham	
G-USAF	T-28C Trojan	M. B. Walker	
G-USTO	Beech A24R Musketeer	E. Perrin Ltd (G-AYPA)	
G-USTY	FRED Srs 2	S. Styles	
G-VAGA	PA-15 Vagabond	Pyrochem Ltd/White Waltham	
G-VALE	AT-6C Harvard 11A (8810677)	Kayvale Finance Ltd (G-RBAC)/Shobdon	
G-VAMP	Thunder Ax6-56 balloon	Thunder Balloons Ltd *Vamp*	
G-VANG	AB-206B JetRanger 3	Skyhook Lifting Ltd (G-BIZA)	
G-VAUN	Cessna 340	F. E. Peacock & Son (Thorney) Ltd	
G-VEGL	Aviamilano F.8L Falco II	B. C. Davies & R. N. Crosland	
G-VEZE	Rutan Vari-Eze	P. J. Henderson	
G-VICK	PA-31 Turbo Navajo	Howard Richard & Co Ltd (G-AWED)	
G-VIEW	Vinter-Wallis WA-116/100	W. Vinten Ltd	
G-VIKE	Bellanca 1730A Viking	E. T. Sutherland & Son Ltd/Netherthorpe	
G-VIKI	Cessna 402B	Glos-Air Services Ltd (G-BARW)/ Bournemouth	
G-VIST	PA-30 Twin Comanche 160	B. P. Paine & ptnrs (G-AVHZ)	
G-VITE	Robin R.1180T	Trans Global Aviation Supply Co Ltd/ Denham	
G-VIVA	Thunder Ax7-65 balloon	G. Edwards *Dopey*	
G-VIZZ	Sportavia RS.180 Sportsman	Executive Air Sport Ltd/Exeter	
G-VMDE	Cessna P.210N	V. S. Evans & Horne & Sutton Ltd/ Cranfield	
G-VNPP	Hughes 369MH	Flintgrange Ltd (G-BDKL)	
G-VPTO	Evans VP-2	J. Cater	
G-VRES	Beech A200 Super King Air	Vernair Transport Services/Liverpool	
G-VSOP	Cameron SS balloon	J. R. Parkington & Co Ltd	
G-VTII	D.H.115 Vampire T.11 (WZ507)	J. Turnbull & ptnrs	
G-VTOL	H.S. Harrier T52	British Aerospace/Dunsfold	
G-WAAC	Cameron N-56 balloon	Advertising Balloon Co	
G-WAGY	Cessna F.172N	J. B. Wagstaff/E. Midlands	
G-WARD	Taylor JT.1 Monoplane	G. & G. D. Ward	
G-WARM	Bell 206L-1 LongRanger	Warmco (Manchester) Ltd	
G-WASP	Brantly B.2B	P. A. Taylor (G-ASXE)	
G-WELD	Hughes 369HS	Uni-Weld Ltd (G-FROG)	
G-WEND	PA-28RT-201 Arrow IV	Trent Insulations Ltd	
G-WERY	SOCATA TB.20 Trinidad	G. J. Werry/Manston	
G-WEST	Agusta A.109A	Westland Helicopters Ltd/Yeovil	
G-WETI	Cameron N-31 balloon	J. M. Albery	
G-WHIT	Westland Bell 47G-3B1	C. G. Whittaker Ltd/Doncaster	
G-WHIZ	Pitts S-1 Special	K. M. McLeod	
G-WHIZ	V.732 Viscount (fuselage only) ★	S. Wales Museum/Rhoose (G-ANRS)	
G-WICH	FRED Srs 2	R. H. Hearn	
G-WICK	Partenavia P.68B	Cillam Holdings Ltd (G-BGFZ)/ Shoreham	
G-WILY	Rutan Long-Eze	W. S. Allen	
G-WINE	Thunder Ax7-77Z balloon	Thunder Balloons Ltd	
G-WISC	BAe.146-200	British Aerospace/Hatfield	
G-WITT	PA-31P Navajo	C. G. Whittaker (G-BBRL) Ltd/Doncaster	
G-WIXY	Mudry/CAARP CAP.10B	G. Tanner & P. O. Wicks Ltd/ Andrewsfield	
G-WIZZ	AB-206B JetRanger 2	T. Robinson/Norwich	
G-WJMN	R. Commander 114	Shoreham Flight Simulation Ltd/ Bournemouth	
G-WMCC	BAe Jetstream 3102-01	Birmingham Executive Airways Ltd (G-TALL)	
G-WOLF	PA-28 Cherokee 140	H. Rea	
G-WOLL	G.164A Ag-Cat	Norfolk Aerial Spraying Ltd (G-AYTM)	
G-WOOD	Beech 95-B55 Baron	Woods Management Services Ltd (G-AYID)/Fairoaks	

153

Notes	Reg.	Type	Owner or Operator
	G-WOSP	Bell 206B JetRanger 3	Burnthills Aviation Ltd/Glasgow
	G-WOTG	BN-2T Islander	Pilatus BN Ltd (G-BJYT)/Bembridge
	G-WPUI	Cessna P.172D	J. Davey (G-AXPI)
	G-WREN	Pitts S-2A Special	P. Meeson/Booker
	G-WROY	PA-32RT-300T Turbo Lance II	R. L. West (G-WRAY)
	G-WSKY	Enstrom F-280C Shark	Skyline Helicopters Ltd (G-BEEK)
	G-WSSC	PA-31-350 Navajo Chieftain	Spacegrand Ltd/Blackpool
	G-WSSL	PA-31-350 Navajo Chieftain	G. W. Sparrow & Sons Ltd/Bristol
	G-WTVB	Cessna 404 Titan	Euroair Transport Ltd/Biggin Hill
	G-WTVC	Cessna 404 Titan	Hay & Co Ltd/Lerwick
	G-WULF	Focke-Wulf Fw.190 (O4)	A. C. Walker & ptnrs/Elstree
	G-WULL	AA-5A Cheetah	Canonbury Wine Ltd
	G-WWII	V.S. Spitfire 18 (SM832)	D. W. Arnold & ptnrs/Blackbushe
	G-WWUK	Enstrom F-28A-UK	Wickwell (UK) Ltd (G-BFFN)
	G-WYMP	Cessna F.150J	R. Bolt & ptnrs (G-BAGW)/Sherburn
	G-WYTE	Bell 47G-2A-1	M. G. White
	G-WZZZ	Colt AS-42 balloon	Hot-Air Balloon Co Ltd
	G-XCUB	PA-18-150 Super Cub	W. G. Fisher/Sandown
	G-XTWO	EMB-121A Xingu II	C.S.E Aviation Ltd (G-XING)/Kidlington
	G-YIII	Cessna F.150L	Sherburn Aero Club Ltd
	G-YNOT	D.62B Condor	A. Littlefair (G-AYFH)
	G-YORK	Cessna F.172M	Sherburn Aero Club Ltd
	G-YPSY	Andreasson BA-4B	H. P. Burrill
	G-YROS	Bensen B.80-D	J. M. Montgomerie
	G-YTWO	Cessna F.172M	Sherburn Aero Club Ltd
	G-YULL	PA-28 Cherokee 180E	Lansdowne Chemical Co (G-BEAJ)/Kidlington
	G-ZERO	AA-5B Tiger	Service Photography & Display Ltd/Biggin Hill
	G-ZIPI	Robin DR.400/180	Stahl Engineering Co Ltd/Headcorn
	G-ZIPP	Cessna E.310Q	Bank Farm Ltd (G-BAYU)
	G-ZIPS	Learjet 35A	Yewlands Executive Transport Ltd (G-ZONE)
	G-ZLIN	Z.526 Trener Master	G. C. Masterson (G-BBCR)
	G-ZSOL	Zlin Z.50L	R. N. Goode/Kemble
	G-ZUMP	Cameron N-77 balloon	M. J. Allen Gazump
	G-ZZIM	Rutan Laser 200	J. G. M. Heathcote
	G-ZZZZ	Point Maker Mk. 1 balloon	M. J. Walkelin

Toy Balloons

Reg.	Type	Owner or Operator	Notes
G-FYAA	Osprey Mk 4D	C. Wilson	
G-FYAB	Osprey Mk 4B	M. R. Wilson	
G-FYAC	Portswood Mk XVI	J. D. Hall	
G-FYAD	Portswood Mk XVI	J. D. Hall	
G-FYAE	Portswood Mk XVI	J. D. Hall	
G-FYAF	Portswood Mk XVI	J. D. Hall	
G-FYAG	Portswood Mk XVI	J. D. Hall	
G-FYAH	Portswood Mk XVI	J. D. Hall	
G-FYAI	Portswood Mk XVI	J. D. Hall	
G-FYAJ	Kelsey	P. J. Kelsey	
G-FYAK	European E.21	J. E. Christopher	
G-FYAL	Osprey Mk 4E2	J. Goodman	
G-FYAM	Osprey Mk 4E2	P. Goodman	
G-FYAN	Williams	M. D. Williams	
G-FYAO	Williams	M. D. Williams	
G-FYAP	Williams Mk 2	G. E. Clarke	
G-FYAR	Williams Mk 2	S. T. Wallbank	
G-FYAS	Osprey Mk 4H2	K. B. Miles	
G-FYAT	Osprey Mk 4D	S. D. Templeman	
G-FYAU	Williams MK 2	P. Bowater	
G-FYAV	Osprey Mk 4E2	C. D. Egan & C. Stiles	
G-FYAW	Portswood Mk XVI	R. S. Joste	
G-FYAX	Osprey Mk 4B	S. A. Dalmas & P. G. Tarr	
G-FYAY	Osprey Mk 1E	M. K. Levenson	
G-FYAZ	Osprey Mk 4D2	M. A. Roblett	
G-FYBA	Portswood Mk XVI	C. R. Rundle	
G-FYBB	Portswood Mk XVI	A. P. Chown	
G-FYBC	Portswood Mk XVI	S. A. Hassell	
G-FYBD	Osprey Mk 1E	M. Vincent	
G-FYBE	Osprey Mk 4D	M. Vincent	
G-FYBF	Osprey Mk V	M. Vincent	
G-FYBG	Osprey Mk 4G2	M. Vincent	
G-FYBH	Osprey Mk 4G	M. Vincent	
G-FYBI	Osprey Mk 4H	M. Vincent	
G-FYBJ	Osprey Mk 3B	M. J. Sheather	
G-FYBK	Osprey Mk 4G2	A. G. Coe & S. R. Burgess	
G-FYBL	Osprey Mk 4D	P. A. Tilley	
G-FYBM	Osprey Mk 4G	P. C. Anderson	
G-FYBN	Osprey Mk 4G2	M. Ford	
G-FYBO	Osprey Mk 4B	D. Eaves	
G-FYBP	European E.84PW	D. Eaves	
G-FYBR	Osprey Mk 4G2	N. A. Partridge	
G-FYBS	Portswood Mk XVI	M. J. Sheather	
G-FYBT	Portswood Mk XVI	M. Hazelwood	
G-FYBU	Portswood Mk XVI	M. A. Roblett	
G-FYBV	Osprey Mk 4D2	D. I. Garrod	
G-FYBW	Osprey Mk 4D	N. I. McAllen	
G-FYBX	Porstwood Mk XVI	I. Chadwick	
G-FYBY	Osprey Mk 4D	K. H. Turner	
G-FYBZ	Osprey Mk 1E	S. J. Showbridge	
G-FYCA	Osprey Mk 4D	R. G. Crewe	
G-FYCB	Osprey Mk 4B	I. R. Hemsley	
G-FYCC	Osprey Mk 4G2	A. Russell	
G-FYCD	BHMED	D. Meades	
G-FYCE	Portswood Mk XVI	R. S. Joste	
G-FYCF	Portswood Mk XVI	R. S. Joste	
G-FYCG	Portswood Mk XVI	R. S. Joste	
G-FYCH	Swan Mk 1	R. S. Joste	
G-FYCI	Portswood Mk XVI	R. S. Joste	
G-FYCJ	Osprey Mk 4H2	A. G. Coe & S. R. Burgess	
G-FYCK	Lovell Mk 1	G. P. Lovell	
G-FYCL	Osprey Mk 4G	P. J. Rogers	
G-FYCM	Osprey Mk 7	K. R. Bundy	
G-FYCN	Osprey Mk 4D	C. F. Chipping	
G-FYCO	Osprey Mk 4B	C. F. Chipping	
G-FYCP	Osprey Mk 1E	C. F. Chipping	
G-FYCR	Osprey MK 4D	C. F. Chipping	

Notes	Reg.	Type	Owner or Operator
	G-FYCS	Portswood Mk XVI	S. McDonald
	G-FYCT	Osprey Mk 4D	S. T. Wallbank
	G-FYCU	Osprey Mk 4D	G. M. Smith
	G-FYCV	Osprey Mk 4D	M. Thomson
	G-FYCW	Osprey Mk 4D	M. L. Partridge
	G-FYCX	Jefferson Mk IV	J. R. Sumner
	G-FYCY	Osprey Mk 4G	R. S. Wordam
	G-FYCZ	Osprey Mk 4D2	P. Middleton
	G-FYDA	Atom	H. C. Saffrey
	G-FYDB	European E.84EL	D. Eaves
	G-FYDC	European EDH-1	D. Eaves & H. Goddard
	G-FYDD	Osprey Mk 4D	A. C. Mitchell
	G-FYDE	Osprey Mk 4D	P. F. Mitchell
	G-FYDF	Osprey Mk 4D	K. A. Jones
	G-FYDG	Osprey Mk 4D	M. D. Williams
	G-FYDH	Premier Voyage	H. C. Saffrey
	G-FYDI	Williams Westwind Two	M. D. Williams
	G-FYDJ	Osprey Mk 4D	A. P. Chown & S. A. Hassell
	G-FYDK	Williams Westwind Two	M. D. Williams
	G-FYDL	—	—
	G-FYDM	Williams Westwind Four	M. D. Williams
	G-FYDN	European 8C	P. D. Ridout
	G-FYDO	Osprey Mk 4D	N. L. Scallan
	G-FYDP	Williams Westwind Three	M. D. Williams
	G-FYDR	European 118	P. F. Mitchell
	G-FYDS	Osprey Mk 4D	N. L. Scallan
	G-FYDT	Viking Warrior Mk 1	D. G. Tomlin
	G-FYDU	Osprey Mk 4D	J. R. Moody
	G-FYDV	Osprey Mk 4D	A. J. Jackson
	G-FYDW	Osprey Mk 4B	R. A. Balfre
	G-FYDX	Osprey Mk 4B	G. T. Young
	G-FYDY	Osprey Mk 4B	P. S. Flanagan
	G-FYDZ	Portswood Mk XVI	S. M. Chance
	G-FYEA	Osprey Mk 4B	S. M. Chance
	G-FYEB	Rango Rega	N. H. Ponsford
	G-FYEC	Osprey Mk 4B	T. R. Spruce
	G-FYED	—	—
	G-FYEE	Osprey Mk 4B	T. R. Spruce
	G-FYEF	Portswood Mk XVI	T. R. Spruce
	G-FYEG	Osprey Mk 1C	P. E. Prime
	G-FYEH	European EJ.1	R. S. Wareham
	G-FYEI	Portswood Mk XVI	A. Russell
	G-FYEJ	Rango NA.24	N. H. Ponsford
	G-FYEK	Unicorn UE.1C	D. & D. Eaves
	G-FYEL	European E.84Z	D. Eaves
	G-FYEO	Eagle Mk.1	M. E. Scallon
	G-FYEP	Boing 746-200A	S. M. Colville & D. J. Hall
	G-FYER	Osprey Mk.4B	S. J. Menges
	G-FYES	Osprey Mk 2 SJM	S. J. Menges
	G-FYET	Markmite Mk 2	M. W. Mabey & M. Davies
	G-FYEU	Rango N.8	R. G. Scathdee
	G-FYEV	Osprey Mk.1C	M. E. Scallen
	G-FYEW	Saturn Mk 2A balloon	M. J. Sheather
	G-FYEY	Largess balloon	S. J. Menges
	G-FYEZ	Firefly Mk 1 balloon	M. E. & N. L. Scallan
	G-FYFA	European E.84LD balloon	D. Goddard & D. Eaves
	G-FYFB	Osprey Mk 1E	K. Marsh
	G-FYFC	European E.84NZ	R. MacPherson
	G-FYFD	Osprey.Mk 2CM	M. Carp
	G-FYFE	Osprey Mk 2GB	G. Bone
	G-FYFF	Osprey Mk 2SW	S. Willis
	G-FYFG	European E.84DE	D. Eaves
	G-FYFH	European E.84DS	D. Eaves
	G-FYFI	European E.84DS	M. Stelling
	G-FYFJ	Westland 2	P. Feasey
	G-FYFK	Westland 2	D. Feasey
	G-FYFL	Osprey Mk 2CL	C. Kennedy

Microlights

Reg.	Type	Owner or Operator	Notes
G-MBAA	Hiway Skytrike Mk 2	Hiway Hang Gliders Ltd	
G-MBAB	Hovey Whing-Ding II	R. F. Morton	
G-MBAC	Pterodactyl Srs 2	D. L. Giles	
G-MBAD	Weedhopper JC-24A	M. Stott	
G-MBAE	Lazair	H. A. Leek	
G-MBAF	R. J. Swift 3	C. G. Wrzesien	
G-MBAG	Skycraft Scout	B. D. Jones	
G-MBAH	Harker D. H.	D. Harker	
G-MBAI	Typhoon Tripacer 250	C. J. & K. Yarrow	
G-MBAJ	Chargus T.250	V. F. Potter	
G-MBAK	Eurowing Spirit	J. S. Potts	
G-MBAL	Hiway Demon	M. Blewitt	
G-MBAM	Skycraft Scout 2	Air Vitesse Ltd	
G-MBAN	American Aerolights Eagle	R. W. Millward	
G-MBAO	Rotec Rally 2B	R. Mayo	
G-MBAP	Rotec Rally 2B	P. D. Lucas	
G-MBAR	Skycraft Scout	L. Chiappi	
G-MBAS	Typhoon Tripacer 250	T. J. Birkbeck	
G-MBAT	Hiway Skytrike	M. R. Gardiner	
G-MBAU	Hiway Skytrike	M. R. Gardiner	
G-MBAV	Weedhopper	L. F. Smith	
G-MBAW	Pterodactyl	J. C. K. Soardifield	
G-MBAX	Hiway Skytrike	D. Clarke	
G-MBAY	Skycraft Scout	J. Colloff & G. T. Wilkinson	
G-MBAZ	Rotec Rally 2B	Western Skysports Ltd	
G-MBBA	Ultraflight Lazair	P. Roberts	
G-MBBB	Skycraft Scout 2	A. J. & B. Chalkley	
G-MBBC	Chargus T.250	R. R. G. Close-Smith	
G-MBBD	Pterodactyl	R. Penford	
G-MBBE	Striplin Skyranger	A. S. Coombes	
G-MBBF	Chargus Titan 38	Chargus Gliding Co	
G-MBBG	Weedhopper JC-24B	F. S. Beckett	
G-MBBH	Flexiform Sealander 160	J. A. Evans	
G-MBBI	Ultraflight Mirage	B. H. Trunkfield & A. A. Howard	
G-MBBJ	Hiway Demon Trike	E. B. Jones	
G-MBBK	Ultraflight Mirage	M. G. Selley	
G-MBBL	Lightning Microlight	I. M. Grayland	
G-MBBM	Eipper Quicksilver MX	J. Brown	
G-MBBN	Eagle Microlight	S. Taylor & D. Williams	
G-MBBO	Rotec Rally 2B	A. J. Doggett	
G-MBBP	Chotia Weedhopper	G. L. Moon	
G-MBBR	Weedhopper JC-24B	J. G. Wallers	
G-MBBS	Chargus T.250	P. R. De Fraine	
G-MBBT	Tripacer 330	The Post Office	
G-MBBU	Savage Microlight	R. Venton-Walters	
G-MBBV	Rotec Rally 2B	Blois Aviation Ltd	
G-MBBW	Flexiform Hilander	R. J. Hamilton	
G-MBBX	Chargus Skytrike	S. A. Geary	
G-MBBY	Flexiform Sealander	J. E. Halsall	
G-MBBZ	Volmer Jensen VJ-24W	D. G. Cook	
G-MBCA	Chargus Cyclone T.250	E. M. Jelonek	
G-MBCB	Lightning Microlight	P. G. Huxham	
G-MBCD	La Mouette Atlas	M. G. Dean	
G-MBCE	Eagle Rainbow	I. H. Lewis	
G-MBCF	Fledgeling Microlight	T. C. N. Carroll	
G-MBCG	Tripacer T.250	A. G. Parkinson	
G-MBCH	Hiway Skytrike	R. Carr	
G-MBCI	Hiway Skytrike	J. R. Bridge	
G-MBCJ	Mainair Sports Tri-Flyer	J. R. North	
G-MBCK	Eipper Quicksilver MX	G. W. Rowbotham	
G-MBCL	Hiway Demon Triflyer	B. R. Underwood	
G-MBCM	Hiway Demon 175	D. M. Mudie	
G-MBCN	Hiway Super Scorpion	M. J. Hadland	
G-MBCO	Flexiform Sealander Buggy	P. G. Kavanagh	
G-MBCP	Flexiform Sealander Triflyer	J. B. Wincott	
G-MBCR	Ultraflight Mirage	B. N. Bower	
G-MBCS	Eagle Microlight	Pleasurecraft Ltd	

Notes	Reg.	Type	Owner or Operator
	G-MBCT	Eagle Microlight	Pleasurecraft Ltd
	G-MBCU	Eagle Microlight	J. L. May
	G-MBCV	Lightning Microlight	C. J. Greasley
	G-MBCW	Hiway Demon 175	C. Foster & S. B. Elwis
	G-BMCX	Hornet Microlight	M. J. Ashley-Rogers
	G-MBCY	Eagle Microlight	R. D. Chiles
	G-MBCZ	Chargus Skytrike 160	R. M. Sheppard
	G-MBDA	Rotec Rally 2B	Blois Aviation Ltd
	G-MBDB	Typhoon Microlight	D. J. Smith
	G-MBDC	Hornet Microlight	R. R. Wolfenden & G. Priestley
	G-MBDD	Skyhook Skytrike	J. H. Clarke & R. M. Larrimore
	G-MBDE	Flexiform Skytrike	R. W. Chatterton
	G-MBDF	Rotec Rally 2B	J. R. & B. T. Jordan
	G-MBDG	Eurowing Goldwing	N. W. Beadle & ptnrs
	G-MBDH	Hiway Demon Triflyer	A. T. Delaney
	G-MBDI	Flexiform Sealander	K. Bryan
	G-MBDJ	Flexiform Sealander Triflyer	L. H. Phillips
	G-MBDK	Typhoon Triflyer	D. J. Atkinson
	G-MBDL	Lone Ranger Microlight	Aero & Engineering Services Ltd
	G-MBDM	Southdown Sigma Trike	A. R. Prentice
	G-MBDN	Hornet Atlas	K. R. Wilson
	G-MBDO	Flexiform Sealander Trike	K. Kerr
	G-MBDP	Flexiform Sealander Skytrike	D. Mackillop
	G-MBDR	U.A.S. Stormbuggy	J. S. Long
	G-MBDT	Eagle Microlight	I. D. Stokes
	G-MBDU	Chargus Titan 38	Property Associates Ltd
	G-MBDV	Pterodactyl Microlight	D. J. Thomas
	G-MBDW	Tripacer Skytrike A	J. T. Meager
	G-MBDX	Electra Eagle	Ardenco Ltd
	G-MBDY	Weedhopper 2	G. N. Mayes
	G-MBDZ	Eipper Quicksilver MX	M. Risdale
	G-MBEA	Hornet Nimrod	B. Berry
	G-MBEB	Hiway Skytrike 250	R. MacDonald
	G-MBEC	Hiway Super Scorpion	C. S. Wates
	G-MBED	Chargus Titan 38	R. K. Parry
	G-MBEE	Hiway Super Scorpion Skytrike 160	P. H. Risdale & ptnrs
	G-MBEF	Eipper Quicksilver MX	Pegasus Ltd
	G-MBEG	Eipper Quicksilver MX	Pegasus Ltd
	G-MBEH	Electra Eagle	Pegasus Ltd
	G-MBEI	Electra Eagle	Pegasus Ltd
	G-MBEJ	Electra Eagle	D. J. Royce & C. R. Gale
	G-MBEK	Electra Eagle	Pegasus Ltd
	G-MBEL	Electra Eagle	J. R. Fairweather
	G-MBEM	Electra Eagle	Pegasus Ltd
	G-MBEN	Eipper Quicksilver MX	Pegasus Ltd
	G-MBEO	Flexiform Sealander	H. W. Williams
	G-MBEP	American Eagle	R. W. Lavender
	G-MBER	Skyhook Sailwings TR-1	Skyhook Sailwings Ltd
	G-MBES	Skyhook Sailwings TR-2	Skyhook Sailwings Ltd
	G-MBET	Micro Mistral Trainer	J. W. V. Edmunds
	G-MBEU	Hiway Demon T.250	D. R. Gazey
	G-MBEV	Chargus Titan 38	A. K. Hatenboer
	G-MBEW	Solar Buggy	F. W. Dakin
	G-MBEZ	Pterodactyl Ptraveller II	P. A. Smith
	G-MBFA	Hiway Skytrike 250	P. S. Jones
	G-MBFD	Gemini Hummingbird	Micro Aviation Ltd
	G-MBFE	Eagle Rainbow	P. W. Cole
	G-MBFF	Hiway Scorpion	H. Redwin
	G-MBFG	Skyhook Sabre	A. H. Trapp
	G-MBFH	Hiway Skytrike	P. Baldwin
	G-MBFI	Hiway Skytrike II	J. R. Brabbs
	G-MBFJ	Chargus Typhoon T.250	A. W. Knowles
	G-MBFK	Hiway Demon	K. T. Vinning
	G-MBFL	Hiway Demon	J. C. Houghton
	G-MBFM	Hiway Hang Glider	G. P. Kimmons & T. V. O. Mahony
	G-MBFN	Hiway Skytrike II	A. Raynor
	G-MBFO	Eipper Quicksilver MX	M. L. Desoutter
	G-MBFP	Hiway Scorpion	J. G. Beesley
	G-MBFR	American Eagle	W. G. Bradley
	G-MBFS	American Electraflyer Eagle	R. Fox

Reg.	Type	Owner or Operator	Notes
G-MBFT	Sigma 12 Meter	D. P. Watts	
G-MBFU	Ultra Sports Tripacer	T. H. J. Prowse	
G-MBFV	Comet Skytrike	R. Willis	
G-MBFW	Hiway Skytrike	B. Bayes	
G-MBFX	Hiway Skytrike 250	Noel Whittall Ltd	
G-MBFY	Mirage II	J. P. Metcalf	
G-MBFZ	M. S. S. Goldwing	I. T. Barr	
G-MBGA	Typhoon Tri-Flyer 250	A. L. Rogers	
G-MBGB	American Eagle	J. C. Miles	
G-MBGC	—	—	
G-MBGD	Pterodactyl 430C Replica	C. Wilkinson	
G-MBGE	Hiway Scorpion Trike	J. A. Rudd	
G-MBGF	Twamley Trike	R. W. Twamley	
G-MBGG	Chargus Titan 38	A. G. Doubtfire	
G-MBGH	Chargus T.250	A. G. Doubtfire	
G-MBGI	Chargus Titan 38	A. G. Doubtfire	
G-MBGJ	Hiway Skytrike Mk 2	J. R. Edwards	
G-MBGK	Electra Flyer Eagle	R. J. Osbourne	
G-MBGL	Flexiform Sealander Skytrike	H. Field	
G-MBGM	Eipper Quicksilver MX	G. G. Johnson	
G-MBGN	Weedhopper Model A	D. Roberts	
G-MBGO	American Eagle	I. Willsher	
G-MBGP	Typhoon Skytrike	M. F. R. Collett	
G-MBGR	Catto Goldwing Canard	I. D. Stokes	
G-MBGS	Rotec Rally 2B	P. C. Bell	
G-MBGT	American Eagle	D. C. Lloyd	
G-MBGV	Skyhook Cutlass	D. M. Parsons	
G-MBGW	Hiway Skytrike	G. W. R. Cooke	
G-MBGX	Lightning	R. B. D. Baker	
G-MBGY	Hiway Demon Skytrike	W. Hopkins	
G-MBGZ	American Eagle	J. K. Davies	
G-MBHA	Trident Trike	P. Jackson	
G-MBHB	Cenrair Moto Delta G-11	R. Leech & J. Earley	
G-MBHC	Chargus Lightning T.250	R. E. Worth	
G-MBHD	Hiway Vulcan Trike	D. Kiddy	
G-MBHE	American Eagle	D. K. W. Paterson	
G-MBHF	Pterodactyl Ptraveller	D. B. Girry	
G-MBHH	Flexiform Sealander Skytrike	G. J. Norris	
G-MBHI	Tripacer 250 Kamouette Atlas	P. T. Anstey	
G-MBHJ	Hornet	M. K. Gill	
G-MBHK	Flexiform Skytrike	G. Barfoot	
G-MBHL	Skyhook Skytrike	C. R. Brêwitt	
G-MBHM	Weedhopper	J. Hopkinson	
G-MBHN	Weedhopper	S. Hopkinson	
G-MBHO	Skyhook Super Sabre Trike	A. Bielawski	
G-MBHP	American Eagle II	P. V. Trollope & H. Caldwell	
G-MBHR	Flexiform Skytrike	Y. P. Osbourne	
G-MBHS	Flexiform Skysails	M. V. Rainford & J. Hardy	
G-MBHT	Chargus T.250	S. F. Dawe	
G-MBHU	Flexiform Hilander Skytrike	R. M. Strange	
G-MBHV	Pterodactyl Ptraveller	H. Partridge	
G-MBHW	American Eagle	P. D. Lloyd-Davies	
G-MBHX	Pterodactyl Ptraveller	W. F. Tremayne	
G-MBHZ	Pterodactyl Ptraveller	T. Deeming	
G-MBIA	Flexiform Sealander Skytrike	Stafford Meadowcroft	
G-MBIB	Mainair Flexiform Sealander	A. D. Pearson	
G-MBIC	Hill Hummer	B. K. Price	
G-MBID	American Eagle	D. A. Campbell	
G-MBIE	Flexiform Striker	Flying Machine (Circa 1910) Ltd	
G-MBIF	American Eagle	Flying Machine (Circa 1910) Ltd	
G-MBIG	American Eagle	L. W. Cload	
G-MBIH	Flexiform Skytrike	M. Hurtley	
G-MBII	Hiway Skytrike	G. A. Archer & V. Nordigian	
G-MBIJ	Solar Typhoon Skytrike	D. Johnson	
G-MBIK	Skycraft Scout	D. K. McDonald	
G-MBIL	Scorpion 1	D. V. Collier	
G-MBIM	American Sea Eagle	J. E. M. Barnatt-Millins	
G-MBIN	Skycraft Sea Scout	I. F. Kerr	
G-MBIO	American Eagle Z Drive	B. J. C. Hill	
G-MBIP	Gemini Hummingbird	Micro Aviation Ltd	
G-MBIR	Gemini Hummingbird	Micro Aviaion Ltd	

Notes	Reg.	Type	Owner or Operator
	G-MBIS	American Eagle	I. R. Bendall
	G-MBIT	Hiway Demon Skytrike	Kuernaland (UK) Ltd
	G-MBIU	Wills Microlight	M. E. Wills
	G-MBIV	Flexiform Skytrike	E. J. & P. T. Orritt
	G-MBIW	Hiway Demon Tri-Flyer Skytrike	Mainair Sports Ltd
	G-MBIX	Ultra Sports	D. Little
	G-MBIY	Ultra Sports	E. M. Woods
	G-MBIZ	Mainair Tri-Flyer	E. F. Clapham & ptnrs
	G-MBJA	Catto Goldwing	A. A. Mol
	G-MBJB	Hiway Skytrike Mk II	P. Cooper
	G-MBJC	American Eagle	R. Jenkins
	G-MBJD	American Eagle	R. W. F. Boarder
	G-MBJE	Chargus	M. E. Glanvill
	G-MBJF	Hiway Skytrike Mk II	A. P. Clark
	G-MBJG	Airwave Nimrod	IOW Microlight Club Training Centre
	G-MBJH	Chargus Titan	IOW Microlight Club Training Centre
	G-MBJI	Ecorpion	Robert Montgomery Ltd
	G-MBJJ	Mirage Mk II	J. F. H. James
	G-MBJK	American Eagle	A. W. Gardner
	G-MBJL	Airwave Hornet	J. S. R. Moodie
	G-MBJM	Striplin Lone Ranger	C. K. Brown
	G-MBJN	Electra Eagle	Manx Eagle Club
	G-MBJO	Birdman Cherokee	R. J. Garland
	G-MBJP	Hiway Skytrike	L. A. Seers
	G-MBJR	American Eagle	M. P. Skelding
	G-MBJS	Mainair Tri-Flyer	T. W. Taylor
	G-MBJT	Hiway Skytrike II	R. A. Kennedy
	G-MBJU	Eagle	J. Basford
	G-MBJV	Rotec Rally 2B	C. J. G. Welch
	G-MBJW	Hiway Demon Mk II	D. J. Walter
	G-MBJX	Hiway Super Scorpion	R. W. Mitchell & J. A. McIntosh
	G-MBJY	Rotec Rally 2B	C. R. V. Hitch
	G-MBJZ	Catto CP.16	Neville Chamberlain Ltd
	G-MBKA	Mistral Trainer	Tricraft Ltd
	G-MBKB	Pterodactyl Ptraveller	W. H. Foddy
	G-MBKC	Lightning	D. A. Izod
	G-MBKD	Chargus Vortex 120P-T.250	T. Knight
	G-MBKE	Catto CP.16	R. S. Tuberville
	G-MBKF	Striplin Skyranger	P. R. Botterill
	G-MBKG	Batchelor-Hunt Skytrike	M. J. Batchelor & ptnrs
	G-MBKH	Southdown Skytrike	P. H. Milward
	G-MBKI	Solar Typhoon	S. T. Jones
	G-MBKJ	Chargus TS.440 Titan 38	Westair Microlights
	G-MBKK	Pterodactyl Ascender	T. D. Baker
	G-MBKL	Hiway Demon Skytrike	D. C. Bedding
	G-MBKM	Weedhopper	P. G. Walton
	G-MBKN	Chargus TS.440 Titan	Chargus Gliding Co Ltd
	G-MBKO	Chargus TS.440 Titan	Chargus Gliding Co Ltd
	G-MBKP	Hiway Skytrike 160	R. A. Davies
	G-MBKR	Hiway Skytrike	C. J. Macey
	G-MBKS	Hiway Skytrike 160	J. H. M. Houldridge
	G-MBKT	Mitchell Wing B.10	T. Beckett
	G-MBKU	Hiway Demon Skytrike	P. W. Twizell
	G-MBKV	Cappo Goldwing	J. Bell
	G-MBKW	Pterodactyl Ptraveller	R. C. H. Russell
	G-MBKY	American Eagle	B. Fussell
	G-MBKZ	Hiway Skytrike	S. I. Harding
	G-MBLA	Flexiform Skytrike	F. A. Prescott
	G-MBLB	Eipper Quicksilver MX	Southern Microlight Centre Ltd
	G-MBLD	Flexiform Striker	D. H. McGovern
	G-MBLE	Hiway Demon Skytrike II	R. E. Harvey
	G-MBLF	Hiway Demon 195 Tri Pacer	A. P. Rostron
	G-MBLG	Chargus Titan T.38	P. R. F. Glenville
	G-MBLH	Flexwing Trike Hornet	A. Brown
	G-MBLJ	Eipper Quicksilver MX	Flylight South East
	G-MBLK	Puma Microlight	D. J. Lewis
	G-MBLM	Hiway Skytrike	W. N. Natson
	G-MBLN	Pterodactyl Ptraveller	H. C. Mason
	G-MBLO	Sealander Skytrike	I. N. Caldwell
	G-MBLP	Pterodactyl Ptraveller	R. N. Greenshields
	G-MBLR	Ultrasports Tripacer	B. J. Farrell

Reg.	Type	Owner or Operator	Notes
G-MBLS	Mistral	I. D. Stokes	
G-MBLT	Chargus TS.440 Titan	I. K. Alderman	
G-MBLU	Lightning L.195 Skytrike	R. J. Honey	
G-MBLV	Ultrasports Hybrid	Midway Microlites	
G-MBLW	Hiway Scorpion	J. Davies	
G-MBLX	Euro-Wing Goldwing	W. B. Thomas	
G-MBLY	Flexiform Sealander Trike	J. Clithero	
G-MBLZ	Scorpion	J. P. Bennett-Snewin	
G-MBMA	Eipper Quicksilver MX	M. Maxwell	
G-MBMB	Scorpion	D. A. Bennett	
G-MBMC	Waspair Tomcat	F. D. Buckle	
G-MBMD	Euro-Wing CP.16	S. Dorrance	
G-MBME	American Eagle Z Drive	Perme Westcott Flying Club	
G-MBMF	Rotec Rally 2B	J. G. Woods	
G-MBMG	Rotec Rally 2B	J. R. Pyper	
G-MBMH	Eagle	M. S. Scott	
G-MBMI	Chargus T.440	G. Durbin	
G-MBMJ	Tri-Flyer	P. A. Gardner	
G-MBMK	Weedhopper Model B	P. W. Grange	
G-MBML	American Aerolights Zenoah Eagle	R. C. Jones	
G-MBMM	—	—	
G-MBMN	Skyhook Silhouette	A. D. F. Clifford	
G-MBMO	Hiway Skytrike 160	I. G. Cole	
G-MBMP	Mitchell Wing B.10	J. Pavelin	
G-MBMR	Ultrasports Tripacer Typhoon	L. Mills	
G-MBMS	Hornet	B. Berry	
G-MBMT	Mainair Tri-Flyer	T. R. Yeomans	
G-MBMU	Euro-Wing Microlight	P. R. Wason	
G-MBMV	Chargus TS.440 Titan 38	R. N. Preston	
G-MBMW	Solar Wings Typhoon	P. Cunliffe	
G-MBMY	Pterodactyl Fledge	G. Clarke	
G-MBMZ	U.A.S. Trike	T. D. Otho-Briggs	
G-MBNA	American Aerolights Eagle	N. D. Hall	
G-MBNB	Southdown Sailwings Lightning	R. H. Persad	
G-MBNC	Southdown Sailwings Puma	Southern Airsports Ltd	
G-MBND	Skyhook Sailwings SK TR.2	Eastern Microlight Aircraft Centre Ltd	
G-MBNE	Southern Airsports Scorpion	Eastern Microlight Aircraft Centre Ltd	
G-MBNF	American Aerolights Eagle	D. Read	
G-MBNG	Hiway Demon Skytrike	C. J. Clayson	
G-MBNH	Southern Airsports Scorpion	R. F. Thomas	
G-MBNI	Typhoon Tri Pacer	B. Smith	
G-MBNJ	Eipper Quicksilver MX	C. Lamb	
G-MBNK	American Aerolights Eagle	R. Moss	
G-MBNL	Hiway Skytrike C.2	K. V. Shail & H. W. Preston	
G-MBNM	American Aerolights Eagle	D. W. J. Orchard	
G-MBNN	Mk 1 Gazelle	N. A. Pitcher	
G-MBNO	—	—	
G-MBNP	Euro-Wing CP.16	M. H. C. Bishop	
G-MBNR	Flexiform Skysails Striker	D. T. Kaberry	
G-MBNS	—	—	
G-MBNT	American Aerolights Eagle	M. D. O'Brien	
G-MBNU	Hilander/Hiway Skytrike	D. Wilson & I. Williams	
G-MBNV	Sheffield Aircraft Skytrike	D. L. Buckley	
G-MBNW	Flexwing Microlight	J. T. Meagher	
G-MBNX	Solar Storm	F. Kratky	
G-MBNY	Steer Terror Fledge II	M. J. Steer	
G-MBNZ	Hiway Skytrike Demon	E. Battersea & J. Paige	
G-MBOA	Flexiform Hilander	A. F. Stafford	
G-MBOB	American Aerolights Eagle	N. J. Oldacres	
G-MBOC	Ultrasports Tripacer 250	R. D. Watton	
G-MBOD	American Aerolights Eagle	M. A. Ford & ptnrs	
G-MBOE	Solar Wing Typhoon Trike	M. J. Phizacklea	
G-MBOF	Jackdaw Microlight	L. G. Pakes	
G-MBOG	Flexiform Sealander	C. T. Richards	
G-MBOH	Microlight Engineering Mistral	D. L. B. Holliday	
G-MBOI	Ultralight Flight Mirage II	H. I. Jones	
G-MBOJ	Pterodactyl Pfledgling	S. P. Dewhurst	
G-MBOK	Dunstable Microlight	W. E. Brooks	
G-MBOL	Pterodactyl 360 SAX	R. Naylor	
G-MBOM	Hiway Hilander	P. H. Beaumont	

Notes	Reg.	Type	Owner or Operator
	G-MBON	Euro-Wing Goldwing Canard	A. H. Dunlop
	G-MBOO	—	—
	G-MBOP	Hiway Demon Skytrike	R. E. Holden
	G-MBOR	Chotia 460B Weedhopper	D. J. Whysall
	G-MBOS	Hiway Super Scorpion	C. Montgomery
	G-MBOT	Hiway 250 Skytrike	J. R. G. Swales
	G-MBOU	Aircraft (Sales) Scout	T. Spiers
	G-MBOV	Southdown Lightning Trike	J. Messenger
	G-MBOW	Solar Wing Typhoon	R. Luke
	G-MBOX	American Aerolights Eagle	J. S. Paine
	G-MBOY	—	
	G-MBPA	Weedhopper Srs 2	C. H. & P. B. Smith
	G-MBPB	Pterodactyl Ptraveller	P. E. Bailey
	G-MBPC	American Aerolights Eagle	Aerial Imaging Systems Ltd
	G-MBPD	American Aerolights Eagle	R. G. Harris & K. Hall
	G-MBPE	Ultrasports Trike	L. W. Humphreys
	G-MBPF	Southern Aerosports Scorpion	R. L. Wadley
	G-MBPG	Hunt Skytrike	J. A. Hunt
	G-MBPH	—	
	G-MBPI	MEA Mistral Trainer	M. J. Kenniston
	G-MBPJ	Moto-Delta	J. B. Jackson
	G-MBPK	—	
	G-MBPL	Hiway Demon	R. M. Strange
	G-MBPM	Eurowing Goldwing	A. B. Paton & ptnrs
	G-MBPN	American Aerolights Eagle	N. O. G. & P. C. Wooler
	G-MBPO	Volnik Arrow	N. A. Seymour
	G-MBPP	American Aerolights Eagle	D. C. North
	G-MBPR	American Aerolights Eagle	P. Kift
	G-MBPS	Gryphon Willpower	A. B. Willgress
	G-MBPT	Hiway Demon	K. M. Simpson
	G-MBPU	Hiway Demon	D. S. Simpson
	G-MBPV	—	
	G-MBPW	Weedhopper	D. H. Whisker
	G-MBPX	Eurowing Goldwing	W. R. Haworth & V. C. Cannon
	G-MBPY	Ultrasports Tripacer Flexwing	P. A. Joyce
	G-MBPZ	Flexiform Striker	C. Harris
	G-MBRA	Catto CP.16	J. Brown
	G-MBRB	—	
	G-MBRC	Skycraft Scout Mk 3A	Skycraft (UK) Ltd
	G-MBRD	American Aerolights Eagle	D. R. Gibbons
	G-MBRE	Skycraft Scout	R. G. Buck
	G-MBRF	Weedhopper 460C	L. R. Smith
	G-MBRG	—	
	G-MBRH	Ultralight Mirage Mk II	R. A. L. Hubbard
	G-MBRI	—	
	G-MBRJ	—	
	G-MBRK	Huntair Pathfinder	British Air Ferries Ltd
	G-MBRL	—	
	G-MBRM	Hiway Demon	S. D. Hicks & ptnrs
	G-MBRN	Hiway Demon 175	R. A. Nicholls
	G-MBRO	Hiway Skytrike 160	R. J. Hughes
	G-MBRP	American Aerolights Eagle	F. G. Rainbow
	G-MBRR	—	
	G-MBRS	American Aerolights Eagle	R. W. Chatterton
	G-MBRU	Skyhook Microlight	T. J. McLauchlan
	G-MBRV	Eurowing Goldwing	J. H. G. Lywood & A. A. Boyle
	G-MBRW	—	
	G-MBRX	—	
	G-MBRY	—	
	G-MBRZ	Hiway Vulcan 250	A. C. Snowling
	G-MBSA	UltraLight Flight Mirage II	M. J. Laxton
	G-MBSB	UltraLight Flight Mirage II	Windsports Centre
	G-MBSC	UltraLight Flight Mirage II	M. E. Hollis
	G-MBSD	Ultrasports Puma	Breen Aviation Ltd
	G-MBSF	UltraLight Flight Mirage II	A. J. Horne
	G-MBSG	UltraLight Flight Mirage II	P. E. Owen
	G-MBSI	American Aerolights Eagle	M. Day
	G-MBSN	American Aerolights Eagle	D. Duckworth
	G-MBSS	Ultrasports Puma 2	Swancar
	G-MBSU	Ultralight Flight Mirage II	R. Lynn
	G-MBSW	Ultralight Flight Mirage II	G. Clare

Reg.	Type	Owner or Operator	Notes
G-MBTA	Solar Buggy 5 Mk 2	N. & D. McEwan	
G-MBTB	Davies Tri-Flyer S	S. Davies	
G-MBTC	Weedhopper	B. Barrass	
G-MBTD	Solar Wings Cherokee 250 Trike	R. D. Yaxley	
G-MBTE	Hornet Dual Trainer Trike	A. B. Greenbank	
G-MBTF	Mainair Tri-Flyer Skytrike	Mainair Sports Ltd	
G-MBTG	Mainair Tri-Flyer 2 Seat Skytrike	Mainair Sports Ltd	
G-MBTH	Whittaker MW.4	J. M. Miller	
G-MBTI	Hovey Whing Ding	A. Carr & R. Saddington	
G-MBTJ	Solar Wings Microlight	J. Swingler	
G-MBTK	Vortex 120P Triflyer	B. R. Beer	
G-MBTL	Super Scorpion	C. S. Beer	
G-MBTM	—	—	
G-MBTN	Mitchell Wing B.10	N. F. James	
G-MBTO	Mainair Demon 250	N. Huxtable	
G-MBTP	Hiway Demon	S. E. Huxtable	
G-MBTR	Skyhook Microlight	R. Smith	
G-MBTS	—	—	
G-MBTT	Ultrasports Typhoon 330	T. R. Aspinall	
G-MBTU	Cloudhopper Mk II	P. C. Lovegrove	
G-MBTV	Ultraflight Tomcat	M. C. Latham	
G-MBTW	Raven Vector 600	L. A. J. Parren	
G-MBTX	Hornet	A. F. Holdsworth	
G-MBTY	American Aerolights Eagle	Southall College of Technology	
G-MBTZ	Huntair Pathfinder	G. M. Hayden	
G-MBUA	—	—	
G-MBUB	Horne Sigma Skytrike	L. G. Horne	
G-MBUC	Huntair Pathfinder	Huntair Ltd	
G-MBUD	Skycraft Scout Mk III	R. J. Adams	
G-MBUE	Micro-Bipe	Herveport Ltd	
G-MBUG	Southern Aerosports Scorpion Twin	Flyflight Southeast	
G-MBUH	Hiway Skytrike	R. Crosthwaite	
G-MBUI	Skycraft Scout Mk I	G. C. Martin	
G-MBUJ	Rotec Rally 2B	L. T. Swallham	
G-MBUK	Mainair 330 Tri Pacer	J. D. Bridge	
G-MBUL	American Aerolights Eagle	Nottingham Offshore Marine	
G-MBUO	Southern Aerosports Scorpion	I. C. Vanner	
G-MBUP	Hiway Skytrike	D. H. & J. Shrimpton	
G-MBUS	MEA Mistral	F. G. Johnson Ltd	
G-MBUT	Flexwing	J. N. Wrigley	
G-MBUU	Mainair Triflyer	G. E. Edwards	
G-MBUV	Huntair Pathfinder	S. Montandon	
G-MBUW	Skyhook Sabre Trike	D. F. Soul	
G-MBUX	Pterodactyl Ptraveller	J. J. Harris	
G-MBUY	American Aerolights Eagle	Nottingham Offshore Marine	
G-MBUZ	Skycraft Scout Mk II	K. C. & C. W. Rolph	
G-MBVA	Volmer Jensen VJ-23E	D. P. Eichorn	
G-MBVB	Ultralight Flight Mirage II	R. Brewer	
G-MBVC	American Aerolights Eagle	E. M. Salt	
G-MBVE	Hiway 160 Valmet	T. J. Daly	
G-MBVF	Hornet	P. D. Hopkins	
G-MBVG	American Aerolights Eagle	Cipher Systems Ltd	
G-MBVH	Mainair Triflyer Striker	M. A. Lomas	
G-MBVI	Hiway 250 Skytrike	D. L. B. Holliday	
G-MBVJ	Skyhook Trike	F. M. Ripley	
G-MBVK	Ultralight Flight Mirage II	R. Braxton	
G-MBVL	Southern Aerosports Scorpion	R. H. Wentham	
G-MBVM	—	—	
G-MBVO	Hovey Whing Ding	J. Labouchere	
G-MBVP	Triflyer 330 Striker	P. M. Wiles	
G-MBVR	Rotec Rally 2B	J. F. Bishop	
G-MBVS	Hiway Skytrike	G. J. Foard	
G-MBVT	American Aerolights Eagle	D. Cracknell	
G-MBVU	Flexiform Sealander Triflyer	R. S. T. Sears	
G-MBVV	Hiway Skytrike	I. Shulver	
G-MBVW	Skyhook TR.2	Oban Divers Ltd	
G-MBVX	Power Fledge	D. G. Tigwell	
G-MBVY	Eipper Quicksilver MX	J. Moss	
G-MBVZ	Hornet Trike 250	R. F. Southcott	
G-MBWA	American Aerolights Eagle	S. Pizzey	

Notes	Reg.	Type	Owner or Operator
	G-MBWB	Hiway Skytrike	C. K. Board
	G-MBWD	Rotec Rally 2B	A. Craw
	G-MBWE	American Aerolights Eagle	R. H. Tombs
	G-MBWF	Triflyer Striker	G. A. Archer
	G-MBWG	Huntair Pathfinder	J. Morris
	G-MBWH	Designability Duet I	Designability Ltd
	G-MBWI	Microlight Lafayette Mk.1	F. W. Harrington
	G-MBWK	Mainair Triflyer	G. C. Weighwell
	G-MBWL	Huntair Pathfinder	M. L. Powell
	G-MBWM	American Aerolights Eagle	J. N. B. Mourant
	G-MBWN	American Aerolights Eagle	J. N. B. Mourant
	G-MBWO	Hiway Demon Skytrike	J. T. W. J. Edwards
	G-MBWP	Ultrasports Trike	E. Craven
	G-MBWR	Hornet	B. D. Jones
	G-MBWS	Turley Vector 600	J. L. Sanders
	G-MBWT	Huntair Pathfinder	D. G. Gibson
	G-MBWU	Hiway Demon Skytrike	J. J. Woollen
	G-MBWW	Southern Aerosports Scorpion	Twinflight Ltd
	G-MBWX	Southern Aerosports Scorpion	Twinflight Ltd
	G-MBWY	American Aerolights Eagle	C. Carber
	G-MBWZ	Breen Eagle	B. Busby
	G-MBXA	Southern Aerosports Scorpion	Osprey Aviation Ltd
	G-MBXB	Southdown Sailwings Puma	Peninsula Flight Ltd
	G-MBXC	Eurowing Goldwing	A. J. J. Bartak
	G-MBXD	Huntair Pathfinder	R. J. Woodland
	G-MBXE	Hiway Skytrike	T. A. Harlow
	G-MBXF	Hiway Skytrike	J. Robinson
	G-MBXG	Mainair Triflyer	R. Bailey
	G-MBXH	Southdown Sailwings Puma	A. Milne
	G-MBXI	Hiway Skytrike	R. M. A. Nickell
	G-MBXJ	Hiway Demon Skytrike	A. Roder
	G-MBXK	Ultrasports Puma	P. W. Robinson
	G-MBXL	Eipper Quicksilver MX2	Flying Machines (Circa 1910) Ltd
	G-MBXM	American Aerolights Eagle	I. M. Willsher
	G-MBXN	Southdown Sailwings Lighting	T. W. Robinson
	G-MBXO	Trident	M. I. Watson
	G-MBXP	Hornet Skytrike	M. J. Phizacklea
	G-MBXR	Hiway Skytrike 150	G. W. Welford
	G-MBXS	Electra Floater	R. G. Hooker
	G-MBXT	Eipper Quicksilver MX2	S. W. Kibble
	G-MBXU	Rotec Rally 2B	M. Cowan & J. K. Cook
	G-MBXW	Hiway Trike	N. G. Arthur
	G-MBXX	Ultralight Flight Mirage II	Newell Aircraft & Tool Co Ltd
	G-MBXY	Hornet	C. Leach
	G-MBXZ	Skyhook TR2	Dennar Engineering Ltd
	G-MBYA	Southern Aerosports Scorpion	Inkerman Microlight Sales Ltd
	G-MBYB	—	—
	G-MBYC	—	—
	G-MBYD	American Aerolights Eagle	J. M. Hutchinson
	G-MBYE	Eipper Quicksilver MX	M. J. Beeby
	G-MBYF	Skyhook TR2	G. S. Stokes
	G-MBYG	—	
	G-MBYH	Hill Hummer	W. E. Gillham
	G-MBYI	Lazair	A. M. Fleming
	G-MBYJ	Hiway Super Scorpion IIC	P. M. Lang
	G-MBYK	Huntair Pathfinder	W. E. Lambert
	G-MBYL	Huntair Pathfinder 330	D. B. White
	G-MBYM	Eipper Quicksilver MX	J. Wibberley
	G-MBYN	Livesey Super-Fly	D. M. Livesey
	G-MBYO	American Aerolights Eagle	B. J. & M. G. Ferguson
	G-MBYP	Hornet 440cc Flexwing Cutlass	T. J. B. Daly
	G-MBYR	American Aerolights Eagle	F. Green & G. McCready
	G-MBYS	Ultralight Flight Mirage II	Breen Aviation Ltd
	G-MBYT	Ultralight Flight Mirage II	L. J. Perring
	G-MBYU	American Aerolights Eagle	F. L. Wiseman
	G-MBYV	Hiway Demon	I. T. Ferguson
	G-MBYW	Magpie	R. Levi
	G-MBYX	American Aerolights Eagle	T. J. Shepherd
	G-MBYY	Southern Aerosports Scorpion	D. J. Lovell
	G-MBYZ	American Aerolights Eagle	N. J. Mackay

Reg.	Type	Owner or Operator	Notes
G-MBZA	Ultrasports Tripacer 330	M. A. Rigler	
G-MBZB	Hiway Skytrike	R. Davies	
G-MBZC	Mainair Solarwings Typhoon	I. Rawson	
G-MBZD	Hiway Volmet 160cc	G. G. Williams	
G-MBZE	Southdown Lighting	P. A. Lee	
G-MBZF	American Aerolights Eagle	G. Calder & A. C. Bernard	
G-MBZG	Twinflight Scorpion 2 seat	H. T. Edwards	
G-MBZH	Eurowing Goldwing	M. I. M. Smith	
G-MBZI	Eurowing Goldwing	R. C. Forsyth	
G-MBZJ	Ultrasports Puma	A. Barnish	
G-MBZK	Ultrasports Tripacer 250	R. Alistair	
G-MBZL	Weedhopper	A. R. Prior	
G-MBZM	Ultralight Sealander Stormbuggy	S. Comber & A. Crabtree	
G-MBZN	Ultrasports Puma	Taurus Aviation Ltd	
G-MBZO	Mainair Triflyer 330	J. Baxendale	
G-MBZP	Skyhook TR2	Army Hang Gliding School	
G-MBZR	Eipper Quicksilver MX	R. Gill	
G-MBZS	Ultrasports Puma	K. T. Venning	
G-MBZT	Solarwings Skytrike	S. Hetherton	
G-MBZU	Skyhook Sabre C	G. N. Beyer-Kay	
G-MBZV	American Aerolights Eagle	G. Borrell	
G-MBZW	American Aerolights Eagle	M. J. Pugh	
G-MBZX	American Aerolights Eagle	M. J. Johnson	
G-MBZY	Waspair Tom Cat HM.81	A. C. Wendelken	
G-MBZZ	Scorpion	P. J. Harlow	
G-MJAA	Ultrasports Tripacer	A. R. Wells	
G-MJAB	Ultrasports Skytrike	I. W. Kemsley	
G-MJAC	American Aerolights Eagle 3	P. R. Fellden	
G-MJAD	Eipper Quicksilver MX	K. Cheesewright	
G-MJAE	American Aerolights Eagle	F. L. Wiseman	
G-MJAF	Ultrasports Puma 440	J. Sharp	
G-MJAG	Skyhook TR1	G. H. Marshall & M. B. Tomlinson	
G-MJAH	Eagle 1A	R. L. Arscott	
G-MJAI	American Aerolights Eagle	Leisure Flight Ltd	
G-MJAJ	Eurowing Goldwing	C. R. Gale & D. J. Royce	
G-MJAK	Hiway Demon	F. C. Potter	
G-MJAL	Skycraft Scout 3	D. H. Simmonds	
G-MJAM	Eipper Quicksilver MX	J. C. Larkin	
G-MJAN	Hiway Skytrike	R. A. V. Pendelbury & F. Dawson	
G-MJAO	Hiway Skytrike	F. Lodge	
G-MJAP	Hiway 160	N. A. Bray	
G-MJAR	Chargus Titan	Quest Air Ltd	
G-MJAS	—		
G-MJAT	Hiway Demon Skytrike	W. Davies	
G-MJAU	Hiway Skytrike 244cc	A. P. Cross	
G-MJAV	Hiway Demon Skytrike 244cc	B. G. Wilding	
G-MJAW	Typhoon Nicholls 250	M. R. Nicholls	
G-MJAX	American Aerolights Eagle	J. P. Simpson & C. W. Mellard	
G-MJAY	Eurowing Goldwing	J. F. White	
G-MJAZ	Raven Vector 610	P. Shoemaker	
G-MJBA	Raven Vector 610	Raven Leisure Industries Ltd	
G-MJBB	Raven Vector 610	Raven Leisure Industries Ltd	
G-MJBC	Raven Vector 610	Raven Leisure Industries Ltd	
G-MJBD	Raven Vector 610	Raven Leisure Industries Ltd	
G-MJBE	Scout X	Newell Aircraft & Tool Co Ltd	
G-MJBF	Southdown Lightning Tripacer	D. J. Godwin	
G-MJBG	Mainair Solarwings Typhoon	A. J. M. Berry	
G-MJBH	American Aerolights Eagle	P. Smith	
G-MJBI	Eipper Quicksilver MX	A. S. Reid	
G-MJBJ	—	—	
G-MJBK	—	—	
G-MJBL	American Aerolights Eagle	B. W. Olley	
G-MJBM	Catto CP.16	A. H. Milne	
G-MJBN	American Aerolights Eagle	D. Darke	
G-MJBO	Bell Microlight Type A	G. Bell	
G-MJBP	Eurowing Catto CP.16	I. Wilson	
G-MJBR	Eipper Quicksilver MX	J. Dilks	
G-MJBS	Ultralight Stormbuggy	G. I. Sargeant	
G-MJBT	Eipper Quicksilver MX	N. C. Butcher & D. Jagger	

Notes	Reg.	Type	Owner or Operator
	G-MJBV	American Aerolights Eagle	P. A. Ellis
	G-MJBW	American Aerolights Eagle	J. D. Penman
	G-MJBX	Pterodactyl Ptraveller	R. E. Hawkes
	G-MJBY	Rotec Rally 2B	B. Eastwood
	G-MJBZ	Huntair Pathfinder	P. S. C. Comina
	G-MJCA	Skyhook Sabre	B. G. Axworthy
	G-MJCB	Hornet 330	A. C. Aspden & ptnrs
	G-MJCC	Ultrasports Puma	Airsports Aviation Ltd
	G-MJCD	Sigma Tetley Skytrike	N. L. Betts & B. Tetley
	G-MJCE	Ultrasports Puma	R. G. Calvert
	G-MJCF	Maxair Hummer	Southern Microlight Centre Ltd
	G-MJCG	S.M.C. Flyer Mk 1	Southern Microlight Centre Ltd
	G-MJCH	Ultralight Flight Mirage II	Southern Microlight Centre Ltd
	G-MJCI	Flexiform Firefly Dual	H. Kruchek
	G-MJCJ	Hiway Spectrum	J. F. Mayes
	G-MJCK	Southern Aerosports Scorpion	S. L. Moss
	G-MJCL	Eipper Quicksilver MX	R. F. Witt
	G-MJCM	S.M.C. Flyer Mk 1	P. L. Gooch
	G-MJCN	S.M.C. Flyer Mk 1	C. W. Merriam
	G-MJCO	Striplin Lone Ranger	J. G. Wellans
	G-MJCP	—	—
	G-MJCR	American Aerolights Eagle	R. F. Hinton
	G-MJCS	EFS Pterodactyl	D. W. Evans
	G-MJCT	Hiway Skytrike	C. Ager
	G-MJCU	Tarjani	S. C. Goozes
	G-MJCV	Southern Flyer Mk 1	G. N. Harris
	G-MJCW	Hiway Super Scorpion	M. G. Sheppard
	G-MJCX	American Aerolights Eagle	S. C. Weston
	G-MJCY	Eurowing Goldwing	A. E. Dewdeswell
	G-MJCZ	Southern Aerosports Scorpion 2	C. Baldwin
	G-MJDA	Hornet Trike Executive	W. J. Barnes
	G-MJDB	Birdman Cherokee	J. K. Cook
	G-MJDC	Mainair Tri-Flyer Dual	J. K. Cross
	G-MJDD	—	
	G-MJDE	Huntair Pathfinder	E. H. Gould
	G-MJDF	Tripacer 250cc Striker	J. Haigh
	G-MJDG	Hornet Supertrike	R. A. Shreeve
	G-MJDH	Huntair Pathfinder	Hewland Engineering Ltd
	G-MJDI	Southern Flyer Mk 1	N. P. Day
	G-MJDJ	Hiway Skytrike Demon	R. J. A. Reid
	G-MJDK	American Aerolights Eagle	P. A. McPherson & ptnrs
	G-MJDL	American Aerolights Eagle	M. T. Edwards
	G-MJDM	Skycraft Scout Mk III	Skycraft (UK) Ltd
	G-MJDN	Skyhook Single Seat	G. Morgan
	G-MJDO	Southdown Lightning	N. G. S. Ltd
	G-MJDP	Eurowing Goldwing	R. Simpson
	G-MJDR	Hiway Demon Skytrike	P. J. Bullock
	G-MJDS	Eipper Quicksilver MX2	Microlight Airsport Services Ltd
	G-MJDT	Eipper Quicksilver MX2	R. E. Derbyshire
	G-MJDU	Eipper Quicksilver MX2	Microlight Airsport Services Ltd
	G-MJDV	Skyhook TR-1	R. Mason
	G-MJDW	Eipper Quicksilver MX	Remus International Ltd
	G-MJDX	Moyes Mega II	P. H. Davies
	G-MJDY	Ultrasports Solarwings	G. I. Simons
	G-MJDZ	Chargus Cyclone	M. G. Drinkwell
	G-MJEA	Flexiform Striker	S. J. O'Neill
	G-MJEB	—	
	G-MJEC	Ultrasports Puma	A. C. Stamp
	G-MJED	Eipper Quicksilver MX	R. Haslam
	G-MJEE	Mainair Triflyer Trike	M. F. Eddington
	G-MJEF	Gryphon 180	F. C. Coulson
	G-MJEG	Eurowing Goldwing	G. J. Stamper
	G-MJEH	Rotec Rally 2B	Blois Aviation Ltd
	G-MJEI	Breen Eagle	A. Moss
	G-MJEJ	Breen Eagle	J. Cole
	G-MJEK	Hiway Demon 330 Skytrike	P. S. Nelson
	G-MJEL	Stratos Trike	G. M. Driskell
	G-MJEM	Skytrike	R. G. Griffin
	G-MJEN	Eurowing Catto CP.16	A. D. G. Wright
	G-MJEO	American Aerolights Eagle	A. M. Shaw
	G-MJEP	Pterodactyl Ptraveller	G. H. Liddle

Reg.	Type	Owner or Operator	Notes
G-MJER	Flexiform Striker	D. S. Simpson	
G-MJES	Stratos Prototype 3 Axis 1	Stratos Aviation Ltd	
G-MJET	Stratos Prototype 3 Axis 1	Stratos Aviation Ltd	
G-MJEU	Hiway Skytrike	P. Best	
G-MJEV	Flexiform Striker	C. Scoble	
G-MJEW	Electraflyer Eagle	R. C. Wright	
G-MJEX	Eipper Quicksilver MX	M. J. Sundaram	
G-MJEY	Southdown Lightning	P. M. Coppola	
G-MJEZ	Raven Vector 600	P. A. Smith	
G-MJFB	Flexiform Striker	A. J. Ketchen	
G-MJFD	Ultrasports Tripacer	R. N. O. Kingsbury	
G-MJFE	Hiway Scorpion	N. A. Fisher	
G-MJFF	Huntair Pathfinder	S. R. L. Eversfield & ptnrs	
G-MJFG	Eurowing Goldwing	J. G. Aspinall & H. R. Marsden	
G-MJFH	Eipper Quicksilver MX	T. J. Drummond & ptnrs	
G-MJFI	Flexiform Striker	M. R. Parr	
G-MJFJ	Hiway Skytrike	J. Hollings	
G-MJFK	Flexiform Skytrike Dual	J. Hollings	
G-MJFL	Flexiform Skytrike Dual	J. Hollings	
G-MJFM	Huntair Pathfinder	M. Lister	
G-MJFN	Huntair Pathfinder	Times Newspapers Ltd	
G-MJFP	American Aerolights Eagle	D. A. Culpitt	
G-MJFR	American Aerolights Eagle	H. G. Smith	
G-MJFS	American Aerolights Eagle	P. R. A. Elliston	
G-MJFT	American Aerolights Eagle	D. S. McMullen	
G-MJFV	Ultrasports Puma	P. M. Kift	
G-MJFW	Ultrasports Puma	J. McCarthy	
G-MJFX	Skyhook TR-1	Skyhook Sailwings Ltd	
G-MJFY	Hornet 250	J. Bates	
G-MJFZ	Hiway Demon Skytrike	J. A. Lowie	
G-MJGA	Hiway Skytrike 160	J. H. Wadsworth	
G-MJGB	American Aerolights Eagle	N. P. Day	
G-MJGC	Hornet	K. Page	
G-MJGD	Huntair Pathfinder	Breen Aviation Ltd	
G-MJGE	Eipper Quicksilver MX	D. Brown	
G-MJGF	Poisestar Aelus Mk 1	Poisestar Ltd	
G-MJGG	Skyhook TR-1	R. Pritchard	
G-MJGH	Flexiform Skytrike	P. Newman	
G-MJGI	Eipper Quicksilver MX	J. M. Hayer & J. R. Wilman	
G-MJGJ	American Aerolights Eagle	B. J. Houlihan	
G-MJGK	Eurowing Goldwing	R. Haslam	
G-MJGL	Chargus Titan 38	R. H. Persad	
G-MJGM	Hiway Demon 195 Skytrike	J. M. Creasey	
G-MJGN	Greenslade Monotrike	P. G. Greenslade	
G-MJGO	Avon Skytrike	B. R. Barnes	
G-MJGP	Hiway Demon Skytrike	G. I. J. Thompson	
G-MJGR	Hiway Demon Skytrike	H. L. Clarke	
G-MJGS	American Aerolights Eagle	P. D. Griffiths	
G-MJGT	Skyhook Cutlass Trike	T. Silvester	
G-MJGU	Pterodactyl Mk 1	J. Pemberton	
G-MJGV	Eipper Quicksilver MX2	Southwest Airsports Ltd	
G-MJGW	Solar Wings Trike	D. J. D. Beck	
G-MJGX	—		
G-MJGZ	Mainair Triflyer 330	J. F. Bennett	
G-MJHA	Hiway Skytrike	P. R. O'Connor	
G-MJHB	Sky Ranger	Aero & Engineering Services Ltd	
G-MJHC	Ultrasports Tripacer 330	G. van Der Gaag	
G-MJHD	Campbell-Jones Prototype	M. A. Campbell-Jones	
G-MJHE	Hiway Demon Skytrike	G. Harrison	
G-MJHF	Skyhook Sailwing Trike	R. A. Watering	
G-MJHG	Huntair Pathfinder 330	A. Nice	
G-MJHH	Soleair Dactyl	C. N. Giddings	
G-MJHI	Soleair Dactyl	S. B. Giddings	
G-MJHJ	Redwing G.W.W.1	G. W. Wickington	
G-MJHK	Hiway Demon 195	B. Richardson	
G-MJHL	Mainair Triflyer Mk II	D. G.Jones	
G-MJHM	Ultrasports	J. Richardson	
G-MJHN	American Aerolights Eagle	P. K. Ewens	
G-MJHO	Bumble Bee Srs 1	C. R. Shilling	
G-MJHP	American Aerolights Eagle	B. A. G. Scott & ptnrs	
G-MJHR	Southdown Lightning	G. N. Sugg	

Notes	Reg.	Type	Owner or Operator
	G-MJHS	American Aerolights Eagle	R. M. Bacon
	G-MJHT	Eurowing Goldwing	J. D. Penman
	G-MJHU	Eipper Quicksilver MX	P. J. Hawcock & ptnrs
	G-MJHV	Hiway Demon 250	A. G. Griffiths
	G-MJHW	Ultrasports Puma 1	P. & C. Crayfourd
	G-MJHX	Eipper Quicksilver MX	G. J. Pill
	G-MJHY	American Aerolights Eagle	J. T. H. McAlpine
	G-MJHZ	Southdown Sailwings	R. R. Saunt
	G-MJIA	Flexiform Striker	B. J. Wood
	G-MJIB	Hornet 250	S. H. Williams
	G-MJIC	Ultrasports Puma 330	Taurus Aviation Ltd
	G-MJID	Southdown Sailwings Puma DS	M. H. Palmer
	G-MJIE	Perrills Tuphoon	T. R. N. Perey
	G-MJIF	Mainair Triflyer	D. P. Fiske
	G-MJIG	Hiway Demon Skytrike	Viscount Lowther
	G-MJIH	Ultrasports Tripacer	A. R. Currah
	G-MJII	American Aerolights Eagle	M. Flitman
	G-MJIJ	Ultrasports Tripacer 250	D. H. Targett
	G-MJIK	Southdown Sailwings Lightning	J. F. Chithalan
	G-MJIL	Mitchell B.10	D. S. & R. M. Bremner
	G-MJIM	Skyhook Cutlass	P. Rayner
	G-MJIN	Hiway Skytrike	P. W. Harding
	G-MJIO	American Aerolights Eagle	R. Apps & J. Marshall
	G-MJIP	Wheeler Scout Mk 33A	A. V. Wilson
	G-MJIR	Eipper Quicksilver MX	J. Tuttiett
	G-MJIS	—	
	G-MJIT	Hiway Skytrike	F. A. Mileham & D. W. B. Hatch
	G-MJIU	Eipper Quicksilver MX	O. W. A. Church
	G-MJIV	Pterodactyl Ptraveller	G. E. Fowles
	G-MJIW	Southdown Lightning	A. R. Hughes
	G-MJIX	Flexiform Hilander	S. Wells & A. Gist
	G-MJIY	Flexiform Voyager	C. & R. J. Sims
	G-MJIZ	Southdown Lightning	J. Stokes
	G-MJJA	Huntair Pathfinder	Quest Air Ltd
	G-MJJB	Eipper Quicksilver MX	J. W. V. Adkins
	G-MJJC	Eipper Quicksilver MX2	A. Brabiner
	G-MJJD	Birdman Cherokee	B. J. Sanderson
	G-MJJE	Douglas Type 1	R. A. Douglas
	G-MJJF	Sealey	J. G. Sealey
	G-MJJG	Southdown Lightning	Southdown Sailwings Ltd
	G-MJJI	Skyrider	R. H. Mackinder
	G-MJJJ	Moyes Knight	R. J. Broomfield
	G-MJJK	Eipper Quicksilver MX2	B. Harrison
	G-MJJL	Solar Wings Storm	P. Wharton
	G-MJJM	Birdman Cherokee Mk 1	R. J. Wilson
	G-MJJN	Ultrasports Puma	J. E. Laidler
	G-MJJO	Flexiform Skytrike Dual	J. D. Hall
	G-MJJP	American Aerolights Eagle	Flying Machines (Circa 1910) Ltd
	G-MJJR	Huntair Pathfinder 330	J. Hannibal
	G-MJJS	Micro Aviation Swallow	D. Corrigan
	G-MJJT	Huntair Pathfinder	Macpara Ltd
	G-MJJU	Hiway Demon	M. R. Starling
	G-MJJV	Skycraft Scout	C. G. Johes
	G-MJJW	Chargus Kilmarnock	J. S. Potts
	G-MJJX	Hiway Skytrike	D. Bosomworth
	G-MJJY	Tirith Firefly	Tirith Ltd
	G-MJJZ	Hiway Demon 175 Skytrike	B. C. Williams
	G-MJKA	Skyhook Sabre Trike	E. James
	G-MJKB	Striplin Skyranger	A. P. Booth
	G-MJKC	Triflyer 330 Striker	G. J. Latham
	G-MJKD	—	
	G-MJKE	Mainair Triflyer 330	J. S. Walton
	G-MJKF	Hiway Demon	W. G. Reynolds
	G-MJKG	John Ivor Skytrike	R. C. Wright
	G-MJKH	—	—
	G-MJKI	—	—
	G-MJKJ	—	—
	G-MJKK	Huntair Pathfinder	A. Leaney & ptnrs
	G-MJKL	Ultrasports Puma	A. Tremer
	G-MJKM	Chargus Titan TS.440/38	Hiway Flight Services Ltd
	G-MJKN	Hiway Demon	Hiway Flight Services Ltd

Reg.	Type	Owner or Operator	Notes
G-MJKO	Goldmark 250 Skytrike	W. E. Bray	
G-MJKP	Hiway Super Scorpion	M. Horsfall	
G-MJKR	Rotec Rally 2B	H. Banks	
G-MJKS	Mainair Triflyer	P. Sutton	
G-MJKT	Hiway Super Scorpion	K. J. Morris	
G-MJKU	Hiway Demon 175	R. D. Middleton	
G-MJKV	Hornet	C. Parkinson	
G-MJKW	Maxair Hummer TX	D. Roberts	
G-MJKX	Ultralight Skyrider Phantom	Skyrider Airsports	
G-MJKY	Hiway Skytrike	M. Dearsley	
G-MJLA	Ultrasports Puma 2	Michael Gardner Ltd	
G-MJLB	Ultrasports Puma 2	Breen Aviation Ltd	
G-MJLC	American Aerolights Double Eagle	Ardenco Ltd	
G-MJLD	Skycraft Scout Mk III	M. Buchanan-Jones	
G-MJLE	Rooster 2 Type 5	J. Lee	
G-MJLF	Southern Microlight Trike	A. Sebhi	
G-MJLG	Hiway Skytrike Mk II	P. Crossman	
G-MJLH	American Aerolights Eagle 2	A. Cussins	
G-MJLI	Hiway Demon Skytrike	A. K. Coveney	
G-MJLJ	Flexiform Sealander	Questair Ltd	
G-MJLK	Dragonfly 250-II	G. Carter	
G-MJLL	Hiway Demon Skytrike	D. Hines	
G-MJLN	Southern Microlight Gazelle	R. Rossiter	
G-MJLO	Coldmarque Skytrike	R. Knowles	
G-MJLP	Nib II Vertigo	W. Niblett	
G-MJLR	Skyhook SK-1	T. Moore	
G-MJLS	Rotec Rally 2B	G. Messenger	
G-MJLT	American Aerolights Eagle	P. de Vere Hunt	
G-MJLU	Skyhook	E. Battersea & ptnrs	
G-MJLV	Eipper Quicksilver MX	W. Wade-Gery	
G-MJLW	Chargus Titan	C. Ellison	
G-MJLX	Rotec Rally 2B	J. Houldenshaw	
G-MJLY	American Aerolights Eagle	A. H. Read	
G-MJLZ	Hiway Demon Skytrike	K. James	
G-MJMA	Hiway Demon	J. C. Carpenter	
G-MJMB	Weedhopper	C. Slater	
G-MJMC	Huntair Pathfinder	R. Griffiths	
G-MJMD	Hiway Demon Skytrike	D. Cussen	
G-MJME	Ultrasports Tripacer Mega II	J. Fleet	
G-MJMF	—	—	
G-MJMG	Weedhopper	S. Reynolds	
G-MJMH	American Aerolights Eagle	D. Crowson	
G-MJMI	Skyhook Sabre	G. Foxall	
G-MJMJ	Skycraft Scout III	R. Mitchell	
G-MJMK	Ultrasports Tripacer	M. F. J. Shipp	
G-MJML	Weedhopper D	V. Dixon	
G-MJMM	Chargus Vortex	D. Gwenin	
G-MJMN	Mainair Trike	D. Harrison	
G-MJMO	Lancashire Microlight Striker	N. Heap	
G-MJMP	Eipper Quicksilver MX	Microlight Aerosports Services Ltd	
G-MJMR	Mainair Trike	D. Randle	
G-MJMS	Hiway Skytrike	E. E. Williams	
G-MJMT	Hiway Demon Skytrike	R. Chiappa	
G-MJMU	Hiway Demon	J. Hall	
G-MJMV	Vulcan 2	R. Rawcliffe	
G-MJMW	Eipper Quicksilver MX2	R. & J. Dover	
G-MJMX	Ultrasports Tripacer	R. MacDonald	
G-MJMY	Kolb Flyer Srs 1	W. Sawney	
G-MJMZ	Robertson Ultralight B1-RD	Southwest Aviation	
G-MJNA	Mainair Triflyer	M. T. Byrne	
G-MJNB	Hiway Skytrike	G. Hammond	
G-MJNC	Hiway Demon Skytrike	T. Gdaniec	
G-MJND	Mainair Triflyer	G. Popplewell	
G-MJNE	Hornet Supreme Dual Trike	Hornet Microlights	
G-MJNF	Harmsworth Trike	C. C. Harmsworth	
G-MJNG	Eipper Quicksilver MX	R. Briggs-Price	
G-MJNH	Skyhook Cutlass Trike	B. M. Marsh	
G-MJNI	Hornet Sabre	T. M. Carter	
G-MJNJ	Typhoon	M. R. Gregory	
G-MJNK	Hiway Skytrike	R. Blenkey	
G-MJNL	American Aerolights Eagle	N. J. Williams	

Notes	Reg.	Type	Owner or Operator
	G-MJNM	American Aerolights Double Eagle	E. G. Cullen
	G-MJNN	—	—
	G-MJNO	American Aerolights Double Eagle	R. S. Martin & J. L. May
	G-MJNP	American Aerolights Eagle	M. P. Harper & P. A. George
	G-MJNR	Ultralight Solar Buggy	D. J. Smith
	G-MJNS	—	
	G-MJNT	Hiway Skytrike	P. R. Allery
	G-MJNU	Skyhook Cutlass	D. M. Camm
	G-MJNV	Eipper Quicksilver MX	W. Toulmin
	G-MJNW	Skyhook Silhouette	R. Hamilton
	G-MJNX	Eipper Quicksilver MX	R. Hurley
	G-MJNY	Skyhook Sabre Trike	P. Ratcliffe
	G-MJNZ	Skyhook Sabre Trike	R. Huthison
	G-MJOA	Chargus T.250 Vortex	R. J. Ridgway
	G-MJOB	Skyhook Cutlass CD Trike	S. S. Broadbent
	G-MJOC	Huntair Pathfinder	N. P. Thompson
	G-MJOD	Rotec Rally 2B	A. J. Capel & K. D. Halsey
	G-MJOE	Eurowing Goldwing	Leisure Flight Ltd
	G-MJOF	Eipper Quicksilver MX	S. M. Wellband
	G-MJOG	American Aerolights Eagle	J. B. Rush
	G-MJOH	Flexiform Striker	R. J. Butler
	G-MJOI	Hiway Demon	M. J. Coppel
	G-MJOJ	Flexiform Skytrike	D. Haynes
	G-MJOK	Triflyer 250	S. Pike & K. Fagan
	G-MJOL	Skyhook Cutlass	K. W. E. Brunnenkant
	G-MJOM	Southdown Puma 40F	Peninsula Flight Ltd
	G-MJON	Southdown Puma 40F	Peninsula Flight Ltd
	G-MJOO	Southdown Puma 40F	D. J. England
	G-MJOP	Southdown Puma 40F	Peninsula Flight Ltd
	G-MJOR	Solair Phoenix	Soleair Aviation
	G-MJOS	Southdown Lightning 170	D. C. Sollom & P. S. Lund
	G-MJOT	Airwave Nimrod	W. G. Lamyman
	G-MJOU	Hiway Demon 175	H. Phipps
	G-MJOV	Solarwings Typhoon	R. H. Lawson
	G-MJOW	Eipper Quicksilver MX	P. N. Haigh
	G-MJOX	Solar Wings Typhoon	L. Johnston
	G-MJOY	Eurowing CP.16	J. P. B. Chilton
	G-MJOZ	—	
	G-MJPA	Rotec Rally 2B	A. Troughton
	G-MJPB	Ladybird	W. L. Marvel
	G-MJPC	American Aerolights Double Eagle	P. H. Hard
	G-MJPD	Hiway Demon Skytrike	T. D. Adamson
	G-MJPE	Hiway Demon Skytrike	D. Hill
	G-MJPF	American Aerolights Eagle 430R	A. E. F. McClintock
	G-MJPG	American Aerolights Eagle 430R	C. J. W. Marriott
	G-MJPH	Huntair Pathfinder	A. J. Lambert
	G-MJPI	Flexiform Striker	M. William
	G-MJPJ	Flexiform Dual Trike 440	M. D. Phillips & ptnrs
	G-MJPK	Hiway Vulcan	R. G. Darcy
	G-MJPL	Birdman Cherokee	P. A. Leach
	G-MJPM	Huntair Pathfinder	Swift Systems Ltd
	G-MJPN	Mitchell B10	T. Wilford
	G-MJPO	Eurowing Goldwing	M. Merryman
	G-MJPP	Hiway Super Scorpion	K. L. Mercer
	G-MJPR	Birdman Cherokee 250	R. J. Shaeffer
	G-MJPS	American Aerolights Eagle 430R	Peter Symonds & Co
	G-MJPT	Dragon	Fly-In Ltd
	G-MJPU	—	
	G-MJPV	Eipper Quicksilver MX	J. B. Walker
	G-MJPW	Mainair Merlin	G. Deegan
	G-MJPX	Hiway Demon	R. Todd
	G-MJPY	American Aerolights Eagle	N. J. Grant
	G-MJPZ	American Aerolights Eagle	A. T. Croy
	G-MJRA	Hiway Demon	P. Richardson & J. Martin
	G-MJRB	Eurowing Goldwing	J. S. Pyke

Reg.	Type	Owner or Operator	Notes
G-MJRC	Eipper Quicksilver MX	R. W. Bunting	
G-MJRD	Gaze	M. Gaze	
G-MJRE	Hiway Demon	Elmstone Construction Ltd	
G-MJRF	Super Scorpion	G. J. Sargent	
G-MJRG	Ultrasports Puma	G. J. Slater	
G-MJRH	Hiway Skytrike	G. P. Foyle	
G-MJRI	American Aerolights Eagle	N. N. Brown	
G-MJRJ	Hiway Demon 175 Skytrike	M. Tomlinson	
G-MJRK	Flexiform Striker	B. J. Bishop	
G-MJRL	Eurowing Goldwing	H. G. I. Goodheart	
G-MJRM	Dragon	Fly-In Ltd	
G-MJRN	Flexiform Striker	M. J. Sinnett	
G-MJRO	Eurowing Goldwing	I. D. Stokes	
G-MJRP	Mainair Triflyer 330	P. E. Blyth	
G-MJRR	Striplin Skyranger Srs 1	J. R. Reece	
G-MJRS	Eurowing Goldwing	J. G. Beesley	
G-MJRT	Southdown Lightning DS	T. J. Franklin	
G-MJRU	Sopwith Tiger Cub 440	P. Johnson	
G-MJRV	Eurowing Goldwing	D. N. Williams	
G-MJRX	Ultrasports Puma II	E. M. Woods	
G-MJRY	MBA Super Tiger Cub 440	Vintage Displays & Training Services Ltd	
G-MJRZ	MBA Super Tiger Cub 440	Vintage Displays & Training Services Ltd	
G-MJSA	Mainair 2-Seat Trike	F. Lodge	
G-MJSB	Eurowing Catto CP.16	Independent Business Forms (Scotland) Ltd	
G-MJSC	American Aerolights Eagle	E. McGuiness	
G-MJSD	Rotec Rally 2B Srs 1	K. J. Dickson	
G-MJSE	Skyrider Airsports Phantom	Skyrider Airsports	
G-MJSF	Skyrider Airsports Phantom	Skyrider Airsports	
G-MJSG	Solar Wings Typhoon	C. A. Kevern	
G-MJSH	American Aerolights Eagle	J. Walsom	
G-MJSI	Huntair Pathfinder	Huntair Ltd	
G-MJSK	Skyhook Sabre	G. E. Coole	
G-MJSL	Dragon 200	Dragon Light Aircraft Co Ltd	
G-MJSM	Weedhopper B	J. R. Bancroft	
G-MJSN	Flexiform Sealander	D. G. Hill	
G-MJSO	Hiway Skytrike	T. J. Trew	
G-MJSP	MBA Super Tiger Cub 440	J. W. E. Romain	
G-MJSR	Flexiform Micro-Trike II	P. G. Kavanagh	
G-MJSS	American Aerolights Eagle	G. N. S. Farrant	
G-MJST	Pterodactyl Ptraveller	G. C. Sutton	
G-MJSU	MBA Tiger Cub	R. J. Adams	
G-MJSV	MBA Tiger Cub	R. J. Adams	
G-MJSW	Eipper Quicksilver MX	Fairwood Aviation Ltd	
G-MJSX	Simplicity Microlight	N. Smith	
G-MJSY	Eurowing Goldwing	A. J. Rex	
G-MJSZ	D.H. Wasp	D. Harker	
G-MJTA	Flexiform Striker	J. V. George	
G-MJTB	Eipper Quicksilver MX	R. F. G. King	
G-MJTC	Solar Wings Typhoon	J. W. Highton	
G-MJTD	Gardner T-M Scout	D. Gardner	
G-MJTE	Skyrider Airsports Phantom	Skyrider Airsports	
G-MJTF	Gryphon Wing	A. T. Armstrong	
G-MJTG	Sky Ranger	Aero & Engineering Ltd	
G-MJTH	S.M.D. Gazelle	R. B. Best	
G-MJTI	Huntair Pathfinder II	Huntair Ltd	
G-MJTJ	Weedhopper	M. J. Blanchard	
G-MJTK	American Aerolights Eagle	N. R. MacRae	
G-MJTL	Aerostructure Pipistrelle 2B	Southdown Aero Services Ltd	
G-MJTM	Aerostructure Pipistrelle 2B	Southdown Aero Services Ltd	
G-MJTN	Eipper Quicksilver MX	D. A. H. Clarke	
G-MJTO	Duet Srs 1	Jordan Aviation Ltd	
G-MJTP	Flexiform Striker	A. J. Dawson & J. P. Hunt	
G-MJTR	Southdown Puma DS Mk 1	V. E. J. Smith	
G-MJTS	Skyhook TR-1	A. de F. Medonca	
G-MJTT	Dragon Srs 150	Dragon Light Aircraft Co Ltd	
G-MJTU	Skyhook Cutlass 185	P. D. Wade	
G-MJTV	Chargus Titan	B. K. Harrison	
G-MJTW	Eurowing Trike	B. K. Harrison	

Notes	Reg.	Type	Owner or Operator
	G-MJTX	Skyrider Phantom	R. E. Derbyshire
	G-MJTY	Huntair Pathfinder	C. H. Smith
	G-MJTZ	Skyrider Airsports Phantom	M. B. Stoner
	G-MJUA	MBA Super Tiger Cub	M. Ward
	G-MJUB	MBA Tiger Cub 440	C. C. Butt
	G-MJUC	MBA Tiger Cub 440	R. R. Hawkes
	G-MJUD	Southdown Puma 440	North of England Microlight School
	G-MJUE	Southdown Puma	J. P. Nicklin
	G-MJUF	MBA Super Tiger Cub 440	M. P. Chetwyn-Talbot
	G-MJUG	Huntair Pathfinder II	Huntair Ltd
	G-MJUH	MBA Tiger Cub 440	J. E. Johnes
	G-MJUI	Flexiform Striker	L. M. R. E. Bailey
	G-MJUJ	Eipper Quicksilver MX II	Microlight Airsport Services Ltd
	G-MJUK	Eipper Quicksilver MX II	Microlight Airsport Services Ltd
	G-MJUL	Southdown Puma Sprint	K. T. Vinning
	G-MJUM	Flexiform Striker	A. P. Smith
	G-MJUN	Hiway Skytrike	A. Donohue
	G-MJUO	Eipper Quicksilver MX II	Border Aviation Ltd
	G-MJUP	Weedhopper B	R. A. P. Cox
	G-MJUR	Skyrider Airsports Phantom	J. Hannibal
	G-MJUS	MBA Tiger Cub 440	H. Jenks
	G-MJUT	Eurowing Goldwing	D. L. Eite
	G-MJUU	Eurowing Goldwing	B. A. Akiens
	G-MJUV	Huntair Pathfinder	B. E. Francis
	G-MJUW	MBA Tiger Cub 440	G. R. Fountain
	G-MJUX	—	—
	G-MJUY	Eurowing Goldwing	J. E. M. Barnatt-Millns
	G-MJUZ	Dragon Srs 150	J. R. Fairweather
	G-MJVA	—	
	G-MJVB	Skyhook TR-2	Skyhook Sailwings Ltd
	G-MJVC	Hiway Skytrike	G. C. Martin
	G-MJVE	Hybred Skytrike	M. Dale
	G-MJVF	CFM Shadow	D. G. Cook
	G-MJVG	Hiway Skytrike	R. Houseman
	G-MJVH	American Aerolights Eagle	M. S. Whitton
	G-MJVI	Rooster 1 Srs 4	J. M. Lee
	G-MJVJ	Striker Wing	Hornet Microlight
	G-MJVK	Silhouette Wing	A. J. Willcox
	G-MJVL	Flexiform Striker	H. Phipps
	G-MJVM	—	
	G-MJVN	Ultrasports Puma 440	P. B. Robinson
	G-MJVO	American Aerolights Eagle	T. J. Mangat
	G-MJVP	Eipper Quicksilver MX II	G. Barker
	G-MJVR	Flexiforn Striker	L. A. Humphreys
	G-MJVS	Hiway Super Scorpion	T. C. Harrold
	G-MJVT	Eipper Quicksilver MX	A. M. Reid
	G-MJVU	—	
	G-MJVV	Hornet Supreme Dual	D. Atkinson & C. B. Mills
	G-MJVW	Airwave Nimrod	T. P. Mason
	G-MJVX	Skyrider Airsports Phantom	J. A. Grindley
	G-MJVY	Dragon Srs 150	Border Aviation Ltd
	G-MJVZ	Hiway Demon Tripacer	E. W. P. Van Zeller
	G-MJWA	—	
	G-MJWB	Eurowing Goldwing	A. R. Slee
	G-MJWC	Paraglide Fabric Self Inflating Wing	O. W. Neumark
	G-MJWD	Solar Wings Typhoon XL	A. R. Hughes
	G-MJWE	Hiway Demon	R. W. Davies
	G-MJWF	MBA Tiger Cub 440	B. R. Hunter
	G-MJWG	MBA Tiger Cub 440	D. H. Carter
	G-MJWH	—	—
	G-MJWI	Flexiform Striker	R. W. Twamley
	G-MJWJ	MBA Tiger Cub 440	H. A. Bromiley
	G-MJWK	Huntair Pathfinder	J. W. Keenan
	G-MJWL	—	—
	G-MJWN	—	—
	G-MJWN	Flexiform Striker	A. N. Baumber
	G-MJWO	Hiway Skytrike	T. Watson
	G-MJWP	MBA Tiger Cub 440	S. May
	G-MJWR	MBA Tiger Cub 440	J. L. Burton
	G-MJWS	Eurowing Goldwing	J. W. Salter & R. J. Bell

Reg.	Type	Owner or Operator	Notes
G-MJWT	American Aerolights Eagle	D. S. Baber	
G-MJWU	Hummer TX	D. Dugdale	
G-MJWV	Southdown Puma MS	S. Bond	
G-MJWW	MBA Super Tiger Cub 440	Midland Ultralights Ltd	
G-MJWX	Flexiform Striker	C. D. Batley	
G-MJWY	Flexiform Striker	G. J. Ford	
G-MJWZ	—	—	
G-MJXA	Flexiform Striker	B. Barlow	
G-MJXB	Eurowing Goldwing	A. W. Odell	
G-MJXC	Mitchell Wing B10	A. C. Dommett	
G-MJXD	MBA Tiger Cub 440	W. L. Rogers	
G-MJXE	Hiway Demon	H. Sykes	
G-MJXF	MBA Tiger Cub 440	E. J. Hadley	
G-MJXG	Flexiform Striker	D. W. Barnes	
G-MJXH	Mitchell Wing B10	M. M. Ruck	
G-MJXI	Flexiform Striker	A. P. Pearson	
G-MJXJ	MBA Tiger Cub 440	J. L. Ellis	
G-MJXL	MBA Tiger Cub 440	M. J. Lister	
G-MJXM	—	—	
G-MJXN	American Aerolights Eagle	C. H. Middleton	
G-MJXO	Middleton CM.5	C. H. Middleton	
G-MJXP	—	—	
G-MJXR	Huntair Pathfinder II	Huntair Ltd	
G-MJXS	Huntair Pathfinder II	Huntair Ltd	
G-MJXT	Phoenix Falcon 1	Phoenix Aircraft Co	
G-MJXU	MBA Tiger Cub 440	Radio West Ltd	
G-MJXV	Flexiform Striker	H. Unsworth	
G-MJXW	Southdown Sigma	C. J. Tansley	
G-MJXX	Flexiform Striker	R. T. Lancaster	
G-MJXY	Hiway Demon Skytrike	C. Russell	
G-MJXZ	Hiway Demon	R. P. Franks	
G-MJYA	—	—	
G-MJYB	Eurowing Goldwing	D. A. Farnworth	
G-MJYC	—	—	
G-MJYD	MBA Tiger Cub 440	M. L. Smith	
G-MJYE	Southdown Lightning Trike	G. Popplewell	
G-MJYF	—	—	
G-MJYG	Skyhook Orion Canard	Skyhook Sailwings Ltd	
G-MJYH	Skyhook 3 Axis Prototype	Skyhook Sailwings Ltd	
G-MJYI	Mainair Triflyer	M. J. Johnson	
G-MJYJ	MBA Tiger Cub 440	M. F. Collett	
G-MJYK	Noble Hardman Snowbird	Noble Hardman Aviation Ltd	
G-MJYL	Airwave Nimrod	R. Bull	
G-MJYM	—	—	
G-MJYN	Mainair Triflyer 440	D. P. Fiske	
G-MJYO	Mainair Triflyer 330	Mainair Sports Ltd	
G-MJYP	Mainair Triflyer 440	Mainair Sports Ltd	
G-MJYR	—	—	
G-MJYS	—	—	
G-MJYT	—	—	
G-MJYU	Mainair Triflyer	R. Clegg	
G-MJYV	—	—	
G-MJYW	Wasp Gryphon III	P. D. Lawrence	
G-MJYX	Mainair Triflyer	R. K. Birlison	
G-MJYY	Hiway Demon	N. H. Martin	
G-MJYZ	Flexiform Striker	R. W. Ashton	
G-MJZA	MBA Tiger Cub	C. R. Barsby	
G-MJZB	Flexiform Striker Dual	P. Cunningham	
G-MJZC	MBA Tiger Cub 440	P. G. Walton	
G-MJZD	—	—	
G-MJZE	MBA Tiger Cub 440	D. Ridley & ptnrs	
G-MJZF	La Mouette Atlas 16	W. R. Crew	
G-MJZG	Mainair Triflyer 440	G. J. Foard	
G-MJZH	Southdown Lightning 195	B. F. Crick	
G-MJZI	Eurowing Goldwing	A. J. Sharpe	
G-MJZJ	Hiway Cutlass Skytrike	G. D. H. Sandlin	
G-MJZK	—	—	
G-MJZL	Eipper Quicksilver MX II	E. E. White	
G-MJZM	MBA Tiger Cub 440	F. M. Ward	
G-MJZN	Pterodactyl	C. J. Blundell	
G-MJZO	Flexiform Striker	B. H. Ness	

173

Notes	Reg.	Type	Owner or Operator
	G-MJZP	MBA Tiger Cub 440	Herts & Cambs Biplanes Ltd
	G-MJZR	Eurowing Zephyr 1	Eurowing Ltd
	G-MJZS	—	
	G-MJZT	Flexiform Striker	J. Whitehouse
	G-MJZU	Flexiform Striker	G. J. Foard
	G-MJZV	Micro 5	D. M. Livesey
	G-MJZW	Eipper Quicksilver MX II	W. Smith & ptnrs
	G-MJZX	Hummer TX	K. T. G. Smith
	G-MJZY	Gold Marque Shadow	P. W. Fathers
	G-MJZZ	Skyhook Cutlass	J. Bradbury & D. F. Coles
	G-MMAA	Dragon Srs 150	Dragon Light Aircraft Co Ltd
	G-MMAB	Dragon Srs 150	Dragon Light Aircraft Co Ltd
	G-MMAC	Dragon Srs 150	Dragon Light Aircraft Co Ltd
	G-MMAD	Dragon Srs 150	Dragon Light Aircraft Co Ltd
	G-MMAE	Dragon Srs 150	Dragon Light Aircraft Co Ltd
	G-MMAF	Dragon Srs 150	Cambrian Aviation Ltd
	G-MMAG	MBA Tiger Cub 440	W. R. Tull
	G-MMAH	Eipper Quicksilver MX II	T. E. McDonald
	G-MMAI	Dragon Srs 150	Blois Aviation Ltd
	G-MMAJ	Southdown Puma Sprint	M. L. Smith
	G-MMAK	MBA Tiger Cub 440	J. R. Watts
	G-MMAL	Flexiform Striker Dual	D. H. McGovern
	G-MMAM	MBA Tiger Cub 440	S. B. Churchill
	G-MMAN	Flexiform Striker	E. Dean
	G-MMAO	—	
	G-MMAP	Hummer TX	O. C. Davies
	G-MMAR	—	—
	G-MMAS	—	—
	G-MMAT	—	—
	G-MMAU	—	
	G-MMAV	American Aerolights Eagle	Aeri-Visual Ltd
	G-MMAW	Mainair Rapier	T. Green
	G-MMAX	Flexiform Striker	R. J. Garland
	G-MMAY	Magic Nimrod Wing	R. E. Patterson
	G-MMAZ	Southdown Puma Sprint	M. A. P. Bull
	G-MMBA	Hiway Super Scorpion	P. Dook
	G-MMBB	American Aerolights Eagle	Microlight Aviation (UK) Ltd
	G-MMBC	Hiway Super Scorpion	A. T. Grain
	G-MMBD	Spectrum 330	J. Hollings
	G-MMBE	MBA Tiger Cub 440	R. J. B. Jordan & R. W. Pearce
	G-MMBF	American Aerolights Eagle	N. V. Middleton
	G-MMBG	Chargus Cyclone	P. N. Long
	G-MMBH	MBA Super Tiger Cub 440	C. H. Jennings & J. F. Howesman
	G-MMBI	—	
	G-MMBJ	Solar Wings Typhoon	R. F. Barber
	G-MMBK	American Aerolights Eagle	B. M. Quinn
	G-MMBL	Southdown Puma	A. J. M. Berry
	G-MMBM	La Mouette Azure	A. Christian
	G-MMBN	Eurowing Goldwing	J. E. Andrew
	G-MMBO	—	
	G-MMBP	Hiway Super Scorpion 2	B. C. Pocklington
	G-MMBR	Hiway Demon 175	S. S. M. Turner
	G-MMBS	Flexiform Striker	J. Tate & R. Collinson
	G-MMBT	MBA Tiger Cub 440	G. M. & C. M. Booth
	G-MMBU	Eipper Quicksilver MX II	C. Crawford
	G-MMBV	Huntair Pathfinder	M. P. Phillipe
	G-MMBW	MBA Tiger Cub 440	J. C. Miles
	G-MMBX	MBA Tiger Cub 440	Fox Brothers Blackpool Ltd
	G-MMBY	Solar Wings Typhoon	Solar Wings Ltd
	G-MMBZ	Solar Wings Typhoon P	D. S. Raymond
	G-MMCA	Solar Wings Storm	P. B. Curnell
	G-MMCB	Huntair Pathfinder	Horizon Aerosails
	G-MMCC	American Aerolights Eagle	Microlight Aviation (UK) Ltd
	G-MMCD	Southdown Lightning DS	Microlight Services
	G-MMCE	MBA Tiger Cub 440	M. K. Dring
	G-MMCF	—	
	G-MMCG	Eipper Quicksilver MX I	Microlight Airsport Services Ltd
	G-MMCH	Southdown Lightning Phase II	R. S. Andrew
	G-MMCI	Southdown Puma Sprint	D. M. Parsons
	G-MMCJ	—	—

Reg.	Type	Owner or Operator	Notes
G-MMCK	Stewkie Aer-O-Ship LTA	K. Stewart	
G-MMCL	Stewkie Aer-O-Ship HAA	K. Stewart	
G-MMCM	Southdown Puma Sprint	C. Montgomery	
G-MMCN	Solar Wings Storm	A. P. S. Presland	
G-MMCO	Southdown Sprint	R. J. O. Walker	
G-MMCP	Southdown Lightning	J. D. Haslam	
G-MMCR	Eipper Quicksilver MX	T. L. & B. L. Holland	
G-MMCS	—	—	
G-MMCT	Hiway Demon	R. G. Gray	
G-MMCU	Dragon Srs 150	Dragon Light Aircraft Co Ltd	
G-MMCV	Solar Wings Typhoon III	S. N. Pugh	
G-MMCW	Southdown Puma Sprint	S. Palmer	
G-MMCX	MBA Super Tiger Cub 440	D. Harkin	
G-MMCY	Flexiform Striker	A. P. White	
G-MMCZ	Flexiform Striker	T. G. Elmhirst	
G-MMDA	Mitchell Wing B-10	H. F. French	
G-MMDB	La Mouette Atlas	D. L. Bowtell	
G-MMDC	Eipper Quicksilver MXII	M. Risdale & C. Lamb	
G-MMDD	Huntair Pathfinder	Microlight Aviation (UK) Ltd	
G-MMDE	Solar Wings Typhoon *	D. E. Smith	
G-MMDF	Southdown Lightning Phase II	P. Kelly	
G-MMDG	Eurowing Goldwing	Edgim Ltd	
G-MMDH	Manta Fledge 2B	R. G. Hooker	
G-MMDI	Hiway Super Scorpion	R. E. Hodge	
G-MMDJ	Solar Wings Typhoon	D. Johnson	
G-MMDK	Flexiform Striker	R. R. Wasson	
G-MMDL	Dragon Srs 150	Dragon Light Aircraft Co Ltd	
G-MMDM	MBA Tiger Cub 440	D. Marsh	
G-MMDN	Flexiform Striker	D. E. Richards	
G-MMDO	Southdown Sprint	E. Barfoot	
G-MMDP	Southdown Sprint	R. E. Derbyshire	
G-MMDR	Huntair Pathfinder II	M. Shapland	
G-MMDS	—	—	
G-MMDT	Flexiform Striker	P. G. Rawson	
G-MMDU	MBA Tiger Cub 440	P. Flynn	
G-MMDV	Ultrasports Panther	E. M. Woods & D. Little	
G-MMDW	Pterodactyl Pfledgling	R. C. Wright	
G-MMDX	Solar Wings Typhoon	E. J. Lloyd	
G-MMDY	Southdown Puma Sprint	A. M. Brooks	
G-MMDZ	Flexiform Dual Strike	D. C. Sagger-Thomas	
G-MMEA	MBA Tiger Cub 440	Border Aviation Ltd	
G-MMEB	Hiway Super Scorpion	A. A. Ridgway	
G-MMEC	Southdown Puma DS	A. E. Wilson	
G-MMED	—	—	
G-MMEE	American Aerolights Eagle	G. R. Bell & J. D. Bailey	
G-MMEF	Hiway Super Scorpion	J. H. Cooling	
G-MMEG	Eipper Quicksilver MX	W. K. Harris	
G-MMEH	—	—	
G-MMEI	Hiway Demon	K. May	
G-MMEJ	Flexiform Striker	R. Calwood	
G-MMEK	Solar Wings Typhoon XL2	C. Draper	
G-MMEL	Solar Wings Typhoon XL2	D. Rigden	
G-MMEM	Solar Wings Typhoon XL2	Wyndham Wade Ltd	
G-MMEN	Solar Wings Typhoon XL2	I. M. Rapley	
G-MMEO	Southdown Puma	G. Borrell	
G-MMEP	MBA Tiger Cub 440	P. M. Yeoman & D. Freestone-Barks	
G-MMER	—	—	
G-MMES	—	—	
G-MMET	Skyhook Sabre TR-1 Mk II	D. Sims	
G-MMEU	MBS Tiger Cub 440	R. Taylor	
G-MMEV	American Aerolights Eagle	J. G. Jennings	
G-MMEW	MBA Tiger Cub 440	V. N. Baker	
G-MMEX	Solar Wings Sprint	P. W. Robinson	
G-MMEY	MBA Tiger Cub 440	M. G. Selley	
G-MMEZ	—	—	
G-MMFA	—	—	
G-MMFB	Flexiform Striker	Flexiform Sky Sails	
G-MMFC	Flexiform Striker	Flexiform Sky Sails	
G-MMFD	Flexiform Striker	B. J. Wood	
G-MMFE	Flexiform Striker	Flexiform Sky Sails	
G-MMFF	Flexiform Striker	Flexiform Sky Sails	

Notes	Reg.	Type	Owner or Operator
	G-MMFG	Flexiform Striker	Flexiform Sky Sails
	G-MMFH	Flexiform Striker	Flexiform Sky Sails
	G-MMFI	Flexiform Striker	Flexiform Sky Sails
	G-MMFJ	Flexiform Striker	Flexiform Sky Sails
	G-MMFK	Flexiform Striker	Flexiform Sky Sails
	G-MMFL	Flexiform Striker	J. G. McNally
	G-MMFM	Piranha Srs 200	G. A. Brown
	G-MMFN	MBA Tiger Cub 440	R. L. Barnett
	G-MMFP	MBA Tiger Cub 440	R. J. Adams
	G-MMFR	MBA Tiger Cub 440	R. J. Adams
	G-MMFS	MBA Tiger Cub 440	P. J. Hodgkinson
	G-MMFT	MBA Tiger Cub 440	E. Barfoot
	G-MMFW	Skyhook Cutlass Wing	W. Chapel
	G-MMFX	MBA Tiger Cub 440	J. W. E. Romain
	G-MMGA	Bass Gosling	G. J. Bass
	G-MMGB	Southdown Puma Sprint	G. Breen
	G-MMGE	Hiway Super Scorpion	N. R. D'Urso
	G-MMGF	MBA Tiger Cub 440	J. Ford-Dunn
	G-MMGH	Flexiform Dual Striker	J. Whitehouse
	G-MMGI	Flexiform Dual Striker	M. Hurtley
	G-MMGJ	MBA Tiger Cub 440	J. Laidler
	G-MMGK	Skyhook Hiway Silhouette	N. E. Smith
	G-MMGL	MBA Tiger Cub 440	A. R. Cornelius
	G-MMGO	MBA Tiger Cub 440	T. J. Court
	G-MMIC	Luscombe Vitality	Luscombe Aircraft Ltd
	G-MMIJ	Airwave Merlin	R. W. Evans
	G-MMIN	Luscombe Vitality	Luscombe Aircraft Ltd
	G-MMJA	Mitchell Wing B-10	J. Abbott
	G-MMJC	Southdown Sprint	J. C. Lloyd
	G-MMJD	Southdown Puma Sprint	J. Doswell
	G-MMJG	Flexiform Striker	J. G. Teague
	G-MMJH	Southdown Puma Sprint	J. Hollings
	G-MMJL	Flexiform 1 + 1 Sealander	J. S. Long
	G-MMJR	MBA Tiger Cub 440	J. F. Ratcliffe
	G-MMJW	Southdown Puma Sprint	J. M. Wassmer
	G-MMKS	Southdown Puma Sprint	J. K. Cross
	G-MMKT	MBA Tiger Cub 440	K. N. Townsend
	G-MMLC	Scaled Composites 97M	Group Lotus Car Co Ltd
	G-MMMS	MBA Tiger Cub 440	M. H. D. Soltau
	G-MMNH	Dragon Srs 150	Air Consultants
	G-MMOF	MBA Tiger Cub 440	Sunderland Parachute Centre
	G-MMON	Microflight Monarch	Microflight
	G-MMPM	Ulstrasports Puma 330	P. J. Martin
	G-MMPR	Dragon Srs 150	P. N. B. Rosenfeld
	G-MMRF	MBA Tiger Cub 440	Fox Bros (Blackpool) Ltd
	G-MMRS	Dragon Srs 150	R. H. W. Strange
	G-MMSB	Huntair Pathfinder II	S. R. Baugh
	G-MMUG	Mainair Triflyer	G. C. Baird
	G-MMUM	MBA Tiger Cub 440	N. C. Butcher
	G-MMZZ	Hill Hummer	Microflight Ltd
	G-MNDK	Southdown Puma Sprint	D. Kerr
	G-MNJG	Southdown Puma Sprint MS	J. V. George
	G-MNPR	Hiway Demon 175	P. Robinson
	G-MNRD	Ultraflight Lazair	D. W. & M. F. Briggs
	G-MNSB	Southdown Puma Sprint	S. Baker

Military to Civil Cross-Reference

Serial carried	Civil identity	Serial carried	Civil identity
04 (Luftwaffe)	G-WULF	N3788	G-AKPF
14 (Luftwaffe)	G-BJZZ	N4877 (VX-F)	G-AMDA
26 (US)	G-BAVO	N5180	G-EBKY
45 (Aeronavale)	G-BHFG	N5182	G-APUP
75	G-AFDX	N5430	G-BHEW
92 (31-GW FrAF)	G-BJGW	N6452	G-BIAU
120 (Fr AF)	G-AZGC	N6532	G-ANTS
164 (USN)	G-BKGL	N6848	G-BALX
168	G-BFDE	N6985	G-AHMN
385 (RCAF)	G-BGPB	N9191	G-ALND
422-15	G-AVJO	N9238	G-ANEL
1049	G-BJCL	N9389	G-ANJA
2345	G-ATVP	N9508	G-APCU
2807 (VE-111 USN)	G-BHTH	N9510	G-AOEL
3066	G-AETA	P-122 (RDanAF)	G-ALUL
3398	G-BFYO	P3308 (UP-A)	G-AWLW
4253/18	G-BFPL	P6382	G-AJRS
5894	G-BFVH	P7350 (SH-D)	G-AWIJ
7198/19	G-AANJ	R1914	G-AHUJ
8449M	G-ASWJ	R4959	G-ARAZ
18393 (C.A.F.)	G-BCYK	R5086	G-APIH
2-7767	G-BIHW	R7524	G-AIWA
133854	G-SUES	S1287	G-BEYB
315509 (USAAF)	G-BHUB	S3398 (2)	G-BFYO
329417 (USAAF)	G-BDHK	T5424	G-AJOA
329601 (D-44 USAAF)	G-AXHR	T5493	G-ANEF
454537 (04-J)	G-BFDL	T5854	G-ANKK
461748	G-BHDK	T6645	G-AIIZ
472216	G-BIXL	T6818	G-ANKT
479865 (A-44)	G-BHPK	T7187	G-AOBX
485784 (YB-E)	G-BEDF	T7281	G-ARTL
542447	G-SCUB	T7404	G-ANMV
542474 (R-184)	G-PCUB	T7997	G-AOBH
8810677	G-VALE	T7909	G-ANON
A16-199 (SF-R RAAF)	G-BEOX	T9707	G-AKKR
A8226	G-BIDW	T9738	G-AKAT
B1807	G-EAVX	U-142 (Swiss AF)	G-BONE
B7270	G-BFCZ	V3388	G-AHTW
D5397/17	G-BFXL	V9281 (RU-M)	G-BCWL
C1701	G-AWYY	V9441 (AR-A)	G-AZWT
C1904	G-PFAP	Z2033	G-ASTL
D8096 (D)	G-AEPH	Z7197	G-AKZN
E-15 (RNethAF)	G-BIYU	AP507 (KX-P)	G-ACWP
E449	G-EBKN	AR213 (QG-A)	G-AIST
E3404	G-ACNB	AR501 (NN-D)	G-AWII
F904	G-EBIA	BB814	G-AFWI
F938	G-EBIC	BS676 (K-U)	G-KUKU
F939 (6)	G-EBIB	DE208	G-AGYU
F1425 (17)	G-BEFR	DE363	G-ANFC
F4650	G-BDWJ	DE623	G-ANFI
F5447	G-BKER	DE992	G-AXXV
F8614	G-AWAU	DF130	G-BACK
G-29-1 (Class B)	G-APRJ	DF155	G-ANFV
G-48-1 (Class B)	G-ALSX	DF198	G-BBRB
H2311	G-ABAA	DG590	G-ADMW
J-108 (Swiss AF)	G-BJAX	DR613	G-AFJB
J9941 (57)	G-ABMR	EM903	G-APBI
K-33 (USAAF)	G-BJLH	FE992	G-BDAM
K123	G-EACN	FT229	G-AZKI
K1786	G-AFTA	FT239	G-BIWX
K2567	G-MOTH	FT323	G-AZSC
K2572	G-AOZH	FT391	G-AZBN
K3215	G-AHSA	FX301 (FD-NQ)	G-JUDI
K4235	G-AHMJ	HB751	G-BCBL
L2301	G-AIZG	LB312	G-AHXE
L8032	G-AMRK	LS326	G-AJVH
N1854	G-AIBE	LZ766	G-ALCK

Serial carried	Civil identity	Serial carried	Civil identity
MC280	G-TEAC	WG348	G-BBMV
MD497	G-ANLW	WG350	G-BCYE
MH434 (AC-S)	G-ASJV	WG422	G-BFAX
ML417	G-BJSG	WG719	G-BRMA
MP425	G-AITB	WJ358	G-ARYD
MT360	G-AKWT	WJ897	G-BDFT
MT438	G-AREI	WJ945	G-BEDV
MT818 (G-M)	G-AIDN	WL626	G-BHDD
MV293	G-SPIT	WP321	G-BRFC
MV370 (AV-L)	G-FXIV	WP790	G-BBNC
MW100	G-AGNV	WP808	G-BDEU
NF875	G-AGTM	WP857	G-BDRJ
NH749 (L)	G-MXIV	WP977	G-BHRD
NJ695	G-AJXV	WT933	G-ALSW
NJ703	G-AKPI	WV493	G-BDYG
NM140	G-APGL	WV783	G-ALSP
NM181	G-AZGZ	WW397 (N-E)	G-BKHP
NP181	G-AOAR	WZ507	G-VTII
NP184	G-ANYP	WZ672	G-BDER
NP303	G-ANZJ	WZ711	G-AVHT
NX611	G-ASXX	WZ868	G-BCIW
PG617	G-AYVY	XB733	G-ATBF
PG651	G-AYUX	XF690	G-BGKA
RG333	G-AIEK	XF785	G-ALBN
RG333	G-AKEZ	XF836 (J-G)	G-AWRY
RH377	G-ALAH	XG452	G-BRMB
RH378	G-AJOE	XG547	G-HAPR
RL962	G-AHED	XJ348	G-NAVY
RM221	G-ANXR	XJ389	G-AJJP
RM619 (AP-D)	G-ALGT	XK417	G-AVXY
RR299 (HT-E)	G-ASKH	XK655	G-AMXA
RS709	G-MOSI	XL717	G-AOXG
SM832	G-WWII	XM553	G-AWSV
SM969	G-BRAF	XM556	G-HELI
TA634	G-AWJV	XM685	G-AYZJ
TA719	G-ASKC	XP279	G-BWKK
TJ569	G-AKOW	XP282	G-BGTC
TW439	G-ANRP	XP355	G-BEBC
VL348	G-AVVO	XR240	G-BDFH
VL349	G-AWSA	XR241	G-AXRR
VM360	G-APHV	XR267	G-BJXR
VR249	G-APIY	XR269	G-BDXY
VS356	G-AOLU	XR363	G-OHCA
VS610	G-AOKL	XR365	G-HLFT
VS623	G-AOKZ	XS101	G-GNAT
VX302 (77-M)	G-BCOV	F+IS (Luftwaffe)	G-BIRW
VZ728	G-AGOS	AT+JX (Luftwaffe)	G-ATJX
WA576	G-ALSS	AX+IH (Luftwaffe)	G-AXIH
WA577	G-ALST	BA+AY (Luftwaffe)	G-BAAY
WB763	G-BBMR	BU+CK (Luftwaffe)	G-BUCK
WD363	G-BCIH	RF+16 (Luftwaffe)	G-PTWO
WD413	G-BFIR	6J+PR (Luftwaffe)	G-AWHB
WE569	G-ASAJ	7A+WN (Luftwaffe)	G-AZMH
WF133	G-BIDN	N8+AA (Luftwaffe)	G-BFHD
WG307	G-BCYJ	N9+AA (Luftwaffe)	G-BECL
WG316	G-BCAH	① (Russian AF)	G-KYAK

XJ348   D.H.104 Sea Devon C.20, civil identity G-NAVY.

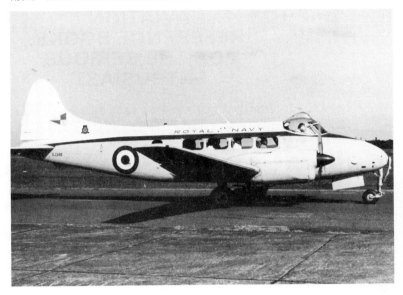

G-KYAK   Yakolev C-11 in Russian colours.

Overseas Airliner Registrations

(Aircraft included in this section are those most likely to be seen at UK airports on scheduled or charter services.)

A40 (Oman)

Reg.	Type	Owner or Operator	Notes
A40-TT	L-1011-385 TriStar 200	Gulf Air	
A40-TV	L-1011-385 TriStar 100	Gulf Air	
A40-TW	L-1011-385 TriStar 100	Gulf Air	
A40-TX	L-1011-385 TriStar 100	Gulf Air	
A40-TY	L-1011-385 TriStar 100	Gulf Air	
A40-TZ	L-1011-385 TriStar 100	Gulf Air	

Note: Gulf Air also operates TriStar 200s N92TA and N92TB.

AP (Pakistan)

AP-AWU	Boeing 707-373C	Pakistan International Airlines	
AP-AWY	Boeing 707-340C	Pakistan International Airlines	
AP-AXA	Boeing 707-340C	Pakistan International Airlines	
AP-AXC	Douglas DC-10-30	Pakistan International Airlines	
AP-AXD	Douglas DC-10-30	Pakistan International Airlines	
AP-AXG	Boeing 707-340C	Pakistan International Airlines	
AP-AYM	Douglas DC-10-30	Pakistan International Airlines	
AP-AYV	Boeing 747-282B	Pakistan International Airlines	
AP-AYW	Boeing 747-282B	Pakistan International Airlines	
AP-AZW	Boeing 707-351B	Pakistan International Airlines	
AP-BAA	Boeing 707-351B	Pakistan International Airlines	
AP-BAK	Boeing 747-240B	Pakistan International Airlines	
AP-BAT	Boeing 747-240B	Pakistan International Airlines	
AP-BBK	Boeing 707-323C	Pakistan International Airlines	
AP-BBL	Douglas DC-10-30	Pakistan International Airlines	

B (China)

B-2402	Boeing 707-3J6B	CAAC	
B-2404	Boeing 707-3J6B	CAAC	
B-2406	Boeing 707-3J6B	CAAC	
B-2408	Boeing 707-3J6B	CAAC	
B-2410	Boeing 707-3J6C	CAAC	
B-2412	Boeing 707-3J6C	CAAC	
B-2414	Boeing 707-3J6C	CAAC	
B-2416	Boeing 707-3J6C	CAAC	
B-2418	Boeing 707-3J6C	CAAC	
B-2420	Boeing 707-3J6C	CAAC	
B-2442	Boeing 747SP-J6	CAAC	
B-2444	Boeing 747SP-J6	CAAC	

Note: CAAC also operates Boeing 747SP-J6 N1304E.

C-F and C-G (Canada)

Notes	Reg.	Type	Owner or Operator
	C-FCPO	Douglas DC-8-63	Worldways Canada
	C-FCPP	Douglas DC-8-63	Worldways Canada
	C-FCPQ	Douglas DC-8-63	Worldways Canada
	C-FCPR	Douglas DC-8-63	Worldways Canada
	C-FCRA	Boeing 747-217B (741)	CP Air *Empress of Japan*
	C-FCRB	Boeing 747-217B (742)	CP Air *Empress of Canada*
	C-FCRD	Boeing 747-217B (743)	CP Air *Empress of Australia*
	C-FCRE	Boeing 747-217B (744)	CP Air *Empress of Italy*
	C-FDJC	Boeing 747-1D1 (399)	Wardair Canada *Phil Garratt*
	C-FFUN	Boeing 747-1D1 (398)	Wardair Canada *Romeo Vachan*
	C-FPWN	L-100-20 Hercules (383)	Pacific Western
	C-FTIK	Douglas DC-8-73AF (867)	Air Canada
	C-FTIO	Douglas DC-8-63AF (871)	Air Canada
	C-FTIP	Douglas DC-8-73AF (872)	Air Canada
	C-FTIQ	Douglas DC-8-63AF (873)	Air Canada
	C-FTIR	Douglas DC-8-63AF (874)	Air Canada
	C-FTIS	Douglas DC-8-63AF (875)	Air Canada
	C-FTJL	Douglas DC-8-54F (812)	Air Canada
	C-FTND	L.1011-385 TriStar 100 (504)	Air Canada
	C-FTNI	L.1011-385 TriStar 100 (509)	Air Canada
	C-FTNJ	L.1011-385 TriStar 100 (510)	Air Canada
	C-FTNK	L.1011-385 TriStar 100 (511)	Air Canada
	C-FTNL	L.1011-385 TriStar 100 (512)	Air Canada
	C-FTOA	Boeing 747-133 (301)	Air Canada
	C-FTOB	Boeing 747-133 (302)	Air Canada
	C-FTOC	Boeing 747-133 (303)	Air Canada
	C-FTOD	Boeing 747-133 (304)	Air Canada
	C-FTOE	Boeing 747-133 (305)	Air Canada
	C-GAGA	Boeing 747-233B (306)	Air Canada
	C-GAGB	Boeing 747-233B (307)	Air Canada
	C-GAGF	L.1011-385 TriStar 500 (551)	Air Canada
	C-GAGG	L.1011-385 TriStar 500 (552)	Air Canada
	C-GAGH	L.1011-385 TriStar 500 (553)	Air Canada
	C-GAGI	L.1011-385 TriStar 500 (554)	Air Canada
	C-GAGJ	L.1011-385 TriStar 500 (555)	Air Canada
	C-GAGK	L.1011-385 TriStar 500 (556)	Air Canada
	C-GCPC	Douglas DC-10-30 (901)	CP Air *Empress of Amsterdam*
	C-GCPD	Douglas DC-10-30 (902)	CP Air *Empress of Sydney*
	C-GCPE	Douglas DC-10-30 (903)	CP Air *Empress of Milan*
	C-GCPI	Douglas DC-10-30 (907)	CP Air *Empress of Honolulu*
	C-GCPJ	Douglas DC-10-30 (908)	CP Air *Empress of Rome*
	C-GFHX	Douglas DC-10-30 (103)	Wardair Canada *S. R. McMilland*
	C-GFLG	Boeing 707-365C	Worldways Canada
	C-GHPW	L-100-30 Hercules (387)	North West Territorial Airways
	C-GXRA	Boeing 747-211B (397)	Wardair Canada *Herbert Hollick Kenyon*
	C-GXRB	Douglas DC-10-30 (101)	Wardair Canada *C. H. Punch Dickens*
	C-GXRC	Douglas DC-10-30 (102)	Wardair Canada *W. R. Wop May*
	C-GXRD	Boeing 747-211B (396)	Wardair Canada *H. A. Doc Oakes*

Note: Airline fleet number carried on aircraft is shown in parenthesis.

CCCP (Russia)

All aircraft listed are operated by Aeroflot. The registrations are prefixed by CCCP in each case.

Reg.	Type	Notes	Reg.	Type	Notes
65001	Tu-134A		65090	Tu-134A	
65004	Tu-134A		65095	Tu-134A	
65005	Tu-134A		65096	Tu-134A	
65008	Tu-134A		65098	Tu-134A	
65009	Tu-134A		65100	Tu-134A	
65010	Tu-134A		65101	Tu-134A	
65011	Tu-134A		65105	Tu-134A	
65013	Tu-134A		65107	Tu-134A	
65014	Tu-134A		65109	Tu-134A	
65015	Tu-134A		65112	Tu-134A	
65017	Tu-134A		65113	Tu-134A	
65018	Tu-134A		65114	Tu-134A	
65020	Tu-134A		65118	Tu-134A	
65021	Tu-134A		65119	Tu-134A	
65023	Tu-134A		65120	Tu-134A	
65024	Tu-134A		65123	Tu-134A	
65025	Tu-134A		65132	Tu-134A	
65027	Tu-134A		65134	Tu-134A	
65028	Tu-134A		65135	Tu-134A	
65030	Tu-134A		65136	Tu-134A	
65031	Tu-134A		65140	Tu-134A	
65032	Tu-134A		65145	Tu-134A	
65034	Tu-134A		65600	Tu-134	
65035	Tu-134A		65601	Tu-134	
65036	Tu-134A		65602	Tu-134	
65037	Tu-134A		65603	Tu-134	
65038	Tu-134A		65604	Tu-134	
65039	Tu-134A		65605	Tu-134	
65040	Tu-134A		65606	Tu-134	
65042	Tu-134A		65607	Tu-134	
65043	Tu-134A		65608	Tu-134	
65044	Tu-134A		65609	Tu-134	
65045	Tu-134A		65610	Tu-134	
65046	Tu-134A		65611	Tu-134	
65047	Tu-134A		65612	Tu-134	
65048	Tu-134A		65613	Tu-134	
65049	Tu-134A		65614	Tu-134	
65050	Tu-134A		65615	Tu-134	
65051	Tu-134A		65616	Tu-134	
65052	Tu-134A		65617	Tu-134	
65053	Tu-134A		65618	Tu-134	
65055	Tu-134A		65619	Tu-134	
65056	Tu-134A		65620	Tu-134	
65058	Tu-134A		65621	Tu-134	
65059	Tu-134A		65622	Tu-134	
65060	Tu-134A		65623	Tu-134	
65061	Tu-134A		65624	Tu-134A	
65062	Tu-134A		65625	Tu-134	
65065	Tu-134A		65626	Tu-134A	
65066	Tu-134A		65627	Tu-134	
65069	Tu-134A		65628	Tu-134	
65070	Tu-134A		65629	Tu-134	
65071	Tu-134A		65630	Tu-134	
65072	Tu-134A		65631	Tu-134	
65074	Tu-134A		65632	Tu-134	
65075	Tu-134A		65633	Tu-134	
65076	Tu-134A		65634	Tu-134	
65077	Tu-134A		65635	Tu-134	
65078	Tu-134A		65636	Tu-134	
65080	Tu-134A		65637	Tu-134	
65082	Tu-134A		65638	Tu-134	
65083	Tu-134A		65639	Tu-134	
65085	Tu-134A		65640	Tu-134	
65086	Tu-134A		65641	Tu-134	
65088	Tu-134A		65642	Tu-134	
65089	Tu-134A		65643	Tu-134	

Notes	Reg.	Type	Notes	Reg.	Type
	65644	Tu-134A		65748	Tu-134A
	65645	Tu-134A		65749	Tu-134A
	65646	Tu-134A		65753	Tu-134A
	65647	Tu-134A		65757	Tu-134A
	65648	Tu-134A		65761	Tu-134A
	65649	Tu-134A		65762	Tu-134A
	65650	Tu-134A		65764	Tu-134A
	65651	Tu-134A		65765	Tu-134A
	65652	Tu-134A		65766	Tu-134A
	65653	Tu-134A		65769	Tu-134A
	65654	Tu-134A		65770	Tu-134A
	65655	Tu-134A		65771	Tu-134A
	65656	Tu-134A		65777	Tu-134A
	65657	Tu-134A		65780	Tu-134A
	65658	Tu-134A		65781	Tu-134A
	65659	Tu-134A		65782	Tu-134A
	65660	Tu-134A		65783	Tu-134A
	65661	Tu-134A		65784	Tu-134A
	65662	Tu-134A		65785	Tu-134A
	65663	Tu-134A		65789	Tu-134A
	65664	Tu-134A		65790	Tu-134A
	65665	Tu-134A		65791	Tu-134A
	65666	Tu-134A		65792	Tu-134A
	65667	Tu-134A		65794	Tu-134A
	65668	Tu-134A		65796	Tu-134A
	65669	Tu-134A		65801	Tu-134A
	65670	Tu-134A		65802	Tu-134A
	65671	Tu-134A		65804	Tu-134A
	65672	Tu-134A		65806	Tu-134A
	65673	Tu-134A		65810	Tu-134A
	65674	Tu-134A		65811	Tu-134A
	65675	Tu-134A		65812	Tu-134A
	65676	Tu-134A		65815	Tu-134A
	65677	Tu-134A		65816	Tu-134A
	65678	Tu-134A		65817	Tu-134A
	65679	Tu-134A		65818	Tu-134A
	65680	Tu-134A		65820	Tu-134A
	65683	Tu-134A		65821	Tu-134A
	65687	Tu-134A		65822	Tu-134A
	65689	Tu-134A		65823	Tu-134A
	65690	Tu-134A		65825	Tu-134A
	65691	Tu-134A		65828	Tu-134A
	65692	Tu-134A		65829	Tu-134A
	65694	Tu-134A		65830	Tu-134A
	65696	Tu-134A		65831	Tu-134A
	65697	Tu-134A		65832	Tu-134A
	65705	Tu-134A		65833	Tu-134A
	65706	Tu-134A		65834	Tu-134A
	65707	Tu-134A		65836	Tu-134A
	65711	Tu-134A		65837	Tu-134A
	65713	Tu-134A		65839	Tu-134A
	65714	Tu-134A		65840	Tu-134A
	65717	Tu-134A		65841	Tu-134A
	65718	Tu-134A		65843	Tu-134A
	65727	Tu-134A		65844	Tu-134A
	65728	Tu-134A		65845	Tu-134A
	65729	Tu-134A		65848	Tu-134A
	65730	Tu-134A		65851	Tu-134A
	65731	Tu-134A		65852	Tu-134A
	65732	Tu-134A		65853	Tu-134A
	65733	Tu-134A		65854	Tu-134A
	65734	Tu-134A		65857	Tu-134A
	65735	Tu-134A		65861	Tu-134A
	65739	Tu-134A		65862	Tu-134A
	65741	Tu-134A		65863	Tu-134A
	65742	Tu-134A		65864	Tu-134A
	65743	Tu-134A		65865	Tu-134A
	65744	Tu-134A		65866	Tu-134A
	65745	Tu-134A		65867	Tu-134A
	65746	Tu-134A		65868	Tu-134A
	65747	Tu-134A		65869	Tu-134A

Reg.	Type	Notes	Reg.	Type	Notes
65870	Tu-134A		85033	Tu-154	
65871	Tu-134A		85034	Tu-154	
65872	Tu-134A		85035	Tu-154	
65873	Tu-134A		85037	Tu-154	
65874	Tu-134A		85038	Tu-154	
65877	Tu-134A		85039	Tu-154	
65878	Tu-134A		85040	Tu-154	
65879	Tu-134A		85041	Tu-154	
65880	Tu-134A		85042	Tu-154	
65881	Tu-134A		85043	Tu-154	
65882	Tu-134A		85044	Tu-154	
65883	Tu-134A		85047	Tu-154	
65884	Tu-134A		85048	Tu-154	
65886	Tu-134A		85050	Tu-154	
65888	Tu-134A		85051	Tu-154	
65890	Tu-134A		85052	Tu-154	
65891	Tu-134A		85053	Tu-154	
65892	Tu-134A		85054	Tu-154	
65893	Tu-134A		85055	Tu-154	
65894	Tu-134A		85057	Tu-154	
65895	Tu-134A		85058	Tu-154A	
65898	Tu-134A		85060	Tu-154A	
65899	Tu-134A		85061	Tu-154A	
65903	Tu-134A		85062	Tu-154A	
65950	Tu-134A		85063	Tu-154A	
65951	Tu-134A		85064	Tu-154A	
65952	Tu-134A		85065	Tu-154A	
65953	Tu-134A		85066	Tu-154A	
65954	Tu-134A		85067	Tu-154A	
65955	Tu-134A		85068	Tu-154A	
65957	Tu-134A		85069	Tu-154A	
65960	Tu-134A		85070	Tu-154A	
65961	Tu-134A		85071	Tu-154A	
65962	Tu-134A		85072	Tu-154A	
65963	Tu-134A		85074	Tu-154A	
65964	Tu-134A		85075	Tu-154A	
65965	Tu-134A		85076	Tu-154A	
65967	Tu-134A		65080	Tu-154A	
65969	Tu-134A		85081	Tu-154A	
65970	Tu-134A		85082	Tu-154A	
65971	Tu-134A		85083	Tu-154A	
65972	Tu-134A		85084	Tu-154A	
65973	Tu-134A		85085	Tu-154A	
65974	Tu-134A		85086	Tu-154A	
65975	Tu-134A		85088	Tu-154A	
65976	Tu-134A		85090	Tu-154A	
85000	Tu-154		85091	Tu-154A	
85001	Tu-154		85092	Tu-154B	
85005	Tu-154		85093	Tu-154A	
85006	Tu-154		85094	Tu-154A	
85007	Tu-154		85095	Tu-154A	
85008	Tu-154		85096	Tu-154B-1	
85009	Tu-154		85097	Tu-154B-1	
85010	Tu-154		85098	Tu-154A	
85011	Tu-154		85099	Tu-154A	
85012	Tu-154		85100	Tu-154A	
85013	Tu-154		85101	Tu-154A	
85014	Tu-154		85102	Tu-154A	
85016	Tu-154		85103	Tu-154A	
85017	Tu-154		85104	Tu-154A	
85018	Tu-154		85105	Tu-154A	
85019	Tu-154		85106	Tu-154B	
85021	Tu-154		85107	Tu-154A	
85022	Tu-154		85108	Tu-154A	
85024	Tu-154		85109	Tu-154B	
85025	Tu-154		85110	Tu-154B	
85028	Tu-154		85111	Tu-154A	
85029	Tu-154		85112	Tu-154A	
85030	Tu-154		85113	Tu-154A	
85031	Tu-154		85114	Tu-154A	
85032	Tu-154		85115	Tu-154A	

Notes	Reg.	Type	Notes	Reg.	Type
	85116	Tu-154A		85192	Tu-154B
	85117	Tu-154A		85193	Tu-154B
	85118	Tu-154B		85194	Tu-154B
	85119	Tu-154A		85195	Tu-154B
	85120	Tu-154B		85196	Tu-154B
	85121	Tu-154B		85197	Tu-154B
	85122	Tu-154B		85198	Tu-154B
	85123	Tu-154B		85199	Tu-154B
	85124	Tu-154B		85200	Tu-154B
	85125	Tu-154B		85201	Tu-154B
	85126	Tu-154B		85202	Tu-154B
	85129	Tu-154B		85203	Tu-154B
	85130	Tu-154B		85204	Tu-154B
	85131	Tu-154B		85205	Tu-154B
	85132	Tu-154B		85206	Tu-154B
	85133	Tu-154B		85207	Tu-154B
	85134	Tu-154B		85210	Tu-154B
	85135	Tu-154B		85211	Tu-154B
	85136	Tu-154B		85212	Tu-154B
	85137	Tu-154B		85213	Tu-154B
	85138	Tu-154B		85214	Tu-154B
	85139	Tu-154B		85215	Tu-154B
	85140	Tu-154B		85216	Tu-154B
	85141	Tu-154B		85217	Tu-154B
	85142	Tu-154B		85218	Tu-154B
	85143	Tu-154B		85219	Tu-154B
	85145	Tu-154B		85220	Tu-154B
	85146	Tu-154B		85221	Tu-154B
	85147	Tu-154B		85222	Tu-154B
	85148	Tu-154B		85223	Tu-154B
	85149	Tu-154B		85226	Tu-154B
	85150	Tu-154B		85227	Tu-154B
	85151	Tu-154B		85228	Tu-154B
	85152	Tu-154B		85229	Tu-154B
	85153	Tu-154B		85230	Tu-154B
	85154	Tu-154B		85231	Tu-154B
	85155	Tu-154B		85232	Tu-154B
	85156	Tu-154B		85233	Tu-154B
	85157	Tu-154B		85234	Tu-154B
	85158	Tu-154B		85235	Tu-154B
	85160	Tu-154B		85236	Tu-154B
	85162	Tu-154B		85237	Tu-154B
	85163	Tu-154B		85238	Tu-154B
	85164	Tu-154B		85240	Tu-154B
	85165	Tu-154B		85241	Tu-154B
	85166	Tu-154B		85242	Tu-154B
	85167	Tu-154B		85243	Tu-154B
	85168	Tu-154B		85244	Tu-154B
	85169	Tu-154B		85245	Tu-154B
	85170	Tu-154B		85246	Tu-154B
	85171	Tu-154B		85247	Tu-154B
	85172	Tu-154B		85248	Tu-154B
	85173	Tu-154B		85249	Tu-154B
	85174	Tu-154B		85250	Tu-154B
	85175	Tu-154B		85251	Tu-154B
	85176	Tu-154B		85252	Tu-154B
	85177	Tu-154B		85253	Tu-154B
	85178	Tu-154B		85254	Tu-154B
	85179	Tu-154B		85255	Tu-154B
	85180	Tu-154B		85256	Tu-154B
	85181	Tu-154B		85257	Tu-154B
	85182	Tu-154B		85259	Tu-154B
	85183	Tu-154B		85260	Tu-154B
	85184	Tu-154B		85261	Tu-154B
	85185	Tu-154B		85263	Tu-154B
	85186	Tu-154B		85264	Tu-154B
	85187	Tu-154B		85265	Tu-154B
	85188	Tu-154B		85267	Tu-154B
	85189	Tu-154B		85268	Tu-154B
	85190	Tu-154B		85269	Tu-154B
	85191	Tu-154B		85270	Tu-154B

Reg.	Type	Notes	Reg.	Type	Notes
85271	Tu-154B		85359	Tu-154B	
85272	Tu-154B		85362	Tu-154B	
85273	Tu-154B		85363	Tu-154B	
85274	Tu-154B		85364	Tu-154B	
85275	Tu-154B		85365	Tu-154B	
85276	Tu-154B		85366	Tu-154B	
85277	Tu-154B		85367	Tu-154B	
85278	Tu-154B		85368	Tu-154B	
85279	Tu-154B		85372	Tu-154B	
85280	Tu-154B		85374	Tu-154B	
85281	Tu-154B		85375	Tu-154B	
85282	Tu-154B		85376	Tu-154B	
85283	Tu-154B		85377	Tu-154B	
85284	Tu-154B		85378	Tu-154B	
85285	Tu-154B		85379	Tu-154B	
85286	Tu-154B		85381	Tu-154B	
85287	Tu-154B		85382	Tu-154B	
85288	Tu-154B		85385	Tu-154B	
85290	Tu-154B		85390	Tu-154B	
85291	Tu-154B		85395	Tu-154B	
85292	Tu-154B		85396	Tu-154B	
85293	Tu-154B		85397	Tu-154B	
85294	Tu-154B		85398	Tu-154B	
85295	Tu-154B		85399	Tu-154B	
85296	Tu-154B		85400	Tu-154B	
85297	Tu-154B		85402	Tu-154B	
85298	Tu-154B		85407	Tu-154B	
85299	Tu-154B		85409	Tu-154B	
85300	Tu-154B		85410	Tu-154B	
85301	Tu-154B		85411	Tu-154B	
85302	Tu-154B		85412	Tu-154B	
85303	Tu-154B		85413	Tu-154B	
85304	Tu-154B		85414	Tu-154B	
85305	Tu-154B		85418	Tu-154B	
85306	Tu-154B		85423	Tu-154B	
85307	Tu-154B		85424	Tu-154B	
85308	Tu-154B		85431	Tu-154B	
85309	Tu-154B		85432	Tu-154B	
85310	Tu-154B		85436	Tu-154B-2	
85311	Tu-154B		85437	Tu-154B	
85312	Tu-154B		85438	Tu-154B	
85313	Tu-154B		85441	Tu-154B	
85314	Tu-154B		85455	Tu-154B	
85316	Tu-154B		85459	Tu-154B	
85317	Tu-154B		85460	Tu-154B	
85318	Tu-154B		85462	Tu-154B	
85319	Tu-154B		85472	Tu-154B	
85322	Tu-154B		85476	Tu-154B	
85323	Tu-154B		85478	Tu-154B	
85328	Tu-154B		85479	Tu-154B	
85239	Tu-154B		85486	Tu-154B	
85330	Tu-154B		85490	Tu-154B	
85331	Tu-154B		85491	Tu-154B	
85332	Tu-154B		85494	Tu-154B	
85334	Tu-154B		85495	Tu-154B	
85335	Tu-154B		85496	Tu-154B	
85336	Tu-154B		85497	Tu-154B	
85337	Tu-154B		85498	Tu-154B	
85338	Tu-154B		85499	Tu-154B	
85339	Tu-154B		85503	Tu-154B	
85340	Tu-154B		85504	Tu-154B	
85346	Tu-154B		85510	Tu-154B-2	
85347	Tu-154B		85513	Tu-154B	
85349	Tu-154B		85518	Tu-154B	
85350	Tu-154B		85519	Tu-154B	
85353	Tu-154B		85525	Tu-154B	
85354	Tu-154B		85526	Tu-154B	
85355	Tu-154B		85530	Tu-154B-2	
85356	Tu-154B		85531	Tu-154B-2	
85357	Tu-154B		85535	Tu-154B	
85358	Tu-154B		85542	Tu-154B-2	

Notes	Reg.	Type	Notes	Reg.	Type
	85544	Tu-154B-2		86478	IL-62M
	85545	Tu-154B		86479	IL-62M
	85552	Tu-154B-2		86480	IL-62M
	85553	Tu-154B		86481	IL-62M
	85554	Tu-154B		86482	IL-62M
	85555	Tu-154B		86483	IL-62M
	85556	Tu-154B		86484	IL-62M
	85557	Tu-154B		86485	IL-62M
	85558	Tu-154B		86486	IL-62M
	85559	Tu-154B		86487	IL-62M
	85560	Tu-154B		86488	IL-62M
	85561	Tu-154B		86489	IL-62M
	85562	Tu-154B		86490	IL-62M
	85563	Tu-154B		86491	IL-62M
	85564	Tu-154B		86492	IL-62M
	85565	Tu-154B		86493	IL-62M
	85566	Tu-154B		86494	IL-62M
	85567	Tu-154B		86496	IL-62M
	85568	Tu-154B		86497	IL-62M
	85569	Tu-154B		86498	IL-62M
	85570	Tu-154B		86499	IL-62M
	85571	Tu-154B		86500	IL-62M
	85572	Tu-154B		86501	IL-62M
	85573	Tu-154B		86502	IL-62M
	85574	Tu-154B		86504	IL-62M
	85575	Tu-154B		86506	IL-62M
	85576	Tu-154B		86507	IL-62M
	85577	Tu-154B		86508	IL-62M
	85578	Tu-154B		86509	IL-62M
	85579	Tu-154B		86510	IL-62M
	85580	Tu-154B		86511	IL-62M
	86000	IL-86		86512	IL-62M
	86002	IL-86		86513	IL-62M
	86003	IL-86		86514	IL-62M
	86004	IL-86		86515	IL-62M
	86005	IL-86		86517	IL-62M
	86006	IL-86		86518	IL-62M
	86007	IL-86		86520	IL-62M
	86008	IL-86		86522	IL-62M
	86009	IL-86		86523	IL-62M
	86010	IL-86		86524	IL-62M
	86012	IL-86		86530	IL-62M
	86015	IL-86		86531	IL-62M
	86022	IL-86		86532	IL-62M
	86025	IL-86		86533	IL-62M
	86050	IL-86		86534	IL-62M
	86054	IL-86		86605	IL-62
	86450	IL-62		86606	IL-62
	86451	IL-62		86607	IL-62M
	86452	IL-62M		86608	IL-62
	86453	IL-62M		86609	IL-62
	86454	IL-62M		86610	IL-62
	86455	IL-62M		86611	IL-62
	86656	IL-62M		86612	IL-62
	86457	IL-62M		86613	IL-62
	86458	IL-62M		86614	IL-62M
	86459	IL-62M		86615	IL-62
	86460	IL-62		86616	IL-62
	86461	IL-62		86617	IL-62
	86462	IL-62M		86618	IL-62M
	86463	IL-62M		86619	IL-62
	86464	IL-62M		86620	IL-62M
	86465	IL-62M		86621	IL-62M
	86469	IL-62M		86622	IL-62M
	86471	IL-62M		86623	IL-62M
	86472	IL-62M		86624	IL-62
	86473	IL-62M		86648	IL-62
	86474	IL-62M		86649	IL-62
	86475	IL-62M		86650	IL-62
	86476	IL-62M		86652	IL-62
	86477	IL-62M		86653	IL-62

Reg.	Type	Notes	Reg.	Type	Notes
86654	IL-62		86681	IL-62	
86655	IL-62		86682	IL-62	
86656	IL-62M		86683	IL-62	
86657	IL-62		86684	IL-62	
86658	IL-62M		86685	IL-62	
86659	IL-62		86686	IL-62	
86661	IL-62		86687	IL-62	
86662	IL-62		86688	IL-62	
86663	IL-62		86689	IL-62	
86664	IL-62		86690	IL-62	
86665	IL-62		86691	IL-62	
86666	IL-62		86692	IL-62M	
86667	IL-62		86693	IL-62M	
86668	IL-62		86694	IL-62	
86669	IL-62		86695	IL-62	
86670	IL-62		86696	IL-62	
86671	IL-62		86697	IL-62	
86672	IL-62		86698	IL-62	
86673	IL-62M		86699	IL-62	
86674	IL-62		86700	IL-62M	
86675	IL-62		86701	IL-62M	
86676	IL-62		86702	IL-62M	
86677	IL-62		86703	IL-62	
86678	IL-62		86704	IL-62	
86679	IL-62		86705	IL-62M	
86680	IL-62				

CN (Morocco)

Reg.	Type	Owner or Operator	Notes
CN-CCF	Boeing 727-2B6	Royal Air Maroc *Fez*	
CN-CCG	Boeing 727-2B6	Royal Air Maroc *l'Oiseau de la Providence*	
CN-CCH	Boeing 727-2B6	Royal Air Maroc *Marrakesh*	
CN-CCW	Boeing 727-2B6	Royal Air Maroc *Agadir*	
CN-RMI	Boeing 737-2B6	Royal Air Maroc *El Ayoun*	
CN-RMJ	Boeing 737-2B6	Royal Air Maroc *Oujda*	
CN-RMK	Boeing 737-2B6	Royal Air Maroc *Smara*	
CN-RML	Boeing 737-2B6	Royal Air Maroc	
CN-RMM	Boeing 737-2B6C	Royal Air Maroc	
CN-RMN	Boeing 737-2B6C	Royal Air Maroc	
CN-RMO	Boeing 727-2B6	Royal Air Maroc	
CN-RMP	Boeing 727-2B6	Royal Air Maroc	
CN-RMQ	Boeing 727-2B6	Royal Air Maroc	
CN-RMR	Boeing 727-2B6	Royal Air Maroc	
CN-RMS	Boeing 727-2B6	Royal Air Maroc	

CS (Portugal)

CS-TBC	Boeing 707-382B	TAP — Air Portugal *Cidade de Luanda*	
CS-TBD	Boeing 707-382B	TAP — Air Portugal *Mocambique*	
CS-TBF	Boeing 707-382B	TAP — Air Portugal *Vasco de Gama*	
CS-TBG	Boeing 707-382B	TAP — Air Portugal *Fernao de Magalhaes*	
CS-TBI	Boeing 707-399C	TAP — Air Portugal *D. Joao de Castro*	
CS-TBJ	Boeing 707-373C	TAP — Air Portugal *Lisboa*	
CS-TBK	Boeing 727-82	TAP — Air Portugal *Acores*	
CS-TBL	Boeing 727-82	TAP — Air Portugal *Madeira*	
CS-TBM	Boeing 727-82	TAP — Air Portugal *Algarve*	
CS-TBN	Boeing 727-82QC	TAP — Air Portugal *Porto*	

Notes	Reg.	Type	Owner or Operator
	CS-TBO	Boeing 727-82QC	TAP — Air Portugal *Costa do Sol*
	CS-TBP	Boeing 727-82	TAP — Air Portugal *Cabo Verde*
	CS-TBQ	Boeing 727-172C	TAP — Air Portugal *Bissau*
	CS-TBS	Boeing 727-282	TAP — Air Portugal *Gago Coutinho*
	CS-TBT	Boeing 707-3F5C	TAP — Air Portugal *Humberto Delgado*
	CS-TBU	Boeing 707-3F5C	TAP — Air Portugal *Jaime Cortesao*
	CS-TBW	Boeing 727-282	TAP — Air Portugal *Coimbra*
	CS-TBX	Boeing 727-282	TAP — Air Portugal *Faro*
	CS-TBY	Boeing 727-282	TAP — Air Portugal *Amadora*
	CS-TEA	L.1011-385 TriStar 500	TAP — Air Portugal *Luis de Gamoa*
	CS-TEB	L.1011-385 TriStar 500	TAP — Air Portugal *Infante D. Henrique*
	CS-TEC	L.1011-385 TriStar 500	TAP — Air Portugal *Gaco Coutinho*
	CS-TED	L.1011-385 TriStar 500	TAP — Air Portugal *Bartolomeode Gusmao*
	CS-TEE	L.1011-385 TriStar 500	TAP — Air Portugal *Santa Lisboa*
	CS-TEK	Boeing 737-282	TAP — Air Portugal *Ponta Delgardo*
	CS-TEL	Boeing 737-282	TAP — Air Portugal *Funchal*
	CS-TEM	Boeing 737-282	TAP — Air Portugal *Sutubal*
	CS-TEN	Boeing 737-282	TAP — Air Portugal *Braga*
	CS-TEO	Boeing 737-282	TAP — Air Portugal *Evora*
	CS-TEP	Boeing 737-282	TAP — Air Portugal *Oporto*
	CS-TEQ	Boeing 737-282C	TAP — Air Portugal *Vila Real*
	CS-TJA	Boeing 747-282B	TAP — Air Portugal *Portugal*
	CS-TJB	Boeing 747-282B	TAP — Air Portugal *Brasil*

CU (Cuba)

	CU-T1208	Illyushin IL-62M	Cubana *Capt Wifredo Perez*
	CU-T1209	Ilyushin IL-62M	Cubana
	CU-T1215	Ilyushin IL-62M	Cubana
	CU-T1216	Ilyushin IL-62M	Cubana
	CU-T1217	Ilyushin IL-62M	Cubana
	CU-T1218	Ilyushin IL-62M	Cubana
	CU-T1225	Ilyushin IL-62M	Cubana
	CU-T1226	Ilyushin IL-62M	Cubana

D (German Federal Republic)

 LTU Hapag-Lloyd Lufthansa Condor Flugdienst

	D-ABAP	S.E.210 Caravelle 10-R	Special Air Transport
	D-ABAV	S.E.210 Caravelle 10-R	Special Air Transport
	D-ABAW	S.E.210 Caravelle 10-R	Special Air Transport
	D-ABBE	Boeing 737-230C	Lufthansa
	D-ABCE	Boeing 737-230C	Lufthansa
	D-ABCI	Boeing 727-230	Lufthansa *Karlsruhe*
	D-ABDE	Boeing 737-230C	Lufthansa
	D-ABDI	Boeing 727-230	Lufthansa *Lübeck*
	D-ABFA	Boeing 737-230	Lufthansa *Regensburg*
	D-ABFB	Boeing 737-230	Lufthansa *Flensburg*
	D-ABFC	Boeing 737-230	Lufthansa *Würzburg*
	D-ABFD	Boeing 737-230	Lufthansa *Bamberg*
	D-ABFE	Boeing 737-230C	Lufthansa
	D-ABFF	Boeing 737-230	Lufthansa *Gelsenkirchen*
	D-ABFH	Boeing 737-230	Lufthansa *Pforzheim*
	D-ABFI	Boeing 727-230	Lufthansa *Münster*
	D-ABFK	Boeing 737-230	Lufthansa *Wuppertal*
	D-ABFL	Boeing 737-230	Lufthansa *Coburg*
	D-ABFM	Boeing 737-230	Lufthansa *Osnabrück*
	D-ABFN	Boeing 737-230	Lufthansa *Kempton*
	D-ABFP	Boeing 737-230	Lufthansa *Offenbach*
	D-ABFR	Boeing 737-230	Lufthansa *Solingen*

Reg.	Type	Owner or Operator	Notes
D-ABFS	Boeing 737-230	Lufthansa *Oldenburg*	
D-ABFT	Boeing 737-230	Condor Flugdienst	
D-ABFU	Boeing 737-230	Lufthansa *Mülheim a.d.R*	
D-ABFW	Boeing 737-230	Lufthansa *Wolfsberg*	
D-ABFX	Boeing 737-230	Lufthansa *Tübingen*	
D-ABFY	Boeing 737-230	Lufthansa *Göttingen*	
D-ABFZ	Boeing 737-230	Lufthansa *Wilhelmshaven*	
D-ABGE	Boeing 737-230C	Lufthansa	
D-ABGI	Boeing 727-230	Lufthansa *Leverkusen*	
D-ABHA	Boeing 737-230	Lufthansa *Koblenz*	
D-ABHB	Boeing 737-230	Lufthansa *Goslar*	
D-ABHC	Boeing 737-230	Lufthansa *Friedrichshafen*	
D-ABHD	Boeing 737-230	Condor Flugdienst	
D-ABHE	Boeing 737-230C	Lufthansa	
D-ABHF	Boeing 737-230	Lufthansa *Heilbronn*	
D-ABHH	Boeing 737-230	Lufthansa *Marburg*	
D-ABHI	Boeing 727-230	Lufthansa *Mönchengladbach*	
D-ABHK	Boeing 737-230	Lufthansa *Bayreuth*	
D-ABHL	Boeing 737-230	Lufthansa *Worms*	
D-ABHM	Boeing 737-230	Lufthansa *Landshut*	
D-ABHN	Boeing 737-230	Lufthansa *Trier*	
D-ABHP	Boeing 737-230	Lufthansa *Erlangen*	
D-ABHR	Boeing 737-230	Lufthansa *Darmstadt*	
D-ABHS	Boeing 737-230	Lufthansa *Remscheid*	
D-ABHT	Boeing 737-230	Condor Flugdienst	
D-ABHU	Boeing 737-230	Lufthansa *Konstanz*	
D-ABHW	Boeing 737-230	Lufthansa *Baden Baden*	
D-ABHX	Boeing 737-230	Condor Flugdienst	
D-ABKA	Boeing 727-230	Lufthansa *Heidelberg*	
D-ABKB	Boeing 727-230	Lufthansa *Augsburg*	
D-ABKC	Boeing 727-230	Lufthansa *Braunschweig*	
D-ABKD	Boeing 727-230	Lufthansa *Freiburg*	
D-ABKE	Boeing 727-230	Lufthansa *Mannheim*	
D-ABKF	Boeing 727-230	Lufthansa *Saarbrücken*	
D-ABKG	Boeing 727-230	Lufthansa *Kassel*	
D-ABKH	Boeing 727-230	Lufthansa *Kiel*	
D-ABKI	Boeing 727-230	Lufthansa *Bremerhaven*	
D-ABKJ	Boeing 727-230	Lufthansa *Wiesbaden*	
D-ABKK	Boeing 727-230	Condor Flugdienst	
D-ABKL	Boeing 727-230	Condor Flugdienst	
D-ABKM	Boeing 727-230	Lufthansa *Hagen*	
D-ABKN	Boeing 727-230	Lufthansa *Ulm*	
D-ABKP	Boeing 727-230	Lufthansa *Krefeld*	
D-ABKQ	Boeing 727-230	Lufthansa *Mainz*	
D-ABKR	Boeing 727-230	Lufthansa *Bielefeld*	
D-ABKS	Boeing 727-230	Lufthansa *Oberhausen*	
D-ABKT	Boeing 727-230	Lufthansa *Aachen*	
D-ABLI	Boeing 727-230	Lufthansa *Ludwigshafen a.Rh.*	
D-ABMI	Boeing 727-230	Condor Flugdienst	
D-ABNI	Boeing 727-230	Condor Flugdienst	
D-ABPI	Boeing 727-230	Condor Flugdienst	
D-ABQI	Boeing 727-230	Lufthansa *Hildesheim*	
D-ABRI	Boeing 727-230	Lufthansa *Esslingen*	
D-ABSI	Boeing 727-230	Lufthansa *Hof*	
D-ABTI	Boeing 727-230	Condor Flugdienst	
D-ABUA	Boeing 707-330C	German Cargo	
D-ABUE	Boeing 707-330C	German Cargo	
D-ABUI	Boeing 707-330C	German Cargo	
D-ABUL	Boeing 707-330B	Lufthansa *Duisburg*	
D-ABUM	Boeing 707-330B	Lufthansa	
D-ABUO	Boeing 707-330C	German Cargo	
D-ABVI	Boeing 727-230	Condor Flugdienst	
D-ABWI	Boeing 727-230	Condor Flugdienst	
D-ABYJ	Boeing 747-230B	Lufthansa *Hessen*	
D-ABYK	Boeing 747-230B	Lufthansa *Rheinland-Pfalz*	
D-ABYL	Boeing 747-230B	Lufthansa *Saarland*	
D-ABYM	Boeing 747-230B	Lufthansa *Schleswig-Holstein*	
D-ABYN	Boeing 747-230B	Lufthansa *Baden-Wurttemberg*	
D-ABYO	Boeing 747-230F	Lufthansa *America*	
D-ABYP	Boeing 747-230B	Lufthansa *Niedersachen*	
D-ABYQ	Boeing 747-230B	Lufthansa *Bremen*	

Notes	Reg.	Type	Owner or Operator
	D-ABYR	Boeing 747-230B	Lufthansa *Nordrhein-Westfalen*
	D-ABYS	Boeing 747-230B	Lufthansa *Bayern*
	D-ABYT	Boeing 747-230B	Lufthansa *Hamburg*
	D-ABYU	Boeing 747-230F	Lufthansa *Asia*
	D-ABYW	Boeing 747-230B	Lufthansa *Berlin*
	D-ABYX	Boeing 747-230B	Lufthansa *Köln*
	D-ABYY	Boeing 747-230B	Lufthansa *München*
	D-ADAO	Douglas DC-10-30	Lufthansa *Düsseldorf*
	D-ADBO	Douglas DC-10-30	Lufthansa *Bochum*
	D-ADCO	Douglas DC-10-30	Lufthansa *Frankfurt*
	D-ADDO	Douglas DC-10-30	Lufthansa
	D-ADFO	Douglas DC-10-30	Lufthansa *Duisburg*
	D-ADGO	Douglas DC-10-30	Lufthansa *Bonn*
	D-ADHO	Douglas DC-10-30	Lufthansa *Hannover*
	D-ADJO	Douglas DC-10-30	Lufthansa *Essen*
	D-ADKO	Douglas DC-10-30	Lufthansa *Stuttgart*
	D-ADLO	Douglas DC-10-30	Lufthansa *Nurnberg*
	D-ADMO	Douglas DC-10-30	Lufthansa *Dortmund*
	D-ADPO	Douglas DC-10-30	Condor Flugdienst
	D-ADQO	Douglas DC-10-30	Condor Flugdienst
	D-ADSO	Douglas DC-10-30	Condor Flugdienst
	D-ADUA	Douglas DC-8-73	German Cargo
	D-ADUE	Douglas DC-8-73	German Cargo
	D-ADUI	Douglas DC-8-73	German Cargo
	D-ADUO	Douglas DC-8-73	German Cargo
	D-AERE	L.1011-385 TriStar 1	LTU
	D-AERI	L.1011-385 TriStar 1	LTU
	D-AERL	L.1011-385 TriStar 500	LTU
	D-AERM	L.1011-385 TriStar 1	LTU
	D-AERN	L.1011-385 TriStar 1	LTU
	D-AERP	L.1011-385 TriStar 1	LTU
	D-AERT	L.1011-385 TriStar 500	LTU
	D-AERU	L.1011-385 TriStar 100	LTU
	D-AHLB	A.300B4 Airbus	Hapag-Lloyd
	D-AHLC	A.300B4 Airbus	Hapag-Lloyd
	D-AHLF	Boeing 737-2K5	Hapag-Lloyd
	D-AHLG	Boeing 737-2K5	Hapag-Lloyd
	D-AHLH	Boeing 737-2K5	Hapag-Lloyd
	D-AHLI	Boeing 737-2K5	Hapag-Lloyd
	D-AHLN	Boeing 727-81	Hapag-Lloyd
	D-AHLS	Boeing 727-89	Hapag-Lloyd
	D-AHLT	Boeing 727-2K5	Hapag-Lloyd
	D-AHLU	Boeing 727-2K5	Hapag-Lloyd
	D-AIAB	A.300B2 Airbus	Lufthansa *Rüdesheim am Rhein*
	D-AIAC	A.300B2 Airbus	Lufthansa *Lüneburg*
	D-AIAD	A.300B2 Airbus	Lufthansa *Westerland/Sylt*
	D-AIAE	A.300B2 Airbus	Lufthansa *Neustadt an der Weinstrasse*
	D-AIAF	A.300B2 Airbus	Lufthansa
	D-AIBA	A.300B4 Airbus	Lufthansa *Rothenburg ob der Tauber*
	D-AIBB	A.300B4 Airbus	Lufthansa *Freudenstadt/Schwarzwald*
	D-AIBC	A.300B4 Airbus	Lufthansa
	D-AIBD	A.300B4 Airbus	Lufthansa *Erbach/Odenwald*
	D-AIBF	A.300B4 Airbus	Lufthansa *Krohnberg/Taunus*
	D-AICA	A.310-203 Airbus	Lufthansa
	D-AICB	A.310-203 Airbus	Lufthansa
	D-AICC	A.310-203 Airbus	Lufthansa *Kaiserslauten*
	D-AICD	A.310-203 Airbus	Lufthansa *Philamonie Hamburg*
	D-AICF	A.310-203 Airbus	Lufthansa
	D-AICH	A.310-203 Airbus	Lufthansa
	D-AICK	A.310-203 Airbus	Lufthansa
	D-AICL	A.310-203 Airbus	Lufthansa
	D-AICM	A.310-203 Airbus	Lufthansa
	D-	A.310-203 Airbus	Lufthansa
	D-	A.310-203 Airbus	Lufthansa
	D-	A.310-203 Airbus	Lufthansa
	D-AJAA	Boeing 727-2K2	Jetair
	D-	Boeing 757-2G5	Luftransport Sud
	D-	Boeing 757-2G5	Luftransport Sud
	D-ALLA	Douglas DC-9-32	Aero Lloyd
	D-ALLB	Douglas DC-9-32	Aero Lloyd
	D-ALLC	Douglas DC-9-32	Aero Lloyd

Reg.	Type	Owner or Operator	Notes
D-AMAP	A.300B4 Airbus	Hapag-Lloyd	
D-AMAX	A.300B4 Airbus	Hapag-Lloyd	
D-AMAY	A.300B4 Airbus	Hapag-Lloyd	
D-BAKA	F.27 Friendship Mk 100	WDL	
D-BAKI	F.27 Friendship Mk 100	WDL	
D-BAKU	F.27 Friendship Mk 200	WDL	

DDR (German Democratic Republic)

DDR-SCB	Tupolev Tu-134	Interflug	
DDR-SCE	Tupolev Tu-134	Interflug	
DDR-SCF	Tupolev Tu-134	Interflug	
DDR-SCG	Tupolev Tu-134	Interflug	
DDR-SCH	Tupolev Tu-134	Interflug	
DDR-SCI	Tupolev Tu-134A	Interflug	
DDR-SCK	Tupolev Tu-134A	Interflug	
DDR-SCL	Tupolev Tu-134A	Interflug	
DDR-SCN	Tupolev Tu-134A	Interflug	
DDR-SCO	Tupolev Tu-134A	Interflug	
DDR-SCP	Tupolev Tu-134A	Interflug	
DDR-SCR	Tupolev Tu-134A	Interflug	
DDR-SCS	Tupolev Tu-134A	Interflug	
DDR-SCT	Tupolev Tu-134A	Interflug	
DDR-SCU	Tupolev Tu-134A	Interflug	
DDR-SCV	Tupolev Tu-134A	Interflug	
DDR-SCW	Tupolev Tu-134A	Interflug	
DDR-SCX	Tupolev Tu-134A	Interflug	
DDR-SCY	Tupolev Tu-134A	Interflug	
DDR-SCZ	Tupolev Tu-134	Interflug	
DDR-SDC	Tupolev Tu-134A	Interflug	
DDR-SDE	Tupolev Tu-134A	Interflug	
DDR-SDF	Tupolev Tu-134A	Interflug	
DDR-SDG	Tupolev Tu-134A	Interflug	
DDR-SDH	Tupolev Tu-134A	Interflug	
DDR-SDI	Tupolev Tu-134A	Interflug	
DDR-SDK	Tupolev Tu-134A	Interflug	
DDR-SDL	Tupolev Tu-134A	Interflug	
DDR-SDM	Tupolev Tu-134A	Interflug	
DDR-SDN	Tupolev Tu-134A	Interflug	
DDR-SDO	Tupolev Tu-134A	Interflug	
DDR-SDP	Tupolev Tu-134A	Interflug	
DDR-SDR	Tupolev Tu-134A	Interflug	
DDR-SDS	Tupolev Tu-134A	Interflug	
DDR-SDT	Tupolev Tu-134A	Interflug	
DDR-STA	Ilyushin IL-18D	Interflug	
DDR-STB	Ilyushin IL-18D	Interflug	
DDR-STC	Ilyushin IL-18D	Interflug	
DDR-STD	Ilyushin IL-18D	Interflug	
DDR-STE	Ilyushin IL-18D	Interflug	
DDR-STF	Ilyushin IL-18D	Interflug	
DDR-STG	Ilyushin IL-18D	Interflug	
DDR-STH	Ilyushin IL-18D	Interflug	
DDR-STI	Ilyushin IL-18D	Interflug	
DDR-STK	Ilyushin IL-18D	Interflug	
DDR-STM	Ilyushin IL-18D	Interflug	
DDR-STN	Ilyushin IL-18D	Interflug	
DDR-STO	Ilyushin IL-18D	Interflug	
DDR-STP	Ilyushin IL-18D	Interflug	

EC (Spain)

Notes	Reg.	Type	Owner or Operator
	EC-AUM	Douglas DC-8-52	Aviaco *Zurbaran*
	EC-BIG	Douglas DC-9-32	Iberia *Villa de Madrid*
	EC-BIH	Douglas DC-9-32	Iberia *Ciudad de Barcelona*
	EC-BIJ	Douglas DC-9-32	Iberia *Santa Cruz de Tenerife*
	EC-BIK	Douglas DC-9-32	Aviaco *Castillo de Guanapa*
	EC-BIL	Douglas DC-9-32	Iberia *Ciudad de Zaragoza*
	EC-BIM	Douglas DC-9-32	Iberia *Ciudad de Santander*
	EC-BIN	Douglas DC-9-32	Iberia *Palma de Mallorca*
	EC-BIO	Douglas DC-9-32	Iberia *Villa de Bilbao*
	EC-BIP	Douglas DC-9-32	Aviaco *Castillo de Monteagudo*
	EC-BIQ	Douglas DC-9-32	Aviaco *Castillo de Argueso*
	EC-BIR	Douglas DC-9-32	Iberia *Ciudad de Valencia*
	EC-BIS	Douglas DC-9-32	Iberia *Ciudad de Alicante*
	EC-BIT	Douglas DC-9-32	Iberia *Ciudad de San Sebastian*
	EC-BIU	Douglas DC-9-32	Iberia *Ciudad de Oviedo*
	EC-BJD	CV-990A Coronado	Spantax
	EC-BMY	Douglas DC-8-63CF	Aviaco *Puerto de la Cruz*
	EC-BMZ	Douglas DC-8-63CF	Iberia *Los Madrazo*
	EC-BPF	Douglas DC-9-32	Iberia *Ciudad de Almeria*
	EC-BPG	Douglas DC-9-32	Iberia *Ciudad de Vigo*
	EC-BPH	Douglas DC-9-32	Iberia *Ciudad de Gerona*
	EC-BQA	CV-990A Coronado	Spantax
	EC-BQS	Douglas DC-8-63	Aviaco *Claudio Coello*
	EC-BQT	Douglas DC-9-32	Iberia *Ciudad de Murcia*
	EC-BQU	Douglas DC-9-32	Iberia *Ciudad de la Coruna*
	EC-BQV	Douglas DC-9-32	Iberia *Ciudad de Ibiza*
	EC-BQX	Douglas DC-9-32	Iberia *Ciudad de Valladolid*
	EC-BQY	Douglas DC-9-32	Iberia *Ciudad de Cordoba*
	EC-BQZ	Douglas DC-9-32	Iberia *Ciudad de Santa Cruz de la Palma*
	EC-BRQ	Boeing 747-256B	Iberia *Calderon de la Barca*
	EC-BSD	Douglas DC-8-63	Aviaco *Cala Galdana*
	EC-BSE	Douglas DC-8-63	Aviaco *Playa de las Canteras*
	EC-BYD	Douglas DC-9-32	Iberia *Ciudad de Arrecife de Lanzarote*
	EC-BYE	Douglas DC-9-32	Iberia *Ciudad de Mahon*
	EC-BYF	Douglas DC-9-32	Iberia *Ciudad de Granada*
	EC-BYG	Douglas DC-9-32	Iberia *Ciudad de Pamplona*
	EC-BYH	Douglas DC-9-32	Aviaco *Castillo de Butron*
	EC-BYI	Douglas DC-9-32	Iberia *Ciudad de Vitoria*
	EC-BYJ	Douglas DC-9-32	Iberia *Ciudad de Salamanca*
	EC-BYK	Douglas DC-9-33RC	Iberia *Ciudad de Badajoz*
	EC-BYL	Douglas DC-9-33RC	Iberia *Ciudad de Albacete*
	EC-BYM	Douglas DC-9-33RC	Iberia *Ciudad de Cangas de Onis*
	EC-BYN	Douglas DC-9-33RC	Iberia *Ciudad de Caceres*
	EC-BZO	CV-990A Coronado	Spantax
	EC-BZP	CV-990A Coronado	Spantax
	EC-CAI	Boeing 727-256	Iberia *Castilla la Neuva*
	EC-CAJ	Boeing 727-256	Iberia *Cataluna*
	EC-CAK	Boeing 727-256	Iberia *Aragon*
	EC-CBA	Boeing 727-256	Iberia *Vascongadas*
	EC-CBB	Boeing 727-256	Iberia *Valencia*
	EC-CBC	Boeing 727-256	Iberia *Navarra*
	EC-CBD	Boeing 727-256	Iberia *Murcia*
	EC-CBE	Boeing 727-256	Iberia *Leon*
	EC-CBF	Boeing 727-256	Iberia *Gran Canaria*
	EC-CBG	Boeing 727-256	Iberia *Extremadura*
	EC-CBH	Boeing 727-256	Iberia *Galicia*
	EC-CBI	Boeing 727-256	Iberia *Asturias*
	EC-CBJ	Boeing 727-256	Iberia *Andalucia*
	EC-CBK	Boeing 727-256	Iberia *Baleares*
	EC-CBL	Boeing 727-256	Iberia *Tenerife*
	EC-CBM	Boeing 727-256	Iberia *Castilla la Vieja*
	EC-CBO	Douglas DC-10-30	Iberia *Costa del Sol*
	EC-CBP	Douglas DC-10-30	Iberia *Costa Dorada*
	EC-CCF	Douglas DC-8-61CF	Spantax

D-ALLA Douglas DC-9-32 of Aero Lloyd.

D-BAKA F.27 Friendship 100 of WDL.

EI-BMF   F.8L Falco.

Reg.	Type	Owner or Operator	Notes
EC-CCG	Douglas DC-8-61CF	Spantax	
EC-CEZ	Douglas DC-10-30	Iberia *Costa del Azahar*	
EC-CFA	Boeing 727-256	Iberia *Jerez Xeres Sherry*	
EC-CFB	Boeing 727-256	Iberia *Rioja*	
EC-CFC	Boeing 727-256	Iberia *Tarragona*	
EC-CFD	Boeing 727-256	Iberia *Montilla Moriles*	
EC-CFE	Boeing 727-256	Iberia *Penedes*	
EC-CFF	Boeing 727-256	Iberia *Valdepenas*	
EC-CFG	Boeing 727-256	Iberia *La Mancha*	
EC-CFH	Boeing 727-256	Iberia *Priorato*	
EC-CFI	Boeing 727-256	Iberia *Carinena*	
EC-CFK	Boeing 727-256	Iberia *Riberio*	
EC-CGN	Douglas DC-9-32	Aviaco *Martin Alonso Pinzon*	
EC-CGO	Douglas DC-9-32	Aviaco *Pedro Alonso Nino*	
EC-CGP	Douglas DC-9-32	Aviaco *Juan Sebastian Elcano*	
EC-CGQ	Douglas DC-9-32	Aviaco *Alonso de Ojeda*	
EC-CGR	Douglas DC-9-32	Aviaco *Francisco de Orellana*	
EC-CGY	Douglas DC-9-14	Spantax	
EC-CGZ	Douglas DC-9-14	Spantax	
EC-CID	Boeing 727-256	Iberia *Malaga*	
EC-CIE	Boeing 727-256	Iberia *Esparragosa*	
EC-CIZ	S.E.210 Caravelle 10R	Hispania	
EC-CLB	Douglas DC-10-30	Iberia *Costa Blanca*	
EC-CLD	Douglas DC-9-32	Aviaco *Hernando de Soto*	
EC-CLE	Douglas DC-9-32	Aviaco *Jaun Ponce de Leon*	
EC-CPI	S.E.210 Caravelle 10R	Hispania	
EC-CNF	CV-990A Coronado	Spantax	
EC-CNH	CV-990A Coronado	Spantax	
EC-CQM	Douglas DC-8-54F	Aviaco	
EC-CSJ	Douglas DC-10-30	Iberia *Costa de la Luz*	
EC-CSK	Douglas DC-10-30	Iberia *Cornisa Cantabrica*	
EC-CTR	Douglas DC-9-34CF	Aviaco *Hernan Cortes*	
EC-CTS	Douglas DC-9-34CF	Aviaco *Francisco Pizarro*	
EC-CTT	Douglas DC-9-34CF	Aviaco *Pedro de Valdivia*	
EC-CTU	Douglas DC-9-34CF	Aviaco *Pedro de Alvarado*	
EC-CYI	S.E.210 Caravelle 10R	Hispania	
EC-CZE	Douglas DC-8-61	Spantax	
EC-DBE	Douglas DC-8-55F	Aviaco *El Greco*	
EC-DCC	Boeing 727-256	Iberia *Albarino*	
EC-DCD	Boeing 727-256	Iberia *Chacoli*	
EC-DCE	Boeing 727-256	Iberia *Mentrida*	
EC-DCN	S.E.210 Caravelle 10R	Hispania	
EC-DDU	Boeing 727-256	Iberia *Alhambra de Granada*	
EC-DDV	Boeing 727-256	Iberia *Acueducto de Segovia*	
EC-DDX	Boeing 727-256	Iberia *Monasterio de Poblet*	
EC-DDY	Boeing 727-256	Iberia *Cuevas de Altamira*	
EC-DDZ	Boeing 727-256	Iberia *Murallas de Avila*	
EC-DEA	Douglas DC-10-30	Iberia *Rias Gallegas*	
EC-DEM	Douglas DC-8-55F	Aviaco *Goya*	
EC-DGB	Douglas DC-9-34	Aviaco *Castillo de Javier*	
EC-DGC	Douglas DC-9-34	Aviaco *Castillo de Sotomayor*	
EC-DGD	Douglas DC-9-34	Aviaco *Castillo de Arcos*	
EC-DGE	Douglas DC-9-34	Aviaco *Castillo de Bellver*	
EC-DHZ	Douglas DC-10-30	Iberia *Costas Canarias*	
EC-DIA	Boeing 747-256B	Iberia *Tirso de Molina*	
EC-DIB	Boeing 747-256B	Iberia *Cervantes*	
EC-DIR	Douglas DC-9-14	Spantax	
EC-DLC	Boeing 747-256B	Iberia *Francisco de Quevedo*	
EC-DLD	Boeing 747-256B	Iberia *Lupe de Vega*	
EC-DLE	A.300B4 Airbus	Iberia *Doana*	
EC-DLF	A.300B4 Airbus	Iberia *Canadas del Teide*	
EC-DLG	A.300B4 Airbus	Iberia *Tablas de Daimiel*	
EC-DLH	A.300B4 Airbus	Iberia *Aigues Tortes*	
EC-DNP	Boeing 747-256B	Iberia *Juan Ramon Jimenez*	
EC-DNQ	A.300B4 Airbus	Iberia *Islas Cies*	
EC-DNR	A.300B4 Airbus	Iberia *Ordesa*	
EC-DQQ	Douglas DC-9-32	Spantax	
EC-DTR	Boeing 737-2K5	Spantax	
EC-	Boeing 737-2K5	Spantax	
EC-	Boeing 737-	Spantax	
EC-	Boeing 737-	Spantax	

EI (Republic of Ireland)

Including complete current Irish Civil Register

Notes	Reg.	Type	Owner or Operator
	EI-ADV	PA-12 Super Cruiser	R. E. Levis
	EI-AFF	B.A. Swallow 2 ★	J. McCarthy
	EI-AFK	D.H.84 Dragon (EI-ABI) ★	Aer Lingus-Irish
	EI-AFN	B.A. Swallow 2 ★	J. McCarthy
	EI-AGB	Miles M.38 Messenger 4 ★	J. McLoughlin
	EI-AGD	Taylorcraft Plus D ★	H. Wolf
	EI-AGJ	J/I Autocrat	W. G. Rafter
	EI-AHA	D.H.82A Tiger Moth ★	J. H. Maher
	EI-AHR	D.H.C.1 Chipmunk 22 ★	C. Lane
	EI-AKM	Piper J-3C-65 Cub	Setanta Flying Group
	EI-ALH	Taylorcraft Plus D	N. Reilly
	EI-ALP	Avro 643 Cadet	J. C. O'Loughlin
	EI-ALU	Avro 631 Cadet	M. P. Cahill
	EI-AMK	J/I Autocrat	Irish Aero Club
	EI-AMO	J/IB Aiglet	R. Hassett
	EI-AMY	J/IN Alpha	Meath Flying Group Ltd
	EI-AND	Cessna 175A	Jack Braithwaite (Ireland) Ltd
	EI-ANE	BAC One-Eleven 208AL	Aer Lingus St Mel
	EI-ANF	BAC One-Eleven 208AL	Aer Lingus St Malachy
	EI-ANG	BAC One-Eleven 208AL	Aer Lingus St Declan
	EI-ANH	BAC One-Eleven 208AL	Aer Lingus St Ronan
	EI-ANT	Champion 7ECA Citabria	Setanta Flying Group
	EI-AOB	PA-28 Cherokee 140	Oscar Bravo Flying Cbub
	EI-AOD	Cessna 182J Skylane	Oscar Delta Flying Training Co Ltd
	EI-AOK	Cessna F.172G	R. J. Cloughley & N. J. Simpson
	EI-AOO	Cessna 150E	R. Hassett
	EI-AOP	D.H.82A Tiger Moth	Dublin Tiger Group
	EI-AOS	Cessna 310B	Joyce Aviation Ltd
	EI-APF	Cessna F.150F	L. O. Kennedy
	EI-APS	Schleicher ASK 14	G. W. Connolly & M. Slazenger
	EI-APT	Fokker D.VII/65 Replica	Blue Max Aviation Ltd
	EI-APU	Fokker D.VII/65 Replica	Blue Max Aviation Ltd
	EI-APV	Fokker D.VII/65 Replica	Blue Max Aviation Ltd
	EI-APW	Fokker Dr.1 Replica	Blue Max Aviation Ltd
	EI-ARA	SE.5A Replica	Blue Max Aviation Ltd
	EI-ARB	SE.5A Replica	Blue Max Aviation Ltd
	EI-ARC	Pfalz D.III Replica	Blue Max Aviation Ltd
	EI-ARE	Stampe SV.4C	Blue Max Aviation Ltd
	EI-ARF	Caudron C.277 Luciole	Blue Max Aviation Ltd
	EI-ARH	Currie Wot/S.E.5 Replica	L. Garrison
	EI-ARI	Currie Wot/S.E.5 Replica	Blue Max Aviation Ltd
	EI-ARJ	Currie Wot/S.E.5 Replica	Blue Max Aviation Ltd
	EI-ARK	Currie Wot/S.E.5 Replica	Blue Max Aviation Ltd
	EI-ARL	Currie Wot/S.E.5 Replica	Blue Max Aviation Ltd
	EI-ARM	Currie Wot/S.E.5 Replica	L. Garrison
	EI-ARW	Jodel D.R.1050	M. Mannion
	EI-ASA	Boeing 737-248	Aer Lingus St Jarlath
	EI-ASB	Boeing 737-248	Aer Lingus St Albert
	EI-ASC	Boeing 737-248C	Aer Lingus St Macartan
	EI-ASD	Boeing 737-248C	Aer Lingus St Ide
	EI-ASE	Boeing 737-248C	Aer Lingus St Fachtna
	EI-ASF	Boeing 737-248	Aer Lingus St Nathy
	EI-ASG	Boeing 737-248	Aer Lingus St Cormack
	EI-ASH	Boeing 737-248	Aer Lingus St Eugene
	EI-ASI	Boeing 747-148	Aer Lingus St Colmcille
	EI-ASJ	Boeing 747-148	Aer Lingus St Patrick
	EI-ASL	Boeing 737-248C	Aer Lingus St Killian
	EI-ASO	Boeing 707-349C	Libyan Arab Airlines
	EI-AST	Cessna F.150H	Liberty Flying Club Group
	EI-ATH	Cessna F.150J	Hibernian Flying Club
	EI-ATJ	B.121 Pup I	Wexford Aero Club
	EI-ATK	PA-28 Cherokee 140	Mayo Flying Club Ltd
	EI-ATS	M.S.880B Rallye Club	O. Bruton & G. Farrar
	EI-AUC	Cessna FA.150K Aerobat	Flying Fifteen Aero Club Ltd
	EI-AUD	M.S.880B Rallye Club	Kilkenny Flying Club Ltd

Reg.	Type	Owner or Operator	Notes
EI-AUE	M.S.880B Rallye Club	Slievenamon Air Ltd	
EI-AUG	M.S.894 Rallye Minerva 220	Weston Ltd	
EI-AUJ	M.S.880B Rallye Club	P. Mulhall	
EI-AUM	J/I Autocrat	J. G. Rafter	
EI-AUO	Cessna FA.150K Aerobat	Kerry Aero Club	
EI-AUP	M.S.880B Rallye Club	Limerick Flying Club	
EI-AUT	Forney F-1A Aircoupe	Joyce Aviation Ltd	
EI-AUV	PA-23 Aztec 250	Shannon Executive Aviation	
EI-AUY	Morane-Saulnier M.S.502	Historical Aircraft Preservation Group	
EI-AVB	Aeronca 7AC Champion	G. G. Bracken	
EI-AVC	Cessna F.337F	Iona National Airways	
EI-AVL	J/5F Aiglet	G. E. Flood	
EI-AVM	Cessna F.150L	Victor Mike Flying Group	
EI-AVN	Hughes 369HM	Helicopter Maintenance Ltd	
EI-AVU	Stampe SV.4C	R. McDowell	
EI-AWA	Bell 206B JetRanger 2	Helicopter Maintenance Ltd	
EI-AWE	Cessna F.150M	Third Flight Group	
EI-AWH	Cessna 210J	M. O'Donnell & ptnrs	
EI-AWM	BN-2A Islander	Aer Arann	
EI-AWP	D.H.82A Tiger Moth	A. Lyons	
EI-AWR	Malmo MFI-9 Junior	M. Nesbitt & S. Duighan	
EI-AWU	M.S.880B Rallye Club	Longford Aviation Ltd	
EI-AWW	Cessna 414	T. Farrington	
EI-AYA	M.S.880B Rallye Club	Dundalk Aero Club Ltd	
EI-AYB	GY-80 Horizon 180	Westwing Flying Group	
EI-AYD	AA-5 Traveler	K. Walters	
EI-AYF	Cessna FRA.150L	Garda Flying Club	
EI-AYI	M.S.880B Rallye Club	Irish Air Training Group	
EI-AYK	Cessna F.172M	J. Martyn & J. Hession	
EI-AYL	A.109 Airedale	J. Ronan	
EI-AYN	BN-2A Islander	Aer Arann	
EI-AYO	Douglas DC-3A ★	Science Museum, Wroughton	
EI-AYR	Schleicher ASK-16	Kilkenny Airport Ltd	
EI-AYS	PA-22 Colt 108	Messrs Skelly & Hall	
EI-AYT	M.S.894A Rallye Minerva	R. C. Cunningham	
EI-AYV	M.S.892A Rallye Commodore 150	P. Murtagh	
EI-AYW	PA-23 Aztec 250	Chutewell International Ltd	
EI-AYY	Evans VP-1	M. Donoghue	
EI-BAB	M.S.894E Rallye Minerva	J. Phelan	
EI-BAF	Thunder Ax6-56 balloon	W. G. Woollett	
EI-BAJ	Stampe SV-4C	Dublin Tiger Group	
EI-BAO	Cessna F.172G	Kingdom Air Ltd	
EI-BAR	Thunder Ax8-105 balloon	J. Burke & V. Hourihane	
EI-BAS	Cessna F.172M	Iona National Airways Ltd	
EI-BAT	Cessna F.150M	20th Air Training Co Ltd	
EI-BAU	Stampe SV.4C	S. P. O'Carroll	
EI-BAV	PA-22 Colt 108	J. P. Montcalm	
EI-BAY	Cameron V-77 balloon	F. N. Lewis	
EI-BBC	PA-28 Cherokee 180C	The Cherokee Group	
EI-BBD	Evans VP-1	Volksplane Group	
EI-BBE	7FC Tri-Traveler (tailwheel)	Aeronca Flying Group	
EI-BBG	M.S.880B Rallye Club	Weston Ltd	
EI-BBI	M.S.892 Rallye Commodore	Kilkenny Airport Ltd	
EI-BBJ	M.S.880B Rallye Club	Weston Ltd	
EI-BBK	A.109 Airedale	H. S. Igoe	
EI-BBL	R. Turbo 690A Commander	The Earl of Granard	
EI-BBM	Cameron O-65 balloon	Dublin Ballooning Club	
EI-BBN	Cessna F.150M	Sligo N.W. Aero Club	
EI-BBO	M.S.893E Rallye 180GT	J. G. Lacey & ptnrs	
EI-BBV	Piper J-3C-65 Cub	F. Cronin	
EI-BBW	M.S.894A Rallye Minerva	J. J. Ladbrook	
EI-BCE	BN-2A-26 Islander	Aer Arann	
EI-BCF	Bensen B.8M	T. A. Brennan	
EI-BCH	M.S.892A Rallye Commodore 150	The Condor Group	
EI-BCJ	F.8L Falco 1 Srs 3	D. Kelly	
EI-BCK	Cessna F.172K	Iona National Airways	
EI-BCL	Cessna 182P	Iona National Airways	
EI-BCM	Piper J-3C-65 Cub	Kilmoon Flying Group	
EI-BCN	Piper J-3C-65 Cub	Snowflake Flying Group	

Notes	Reg.	Type	Owner or Operator
	EI-BCO	Piper J-3C-65 Cub	J. Molloy
	EI-BCR	Boeing 737-281	Aer Lingus *Sir Oliver Plunkett*
	EI-BCS	M.S.880B Rallye Club	J. Murphy
	EI-BCT	Cessna 411A	Air Surveys International
	EI-BCU	M.S.880B Rallye Club	Weston Ltd
	EI-BCV	Cessna F.150M	Hibernian Flying Club Ltd
	EI-BCW	M.S.880B Rallye Club	H. Clarke
	EI-BCY	Beech 200 Super King Air (232)	Minister of Defence
	EI-BDH	M.S.880B Rallye Club	Munster Wings Ltd
	EI-BDK	M.S.880B Rallye Club	Limerick Flying Club Ltd
	EI-BDL	Evans VP-2	J. Duggan
	EI-BDM	PA-23 Aztec 250D	Executive Air Services
	EI-BDO	Cessna F.152	Iona National Airways
	EI-BDP	Cessna 182P	182 Flying Group
	EI-BDR	PA-28 Cherokee 180	Cork Flying Club
	EI-BDY	Boeing 737-2E1	Aer Lingus Teo
	EI-BEA	M.S.880B Rallye 100ST	Weston Ltd
	EI-BEB	Boeing 737-248	Aer Lingus Teo *St Eunan*
	EI-BEC	Boeing 737-248	Aer Lingus Teo
	EI-BED	Boeing 747-130	Aer Linte Eireann Teo *St Kieran*
	EI-BEE	Boeing 737-281	Aer Lingus Teo *St Cronin*
	EI-BEF	Boeing 737-281	Aer Tara Ltd
	EI-BEH	Short SD3-30	Aer Lingus Teo
	EI-BEI	—	Aer Lingus Teo
	EI-BEJ	—	Aer Lingus Teo
	EI-BEK	—	Aer Lingus Teo
	EI-BEL	—	Aer Lingus Teo
	EI-BEM	—	Aer Lingus Teo
	EI-BEN	Piper J-3C-65 Cub	Capt J. J. Sullivan
	EI-BEO	Cessna 310Q	Iona National Airways
	EI-BEP	M.S.892A Rallye Commodore	H. Lynch & J. O'Leary
	EI-BET	Cessna F.337G	K. Walters
	EI-BEY	Naval N3N-3	Huntley & Huntley Ltd
	EI-BFB	M.S.880B Rallye 100ST	Weston Ltd
	EI-BFC	Boeing 737-2H4	Air Tara Ltd
	EI-BFE	Cessna F.150G	Joyce Aviation Ltd
	EI-BFF	Beech A.23 Musketeer	A. Cody
	EI-BFH	Bell 212	Irish Helicopters Ltd
	EI-BFI	M.S.880B Rallye 100ST	J. O'Neill
	EI-BFJ	Beech A.200 Super King Air (234)	Minister of Defence
	EI-BFM	M.S.893E Rallye 235GT	M. Orr
	EI-BFO	Piper J-3C-90 Cub	M. Slattery
	EI-BFP	M.S.800B Rallye 100ST	Weston Ltd
	EI-BFR	M.S.880B Rallye 100ST	Galway Flying Club
	EI-BFS	FRED Srs 2	G. J. McGlennon
	EI-BFT	Beech A200 Super King Air	Avair Ltd
	EI-BFU	—	—
	EI-BFV	M.S.880B Rallye 100ST	Ormond Flying Club
	EI-BGA	M.S.880B Rallye 100ST	T. Daly
	EI-BGB	M.S.880B Rallye 100ST	G. N. Atkinson
	EI-BGC	M.S.880B Rallye Club	P. Moran
	EI-BGD	M.S.880B Rallye Club	S. O'Rourke
	EI-BGF	PA-28R Cherokee Arrow 180	Arrow Group
	EI-BGG	M.S.893 Rallye 180GT	C. Weldon
	EI-BGH	Cessna F.172N	Iona National Airways
	EI-BGI	Cessna F.152	Iona National Airways
	EI-BGJ	Cessna F.152	Kerry Aero Club
	EI-BGK	Cessna P206D	Shannon Executive Aviation
	EI-BGL	R. Turbo Commander 690B	Flightline Ltd
	EI-BGN	M.S.880B Rallye Club	Rathcoole Flying Group Ltd
	EI-BGO	Canadair CL-44D-4J	Aer Turas Teo
	EI-BGP	Cessna 414A	Iona National Airways
	EI-BGS	M.S.893B Rallye 180GT	M. Farrelly
	EI-BGT	Colt 77A balloon	K. Haugh
	EI-BGU	M.S.880B Rallye Club	M. F. Neary
	EI-BGV	AA-5 Traveler	J. Crowe
	EI-BHA	Beech A200 Super King Air	Avair Ltd
	EI-BHB	M.S.887 Rallye 125	C. Burns
	EI-BHC	Cessna F.177RG	P. J. McGuire & B. Palfrey
	EI-BHD	M.S.893E Rallye 180GT	Epic Flying Group

Reg.	Type	Owner or Operator	Notes
EI-BHF	M.S.892A Rallye Commodore 150	B. Mullen	
EI-BHG	Beech 200 Super King Air	Avair Ltd	
EI-BHH	Cessna FRA.150L	T. F. Joyce & A. J. Conran	
EI-BHI	Bell 206B JetRanger 2	J. Mansfield	
EI-BHK	M.S.880B Rallye Club	J. Lawlor & B. Lyons	
EI-BHL	Beech E90 King Air	Stewart Singlam Fabrics Ltd	
EI-BHM	Cessna 337E	The Ross Flying Group	
EI-BHN	M.S.893A Rallye Commodore	K. O'Driscoll & ptnrs	
EI-BHO	Sikorsky S-61N	Irish Helicopters Ltd	
EI-BHP	M.S.893A Rallye Commodore	Wicklow Flying Group	
EI-BHT	Beech 77 Skipper	Hibernian Flying Club	
EI-BHV	Champion 7EC Traveler	Condor Group	
EI-BHW	Cessna F.150F	B. A. Carpenter	
EI-BHY	M.S.892E Rallye Commodore	D. Killian	
EI-BIC	Cessna F.172N	Oriel Flying Group Ltd	
EI-BID	PA-18 Super Cub 95	D. MacCarthy	
EI-BIE	Cessna FA.152	D. F. McEllin	
EI-BIF	M.S.894 Rallye Minerva 235	Empire Enterprises Ltd	
EI-BIG	Zlin 526	P. von Lonkhuyzen	
EI-BIJ	AB-206B JetRanger 2	Irish Helicopters Ltd	
EI-BIK	PA-18-180 Super Cub	Dublin Gliding Club	
EI-BIL	Beech A35 Bonanza	W. J. Phelan	
EI-BIM	M.S.880B Rallye Club	D. Millar	
EI-BIN	Cessna F.172N	Iona National Airways Ltd	
EI-BIO	Piper J-3C-65 Cub	Monasterevin Flying Club	
EI-BIP	Beech 200 Super King Air	Avair Ltd	
EI-BIR	Cessna F.172M	P. O'Reilly	
EI-BIS	Robin R.1180TD	Robin Aiglon Group	
EI-BIT	M.S.887 Rallye 125	Tango Flying Group	
EI-BIU	Robin R.2112A	Bruton Aircraft Engineering Ltd	
EI-BIV	Bellanca 8KCAB Citabria	Aerocrats Flying Group	
EI-BIW	M.S.880B Rallye Club	E. J. Barr	
EI-BJA	Cessna FRA.150L	Joyce Aviation Ltd	
EI-BJC	Aeronca 7AC Champion	R. J. Bentley	
EI-BJE	Boeing 737-275	Air Tara Ltd (leased to Nigeria Airways)	
EI-BJF	AA-5 Traveler	P. Mercer & ptnrs	
EI-BJG	Robin R.1180	N. Hanley	
EI-BJH	Nipper T.66 Srs 3	S. T. O'Rourke	
EI-BJJ	Aeronca 15AC Sedan	A. A. Alderdice & S. H. Boyd	
EI-BJK	M.S.880B Rallye 110ST	Barton Ltd	
EI-BJL	Cessna 550 Citation II	Helicopter Maintenance Ltd	
EI-BJM	Cessna A.152	Leinster Aero Club	
EI-BJN	Cessna 500 Citation	Tool & Mould Steel (Ireland) Ltd	
EI-BJO	Cessna R.172K	P. Hogan & G. Ryder	
EI-BJP	Boeing 737-275C	Air Tara Ltd	
EI-BJS	AA-5B Tiger	A. Killian & C. Pearce	
EI-BJT	PA-38-112 Tomahawk	Westair	
EI-BJV	AB-206B JetRanger 3	J. Kelly	
EI-BJW	D.H.104 Dove 6	S. J. Filhol Ltd	
EI-BJY	Beech 200 Super King Air	Avair Ltd	
EI-BKA	Pitts S-2A Special	A. Wignall	
EI-BKC	Aeronca 115AC Sedan	G. Treacy	
EI-BKD	Mooney M.20J	Limerick Warehousing Ltd	
EI-BKE	M.S.885 Super Rallye	C. Brady & G. Groom	
EI-BKF	Cessna F.172H	M. & M. C. Veale	
EI-BKK	Taylor JT.1 Monoplane	F. J. Hoysted	
EI-BKL	Cessna FR.172F	Irish Parachute Club	
EI-BKM	Zenith CH.200	B. McGann	
EI-BKN	M.S.880B Rallye 100ST	Weston Ltd	
EI-BKP	Zenith CH.200	L. McEnteggart	
EI-BKS	Eipper Quicksilver	Irish Microlight Ltd	
EI-BKT	AB-206B JetRanger 3	Irish Helicopters Ltd	
EI-BKU	M.S.892A Rallye Commodore	T. Maguire	
EI-BKY	Beech 99	Avair Ltd	
EI-BLA	PA-23 Aztec 250	National Aluminium Ltd	
EI-BLB	Stampe SV-4C	J. E. Hutchinson & R. A. Stafford	
EI-BLD	Bolkow Bo 105C	Irish Helicopters Ltd	
EI-BLE	Eipper Microlight	R. P. St George-Smith	
EI-BLF	Hiway Demon	F. Warren	
EI-BLG	AB.206B JetRanger 3	Anglo Irish Meat Co Ltd	

Notes	Reg.	Type	Owner or Operator
	EI-BLH	Cessna 421C	A. D. D. Rogers
	EI-BLI	Beech C90 King Air	Avair Ltd
	EI-BLJ	Cessna T.210H	N. V. Lott Ltd
	EI-BLK	PA-28-181 Archer II	J. J. Sundival
	EI-BLL	Cessna F.172P	J. J. Spollen
	EI-BLM	Hiway Skytrike II/MSD	R. Hudson
	EI-BLN	Eipper Quicksilver MX	O. J. Conway & B. Daffy
	EI-BLO	Catto CP.16	R. W. Hall
	EI-BLP	Short SD3-30	Avair Ltd
	EI-BLR	PA-34-200T Seneca II	R. Paris
	EI-BLS	Cessna 150M	Phoenix Flying Ltd
	EI-BLU	Evans VP-1	A. Bailey
	EI-BLW	PA-23 Aztec 250	Shannon Executive Aviation
	EI-BLY	Sikorsky S-61N	Irish Helicopters Ltd
	EI-BMA	M.S.880B Rallye Club	CTC Group
	EI-BMB	M.S.880B Rallye 100T	C. Scott
	EI-BMC	Hiway Demon Skytrike	S. Pallister
	EI-BMD	Eagle Microlight	E. Fitzgerald
	EI-BMF	F.8L Falco	M. Slazenger
	EI-BMH	M.S.880B Rallye Club	N. J. Bracken
	EI-BMI	SOCATA TB.9 Tampico	Weston Ltd
	EI-BMJ	M.S.893A Rallye Club	Galway Flying Club
	EI-BMK	Cessna 310Q	Iona National Airways Ltd
	EI-BML	PA-23 Aztec 250	Bruton Aircraft Engineering Ltd
	EI-BMM	Cessna F.152 II	Iona National Airways Ltd
	EI-BMN	Cessna F.152 II	Iona National Airways Ltd
	EI-BMO	Robin R.2160	The Robin Group
	EI-BMR	Southdown Puma	R. Hudson
	EI-BMS	Cessna F.177RG	A. M. Smyth
	EI-BMT	AA-5B Tiger	T. Drury
	EI-BMU	Monnet Sonerai II	P. Forde & D. Connaire
	EI-BMV	AA-5 Traveler	D. M. Lummes
	EI-BMW	Vulcan Air Trike	L. Maddock
	EI-BMY	Boeing 737-2L9	Air Tara Ltd
	EI-BNA	Douglas DC-8-63CF	Air Turas
	EI-BNB	Lake LA-4-200 Buccaneer	L. McNamara & M. Ledwith
	EI-BNC	Cessna F.152	Iona National Airlines
	EI-BND	Conroy CL-44-0	HeavyLift Cargo Airlines Ltd/Stansted
	EI-BNE	Helio HT-295 Super Courier	Huntley & Huntley Ltd
	EI-BNF	Goldwing Canard	T. Morelli
	EI-BNG	M.S.892A Rallye Commodore	B. A. Carpenter
	EI-BNH	Hiway Skytrike	M. Martin
	EI-BNI	Bell 412	Vellare Ltd
	EI-BNJ	Evans VP-2	G. A. Cashman
	EI-BNK	Cessna U.206F	Irish Parachute Club Ltd
	EI-BNL	Rand KR-2	K. Hayes
	EI-BNM	Short SD3-30	Avair Ltd
	EI-BNN	SC.7 Skyvan	B. A. Carpenter
	EI-BNO	AS.350B Ecureuil	M. V. O'Brien
	EI-BNP	Rotorway 133	R. L. Renfroe
	EI-BNR	AA-5 Traveler	Victor Mike Flying Group
	EI-BNT	—	
	EI-BNU	M.S.880B Rallye Club	P. A. Doyle
	EI-BNV	PA-23 Aztec 250	Epic Flying Group Ltd
	EI-BNY	SNIAS SN.601 Corvette	Flightline Ltd
	EI-BOA	Pterodactyl Ptraveller	A. Murphy
	EI-BOB	Nimrod 165	K. B. O'Regan
	EI-BOD	Cessna 210F	P. Parke
	EI-BOE	SOCATA TB.10 Tobago	E. L. Symmons
	EI-BOF	SOCATA TB.10 Tobago	J. Condron
	EI-BOH	Eipper Quicksilver	L. Leech
	EI-BOI	Cessna F.150G	D. Hillary & S. Burke
	EI-BOJ	Boeing 737-2L9	Air Tara Ltd
	EI-BOK	—	—
	EI-BOL	PA-31 Turbo Navajo	National Aluminium (Manufacturing) Ltd
	EI-BOM	—	—
	EI-BON	—	—
	EI-BOO	—	—
	EI-BOP	—	—

EL (Liberia)

Reg.	Type	Owner or Operator	Notes
EL-AJA	Boeing 707-321C	Liberia World Airlines	

EP (Iran)

EP-IAA	Boeing 747SP-86	Iran Air *Fars*	
EP-IAB	Boeing 747SP-86	Iran Air *Kurdistan*	
EP-IAC	Boeing 747SP-86	Iran Air *Khuzestan*	
EP-IAD	Boeing 747SP-86	Iran Air	
EP-IAG	Boeing 747-286B	Iran Air *Azarabadegan*	
EP-IAH	Boeing 747-286B	Iran Air *Khorasan*	
EP-IAM	Boeing 747-186B	Iran Air	
EP-ICA	Boeing 747-2J9F	Iran Air	
EP-ICB	Boeing 747-2J9F	Iran Air	
EP-IRJ	Boeing 707-321B	Iran Air	
EP-IRK	Boeing 707-321C	Iran Air	
EP-IRL	Boeing 707-386C	Iran Air *Apadana*	
EP-IRM	Boeing 707-386C	Iran Air *Ekbatana*	
EP-IRN	Boeing 707-386C	Iran Air *Pasargad*	
EP-NHD	Boeing 747-131	Iran Air	
EP-NHK	Boeing 747-131	Iran Air	

ET (Ethiopia)

ET-AAH	Boeing 720-060B	Ethiopian Airlines *White Nile*	
ET-ABP	Boeing 720-060B	Ethiopian Airlines	
ET-ACQ	Boeing 707-379C	Ethiopian Airlines	
ET-AFA	Boeing 720-024B	Ethiopian Airlines	
ET-AFB	Boeing 720-024B	Ethiopian Airlines	
ET-AFK	Boeing 720-024B	Ethiopian Airlines	
ET-AIE	Boeing 767-260	Ethiopian Airlines	
ET-AIF	Boeing 767-260	Ethiopian Airlines	

F (France)

F-BEIG	Douglas DC-3	Normandie Air Services	
F-BIEM	Beech 99	Air Limousin	
F-BIUK	F.27 Friendship Mk 100	Uni-Air	
F-BJEN	S.E.210 Caravelle 10B	Air Charter International	
F-BJTU	S.E.210 Caravelle 10B	Air Charter International	
F-BMKS	S.E.210 Caravelle 10B	Air Charter International	
F-BNKC	S.E.210 Caravelle 10B	Altair	
F-BNKG	S.E.210 Caravelle III	Altair	
F-BNOG	S.E.210 Caravelle 12	Air Inter	
F-BNOH	S.E.210 Caravelle 12	Air Inter	
F-BOJA	Boeing 727-228	Air France	
F-BOJB	Boeing 727-228	Air France	

Notes	Reg.	Type	Owner or Operator
	F-BOJC	Boeing 727-228	Air France
	F-BOJD	Boeing 727-228	Air France
	F-BOJE	Boeing 727-228	Air France
	F-BOJF	Boeing 727-228	Air France
	F-BPJG	Boeing 727-228	Air France
	F-BPJH	Boeing 727-228	Air France
	F-BPJI	Boeing 727-228	Air France
	F-BPJJ	Boeing 727-228	Air France
	F-BPJK	Boeing 727-228	Air France
	F-BPJL	Boeing 727-228	Air France
	F-BPJM	Boeing 727-228	Air France
	F-BPJN	Boeing 727-228	Air France
	F-BPJO	Boeing 727-228	Air France
	F-BPJP	Boeing 727-228	Air France
	F-BPJQ	Boeing 727-228	Air France
	F-BPJR	Boeing 727-228	Air France
	F-BPJS	Boeing 727-228	Air France
	F-BPJT	Boeing 727-228	Air France
	F-BPJU	Boeing 727-214	Air Charter International
	F-BPJV	Boeing 727-214	Air Charter International
	F-BPNA	F.27 Friendship Mk 500	Air Inter
	F-BPNB	F.27 Friendship Mk 500	Air Inter
	F-BPNC	F.27 Friendship Mk 500	Air Inter
	F-BPND	F.27 Friendship Mk 500	Air Inter
	F-BPNE	F.27 Friendship Mk 500	Air Inter
	F-BPNG	F.27 Friendship Mk 500	Brit Air
	F-BPNH	F.27 Friendship Mk 500	Air Inter
	F-BPNI	F.27 Friendship Mk 500	Brit Air
	F-BPNJ	F.27 Friendship Mk 500	Air Inter
	F-BPPA	Aero Spacelines Guppy-201	Airbus Industrie *Airbus Skylink 2*
	F-BPUA	F.27 Friendship Mk 500	Air France
	F-BPUB	F.27 Friendship Mk 500	Air France
	F-BPUC	F.27 Friendship Mk 500	Air France
	F-BPUD	F.27 Friendship Mk 500	Air France
	F-BPUE	F.27 Friendship Mk 500	Air France
	F-BPUF	F.27 Friendship Mk 500	Air France
	F-BPUG	F.27 Friendship Mk 500	Air France
	F-BPUH	F.27 Friendship Mk 500	Air France
	F-BPUI	F.27 Friendship Mk 500	Air France
	F-BPUJ	F.27 Friendship Mk 500	Air France
	F-BPUK	F.27 Friendship Mk 500	Air France
	F-BPUL	F.27 Friendship Mk 500	Air France
	F-BPVA	Boeing 747-128	Air France
	F-BPVB	Boeing 747-128	Air France
	F-BPVC	Boeing 747-128	Air France
	F-BPVD	Boeing 747-128	Air France
	F-BPVE	Boeing 747-128	Air France
	F-BPVF	Boeing 747-128	Air France
	F-BPVG	Boeing 747-128	Air France
	F-BPVH	Boeing 747-128	Air France
	F-BPVJ	Boeing 747-128	Air France
	F-BPVK	Boeing 747-128	Air France
	F-BPVL	Boeing 747-128	Air France
	F-BPVM	Boeing 747-128	Air France
	F-BPVN	Boeing 747-128	Air France
	F-BPVO	Boeing 747-228F	Air France
	F-BPVP	Boeing 747-128	Air France
	F-BPVQ	Boeing 747-128	Air France
	F-BPVR	Boeing 747-228F	Air France
	F-BPVS	Boeing 747-228B	Air France
	F-BPVT	Boeing 747-228B	Air France
	F-BPVV	Boeing 747-228F	Air France
	F-BPVX	Boeing 747-228B	Air France
	F-BPVY	Boeing 747-228B	Air France
	F-BPVZ	Boeing 747-228F	Air France
	F-BRGU	S.E.210 Caravelle VI-N	Minerve
	F-BRNI	Beech 70 Queen Air	Lucas Air Transport
	F-BSGT	Boeing 707-321B	Pointair
	F-BSUM	F.27 Friendship Mk 500	Air France
	F-BSUN	F.27 Friendship Mk 500	Air France

Reg.	Type	Owner or Operator	Notes
F-BSUO	F.27 Friendship Mk 500	Air France	
F-BTAU	D.H.C.6 Twin Otter	Air Limousin	
F-BTGV	Aero Spacelines Guppy-201	Airbus Industrie	
		Airbus Skylink 1	
F-BTOA	S.E.210 Caravelle 12	Air Inter	
F-BTOB	S.E.210 Caravelle 12	Air Inter	
F-BTOC	S.E.210 Caravelle 12	Air Inter	
F-BTOD	S.E.210 Caravelle 12	Air Inter	
F-BTOE	S.E.210 Caravelle 12	Air Inter	
F-BTSC	Concorde 101	Air France	
F-BTSD	Concorde 101	Air France	
F-BTTA	Mercure 100	Air Inter	
F-BTTB	Mercure 100	Air Inter	
F-BTTC	Mercure 100	Air Inter	
F-BTTD	Mercure 100	Air Inter	
F-BTTE	Mercure 100	Air Inter	
F-BTTF	Mercure 100	Air Inter	
F-BTTG	Mercure 100	Air Inter	
F-BTTH	Mercure 100	Air Inter	
F-BTTI	Mercure 100	Air Inter	
F-BTTJ	Mercure 100	Air Inter	
F-BUAE	A.300B2 Airbus	Air Inter	
F-BUAF	A.300B2 Airbus	Air Inter	
F-BUAG	A.300B2 Airbus	Air Inter	
F-BUAH	A.300B2 Airbus	Air Inter	
F-BUAI	A.300B2 Airbus	Air Inter	
F-BUAJ	A.300B2 Airbus	Air Inter	
F-BUAK	A.300B2 Airbus	Air Inter	
F-BUAL	A.300B2 Airbus	Air Inter	
F-BUAM	A.300B2 Airbus	Air Inter	
F-BUTI	F-28 Fellowship 1000	T.A.T.	
F-BUZC	S.E.210 Caravelle VI-R	Minerve	
F-BVFA	Concorde 101	Air France	
F-BVFB	Concorde 101	Air France	
F-BVFC	Concorde 101	Air France	
F-BVFD	Concorde 101	Air France	
F-BVFF	Concorde 101	Air France	
F-BVFG	Nord 262A	Air Limousin	
F-BVFJ	Nord 262A	Air Limousin	
F-BVFP	HPR-7 Herald 214	Trans Azur Aviation	
F-BVGA	A.300B2 Airbus	Air France	
F-BVGB	A.300B2 Airbus	Air France	
F-BVGC	A.300B2 Airbus	Air France	
F-BVGD	A.300B2 Airbus	Air Inter	
F-BVGE	A.300B2 Airbus	Air Inter	
F-BVGF	A.300B2 Airbus	Air Inter	
F-BVGG	A.300B4 Airbus	Air France	
F-BVGH	A.300B4 Airbus	Air France	
F-BVGI	A.300B4 Airbus	Air France	
F-BVGJ	A.300B4 Airbus	Air France	
F-BVGL	A.300B4 Airbus	Air France	
F-BVGM	A.300B4 Airbus	Air France	
F-BVGN	A.300B4 Airbus	Air France	
F-BVGO	A.300B4 Airbus	Air France	
F-BVGP	A.300B4 Airbus	Air France	
F-BVGQ	A.300B4 Airbus	Air France	
F-BVGR	A.300B4 Airbus	Air France	
F-BVGS	A.300B4 Airbus	Air France	
F-BVGT	A.300B4 Airbus	Air France	
F-BVPZ	S.E.210 Caravelle VI-N	Corse Air *Golfe de Porto Vecchio*	
F-BVSF	S.E.210 Caravelle VI-N	Corse Air	
F-BYAB	F.27 Friendship Mk 400	T.A.T.	
F-BYAI	S.E.210 Caravelle VI-N	Corse Air	
F-BYAO	F.27 Friendship Mk 100	Uni-Air	
F-BYAP	F.27 Friendship Mk 100	Brit Air	
F-BYAT	S.E.210 Caravelle VI-N	Corse Air	
F-BYCD	S.E.210 Caravelle VI-N	Europe Aero Service *Ile de France*	
F-BYCN	Boeing 707-321C (Cargo)	Air France	
F-BYCO	Boeing 707-321C (Cargo)	Air France	
F-BYCP	Boeing 707-321C (Cargo)	Air France	
F-BYCU	Douglas DC-3	Stellair	

Notes	Reg.	Type	Owner or Operator
	F-BYCY	S.E.210 Caravelle VI-N	Corse Air
	F-BYFM	Douglas DC-8-53	Minerve
	F-GAOT	F.27 Friendship Mk 100	Uni-Air
	F-GAPA	S.E.210 Caravelle VI-R	Minerve
	F-GATP	S.E.210 Caravelle 10B	Minerve
	F-GATZ	S.E.210 Caravelle VI-N	Minerve
	F-GBBR	F.28 Fellowship 1000	T.A.T.
	F-GBBS	F.28 Fellowship 1000	T.A.T.
	F-GBBT	F.28 Fellowship 1000	T.A.T.
	F-GBBX	F.28 Fellowship 1000	T.A.T.
	F-GBEA	A.300B2 Airbus	Air France
	F-GBEB	A.300B2 Airbus	Air France
	F-GBEC	A.300B2 Airbus	Air France
	F-GBGA	EMB-110P2 Bandeirante	Brit Air
	F-GBLE	EMB-110P2 Bandeirante	Brit Air
	F-GBMG	EMB-110P2 Bandeirante	Brit Air
	F-GBMJ	S.E.210 Caravelle VI-N	Europe Aero Service *Valentinois*
	F-GBMK	S.E.210 Caravelle VI-N	Europe Aero Service *Rousillon*
	F-GBRM	EMB-110P2 Bandeirante	Brit Air
	F-GBRQ	FH.227B Friendship	T.A.T.
	F-GBRU	F.27J Friendship	T.A.T.
	F-GBRV	F.27J Friendship	T.A.T.
	F-GBTO	SA.226TC Metro II	Cie Aèrienne du Languedoc
	F-GBYA	Boeing 737-228	Air France
	F-GBYB	Boeing 737-228	Air France
	F-GBYC	Boeing 737-228	Air France
	F-GBYD	Boeing 737-228	Air France
	F-GBYE	Boeing 737-228	Air France
	F-GBYF	Boeing 737-228	Air France
	F-GBYG	Boeing 737-228	Air France
	F-GBYH	Boeing 737-228	Air France
	F-GBYI	Boeing 737-228	Air France
	F-GBYJ	Boeing 737-228	Air France
	F-GBYK	Boeing 737-228	Air France
	F-GBYL	Boeing 737-228	Air France
	F-GCBA	Boeing 747-228B	Air France
	F-GCBC	Boeing 747-228B	Air France
	F-GCDA	Boeing 727-228	Air France
	F-GCDB	Boeing 727-228	Air France
	F-GCDC	Boeing 727-228	Air France
	F-GCDD	Boeing 727-228	Air France
	F-GCDE	Boeing 727-228	Air France
	F-GCDF	Boeing 727-228	Air France
	F-GCDG	Boeing 727-228	Air France
	F-GCDH	Boeing 727-228	Air France
	F-GCDI	Boeing 727-228	Air France
	F-GCFC	FH.227B Friendship	T.A.T.
	F-GCFE	SA.226TC Metro II	Cie Aérienne du Langudoc
	F-GCGH	FH.227B Friendship	T.A.T.
	F-GCGQ	Boeing 727-227	Europe Aero Service *Normandie*
	F-GCJL	Boeing 737-222	Euralair
	F-GCJO	FH.227B Friendship	T.A.T.
	F-GCJT	S.E.210 Caravelle 10B	Europe Aero Service *Bretagne*
	F-GCLA	EMB-110P2 Bandeirante	Lucas Air Transport
	F-GCLL	Boeing 737-222	Euralair
	F-GCLM	FH.227B Friendship	T.A.T.
	F-GCLN	FH.227B Friendship	T.A.T.
	F-GCLO	FH.227B Friendship	T.A.T.
	F-GCMV	Boeing 727-2X3	Air Charter International
	F-GCMX	Boeing 727-2X3	Air Charter International
	F-GCPG	SA.226TC Metro II	Cie Aérienne du Languedoc
	F-GCPS	FH.227B Friendship	T.A.T.
	F-GCPT	FH.227B Friendship	T.A.T.
	F-GCPU	FH.227B Friendship	T.A.T.
	F-GCPV	FH.227B Friendship	T.A.T.
	F-GCPX	FH.227B Friendship	T.A.T.
	F-GCPY	FH.227B Friendship	T.A.T.
	F-GCPZ	FH.227B Friendship	T.A.T.
	F-GCSL	Boeing 737-222	Euralair
	F-GCTE	SA.226TC Metro II	Cie Aérienne du Languedoc
	F-GCVI	S.E.210 Caravelle 12	Air Inter

F-BJEN   S.E.210 Caravelle 10B of Air Charter International.

207

HA-LCB   Tupolev Tu-154B of Malev.

HB-IPA   Airbus A.310.221 of Swissair.

Reg.	Type	Owner or Operator	Notes
F-GCVJ	S.E.210 Caravelle 12	Air Inter	
F-GCVK	S.E.210 Caravelle 12	Air Inter	
F-GCVL	S.E.210 Caravelle 12	Air Inter	
F-GCVM	S.E.210 Caravelle 12	Air Inter	
F-GDAQ	L-100-30 Hercules	Sfair	
F-GDFC	F.28 Fellowship 4000	T.A.T.	
F-GDFD	F.28 Fellowship 4000	T.A.T.	
F-GDFY	S.E.210 Caravelle 10B	Air Charter International	
F-GDFZ	S.E.210 Caravelle 10B	Air Charter International	
F-GDJK	Douglas DC-10-30	Lineas Aereas de Mocambique	
F-GDJM	Douglas DC-8-62CF	Minerve	
F-GDJU	S.E.210 Caravelle 10B	Europe Aero Service	
F-GDMR	SA.226TC Metro II	Cie Aérienne du Languedoc	
F-GDPM	Douglas DC-8-53	Minerve	
F-GDPS	Douglas DC-8-61	Pointair	
F-GDSG	UTA Super Guppy	Airbus Industrie	
F-GEAI	UTA Super Guppy	Airbus Industrie	

Note: Air France also operates six more Boeing 747s which retain the US registrations N1252E, N1289E, N1305E, N4506H, N4508E and N4544F. Corse Air also operates Caravelle TZ-ADS on lease.

HA (Hungary)   MALÉV

HA-LBE	Tupolev Tu-134	Malev	
HA-LBF	Tupolev Tu-134	Malev	
HA-LBG	Tupolev Tu-134	Malev	
HA-LBH	Tupolev Tu-134	Malev	
HA-LBI	Tupolev Tu-134A	Malev	
HA-LBK	Tupolev Tu-134A	Malev	
HA-LBN	Tupolev Tu-134A	Malev	
HA-LBO	Tupolev Tu-134A	Malev	
HA-LBP	Tupolev Tu-134A	Malev	
HA-LBR	Tupolev Tu-134A	Malev	
HA-LCA	Tupolev Tu-154B	Malev	
HA-LCB	Tupolev Tu-154B	Malev	
HA-LCE	Tupolev Tu-154B	Malev	
HA-LCG	Tupolev Tu-154B	Malev	
HA-LCH	Tupolev Tu-154B	Malev	
HA-LCM	Tupolev Tu-154B	Malev	
HA-LCN	Tupolev Tu-154B	Malev	
HA-LCO	Tupolev Tu-154B	Malev	
HA-LCP	Tupolev Tu-154B	Malev	
HA-LCR	Tupolev Tu-154B	Malev	

HB (Switzerland)   swissair

BALAIR

HB-AHA	Saab-Fairchild 340	Crossair	
HB-AHB	Saab-Fairchild 340	Crossair	
HB-AHC	Saab-Fairchild 340	Crossair	
HB-AHD	Saab-Fairchild 340	Crossair	
HB-AHE	Saab-Fairchild 340	Crossair	
HB-AHF	Saab-Fairchild 340	Crossair	
HB-AHG	Saab-Fairchild 340	Crossair	
HB-AHH	Saab-Fairchild 340	Crossair	
HB-AHI	Saab-Fairchild 340	Crossair	
HB-AHK	Saab-Fairchild 340	Crossair	
HB-ICI	S.E.210 Caravelle 10-R	CTA	
HB-ICN	S.E.210 Caravelle 10-R	CTA *Ville de Genève*	
HB-ICO	S.E.210 Caravelle 10-R	CTA *Romandie*	
HB-ICQ	S.E.210 Caravelle 10-R	CTA	

Notes	Reg.	Type	Owner or Operator
	HB-IDI	Douglas DC-8-62	Swissair *Solothurn*
	HB-IDL	Douglas DC-8-62	Swissair
	HB-IDO	Douglas DC-9-32	Swissair *Genève-Cointrin*
	HB-IDP	Douglas DC-9-32	Swissair *Basel-Land*
	HB-IDT	Douglas DC-9-34	Balair
	HB-IDZ	Douglas DC-8-63PF	Balair
	HB-IFH	Douglas DC-9-32	Swissair *Baden*
	HB-IFU	Douglas DC-9-32	Swissair *Chur*
	HB-IFV	Douglas DC-9-32	Swissair *Bülach*
	HB-IFW	Douglas DC-9-33F	Swissair *Payerne*
	HB-IFZ	Douglas DC-9-33F	Balair
	HB-IGA	Boeing 747-257B	Swissair *Geneve*
	HB-IGB	Boeing 747-257B	Swissair *Zurich*
	HB-IGC	Boeing 747-357	Swissair *Bern*
	HB-IGD	Boeing 747-357	Swissair *Basel*
	HB-IGG	Boeing 747-357	Swissair
	HB-IHC	Douglas DC-10-30	Swissair *Luzern*
	HB-IHD	Douglas DC-10-30	Swissair *Thurgau*
	HB-IHE	Douglas DC-10-30	Swissair *Vaud*
	HB-IHF	Douglas DC-10-30	Swissair *Nidwalden*
	HB-IHG	Douglas DC-10-30	Swissair *Graubünden*
	HB-IHH	Douglas DC-10-30	Swissair *Schaffhausen*
	HB-IHI	Douglas DC-10-30	Swissair *Fribourg*
	HB-IHK	Douglas DC-10-30	Balair
	HB-IHL	Douglas DC-10-30ER	Swissair *Ticino*
	HB-IHM	Douglas DC-10-30ER	Swissair *Valais-Wallis*
	HB-IHN	Douglas DC-10-30ER	Swissair *St Gallen*
	HB-IHO	Douglas DC-10-30ER	Swissair *Uri*
	HB-IKF	Douglas DC-9-51	Alisarda (Italy)
	HB-IKG	Douglas DC-9-51	Alisarda (Italy)
	HB-IKH	Douglas DC-9-51	Alisarda (Italy)
	HB-INA	Douglas DC-9-81	Swissair *Obwalden*
	HB-INB	Douglas DC-9-81	Balair
	HB-INC	Douglas DC-9-81	Swissair
	HB-IND	Douglas DC-9-81	Swissair *Zug*
	HB-INE	Douglas DC-9-81	Swissair *Rümlang*
	HB-INF	Douglas DC-9-81	Swissair *Appenzell a.Rh.*
	HB-ING	Douglas DC-9-81	Swissair *Glarus*
	HB-INH	Douglas DC-9-81	Swissair *Winterthur*
	HB-INI	Douglas DC-9-81	Swissair *Kloten*
	HB-INK	Douglas DC-9-81	Swissair *Opfikon*
	HB-INL	Douglas DC-9-81	Swissair *Jura*
	HB-INM	Douglas DC-9-81	Swissair *Lausanne*
	HB-INN	Douglas DC-9-81	Swissair *Appenzell i.Rh.*
	HB-INO	Douglas DC-9-81	Swissair *Bellinzona*
	HB-INP	Douglas DC-9-81	Swissair *Oberglatt*
	HB-IPA	A.310-221 Airbus	Swissair *Aargau*
	HB-IPB	A.310-221 Airbus	Swissair *Neuchatel*
	HB-IPC	A.310-221 Airbus	Swissair *Schwyz*
	HB-IPD	A.310-221 Airbus	Swissair *Solothurn*
	HB-IPE	A.310-221 Airbus	Swissair
	HB-IPF	A.310-221 Airbus	Swissair
	HB-IPG	A.310-221 Airbus	Swissair
	HB-ISK	Douglas DC-9-51	Swissair *Höri*
	HB-ISL	Douglas DC-9-51	Swissair *Köniz*
	HB-ISM	Douglas DC-9-51	Swissair *Wettingen*
	HB-ISN	Douglas DC-9-51	Swissair *Sion*
	HB-ISO	Douglas DC-9-51	Swissair *Bienne*
	HB-IST	Douglas DC-9-51	Swissair *Aarau*
	HB-ISU	Douglas DC-9-51	Swissair *Bachenbülach*
	HB-ISV	Douglas DC-9-51	Swissair *Winkel*
	HB-ISW	Douglas DC-9-51	Swissair *Dubendorf*
	HB-LLD	SA.227AC Metro III	Crossair
	HB-LLE	SA.227AC Metro III	Crossair
	HB-LLF	SA.227AC Metro III	Crossair
	HB-LNA	SA.227AC Metro III	Crossair
	HB-LNB	SA.227AC Metro III	Crossair
	HB-LNC	SA.227AC Metro III	Crossair
	HB-LND	SA.227AC Metro III	Crossair
	HB-LNE	SA.227AC Metro III	Crossair

Reg.	Type	Owner or Operator	Notes
HB-LNO	SA.227AC Metro III	Crossair	

Note: Swissair also operates two Boeing 747-357s which retain their US registrations N221GE and N221GF.

HL (Korea)

HL7406	Boeing 707-3B5C	Korean Air Lines	
HL7425	Boeing 707-373C	Korean Air Lines	
HL7427	Boeing 707-321C	Korean Air Lines	
HL7431	Boeing 707-321C	Korean Air Lines	
HL7432	Boeing 707-338C	Korean Air Lines	
HL7433	Boeing 707-338C	Korean Air Lines	
HL7435	Boeing 707-321B	Korean Air Lines	
HL7452	Boeing 747-2B5F	Saudia — Saudi Arabian Airlines	
HL7459	Boeing 747-2B5F	Saudia — Saudi Arabian Airlines	

HS (Thailand)

HS-TGA	Boeing 747-2D7B	Thai Airways International *Visuthakasatriya*	
HS-TGB	Boeing 747-2D7B	Thai Airways International *Sirisobhakya*	
HS-TGC	Boeing 747-2D7B	Thai Airways International *Dararasmi*	
HS-TGF	Boeing 747-2D7B	Thai Airways International *Phimara*	
HS-TGG	Boeing 747-2D7B	Thai Airways International *Sriwanna*	
HS-TGS	Boeing 747-2D7B	Thai Airways International	
HS-TGZ	Douglas DC-8-63	Icelandair	

HZ (Saudi Arabia)

HZ-AHA	L.1011-385 TriStar 200	Saudia — Saudi Arabian Airlines	
HZ-AHB	L.1011-385 TriStar 200	Saudia — Saudi Arabian Airlines	
HZ-AHC	L.1011-385 TriStar 200	Saudia — Saudi Arabian Airlines	
HZ-AHD	L.1011-385 TriStar 200	Saudia — Saudi Arabian Airlines	
HZ-AHE	L.1011-385 TriStar 200	Saudia — Saudi Arabian Airlines	
HZ-AHF	L.1011-385 TriStar 200	Saudia — Saudi Arabian Airlines	
HZ-AHG	L.1011-385 TriStar 200	Saudia — Saudi Arabian Airlines	
HZ-AHH	L.1011-385 TriStar 200	Saudia — Saudi Arabian Airlines	
HZ-AHI	L.1011-385 TriStar 200	Saudia — Saudi Arabian Airlines	
HZ-AHJ	L.1011-385 TriStar 200	Saudia — Saudi Arabian Airlines	
HZ-AHL	L.1011-385 TriStar 200	Saudia — Saudi Arabian Airlines	
HZ-AHM	L.1011-385 TriStar 200	Saudia — Saudi Arabian Airlines	
HZ-AHN	L.1011-385 TriStar 200	Saudia — Saudi Arabian Airlines	
HZ-AHO	L.1011-385 TriStar 200	Saudia — Saudi Arabian Airlines	
HZ-AHP	L.1011-385 TriStar 200	Saudia — Saudi Arabian Airlines	
HZ-AHQ	L.1011-385 TriStar 200	Saudia — Saudi Arabian Airlines	
HZ-AHR	L.1011-385 TriStar 200	Saudia — Saudi Arabian Airlines	
HZ-AIA	Boeing 747-168B	Saudia — Saudi Arabian Airlines	
HZ-AIB	Boeing 747-168B	Saudia — Saudi Arabian Airlines	
HZ-AIC	Boeing 747-168B	Saudia — Saudi Arabian Airlines	
HZ-AID	Boeing 747-168B	Saudia — Saudi Arabian Airlines	
HZ-AIE	Boeing 747-168B	Saudia — Saudi Arabian Airlines	
HZ-AIF	Boeing 747SP-68	Saudia — Saudi Arabian Airlines	
HZ-AIG	Boeing 747-168B	Saudia — Saudi Arabian Airlines	
HZ-AIH	Boeing 747-168B	Saudia — Saudi Arabian Airlines	

Notes	Reg.	Type	Owner or Operator
	HZ-AII	Boeing 747-168B	Saudia — Saudi Arabian Airlines
	HZ-AIJ	Boeing 747SP-68	Saudia — Saudi Arabian Airlines

Note: Saudia also operates DC-8s leased from Overseas National and Boeing 747-2B5Fs HL7452 and HL7459 on lease from Korean Airlines.

I (Italy) — **Alitalia**

	Reg.	Type	Owner or Operator
	I-ATIA	Douglas DC-9-32	Aero Trasporti Italiani (ATI) *Polluce*
	I-ATIE	Douglas DC-9-32	Aero Trasporti Italiani (ATI)
	I-ATIH	Douglas DC-9-32	Aermediterranea *Lido degli Estensi*
	I-ATIJ	Douglas DC-9-32	Aero Trasporti Italiani (ATI)
	I-ATIK	Douglas DC-9-32	Aero Trasporti Italiani (ATI) *Sardegna*
	I-ATIO	Douglas DC-9-32	Aero Trasporti Italiani (ATI)
	I-ATIQ	Douglas DC-9-32	Aermediterranea *Sila*
	I-ATIU	Douglas DC-9-32	Aero Trasporti Italiani (ATI)
	I-ATIW	Douglas DC-9-32	Aero Trasporti Italiani (ATI) *Lazio*
	I-ATIX	Douglas DC-9-32	Aero Trasporti Italiani (ATI) *Calabria*
	I-ATIY	Douglas DC-9-32	Aero Trasporti Italiani (ATI) *Lombardia*
	I-ATJA	Douglas DC-9-32	Aero Trasporti Italiani (ATI)
	I-ATJB	Douglas DC-9-32	Aermediterranea *Riviera del Conero*
	I-BUSB	A.300B4 Airbus	Alitalia *Tiziano*
	I-BUSC	A.300B4 Airbus	Alitalia *Botticelli*
	I-BUSD	A.300B4 Airbus	Alitalia *Caravaggio*
	I-BUSF	A.300B4 Airbus	Alitalia *Tintoretto*
	I-BUSG	A.300B4 Airbus	Alitalia *Canaletto*
	I-BUSH	A.300B4 Airbus	Alitalia *Mantegua*
	I-BUSJ	A.300B4 Airbus	Alitalia *Tiepolo*
	I-BUSL	A.300B4 Airbus	Alitalia *Pinturicchia*
	I-DAWA	Douglas DC-9-82	Alitalia *Roma*
	I-DAWB	Douglas DC-9-82	Alitalia *Cagliari*
	I-DAWC	Douglas DC-9-82	Alitalia *Campobasso*
	I-DAWD	Douglas DC-9-82	Alitalia *Catanzaro*
	I-DAWE	Douglas DC-9-82	Alitalia *Milano*
	I-DAWF	Douglas DC-9-82	Alitalia *Firenze*
	I-DAWG	Douglas DC-9-82	Alitalia *L'Aquila*
	I-DAWH	Douglas DC-9-82	Alitalia
	I-DAWI	Douglas DC-9-82	Alitalia *Ancona*
	I-DAWJ	Douglas DC-9-82	Alitalia
	I-DAWL	Douglas DC-9-82	Alitalia
	I-DAWM	Douglas DC-9-82	Alitalia
	I-DAWN	Douglas DC-9-82	Alitalia
	I-DAWO	Douglas DC-9-82	Alitalia *Bari*
	I-DAWP	Douglas DC-9-82	Alitalia
	I-DAWQ	Douglas DC-9-82	Alitalia
	I-DAWR	Douglas DC-9-82	Alitalia
	I-DAWS	Douglas DC-9-82	Alitalia
	I-DAWT	Douglas DC-9-82	Alitalia
	I-DAWU	Douglas DC-9-82	Alitalia *Bologna*
	I-DEMC	Boeing 747-243B	Alitalia *Taormina*
	I-DEMD	Boeing 747-243B	Alitalia *Cortina d'Ampezzo*
	I-DEMF	Boeing 747-243B	Alitalia *Portofino*
	I-DEMG	Boeing 747-243B	Alitalia *Cervinia*
	I-DEML	Boeing 747-243B	Alitalia *Sorrento*
	I-DEMN	Boeing 747-243B	Alitalia *Portocervo*
	I-DEMP	Boeing 747-243B	Alitalia *Capri*
	I-DEMR	Boeing 747-243B	Alitalia *Stresa*
	I-DEMS	Boeing 747-243B	Alitalia *Monte Argentario*
	I-DIBC	Douglas DC-9-32	Alitalia *Isola di Lampedusa*
	I-DIBD	Douglas DC-9-32	Alitalia *Isola di Montecristo*
	I-DIBJ	Douglas DC-9-32	Alitalia *Isola della Capraia*
	I-DIBN	Douglas DC-9-32	Alitalia *Isola della Palmaria*
	I-DIBO	Douglas DC-9-32	Aermediterranea *Conca d'Ora*
	I-DIBQ	Douglas DC-9-32	Alitalia *Isola di Pianosa*
	I-DIKC	Douglas DC-9-32	Alitalia *Isola di Ponza*
	I-DIKM	Douglas DC-9-32	Aero Trasporti Italiani (ATI) *Positano*

Reg.	Type	Owner or Operator	Notes
I-DIKN	Douglas DC-9-32	Aero Trasporti Italiani (ATI)	
I-DIKP	Douglas DC-9-32	Aero Trasporti Italiani (ATI)	
I-DIKR	Douglas DC-9-32	Aero Trasporti Italiani (ATI) *Piemonte*	
I-DIKS	Douglas DC-9-32	Aermediterranea *Isola di Filicudi*	
I-DIKT	Douglas DC-9-32	Aermediterranea *Isola d'Ustica*	
I-DIKV	Douglas DC-9-32	Alitalia *Isola di Vulcano*	
I-DIKY	Douglas DC-9-32	Aero Trasporti Italiani (ATI) *Sicilia*	
I-DIKZ	Douglas DC-9-32	Alitalia *Isola di Linosa*	
I-DIRA	Boeing 727-243	Alitalia *Citta di Gubbio*	
I-DIRB	Boeing 727-243	Alitalia *Citta di Siracusa*	
I-DIRC	Boeing 727-243	Alitalia *Citta di Aosta*	
I-DIRD	Boeing 727-243	Alitalia *Citta di Bergamo*	
I-DIRF	Boeing 727-243	Alitalia *Citta di Lecce*	
I-DIRG	Boeing 727-243	Alitalia *Citta di Urbino*	
I-DIRI	Boeing 727-243	Alitalia *Citta di Siena*	
I-DIRJ	Boeing 727-243	Alitalia *Citta di Verona*	
I-DIRL	Boeing 727-243	Alitalia *Citta di Viterbo*	
I-DIRM	Boeing 727-243	Alitalia *Citta di Genova*	
I-DIRN	Boeing 727-243	Alitalia *Citta di Aquileila*	
I-DIRO	Boeing 727-243	Alitalia *Citta di Amalfi*	
I-DIRP	Boeing 727-243	Alitalia *Citta di Ivrea*	
I-DIRQ	Boeing 727-243	Alitalia *Citta di Sassari*	
I-DIRR	Boeing 727-243	Alitalia *Citta di Trento*	
I-DIRS	Boeing 727-243	Alitalia *Citta di Sulmona*	
I-DIRT	Boeing 727-243	Alitalia *Citta di Matera*	
I-DIRU	Boeing 727-243	Alitalia *Citta di Ravenna*	
I-DIZA	Douglas DC-9-32	Alitalia *Isola di Palmarola*	
I-DIZB	Douglas DC-9-32	Aero Trasporti Italiani (ATI)	
I-DIZC	Douglas DC-9-32	Aero Trasporti Italiani (ATI)	
I-DIZE	Douglas DC-9-32	Aero Trasporti Italiani (ATI)	
I-DIZF	Douglas DC-9-32	Aermediterranea *Dolomiti*	
I-DIZI	Douglas DC-9-32	Aero Trasporti Italiani (ATI)	
I-DIZO	Douglas DC-9-32	Aero Trasporti Italiani (ATI) *Liguria*	
I-DIZU	Douglas DC-9-32	Aero Trasporti Italiani (ATI)	
I-DYNB	Douglas DC-10-30	Alitalia *Giotto di Bondone*	
I-DYNC	Douglas DC-10-30	Alitalia *Luigi Pirandello*	
I-GISE	S.E.210 Caravelle III	Altair *Citta di Civago*	
I-GISI	S.E.210 Caravelle III	Altair	
I-S	Douglas DC-9-82	Alisarda	
I-S	Douglas DC-9-82	Alisarda	

Note: Alisarda also uses DC-9s which retain their Swiss registrations HB-IKF, HB-IKG and HB-IKH. Altair uses a Caravelle which carries its French registration F-BHRS. Alitalia is in the process of changing its DC-9 fleet. Nine of its DC-9-32s have been reregistered N901DC, N902DC, N903DC, N904DC, N905DC, N906DC, N2786S, N2786T and N4326S. These will gradually be replaced by Srs 82s.

J2 (Djibouti)

J2-KAD	Boeing 727-21C	Air Djibouti	

JA (Japan)

JA8036	Douglas DC-8-62AF	Japan Air Lines	
JA8044	Douglas DC-8-62AF	Japan Air Lines	
JA8055	Douglas DC-8-62AF	Japan Air Lines	
JA8101	Boeing 747-146	Japan Air Lines	
JA8104	Boeing 747-246B	Japan Air Lines	
JA8105	Boeing 747-246B	Japan Air Lines	
JA8106	Boeing 747-246B	Japan Air Lines	
JA8107	Boeing 747-146A	Japan Air Lines	
JA8108	Boeing 747-246B	Japan Air Lines	

Notes	Reg.	Type	Owner or Operator
	JA8110	Boeing 747-246B	Japan Air Lines
	JA8111	Boeing 747-246B	Japan Air Lines
	JA8112	Boeing 747-146A	Japan Air Lines
	JA8113	Boeing 747-246B	Japan Air Lines
	JA8114	Boeing 747-246B	Japan Air Lines
	JA8115	Boeing 747-146A	Japan Air Lines
	JA8116	Boeing 747-146A	Japan Air Lines
	JA8122	Boeing 747-246B	Japan Air Lines
	JA8123	Boeing 747-246F	Japan Air Lines
	JA8125	Boeing 747-246B	Japan Air Lines
	JA8127	Boeing 747-246B	Japan Air Lines
	JA8128	Boeing 747-146A	Japan Air Lines
	JA8129	Boeing 747-246B	Japan Air Lines
	JA8130	Boeing 747-246B	Japan Air Lines
	JA8131	Boeing 747-246B	Japan Air Lines
	JA8132	Boeing 747-246F	Japan Air Lines
	JA8140	Boeing 747-246B	Japan Air Lines
	JA8141	Boeing 747-246B	Japan Air Lines
	JA8142	Boeing 747-146B	Japan Air Lines
	JA8143	Boeing 747-146B	Japan Air Lines
	JA8144	Boeing 747-246F	Japan Air Lines
	JA8149	Boeing 747-246B	Japan Air Lines
	JA8150	Boeing 747-246B	Japan Air Lines
	JA8151	Boeing 747-246F	Japan Air Lines
	JA8154	Boeing 747-246B	Japan Air Lines
	JA8155	Boeing 747-246B	Japan Air Lines
	JA8161	Boeing 747-246B	Japan Air Lines
	JA8162	Boeing 747-246B	Japan Air Lines
	JA8534	Douglas DC-10-40	Japan Air Lines
	JA8535	Douglas DC-10-40	Japan Air Lines
	JA8538	Douglas DC-10-40	Japan Air Lines
	JA8539	Douglas DC-10-40	Japan Air Lines
	JA8541	Douglas DC-10-40	Japan Air Lines
	JA8542	Douglas DC-10-40	Japan Air Lines
	JA8543	Douglas DC-10-40	Japan Air Lines
	JA8544	Douglas DC-10-40	Japan Air Lines
	JA8545	Douglas DC-10-40	Japan Air Lines
	JA8547	Douglas DC-10-40	Japan Air Lines

Note: Japan Air Lines also operated a Boeing 747-221F which retains its US registration N211JL and two 747-346s N212JL and N213JL.

JY (Jordan)

	JY-ADP	Boeing 707-3D3C	Alia — The Royal Jordanian Airline *City of Amman*
	JY-AEB	Boeing 707-384C	Alia — The Royal Jordanian Airline
	JY-AEC	Boeing 707-384C	Sierra Leone Airlines
	JY-AES	Boeing 707-321C	Alia — The Royal Jordanian Airline
	JY-AFA	Boeing 747-2D3B	Alia — The Royal Jordanian Airline *Prince Ali*
	JY-AFB	Boeing 747-2D3B	Alia — The Royal Jordanian Airline *Princess Haya*
	JY-AFS	Boeing 747-2D3B	Alia — The Royal Jordanian Airline *Prince Hamzah*
	JY-AGA	L.1011-385 TriStar 500	Alia — The Royal Jordanian Airline *Abas Bin Firnas*
	JY-AGB	L.1011-385 TriStar 500	Alia — The Royal Jordanian Airline *Ibn Batouta*
	JY-AGC	L.1011-385 TriStar 500	Alia — The Royal Jordanian Airline
	JY-AGD	L.1011-385 TriStar 500	Alia — The Royal Jordanian Airline
	JY-AGE	L.1011-385 TriStar 500	Alia — The Royal Jordanian Airline
	JY-CAB	Boeing 707-321C	Arab Air Cargo
	JY-CAC	Boeing 707-321C	Arab Air Cargo

LN (Norway)

FRED OLSEN AIRTRANSPORT

Reg.	Type	Owner or Operator	Notes
LN-AEO	Boeing 747-283B	S.A.S.	
LN-AET	Boeing 747-283B	S.A.S.	
LN-BWG	Convair 580	Nor-Fly	
LN-BWN	Convair 580	Nor-Fly	
LN-FOG	L-188AF Electra	Fred Olsen Airtransport	
LN-FOH	L-188AF Electra	Fred Olsen Airtransport	
LN-FOI	L-188CF Electra	Fred Olsen Airtransport	
LN-KLK	Convair 440	Nor-Fly	
LN-MAP	Convair 440	Nor-Fly	
LN-MOF	Douglas DC-8-63	S.A.S. *Tyra Viking*	
LN-MOW	Douglas DC-8-62	*S.A.S. Roald Viking*	
LN-NPB	Boeing 737-2R4C	Busy Bee	
LN-NPC	F-27 Friendship Mk 100	Busy Bee	
LN-NPH	F.27 Friendship Mk 300	Busy Bee	
LN-NPI	F.27 Friendship Mk 100	Busy Bee	
LN-NPM	F.27 Friendship Mk 100	Busy Bee	
LN-RCA	A.300B4 Airbus	S.A.S. Scanair *Snorre Viking*	
LN-RKA	Douglas DC-10-30	S.A.S. *Olav Viking*	
LN-RKB	Douglas DC-30-30	S.A.S. *Haakon Viking*	
LN-RLA	Douglas DC-9-41	S.A.S. *Are Viking*	
LN-RLB	Douglas DC-9-41	S.A.S. *Arne Viking*	
LN-RLC	Douglas DC-9-41	S.A.S. *Gunnar Viking*	
LN-RLD	Douglas DC-9-41	S.A.S. *Torleif Viking*	
LN-RLH	Douglas DC-9-41	S.A.S. *Einar Viking*	
LN-RLJ	Douglas DC-9-41	S.A.S. *Stein Viking*	
LN-RLK	Douglas DC-9-41	S.A.S. *Erling Viking*	
LN-RLL	Douglas DC-9-21	S.A.S. *Guttorm Viking*	
LN-RLN	Douglas DC-9-41	S.A.S. *Halldor Viking*	
LN-RLO	Douglas DC-9-21	S.A.S. *Gunder Viking*	
LN-RLP	Douglas DC-9-41	S.A.S. *Froste Viking*	
LN-RLS	Douglas DC-9-41	S.A.S. *Asmund Viking*	
LN-RLT	Douglas DC-9-41	S.A.S. *Audun Viking*	
LN-RLU	Douglas DC-9-41	S.A.S. *Eivind Viking*	
LN-RLW	Douglas DC-9-33AF	S.A.S. *Rand Viking*	
LN-RLX	Douglas DC-9-41	S.A.S. *Sote Viking*	
LN-RLZ	Douglas DC-9-41	S.A.S. *Bodvar Viking*	
LN-SUA	Boeing 737-205C	Braathens SAFE *Halvdan Svarte*	
LN-SUB	Boeing 737-205	Braathens SAFE *Magnus Den Gode*	
LN-SUC	F.28 Fellowship 1000	Braathens SAFE *Olav Kyrre*	
LN-SUD	Boeing 737-205	Braathens SAFE *Olav Tryggvason*	
LN-SUE	F.27 Friendship Mk 100	Busy Bee	
LN-SUF	F.27 Friendship Mk 100	Busy Bee	
LN-SUG	Boeing 737-205	Braathens SAFE *Harald Harfagre*	
LN-SUH	Boeing 737-205	Braathens SAFE *Sigurd Jorsalfar*	
LN-SUI	Boeing 737-205	Braathens SAFE *Haakon den Gode*	
LN-SUK	Boeing 737-205	Braathens SAFE *Olav Haraldsson*	
LN-SUL	F.27 Friendship Mk 100	Busy Bee	
LN-SUM	Boeing 737-205	Braathens SAFE *Magnus Lagaboter*	
LN-SUN	F.28 Fellowship 1000	Braathens SAFE *Haakon Sverresson*	
LN-SUO	F.28 Fellowship 1000	Braathens SAFE *Magnus Barfot*	
LN-SUP	Boeing 737-205	Braathens SAFE *Haakon IV Hakonsson*	
LN-SUS	Boeing 737-205	Braathens SAFE *Haakon V Magnusson*	
LN-SUT	Boeing 737-205	Braathens SAFE *Oystein Magnusson*	
LN-SUV	Boeing 767-205	Braathens	
LN-SUW	Boeing 767-205	Bratthens	
LN-SUX	F.28 Fellowship 1000	Braathens SAFE *Harald Hardrade*	

Note: S.A.S. also operates two Boeing 747-283Bs which retain their US registrations
N4501Q and N4502R and DC-9-51 YU-AJU from Inex Adria.

LV (Argentina)

Notes	Reg.	Type	Owner or Operator
	LV-MLO	Boeing 747-287B	Metro International
	LV-MLP	Boeing 747-287B	Aerolineas Argentinas
	LV-MLR	Boeing 747-287B	Aerolineas Argentinas
	LV-OEP	Boeing 747-287B	Aerolineas Argentinas
	LV-OOZ	Boeing 747-287B	Aerolineas Argentinas
	LV-OPA	Boeing 747-287B	Aerolineas Argentinas

Note: Services to the UK are suspended.

LX (Luxembourg)

	LX-DCV	Boeing 747-2R7F	Cargolux *City of Luxembourg*
	LX-ECV	Boeing 747-2R7F	Cargolux *City of Esch sur Alzette*
	LX-LGA	F.27 Friendship Mk 100	Luxair *Prince Henri*
	LX-LGB	F.27 Friendship Mk 100	Luxair *Prince Jean*
	LX-LGD	F.27 Friendship Mk 400	Luxair *Princess Margaretha*
	LX-LGH	Boeing 737-2C9	Luxair *Prince Guillaume*
	LX-LGI	Boeing 737-2C9	Luxair *Princess Marie-Astrid*
	LX-LGS	Boeing 707-344C	Luxavia
	LX-LGT	Boeing 707-344C	Luxavia

Note: Cargolux also operates DC-8-63CF TF-BCV.

LZ (Bulgaria)

	LZ-BEA	Ilyushin IL-18D	Balkan Bulgarian Airlines
	LZ-BEK	Ilyushin IL-18V	Balkan Bulgarian Airlines
	LZ-BEL	Ilyushin IL-18V	Balkan Bulgarian Airlines
	LZ-BEO	Ilyushin IL-18D	Balkan Bulgarian Airlines
	LZ-BEP	Ilyushin IL-18V	Balkan Bulgarian Airlines
	LZ-BET	Ilyushin IL-18D	Balkan Bulgarian Airlines
	LZ-BEV	Ilyushin IL-18V	Balkan Bulgarian Airlines
	LZ-BTA	Tupolev Tu-154B	Balkan Bulgarian Airlines
	LZ-BTC	Tupolev Tu-154B	Balkan Bulgarian Airlines
	LZ-BTD	Tupolev Tu-154B	Balkan Bulgarian Airlines
	LZ-BTE	Tupolev Tu-154B	Balkan Bulgarian Airlines
	LZ-BTF	Tupolev Tu-154B	Balkan Bulgarian Airlines
	LZ-BTG	Tupolev Tu-154B	Balkan Bulgarian Airlines
	LZ-BTJ	Tupolev Tu-154B	Balkan Bulgarian Airlines
	LZ-BTK	Tupolev Tu-154B	Balkan Bulgarian Airlines
	LZ-BTL	Tupolev Tu-154B	Balkan Bulgarian Airlines
	LZ-BTM	Tupolev Tu-154B	Balkan Bulgarian Airlines
	LZ-BTO	Tupolev Tu-154B	Balkan Bulgarian Airlines
	LZ-BTP	Tupolev Tu-154B	Balkan Bulgarian Airlines
	LZ-BTR	Tupolev Tu-154B	Balkan Bulgarian Airlines
	LZ-BTS	Tupolev Tu-154B	Balkan Bulgarian Airlines
	LZ-BTT	Tupolev Tu-154B	Balkan Bulgarian Airlines
	LZ-BTU	Tupolev Tu-154B	Balkan Bulgarian Airlines
	LZ-BTV	Tupolev Tu-154B	Balkan Bulgarian Airlines
	LZ-TUA	Tupolev Tu-134	Balkan Bulgarian Airlines
	LZ-TUC	Tupolev Tu-134	Balkan Bulgarian Airlines
	LZ-TUD	Tupolev Tu-134	Balkan Bulgarian Airlines
	LZ-TUE	Tupolev Tu-134	Balkan Bulgarian Airlines
	LZ-TUF	Tupolev Tu-134	Balkan Bulgarian Airlines

Reg.	Type	Owner or Operator	Notes
LZ-TUK	Tupolev Tu-134A	Balkan Bulgarian Airlines	
LZ-TUL	Tupolev Tu-134A	Balkan Bulgarian Airlines	
LZ-TUM	Tupolev Tu-134A	Balkan Bulgarian Airlines	
LZ-TUN	Tupolev Tu-134A	Balkan Bulgarian Airlines	
LZ-TUO	Tupolev Tu-134	Balkan Bulgarian Airlines	
LZ-TUP	Tupolev Tu-134A	Balkan Bulgarian Airlines	
LZ-TUR	Tupolev Tu-134A	Balkan Bulgarian Airlines	
LZ-TUS	Tupolev Tu-134A	Balkan Bulgarian Airlines	

N (USA)

 TRANSAMERICA   ALASKA INTERNATIONAL AIR

 DELTA AIR LINES

 WORLD    CAPITOL INTERNATIONAL AIRWAYS

N10ST	L-100-30 Hercules	Transamerica Airlines	
N11ST	L-100-30 Hercules	Transamerica Airlines	
N12ST	L-100-30 Hercules	Transamerica Airlines	
N15ST	L-100-30 Hercules	Transamerica Airlines	
N16ST	L-100-30 Hercules	Transamerica Airlines	
N18ST	L-100-30 Hercules	Transamerica Airlines	
N19ST	L-100-30 Hercules	Transamerica Airlines	
N20ST	L-100-30 Hercules	Transamerica Airlines	
N21ST	L-100-30 Hercules	Transamerica Airlines	
N23ST	L-100-30 Hercules	Transamerica Airlines	
N24ST	L-100-30 Hercules	Transamerica Airlines	
N63AF	Boeing 737-222	Pan Am *Clipper Schoneberg*	
N64AF	Boeing 737-222	Pan Am *Clipper Spandau*	
N67AF	Boeing 737-222	Pan Am *Clipper Templehof*	
N68AF	Boeing 737-222	Pan Am *Clipper Zehlendorf*	
N69AF	Boeing 737-222	Pan Am *Clipper Charlottenburg*	
N80NA	Douglas DC-10-30	American Airlines	
N81NA	Douglas DC-10-30	American Airlines	
N82NA	Douglas DC-10-30	American Airlines	
N83NA	Douglas DC-10-30	American Airlines	
N84NA	Douglas DC-10-30	Pan Am *Clipper Glory of the Skies*	
N92TA	L-1011-385 TriStar 100	Gulf Air	
N92TB	L-1011-385 TriStar 100	Gulf Air	
N101AK	L-100-30 Hercules	Alaska International Air	
N103WA	Douglas DC-10-30CF	World Airways	
N104AK	L-100-30 Hercules	Alaska International Air	
N104WA	Douglas DC-10-30CF	World Airways	
N105WA	Douglas DC-10-30CF	World Airways	
N106AK	L-100-30 Hercules	Alaska International Air	
N106WA	Douglas DC-10-30CF	World Airways	
N107AK	L-100-30 Hercules	Alaska International Air	
N107WA	Douglas DC-10-30CF	World Airways	
N108AK	L-100-30 Hercules	Alaska International Air	
N108WA	Douglas DC-10-30CF	World Airways	
N109RD	Douglas DC-8-54	Arrow Air	
N109WA	Douglas DC-10-30CF	Air Florida	
N112WA	Douglas DC-10-30CF	World Airways	
N116KB	Boeing 747-312B	Singapore Airlines	
N117KC	Boeing 747-312B	Singapore Airlines	
N118KD	Boeing 747-312B	Singapore Airlines	
N119KE	Boeing 747-312B	Singapore Airlines	
N120KF	Boeing 747-312B	Singapore Airlines	
N121KG	Boeing 747-312B	Singapore Airlines	
N121AE	Canadair CL-44D-4	Air Express International	
N122AE	Canadair CL-44D-4	Air Express International	

Notes	Reg.	Type	Owner or Operator
	N122KH	Boeing 747-312B	Singapore Airlines
	N133TW	Boeing 747-146	Trans World Airlines
	N134TW	Boeing 747-156	Trans World Airlines
	N136AA	Douglas DC-10-30	American Airlines
	N137AA	Douglas DC-10-30	American Airlines
	N138AA	Douglas DC-10-30	American Airlines
	N183AT	Douglas DC-10-10	American Trans Air *City of Indiannapolis*
	N211JL	Boeing 747-221F	Japan Air Lines
	N212JL	Boeing 747-346	Japan Air Lines
	N213JL	Boeing 747-346	Japan Air Lines
	N221GE	Boeing 747-357	Swissair *Geneve*
	N221GF	Boeing 747-357	Swissair *Zurich*
	N345HC	Douglas DC-10-30ER	Finnair
	N356AS	Boeing 747-143	Overseas National Airways
	N358AS	Boeing 747-243B	Overseas National Airways
	N380PA	Boeing 737-275	Pan Am *Clipper Neukölln*
	N381PA	Boeing 737-275	Pan Am *Clipper Wedding*
	N382PA	Boeing 737-214	Pan Am *Clipper Kreuzberg*
	N383PA	Boeing 737-2A9C	Pan Am *Clipper Steglitz*
	N385PA	Boeing 737-2Q9	Pan Am *Clipper Berlin*
	N387PA	Boeing 737-296	Pan Am *Clipper Tiergarten*
	N388PA	Boeing 737-296	Pan Am *Clipper Reinickendorf*
	N389PA	Boeing 737-296	Pan Am *Clipper Frankfurt*
	N480GX	Boeing 747-130	Overseas National Airways
	N529PA	Boeing 747SP-27	Pan Am *Clipper America*
	N530PA	Boeing 747SP-21	Pan Am *Clipper Mayflower*
	N531PA	Boeing 747SP-21	Pan Am *Clipper Freedom*
	N532PA	Boeing 747SP-21	Pan Am *Clipper Constitution*
	N533PA	Boeing 747SP-21	Pan Am *Clipper San Francisco*
	N534PA	Boeing 747SP-21	Pan Am *Clipper Great Republic*
	N536PA	Boeing 747SP-21	Pan Am *Clipper Lindbergh*
	N537PA	Boeing 747SP-21	Pan Am *Clipper Washington*
	N538PA	Boeing 747SP-21	Pan Am *Clipper Plymouth Rock*
	N539PA	Boeing 747SP-21	Pan Am *Clipper Liberty Bell*
	N540PA	Boeing 747SP-21	Pan Am *China Clipper*
	N601US	Boeing 747-151	Northwest Orient
	N602PE	Boeing 747-227B	People Express
	N602US	Boeing 747-151	Northwest Orient
	N603US	Boeing 747-151	Northwest Orient
	N604US	Boeing 747-151	Northwest Orient
	N605US	Boeing 747-151	Northwest Orient
	N606US	Boeing 747-151	Northwest Orient
	N607US	Boeing 747-151	Northwest Orient
	N608US	Boeing 747-151	Northwest Orient
	N609US	Boeing 747-151	Northwest Orient
	N610US	Boeing 747-151	Northwest Orient
	N611US	Boeing 747-251B	Northwest Orient
	N612US	Boeing 747-251B	Northwest Orient
	N613US	Boeing 747-251B	Northwest Orient
	N614US	Boeing 747-251B	Northwest Orient
	N615US	Boeing 747-251B	Northwest Orient
	N616US	Boeing 747-251F	Northwest Orient
	N617US	Boeing 747-251F	Northwest Orient
	N618US	Boeing 747-251F	Northwest Orient
	N619US	Boeing 747-251F	Northwest Orient
	N620US	Boeing 747-135	Northwest Orient
	N621US	Boeing 747-135	Northwest Orient
	N622US	Boeing 747-251B	Northwest Orient
	N623US	Boeing 747-251B	Northwest Orient
	N624US	Boeing 747-251B	Northwest Orient
	N625US	Boeing 747-251B	Northwest Orient
	N626US	Boeing 747-251B	Northwest Orient
	N627US	Boeing 747-251B	Northwest Orient
	N628US	Boeing 747-251B	Northwest Orient
	N629US	Boeing 747-251F	Northwest Orient
	N630US	Boeing 747-2J9F	Northwest Orient
	N631US	Boeing 747-251B	Northwest Orient
	N632US	Boeing 747-251B	Northwest Orient
	N633US	Boeing 747-227B	Northwest Orient
	N634US	Boeing 747-227B	Northwest Orient
	N651TF	Boeing 707-351B	Jet 24

N385PA   Boeing 757-209 of Pan Am.

Reg.	Type	Owner or Operator	Notes
N652PA	Boeing 747-121	Pan Am *Clipper Mermaid*	
N653PA	Boeing 747-121	Pan Am *Clipper Pride of the Ocean*	
N655PA	Boeing 747-121	Pan Am *Clipper Sea Serpent*	
N656PA	Boeing 747-121	Pan Am *Clipper Empress of the Seas*	
N657PA	Boeing 747-121	Pan Am *Clipper Seven Seas*	
N659PA	Boeing 747-121	Pan Am *Clipper Plymouth Rock*	
N707AD	Boeing 707-327C	Arrow Air	
N707JJ	Boeing 707-324C	Arrow Air	
N707ME	Boeing 707-338C	Arrow Air	
N707PD	Boeing 707-347C	Arrow Air	
N707SH	Boeing 707-324C	Arrow Air	
N720GS	Boeing 707-321C	Pan Aviation	
N722GS	Boeing 707-321C	Pan Aviation	
N723GS	Boeing 707-355C	Pan Aviation	
N728PA	Boeing 747-212B	Pan Am *Clipper Water Witch*	
N729PA	Boeing 747-212B	Pan Am	
N730PA	Boeing 747-212B	Pan Am	
N731PA	Boeing 747-121	Pan Am *Clipper Ocean Express*	
N732PA	Boeing 747-121	Pan Am *Clipper Ocean Telegraph*	
N733PA	Boeing 747-121	Pan Am *Clipper Pride of the Sea*	
N734PA	Boeing 747-121	Pan Am *Clipper Champion of the Seas*	
N735PA	Boeing 747-121	Pan Am *Clipper Spark of the Ocean*	
N737PA	Boeing 747-121	Pan Am *Clipper Ocean Herald*	
N739PA	Boeing 747-121	Pan Am *Clipper Maid of the Seas*	
N740PA	Boeing 747-121	Pan Am *Clipper Ocean Pearl*	
N741PA	Boeing 747-121	Pan Am *Clipper Sparkling Wave*	
N741PR	Boeing 747-2F6B	Philippine Airlines	
N741TV	Boeing 747-271C	Transamerica Airlines	
N742PA	Boeing 747-121	Pan Am *Clipper Neptune's Car*	
N742PR	Boeing 747-2F6B	Philippine Airlines	
N742TV	Boeing 747-271C	Transamerica Airlines	
N743PA	Boeing 747-121	Pan Am *Clipper Black Sea*	
N743PR	Boeing 747-2F6B	Philippine Airlines	
N743TV	Boeing 747-271C	Transamerica Airlines	
N744PA	Boeing 747-121	Pan Am *Clipper Ocean Spray*	
N744PR	Boeing 747-2F6B	Philippine Airlines	
N747BC	Boeing 747-212B	Nigerian Airways	
N747PA	Boeing 747-121	Pan Am *Clipper Juan J. Trippe*	
N747WR	Boeing 747-273C	World Airways	
N748PA	Boeing 747-121	Pan Am *Clipper Crest of the Wave*	
N748WA	Boeing 747-273C	World Airways	
N749PA	Boeing 747-121	Pan Am *Clipper Gem of the Ocean*	
N750PA	Boeing 747-121	Pan Am *Clipper Neptune's Favorite*	
N751DA	L-1011-385 TriStar 500	Delta Air Lines	
N751PA	Boeing 747-121	Pan Am *Clipper Gem of the Seas*	
N752DA	L-1011-385 TriStar 500	Delta Air Lines	
N753DA	L-1011-385 TriStar 500	Delta Air Lines	
N753PA	Boeing 747-121	Pan Am *Clipper Queen of the Seas*	
N754PA	Boeing 747-121	Pan Am *Clipper Ocean Rover*	
N755PA	Boeing 747-121	Pan Am *Clipper Sovereign of the Seas*	
N770PA	Boeing 747-121	Pan Am *Clipper Queen of the Pacific*	
N772FT	Douglas DC-8-63CF	Flying Tiger Line	
N773FT	Douglas DC-8-63CF	Flying Tiger Line	
N776FT	Douglas DC-8-63CF	Flying Tiger Line	
N778PA	Boeing 707-139B	Maof Airlines	
N781FT	Douglas DC-8-63CF	Flying Tiger Line	
N783FT	Douglas DC-8-63AF	Air India Cargo	
N790FT	Douglas DC-8-63AF	Flying Tiger Line	
N791FT	Douglas DC-8-63CF	Flying Tiger Line	
N792FT	Douglas DC-8-63CF	Flying Tiger Line	
N795FT	Douglas DC-8-63CF	Flying Tiger Line	
N796FT	Douglas DC-8-63CF	Flying Tiger Line	
N797FT	Douglas DC-8-63CF	Flying Tiger Line	
N798FT	Douglas DC-8-63CF	Flying Tiger Line	
N801WA	Douglas DC-8-63CF	World Airways	
N803FT	Boeing 747-132F	Flying Tiger Line	
N804FT	Boeing 747-132F	Flying Tiger Line	
N805FT	Boeing 747-132F	Flying Tiger Line	
N805WA	Douglas DC-8-63CF	Capitol Air	
N806FT	Boeing 747-249F	Flying Tiger Line *Robert W. Prescott*	
N807FT	Boeing 747-249F	Flying Tiger Line *Thomas Haywood*	

Notes	Reg.	Type	Owner or Operator
	N808FT	Boeing 747-249F	Flying Tiger Line *William E. Bartlett*
	N810FT	Boeing 747-249F	Flying Tiger Line *Clifford G. Groh*
	N811EV	Douglas DC-8-63CF	Evergreen International Airlines
	N811FT	Boeing 747-245F	Flying Tiger Line
	N812FT	Boeing 747-245F	Flying Tiger Line
	N813FT	Boeing 747-245F	Flying Tiger Line
	N814FT	Boeing 747-245F	Flying Tiger Line
	N815FT	Boeing 747-245F	Flying Tiger Line *W. Henry Renniger*
	N816FT	Boeing 747-245F	Flying Tiger Line *Henry L. Heguy*
	N817FT	Boeing 747-121F	Flying Tiger Line
	N818FT	Boeing 747-121F	Flying Tiger Line
	N819FT	Boeing 747-121F	Flying Tiger Line
	N820FT	Boeing 747-121F	Flying Tiger Line
	N863FT	Douglas DC-8-61CF	Flying Tiger Line
	N864FT	Douglas DC-8-61CF	Flying Tiger Line
	N865F	Douglas DC-8-63CF	Saudia — Saudi Arabian Airlines
	N867FT	Douglas DC-8-61CF	Pacific East Air
	N868FT	Douglas DC-8-61CF	Flying Tiger Line
	N870TV	Douglas DC-8-63CF	Transamerica Airlines
	N871TV	Douglas DC-8-63CF	Transamerica Airlines
	N872TV	Douglas DC-8-63CF	Transamerica Airlines
	N901DC	Douglas DC-9-32	Alitalia *Isola di Capri*
	N901PA	Boeing 747-123F	Pan Am *Clipper Telegraph*
	N902DC	Douglas DC-9-32	Alitalia *Isola d'Elba*
	N902JW	Douglas DC-10-10	Arrow Air
	N902PA	Boeing 747-132	Pan Am *Clipper Seaman's Bridge*
	N902R	Douglas DC-8-55	Overseas National Airways
	N903DC	Douglas DC-9-32	Alitalia *Isola di Murano*
	N904DC	Douglas DC-9-32	Alitalia *Isola di Pantellaria*
	N904PA	Boeing 747-221F	Pan Am *Clipper Industry*
	N905DC	Douglas DC-9-32	Alitalia *Isola d'Ischia*
	N905WA	Douglas DC-10-10	Capitol Air
	N906DC	Douglas DC-9-32	Alitalia *Isola del Giglio*
	N906R	Douglas DC-8-63CF	Air India Cargo
	N907CL	Douglas DC-8-63CF	Capitol Air
	N910CL	Douglas DC-8-63CF	Capitol Air
	N910R	Douglas DC-8-55	Saudia — Saudi Arabian Airlines
	N912R	Douglas DC-8-61	Overseas National Airways
	N914CL	Douglas DC-8-61	Capitol Air
	N915CL	Douglas DC-8-61	Capitol Air
	N915R	Douglas DC-8-61	Saudia — Saudi Arabian Airlines
	N916CL	Douglas DC-10-10	Capitol Air
	N916R	Douglas DC-8-55	Icelandair
	N917CL	Douglas DC-10-10	Arrow Air
	N917R	Douglas DC-8-71	Overseas National Airways
	N918CL	Douglas DC-8-51	Capitol Air
	N919CL	Douglas DC-8-73CF	Arrow Air
	N920CL	Douglas DC-8-63PF	Arista International *Karo*
	N921R	Douglas DC-8-63CF	Overseas National Airways
	N922CL	Douglas DC-8-62	Capitol Air
	N923CL	Douglas DC-8-62	Capitol Air
	N1252E	Boeing 747-228B	Air France
	N1289E	Boeing 747-228B	Air France
	N1295E	Boeing 747-206B	K.L.M. *The Ganges*
	N1298E	Boeing 747-206B	K.L.M. *The Indus*
	N1304E	Boeing 747SP-J6	CAAC
	N1305E	Boeing 747-228B	Air France
	N1309E	Boeing 747-206B	K.L.M. *Admiral Richard E. Byrd*
	N1805	Douglas DC-8-62	Rich International Airways
	N1808E	Douglas DC-8-62	Rich International Airways
	N2674U	Douglas DC-8-63CF	Arrow Air
	N2786S	Douglas DC-9-32	Alitalia *Isola di Giannutri*
	N2786T	Douglas DC-9-32	Alitalia *Isola di Panarea*
	N2941W	Boeing 737-2K5	Air Berlin
	N3140D	L.1011 TriStar 500	B.W.I.A.
	N3238N	Boeing 707-329C	Jet 24
	N3238S	Boeing 707-329C	Jet 24
	N3931A	Douglas DC-8-62CF	Sea & Sun Aviation
	N3931G	Douglas DC-8-62CF	Pacific East Air
	N4326S	Douglas DC-9-32	Alitalia *Isola di Lipari*
	N4501Q	Boeing 747-283B	S.A.S. *Dan Viking*

Reg.	Type	Owner or Operator	Notes
N4502R	Boeing 747-283B	S.A.S. *Huge Viking*	
N4506H	Boeing 747-228B	Air France	
N4508E	Boeing 747-228F	Air France	
N4548M	Boeing 747-306	K.L.M. *Sir Frank Whittle*	
N4703U	Being 747-122	United Airlines *William M. Allen*	
N4726U	Boeing 747-122	United Airlines	
N4717U	Boeing 747-122	United Airlines *Edward E. Carlson*	
N4720U	Boeing 747-122	United Airlines	
N4727U	Boeing 747-122	United Airlines	
N4864T	Douglas DC-8-63CF	Evergreen International Airlines	
N4865T	Douglas DC-8-73CF	Transamerica Airlines	
N4866T	Douglas DC-8-73CF	Transamerica Airlines	
N4867T	Douglas DC-8-63CF	Transamerica Airlines	
N4868T	Douglas DC-8-63CF	Transamerica Airlines	
N4869T	Douglas DC-8-63CF	Transamerica Airlines	
N4902W	Boeing 737-210C	Pan Am *Clipper Wilmersdorf*	
N6161A	Douglas DC-8-63CF	Arrow Air	
N6162A	Douglas DC-8-63CF	Arrow Air	
N7035T	L.1011 TriStar 100	Trans World Airlines	
N7036T	L.1011 TriStar 100	Trans World Airlines	
N7515A	Boeing 707-123B	American Trans Air	
N7554A	Boeing 707-123B	American Trans Air	
N7570A	Boeing 707-123B	American Trans Air	
N7573A	Boeing 707-123B	American Trans Air	
N7589A	Boeing 707-123B	American Trans Air	
N7597A	Boeing 707-323C	American Trans Air	
N7599A	Boeing 707-323C	American Trans Air	
N7984S	L-100-20 Hercules	Southern Air Transport	
N8034T	L.1011 TriStar 100	Trans World Airlines	
N8075U	Douglas DC-8-61	Arrow Air	
N8416	Boeing 707-323C	American Trans Air	
N8763	Douglas DC-8-61	Airlift International	
N8764	Douglas DC-8-61	Airlift International	
N8765	Douglas DC-8-61	Airlift International	
N8766	Douglas DC-8-61	Saudia — Saudi Arabian Airlines	
N8968U	Douglas DC-8-62	Arrow Air	
N8969U	Douglas DC-8-62	Arrow Air	
N8974U	Douglas DC-8-62	Arrow Air	
N9232R	L-100-30 Hercules	Southern Air Transport	
N9266R	L-100-20 Hercules	Southern Air Transport	
N17125	Boeing 747-136	Trans World Airlines	
N17126	Boeing 747-136	Trans World Airlines	
N18712	Boeing 707-331B	Maof Airlines	
N31019	L.1011-385 TriStar 50	Trans World Airlines	
N31023	L.1011-385 TriStar 50	Trans World Airlines	
N31024	L.1011-385 TriStar 50	Trans World Airlines	
N31029	L.1011-385 TriStar 100	Trans World Airlines	
N31030	L.1011-385 TriStar 100	Trans World Airlines	
N31031	L.1011-385 TriStar 100	Trans World Airlines	
N31032	L.1011-385 TriStar 100	Trans World Airlines	
N31033	L.1011-385 TriStar 100	Trans World Airlines	
N39305	Douglas DC-8-62	Pacific East Air	
N39307	Douglas DC-8-62	Sea & Sun Aviation	
N41020	L.1011-385 TriStar 50	Trans World Airlines	
N53110	Boeing 747-131	Trans World Airlines	
N53116	Boeing 747-131	Trans World Airlines	
N57202	Boeing 747SP-31	Trans World Airlines	
N57203	Boeing 747SP-31	Trans World Airlines	
N58201	Boeing 747SP-31	Trans World Airlines	
N70723	Boeing 737-297	Pan Am	
N70724	Boeing 737-297	Pan Am	
N81025	L.1011-385 TriStar 100	Trans World Airlines	
N81026	L.1011-385 TriStar 100	Trans World Airlines	
N81027	L.1011-385 TriStar 50	Trans World Airlines	
N81028	L.1011-385 TriStar 100	Trans World Airlines	
N93104	Boeing 747-131	Trans World Airlines	
N93105	Boeing 747-131	Trans World Airlines	
N93106	Boeing 747-131	Trans World Airlines	
N93107	Boeing 747-131	Trans World Airlines	
N93108	Boeing 747-131	Trans World Airlines	
N93109	Boeing 747-131	Trans World Airlines	

Notes	Reg.	Type	Owner or Operator
	N93115	Boeing 747-131	Trans World Airlines
	N93117	Boeing 747-131	Trans World Airlines
	N93119	Boeing 747-131	Trans World Airlines

Note: Arista International operates DC-8-62 SE-DBI on lease from S.A.S., and Metro International operates Boeing 747-287B LV-MLO on lease from Aerolineas Argentinas.

OD (Lebanon)

	OD-AFD	Boeing 707-3B4C	Middle East Airlines
	OD-AFE	Boeing 707-3B4C	Middle East Airlines
	OD-AFL	Boeing 720-023B	Middle East Airlines
	OD-AFM	Boeing 720-023B	Middle East Airlines
	OD-AFN	Boeing 720-023B	Middle East Airlines
	OD-AFQ	Boeing 720-023B	Middle East Airlines
	OD-AFS	Boeing 720-023B	Middle East Airlines
	OD-AFY	Boeing 707-327C	Trans Mediterranean Airways
	OD-AFZ	Boeing 720-023B	Middle East Airlines
	OD-AGB	Boeing 720-023B	Middle East Airlines
	OD-AGD	Boeing 707-323C	Trans Mediterranean Airways
	OD-AGF	Boeing 720-047B	Middle East Airlines
	OD-AGH	Boeing 747-2B4B	Middle East Airlines
	OD-AGI	Boeing 747-2B4B	Middle East Airlines
	OD-AGJ	Boeing 747-2B4B	Middle East Airlines
	OD-AGO	Boeing 707-321C	Trans Mediterranean Airways
	OD-AGP	Boeing 707-321C	Trans Mediterranean Airways
	OD-AGQ	Boeing 720-047B	Middle East Airlines
	OD-AGR	Boeing 720-047B	Middle East Airlines
	OD-AGS	Boeing 707-331C	Trans Mediterranean Airways
	OD-AGU	Boeing 707-347C	Middle East Airlines
	OD-AGV	Boeing 707-347C	Middle East Airlines
	OD-AGX	Boeing 707-327C	Trans Mediterranean Airways
	OD-AGY	Boeing 707-327C	Trans Mediterranean Airways
	OD-AGZ	Boeing 707-327C	Trans Mediterranean Airways
	OD-AHB	Boeing 707-323C	Middle East Airlines
	OD-AHC	Boeing 707-323C	Middle East Airlines
	OD-AHD	Boeing 707-323C	Middle East Airlines
	OD-AHE	Boeing 707-323C	Middle East Airlines
	OD-	A.310-221 Airbus	Middle East Airlines
	OD-	A.310-221 Airbus	Middle East Airlines

OE (Austria) *AUSTRIAN AIRLINES*

	OE-HLS	D.H.C. 7-102 Dash Seven	Tyrolean Airways *Stadt Innsbruck*
	OE-HLT	D.H.C. 7-102 Dash Seven	Tyrolean Airways *Stadt Wien*
	OE-LDF	Douglas DC-9-32	Austrian Airlines *Salzburg*
	OE-LDG	Douglas DC-9-32	Austrian Airlines *Tirol*
	OE-LDH	Douglas DC-9-32	Austrian Airlines *Vorarlberg*
	OE-LDI	Douglas DC-9-32	Austrian Airlines *Bregenz*
	OE-LDK	Douglas DC-9-51	Austrian Airlines *Graz*
	OE-LDL	Douglas DC-9-51	Austrian Airlines *Linz*
	OE-LDM	Douglas DC-9-51	Austrian Airlines *Klagenfurt*
	OE-LDN	Douglas DC-9-51	Austrian Airlines *Innsbruck*
	OE-LDO	Douglas DC-9-51	Austrian Airlines *Eisenstädt*
	OE-LDP	Douglas DC-9-81	Austrian Airlines *Niederösterreich*
	OE-LDR	Douglas DC-9-81	Austrian Airlines *Wien*
	OE-LDS	Douglas DC-9-81	Austrian Airlines *Burgenland*
	OE-LDT	Douglas DC-9-81	Austrian Airlines *Kärnten*
	OE-LDU	Douglas DC-9-81	Austrian Airlines *Steiermark*

Reg.	Type	Owner or Operator	Notes
OE-LDV	Douglas DC-9-81	Austrian Airlines *Oberösterreich*	
OE-LDW	Douglas DC-9-81	Austrian Airlines *Salzburg*	
OE-LDX	Douglas DC-9-81	Austrian Airlines *Tirol*	
OE-LDY	Douglas DC-9-81	Austrian Airlines *Vorarlberg*	
OE-LDZ	Douglas DC-9-81	Austrian Airlines *Bregenz*	

Note: Austrian Airlines is in the process of replacing its DC-9-32s with Series 81s.

OH (Finland)

OH-KDM	Douglas DC-8-51	Kar Air	
OH-LFZ	Douglas DC-8-62	Finnair *Jean Sibelius*	
OH-LHA	Douglas DC-10-30	Finnair *Iso Antti*	
OH-LHB	Douglas DC-10-30	Finnair	
OH-LHD	Douglas DC-10-30ER	Finnair	
OH-LMN	Douglas DC-9-82	Finnair	
OH-LMO	Douglas DC-9-82	Finnair	
OH-LMP	Douglas DC-9-82	Finnair	
OH-LNB	Douglas DC-9-41	Finnair	
OH-LNC	Douglas DC-9-41	Finnair	
OH-LND	Douglas DC-9-41	Finnair	
OH-LNE	Douglas DC-9-41	Finnair	
OH-LNF	Douglas DC-9-41	Finnair	
OH-LYD	Douglas DC-9-14	Finnair	
OH-LYE	Douglas DC-9-14	Finnair	
OH-LYH	Douglas DC-9-15MC	Finnair	
OH-LYI	Douglas DC-9-15MC	Finnair	
OH-LYN	Douglas DC-9-51	Finnair	
OH-LYO	Douglas DC-9-51	Finnair	
OH-LYP	Douglas DC-9-51	Finnair	
OH-LYR	Douglas DC-9-51	Finnair	
OH-LYS	Douglas DC-9-51	Finnair	
OH-LYT	Douglas DC-9-51	Finnair	
OH-LYU	Douglas DC-9-51	Finnair	
OH-LYV	Douglas DC-9-51	Finnair	
OH-LYW	Douglas DC-9-51	Finnair	
OH-LYX	Douglas DC-9-51	Finnair	
OH-LYY	Douglas DC-9-51	Finnair	
OH-LYZ	Douglas DC-9-51	Finnair	

Note: Finnair also operates a DC-10-30 which retains its US registration N345HC.

OK (Czechoslovakia)

OK-ABD	Ilyushin IL-62	Ceskoslovenske Aerolinie *Kosice*	
OK-AFA	Tupolev Tu-134A	Ceskoslovenske Aerolinie	
OK-AFB	Tupolev Tu-134A	Ceskoslovenske Aerolinie	
OK-CFC	Tupolev Tu-134A	Ceskoslovenske Aerolinie	
OK-CFE	Tupolev Tu-134A	Ceskoslovenske Aerolinie	
OK-CFF	Tupolev Tu-134A	Ceskoslovenske Aerolinie	
OK-CFG	Tupolev Tu-134A	Ceskoslovenske Aerolinie	
OK-CFH	Tupolev Tu-134A	Ceskoslovenske Aerolinie	
OK-DBE	Ilyushin IL-62	Ceskoslovenske Aerolinie *Brno*	
OK-DFI	Tupolev Tu-134A	Ceskoslovenske Aerolinie	
OK-EBG	Ilyushin IL-62	Ceskoslovenske Aerolinie *Banska Bystrica*	
OK-EFJ	Tupolev Tu-134A	Ceskoslovenske Aerolinie	
OK-EFK	Tupolev Tu-134A	Ceskoslovenske Aerolinie	

Notes	Reg.	Type	Owner or Operator
	OK-FBF	Ilyushin IL-62	Ceskoslovenske Aerolinie
	OK-GBH	Ilyushin IL-62	Ceskoslovenske Aerolinie *Usti Nad Labem*
	OK-HFL	Tupolev Tu-134A	Ceskoslovenske Aerolinie
	OK-HFM	Tupolev Tu-134A	Ceskoslovenske Aerolinie
	OK-IFN	Tupolev Tu-134A	Ceskoslovenske Aerolinie
	OK-JBI	Ilyushin IL-62M	Ceskoslovenske Aerolinie *Plzen*
	OJ-JBJ	Ilyushin IL-62M	Ceskoslovenske Aerolinie *Hradec Kralové*
	OK-KBK	Ilyushin IL-62M	Ceskoslovenske Aerolinie *Ceske Budejovice*
	OK-YBA	Ilyushin IL-62	Ceskoslovenske Aerolinie *Praha*
	OK-YBB	Ilyushin IL-62	Ceskoslovenske Aerolinie *Bratislava*
	OK-ZBC	Ilyushin IL-62	Ceskoslovenske Aerolinie *Ostrava*

OO (Belgium)

Notes	Reg.	Type	Owner or Operator
	OO-DTA	FH-227B Friendship	Sabena
	OO-DTC	FH-227B Friendship	Sabena
	OO-DTD	FH-227B Friendship	Delta Air Transport
	OO-DTE	FH-227B Friendship	Delta Air Transport
	OO-JPI	Swearingen SA226TC Metro II	European Air Transport
	OO-JPK	Swearingen SA226TC Metro II	European Air Transport
	OO-LAW	Swearingen SA226TC Metro III	Sabena/Publi Air
	OO-PLH	Boeing 737-247	Air Belgium
	OO-SBQ	Boeing 737-229	Sobelair
	OO-SBS	Boeing 737-229	Sabena
	OO-SBT	Boeing 737-229	Sobelair
	OO-SBU	Boeing 707-373C	Sobelair
	OO-SCA	A.310-221 Airbus	Sabena
	OO-SCB	A.310-221 Airbus	Sabena
	OO-SCC	A.310-221 Airbus	Sabena
	OO-SDA	Boeing 737-229	Sabena
	OO-SDB	Boeing 737-229	Sabena
	OO-SDC	Boeing 737-229	Sabena
	OO-SDD	Boeing 737-229	Sabena
	OO-SDE	Boeing 737-229	Sabena
	OO-SDF	Boeing 737-229	Sabena
	OO-SDG	Boeing 737-229	Sabena
	OO-SDJ	Boeing 737-229C	Sabena
	OO-SDK	Boeing 737-229C	Sabena
	OO-SDL	Boeing 737-229	Sabena
	OO-SDM	Boeing 737-229	Sabena
	OO-SDN	Boeing 737-229	Sabena
	OO-SDO	Boeing 737-229	Sabena
	OO-SDP	Boeing 737-229C	Sabena
	OO-SDR	Boeing 737-229C	Sabena
	OO-SGA	Boeing 747-129	Sabena
	OO-SGB	Boeing 747-129	Sabena
	OO-SJJ	Boeing 707-329C	Sabena
	OO-SJM	Boeing 707-329C	Sabena
	OO-SJO	Boeing 707-329C	Sabena
	OO-SLA	Douglas DC-10-30CF	Sabena
	OO-SLB	Douglas DC-10-30CF	Sabena
	OO-SLC	Douglas DC-10-30CF	Sabena
	OO-SLD	Douglas DC-10-30CF	Sabena
	OO-SLE	Douglas DC-10-30CF	Sabena
	OO-TED	Boeing 707-131	Trans European Airways *Rena*
	OO-TEF	A.300B1 Airbus	Trans European Airways
	OO-TEH	Boeing 737-2M8	Trans European Airways *Marcus Johannes*
	OO-TEN	Boeing 737-2M8	Trans European Airways
	OO-TEO	Boeing 737-2M8	Trans European Airways *Jonathan*
	OO-WAY	Beech 99	Sabena/Publi-Air

OY (Denmark)

Reg.	Type	Owner or Operator	Notes
OY-APP	Boeing 737-2L9	Maersk Air	
OY-APS	Boeing 737-2L9	Maersk Air	
OY-APU	Boeing 720-051B	Conair	
OY-APV	Boeing 720-051B	Conair	
OY-APW	Boeing 720-051B	Conair	
OY-APY	Boeing 720-051B	Conair	
OY-APZ	Boeing 720-051B	Conair	
OY-DSP	Boeing 720-025	Conair	
OY-KDA	Douglas DC-10-30	S.A.S. *Gorm Viking*	
OY-KGA	Douglas DC-9-41	S.A.S. *Heming Viking*	
OY-KGB	Douglas DC-9-41	S.A.S. *Toste Viking*	
OY-KGC	Douglas DC-9-41	S.A.S. *Helge Viking*	
OY-KGD	Douglas DC-9-21	S.A.S. *Ubbe Viking*	
OY-KGE	Douglas DC-9-21	S.A.S. *Orvar Viking*	
OY-KGF	Douglas DC-9-21	S.A.S. *Rolf Viking*	
OY-KGG	Douglas DC-9-41	S.A.S. *Sune Viking*	
OY-KGH	Douglas DC-9-41	S.A.S. *Eiliv Viking*	
OY-KGI	Douglas DC-9-41	S.A.S. *Bent Viking*	
OY-KGK	Douglas DC-9-41	S.A.S. *Ebbe Viking*	
OY-KGL	Douglas DC-9-41	S.A.S. *Angantyr Viking*	
OY-KGM	Douglas DC-9-41	S.A.S. *Arnfinn Viking*	
OY-KGN	Douglas DC-9-41	S.A.S. *Gram Viking*	
OY-KGO	Douglas DC-9-41	S.A.S. *Holte Viking*	
OY-KGP	Douglas DC-9-41	S.A.S. *Torbern Viking*	
OY-KGR	Douglas DC-9-41	S.A.S. *Holger Viking*	
OY-KGS	Douglas DC-9-41	S.A.S. *Hall Viking*	
OY-KTE	Douglas DC-8-62CF	S.A.S.	
OY-KTF	Douglas DC-8-63	Scanair *Mette Viking*	
OY-KTG	Douglas DC-8-63	S.A.S. *Torodd Viking*	
OY-MBV	Boeing 737-2L9	Maersk Air	
OY-MBW	Boeing 737-2L9	Maersk Air	
OY-MBZ	Boeing 737-2L9	Maersk Air	
OY-SAS	Boeing 727-2J4	Sterling Airways	
OY-SAT	Boeing 727-2J4	Sterling Airways	
OY-SAU	Boeing 727-2J4	Sterling Airways	
OY-SBE	Boeing 727-2J4	Sterling Airways	
OY-SBF	Boeing 727-2J4	Sterling Airways	
OY-SBG	Boeing 727-2J4	Sterling Airways	
OY-STC	S.E.210 Caravelle 10B	Sterling Airways	
OY-STD	S.E.210 Caravelle 10B	Sterling Airways	
OY-STF	S.E.210 Caravelle 10B	Sterling Airways	
OY-STH	S.E.210 Caravelle 10B	Sterling Airways	
OY-STI	S.E.210 Caravelle 10B	Sterling Airways	
OY-STM	S.E.210 Caravelle 10B	Sterling Airways	

Note: S.A.S. also operates two Boeing 747-283Bs which retain their U.S. registrations
N4501Q and N4502R and DC-9-51 YU-AJU from Inex Adria.

PH (Netherlands)

PH-AGA	A.310-202 Airbus	K.L.M. *Rembrandt*	
PH-AGB	A.310-202 Airbus	K.L.M. *Jeroen Bosch*	
PH-AGC	A.310-202 Airbus	K.L.M. *Albert Cuyp*	
PH-AGD	A.310-202 Airbus	K.L.M. *Nicolaas Maes*	
PH-AGE	A.310-202 Airbus	K.L.M. *Jan Steen*	

Notes	Reg.	Type	Owner or Operator
	PH-AGF	A.310-202 Airbus	K.L.M. *Frans Hals*
	PH-AGG	A.310-202 Airbus	K.L.M. *Vincent van Gogh*
	PH-AGH	A.310-202 Airbus	K.L.M. *Peiter de Hoogh*
	PH-BUA	Boeing 747-206B	K.L.M. *The Mississippi*
	PH-BUB	Boeing 747-206B	K.L.M. *The Danube*
	PH-BUC	Boeing 747-206B	K.L.M. *The Amazon*
	PH-BUD	Boeing 747-206B	K.L.M. *The Nile*
	PH-BUE	Boeing 747-206B	K.L.M. *Rio de la Plata*
	PH-BUG	Boeing 747-206B	K.L.M. *The Orinoco*
	PH-BUH	Boeing 747-206B	K.L.M. *Dr Albert Plesman*
	PH-BUI	Boeing 747-206B	K.L.M. *Wilbur Wright*
	PH-BUK	Boeing 747-206B	K.L.M. *Louis Blèriot*
	PH-BUL	Boeing 747-206B	K.L.M. *Charles A. Lindbergh*
	PH-BUM	Boeing 747-206B	K.L.M. *Sir Charles E. Kingsford-Smith*
	PH-BUN	Boeing 747-206B	K.L.M. *Anthony H. G. Fokker*
	PH-BUO	Boeing 747-206B	K.L.M. *The Missouri*
	PH-CHB	F.28 Fellowship 4000	N.L.M. *City of Birmingham*
	PH-CHD	F.28 Fellowship 4000	N.L.M. *City of Maastricht*
	PH-CHF	F.28 Fellowship 4000	N.L.M. *Island of Guernsey*
	PH-CHN	F.28 Fellowship 4000	N.L.M.
	PH-DEB	Douglas DC-8-63	K.L.M. *Christopher Columbus*
	PH-DEC	Douglas DC-8-63	K.L.M. *Marco Polo*
	PH-DED	Douglas DC-8-63	K.L.M. *Leifur Eiriksson*
	PH-DEE	Douglas DC-8-63	K.L.M. *Abel Tasman*
	PH-DEF	Douglas DC-8-63	K.L.M. *Henry Hudson*
	PH-DEH	Douglas DC-8-63	K.L.M. *Vasco de Gama*
	PH-DEK	Douglas DC-8-63	K.L.M. *David Livingstone*
	PH-DEM	Douglas DC-8-63	K.L.M. *James Cook*
	PH-DNC	Douglas DC-9-15	K.L.M. *City of Luxembourg*
	PH-DNG	Douglas DC-9-32	K.L.M. *City of Rotterdam*
	PH-DNH	Douglas DC-9-32	K.L.M. *City of Zurich*
	PH-DNI	Douglas DC-9-32	K.L.M. *City of Istanbul*
	PH-DNK	Douglas DC-9-32	K.L.M. *City of Copenhagen*
	PH-DNL	Douglas DC-9-32	K.L.M. *City of London*
	PH-DNM	Douglas DC-9-33RC	K.L.M. *City of Madrid*
	PH-DNN	Douglas DC-9-33RC	K.L.M. *City of Vienna*
	PH-DNO	Douglas DC-9-33RC	K.L.M. *City of Oslo*
	PH-DNP	Douglas DC-9-33RC	K.L.M. *City of Athens*
	PH-DNR	Douglas DC-9-33RC	K.L.M. *City of Stockholm*
	PH-DNS	Douglas DC-9-32	K.L.M. *City of Arnhem*
	PH-DNT	Douglas DC-9-32	K.L.M. *City of Lisbon*
	PH-DNV	Douglas DC-9-32	K.L.M. *City of Warsaw*
	PH-DNW	Douglas DC-9-32	K.L.M. *City of Moscow*
	PH-DNY	Douglas DC-9-33RC	K.L.M. *City of Paris*
	PH-DOA	Douglas DC-9-32	K.L.M. *City of Utrecht*
	PH-DOB	Douglas DC-9-32	K.L.M. *City of Santa Monica*
	PH-DTA	Douglas DC-10-30	K.L.M. *Johann Sebastian Bach*
	PH-DTB	Douglas DC-10-30	K.L.M. *Ludwig van Beethoven*
	PH-DTC	Douglas DC-10-30	K.L.M. *Frédéric François Chopin*
	PH-DTD	Douglas DC-10-30	K.L.M. *Maurice Ravel*
	PH-DTL	Douglas DC-10-30	K.L.M. *Edvard Hagerup Grieg*
	PH-FKT	F-27 Friendship Mk 600	XP Parcel Service
	PH-KFD	F.27 Friendship Mk 200	N.L.M. *Jan Moll*
	PH-KFE	F.27 Friendship Mk 600	N.L.M. *Jan Dellaert*
	PH-KFG	F.27 Friendship Mk 200	N.L.M. *Koos Abspoel*
	PH-KFI	F.27 Friendship Mk 500	N.L.M. *Bremen*
	PH-KFK	F.27 Friendship Mk 500	N.L.M. *Zestienhoven*
	PH-KFL	F.27 Friendship Mk 500	N.L.M.
	PH-LEX	F-28 Fellowship 4000	T.A.T.
	PH-MAX	Douglas DC-9-32	K.L.M. *City of Rome*
	PH-MBG	Douglas DC-10-30CF	Martinair *Kohoutek*
	PH-MBN	Douglas DC-10-30CF	Martinair *Anthony Ruys*
	PH-MBP	Douglas DC-10-30CF	Martinair *Hong Kong*
	PH-MBT	Douglas DC-10-30CF	Martinair
	PH-MBZ	Douglas DC-9-82	Martinair *Prinses Juiliana*
	PH-MCA	A.310-202 Airbus	Martinair
	PH-MCB	A.310-202CF Airbus	Martinair
	PH-MCD	Douglas DC-9-82	Martinair *Lucien Ruys*
	PH-RAL	Boeing 737-2M8	Rotterdam Airlines *Delfshaven*
	PH-SAD	F.27 Friendship Mk 200	N.L.M. *Evert van Dijk*
	PH-SIX	F.28 Fellowship 6000	Linjeflyg

Reg.	Type	Owner or Operator	Notes
PH-TVC	Boeing 737-2K2C	Transavia *Richard Gordon*	
PH-TVD	Boeing 737-2K2C	Transavia *Charles Conrad*	
PH-TVE	Boeing 737-2K2C	Transavia *Alan Bean*	
PH-TVH	Boeing 737-222	Transavia *Neil Armstrong*	
PH-TVP	Boeing 737-2K2	Transavia	
PH-TVS	Boeing 737-2K2	Transavia	
PH-TVU	Boeing 737-2K2	Transavia	

Note: K.L.M. also operates Boeing 747-206Bs N1295E, N1298E and N1309E and Boeing 747-306 N4548M.

PK (Indonesia)

PK-GSA	Boeing 747-2U3B	Garuda Indonesian Airways *City of Jakarta*	
PK-GSB	Boeing 747-2U3B	Garuda Indonesian Airways *City of Bandung*	
PK-GSC	Boeing 747-2U3B	Garuda Indonesian Airways *City of Medan*	
PK-GSD	Boeing 747-2U3B	Garuda Indonesian Airways *City of Surabaya*	
PK-GSE	Boeing 747-2U3B	Garuda Indonesian Airways *City of Yogyakarte*	
PK-GSF	Boeing 747-2U3B	Garuda Indonesian Airways *City of Denpasar*	

PP (Brazil)

PP-VJH	Boeing 707-320C	VARIG	
PP-VJK	Boeing 707-379C	VARIG	
PP-VJX	Boeing 707-345C	VARIG	
PP-VJY	Boeing 707-345C	VARIG	
PP-VLI	Boeing 707-385C	VARIG	
PP-VLK	Boeing 707-324C	VARIG	
PP-VLL	Boeing 707-324C	VARIG	
PP-VLM	Boeing 707-324C	VARIG	
PP-VLN	Boeing 707-324C	VARIG	
PP-VLO	Boeing 707-324C	VARIG	
PP-VLP	Boeing 707-323C	VARIG	
PP-VMA	Douglas DC-10-30	VARIG	
PP-VMB	Douglas DC-10-30	VARIG	
PP-VMD	Douglas DC-10-30	VARIG	
PP-VMQ	Douglas DC-10-30	VARIG	
PP-VMS	Douglas DC-10-30	VARIG	
PP-VMT	Douglas DC-10-30	VARIG	
PP-VMU	Douglas DC-10-30	VARIG	
PP-VMV	Douglas DC-10-30	VARIG	
PP-VMW	Douglas DC-10-30	VARIG	
PP-VMX	Douglas DC-10-30	VARIG	
PP-VMY	Douglas DC-10-30	VARIG	
PP-VMZ	Douglas DC-10-30	VARIG	

RP (Philippines)

Note: Philippine Airlines operates four Boeing 747s which retain their U.S. registrations N741PR, N742PR, N743PR and N744PR.

S2 (Bangladesh)

 বাংলাদেশ বিমান Bangladesh Biman

Notes	Reg.	Type	Owner or Operator
	S2-ABN	Boeing 707-351C	Bangladesh Biman *City of Shah Jalal*
	S2-ACA	Boeing 707-351C	Bangladesh Biman *Khan Jahan Ali*
	S2-ACE	Boeing 707-351C	Bangladesh Biman *City of Tokyo*
	S2-ACF	Boeing 707-351C	Bangladesh Biman *City of Hazrat Shah Balkhi*
	S2-ACK	Boeing 707-321B	Bangladesh Biman *City of Kuwait*
	S2-ACO	Douglas DC-10-30	Bangladesh Biman *City of Hazrat-Shar Makhdoom (R.A.)*
	S2-ACP	Douglas DC-10-30	Bangladesh Biman *City of Uhaka*

S7 (Seychelles)

	S7-SIA	Douglas DC-8-53	Seychelles International *Island Bird*

SE (Sweden)

	SE-DAK	Douglas DC-9-41	S.A.S. *Ragnvald Viking*
	SE-DAL	Douglas DC-9-41	S.A.S. *Algot Viking*
	SE-DAM	Douglas DC-9-41	S.A.S. *Starkad Viking*
	SE-DAN	Douglas DC-9-41	S.A.S. *Alf Viking*
	SE-DAO	Douglas DC-9-41	S.A.S. *Asgaut Viking*
	SE-DAP	Douglas DC-9-41	S.A.S. *Torgils Viking*
	SE-DAR	Douglas DC-9-41	S.A.S. *Agnar Viking*
	SE-DAS	Douglas DC-9-41	S.A.S. *Garder Viking*
	SE-DAT	Douglas DC-9-41	S.A.S. *Gissur Viking*
	SE-DAU	Douglas DC-9-41	S.A.S. *Hadding Viking*
	SE-DAW	Douglas DC-9-41	S.A.S. *Gotrik Viking*
	SE-DAX	Douglas DC-9-41	S.A.S. *Helsing Viking*
	SE-DBG	Douglas DC-8-62	S.A.S. *Jorund Viking*
	SE-DBI	Douglas DC-8-62CF	Arista International Airlines *Valerie*
	SE-DBK	Douglas DC-8-63	Scanair *Sigyn Viking*
	SE-DBL	Douglas DC-8-63	Scanair *Bodil Viking*
	SE-DBM	Douglas DC-9-41	S.A.S. *Ossur Viking*
	SE-DBN	Douglas DC-9-33AF	S.A.S. *Sigtrygg Viking*
	SE-DBO	Douglas DC-9-21	S.A.S. *Siger Viking*
	SE-DBP	Douglas DC-9-21	S.A.S. *Rane Viking*
	SE-DBR	Douglas DC-9-21	S.A.S. *Skate Viking*
	SE-DBS	Douglas DC-9-21	S.A.S. *Svipdag Viking*
	SE-DBT	Douglas DC-9-41	S.A.S. *Agne Viking*
	SE-DBU	Douglas DC-9-41	S.A.S. *Hjalmar Viking*
	SE-DBW	Douglas DC-9-41	S.A.S. *Adils Viking*
	SE-DBX	Douglas DC-9-41	S.A.S. *Arnljot Viking*
	SE-DDP	Douglas DC-9-41	S.A.S. *Brun Viking*
	SE-DDR	Douglas DC-9-41	S.A.S. *Atle Viking*
	SE-DDS	Douglas DC-9-41	S.A.S. *Alrik Viking*
	SE-DDT	Douglas DC-9-41	S.A.S. *Amund Viking*
	SE-DDU	Douglas DC-8-62	S.A.S.
	SE-DFD	Douglas DC-10-30	S.A.S. *Dag Viking*
	SE-DFE	Douglas DC-10-30	S.A.S. *Sverker Viking*
	SE-DFK	A.300B4 Airbus	Scanair *Sven Viking*
	SE-DFL	A.300B4 Airbus	S.A.S. *Ingemar Viking*
	SE-DFZ	Boeing 747-283B	S.A.S./Nigeria Airways
	SE-DGA	F.28 Fellowship 1000	Linjeflyg
	SE-DGB	F.28 Fellowship 1000	Linjeflyg
	SE-DGC	F.28 Fellowship 1000	Linjeflyg
	SE-DGD	F.28 Fellowship 4000	Linjeflyg

Reg.	Type	Owner or Operator	Notes
SE-DGE	F.28 Fellowship 4000	Linjeflyg	
SE-DGF	F.28 Fellowship 4000	Linjeflyg	
SE-DGG	F.28 Fellowship 4000	Linjeflyg	
SE-DGH	F.28 Fellowship 4000	Linjeflyg	
SE-DGI	F.28 Fellowship 4000	Linjeflyg	
SE-DGK	F.28 Fellowship 4000	Linjeflyg	
SE-DGL	F.28 Fellowship 4000	Linjeflyg	
SE-DGM	F.28 Fellowship 4000	Linjeflyg	
SE-DGN	F.28 Fellowship 4000	Linjeflyg	
SE-DGO	F.28 Fellowship 4000	Linjeflyg	
SE-DGP	F.28 Fellowship 4000	Linjeflyg	
SE-IEG	F.27 Friendship	Swedair	
SE-IEY	Convair 580	ScanBee	
SE-IGZ	F.27J Friendship	Aerocenter i Växjö	
SE-INA	F.27 Friendship	Swedair	
SE-INB	F.27A Friendship	Swedair	

Note: S.A.S. also operates two Boeing 747-283Bs, which retain their U.S registrations N4501Q and N4502R and DC-9-51 YU-AJU from Inex Adria.

SP (Poland)

SP-LAB	Ilyushin IL-62	Polskie Linie Lotnicze (LOT) *Tadeusz Kosciuszko*	
SP-LAC	Ilyushin IL-62	Polskie Linie Lotnicze (LOT) *Fryderyk Chopin*	
SP-LAD	Ilyushin IL-62	Polskie Linie Lotnicze (LOT) *Kazimierz Pulaski*	
SP-LAE	Ilyushin IL-62	Polskie Linie Lotnicze (LOT) *Henryk Sienkiewicz*	
SP-LAF	Ilyushin IL-62	Polskie Linie Lotnicze (LOT) *Adam Michiewicz*	
SP-LAG	Ilyushin IL-62	Polskie Linie Lotnicze (LOT) *Maria Sklodowska-Curie*	
SP-LBA	Ilyushin IL-62M	Polskie Linie Lotnicze (LOT) *Juliusz Sowacki*	
SP-LBB	Ilyushin IL-62M	Polskie Linie Lotnicze (LOT) *Jgnacy Paderewski*	
SP-LBC	Ilyushin IL-62M	Polskie Linie Lotnicze (LOT) *Joseph Conrad-Korzeniowski*	
SP-LBD	Ilyushin IL-62M	Polskie Linie Lotnicze (LOT)	
SP-LBE	Ilyushin IL-62M	Polskie Linie Lotnicze (LOT)	
SP-LBF	Ilyushin IL-62M	Polskie Linie Lotnicze (LOT)	
SP-LGA	Tupolev Tu-134	Polskie Linie Lotnicze (LOT)	
SP-LGC	Tupolev Tu-134	Polskie Linie Lotnicze (LOT)	
SP-LGD	Tupolev Tu-134	Polskie Linie Lotnicze (LOT)	
SP-LGE	Tupolev Tu-134	Polskie Linie Lotnicze (LOT)	
SP-LHA	Tupolev Tu-134A	Polskie Linie Lotnicze (LOT)	
SP-LHB	Tupolev Tu-134A	Polskie Linie Lotnicze (LOT)	
SP-LHC	Tupolev Tu-134A	Polskie Linie Lotnicze (LOT)	
SP-LHD	Tupolev Tu-134A	Polskie Linie Lotnicze (LOT)	
SP-LHE	Tupolev Tu-134A	Polskie Linie Lotnicze (LOT)	
SP-LHF	Tupolev Tu-134A	Polskie Linie Lotnicze (LOT)	
SP-LHG	Tupolev Tu-134A	Polskie Linie Lotnicze (LOT)	
SP-LSA	Ilyushin IL-18V (Cargo)	Polskie Linie Lotnicze (LOT)	
SP-LSB	Ilyushin IL-18V	Polskie Linie Lotnicze (LOT)	
SP-LSC	Ilyushin IL-18V (Cargo)	Polskie Linie Lotnicze (LOT)	
SP-LSD	Ilyushin IL-18V	Polskie Linie Lotnicze (LOT)	
SP-LSE	Ilyushin IL-18V	Polskie Linie Lotnicze (LOT)	
SP-LSF	Ilyushin IL-18E	Polskie Linie Lotnicze (LOT)	
SP-LSG	Ilyushin IL-18E	Polskie Linie Lotnicze (LOT)	
SP-LSH	Ilyushin IL-18V	Polskie Linie Lotnicze (LOT)	
SP-LSI	Ilyushin IL-18D	Polskie Linie Lotnicze (LOT)	
SP-	Ilyushin IL-86	Polskie Linie Lotnicze (LOT)	

ST (Sudan)

االخطوط الجوية السودانية

SUDAN AIRWAYS

Notes	Reg.	Type	Owner or Operator
	ST-AFA	Boeing 707-3J8C	Sudan Airways
	ST-AFB	Boeing 707-3J8C	Sudan Airways

SU (Egypt)

مصرللطيران

EGYPTAIR

	SU-AOU	Boeing 707-366C	EgyptAir *Khopho*
	SU-APD	Boeing 707-366C	EgyptAir *Khafrah*
	SU-AVX	Boeing 707-366C	EgyptAir *Tutankhamun*
	SU-AVY	Boeing 707-366C	EgyptAir *Akhenaton*
	SU-AVZ	Boeing 707-366C	EgyptAir *Mena*
	SU-AXK	Boeing 707-366C	EgyptAir *Seti I*
	SU-BAO	Boeing 707-351C	EgyptAir
	SU-BBA	Boeing 707-338C	Air Cargo Egypt
	SU-BCA	A.300B4 Airbus	EgyptAir *Horus*
	SU-BCB	A.300B4 Airbus	EgyptAir *Osiris*
	SU-BCC	A.300B4 Airbus	EgyptAir *Nowt*
	SU-BDF	A.300B4 Airbus	EgyptAir
	SU-BDG	A.300B4 Airbus	EgyptAir *Aton*
	SU-DAA	Boeing 707-328C	Zakani Aviation Services
	SU-DAB	Boeing 707-328C	Zakani Aviation Services
	SU-EAA	Boeing 707-138B	EgyptAir
	SU-FAA	Boeing 707-138B	EgyptAir
	SU-FAB	Boeing 707-138B	EgyptAir
	SU-GAA	A.300B4 Airbus	EgyptAir *Isis*
	SU-GAB	A.300B4 Airbus	EgyptAir *Amun*
	SU-GAC	A.300B4 Airbus	EgyptAir

SX (Greece)

OLYMPIC *AIRWAYS*

	SX-BCA	Boeing 737-284	Olympic Airlines *Apollo*
	SX-BCB	Boeing 737-284	Olympic Airlines *Hermes*
	SX-BCC	Boeing 737-284	Olympic Airlines *Hercules*
	SX-BCD	Boeing 737-284	Olympic Airlines *Hephaestus*
	SX-BCE	Boeing 737-284	Olympic Airlines *Dionysus*
	SX-BCF	Boeing 737-284	Olympic Airlines *Poseidin*
	SX-BCG	Boeing 737-284	Olympic Airlines *Phoebus*
	SX-BCH	Boeing 737-284	Olympic Airlines *Triton*
	SX-BCI	Boeing 737-284	Olympic Airlines *Proteus*
	SX-BCK	Boeing 737-284	Olympic Airlines *Nereus*
	SX-BCL	Boeing 737-284	Olympic Airlines *Isle of Thassos*
	SX-BEB	A.300B4 Airbus	Olympic Airways *Odysseus*
	SX-BEC	A.300B4 Airbus	Olympic Airways *Achilles*
	SX-BED	A.300B4 Airbus	Olympic Airways *Telemachos*
	SX-BEE	A.300B4 Airbus	Olympic Airways *Nestor*
	SX-BEF	A.300B4 Airbus	Olympic Airways *Ajax*
	SX-BEG	A.300B4 Airbus	Olympic Airways *Diamedes*
	SX-BEH	A.300B4 Airbus	Olympic Airways *Peleus*
	SX-BEI	A.300B4 Airbus	Olympic Airways *Neoptolemos*
	SX-CBA	Boeing 727-284	Olympic Airways *Mount Olympus*
	SX-CBB	Boeing 727-284	Olympic Airways *Mount Pindos*
	SX-CBC	Boeing 727-284	Olympic Airways *Mount Parnassus*
	SX-CBD	Boeing 727-284	Olympic Airways *Mount Helicon*
	SX-CBE	Boeing 727-284	Olympic Airways *Mount Athos*
	SX-CBF	Boeing 727-284	Olympic Airways *Mount Taygetus*

PK-GSC   Boeing 747-2U3B of Garuda Indonesian Airways.

SU-BDG   Airbus A.300B4-203 of Egyptair.

YU-AKH   Boeing 727-2L8 of Aviogenex.

234

Reg.	Type	Owner or Operator	Notes
SX-DBC	Boeing 707-384C	Olympic Airways *City of Knossos*	
SX-DBD	Boeing 707-384C	Olympic Airways *City of Sparta*	
SX-DBE	Boeing 707-384B	Olympic Airways *City of Pella*	
SX-DBF	Boeing 707-384B	Olympic Airways *City of Mycenae*	
SX-DBO	Boeing 707-351C	Olympic Airways *City of Lindos*	
SX-DBP	Boeing 707-351C	Olympic Airways *City of Thebes*	
SX-OAA	Boeing 747-284B	Olympic Airways *Olympic Zeus*	
SX-OAB	Boeing 747-284B	Olympic Airways *Olympic Eagle*	

TC (Turkey)

TC-JAU	Douglas DC-10-10	Türk Hava Yollari (THY) *Istanbul*	
TC-JAY	Douglas DC-10-10	Türk Hava Yollari (THY) *Izmir*	
TC-JBF	Boeing 727-2F2	Türk Hava Yollari (THY) *Adana*	
TC-JBG	Boeing 727-2F2	Türk Hava Yollari (THY) *Ankara*	
TC-JBJ	Boeing 727-2F2	Türk Hava Yollari (THY) *Diyarbakir*	
TC-JBM	Boeing 727-2F2	Türk Hava Yollari (THY) *Menderes*	
TC-JBS	Boeing 707-321B	Türk Hava Yollari (THY) *Basak*	
TC-JBT	Boeing 707-321B	Türk Hava Yollari (THY) *Baris*	
TC-JBU	Boeing 707-321B	Türk Hava Yollari (THY) *Yurdum*	
TC-JCA	Boeing 727-2F2	Türk Hava Yollari (THY) *Edirne*	
TC-JCB	Boeing 727-2F2	Türk Hava Yollari (THY) *Kars*	
TC-JCC	Boeing 707-321C	Türk Hava Yollari (THY) *Kervan I*	
TC-JCD	Boeing 727-2F2	Türk Hava Yollari (THY) *Sinop*	
TC-JCE	Boeing 727-2F2	Türk Hava Yollari (THY) *Hatay*	
TC-JCF	Boeing 707-321C	Türk Hava Yollari (THY) *Kervan II*	

TF (Iceland)

ICELANDAIR

TF-BCV	Douglas DC-8-63CF	Cargolux	
TF-CCV	Douglas DC-8-63CF	Air India Cargo	
TF-FLB	Douglas DC-8-63CF	Icelandair	
TF-FLC	Douglas DC-8-63CF	Saudia — Saudi Arabian Airlines	
TF-FLE	Douglas DC-8-63CF	Saudia — Saudi Arabian Airlines	
TF-FLG	Boeing 727-185C	Icelandair *Heim Fari*	
TF-FLH	Boeing 727-108C	Icelandair	
TF-FLI	Boeing 727-208	Icelandair *Fronfari*	
TF-FLJ	Boeing 727-155C	Icelandair	
TF-VLJ	Boeing 707-324C	Libyan Arab Airlines	
TF-VLP	Boeing 707-351C	Libyan Arab Airlines	
TV-VLR	Boeing 707-351C	Libyan Arab Airlines	

Note: Icelandair also operates DC-8s HS-TGZ and N916R.

TJ (Cameroon)

TJ-CAA	Boeing 707-3H7C	Cameroon Airlines *La Sanaga*	

TR (Gabon)

TR-LVK	Douglas DC-8-55F	Air Gabon Cargo	

TS (Tunisia)

الخطوط الجوية التونسية
TUNIS AIR

Notes	Reg.	Type	Owner or Operator
	TS-IMA	A.300B4 Airbus	Tunis-Air *Amilcar*
	TS-IOC	Boeing 737-2H3	Tunis-Air *Salammbo*
	TS-IOD	Boeing 737-2H3C	Tunis-Air *Bulla Regia*
	TS-IOE	Boeing 737-2H3	Tunis-Air *Zarzis*
	TS-IOF	Boeing 737-2H3	Tunis-Air *Sousse*
	TS-JHN	Boeing 727-2H3	Tunis-Air *Carthago*
	TS-JHO	Boeing 727-2H3	Tunis-Air *Jerba*
	TS-JHP	Boeing 727-2H3	Tunis-Air *Monastir*
	TS-JHQ	Boeing 727-2H3	Tunis-Air *Tozeur-Nefta*
	TS-JHR	Boeing 727-2H3	Tunis-Air *Bizerte*
	TS-JHS	Boeing 727-2H3	Tunis-Air *Kairouan*
	TS-JHT	Boeing 727-2H3	Tunis-Air *Sidi Bousaid*
	TS-JHU	Boeing 727-2H3	Tunis-Air *Hannibal*
	TS-JHV	Boeing 727-2H3	Tunis-Air *Jugurtha*
	TS-JHW	Boeing 727-2H3	Tunis-Air *Ibn Khaldoun*

TZ (Mali)

	TZ-ADR	Boeing 727-173C	Air Mali
	TZ-ADS	SE.210 Caravelle 10B	Corse Air

VH (Australia)

	VH-EBA	Boeing 747-238B	Qantas Airways *City of Canberra*
	VH-EBB	Boeing 747-238B	Qantas Airways *City of Melbourne*
	VH-EBC	Boeing 747-238B	Qantas Airways *City of Sydney*
	VH-EBD	Boeing 747-238B	Qantas Airways *City of Perth*
	VH-EBE	Boeing 747-238B	Qantas Airways *City of Brisbane*
	VH-EBF	Boeing 747-238B	Qantas Airways *City of Adelaide*
	VH-EBG	Boeing 747-238B	Qantas Airways *City of Hobart*
	VH-EBH	Boeing 747-238B	Qantas Airways *City of Newcastle*
	VH-EBI	Boeing 747-238B	Qantas Airways *City of Darwin*
	VH-EBJ	Boeing 747-238B	Qantas Airways *City of Geelong*
	VH-EBK	Boeing 747-238B	Qantas Airways *City of Wollongong*
	VH-EBL	Boeing 747-238B	Qantas Airways *City of Townsville*
	VH-EBM	Boeing 747-238B	Qantas Airways *City of Parramatta*
	VH-EBN	Boeing 747-238B	Qantas Airways *City of Albury*
	VH-EBO	Boeing 747-238B	Qantas Airways *City of Elizabeth*
	VH-EBP	Boeing 747-238B	Qantas Airways *City of Freemantle*
	VH-EBQ	Boeing 747-238B	Qantas Airways *City of Bunbury*
	VH-EBR	Boeing 747-238B	Qantas Airways *City of Dubbo*
	VH-EBS	Boeing 747-238B	Qantas Airways *City of Longreach*
	VH-ECA	Boeing 747-238B	Qantas Airways *City of Sale*
	VH-ECB	Boeing 747-238B	Qantas Airways *City of Swan Hill*
	VH-ECC	Boeing 747-238B	Qantas Airways *City of Shepparton*
	VH-	Boeing 747-338B	Qantas Airways
	VH-	Boeing 747-338B	Qantas Airways
	VH-	Boeing 747-338B	Qantas Airways

VR-H (Hong Kong)

Reg.	Type	Owner or Operator	Notes
VR-HIA	Boeing 747-267B	Cathay Pacific Airways	
VR-HIB	Boeing 747-267B	Cathay Pacific Airways	
VR-HIC	Boeing 747-267B	Cathay Pacific Airways	
VR-HID	Boeing 747-267B	Cathay Pacific Airways	
VR-HIE	Boeing 747-267B	Cathay Pacific Airways	
VR-HIF	Boeing 747-267B	Cathay Pacific Airways	
VH-HIH	Boeing 747-267B	Cathay Pacific Airways	
VR-HKG	Boeing 747-267B	Cathay Pacific Airways	
VR-HVY	Boeing 747-236F	Cathay Pacific Airways	

VT (India)

VT-DPM	Boeing 707-337B	Air-India *Dhaulagiri*	
VT-DSI	Boeing 707-337B	Air-India *Lhotse*	
VT-DVA	Boeing 707-337B	Air-India *Annapoorna*	
VT-DVB	Boeing 707-337C	Air-India *Kamet*	
VT-DXT	Boeing 707-337C	Air-India *Trishul*	
VT-EBE	Boeing 747-237B	Air-India *Emperor Shahjehan*	
VT-EBN	Boeing 747-237B	Air-India *Emperor Rajendra Chola*	
VT-EBO	Boeing 747-237B	Air-India *Emperor Nikramaditya*	
VT-EDU	Boeing 747-237B	Air-India *Emperor Akbar*	
VT-EFJ	Boeing 747-237B	Air-India *Emperor Chandragupta*	
VT-EFO	Boeing 747-237B	Air-India *Emperor Kanishka*	
VT-EFU	Boeing 747-237B	Air-India *Emperor Krishna Deva*	
VT-EGA	Boeing 747-237B	Air-India *Emperor Samudra Gupto*	
VT-EGB	Boeing 747-237B	Air-India *Emperor Mahendra Varman*	
VT-EGC	Boeing 747-237B	Air-India *Emperor Harsha Vardhuma*	

Note: Air-India Cargo operates two Douglas DC-8-63CFs which retain their registrations N783FT, N906R and TF-CCV.

YA (Afghanistan)

YA-LAS	Douglas DC-10-30	Ariana	

YI (Iraq)

YI-AGE	Boeing 707-370C	Arab Air Cargo	
YI-AGG	Boeing 707-370C	Iraqi Airways	
YI-AGN	Boeing 747-270C	Iraqi Airways	
YI-AGO	Boeing 747-270C	Iraqi Airways	
YI-AGP	Boeing 747-270C	Iraqi Airways	
YI-AIK	Ilyushin IL-76T	Iraqi Airways	
YI-AIL	Ilyushin IL-76T	Iraqi Airways	
YI-AIM	Ilyushin IL-76T	Iraqi Airways	
YI-AIN	Ilyushin IL-76T	Iraqi Airways	
YI-AIP	Ilyushin IL-76T	Iraqi Airways	
YI-AKO	Ilyushin IL-76M	Iraqi Airways	
YI-AKP	Ilyushin IL-76M	Iraqi Airways	
YI-AKQ	Ilyushin IL-76	Iraqi Airways	
YI-AKS	Ilyushin IL-76	Iraqi Airways	

Notes	Reg.	Type	Owner or Operator
	YI-AKT	Ilyushin IL-76M	Iraqi Airways
	YI-AKU	Ilyushin IL-76	Iraqi Airways
	YI-AKV	Ilyushin IL-76M	Iraqi Airways
	YI-AKW	Ilyushin IL-76M	Iraqi Airways
	YI-AKX	Ilyushin IL-76M	Iraqi Airways
	YI-ALL	Ilyushin IL-76M	Iraqi Airways
	YI-ALM	Boeing 747SP-70	Iraqi Airways *Al Qadissiya*
	YI-ALO	Ilyushin IL-76M	Iraqi Airways
	YI-ALP	Ilyushin IL-76M	Iraqi Airways
	YI-ALR	Ilyushin IL-76M	Iraqi Airways
	YI-ALS	Ilyushin IL-76M	Iraqi Airways

YK (Syria)

شركة الطيران العربية السورية
SYRIAN ARAB AIRLINES

	YK-AHA	Boeing 747SP-94	Syrian Arab Airlines *16 Novembre*
	YK-AHB	Boeing 747SP-94	Syrian Arab Airlines *Arab Solidarity*
	YK-ATA	Ilyushin IL-76M	Syrian Arab Airlines
	YK-ATB	Ilyushin IL-76M	Syrian Arab Airlines
	YK-ATC	Ilyushin IL-76T	Syrian Arab Airlines
	YK-ATD	Ilyushin IL-76T	Syrian Arab Airlines

YR (Romania)

	YR-ABA	Boeing 707-3K1C	Tarom
	YR-ABC	Boeing 707-3K1C	Tarom
	YR-ABM	Boeing 707-321C	Tarom
	YR-ABN	Boeing 707-321C	Tarom
	YR-BCB	BAC One-Eleven 424EU	Tarom
	YR-BCE	BAC One-Eleven 424EU	Tarom
	YR-BCG	BAC One-Eleven 401AK	Tarom
	YR-BCH	BAC One-Eleven 402AP	Tarom
	YR-BCI	BAC One-Eleven 525FT	Tarom
	YR-BCJ	BAC One-Eleven 525FT	Tarom
	YR-BCK	BAC One-Eleven 525FT	Tarom
	YR-BCL	BAC One-Eleven 525FT	Tarom
	YR-BCM	BAC One-Eleven 525FT	Tarom
	YR-BCN	BAC One-Eleven 525FT	Tarom
	YR-BCO	BAC One-Eleven 525FT	Tarom
	YR-BCQ	BAC One-Eleven 525RC	Tarom
	YR-BCR	BAC One-Eleven 487GK	Tarom
	YR-BRA	Rombac One-Eleven 560	Tarom
	YR-IMA	Ilyushin IL-18V	Tarom
	YR-IMC	Ilyushin IL-18V	Tarom
	YR-IMD	Ilyushin IL-18V	Tarom
	YR-IME	Ilyushin IL-18V	Tarom
	YR-IMF	Ilyushin IL-18V	Tarom
	YR-IMG	Ilyushin IL-18V	Tarom
	YR-IMH	Ilyushin IL-18V	Tarom
	YR-IMI	Ilyushin IL-18V	Tarom
	YR-IMJ	Ilyushin IL-18D	Tarom
	YR-IML	Ilyushin IL-18D	Tarom
	YR-IMM	Ilyushin IL-18D	Tarom
	YR-IMZ	Ilyushin IL-18V	Tarom
	YR-IRA	Ilyushin IL-62	Tarom
	YR-IRB	Ilyushin IL-62	Tarom
	YR-IRC	Ilyushin IL-62	Tarom
	YR-IRD	Ilyushin IL-62M	Tarom
	YR-IRE	Ilyushin IL-62M	Tarom
	YR-TPA	Tupolev Tu-154B	Tarom

Reg.	Type	Owner or Operator	Notes
YR-TPB	Tupolev Tu-154B	Tarom	
YR-TPC	Tupolev Tu-154B	Tarom	
YR-TPD	Tupolev Tu-154B	Tarom	
YR-TPE	Tupolev Tu-154B	Tarom	
YR-TPF	Tupolev Tu-154B	Tarom	
YR-TPG	Tupolev Tu-154B	Tarom	
YR-TPI	Tupolev Tu-154B	Tarom	
YR-TPJ	Tupolev Tu-154B	Tarom	
YR-TPK	Tupolev Tu-154B	Tarom	
YR-TPL	Tupolev Tu-154B	Tarom	

YU (Yugoslavia)

 INEX ADRIA

AVIOGENEX

Reg.	Type	Owner or Operator	Notes
YU-AGE	Boeing 707-340C	Jugoslovenski Aerotransport	
YU-AGG	Boeing 707-340C	Jugoslovenski Aerotransport	
YU-AGI	Boeing 707-351C	Jugoslovenski Aerotransport	
YU-AGJ	Boeing 707-351C	Jugoslovenski Aerotransport	
YU-AHJ	Douglas DC-9-32	Inex Adria Ariways *Ljubljana*	
YU-AHL	Douglas DC-9-32	Jugoslovenski Aerotransport	
YU-AHM	Douglas DC-9-32	Jugoslovenski Aerotransport *Tivat*	
YU-AHN	Douglas DC-9-32	Jugoslovenski Aerotransport	
YU-AHO	Douglas DC-9-32	Jugoslovenski Aerotransport	
YU-AHP	Douglas DC-9-32	Jugoslovenski Aerotransport	
YU-AHU	Douglas DC-9-32	Jugoslovenski Aerotransport	
YU-AHV	Douglas DC-9-32	Jugoslovenski Aerotransport	
YU-AHW	Douglas DC-9-33CF	Inex Adria Airways *Sarajevo*	
YU-AHX	Tupolev Tu-134A	Aviogenex *Beograd*	
YU-AHY	Tupolev Tu-134A	Aviogenex *Zagreb*	
YU-AJA	Tupolev Tu-134A	Aviogenex *Titograd*	
YU-AJB	Douglas DC-9-32	Inex Adria Airways	
YU-AJD	Tupolev Tu-134A	Aviogenex *Skopje*	
YU-AJF	Douglas DC-9-32	Inex Adria Airways	
YU-AJH	Douglas DC-9-32	Jugoslovenski Aerotransport	
YU-AJI	Douglas DC-9-32	Jugoslovenski Aerotransport	
YU-AJJ	Douglas DC-9-32	Jugoslovenski Aerotransport	
YU-AJK	Douglas DC-9-32	Jugoslovenski Aerotransport	
YU-AJL	Douglas DC-9-32	Jugoslovenski Aerotransport	
YU-AJM	Douglas DC-9-32	Jugoslovenski Aerotransport	
YU-AJT	Douglas DC-9-51	Inex Adria Airways	
YU-AJU	Douglas DC-9-51	Inex Adria Airways *Maribor*/S.A.S.	
YU-AJV	Tupolev Tu-134A	Aviogenex *Mostar*	
YU-AJW	Tupolev Tu-134A	Aviogenex *Pristina*	
YU-AKA	Boeing 727-2H9	Jugoslovenski Aerotransport	
YU-AKB	Boeing 727-2H9	Jugoslovenski Aerotransport	
YU-AKD	Boeing 727-2L8	Aviogenex *Zagreb*	
YU-AKE	Boeing 727-2H9	Jugoslovenski Aerotransport	
YU-AKF	Boeing 727-2H9	Jugoslovenski Aerotransport	
YU-AKG	Boeing 727-2H9	Jugoslovenski Aerotransport	
YU-AKH	Boeing 727-2L8	Aviogenex *Beograd*	
YU-AKI	Boeing 727-2H9	Jugoslovenski Aerotransport	
YU-AKJ	Boeing 727-2H9	Jugoslovenski Aerotransport	
YU-AKK	Boeing 727-2H9	Jugoslovenski Aerotransport	
YU-AKL	Boeing 727-2H9	Jugoslovenski Aerotransport	
YU-AMA	Douglas DC-10-30	Jugoslovenski Aerotransport *Nikola Tesla*	
YU-AMB	Douglas DC-10-30	Jugoslovenski Aerotransport *Edvard Rusijan*	
YU-ANB	Douglas DC-9-82	Inex Adria Airways	
YU-ANC	Douglas DC-9-82	Inex Adria Airways	
YU-ANE	Tupolev Tu-134A	Aviogenex *Novi Sad*	

YV (Venezuela)

Notes	Reg.	Type	Owner or Operator
	YV-133C	Douglas DC-10-30	Viasa
	YV-134C	Douglas DC-10-30	Viasa
	YV-135C	Douglas DC-10-30	Viasa
	YV-136C	Douglas DC-10-30	Viasa
	YV-137C	Douglas DC-10-30	Viasa
	YV-138C	Douglas DC-10-30	Viasa

Z (Zimbabwe)

	Z-WKR	Boeing 707-330B	Air Zimbabwe
	Z-WKS	Boeing 707-330B	Air Zimbabwe
	Z-WKT	Boeing 707-330B	Air Zimbabwe
	Z-WKU	Boeing 707-330B	Air Zimbabwe
	Z-WKV	Boeing 707-330B	Air Zimbabwe
	Z-WMJ	Douglas DC-8-54F	Affretair *Captain Stock Wallek*

ZK (New Zealand)

	ZK-NZV	Boeing 747-219B	Air New Zealand *Aotea*
	ZK-NZW	Boeing 747-219B	Air New Zealand *Tainui*
	ZK-NZX	Boeing 747-219B	Air New Zealand *Takitimu*
	ZK-NZY	Boeing 747-219B	Air New Zealand *Te Arawa*
	ZK-NZZ	Boeing 747-219B	Air New Zealand *Tokomaru*

ZS (South Africa)

	ZS-SAL	Boeing 747-244B	South African Airways *Tafelberg*
	ZS-SAM	Boeing 747-244B	South African Airways *Drakensberg*
	ZS-SAN	Boeing 747-244B	South African Airways *Lebombo*
	ZS-SAO	Boeing 747-244B	South African Airways *Magaliesberg*
	ZS-SAP	Boeing 747-244B	South African Airways *Swartberg*
	ZS-SAR	Boeing 747-244B	South African Airways *Waterberg*
	ZS-SAS	Boeing 747-244B	South African Airways *Helderberg*
	ZS-SAT	Boeing 747-344	South African Airways
	ZS-SAU	Boeing 747-344	South African Airways
	ZS-SPA	Boeing 747SP-44	South African Airways *Matroosberg*
	ZS-SPB	Boeing 747SP-44	South African Airways *Outeniqua*
	ZS-SPC	Boeing 747SP-44	South African Airways *Maluti*
	ZS-SPD	Boeing 747SP-44	South African Airways *Majuba*
	ZS-SPE	Boeing 747SP-44	South African Airways *Hantam*
	ZS-SPF	Boeing 747SP-44	South African Airways *Soutpansberg*

3B (Mauritius)

	3B-NAE	Boeing 707-344B	Air Mauritius *City of Port Louis*
	3B-NAF	Boeing 707-344B	Air Mauritius

3X (Guinea)

	3X-GAZ	Boeing 707-351C	Air Guinee

4R (Sri Lanka)

Reg.	Type	Owner or Operator	Notes
4R-ULA	L.1011-385 TriStar 500	Air Lanka *City of Colombo*	
4R-ULB	L.1011-385 TriStar 500	Air Lanka *City of Jayewardenepura*	
4R-ULC	L.1011-385 TriStar 1	Air Lanka	
4R-ULD	L.1011-385 TriStar 1	Air Lanka	

4W (Yemen)

4W-ACF	Boeing 727-2N8	Yemen Airways	
4W-ACG	Boeing 727-2N8	Yemen Airways	
4W-ACH	Boeing 727-2N8	Yemen Airways	
4W-ACI	Boeing 727-2N8	Yemen Airways	
4W-ACJ	Boeing 727-2N8	Yemen Airways	

4X (Israel)

4X-ATA	Boeing 707-458	El Al	
4X-ATB	Boeing 707-458	El Al	
4X-ATD	Boeing 707-331B	El Al	
4X-ATR	Boeing 707-358B	El Al	
4X-ATS	Boeing 707-358B	El Al	
4X-ATT	Boeing 707-358B	El Al	
4X-ATX	Boeing 707-358C	El Al	
4X-ATY	Boeing 707-358C	Sun d'Or International Airlines	
4X-AXA	Boeing 747-258B	El Al	
4X-AXB	Boeing 747-258B	El Al	
4X-AXC	Boeing 747-258B	El Al	
4X-AXD	Boeing 747-258C	El Al	
4X-AXF	Boeing 747-258C	El Al	
4X-AXG	Boeing 747-258F	El Al	
4X-AXH	Boeing 747-258B	El Al	
4X-AXZ	Boeing 747-124F	El Al	
4X-BAB	Boeing 737-2E7	Arkia	
4X-BMA	Boeing 720-023B	Maof Airlines	
4X-BMB	Boeing 720-023B	Maof Airlines	
4X-EAA	Boeing 767-258	El Al	
4X-EAB	Boeing 767-258	El Al	
4X-EAC	Boeing 767-258	El Al	
4X-EAD	Boeing 767-258	El Al	

Note: Maof Airlines also operates Boeing 707s N778PA and N18712 on lease.

5A (Libya)

5A-DAI	Boeing 727-224	Libyan Arab Airlines	
5A-DAK	Boeing 707-3L5C	Libyan Arab Airlines	
5A-DIA	Boeing 727-2L5	Libyan Arab Airlines	
5A-DIB	Boeing 727-2L5	Libyan Arab Airlines	
5A-DIC	Boeing 727-2L5	Libyan Arab Airlines	
5A-DID	Boeing 727-2L5	Libyan Arab Airlines	
5A-DIE	Boeing 727-2L5	Libyan Arab Airlines	
5A-DIF	Boeing 727-2L5	Libyan Arab Airlines	
5A-DIG	Boeing 727-2L5	Libyan Arab Airlines	
5A-DIH	Boeing 727-2L5	Libyan Arab Airlines	
5A-DII	Boeing 727-2L5	Libyan Arab Airlines	

Notes	Reg.	Type	Owner or Operator
	5A-DIK	Boeing 707-328C	Libyan Arab Airlines
	5A-DJM	Boeing 707-321B	Libyan Arab Airlines
	5A-DLT	Boeing 707-328B	Libyan Arab Airlines

Note: Libyan Arab Airlines also operate Boeing 707s TF-VLJ and TF-VLP on lease.

5B (Cyprus)

	5B-DAG	BAC One Eleven 537GF	Cyprus Airways
	5B-DAH	BAC One Eleven 537GF	Cyprus Airways
	5B-DAJ	BAC One Eleven 537GF	Cyprus Airways
	5B-DAK	Boeing 707-123B	Cyprus Airways
	5B-DAL	Boeing 707-123B	Cyprus Airways
	5B-DAO	Boeing 707-123B	Cyprus Airways
	5B-DAP	Boeing 707-123B	Cyprus Airways
	5B-DAR	A.310-202 Airbus	Cyprus Airways
	5B-DAS	A.310-202 Airbus	Cyprus Airways

5N (Nigeria)

	5N-ABJ	Boeing 707-3F9C	Nigeria Airways
	5N-ABK	Boeing 707-3F9C	Nigeria Airways
	5N-ANN	Douglas DC-10-30	Nigeria Airways
	5N-ANO	Boeing 707-3F9C	Nigeria Airways
	5N-ANR	Douglas DC-10-30	Nigeria Airways
	5N-ARQ	Boeing 707-338C	R.N. Cargo
	5N-ASY	Boeing 707-351C	United Air Services
	5N-AVR	Douglas DC-8-52	Intercontinental Airlines
	5N-AVS	Douglas DC-8-52	Intercontinental Airlines
	5N-AVY	Douglas DC-8-51	Intercontinental Airlines

Note: Nigeria Airways also operates Boeing 747s SE-DFZ and N747BC on lease.

5X (Uganda)

	5X-UAC	Boeing 707-351C	Uganda Airlines
	5X-UBC	Boeing 707-338C	Uganda Airlines *Pearl of Africa*
	5X-UCF	Lockheed L382G Hercules	Uganda Airlines

5Y (Kenya)

 Kenya Airways

	5Y-BBI	Boeing 707-351B	Kenya Airlines
	5Y-BBJ	Boeing 707-351B	Kenya Airlines
	5Y-BBK	Boeing 707-351B	Kenya Airlines
	5Y-BBX	Boeing 720-047B	Kenya Airlines

6Y (Jamaica)

Note: Air Jamaica operates a Boeing 747 on lease from Aer Lingus.

7T (Algeria)

Reg.	Type	Owner or Operator	Notes
7T-VEA	Boeing 727-2D6	Air Algerie *Tassili*	
7T-VEB	Boeing 727-2D6	Air Algerie *Hoggar*	
7T-VED	Boeing 737-2D6C	Air Algerie *Atlas Saharien*	
7T-VEE	Boeing 737-2D6C	Air Algerie *Oasis*	
7T-VEF	Boeing 737-2D6	Air Algerie *Saoura*	
7T-VEG	Boeing 737-2D6	Air Algerie *Monts des Ouleds Neils*	
7T-VEH	Boeing 727-2D6	Air Algerie *Lalla Khadidja*	
7T-VEI	Boeing 727-2D6	Air Algerie *Djebel Amour*	
7T-VEJ	Boeing 737-2D6	Air Algerie *Chrea*	
7T-VEK	Boeing 737-2D6	Air Algerie *Edough*	
7T-VEL	Boeing 737-2D6	Air Algerie *Akfadou*	
7T-VEM	Boeing 727-2D6	Air Algerie *Mont du Ksall*	
7T-VEN	Boeing 737-2D6	Air Algerie *La Soummam*	
7T-VEO	Boeing 737-2D6	Air Algerie *La Titteri*	
7T-VEP	Boeing 727-2D6	Air Algerie *Mont du Tessala*	
7T-VEQ	Boeing 737-2D6	Air Algerie *Le Zaccar*	
7T-VER	Boeing 737-2D6	Air Algerie *Le Souf*	
7T-VES	Boeing 737-2D6C	Air Algerie *Le Tadmaït*	
7T-VET	Boeing 727-2D6	Air Algerie *Georges du Rhumel*	
7T-VEU	Boeing 727-2D6	Air Algerie	
7T-VEV	Boeing 727-2D6	Air Algerie	
7T-VEW	Boeing 727-2D6	Air Algerie	
7T-VEX	Boeing 727-2D6	Air Algerie	
7T-VEY	Boeing 737-2D6	Air Algerie *Rhoufi*	
7T-VEZ	Boeing 737-2T4	Air Algerie	
7T-VJA	Boeing 737-2T4	Air Algerie	
7T-VJB	Boeing 737-2T4	Air Algerie	

9G (Ghana)

9G-ACX	Boeing 707-336C	West Africa Airlines	
9G-ACY	Boeing 707-331C	West Coast Airlines	
9G-ACZ	Boeing 707-336C	—	
9G-ADB	Boeing 707-336B	West Coast Airlines	
9G-ANA	Douglas DC-10-30	Ghana Airways	

9H (Malta)

AIRMALTA⊠

9H-AAK	Boeing 720-047B	Air Malta	
9H-AAL	Boeing 720-047B	Air Malta	
9H-AAN	Boeing 720-040B	Air Malta	
9H-AAO	Boeing 720-047B	Air Malta	
9H-ABA	Boeing 737-2Y5	Air Malta	
9H-ABB	Boeing 737-2Y5	Air Malta	
9H-ABC	Boeing 737-2Y5	Air Malta	

9J (Zambia)

 Zambia Airways

9J-ADY	Boeing 707-349C (Cargo)	Zambia Airways	
9J-AEB	Boeing 707-351C	Zambia Airways	
9J-AEL	Boeing 707-338C	Zambia Airways	
9J-AEQ	Boeing 707-321C (Cargo)	Zambia Airways	

9K (Kuwait)

Notes	Reg.	Type	Owner or Operator
	9K-ACJ	Boeing 707-369C	Kuwait Airways *Wara*
	9K-ACK	Boeing 707-369C	Kuwait Airways *Kadhma*
	9K-ACL	Boeing 707-369C	Kuwait Airways *Al-Jahra*
	9K-ACM	Boeing 707-369C	Kuwait Airways *Failaka*
	9K-ACN	Boeing 707-369C	Kuwait Airways *Burghan*
	9K-ACS	Boeing 707-321C	Kuwait Airways *Gharnada*
	9K-ACX	Boeing 707-311C	Kuwait Airways *Wafra*
	9K-ADA	Boeing 747-269B	Kuwait Airways *Al Sabahiya*
	9K-ADB	Boeing 747-269B	Kuwait Airways *Al Jaberiya*
	9K-ADC	Boeing 747-269B	Kuwait Airways *Al Murbarakiya*
	9K-ADD	Boeing 747-269B	Kuwait Airways *Al Salmiya*
	9K-AHA	A.310-222 Airbus	Kuwait Airways
	9k-AHB	A.310-222 Airbus	Kuwait Airways
	9K-AHC	A.310-222 Airbus	Kuwait Airways
	9K-AHD	A.310-222 Airbus	Kuwait Airways
	9K-AHE	A.310-222 Airbus	Kuwait Airways
	9K-AHF	A.300-600 Airbus	Kuwait Airways
	9K-AHG	A.300-600 Airbus	Kuwait Airways
	9K-AHH	A.300-600 Airbus	Kuwait Airways
	9K-	A.310-222 Airbus	Kuwait Airways
	9K-	A.310-222 Airbus	Kuwait Airways
	9K-	A.310-222 Airbus	Kuwait Airways

9L (Sierra Leone)

Sierra Leone Airways' services between Freetown and London are operated by using Boeing 707 JY-AEC leased from Alia.

9M (Malaysia)

	9M-MHI	Boeing 747-236B	Malaysian Airline System
	9M-MHJ	Boeing 747-236B	Malaysian Airline System

9Q (Zaïre)

	9Q-CKQ	Canadair CL-44-6	Vic Air Cargo
	9Q-CLI	Douglas DC-10-30	Air Zaïre *Mont Ngaliema*
	9Q-CLT	Douglas DC-10-30	Air Zaïre *Mont Ngafula*
	9Q-CLY	Boeing 707-336C	EMZ
	9Q-CQS	Canadair CL-44J	Vic Air Cargo
	9Q-CQU	Canadair CL-44D4	Vic Air Cargo
	9Q-CVG	Boeing 707-329C	Katale Aero Transport

9V (Singapore)

	9V-SKA	Boeing 747-312B	Singapore Airlines
	9V-SQH	Boeing 747-212B	Singapore Airlines
	9V-SQI	Boeing 747-212B	Singapore Airlines

Reg.	Type	Owner or Operator	Notes
9V-SQJ	Boeing 747-212B	Singapore Airlines	
9V-SQK	Boeing 747-212B	Singapore Airlines	
9V-SQL	Boeing 747-212B	Singapore Airlines	
9V-SQM	Boeing 747-212B	Singapore Airlines	
9V-SQN	Boeing 747-212B	Singapore Airlines	
9V-SQO	Boeing 747-212B	Singapore Airlines	
9V-SQP	Boeing 747-212B	Singapore Airlines	
9V-SQQ	Boeing 747-212B	Singapore Airlines	
9V-SQR	Boeing 747-212B	Singapore Airlines	
9V-SQS	Boeing 747-212B	Singapore Airlines	

Note: Singapore Airlines also operates Boeing 747-312Bs N116KB, N117KC, N118KD, N119KE, N120KF, N121KG and N122KH.

9XR (Rwanda)

9XR-JA	Boeing 707-328C	Air Rwanda	

9Y (Trinidad and Tobago)

9Y-TGJ	L.1011 TriStar 500	B.W.I.A. *Flamingo*	
9Y-TGN	L.1011 TriStar 500	B.W.I.A.	
9Y-THA	L.1011 TriStar 500	B.W.I.A.	

Note: B.W.I.A. also operates a TriStar 500 which retains its US registration N3140D.

Radio Frequencies

The frequencies used by the larger airfields/airports are listed below. Abbreviations used: TWR — Tower, APP — Approach, A/G — Air-ground advisory. It is possible for changes to be made from time to time with the frequencies allocated which are all quoted in Megahertz (MHz).

Airfield	TWR	APP	A/G	Airfield	TWR	APP	A/G
Aberdeen	118.1	120.4		Leeds	120.3	123.75	
Aldergrove	118.3	120.0		Leicester			122.25
Alderney	123.6			Little Snoring			122.4
Andrewsfield			130.55	Liverpool	118.1	119.85	
Barton			122.7	Long Marston			130.1
Barrow			123.2	Luton	120.2	129.55	
Bembridge			123.25	Lydd	126.7	120.7	
Biggin Hill	129.4	118.42		Manchester	118.7	119.4	
Birmingham	118.3	120.5		Manston	124.9	126.35	
Blackbushe			122.3	Netherthorpe			123.5
Blackpool	118.4	118.4		Newcastle	119.7	126.35	
Bodmin			122.7	North Denes			120.45
Booker			121.15	Norwich	118.9	119.35	
Bourn			129.8	Panshanger			120.25
Bournemouth	125.6	118.65		Perth	119.8	122.3	
Bristol	120.55	127.75		Plymouth	122.6	123.2	
Cambridge	122.2	123.6		Popham			129.8
Cardiff	121.2	125.85		Prestwick	118.15	120.55	
Carlisle			123.6	Redhill			123.22
Compton Abbas			122.7	Rochester			122.25
Coventry	119.25	119.25		Ronaldsway	118.9	120.85	
Cranfield	123.2	122.85		Sandown			123.5
Crowland			122.6	Seething			122.6
Denham			130.72	Sherburn			122.6
Doncaster			122.9	Shobdon			123.5
Dundee	122.9	122.9		Shoreham	125.4	123.15	
Dunkeswell			123.5	Sibson			122.3
Dunsfold	130.0	122.55		Sleap			122.45
Duxford			123.5	Southampton	118.2	128.85	
East Midlands	124.0	119.65		Southend	119.7	128.95	
Edinburgh	118.7	121.2		Stansted	118.15	126.95	
Elstree			122.4	Stapleford			122.8
Exeter	119.8	128.15		Staverton	125.65		
Fairoaks			123.42	Sumburgh	118.25	123.15	
Felthorpe			123.5	Sunderland	122.7	122.2	
Fenland			123.05	Swansea	119.7		
Filton	124.95	130.85		Swanton Morley	123.5		
Gamston			123.65	Sywell			122.7
Gatwick	124.22	119.6		Tees-side	119.8	118.85	
Glasgow	118.8	119.1		Thruxton			130.45
Goodwood	119.7	122.45		Tollerton			122.8
Guernsey	119.95	128.65		Wellesbourne			130.45
Halfpenny Green			123.0	Weston	122.5		
Hamble	120.65	125.0		White Waltham	122.6		
Hatfield	130.8	123.35		Wick	119.7		
Haverfordwest			122.2	Wickenby			122.45
Hawarden	124.95	123.35		Woodford	122.5	130.05	
Hayes Heliport			123.65	Yeovil	125.4	130.8	
Headcorn			122.0				
Heathrow	118.7	119.2					
	121.0	119.5					
Henstridge			130.27				
Hethal			122.35				
Hucknall			130.8				
Humberside	118.55	123.15					
Ingoldmells			130.45				
Inverness	122.6	122.6					
Ipswich	123.25						
Jersey	119.45	120.3					
Kidlington	119.8	130.3					
Land's End			122.3				
Leavesden	122.15						

Airline Codes

Two character codes are used by airlines to prefix flight numbers in timetables, airport movement boards, etc. Those listed below identify both U.K. and overseas airlines appearing in the book.

Code	Airline	Reg
AA	American A/L	N
AC	Air Canada	C
AE	Air Europe	G
AF	Air France	F
AH	Air Algerie	7T
AI	Air India	VT
AK	Air Bridge	G
AO	Aviaco	EC
AR	Aerolineas Argentinas	LV
AT	Royal Air Maroc	CN
AY	Finnair	OH
AZ	Alitalia	I
BA	British Airways	G
BB	Balair	HB
BC	Brymon Aviation	G
BD	British Midland	G
BF	Alaska Intl Air	N
BG	Bangladesh Biman	S2
BM	ATI	I
BQ	Aermediterranea	I
BR	British Caledonian	G
BS	Busy Bee	LN
BU	Braathens	LN
BW	B.W.I.A.	9Y
BX	Spantax	EC
BY	Britannia	G
BZ	Brit Air	F
CA	CAAC	B
CC	Air Freight Egypt	SU
CL	Capitol Intl A/W	N
CP	CP Air	C
CS	Corse Air	F
CU	Cubana	CU
CV	Cargolux	LX
CX	Cathay Pacific	VR-H
CY	Cyprus A/W	5B
DA	Dan-Air	G
DE	Delta Air Transport	OO
DF	Condor	D
DG	Air Atlantique	G
DK	Scanair	SE
DL	Delta A/L	N
DM	Maersk	OY
DQ	Air Limousin	F
EC	Air Ecosse	G
EI	Aer Lingus	EI
EL	Euralair	F
EN	Genair	G
EO	Euroflite	G
ER	Sun d'Or Intl A/L	4X
ET	Ethiopian A/L	ET
EY	Europe Aero Service	F
EZ	Euroair	G
EZ	Evergreen Intl	N
FC	Fairflight	G
FD	Ford	G
FG	Ariana	YA
FI	Icelandair	TF
FO	Fred Olsen	LN
FQ	Minerve	F
FT	Flying Tiger	N
GA	Garuda	PK
GE	Guernsey A/L	G
GE	German Cargo	D
GF	Gulf Air	A40
GG	Air London	G
GH	Ghana A/W	9G
GI	Air Guinee	3X
GR	Aurigny A/S	G
GT	GB Airways	G
GX	Global Intl	G
HE	Trans European A/W	OO
HF	Hapag-Lloyd	D
HI	Hispania	EC
HN	N.L.M.	PH
HO	TAR	LV
HV	Transavia	PH
HZ	Thurston Aviation	G
IA	Iraq A/W	YI
IF	Interflug	DDR
IG	Alisarda	I
IK	Tradewinds	G
IO	TAT	F
IR	Iran Air	EP
IT	Air Inter	F
IY	Yemen A/W	4W
JE	Manx Airlines	G
JJ	Aviogenex	YU
JL	Japan A/L	JA
JP	Inex Adria	YU
JU	JAT	YU
JW	Arrow Air	N
JY	Jersey European	G
KB	Burnthills Aviation	G
KD	British Island A/L	G
KG	Orion A/W	G
KL	K.L.M.	PH
KM	Air Malta	9H
KQ	Kenya A/W	5Y
KR	Kar-Air	OH
KT	British Airtours	G
KU	Kuwait A/W	9K
KY	W. Africa Aircargo	9G
KZ	Avair	EI
LC	Loganair	G
LF	Linjeflyg	SE
LG	Luxair	LX
LH	Lufthansa	D
LJ	Sierra Leone A/W	9L
LK	Lucas A/T	F
LL	Aero Lloyd	D
LN	Libyan Arab A/L	5A
LO	Polish A/L (LOT)	SP
LP	Air Alpes	F
LS	Express A/S	G
LT	LTU	D
LW	Lauda Air	OE
LX	Crossair	HB
LY	El Al	4X
LZ	Bulgarian A/L	LZ
MA	Malev	HA
ME	Middle East A/L	OD
MH	Malaysian A/L	9M
MK	Air Mauritius	3B
MP	Martinair	PH
MS	Egyptair	SU
NB	Sterling A/W	OY
NP	Heavy Lift	G
NQ	NW Territorial A/W	C
NV	Northern Executive	G
NW	Northwest Orient	N
OA	Olympic A/W	SX
OJ	Maof A/L	4X
OK	Czech A/L	OK
OM	Monarch A/L	G
OO	Sobelair	OO
OS	Austrian A/L	OE
OV	Overseas National	N
OY	Conair	OY
PA	Pan Am	N
PJ	Peregrine A/S	G
PK	Pakistan Intl	AP
PR	Philippine A/L	RP
PW	Pacific Western	C
QC	Air Zaire	9Q
QF	Qantas	VH
QH	Air Florida	N
QK	Aeromaritime	F
QT	Inter City A/L	G
QU	Uganda A/L	5X
QZ	Zambia A/W	9J
RB	Syrian Arab	YK
RD	Airlift Intl	N
RD	Metropolitan A/W	G
RG	Varig	PP
RH	Air Zimbabwe	Z
RJ	Alia	JY
RM	McAlpine	G
RO	Tarom	YR
RU	CTA	HB
SA	South African A/W	ZS
SD	Sudan A/W	ST
SF	Air Charter Intl	F
SJ	Southern A/T	N
SK	S.A.S.	SE OY LN
SM	Altair	I
SN	Sabena	OO
SQ	Singapore A/L	9Q
SR	Swissair	HB
SU	Aeroflot	CCCP
SV	Saudia	HZ
TE	Air New Zealand	ZK
TG	Thai Intl	HS
TK	Turkish A/L	TC
TL	Trans Mediterranean	OD
TP	Air Portugal	CS
TU	Tunis Air	TS
TV	Transamerica	N
TW	TWA	N
UB	Bristow	G
UJ	Air Lanka	4R
UK	Air UK	G
UP	Air Foyle	G
UQ	United African A/L	5A
UW	Air Rwanda	9XR
UY	Cameroon A/L	TJ
VA	Viasa	YV
VF	British Air Ferries	G
VL	Eagle Air	TF
VO	Tyrolean	OE
VQ	Aermediterranea	I
VS	Intercontinental	5N
VY	Air Belgium	OO
WD	Wardair	C
WE	WDL Flugdienst	D
WG	Air Ecosse	G
WN	Norfly	LN
WO	World A/W	N
WT	Nigeria A/W	5N
XF	Spacegrand	G
3A	Air Commuter	G
3T	American Trans Air	N
8R	Rotterdam A/L	PH

British Aircraft Preservation Council Register

The British Aircraft Preservation Council was formed in 1967 to co-ordinate the works of all bodies involved in the preservation, restoration and display of historical aircraft. Membership covers the whole spectrum of national, Service, commercial and voluntary groups, and meetings are held regularly at the bases of member organisations. The Council is able to provide a means of communication, helping to resolve any misunderstandings or duplication of effort. Every effort is taken to encourage the raising of standards of both organisation and technical capacity amongst the member groups to the benfit of everyone interested in aviation. To assist historians, the B.A.P.C. register has been set up and provides an identity for those aircraft which do not qualify for a Service serial or inclusion in the UK Civil Register.

Aircraft on the current B.A.P.C. Register are as follows:

Notes	Reg.	Type	Owner or Operator
	1	Roe Triplane Type IV (replica)	Now G-ARSG
	2	Bristol Boxkite (replica)	Now G-ASPP
	3	Blériot XI	Now G-AANG
	4	Deperdussin monoplane	Now G-AANH
	5	Blackburn monoplane	Now G-AANI
	6	Roe Triplane Type IV (replica)	Manchester Air & Space Museum
	7	Southampton University MPA	The Shuttleworth Trust
	8	Dixon ornithopter	The Shuttleworth Trust
	9	Humber Monoplane (replica)	Fleet Air Arm Museum
	10	Hafner R.11 Revoplane	British Rotorcraft Museum
	11	English Electric Wren	Now G-EBNV
	12	Mignet HM.14 Pou-du-Ciel	Museum of Flight/E. Fortune
	13	Mignet HM.14 Pou-du-Ciel	The Aeroplane Collection Ltd
	14	Addyman standard training glider	N. H. Ponsford
	15	Addyman standard training glider	The Aeroplane Collection Ltd
	16	Addyman ultra-light aircraft	N. H. Ponsford
	17	Woodhams Sprite	The Aeroplane Collection Ltd
	18	Killick MP Gyroplane	N. H. Ponsford
	19	Bristol F.2b	Anne Lindsay
	20	Lee-Richards annular biplane (replica)	Newark Air Musem
	22	Mignet HM.14 Pou-du-Ciel (G-AEOE)	R. M. Mitchell/Holland
	25	Nyborg TGN-111 glider	Midland Air Museum
	26	Auster AOP.9	S. Wales Aircraft Preservation Soc
	27	Mignet HM.14 Pou-du-Ciel	M. J. Abbey
	28	Wright Flyer (replica)	RAF Museum/Cardington
	29	Mignet HM.14 Pou-du-Ciel (G-ADRY)	J. J. Penney/Aberdare
	31	Slingsby T.7 Tutor	S. Wales Aircraft Preservation Soc
	32	Crossley Tom Thumb	Midland Air Museum
	33	DFS.108-49 Grunau Baby 116	Russavia Collection/Duxford
	34	DFS.108-49 Grunau Baby 116	D. Elsdon
	35	EoN primary glider	Russavia Collection
	36	FZG-76 (V.I) (replica)	The Shuttleworth Trust
	37	Blake Bluetit	The Shuttleworth Trust
	38	Bristol Scout replica (A1742)	RAF St Athan
	40	Bristol Boxkite (replica)	Bristol City Museum
	41	B.E.2C (replica) (6232)	RAF St Athan
	42	Avro 504 (replica) (H1968)	RAF St Athan
	43	Mignet HM.14 Pou-du-Ciel	Lincolnshire Aviation Museum
	44	Miles Magister (L6906)	G. H. R. Johnson (G-AKKY)
	45	Pilcher Hawk (replica)	Stanford Hall Museum
	46	Mignet HM.14 Pou-du-Ciel	Alan McKechnie Racing Ltd
	47	Watkins monoplane	RAF St Athan
	48	Pilcher Hawk (replica)	Glasgow Museum of Transport
	49	Pilcher Hawk	Royal Scottish Museum/Edinburgh
	50	Roe Triplane Type 1	Science Museum
	51	Vickers Vimy IV	Science Museum
	52	Lilienthal glider	Science Museum
	53	Wright Flyer (replica)	Science Museum

Reg.	Type	Owner or Operator	Notes
54	JAP-Harding monoplane	Science Museum	
55	Levavasseur Antoinette VII	Science Museum	
56	Fokker E.III	Science Museum	
57	Pilcher Hawk (replica)	Science Museum	
58	Yokosuka MXY-7 Ohka II	Science Museum	
59	Sopwith Camel (replica) (D3419)	RAF St Athan	
60	Murray M.I helicopter	The Aeroplane Collection Ltd	
61	Stewart man-powered ornithopter	Lincolnshire Aviation Museum	
62	Cody Biplane (304)	Science Museum	
63	Hurricane (replica) (L1592)	Torbay Aircraft Museum	
64	Hurricane (replica)	—	
65	Spitfire (replica) (QV-K)	—	
66	Bf 109 (replica)	—	
67	Bf 109 (replica) (14)	Midland Air Museum	
68	Hurricane (replica)	Midland Air Museum	
69	Spitfire (replica)	Torbay Aircraft Museum	
70	Auster AOP.5 (TJ472)	Aircraft Preservation Soc of Scotland	
71	Spitfire (replica) (P9390)	Norfolk & Suffolk Aviation Museum	
72	Hurricane (replica) (V7767)	N. Weald Aircraft Restoration Flight	
73	Hurricane (replica)	Queens Head/Bishops Stortford	
74	Bf 109 (replica)	Torbay Aircraft Museum	
75	Mignet HM.14 Pou-du-Ciel	Nigel Ponsford	
76	Mignet HM.14 Pou-du-Ciel (G-AFFI)	Bomber County Museum/Cleethorpes	
77	Mignet HM.14 Pou-du-Ciel	P. Kirby/Innsworth	
78	Hawker Hind (Afghan)	Now G-AENP	
79	Fiat G.46-4 (ZI-4)	Visionair International	
80	Airspeed Horsa (TL769)	Museum of Army Flying	
81	Hawkridge Dagling	Russavia Collection/Duxford	
82	Hawker Hind (Afghan)	RAF Museum	
83	Kawasaki Ki-100IB	Aerospace Museum/Cosford	
84	Nakajima Ki-46 (Dinah III)	RAF St Athan	
85	Weir W-2 autogyro	Museum of Flight/E. Fortune	
86	de Havilland Tiger Moth (replica)	Yorkshire Aircraft Preservation Soc	
87	Bristol Babe (replica)	Bomber County Museum	
88	Fokker Dr 1 (replica) (102/18)	Fleet Air Arm Museum	
89	Cayley glider (replica)	Manchester Air & Space Museum	
90	Colditz Cock (replica)	Torbay Aircraft Museum	
91	Fieseler Fi 103/FZG.76 (V.I)	Lashenden Air Warfare Museum	
92	Fieseler Fi 103/FZG.76 (V.I)	RAF Museum/Henlow	
93	Fieseler Fi 103/FZG.76 (V.I)	RAF St Athan	
94	Fieseler Fi 103/FZG.76 (V.I)	Aerospace Museum/Cosford	
95	Gizmer autogyro	N.E. Aircraft Museum	
96	Brown helicopter	N.E. Aircraft Museum	
97	Luton L.A.4a Minor	Nene Valley Aviation Soc/Sywell	
98	Yokosuka MXY-7 Ohka II	RAF Museum/Henlow	
99	Yokosuka MXY-7 Ohka II	Aerospace Museum/Cosford	
100	Clarke glider	Science Museum	
101	Mignet HM.14 Pou-du-Ciel	Lincolnshire Aviation Museum	
102	Mignet HM.14 Pou-du-Ciel	W. Sneesby	
103	Pilcher glider (replica)	Personal Plane Services Ltd	
104	Blériot XI (replica)	Now G-AVXV/St Athan	
105	Blériot XI (replica)	Aviodome/Schiphol, Holland	
106	Blériot XI (164)	RAF Museum	
107	Blériot XXVII (433)	RAF Museum	
108	Fairey Swordfish (HS503)	RAF Museum/Henlow	
109	Slingsby Kirby Cadet	RAF Museum/Henlow	
110	Fokker D.VII replica (static) (5125)	Leisure Sport Ltd	
111	Sopwith Triplane replica (static) (N5492)	Leisure Sport Ltd	
112	D.H.2 replica (static) (5964)	Leisure Sport Ltd	
113	S.E.5A replica (static) (B4863)	Leisure Sport Ltd	
114	Vickers Type 60 Viking (static)	Leisure Sport Ltd	
115	Mignet HM.14 Pou-du-Ciel	Essex Aviation Group/Andrewsfield	
116	Santos-Dumont Demoiselle (replica)	Cornwall Aero Park, Helston	
117	B.E.2C (replica)	N. Weald Aircraft Restoration Flight	

Notes	Reg.	Type	Owner or Operator
	118	Albatross D.V. (replica)	N. Weald Aircraft Restoration Flight
	119	Bensen B.7	N.E. Aircraft Museum
	120	Mignet HM.14 Pou-du-Ciel	Bomber County Museum/Cleethorpes
	121	Mignet HM.14 Pou-du-Ciel (G-AEKR)	S. Yorks Aviation Soc
	122	Avro 504 (replica)	British Broadcasting Corp
	123	Vickers FB.5 Gunbus (replica)	British Broadcasting Corp
	124	Lilienthal Glider Type XI (replica)	Science Museum
	125	Clay Cherub	Midland Air Museum
	126	D.31 Turbulent (static)	Midland Air Museum
	127	Halton Jupiter	Shuttleworth Trust
	128	Watkinson Cyclogyroplane Mk IV	British Rotorcraft Museum
	129	Blackburn 1911 Monoplane (replica)	Cornwall Aero Park/Helston
	130	Blackburn 1912 Monoplane (replica)	Cornwall Aero Park/Helston
	131	Pilcher Hawk (replica)	C. Paton
	132	Blériot XI	Aerospace Museum/Cosford
	133	Fokker Dr 1 (replica) (425/17)	Torbay Aircraft Museum
	134	Pitts S-2A static (G-RKSF)	Torbay Aircraft Museum
	135	Bristol M.IC (replica) (C4912)	Leisure Sport Ltd
	136	Deperdussin Seaplane (replica)	Leisure Sport Ltd
	137	Sopwith Baby Floatplane (replica) (8151)	Leisure Sport Ltd
	138	Hansa Brandenburg W.29 Floatplane (replica) (22912)	Leisure Sport Ltd
	139	Fokker Dr 1 (replica) 150/17	Leisure Sport Ltd
	140	Curtiss R3C-2 Floatplane (replica)	Leisure Sport Ltd
	141	Macchi M.39 Floatplane (replica)	Leisure Sport Ltd
	142	SE-5A (replica)	Cornwall Aero Park/Helston
	143	Paxton MPA	R. A. Paxton/Staverton
	144	Weybridge Mercury	Cranwell Gliding Club
	145	Oliver MPA	D. Oliver
	146	Pedal Aeronauts Toucan MPA	Shuttleworth Trust
	147	Bensen B.7	Norfolk & Suffolk Aviation Museum
	148	Hawker Fury II (replica) (K7271)	Aerospace Museum/Cosford
	149	Short S.27 (replica)	Fleet Air Arm Museum
	150	SEPECAT Jaguar GR.1 (replica) (XX718)	RAF Exhibition Flight
	151	SEPECAT Jaguar GR.1 (replica) (XX824)	RAF Exhibition Flight
	152	BAe Hawk T.1 (replica) (XX162)	RAF Exhibition Flight
	153	Westland WG.33	British Rotorcraft Museum
	154	D.31 Turbulent	Lincolnshire Aviation Museum
	155	Panavia Tornado GR.1 (replica) (ZA322)	RAF Exhibition Flight
	156	Supermarine S-6B (replica) (S1595)	Leisure Sport Ltd
	157	Waco CG-4A	Pennine Aviation Museum
	158	Fieseler Fi 103/FZG.76 (V.I)	Joint Bomb Disposal School
	159	Fuji Oka	Joint Bomb Disposal School
	160	Chargus 108 hang glider	Museum of Flight/E. Fortune
	161	Stewart Ornithopter Cappela	Bomber County Museum
	162	Goodhart Newbury Manflier MPA	Science Museum/Wroughton
	163	AFEE 10/42 Rotabuggy (replica)	Wessex Aviation Soc Wimborne
	164	Wight Quadraplane Type 1 (replica)	Wessex Aviation Soc Wimborne
	165	Bristol F.2b	RAF Museum/Cardington
	166	Bristol F.2b	Shuttleworth Trust
	167	S.E.5A replica	Torbay Aircraft Museum
	168	D.H.60G Moth static replica (G-AAAJ)	Hilton Hotel/Gatwick
	169	SEPECAT Jaguar GR.1 static replica (XX110)	No 1 S. of T.T. RAF Halton
	170	Pilcher Hawk (replica)	A. Gourlay
	171	BAe Hawk T.1 (replica) (XX262)	RAF Exhibition Flight/Abingdon
	172	Chargus Midas Super 8 hang glider	Scienc Museum/Wroughton

Reg.	Type	Owner or Operator	Notes
173	Birdman Promotions Grasshopper	Science Museum/Wroughton	
174	Bensen B.7	Science Museum/Wroughton	
175	Volmer VJ-23 Swingwing	Manchester Air & Space Museum	
176	Currie Wot/SE-5A (replica)	S. Yorkshire Aircraft Preservation Soc	
177	Avro 504K (replica) (C1381)	(Stored)/Henlow	
178	Avro 504K (replica) (E373)	(Stored)/Henlow	
179	Sopwith Pup	N. Weald Aircraft Restoration Flight	

Note: Registrations/Serials carried are mostly false identities. MPA = Man Powered Aircraft.

ADDENDA
New in-sequence registrations

Reg.	Type	Owner or Operator	Notes
G-ACOL	D.H.85A Leopard Moth	M. J. Abbott	
G-AVLJ	PA-28 Cherokee 140		
G-AWTS	Beech A23-19A Musketeer	B. A. Dunlop	
G-AXLM	BAC One-Eleven 523FJ	British Aerospace PLC	
G-AXLN	BAC One-Eleven 523FJ	British Aerospace PLC	
G-BDEA	Boeing 707-338C	—	
G-BEVU	BN-2A Mk III-2 Trislander	Airmore Aviation Ltd	
G-BFZV	Cessna F.172H	W. J. Kavanagh	

New out-of-sequence registrations

Reg.	Type	Owner or Operator	Notes
G-BMAR	Short SD3-60	British Midland Airways (G-BLCR)/ E. Midlands	
G-DDCD	D.H.104 Dove 4	C. Daniel (G-ARUM)	
G-FOOD	Beech B200 Super King Air	Airmore Aviation Ltd/Elstree	
G-GWHH	AS.355F Twin Squirrel	Wimpey Homes Holdings Ltd (G-BKUL)	
G-HSKY	Hughes 369HM	Skyline Helicopters Ltd (G-VNPP/ G-BDKL)	
G-ILSE	Corby CJ-1 Starlet	S. Stride	
G-JAJV	Partenavia P.68B	Matthew Royce	
G-MONI	Monnet Moni	R. P. Williams	
G-NITA	PA-28 Cherokee 180	D. R. Greenhill (G-AVVG)	
G-NOEI	AS350B Ecureuil	Colt Car Co Ltd (G-MORR/G-BHIU)	
G-OCAP	Bell 206B JetRanger	Air Hanson Sales Ltd	
G-OPOP	Enstrom F-280C-UK-2 Shark	Environmental Services (Southern) Ltd (G-OFED)	
G-OPSA	BAe.146-100	British Aerospace PLC (G-SSHH/ G-BIAE)	
G-RING	Cessna FR.182	A. Hopper	
G-TIKI	Colt 105A balloon	Lighter-Than-Air Ltd	
G-TIKU	AS.332L Super Puma	Bristow Helicopters Ltd	
G-TIGV	AS.332L Super Puma	Bristow Helicopters Ltd	
G-TRAD	Boeing 707-321C	Tradewinds Ltd (G-BGIS)	
G-WADE	Cessna F.172N	Wade Aviation (G-BHMI)	

New overseas registrations

B-2446	Boeing 747-2J6B	CAAC	
D-AJAB	Boeing 737-2L9	Jetair	
EI-BNT	Cvjetkovic CA.65 Skyfly	B. Tobin & P. G. Ryan	
EI-BOK	PA-23 Aztec 250	K. O'Connor	
EI-BOM	Boeing 737-2T4	Air Tara Ltd	
EI-BON	Boeing 737-2T4	Air Tara Ltd	
EI-BOP	SOCATA Rallye	Limerick Flying Club	
EI-BOR	Bell 222	M. V. O'Brien	
JA8165	Boeing 747-221F	Japan Air Lines	
LZ-TUU	Tupolev Tu-134A	Bulkan Bulgarian Airlines	

N908CL	Douglas DC-8-63	Capitol Air
N909CL	Douglas DC-8-63	Capitol Air
N926CL	Douglas DC-8-63	Capitol Air
N1809E	Douglas DC-8-62	Arrow Air
N4574P	Douglas DC-8-63	Arrow Air
S2-ACQ	Douglas DC-10-30	Bangladesh Biman *City of HZ Shah Jalal (RA)*
S2-ACR	Douglas DC-10-30	Bangladesh Biman
SP-LBG	Ilyushin IL-62M	Polskie Linie Lotnicze (LOT)

Future Allocations Log (In-Sequence)

The grid provides the facility to record future in-sequence registrations as they are issued or seen. To trace a particular code, refer to the left hand column which contains the three letters following the G prefix. The final letter can be found by reading across the columns headed A to Z. For example, the box for G-BLJD is located five rows down (BLJ) and then four across to the D column.

G-	A	B	C	D	E	F	G	H	I	J	K	L	M	N	O	P	R	S	T	U	V	W	X	Y	Z
BLF																									
BLG																									
BLH																									
BLI																									
BLJ																									
BLK																									
BLL																									
BLM																									
BLN																									
BLO																									
BLP																									
BLR																									
BLS																									
BLT																									
BLU																									
BLV																									
BLW																									
BLX																									
BLY																									
BLZ																									
BMA																									
BMB																									
BMC																									
BMD																									
BME																									
BMF																									
BMG																									
BMH																									
BMI																									
BMJ																									
BMK																									
BML																									
BMM																									
	A	B	C	D	E	F	G	H	I	J	K	L	M	N	O	P	R	S	T	U	V	W	X	Y	Z

Credit: *Wal Gandy*

Future Allocations Log (Out-of-Sequence)

This grid can be used to record out-of-sequence registrations as they are issued or seen. The first two columns are provided for the ranges prefixed with G-B, ie from G-BMxx to G-BZxx. The remaining columns cover the sequences from G-Cxxx to G-Zxxx and in this case it is necessary to insert the last three letters in the appropriate section.

G-B	G-B	G-C	G-E	G-G	G-I	G-L	G-N	G-P	G-S	G-U
M	R									
	S									
										G-V
N					G-J					
										G-W
	T									
							G-O			
		G-D	G-F	G-H		G-M		G-R		
	U									
									G-T	
	V									G-X
O										
	W									
					G-K					
										G-Y
	X									
P	Y									
										G-Z
	Z									

254